7th Linguistic Annotation Workshop & Interoperability with Discourse 2013

(LAW VII & ID)

Sofia, Bulgaria
8 – 9 August 2013

ISBN: 978-1-62748-997-3

Printed from e-media with permission by:

Curran Associates, Inc.
57 Morehouse Lane
Red Hook, NY 12571

CURRAN ASSOCIATES INC. proceedings.com

Some format issues inherent in the e-media version may also appear in this print version.

Printed by Curran Associates, Inc. (2013)

Association for Computational Linguistics
209 N. Eighth Street
Stroudsburg, Pennsylvania 18360

Phone: 1-570-476-8006
Fax: 1-570-476-0860

acl@aclweb.org

Additional copies of this publication are available from:

Curran Associates, Inc.
57 Morehouse Lane
Red Hook, NY 12571 USA
Phone: 845-758-0400
Fax: 845-758-2634
Email: curran@proceedings.com
Web: www.proceedings.com

LAW VII & ID

7th Linguistic Annotation Workshop
&
Interoperability with Discourse

Proceedings of the Workshop

August 8-9, 2013
Sofia, Bulgaria

Linguistic Annotation and Interoperability with Discourse – Workshop Overview

The *Linguistic Annotation Workshop* (LAW) is organized annually by the *Association for Computational Linguistics Special Interest Group for Annotation* (ACL SIGANN). It provides a forum to facilitate the exchange and propagation of research results concerned with the annotation, manipulation, and exploitation of corpora; work towards the harmonization and interoperability from the perspective of the increasingly large number of tools and frameworks for annotated language resources; and work towards a consensus on all issues crucial to the advancement of the field of corpus annotation.

The LAW VII & ID mission statement

This year the LAW has been combined with a workshop proposed for ACL 2013 on *Collating Models of Discourse Annotation* (CoMoDA). The aim of CoMoDA was to stimulate debate on and encourage work that proposes methods, frameworks and tools for comparing or aligning the varied types of discourse annotation currently available with the goal of achieving interoperability. CoMoDA proposed to use scholarly text as the testbed for this initiative by introducing a shared task.

While both proposals were accepted as individual workshops, it was considered beneficial to combine them and create a two-day event which would reach out to both communities. Traditionally, the LAW features a theme, which provides a focus point for workshop submissions. More recently, it features also a challenge, which awards papers addressing certain aspects of the theme. We decided that a natural way of combining the two workshops would be to let the CoMoDA agenda guide the theme of the 7th LAW. This is how *LAW VII and Interoperability with Discourse* (LAW VII & ID) came into being.

Thus, the LAW VII & ID workshop accepted papers on all aspects of linguistic annotation and was particularly interested in the comparison and interoperability of different models and techniques used for and in conjunction with discourse annotation, focusing on any of the following goals:

- Creation of new insights within the field of discourse (by juxtaposing two or more points of view as reflected by different annotation schemes or annotation techniques).
- Fostering interoperability between pragmatic and semantic phenomena in discourse, ranging from functional categories (e.g. methods, results, hypotheses, etc.) to traditional discourse relations (connectives, anaphora, metonymies, etc.).
- Connecting syntactic, semantic and pragmatic layers of annotation.
- Working towards a framework, representation standards, tools and methods that will allow the integration and co-existence of current and future discourse-related annotation schemes.

It was decided that the workshop would have a challenge and a shared task to encourage focussed submissions addressing the workshop theme. Any paper which dealt with annotation interoperability or integration automatically qualified for the challenge, while special consideration was given to papers (1) integrating functional discourse annotation from one or more corpora with other types of annotation; and (2) demonstrating how interoperability can increase the understanding of the discourse. The shared task was introduced to provide a testbed of scientific corpora for experimentation with different discourse annotation schemes.

These proceedings include papers presented at LAW VII & ID, held in Sofia, Bulgaria, on 8-9 August 2013.

Overview of accepted papers

LAW VII & ID's call for papers was answered by 48 submissions. After careful review, the Programme Committee accepted 18 long papers, together with ten additional papers to be presented as short talks and/or posters. This year's submissions addressed many topics of interest for resource annotation. Among these, the following topics are strongly represented, and serve as the headers of the different sessions into which LAW VII & ID has been divided:

1. sparse annotations and annotation error correction (three accepted papers),
2. annotation comparison and evaluation (five accepted papers),
3. interoperability and/or discourse — the special theme of the workshop (five accepted papers),
4. discourse annotation (ten papers on this issue included in the proceedings),
5. semantic annotation (six accepted papers), and
6. novel methods in annotation (four papers fall under this category).

While part-of-speech or syntactic tagging do not seem to feature prominently in the above thematic categories, there is actually a considerable amount of work being done on the correction and improvement of part-of-speech and/or syntactic annotations. Papers representative of such work have been included in the session on 'Sparse Annotations & Error Correction'.

The wide range of languages addressed in the accepted papers, the domains for which annotation was performed, as well as the countries of origin of the authors, indicate that this is a very active and lively area globally. As shown by the papers in the workshop proceedings, English is still the language of preference for annotation purposes (11 out of the 38 contributions deal with annotating English data to some extent). None of the papers submitted discussed linguistic annotation for Spanish, despite it being one of the most spoken languages in the world. Russian, while being one of the ten most spoken languages in the world, is not represented either. Interestingly, the ratio of papers representing Turkish is higher than the ratio of papers representing German, inspite of the huge amount of annotation projects and research being carried out in Germany. Asian languages are represented in the workshop by Chinese, Hindi, Indonesian, Japanese and Vietnamese, while Arabic languages are also represented: by Darija (from North-Africa) and Egyptian Arabic. The remaining languages dealt with in the papers are Czech, Danish, French, Italian, Norwegian, Portuguese and Swedish. Having a look at the languages discussed in the workshop papers and the countries where they come from, one can see that a number of non-native English-speaking researchers are working on the annotation of English data. Globalization, research evaluation metrics and the lack of suitable open and/or free resources (amongst other reasons) may be the main explanation for this phenomenon.While not totally surprising or unexpected, this poses some concern for linguistic diversity in annotation and the preservation of these languages in the long run.

The following includes some general observations on the accepted papers. Firstly, most of the semantic and discourse-related annotations of the workshop have been performed manually. This may indicate that existing technologies are not yet mature enough to produce automatic reliable semantic and discourse annotations or the scarcity of resources for producing automated methods. Secondly, only four out of the thirty-eight accepted submissions deal directly with annotation standards and standardization, and only two additional ones provide some kind of (explicit) best practices for annotation. This raises some concern, since it may mean that either (a) people are not aware of the standards being developed for annotation; or (b) the authors do not think these standards are useful for their work. In any case, we believe that some actions should be taken to remedy this situation. Thirdly, only five accepted papers discuss the interoperability topic, despite it being this yearś special theme. We believe this is a major challenge: advances in linguistic research in coming years will require annotations at different levels, and thus providing and querying corpora with such multi-layered information should become the norm. Thus, annotations at different levels and layers will have to interoperate to a great extent, with corpora and resources not conforming to such requirements running the risk of quickly becoming obsolete.

The LAW VII & ID Challenge

To emphasise the need for interoperability in linguistic annotation the LAW VII & ID workshop presented *The LAW Challenge*, an award sponsored by the U.S. National Science Foundation (IIS 0948101 Content of Linguistic Annotation: Standards and Practices (CLASP)) and the ACL Special Interest Group on Annotation (ACL SIGANN). The aim of this year's challenge was to promote the use and collaborative development of open, shared resources, and to identify and promote best practices for annotation interoperability focusing on (but not restricted to) discourse and discourse annotations. The second and third call for papers placed an emphasis on the challenge.

Papers addressing one of the topics below were considered eligible for the challenge award:

1. integration of functional discourse annotation from one or more corpora with other types of annotation;
2. demonstration of how interoperability can increase understanding of the discourse;
3. interoperability or integration between different types of linguistic annotation.

Other evaluation criteria considered in the challenge selection process include:

- innovative use of linguistic information from different discourse annotation layers;
- demonstrable interoperability with at least one other annotation scheme or format developed by others;
- quality of the annotated resource in terms of scheme design, documentation, tool support, etc.;
- open availability of developed resources for community use;
- usability and reusability of the annotation scheme or annotated resource;
- outstanding contribution to the development of annotation best practices.

Based on the above criteria, the winner of the second LAW Challenge was: "Towards a Better Understanding of Discourse: Integrating Multiple Discourse Annotation Perspectives Using UIMA" Authors: Claudiu Mihaila, Georgios Kontonatsios, Riza Theresa Batista-Navarro, Paul Thompson, Ioannis Korkontzelos and Sophia Ananiadou.

This paper addresses interoperability between different types of discourse annotation and also some aspects of the shared task as it uses an extension of U-compare (a graphical UIMA-based workflow platform for combining NLP resources) to compare functional discourse annotations and correlate functional discourse annotations with discourse connectives. This work addresses both annotation interoperability and also how discourse annotations interact with other types of annotation, both in the context of scientific articles and other texts. It offers a framework on which future research can be based to further annotation interoperability and investigate the interaction and synergies between different discourse components.

The winning paper received a monetary award of $2500 towards covering the authors' travel expenses and workshop registration.

The LAW VII & ID Shared Task

In the context of the challenge, we created an optional shared task to promote the comparison, alignment and interoperability of discourse annotation schemes between them and also between other annotation schemes. The shared task aimed to use scientific texts as a testbed to help participants address the goals of the challenge.

A paper was regarded as addressing the shared task when it used scientific papers to explore how discourse annotations interact, considering at least one functional discourse annotation scheme and potentially also other types of discourse annotations.

A platform for the dissemination of scientific corpora was provided, so that the same character offsets were used in each case. Links to the corresponding annotation guidelines, links to annotation tools for discourse annotation and links to visualisation tools were also provided. The corpora made available for the shared task all contain functional annotations. We are interested in how these types of annotations can be combined with traditional discourse relations covering connectives, anaphora, metonymies and such and the resulting synergies.

Collections of scientific texts were made available for download in a shared format, catering for visualizations using brat, a web-based tool for annotation visualisation and editing. Corpora released in comparable formats include:

- The BioScope Corpus,
- The GENIA corpus with meta-knowledge information for bio-events,
- The ART/CoreSC corpus,
- Chemistry AZ-II corpus (annotated with both CoreSC and AZ-II), and
- 3 papers annotated with CoreSC, Meta-Knowledge for bio-events and discourse segments.

A detailed description of the shared task along with the corresponding resources is available at `http://nactem.ac.uk/law7-id/sharedtask.html`.

The effort that went into the preparation of the material for the shared task was unfortunately not rewarded in terms of submissions received; only two papers addressed the shared task, of which only one was accepted for presentation at the workshop. We believe that the main reasons for this were the delay in releasing the shared task data and perhaps not advertising the existence of the shared task enough, since this is a first for the LAW series. The fact that one of the two shared-task related submissions won the challenge award offers some gratification, but we are hoping that more people will be able to contribute to this very interesting topic of comparing, aligning and integrating different types of annotation so as to connect together syntactic, semantic and pragmatic aspects of discourse. For this reason, we have scheduled a two hour session within the workshop itself. We will discuss the shared task and, potentially, also have some hands on experimentation with the data. This will help us envision how it could be explored for future use.

Acknowledgments

We would like to thank SIGANN for its continuing organization of the LAW series, as well as the support of the ACL 2013 workshop committee chairs, Aoife Cahill and Qun Liu. Most of all, we would like to thank all the authors for submitting their papers to the workshop and our program committee members and reviewers for their dedication and informative reviews.

Antonio, Maria and Stefanie – Workshop Chairs

Workshop Chairs (in alphabetical order):

Stefanie Dipper (Ruhr-University Bochum)
Maria Liakata (University of Warwick/European Bioinformatics Institute Cambridge)
Antonio Pareja-Lora (SIC & ILSA, UCM / ATLAS, UNED)

Organizing Committee:

Sophia Ananiadou (University of Manchester)
Cathy Blake (University of Illinois)
Alex Chengyu Fang (City University of Hong Kong)
Chu-Ren Huang (The Hong Kong Polytechnic University)
Nancy Ide (Vassar College)
Piroska Lendvai (Hungarian Academy of Sciences)
Maria Liakata (University of Warwick/European Bioinformatics Institute Cambridge)
Adam Meyers (New York University)
Anika Oellrich (Wellcome Trust Sanger Institute)
Antonio Pareja-Lora (SIC & ILSA, UCM / ATLAS, UNED)
Massimo Poesio (University of Trento)
Sameer Pradhan (BBN Technologies)
Sampo Pyysalo (University of Manchester)
Caroline Sporleder (Trier University)
Manfred Stede (Potsdam University)
Simone Teufel (University of Cambridge)
Anita de Waard (Elsevier Labs)
Fei Xia (University of Washington)
Nianwen Xue (Brandeis University)

Programme Committee:

Sophia Ananiadou (University of Manchester)
Colin Batchelor (Royal Society of Chemistry Publishing)
Cathy Blake (University of Illinois)
Johan Bos (University of Groningen)
Nicoletta Calzolari (ILC/CNR)
Steve Cassidy (Macquarie University)
Christian Chiarcos (University of Frankfurt)
Christopher Cieri (LDC/University of Pennsylvania)
Kevin Bretonnel Cohen (University of Colorado School of Medicine)
Nigel Collier (EMBL-EBI and National Institute of Informatics, Japan)
Stefanie Dipper (Ruhr-University Bochum)
Tomaz Erjavec (Josef Stefan Institute)
Alex Chengyu Fang (City University of Hong Kong)
Vanessa (Wei) Feng (University of Toronto)
Karen Fort (Loria, Équipe Sémagramme)
Yufan Guo (University of Cambridge)
Udo Hahn (Friedrich-Schiller-Universität Jena)
Graeme Hirst (University of Toronto)
Eduard Hovy (Carnegie Mellon University)

Chu-Ren Huang (Hong Kong Polytechnic)
Nancy Ide (Vassar College)
Aravind Joshi (University of Pennsylvania)
Jin-Dong Kim (University of Tokyo)
Valia Kordoni (University of Berlin)
Piroska Lendvai (Hungarian Academy of Sciences)
Maria Liakata (University of Warwick and EMBL-EBI)
Annie Louis (Univerity of Pennsylvania)
Adam Meyers (New York University)
Raheel Nawaz (University of Manchester)
Anika Oellrich (Wellcome Trust Sanger Institute)
Martha Palmer (University of Colorado)
Antonio Pareja-Lora (SIC & ILSA, UCM / ATLAS, UNED)
Massimo Poesio (University of Trento)
Sameer Pradhan (BBN Technologies)
Rashmi Prasad (University of Wisconsin-Milwaukee)
Sampo Pyysalo (University of Manchester)
Dietrich Rebholz-Schuhmann (University of Zurich and EMBL-EBI)
Agnes Sandor (Xerox Labs)
Hagit Shatkay (University of Delaware)
Caroline Sporleder (Trier University)
Manfred Stede (Potsdam University)
Simone Teufel (University of Cambridge)
Paul Thompson (University of Manchester)
Katrin Tomanek (Averbis GmbH/Germany)
Anita de Waard (Elsevier Labs)
Stephen Wan (CSIRO)
Bonnie Webber (University of Edinburgh)
Andreas Witt (IdS Mannheim)
Fei Xia (University of Washington)
Nianwen Xue (Brandeis University)
Heike Zinsmeister (University of Stuttgart)

Invited Speaker:

Christopher Manning, Natural Language Processing Group, Stanford University

Table of Contents

Conference Program

August 8, 2013

8:45-9:00	Opening Remarks
	Session 1.1: Sparse Annotations and Error Correction
9:00-9:40	Christopher Manning (invited talk): Improving the Linguistics of Linguistic Annotation: Opportunities and Limits
9:40–10:05	*Automatic Correction and Extension of Morphological Annotations* Ramy Eskander, Nizar Habash, Ann Bies, Seth Kulick and Mohamed Maamouri
10:05–10:30	*POS Tagging for Historical Texts with Sparse Training Data* Marcel Bollmann
10:30-11:00	Coffee break
	Session 1.2: Comparison and Evaluation of Annotations
11:00–11:07	*Utilizing State-of-the-art Parsers to Diagnose Problems in Treebank Annotation for a Less Resourced Language* Quy Nguyen, Ngan Nguyen and Yusuke Miyao
11:07–11:14	*Influence of preprocessing on dependency syntax annotation: speed and agreement* Arne Skjærholt
11:15–11:40	*Continuous Measurement Scales in Human Evaluation of Machine Translation* Yvette Graham, Timothy Baldwin, Alistair Moffat and Justin Zobel
11:40–12:05	*Entailment: An Effective Metric for Comparing and Evaluating Hierarchical and Non-hierarchical Annotation Schemes* Rohan Ramanath, Monojit Choudhury and Kalika Bali
12:05–12:30	*A Framework for (Under)specifying Dependency Syntax without Overloading Annotators* Nathan Schneider, Brendan O'Connor, Naomi Saphra, David Bamman, Manaal Faruqui, Noah A. Smith, Chris Dyer and Jason Baldridge
12:30-14:00	Lunch

August 8, 2013 (continued)

Session 1.3: Special Theme and Challenge - Interoperability and Discourse

14:00–14:25 *Converting Italian Treebanks: Towards an Italian Stanford Dependency Treebank*
Cristina Bosco, Simonetta Montemagni and Maria Simi

14:25–14:50 *Analyses of the Association between Discourse Relation and Sentiment Polarity with a Chinese Human-Annotated Corpus*
Hen-Hsen Huang, Chi-Hsin Yu, Tai-Wei Chang, Cong-Kai Lin and Hsin-Hsi Chen

14:50-15:15 LAW VII and ID Challenge Award:

Towards a Better Understanding of Discourse: Integrating Multiple Discourse Annotation Perspectives Using UIMA
Claudiu Mihăilă, Georgios Kontonatsios, Riza Theresa Batista-Navarro, Paul Thompson, Ioannis Korkontzelos and Sophia Ananiadou

15:15–15:22 *Making UIMA Truly Interoperable with SPARQL*
Rafal Rak and Sophia Ananiadou

15:22–15:29 *Importing MASC into the ANNIS linguistic database: A case study of mapping GrAF*
Arne Neumann, Nancy Ide and Manfred Stede

15:30-16:00 Coffee break

Session 1.4: Shared-Task

16:00-18:00 Introduction to the task and hands-on work (Maria Lakata and Sampo Pyysalo)

End of Day 1

August 9, 2013

Session 2.1: Discourse Annotation

Session 2.2: Semantic Annotation

August 9, 2013 (continued)

12:30-14:00 Lunch

Session 2.3: Novel Methods in Annotation

14:00–14:25 *The Benefits of a Model of Annotation*
Rebecca J. Passonneau and Bob Carpenter

14:25–14:50 *Ranking the annotators: An agreement study on argumentation structure*
Andreas Peldszus and Manfred Stede

14:50–15:15 *Leveraging Crowdsourcing for Paraphrase Recognition*
Martin Tschirsich and Gerold Hintz

15:15–15:40 *Investigation of annotator's behaviour using eye-tracking data*
Ryu Iida, Koh Mitsuda and Takenobu Tokunaga

15:40-16:00 Coffee break

Session 2.4: Further Discourse Papers; Posters and Demos

16:00–16:07 *Enunciative and modal variations in newswire texts in French: From guideline to automatic annotation*
Marine Damiani and Delphine Battistelli

16:07–16:14 *Annotating the Interaction between Focus and Modality: the case of exclusive particles*
Amália Mendes, Iris Hendrickx, Agostinho Salgueiro and Luciana Ávila

16:15-17:15 Posters and Demos

17:15-17:30 Concluding Remarks

Automatic Correction and Extension of Morphological Annotations

Ramy Eskander, Nizar Habash
Center for Computational Learning Systems, Columbia University
{reskander,habash}@ccls.columbia.edu

Ann Bies, Seth Kulick, Mohamed Maamouri
Linguistic Data Consortium, University of Pennsylvania
{bies,skulick,maamouri}@ldc.upenn.edu

Abstract

For languages with complex morphologies, limited resources and tools, and/or lack of standard grammars, developing annotated resources can be a challenging task. Annotated resources developed under time/money constraints for such languages tend to tradeoff depth of representation with degree of noise. We present two methods for automatic correction and extension of morphological annotations, and demonstrate their success on three divergent Egyptian Arabic corpora.

1 Introduction

Annotated corpora are essential for most research in natural language processing (NLP). For example, the development of treebanks, such as the Penn Treebank and the Penn Arabic Treebank, has been essential in pushing research on part-of-speech (POS) tagging and parsing of English and Arabic (Marcus et al., 1993; Maamouri et al., 2004). The creation of such resources tends to be quite expensive and time consuming: guidelines need to be developed, annotators hired, trained, and regularly evaluated for quality control. For languages with complex morphologies, limited resources and tools, and/or lack of standard grammars, such as any of the Dialectal Arabic (DA) varieties, developing annotated resources can be a challenging task. As a result, annotated resources developed under time/money constraints for such languages tend to tradeoff depth of representation with degree of noise. In the extremes, we find rich morphological representations that may be noisy and inconsistent or simple by highly consistent and reliable annotations that have limited usability. Furthermore, such resources are often developed by different research groups leading to many inconstancies that make pooling these resources not a very easy task.

In this paper, we describe two general techniques to address the limitations of the two types of annotations: corrections of rich noisy annotations and extensions of clean but shallow ones. We present our work on Egyptian Arabic, an important Arabic dialect with limited resources, and rich and ambiguous morphology. Resulting from this effort is the largest Egyptian Arabic corpus annotated in one common representation by pooling resources from three very different sources: a non-final, pre-release version of the ARZ[1] corpora from the Linguistic Data Consortium (LDC) (Maamouri et al., 2012g), the LDC's CallHome Egypt transcripts (Gadalla et al., 1997) and CMU's Egyptian Arabic corpus (CMUEAC) (Mohamed et al., 2012).

Although the paper focuses on Arabic, the basic problem is relevant to other languages, especially spontaneously written colloquial language forms such as those used in social media. The general solutions we propose are language independent given availability of specific language resources.

Next we discuss some related work and relevant linguistic facts (Sections 2 and 3, respectively). Section 4 presents our annotation correction technique; and Section 5 presents out annotation extension technique. Finally, Section 6 presents some statistics on the Egyptian Arabic corpus annotated in one unified representation resulting from our correction and extension work.

2 Related Work

Much work has been done on automatic spelling correction. Both supervised and unsupervised approaches have been used employing a variety of

[1] ARZ is the language code for Egyptian Arabic, http://www-01.sil.org/iso639-3/documentation.asp?id=arz

tools, resources, and heuristics, e.g., morphological analyzers, language models, annotated data and edit-distance measures, respectively (Kukich, 1992; Oflazer, 1996; Shaalan et al., 2003; Hassan et al., 2008; Kolak and Resnik, 2002; Magdy and Darwish, 2006). Our work is different from these approaches in that it extends beyond spelling of word forms to deeper annotations. However, we use some of these techniques to correct not just the words, but also malformed POS tags.

A number of efforts exist on treebank enrichment for many languages including Arabic (Palmer et al., 2008; Hovy et al., 2006; Alkuhlani and Habash, 2011; Alkuhlani et al., 2013). Our morphological extension effort is similar to Alkuhlani et al. (2013)'s work except that they start with tokenizations, reduced POS tags and dependency trees and extend them to full morphological information.

There has been a lot of work on Arabic POS tagging and morphological disambiguation (Habash and Rambow, 2005; Smith et al., 2005; Hajič et al., 2005; Habash, 2010; Habash et al., 2013). The work by Habash et al. (2013) uses one of the resources we improve on in this paper. In their work, they simply attempt to "synchronize" unknown/malformed annotations with the morphological analyzer they use, thus forcing a reading on the word to make the unknown/malformed annotation usable. In our work, we address the cleaning issue directly. We intend to make these automatic corrections and extensions available in the future so that they can be used in future disambiguation tools.

Maamouri et al. (2009) described a set of manual and automatic techniques used to improve on the quality of the Penn Arabic Treebank. Their work is most similar to ours except in the following aspects: we work only on morphology and for dialectal Arabic, whereas their work is primarily on syntax and standard Arabic. Furthermore, the challenge of malformed tags is not a major problem for them, while it is a core problem for us. Furthermore, we work with data that has partial annotations that we extend, while their work was for very rich syntax/morphology annotations.

3 Linguistic Facts

The Arabic language is a collection of variants, most prominent amongst which is Modern Standard Arabic (MSA), the official language of the media and education. The other variants, the Arabic dialects, are the day-to-day native vernaculars spoken in the Arab World. While MSA is the official language, it is not the native language of any modern day Arabic speakers. Their differences from MSA are comparable to the differences between Romance languages and Latin.[2]

Egyptian Arabic poses many challenges for NLP. Arabic in general is a morphologically complex language which includes rich inflectional morphology, expressed both templatically and affixationally, and several classes of attachable clitics. For example, the Egyptian Arabic word وهيكتبوها *wi+ha+yi-ktib-uw+hA*[3] 'and they will write it' has two proclitics (و+ *wi+* 'and' and ه+ *ha+* 'will'), one prefix ي- *yi-* '3rd person', one suffix -و *-uw* 'masculine plural' and one pronominal enclitic +ها *+hA* 'it/her'. The word is considered an inflected form of the lemma *katab* 'write [lit. he wrote]'. An important challenge for NLP work on dialectal Arabic in general is the lack of an orthographic standard. Egyptian Arabic writers are often inconsistent even in their own writing (Habash et al., 2012a), e.g., the future particle ح *Ha* appears as a separate word or as a proclitic ح+/ه+ *Ha+/ha+*, reflecting different pronunciations. Arabic orthography in general drops diacritical marks that mark short vowels and gemination. However in analyses, we want these diacritics to be indicated. Moreover, some letters in Arabic (in general) are often spelled inconsistently which leads to an increase in both sparsity (multiple forms of the same word) and ambiguity (same form corresponding to multiple words), e.g., variants of Hamzated Alif, أ Â or إ Ǎ, are often written without their Hamza (ء '): ا *A*; and the Alif-Maqsura (or dotless Ya) ى ý and the regular dotted Ya ي *y* are often used interchangeably in word final position (El Kholy and Habash, 2010). For the purposes of normalizing the representations used in computational models, we follow the work of Habash et al. (2012a) who devised a *conventional orthography for dialectal Arabic* (CODA) for use in computational processing of Arabic dialects..

An analysis of an Egyptian word for our work consists of a surface form that may not be in

[2]Habash and Rambow (2006) reported that a state-of-the-art MSA morphological analyzer has only 60% coverage of Levantine Arabic verb forms.

[3]Arabic orthographic transliteration is presented in the Habash-Soudi-Buckwalter scheme (Habash et al., 2007):
ا ب ت ث ج ح خ د ذ ر ز س ش ص ض ط ظ ع غ ف ق ك ل م ن ه و ي
A b t θ j H x d ð r z s š S D T Ď ς γ f q k l m n h w y
in addition to ' ء, Â أ, Ǎ إ, Ā آ, ŵ ؤ, ŷ ئ, ħ ة, ý ى.

CODA (henceforth, RAW), a fully diacritized CODA form (henceforth, DIAC), a morpheme split form (henceforth, MORPH), which may slightly differ from the allomorphic DIAC surface forms, a POS tag for each morpheme and stem, and a lemma (henceforth LEM). For instance, the Egyptian Arabic example used above has the following analysis:

RAW	*whyktbuwhA*
DIAC	*wiHayiktibuwhA*
MORPH	*wi+Ha+yi+ktib+uwA+hA*
POS	CONJ+FUT_PART+IV3P+IV +IVSUFF_SUBJ:3P+IVSUFF_DO:3FS
LEM	*katab*

The morphological analyzers we use in the paper, CALIMA (Habash et al., 2012b) and SAMA (Graff et al., 2009), both generate the different levels of representation discussed above.

4 Automatic Morphological Correction

In this section, we present the effort on automatic morphological correction of rich noisy annotations. We next describe the data set we work with and the problems it has. This is followed by a discussion of our approach and results including an error analysis.

4.1 Data

We use a non-final, pre-release version of six manually annotated Egyptian Arabic corpora developed by the LDC, and labeled as "ARZ", parts one through six. The published versions of these corpora (Maamouri et al., 2012a-f) do not include the annotation errors discussed in this paper. Rather, in the official releases of the data from the LDC, such problematic cases with an unknown POS tag sequence (as in the example at the end of Section 4.2) were caught and given a NO_FUNC POS tag instead, in order to allow syntactic annotation of the data to proceed, and in order to meet data publication deadlines. The combined corpus consists of about 274K words. The annotations are very detailed contextually selected morphological analyses that include for each RAW word its LEM, POS, MORPH and DIAC as described earlier. The LDC used the CALIMA[4] Egyptian Arabic morphological analyzer (Habash et al., 2012b) to provide the annotators with sets of analyses to select from.[5] CALIMA's non-lexical morphological coverage (i.e. model of affixes and stem POS combinations) is almost complete; and its lexical entries are of high precision. However, CALIMA lacks some lexical items, i.e., its lexical recall is not perfect – Habash et al. (2012b) report coverage of 84% for basic CALIMA and 92% for CALIMA extended with SAMA (Graff et al., 2009) (henceforth, CALIMA+SAMA or simply the analyzer).[6] Many missing entries are a result of spelling variants that are not modeled in CALIMA. In cases when CALIMA fails to provide analyses or the annotators disagree with all the provided analyses, the annotators enter the information manually or copy and modify CALIMA provided analyses, which sometimes introduces errors.

For the purpose of this work, we consider all analyses in the corpus that are in the CALIMA+SAMA morphological analyzer to be correct. We will not attempt to modify them. Almost 30% of the corpus analyses are *not* in the analyzer, i.e. analyzer out-of-vocabulary (OOV). We discuss next the general patterns of these analyses. We refer to the original corpus analyses as the "Baseline" analyses.

4.2 Patterns of OOV Analyses in Baseline

About 3.3% of all OOV analyses (and 1% of all corpus words) are tagged as TYPOs.[7] We do not address these cases in this paper.

Over half of the POS OOVs (56%) in the pre-release data involve a different category of a nominal (NOUN/NOUN_PROP/ADJ). This is a well known issue even in MSA. The rest of the cases involve incorrect feature combinations such as giving the unaccusative verb اتنفذ *Aitnaf∼ið* 'be performed' the POS PV_PASS (passive perfective).[8] Another example is assigning the feminine singular pronoun دي *diy* the POS DEM_PRON instead of DEM_PRON_FS. Or the imperative verb الغوا *AilguwA* 'cancel [you plural]' the POS CV+CVSUFF_SUBJ:2MS (for 'you masculine singular') instead of the correct CV+CVSUFF_SUBJ:2MP. A tiny percentage of all POS tags in the corpus (0.02%) include case-related variation (e.g. CONJ vs Conj); these add to type sparsity, but are trivial to handle.

[4]Columbia Arabic Language and dIalect Morphological Analyzer

[5]SAMA, the Standard Arabic Morphological Analyzer (Graff et al., 2009), was used to provide the annotators with analyses for the MSA tokens.

[6]In our work, we distinguish between morphological analysis, which refers to producing the various readings of a word out of context, and morphological tagging (or disambiguation), which identifies the appropriate analysis in context.

[7]The rate of TYPO words in the ARZ data is almost 18 times the rate in the MSA PATB data sets.

[8]The inflected verb *Aitnaf∼ið* is the passive voice of the verb with the lemma *naf∼að* or the active voice of the verb with the lemma *Aitnaf∼ið*.

Among LEMs and DIACs, there is considerable variation in the Arabic spelling, particularly involving the spelling of Alif/Hamza forms, the Egyptian long vowels /e:/ and /o:/ and often requiring adjustment to conform to CODA guidelines.[9] The following are some examples. Specific CODA cases include spelling كده *kidah* 'as such' as كدا *kdA* or spelling قوي *qawiy* [pronounced /awi/] 'very' as اوي *Awy*. The preposition فيه *fiyh* 'in it' is incorrectly spelled as *fiyuh* (allomorphic form is incorrect). The word بيت *bayt* 'house' is spelled *biyt* (long vowel spelling error). And finally the interjection لأ *lÂ* 'no!' is spelled as (the implausible form) لء *la'*.

Among LEMs, over 63% of the errors is due to inconsistency in assigning lemmas of punctuation and digit, a trivial challenge. 29% of the cases are spelling errors such as those discussed above. The remaining 10% are due to not following the specific format guidelines of lemmas (e.g., must be singular, uncliticized, and with a sense id number). Among DIACs, almost all of the mismatches are non-CODA-compliant spelling variations. One third is Alif/Hamza forms, and another quarter is long vowel spelling. One eighth involves diacritic choice.

Combinations of these error types occur, of course. One extreme case is the progressive particle prefix *bi*, which should be tagged as bi/PROG_PART, but appears additionally as b/PROG_PART, ba/PROG_PART, bi/PART_PROG, bi/PRO_PART, and bi/FUT_PART.

Example For the rest of this section, we consider the example word حيأجلوا *HyÂjlwA* 'and they will postpone'. Figure 1 contrasts an erroneous analysis in the pre-release data with a corrected version of it. There are multiple problems in this example. First, the POS tag is both internally inconsistent and is inconsistent with the MORPH choice. The POS has a singular subject prefix (IV3MS) and a plural subject suffix (IVSUFF_SUBJ:P); and the plural subject suffix is written using the morpheme (*+uh*), which corresponds to a direct object enclitic. The two morphemes, *+uh* and *+uwA*, are homophonous, which is the most likely cause for this error. Second, the future marker (*Ha+*) is written in a non-CODA-compliant way (*ha+*) in the analysis. And finally, the lemma is malformed, containing multiple extra sense id digits. It is important to point out that there are multiple ways to correct the analysis. For example, it can be *Ha+yi+Âaj~il+uh* FUT_PART+IV3MS+IV+IVSUFF_DO:3MS 'he will postpone it'.[10]

4.3 Approach

Our target is to provide correct morphological analyses for the OOV annotations in the pre-release version of the ARZ corpus. Since not all of the OOV annotations are wrong in principle, we do not force map them all to CALIMA+SAMA in-vocabulary variants, especially for open class categories, where we know CALIMA+SAMA may be deficient. As such, our general solution focuses on correcting closed classes (some stems and all of the affixes) by mapping them to in-vocabulary variants. We also use a set of language-specific preprocessing corrections for common orthographic variations (for all open and closed classes). An important tool we use throughout to rank choices and break ties is modified Levenshtein edit distance.[11]

Next, we present the four steps of our correction process: annotation preprocessing, morpheme-POS correction, lemma correction and surface DIAC generation.

Annotation Preprocessing When first reading the pre-release annotations, we perform a preprocessing step that includes a set of deterministic corrections for common non-CODA-compliant orthographic variations and errors, and POS tagging typos. The corrections apply to the POS tags, lemmas, morphemes and surface forms. Examples of these corrections include the following: reordering diacritics, e.g., *saji~l* → *saj~il*; removing duplicate diacritics, e.g., *saj~iil* → *saj~il*; adjusting Alif-Hamza forms to match the diacritics that fol-

[9]LDC annotators were not asked to comply with CODA guidelines during the annotation task. Therefore, multiple spelling variants for OOV Egyptian Arabic words were to be expected.

[10]Since our approach currently considers words out of context, such a correction is not preferred because it requires more character edits (see Figure 2). We acknowledge this to be a limitation and plan to address it in the future.

[11]The Levenshtein edit distance is defined as the minimum number of single-character edits (insertion, deletion and substitution) required to change one string into the other. For Arabic words and morphemes, we modify the cost of substitutions involving two phonologically or orthographically similar letters to count as half edits. We acquire the list of such letter substitutions from Eskander et al. (2013), who report them as the most frequent source of errors in Egyptian Arabic orthography. We map all diacritic-only morphemes to empty morphemes in both ways at a cost of half edit also. For POS tag edit distance, we use the standard definition of Levenshtein edit distance. Edit cost is an area where a lot of tuning could be done and we plan to explore it in the future.

RAW	هياجلو *hyAjlw*	
Analysis	**Incorrect Annotation**	**Correct Annotation**
DIAC	*hayiÂaj∼iluh*	*HayiÂaj∼iluwA*
MORPH	*ha+yi+Âaj∼il+uh*	*Ha+yi+Âaj∼il+uwA*
POS	FUT_PART+IV3MS+IV+IVSUFF_SUBJ:P	FUT_PART+IV3P+IV+IVSUFF_SUBJ:P
LEM	*Âaj∼ill1*	*Âaj∼il_1*

Figure 1: An incorrect annotation example with a possible correction.

low them, e.g., *ǍaSl* → *ÂaSl*; and POS tag capitalization, e.g., Fut_Part → FUT_PART.

Morpheme-POS Correction For morpheme correction purposes, we define an abstract representation that combines all the closed-class morphemes and POS tags. For open-class stems, we simply use the POS tag. For example, the abstract morpheme representation for the correct version of the word in Figure 1 is *Ha/FUT_PART+yi/IV3P+IV+uwA/IVSUFF_SUBJ:P*. We will refer to this representation as the inflectional morph-tag (IMT).

We build two models for this task. First, we build an IMT language model from the CALIMA+SAMA databases. This models all possible inflections in the analyzer without the open class stems. This model includes 304K sequences. Second, we construct a map from all the seen IMTs in the ARZ corpus to all the in-vocabulary IMTs in the IMT language model. The mapping includes a cost that is based on the edit distance discussed earlier. Figure 2 shows the top mappings for the IMTs in our example. Both models are implemented as finite state machines using the ATT FSM toolkit (Mohri et al., 1998).

The input, possibly incorrect, IMT is converted into an FSM that is then composed with the mapping transducer and the language model automaton to generate a cost-ranked list of mappings. The output for our example is listed in Figure 3. We then replace the input POS and MORPH with the top ranked correction: *Ha/FUT_PART+yi/IV3MS+IV+uh/IVSUFF_SUBJ:P* at a cost of 4.0. The open class stem is not modified.

Lemma Correction We generate a map that includes all the possible lemmas for every possible stem morpheme in CALIMA+SAMA. For a given ARZ word analysis, if the stem morpheme is in CALIMA+SAMA, then we pick the lemma from its corresponding lemma set. When there is more than one possible lemma, we pick the lemma that is closest to the provided pre-release ARZ lemma, based on their string edit distance as defined earlier. If the stem morpheme is not in CALIMA+SAMA (e.g., open class), then we keep the ARZ lemma as it is.

Base IMT Morpheme	Mapped IMT Morphemes	Cost
ha/FUT_PART	Ha/FUT_PART	0.5
	sa/FUT_PART	1.0
yi/IV3MS	yi/IV3MS	0.0
	ya/IV3MS	1.0
	y/IV3MS	1.0
	yu/IV3MS	1.0
	yi/IV3P	2.0
IV	IV	0.0
	PV	1.0
	CV	1.0
uh/IVSUFF_SUBJ:P	uwA/IVSUFF_SUBJ:P	1.5
	na/IVSUFF_SUBJ:FP	3.0

Figure 2: Top mappings for the IMT morphemes ha/FUT_PART, yi/IV3P, IV and uh/IVSUFF_SUBJ:P

Input: *ha/FUT_PART+yi/IV3P+IV+uh/IVSUFF_SUBJ:P*	
FSM Output	**Cost**
Ha/FUT_PART+yi/IV3P+IV+uwA/IVSUFF_SUBJ:P	4.0
Ha/FUT_PART+y/IV3P+IV+uwA/IVSUFF_SUBJ:P	5.0
Ha/FUT_PART+ti/IV2P+IV+uwA/IVSUFF_SUBJ:P	6.0
Ha/FUT_PART+yi/IV3MS+IV+uh/IVSUFF_DO:3MS	6.5
Ha/FUT_PART+yi/IV3MS+IV+kuw/IVSUFF_DO:2P	7.0
Ha/FUT_PART+yi/IV3MS+IV+nA/IVSUFF_DO:1P	7.0
Ha/FUT_PART+tu/IV2P+IV+uwA/IVSUFF_SUBJ:P	7.0
sa/FUT_PART+ya/IV3FP+IV+na/IVSUFF_SUBJ:FP	7.0
sa/FUT_PART+yu/IV3FP+IV+na/IVSUFF_SUBJ:FP	7.0
Ha/FUT_PART+yi/IV3MS+IV+kum/IVSUFF_DO:2P	7.5

Figure 3: Top corrections for the input ha/FUT_PART+yi/IV3P+IV+uh/IVSUFF_SUBJ:P

In our example, the stem morpheme *Âaj∼il/IV* is paired in CALIMA+SAMA with the lemma *Âaj∼il_1*. Accordingly, *Âaj∼il_1* replaces the input pre-release ARZ lemma.

Surface DIAC Generation After correcting the morphemes and POS tags in the input word, we use them to generate a new surface DIAC form. For all the closed-class morphemes and in-vocabulary open-class stems, we use CALIMA+SAMA to identify all the MORPH+POS to DIAC mappings. For open-class stems that are

OOVs, we use their corresponding DIAC form in the input word.[12] This may lead to many possible sequences. We rank them by their edit distance (defined above) to the surface DIAC of the input word.

In our example, this process is rather trivial: every morpheme is paired with only one surface DIAC in the morphological analyzer. The surface DIACs corresponding to *Ha/FUT_PART*, *yi/IV3P*, *Âaj∼il/IV* and *uwA/IVSUFF_SUBJ:P* are *Ha*, *yi*, *Âaj∼il* and *uwA*, respectively. The final combined surface is *HayiÂaj∼iluwA*.

A more interesting example is the word علينا *ςalay+nA* 'upon us' which has the analysis *ςalaý*/PREP+*nA*/PRON_1P. The MORPH stem *ςalaý* has two DIAC forms: *ςalaý* and *ςalay*. The second form is only used when an enclitic is present. It is selected in this example because it has a smaller edit distance to the full word input DIAC form than the surface stem *ςalaý*. In the future, we plan to use more sophisticated generation and detokenization techniques (El Kholy and Habash, 2010).

4.4 Results and Error Analysis

Results We conducted a manual evaluation for 1,000 words from the internal, pre-release ARZ after applying the automatic correction process. This set is a blind test set, i.e., not used as part of the development. The results are listed in Table 1 for the lemmas, POS tags, diacritized morphemes and diacritized surface forms, in addition to the complete morphological analyses (token-based), where the correction output is compared to the pre-release ARZ annotations (the baseline).

The results are listed for different subsets of the data. The first row lists the results considering the complete 1,000 words, where all the in-vocabulary words are considered correct. This is only intended to give an overall estimate of the correctness of the set. The second row lists the results for CALIMA+SAMA OOV words only. The third row is the same as the second, but excluding punctuations, digits and typos. Focusing on the last row, we see that we achieve between 58% and 24% error reduction on different features, and reach almost 40% error reduction on all features combined.

Error Analysis For POS, 99.7% of all the correct cases in the Baseline were not changed. Only one case was changed and it was caused by an error in the input MORPH splits. Of the erroneous cases in the Baseline, 40% were not changed. Among the attempted changes, 71% successfully fixed the baseline problem. Almost all of the failed changes are due to implausible null pronouns in the Baseline that were not handled in the current implementation, which only considered correct null pronouns. We plan to address these in the future. Among the errors that were not addressed, the most common case involves nominal form (41%) followed by hard features to resolve and open class passive-voice inconsistency (each 27%).

Regarding lemmas, 93.9% of all correct baseline lemmas remained correct. In the rest, over-correction attempts resulting from matching the OOV lemma to the wrong in-vocabulary lemma backfired. Around 8.7% of the erroneous baseline lemmas were not modified and 1.6% were modified incorrectly. The rest, 92.8%, were successfully fixed. Almost all of the system errors resulting from changes involve over correction by mapping to incorrect INV lemma forms.

Finally, as for diacritized forms, 96.9% of the correct baseline DIACs remained correct; the rest fell victim to over-correction. Among incorrect baseline cases, 43% remained unchanged; and 45% were fixed; 4% were over-corrected and 8% only partially corrected. Remaining DIAC errors are mostly in open classes where the analyzer recall problems cannot help.

5 Automatic Morphological Extension

In this section, we present the general technique we use to extend shallow annotations. We discuss the data sets, the approach and evaluation results next.

5.1 Data

We conduct our experiments on two different Egyptian Arabic corpora: the CALLHOME Egypt (CHE) corpus (Gadalla et al., 1997) and Carnegie Mellon University Egyptian Arabic corpus (CMUEAC) (Mohamed et al., 2012).

CHE The CHE corpus contains 140 telephone conversation transcripts of about 179K words. Each word is represented by its phonological form and undiacritized Arabic script orthography. The orthography used is quite similar to the CODA standard we use. Being a transcript corpus, it is quite clean and free of spelling variations. We use a technique described in more detail in Habash et

[12]Since the surface DIAC splits are not provided, we determine the exact boundary of the surface DIAC stem by minimizing the edit distance between the prefixing/suffixing morphemes and the full input surface DIAC form.

		Lem	POS	Morph	Diac	POS +Morph	**All**
All words	Baseline	79.8%	93.2%	92.2%	91.1%	87.3%	72.7%
	System	95.7%	95.5%	93.8%	93.6%	91.5%	90.0%
Analyzer OOV	Baseline	47.1%	82.4%	79.7%	76.8%	66.8%	28.4%
	System	88.9%	88.42%	83.9%	83.4%	77.9%	73.9%
Analyzer OOV, no Punc/Digit/Typos	Baseline	71.3%	82.5%	74.1%	69.7%	59.0%	43.0%
	System	88.0%	87.3%	80.5%	79.7%	71.3%	65.3%

Table 1: Accuracy of the automatic morphological correction of internal, pre-release ARZ data.

al. (2012b) to combine the phonological form and undiacritized Arabic script into diacritized Arabic script, i.e. Diac. For example, the undiacritized word عينه *ςynh* 'his eye' is combined with its pronunciation /ςe:nu/ producing the diacritized form *ςaynuh*.

CMUEAC The CMUEAC corpus includes about 23K words that are only annotated for morph splits. The corpus text includes spontaneously written Egyptian Arabic text collected off the web. To use the same example as above, the word عينه *ςynh* 'his eye' is segmented as *ςyn+h* indicating that there is a base word plus an enclitic.

5.2 Approach

Our approach to morphological extension is to automatically annotate the corpus using a very rich morphological tagger, and then use the limited manual annotations to adjust the morphological choice. We use a morphological tagger, MADA-ARZ (Morphological Analysis and Disambiguation for Egyptian Arabic) (Habash et al., 2013). MADA-ARZ produces, for each input word, a contextually ranked list of analyses specifying all the morphological interpretations of that word as provided by the CALIMA+SAMA morphological analyzer.

CHE In the case of CHE, we select the first choice from the ranked list of analyses whose Diac matches the diacritized word in CHE. For example, for the word عينه *ςynh* MADA-ARZ generates 45 different morphological analyses with different lemmas, POS, orthographies and diacritics: *ςayn+uh* 'his eye', *ςay∼in+ah̄* 'sample' and *ςay∼in+uh* 'he appointed him'. The diacritized word *ςayn+uh* allows us to select the following full analysis:

Metric	**CHE**	**CMUEAC**
Lem	97.2	82.0
POS	95.2	79.6
Morph	96.8	77.6
Diac	97.2	78.4
POS+Morph	92.8	74.0
All	92.8	72.0

Table 2: Accuracy of automatic morphological extension of CHE and CMUEAC.

Raw	*Eynh*
Diac	*Eaynuh*
Morph	*Eayn+uh*
POS	NOUN+POSS_PRON_3MS
Lem	*Eayn_1*

Although this example may not require the full power of a tagger, but just the out-of-context analyzer, other cases involving POS ambiguity unrealized through diacritization necessitate the use of a tagger, e.g., the word كاتب *kAtib* can be an ADJ meaning 'writing' or a NOUN meaning 'writer/author'.

CMUEAC In the case of CMUEAC, we select the first choice from the ranked list of analyses whose undiacritized Morph splits match the word tokenization. In the case of the word عينه *ςyn+h*, the tokenization cannot distinguish between the noun reading *ςayn+uh* 'his eye' and the verbal reading *ςay∼in+uh* 'he appointed him'. MADA-ARZ effectively selects in such cases. We expect the performance on CMUEAC to be worse than CHE given the difference in the amount of information between the two corpora.

5.3 Results and Error Analysis

We evaluate the accuracy of the morphological extension process on both CHE and CMUEAC using two 300 word samples that were manually enriched. Table 2 presents the accuracies of the assigned Lems, POS tags, Diac forms and

MORPHS, in addition to the complete morphological analysis. All results are token-based.

CHE CHE analyses have high accuracies ranging between 95.2% and 97.2% for the different analysis features, with the complete analysis having an accuracy of 92.8%. One third of the errors is due to gold diacritization errors in the CHE corpus. 28% of the errors are due to wrong verbal features (person, number and gender) for forms that are not distinguishable in DIAC, e.g., كتبت *katabt* 'I/you wrote' and تكتب *tiktib* 'you write/she writes'. The rest of the errors are because of failure in assigning the correct POS tags for nouns, particles and verbs with percentages of 22%, 11% and 6%, respectively.

CMUEAC CMUEAC analyses have much lower accuracies compared to CHE, ranging between 77.6% and 82.0% for different features, with the complete analysis accuracy at 72.0%. The CMUEAC is much harder to extend for two reasons: the text, being naturally occurring, contains a lot of orthographic noise; and tokenization information is not sufficient to disambiguate many analyses. For CMUEAC, a quarter of the errors is due to gold tokenization errors in the original CMUEAC corpus. Another quarter of the errors results from MADA-ARZ assigning an MSA analysis instead of an Egyptian Arabic analysis.[13] Failure to assign the correct POS tags for particles, verbs and nouns represents 14%, 10% and 7% of the errors, respectively. Other errors are because of wrong verbal features (13%) and wrong diacritization (6%).

As expected, relatively richer annotations (i.e., diacritics) are easier to extend to full morphological information that relatively poorer annotations (i.e., tokenization). Of course, the tradeoff is still there as tokenizations are much easier and cheaper to annotate. We plan to explore the question of what would be an optimal set of poor annotations that can help us extend to the full morphology at high accuracy in the future.

6 Egyptian Corpus

After applying morphological corrections to pre-release ARZ and morphological extensions to CHE and CMUEAC, we have now three big corpora that are automatically adjusted to include the same rich morphological information, that is: lemma, POS tag, diacritized morphemes, and diacritized surface. We combine the three resources together in one morphologically rich corpus that contains about 46K sentences and 447K words, representing 61K unique lemmas. We intend to make these automatic corrections and extensions available in the future to provide extensive support for Egyptian Arabic processing for different purposes.

7 Conclusion and Future Work

We presented two methods for automatic correction and extension of morphological annotations and demonstrated their success on three different Egyptian Arabic corpora, which now have annotations that are automatically adjusted to include the same rich morphological information although at different degrees of quality that correspond to the amount of initial information.

We presented two methods for automatic correction and extension of morphological annotations and demonstrated their success on three different Egyptian Arabic corpora, which now have annotations that are automatically adjusted to include the same rich morphological information although at different degrees of quality that correspond to the amount of initial information.

In the future, we plan to study how to optimize the amount of basic information to annotate manually in order to maximize the benefit of automatic extensions. We also plan to provide feedback to the annotation process to reduce the percentage of errors generated by the annotators, perhaps through a tighter integration of the correction/extension techniques with the annotation process. We also plan on using the cleaned up corpus to extend the existing analyzer for Egyptian Arabic.

Acknowledgment

This paper is based upon work supported by the Defense Advanced Research Projects Agency (DARPA) under contracts No. HR0011-12-C-0014 and HR0011-11-C-0145. Any opinions, findings and conclusions or recommendations expressed in this paper are those of the authors and do not necessarily reflect the views of DARPA. We also would like to thank Emad Mohamed and Kemal Oflazer for providing us with the CMUEAC corpus. We thank Ryan Roth for help with MADA-ARZ. Finally, we thank Owen Rambow, Mona Diab and Warren Churchill for helpful discussions.

[13] MADA-ARZ is trained on a combination of MSA and Egyptian Arabic text and as such may select an MSA analysis in cases that are ambiguous.

References

Sarah Alkuhlani and Nizar Habash. 2011. A Corpus for Modeling Morpho-Syntactic Agreement in Arabic: Gender, Number and Rationality. In *Proceedings of the 49th Annual Meeting of the Association for Computational Linguistics (ACL'11)*, Portland, Oregon, USA.

Sarah Alkuhlani, Nizar Habash, and Ryan Roth. 2013. Automatic morphological enrichment of a morphologically underspecified treebank. In *Proceedings of the 2013 Conference of the North American Chapter of the Association for Computational Linguistics: Human Language Technologies*, pages 460–470, Atlanta, Georgia, June. Association for Computational Linguistics.

Ahmed El Kholy and Nizar Habash. 2010. Techniques for Arabic Morphological Detokenization and Orthographic Denormalization. In *Proceedings of the seventh International Conference on Language Resources and Evaluation (LREC)*, Valletta, Malta.

Ramy Eskander, Nizar Habash, Owen Rambow, and Nadi Tomeh. 2013. Processing spontaneous orthography. In *Proceedings of the 2013 Conference of the North American Chapter of the Association for Computational Linguistics: Human Language Technologies*, pages 585–595, Atlanta, Georgia, June. Association for Computational Linguistics.

Hassan Gadalla, Hanaa Kilany, Howaida Arram, Ashraf Yacoub, Alaa El-Habashi, Amr Shalaby, Krisjanis Karins, Everett Rowson, Robert MacIntyre, Paul Kingsbury, David Graff, and Cynthia McLemore. 1997. CALLHOME Egyptian Arabic Transcripts. In *Linguistic Data Consortium, Philadelphia*.

David Graff, Mohamed Maamouri, Basma Bouziri, Sondos Krouna, Seth Kulick, and Tim Buckwalter. 2009. Standard Arabic Morphological Analyzer (SAMA) Version 3.1. Linguistic Data Consortium LDC2009E73.

Nizar Habash and Owen Rambow. 2005. Arabic Tokenization, Part-of-Speech Tagging and Morphological Disambiguation in One Fell Swoop. In *Proceedings of the 43rd Annual Meeting of the Association for Computational Linguistics (ACL'05)*, pages 573–580, Ann Arbor, Michigan.

Nizar Habash and Owen Rambow. 2006. MAGEAD: A Morphological Analyzer and Generator for the Arabic Dialects. In *Proceedings of the 21st International Conference on Computational Linguistics and 44th Annual Meeting of the Association for Computational Linguistics*, pages 681–688, Sydney, Australia.

Nizar Habash, Abdelhadi Soudi, and Tim Buckwalter. 2007. On Arabic Transliteration. In A. van den Bosch and A. Soudi, editors, *Arabic Computational Morphology: Knowledge-based and Empirical Methods*. Springer.

Nizar Habash, Mona Diab, and Owen Rabmow. 2012a. Conventional Orthography for Dialectal Arabic. In *Proceedings of the Language Resources and Evaluation Conference (LREC)*, Istanbul.

Nizar Habash, Ramy Eskander, and Abdelati Hawwari. 2012b. A Morphological Analyzer for Egyptian Arabic. In *NAACL-HLT 2012 Workshop on Computational Morphology and Phonology (SIGMORPHON2012)*, pages 1–9, Montréal, Canada.

Nizar Habash, Ryan Roth, Owen Rambow, Ramy Eskander, and Nadi Tomeh. 2013. Morphological Analysis and Disambiguation for Dialectal Arabic. In *Proceedings of the 2013 Conference of the North American Chapter of the Association for Computational Linguistics: Human Language Technologies (NAACL-HLT)*, Atlanta, GA.

Nizar Habash. 2010. *Introduction to Arabic Natural Language Processing*. Morgan & Claypool Publishers.

Jan Hajič, Otakar Smrž, Tim Buckwalter, and Hubert Jin. 2005. Feature-based tagger of approximations of functional Arabic morphology. In *Proceedings of the Workshop on Treebanks and Linguistic Theories (TLT)*, Barcelona, Spain.

Ahmed Hassan, Sara Noeman, and Hany Hassan. 2008. Language Independent Text Correction using Finite State Automata. In *Proceedings of the International Joint Conference on Natural Language Processing (IJCNLP 2008)*.

Eduard Hovy, Mitchell Marcus, Martha Palmer, Lance Ramshaw, and Ralph Weischedel. 2006. OntoNotes: The 90% Solution. In *NAACL '06: Proceedings of the Human Language Technology Conference of the NAACL, Companion Volume: Short Papers on XX*, pages 57–60, Morristown, NJ, USA.

Okan Kolak and Philip Resnik. 2002. OCR error correction using a noisy channel model. In *Proceedings of the second international conference on Human Language Technology Research*.

Karen Kukich. 1992. Techniques for Automatically Correcting Words in Text. *ACM Computing Surveys*, 24(4).

Mohamed Maamouri, Ann Bies, Tim Buckwalter, and Wigdan Mekki. 2004. The Penn Arabic Treebank: Building a Large-Scale Annotated Arabic Corpus. In *NEMLAR Conference on Arabic Language Resources and Tools*, pages 102–109, Cairo, Egypt.

Mohamed Maamouri, Ann Bies, and Seth Kulick. 2009. Creating a methodology for large-scale correction of treebank annotation: The case of the arabic treebank. In *MEDAR Second International Conference on Arabic Language Resources and Tools, Egypt*. Citeseer.

Mohamed Maamouri, Ann Bies, Seth Kulick, Sondos Krouna, Dalila Tabassi, and Michael Ciul. 2012a. Egyptian Arabic Treebank DF Part 1 V2.0. LDC catalog number LDC2012E93.

Mohamed Maamouri, Ann Bies, Seth Kulick, Sondos Krouna, Dalila Tabassi, and Michael Ciul. 2012b. Egyptian Arabic Treebank DF Part 2 V2.0. LDC catalog number LDC2012E98.

Mohamed Maamouri, Ann Bies, Seth Kulick, Sondos Krouna, Dalila Tabassi, and Michael Ciul. 2012c. Egyptian Arabic Treebank DF Part 3 V2.0. LDC catalog number LDC2012E89.

Mohamed Maamouri, Ann Bies, Seth Kulick, Sondos Krouna, Dalila Tabassi, and Michael Ciul. 2012d. Egyptian Arabic Treebank DF Part 4 V2.0. LDC catalog number LDC2012E99.

Mohamed Maamouri, Ann Bies, Seth Kulick, Sondos Krouna, Dalila Tabassi, and Michael Ciul. 2012e. Egyptian Arabic Treebank DF Part 5 V2.0. LDC catalog number LDC2012E107.

Mohamed Maamouri, Ann Bies, Seth Kulick, Sondos Krouna, Dalila Tabassi, and Michael Ciul. 2012f. Egyptian Arabic Treebank DF Part 6 V2.0. LDC catalog number LDC2012E125.

Mohamed Maamouri, Sondos Krouna, Dalila Tabessi, Nadia Hamrouni, and Nizar Habash. 2012g. Egyptian Arabic Morphological Annotation Guidelines.

Walid Magdy and Kareem Darwish. 2006. Arabic OCR Error Correction Using Character Segment Correction, Language Modeling, and Shallow Morphology. In *Proceedings of 2006 Conference on Empirical Methods in Natural Language Processing (EMNLP 2006)*, pages 408–414, Sydney, Austrailia.

Mitchell P. Marcus, Beatrice Santorini, and Mary Ann Marcinkiewicz. 1993. Building a large annotated corpus of English: The Penn treebank. *Computational Linguistics*, 19(2):313–330, June.

Emad Mohamed, Behrang Mohit, and Kemal Oflazer. 2012. Annotating and Learning Morphological Segmentation of Egyptian Colloquial Arabic. In *Proceedings of the Language Resources and Evaluation Conference (LREC)*, Istanbul.

Mehryar Mohri, Fernando C. N. Pereira, and Michael Riley. 1998. A rational design for a weighted finite-state transducer library. In D. Wood and S. Yu, editors, *Automata Implementation*, Lecture Notes in Computer Science 1436, pages 144–58. Springer.

Kemal Oflazer. 1996. Error-tolerant finite-state recognition with applications to morphological analysis and spelling correction. *Computational Linguistics*, 22:73–90.

Martha Palmer, Olga Babko-Malaya, Ann Bies, Mona Diab, Mohamed Maamouri, Aous Mansouri, and Wajdi Zaghouani. 2008. A Pilot Arabic Propbank. In *Proceedings of LREC*, Marrakech, Morocco, May.

Khaled Shaalan, Amin Allam, and Abdallah Gomah. 2003. Towards Automatic Spell Checking for Arabic. In *Conference on Language Engineering, ELSE*, Cairo, Egypt.

Noah Smith, David Smith, and Roy Tromble. 2005. Context-Based Morphological Disambiguation with Random Fields. In *Proceedings of the 2005 Conference on Empirical Methods in Natural Language Processing (EMNLP05)*, pages 475–482, Vancouver, Canada.

POS Tagging for Historical Texts with Sparse Training Data

Marcel Bollmann
Department of Linguistics, Ruhr University Bochum
bollmann@linguistics.rub.de

Abstract

This paper presents a method for part-of-speech tagging of historical data and evaluates it on texts from different corpora of historical German (15th–18th century). Spelling normalization is used to preprocess the texts before applying a POS tagger trained on modern German corpora. Using only 250 manually normalized tokens as training data, the tagging accuracy of a manuscript from the 15th century can be raised from 28.65% to 74.89%.

1 Introduction[1]

Part-of-speech (POS) tagging of modern language data is a well-explored field, commonly achieving accuracies around 97% (Brants, 2000; Schmid and Laws, 2008). For historical language varieties, the situation is worse, as specialized taggers are typically not available. As an example, a study by Scheible et al. (2011a) reports an average tagging accuracy of 69.6% for Early Modern German texts. However, with projects to create historical corpora being on the rise (Sánchez-Marco et al., 2010; Scheible et al., 2011b, are recent examples), the need for more accurate tagging methods on these types of data increases.

A common approach for historical texts is to use spelling normalization to map historical wordforms to modern ones (Baron and Rayson, 2008; Jurish, 2010). Manually normalized data was found to improve POS tagging accuracy for a variety of languages such as German, English, and Portuguese, with accuracies between 79% and 91% (Scheible et al., 2011a; Rayson et al., 2007; Hendrickx and Marquilhas, 2011).

[1]I would like to thank the anonymous reviewers for their helpful comments. The research reported here was supported by Deutsche Forschungsgemeinschaft (DFG), Grants DI 1558/4-1 and DI 1558/5-1.

This paper presents results for POS tagging of historical German from 1400 to 1770, classified here as Early New High German (ENHG), using automatic spelling normalization to preprocess the data for a POS tagger trained on modern German corpora. To train the normalization tool, short fragments of a few hundred tokens are used for each text. This approach allows for a better adaptation to the individual spelling characteristics of each text while requiring only small amounts of training data. Additionally, different ways to deal with typical obstacles for processing historical texts (e.g., inconsistent use of punctuation) are compared.

The structure of this paper is as follows. Sec. 2 presents the historical texts used for the evaluation. Sec. 3 describes the approach to normalization, while Sec. 4 discusses problems and results of POS tagging on normalized data. Sec. 5 presents related work, and Sec. 6 concludes.

2 Corpora

This study considers texts from two corpora of historical German: the Anselm corpus (Dipper and Schultz-Balluff, 2013) and the GerManC-GS corpus (Scheible et al., 2011b).

The Anselm corpus consists of more than 50 different versions of a medieval religious treatise written up in various German dialects. As the creation of gold-standard annotations for the corpus is still in progress, only two texts are used here: a manuscript in an Eastern Upper German dialect kept in Melk, Austria; and an Eastern Central German manuscript kept in Berlin. Both manuscripts are dated to the 15th century.

The GerManC-GS corpus aims to be a representative subcorpus of GerManC with additional gold-standard annotations. It contains texts from Early Modern German categorized by genre, region, and time period. For this study, the three texts of the genre "sermon" are used. They are

Corpus	Date	Name	Tokens
Anselm	15c	Berlin	5,399
	15c	Melk	4,783
GerManC-GS	1677	LeichSermon	2,585
	1730	JubelFeste	2,523
	1770	Gottesdienst	2,292

Table 1: Texts used for the evaluation

dated from 1677 to 1770, which makes them considerably newer than the Anselm texts. Table 1 gives an overview of all texts used here.

All texts are manually annotated with normalizations and POS tags. In the normalization layer, tokens are mapped to modern German equivalents. The normalization schemes are not identical, but roughly comparable for both GerManC-GS and Anselm (see Scheible et al. (2011b) and Bollmann et al. (2012) for details). In both corpora, POS tagging follows the STTS tagset (Schiller et al., 1999) without morphological information, though some additional tags were introduced in GerManC-GS. For our evaluation, they are mapped back to standard STTS tags; this mapping only affects 80 tokens from all three texts.

Additionally, both corpora are annotated with modern punctuation and sentence boundaries; however, while modern punctuation is a separate annotation layer in Anselm, there is always a 1:1 correspondence between historical and modern (i.e., normalized) punctuation marks in GerManC-GS.

Finally, both corpora preserve many spelling characteristics of the original manuscripts, e.g., superposition of characters such as *ů*, or abbreviation marks such as the nasal bar (as in *v̄*). Before any further processing, all wordforms are simplified to plain alphabetic characters; e.g., *ů* is mapped to *uo*. For some abbreviation marks in the Anselm corpus, there is no clear "best" simplification: the nasal bar is a prime example here, which should be simplified most appropriately to *e*, *(e)n*, *(e)m*, or nothing, either before or after the letter on which it is placed, depending on context. In these cases, manually defined heuristics were used to guess the most appropriate mapping. As capitalization is not used consistently in the texts, all letters were additionally lowercased.

3 Normalization

Spelling normalization is performed using the Norma tool (Bollmann, 2012). It implements a chain of normalization methods—to the effect that methods further down the chain are only called if previous ones failed to produce a result—in the following order: (1) wordlist mapping; (2) rule-based normalization; and (3) weighted Levenshtein distance.

Wordlist mapping considers simple 1:1 mappings of historical wordforms to modern ones (e.g., *vnd* → *und* "and"), while rule-based normalization applies context-sensitive character rewrite rules (e.g., transform *v* to *u* between a word boundary and *n*) to an input string from left to right. Weighted Levenshtein distance assigns individual weights to character replacements (e.g., *v* → *u*), and performs normalization by retrieving the wordform from a modern lexicon which can be derived from the historical input wordform with the lowest cost, i.e., using a sequence of edit operations with the lowest sum of weights.

3.1 Normalization procedure

All normalization algorithms described above require some kind of parametrization to work (i.e., a wordlist; rewrite rules; Levenshtein weights). These parametrizations are neither hard-coded nor manually defined, but are derived automatically by the Norma tool from a set of manually normalized training data. For this purpose, short samples from the text to be normalized are used; i.e., training set and evaluation set are always disjoint parts of the same text. The reasons for choosing this approach lie in the individual spelling characteristics of the texts—the following examples show excerpts from Berlin, Melk, and LeichSermon, respectively, along with their (gold-standard) normalizations:

(1) *dyn lybes kynt*
dein liebes kind
"your dear child"

(2) *mein liebs chind*
mein liebes kind
"my dear child"

(3) *eins ihrer andern kinder*
eins ihrer anderen kinder
"one of their other children"

Text	Baseline	Normalizations			
		100	250	500	1,000
Berlin	23.05%	68.99%	75.02%	79.14%	81.83%
Melk	39.32%	69.10%	74.39%	75.74%	77.98%
LeichSermon	72.71%	77.96%	80.51%	82.85%	87.23%
JubelFeste	79.47%	88.50%	89.98%	91.87%	93.13%
Gottesdienst	83.41%	93.77%	95.24%	95.27%	95.56%

Table 2: Normalization accuracy after training on *n* tokens and evaluating on 1,000 tokens (average of 10 random training and evaluation sets), compared to the "baseline" score of the full text without any normalization

The first two examples, while both dated to the 15th century, show quite different spellings of the modern *Kind* "child": Ex. (1) shows the frequent use of *y* for modern *ei* or *i(e)*, while Ex. (2) demonstrates the frequent spelling *ch* for *k*. These differences are likely a cause of the different dialectal regions from which the manuscripts originate, but could also be attributed, at least in parts, to individual preferences by the manuscripts' writers. The LeichSermon text from 1677 in Ex. (3), on the other hand, already has the modern German spelling *Kind*.

Given this range of spelling variations, it seems implausible to achieve good normalization results using the same parametrization for each of the texts. Furthermore, for the older manuscripts showing more variation such as in Ex. (1), it is unclear what other training data could be used. The full GerManC-GS consists of texts from 1650 to 1800, while Jurish (2010) uses a corpus of German texts from 1780 to 1880; these texts are all considerably newer, consequently having less spelling variation than the Anselm texts. This lack of appropriate training data applies similarly to all kinds of less-resourced language varieties.

Therefore, while this approach requires slightly more effort for manually normalizing parts of the texts beforehand, it does not depend on the availability of a large training corpus or a specialized tool for the language variety to be processed.

3.2 Evaluation

Normalization is evaluated separately for each text, using a part of that text for training and evaluating on a different part of the same text. To address the question of how much training data is needed, evaluation is performed with different sizes of the training set in a range between 100 and 1,000 tokens. The evaluation set is kept at a fixed size of 1,000 tokens. Normalization accuracy is calculated by taking the average of 10 trials with randomly drawn training and evaluation sets. The results of this evaluation are shown in Table 2.

The baseline score for a text is defined as the percentage of matching tokens between the unmodified, historical text and its gold-standard normalization. There is a clear difference between the Anselm texts, with scores of 23% and 39%, and the GerManC-GS texts, which range from 72% to 83%. This shows that spelling variation affects significantly more wordforms in the Anselm texts. The age of a text is likely to be the main factor for this, as even within the group of GerManC-GS texts, a clear tendency for newer texts to have higher baseline scores can be observed.

Spelling normalization with the Norma tool shows rather positive results even for small training samples: with only 100 tokens used for training, it achieves a normalization accuracy of 69% for the Anselm texts, and raises the score for the GerManC-GS texts by 5–10 percentage points. Using 250 tokens results in another noticeable increase in accuracy, although the relative gain from increasing the training size even further attenuates after this point.

4 Part-of-speech tagging

While spelling normalization can be useful in itself (e.g., for search queries in the corpus), our main focus is on its usefulness for further processing of the data such as part-of-speech tagging. The results presented here were achieved using the RFTagger (Schmid and Laws, 2008) with an increased context size of 10, which we found to perform best on average on our data.

Text	OrigP	ModP	NoP
Berlin	85.78%	87.29%	87.07%
Melk	85.21%	87.76%	87.74%
LeichSermon	81.22%	80.59%	81.04%
JubelFeste	90.41%	90.41%	90.03%
Gottesdienst	93.24%	93.24%	92.27%

Table 3: Tagging accuracy on the gold-standard normalizations (OrigP = original punctuation, ModP = modern punctuation, NoP = no punctuation)

Original	96.85%
Lowercased	96.50%
No punctuation and SB	96.22%
Lowercased + no punctuation and SB	95.74%

Table 4: Tagging accuracy on the combined TIGER/Tüba corpus, using 10-fold CV, evaluated with and without capitalization, punctuation, and sentence boundaries (SB)

4.1 Impact of punctuation

Normalization tries to handle the problem of spelling inconsistencies found in historical language data. However, this is not the only challenge for processing the data with modern POS taggers. There is often no consistent capitalization, which can normally be used as a clue to detect nouns in modern German. This has already led to all wordforms being lowercased for the normalization process. Additionally, punctuation marks are also often used inconsistently or are missing completely: e.g., the Melk manuscript mostly uses virgules (visually resembling a modern slash '/') where modern German would use a full stop, but this is far from a definite rule, and large parts of the Anselm texts feature no punctuation marks at all. This raises the question whether punctuation should be used for POS tagging at all for these texts.

In order to test the impact of punctuation on tagging performance, three scenarios are considered: tagging with original, modern, and no punctuation marks. In order to provide a fairer comparison, instead of using the supplied parameter file for German, we retrain RFTagger on a prepared set of data. For this purpose, the TIGER corpus (Brants et al., 2002) and version 6 of Tüba-D/Z (Telljohann et al., 2004) are used. First, the two corpora are combined—with minor modifications to the POS tags to make them uniform—and lowercased. The combined corpus has a size of more than 1.6 million tokens. Additionally, for the evaluation without punctuation, a separate tagger model is trained on a version of the TIGER/Tüba corpus where all punctuation marks and sentence boundaries have been removed.

Using these tagger models, tagging performance is evaluated on the gold-standard normalizations with different levels of punctuation. The results are shown in Table 3. For better comparability, accuracy was evaluated excluding punctuation marks in all scenarios.

Tagging with modern punctuation or no punctuation is shown to be best in all cases, with the difference between these two scenarios never being statistically significant ($p > 0.05$). For the Anselm texts, using the original punctuation is worse than using none at all. This is not true for GerManC-GS, though the differences are minor; also, original and modern punctuation are identical for the JubelFeste and Gottesdienst texts, showing that they already follow modern German conventions in this regard.

The results show that removing all punctuation marks does not lead to significant losses in POS tagging accuracy. Indeed, for texts with infrequent and/or inconsistent use of punctuation marks, discarding punctuation is shown to be preferable. For these reasons, the tagging approach without punctuation is used for all following experiments.

4.2 Tagging "with handicaps"

So far, the preprocessing of the historical data includes removing all capitalization and punctuation. Consequently, information about sentence boundaries should also be removed, as it cannot easily be derived from texts without (consistent) punctuation. However, POS tagging with these "handicaps" potentially increases the difficulty of the task in general.

To gauge the extent of this effect, an evaluation on modern data was performed using 10-fold cross-validation on the combined TIGER/Tüba corpus, both with and without these artificial modifications. Table 4 shows the results of

Text	Tokens	Original	Automatically normalized				Gold
			100	250	500	1,000	
Berlin	4,719	28.65%	58.68%	74.89%	75.95%	78.03%	87.07%
Melk	4,550	44.70%	69.63%	74.02%	76.24%	78.66%	87.74%
LeichSermon	2,215	67.95%	72.87%	74.63%	75.85%	78.01%	81.04%
JubelFeste	2,137	82.26%	82.64%	83.62%	86.52%	87.74%	90.03%
Gottesdienst	1,953	88.07%	88.84%	90.27%	91.30%	91.65%	92.27%

Table 5: POS tagging accuracy on texts without punctuation and capitalization, for tagging on the original data, the gold-standard normalization, and automatic normalizations using the first *n* tokens as training data

this experiment; tagging accuracy drops from 96.85% to 95.74% when removing capitalization and punctuation. While this change is significant ($p < 0.01$) considering the corpus size, with regard to the effort involved in manually annotating whole texts with modern capitalization and punctuation marks, it seems small enough to make tagging without this information a viable approach for historical data.

4.3 Tagging historical data

POS tagging on the historical texts is evaluated in three different scenarios: first, tagging on the simplified, but otherwise unmodified, original texts; second, tagging on the gold standard normalizations; and third, tagging on texts which have been normalized automatically as described in Sec. 3.

For automatic normalization, the first *n* tokens of a text were used for training the Norma tool, with different values for *n* (cf. Sec. 3.2). Only the remainder of the text has then been automatically processed by Norma. This means that, e.g., for a text with 500 tokens used for training, POS tagging is performed on a version of the text consisting of 500 gold-standard normalizations plus automatically generated normalizations for the remainder of the text. This evaluation method models a typical application scenario, where a tradeoff is made between no manual effort (= tagging on the original) and full manual preprocessing (= tagging on the gold-standard).

Full evaluation results are shown in Table 5. Tagging accuracy roughly correlates with normalization accuracy (cf. Table 2); it tends to be slightly above the normalization score for Anselm and a few points below that score for GerManC-GS. Tagging on the original, historical data is particularly inaccurate for the Anselm texts, with the Berlin text only achieving an accuracy of 28.7%. This again highlights the need for specialized tagging methods on such types of data. The GerManC-GS texts from the 18th century perform much better without normalization, with accuracies up to 88% for the Gottesdienst text. These results mainly confirm the observations that the Anselm texts show much more variety in spelling than the newer texts from GerManC-GS.

Similar to the results for normalization, using only 100 tokens for training is enough to increase tagging accuracy for the Melk text from 45% to 70%. For Berlin, this method results in an even higher relative increase, more than doubling the number of correct POS tags. Results for these texts can be improved further to about 74% when using 250 tokens for training; after this figure, POS tagging seems to profit less from increasing the size of the training set, with accuracies around 78% for a training set of 1,000 tokens.

The GerManC-GS texts, particularly JubelFeste and Gottesdienst, do not benefit as much from a small number of training tokens. With 100 tokens, POS tagging accuracy only increases by 0.38–0.77 percentage points. However, these texts already have a comparatively high baseline to start with (82–88%). As they are already much closer to modern German spelling, fewer wordforms have spelling variations at all; consequently, more training data is required to capture a similar amount of variant wordforms as in the Anselm texts. Indeed, when increasing the training portion to 1,000 tokens, the benefit of spelling normalization becomes more pronounced.

Curiously, for the LeichSermon text, even the gold-standard normalization only achieves 81% accuracy, which is significantly lower than for any other text in the evaluation. This is unexpected, considering that the text is much more recent than Berlin and Melk. The reason for this discrepancy is the frequent use of bible verse numbers in LeichSermon, which are written as numerals followed by a dot and annotated as CARD (cardinal number) in the gold-standard data. In the TIGER corpus and Tüba-D/Z, such numerals are treated as ordinal numbers and tagged as ADJA, leading to a high number of mismatching tags.

4.4 Error analysis

POS tagging results for the historical texts are still considerably worse than those for modern data, even when tagging on gold-standard normalizations (81–92% vs. 95.74%). There are several factors responsible for this.

It is important to observe that even perfectly normalized historical data has different characteristics than modern data, as normalization only affects the spelling of wordforms. One potential source of errors are semantic changes, as shown in Ex. (4) from the LeichSermon text: the wordform *so* is an adverb in modern German, but is frequently used as a relative pronoun (PRELS[2]) in ENHG, which nevers occurs in the training data of the TIGER/Tüba corpus.

(4)	*die*	*faelle*	*so*	*aus*	*schwacheit*
	die	fälle	so	aus	schwachheit
	ART	NN	PRELS	APPR	NN
	geschehen				
	geschehen				
	VVPP				

"the cases which occur out of weakness"

Extinct wordforms are a major problem for the normalization approach. They cannot usually be normalized to a modern wordform by applying spelling changes, but would have to be mapped on a word-by-word basis. However, both GerManC-GS and the normalization layer of Anselm[3] map extinct wordforms to artificial lemmas, which are still useful to identify spelling variants, but impractical for this POS tagging approach. A common example in Melk is *czuhant* "immediately", which is mapped to the artificial lemma *zehant*, but would rather be expressed as *sofort* in modern German:

(5)	*czuhant*	*chust*	*iudas*	*mein*	*chint*
	zehant	küsst	judas	mein	kind
	ADV	VVFIN	NE	PPOSAT	NN

"Immediately, Judas kisses my child"

Finally, a significant number of errors appears to result from limitations of the modern TIGER/Tüba corpus used to train the POS tagger. This corpus is created from newspaper texts, which are typically written in a rather formal style. The Anselm texts, on the other hand, consist of question/answer sets which contain a lot of direct speech. Similarly, the Gottesdienst text is a religious speech which addresses its audience right from the beginning. Ex. (6) shows a phrase that occurs frequently in the Berlin text:

(6)	*sieh*	*anselm*
	VVIMP	NE

"Look, Anselm"

The imperative form *sieh* "look" is used 24 times in the Berlin text, but typically mistagged as a proper noun (NE) despite being correctly normalized. A look at the TIGER/Tüba training data reveals the cause for this: the wordform *sieh* does not occur there at all; only the standard form *siehe* was learned. Imperative verb forms in general are very uncommon in TIGER/Tüba, only making up 397 tokens (0.02%). In comparison, the gold-standard POS annotation of Berlin already contains 43 imperative verb forms (0.91%).

Similarly, the religious texts in Anselm and GerManC-GS often use vocabulary that is rarely used in newspaper text. Ex. (7) shows the finite verb form *verschmähten* "despised/spurned", which has only one occurrence in the TIGER/Tüba corpus where it was used as an adjective instead, inevitably leading to a tagging error.

(7)	*vnd*	*vorsmeten*	*yn*
	und	verschmähten	ihn
	KON	VVFIN	PPER

"and [they] despised him"

These examples show that even if spelling normalization was done perfectly on historical texts, semantic/syntactic variation and domain adaptation of the POS tagger provide further obstacles for achieving higher tagging accuracies.

[2]Actually, GerManC-GS annotates *so* in this example with the new tag PTKREL, which is mapped back to PRELS for reasons of compatibility. As PTKREL is not found in TIGER or Tüba-D/Z, keeping this tag would not solve the problem here, though.

[3]The Anselm corpus provides an additional "modernization" layer which maps extinct forms to actual modern words, but a first evaluation showed that using this layer has a negative impact on overall normalization accuracy.

5 Related work

For automatic spelling normalization, VARD 2 (Baron and Rayson, 2008) is another tool that has been developed for Early Modern English. It has been successfully adapted to other languages, e.g. Portuguese (Hendrickx and Marquilhas, 2011), though previous experiments found it to perform worse than Norma on the Anselm data (Bollmann, 2012). Jurish (2010) presents a normalization method that includes token context, which seems to be the logical next step to further improve normalization results.

POS tagging on normalized data has been tried for the GerManC-GS corpus before with an average accuracy of 79.7% (Scheible et al., 2011a), however, only manual normalization was considered. For English, Rayson et al. (2007) report an accuracy of 89–91% on gold standard normalizations and 85–89% on automatically normalized texts. Hendrickx and Marquilhas (2011) perform a similar evaluation for Portuguese, achieving 86.6% and 83.4% on gold standard and automatic normalizations, respectively.

There are some notable differences, however, between the aforementioned studies and the approach outlined here. Firstly, those studies using automatic normalization methods typically utilize either a much higher amount of training data or some kind of manually crafted resource. VARD, for instance, uses a manually compiled list of spelling variants totalling more than 45,000 entries (Rayson et al., 2005), while Hendrickx and Marquilhas (2011) use a training set of more than 37,000 tokens. While I certainly expect to improve the results in the future by using full texts from the Anselm and/or GerManC-GS corpora as basis for training, this approach might not always be feasible. The approach presented here, requiring only a few hundred tokens for training, seems especially suited for languages where projects to create historical corpora have only been started, and therefore do not have large amounts of previously annotated training material to fall back to.

Secondly, the Anselm texts evaluated here show a much lower baseline than the texts evaluated in other studies. Without normalization, POS tagging accuracy is 82–88% in Rayson et al. (2007), 76.9% in Hendrickx and Marquilhas (2011), and 69.6% for the German data in Scheible et al. (2011a). The texts from Berlin and Melk, on the other hand, perform much worse without the normalization step (28.7% and 44.7%, respectively). This suggests a higher amount of variance in the Anselm data compared to the types of text used in previous studies, making their automatic processing a potentially more challenging problem. Also, annotated data from these studies is less likely to be useful as training data for these texts.

6 Conclusion

I presented an approach to part-of-speech tagging for historical texts that uses spelling normalization as a preprocessing step. Evaluation on texts from Early New High German showed that by manually normalizing 250 tokens of a text and using them as training data, automatic normalization of the remaining text performs well enough to result in a notable increase in POS tagging accuracy. Texts with more spelling variation were shown to benefit more from this approach than texts which are already closer to the modern target language.

For one German manuscript from the 15th century, this method increased tagging accuracy from 28.65% to 74.89%. While this is still far from the accuracy scores reported for modern language data, and also quite a bit worse than tagging on the gold-standard normalization (87.07% for this text), it offers a way to facilitate the (semi-automatic) POS annotation of historical texts with relatively minor effort. Furthermore, as it does not require a sizeable amount of training data, this approach is potentially interesting for less-resourced language varieties in general, assuming some level of graphematic similarity to a well-resourced target language.

Future work should likely consider inclusion of token context for the normalization as proposed by Jurish (2010). Analysis of the POS tagging errors also highlighted some of the problems that remain. Domain-specific differences can negatively impact tagging performance even on perfectly normalized data. Furthermore, spelling normalization cannot account for semantic and syntactic peculiarities of historical language. For a corpus of Old Spanish, this led Sánchez-Marco et al. (2010) to abandon the normalization approach and use a customized POS tagger instead. On the other hand, a study by Dipper (2010) showed that normalization is still beneficial even when retraining a tagger on a corpus of historical data. Future research could try to combine a normalization step with a modified POS tagger to improve the results further.

References

Alistair Baron and Paul Rayson. 2008. VARD 2: A tool for dealing with spelling variation in historical corpora. In *Proceedings of the Postgraduate Conference in Corpus Linguistics*.

Marcel Bollmann, Stefanie Dipper, Julia Krasselt, and Florian Petran. 2012. Manual and semi-automatic normalization of historical spelling – Case studies from Early New High German. In *Proceedings of KONVENS 2012 (LThist 2012 workshop)*, pages 342–350, Vienna, Austria.

Marcel Bollmann. 2012. (Semi-)automatic normalization of historical texts using distance measures and the Norma tool. In *Proceedings of the Second Workshop on Annotation of Corpora for Research in the Humanities (ACRH-2)*, Lisbon, Portugal.

Sabine Brants, Stefanie Dipper, Silvia Hansen, Wolfgang Lezius, and George Smith. 2002. The TIGER treebank. In Erhard Hinrichs and Kiril Simov, editors, *Proceedings of the First Workshop on Treebanks and Linguistic Theories (TLT 2002)*, Sozopol, Bulgaria.

Thorsten Brants. 2000. TnT — a statistical part-of-speech tagger. In *Proceedings of ANLP 2000*, pages 224–231, Seattle, USA.

Stefanie Dipper and Simone Schultz-Balluff. 2013. The Anselm corpus: Methods and perspectives of a parallel aligned corpus. In *Proceedings of the NODALIDA Workshop on Computational Historical Linguistics*.

Stefanie Dipper. 2010. POS-tagging of historical language data: First experiments. In *Proceedings of KONVENS 2010*, pages 117–121, Saarbrücken, Germany.

Iris Hendrickx and Rita Marquilhas. 2011. From old texts to modern spellings: an experiment in automatic normalisation. *JLCL*, 26(2):65–76.

Bryan Jurish. 2010. More than words: using token context to improve canonicalization of historical German. *Journal for Language Technology and Computational Linguistics*, 25(1):23–39.

Paul Rayson, Dawn Archer, and Nicholas Smith. 2005. VARD versus Word. A comparison of the UCREL variant detector and modern spell checkers on english historical corpora. In *Proceedings of Corpus Linguistics 2005*, Birmingham, UK.

Paul Rayson, Dawn Archer, Alistair Baron, Jonathan Culpeper, and Nicholas Smith. 2007. Tagging the bard: Evaluating the accuracy of a modern POS tagger on Early Modern English corpora. In *Proceedings of Corpus Linguistics 2007*, University of Birmingham, UK.

Cristina Sánchez-Marco, Gemma Boleda, Josep Maria Fontana, and Judith Domingo. 2010. Annotation and representation of a diachronic corpus of Spanish. In *Proceedings of the Seventh Conference on International Language Resources and Evaluation*, pages 2713–2718.

Silke Scheible, Richard J. Whitt, Martin Durrell, and Paul Bennett. 2011a. Evaluating an 'off-the-shelf' POS-tagger on Early Modern German text. In *Proceedings of the ACL-HLT 2011 Workshop on Language Technology for Cultural Heritage, Social Sciences, and Humanities (LaTeCH 2011)*, pages 19–23, Portland, Oregon, USA.

Silke Scheible, Richard J. Whitt, Martin Durrell, and Paul Bennett. 2011b. A gold standard corpus of Early Modern German. In *Proceedings of the ACL-HLT 2011 Linguistic Annotation Workshop (LAW V)*, pages 124–128, Portland, Oregon, USA.

Anne Schiller, Simone Teufel, Christine Stöckert, and Christine Thielen. 1999. Guidelines für das Tagging deutscher Textcorpora mit STTS. Technical report.

Helmut Schmid and Florian Laws. 2008. Estimation of conditional probabilities with decision trees and an application to fine-grained POS tagging. In *Proceedings of COLING '08*, Manchester, Great Britain.

Heike Telljohann, Erhard Hinrichs, and Sandra Kübler. 2004. The Tüba-D/Z Treebank: Annotating German with a Context-Free Backbone. In *Proceedings of the Fourth International Conference on Language Resources and Evaluation (LREC 2004)*, pages 2229–2235, Lisbon, Portugal.

Utilizing State-of-the-art Parsers to Diagnose Problems in Treebank Annotation for a Less Resourced Language

Quy T. Nguyen
University of Information Technology, Ho Chi Minh City
quynt@uit.edu.vn

Ngan L.T. Nguyen
National Institute of Informatics, Tokyo
ngan@nii.ac.jp

Yusuke Miyao
National Institute of Informatics, Tokyo
yusuke@nii.ac.jp

Abstract

The recent success of statistical parsing methods has made treebanks become important resources for building good parsers. However, constructing high-quality annotated treebanks is a challenging task. We utilized two publicly available parsers, Berkeley and MST parsers, for feedback on improving the quality of part-of-speech tagging for the Vietnamese Treebank. Analysis of the treebank and parsing errors revealed how problems with the Vietnamese Treebank influenced the parsing results and real difficulties of Vietnamese parsing that required further improvements to existing parsing technologies.

1 Introduction

Treebanks, corpora annotated with syntactic structures, have become more and more important for language processing. The Vietnamese Treebank (VTB) has been built as part of the national project "Vietnamese language and speech processing (VLSP)" to strengthen automatic processing of the Vietnamese language (Nguyen et al., 2009). However, when we trained the Berkeley parser (Petrov et al., 2006) in our preliminary experiment with VTB and evaluated it using the corpus, the parser only achieved an F-score of 72.1%. This percentage was far lower than the state-of-the-art performance reported for the Berkeley parser on the English Penn Treebank of 90.2% (Petrov et al., 2006). There are two possible reasons for this. First, the quality of VTB is not good enough to construct a good parser that included the quality of the annotation scheme, the annotation guidelines, and the annotation process. Second, parsing Vietnamese is a difficult problem on its own, and we need to seek new solutions to this.

Nguyen et al. (2012) proposed methods of improving the annotations of word segmentation (WS) for VTB. They also evaluated different WS criteria in two applications, i.e., machine translation and text classification. This paper focuses on improving the quality of parts-of-speech (POS) annotations by using state-of-the-art parsers to provide feedback for this process.

The difficulties with Vietnamese POS tagging have been recognized by many researchers (Nghiem et al., 2008; Le et al., 2010). There is little consensus as to the methodology for classifying words. Polysemous words, words with the same surface form but having different meanings and grammar functions, are very popular in the Vietnamese language. For example, the word *"cổ"* can be a noun that means *neck/she*, or an adjective that means *ancient* depending on the context. This characteristic makes it difficult to tag POSs for Vietnamese, both manually and automatically.

The rest of this paper is organized as follows: a brief introduction to VTB and its annotation schemes are provided in Section 2. Then, previous work is summarized in Section 3. Section 4 describes our methods of detecting and correcting inconsistencies in POSs in the VTB corpus. Evaluations of these methods are described in Section 5. Finally, Section 6 explains our evaluations of the Berkeley parser and Minimum-Spanning Tree (MST) parser on different versions of the VTB corpus, which were created by using detected inconsistencies. These results from evaluations are considered to be a way of measuring the effect of automatically detected and corrected inconsistencies. We could observe difficulties with Vietnamese that affected the quality of parsers by analyzing the results from parsing.

Our experiences in using state-of-the-art parsers for treebank annotation, which are presented in this paper, should not only benefit the Vietnamese language, but also other languages with similar

Label	Name	Example
N	Common noun	*nhân dân {people}*
Np	Proper noun	*Việt Nam {Vietnam}*
Nc	Classifer noun	*con, cái, bức {*}*
Nu	Unit noun	*mét {meter}*
V	Verb	*ngồi {sit}*
A	Adjective	*tốt {good}*
P	Pronoun	*tôi {I}, hắn {he}*
L	Determiner	*mỗi {every}, những {*}*
M	Number	*một {one}*
R	Adverb	*đã, sẽ, đang {*}*
E	Preposition	*trên {on}*
C	Conjunction	*tuy nhiên {however}*
I	Exclamation	*ôi, chao, a ha {*}*
T	Particle	*ạ, ấy, chăng {*}*
B	Foreign word	*internet, email*
Y	Abbreviation	*APEC, WTO, HIV*
S	Affix	*bất, vô, đa {*}*
X	Other	

Table 1: VTB part-of-speech tag set

characteristics.

2 Brief introduction to VTB

The VTB corpus contains 10.433 sentences (274.266 tokens), semi-manually annotated with three layers of WS, POS tagging, and bracketing. The first annotation is produced for each annotation layer by using automatic tools. Then, the annotators revise these data. The WS and POS annotation schemes were introduced by Nguyen et al. (2012). This section briefly introduces POS tag set and a bracketing annotation scheme.

VTB specifies the 18 different POS tags summarized in Table 1 (Nguyen et al., 2010a). Each unit in this table goes with several example words. English translations of these words are included in braces. However, as we could not find any appropriate English translations for some words, these empty translations have been denoted by asterisks (*).

The VTB corpus is annotated with three syntactic tag types: constituency tags, functional tags, and null-element tags. There are 18 constituency tags in VTB. The functional tags are used to enrich information for syntactic trees, such as where functional tag "SUB" is combined with constituency tag "NP", which is presented as "NP-SUB" to indicate this noun phrase is a subject. There are 17 functional tags in VTB. The head word of a phrase is annotated with functional tag "H".

The phrase structures of Vietnamese include three positions: *<pre-head>*, *<head>*, and *<post-head>* (Vietnamese grammar, 1983; Nguyen et al., 2010c). The head word of the phrase is in the <head> position. The words that are in the <pre-head> and <post-head> positions are modifiers of the head word.

There is a special type of noun in Vietnamese that we have called Nc-noun in this paper. Nc-nouns can be classifier nouns or common nouns depending on their modifiers. For example, the Nc-noun *"con"* is a classifier noun if its modifier is the word *"cá {fish}"* (*"con cá"*, which means a specific fish, similar to *"the fish"* in English). However, the Nc-noun *"con {child}"* is a common noun if its modifier is the word *"ghẻ"* (*"con ghẻ"*, which means *"stepchild"* in English). We found that Nc-nouns always appeared in the head positions of noun phrases by investigating the VTB corpus. There is currently little consensus as to the methodology for annotating Nc-nouns (Hoang, 1998; Nguyen et al., 2010b; Nguyen et al., 2010a).

3 Summarization of previous work

Nguyen et al. (2012) described methods of detecting and correcting WS inconsistencies in the VTB corpus. These methods focused on two types of WS inconsistency, variation and structural inconsistency, which are defined below.

Variation inconsistency: is a sequence of tokens that has more than one way of being segmented in the corpus.

Structural inconsistency: occurs when different sequences have similar structures, and thus should be split in the same way, but are segmented in different ways in the corpus. Nguyen et al. (2012) pointed out three typical cases of structural inconsistency that were analyzed as classifier nouns (Nc), affixes (S), and special characters.

Nguyen et al. (2012) analyzed N-gram sequences and phrase structures to detect WS inconsistencies. Then, the detected WS inconsistencies were classified into several patterns of inconsistencies, parts of which were manually fixed to improve the quality of the corpus. The rest were used to create different versions of the VTB corpus. These data sets were evaluated on automatic WS and its applications to text classification and English-Vietnamese statistical machine translations to find appropriate criteria for automatic WS and its applications.

Their experiments revealed that the VAR_FREQ data set achieved excellent results in these applications. The VAR_FREQ data set was the original VTB corpus with manually corrected structural inconsistencies in special characters and selected segmentations with higher frequencies in all detected variations. Therefore, we used the VAR_FREQ data set in our experiments.

4 Methods of detecting and correcting inconsistencies in POS annotations

We propose two kinds of methods of detecting and correcting inconsistencies. They correspond to two different types of POS inconsistency that we call multi-POS inconsistency (MI) and Nc inconsistency (NcI), which are defined as follows.

Multi-POS inconsistency: is a word that is not Nc-noun and has more than one POS tag at each position in each phrase category.

Nc inconsistency: is a sequence of Nc-noun and modifier, in which Nc-noun has more than one way of POS annotation in the VTB corpus.

We separated the POS inconsistencies into these two types of inconsistencies because Nc-nouns are special types of words in Vietnamese. The methods of detecting and correcting NcIs were language-specific methods developed based on the characteristics of Vietnamese. However, as the methods for MIs are rather general, they can be applied to other languages.

4.1 General method for multi-POS inconsistencies

Detection method (MI_DM)

Our main problem was to distinguish MIs from polysemous words, since polysemous words should not be considered inconsistent annotations. Our method was based on the position of words in phrases and phrase categories. This idea resulted from the observation that polysemous words have many POS tags; however, each word usually has only one true POS tag at each position in each phrase category. For example, when a phrase category is a verb phrase, the word *"can"* in the pre-head position of the verb phrase *"(VP (MD can) (VB can))"* should be a modal, but the word *"can"* in the head position should be a verb. Further, the word *"cut"* in the head position of a noun phrase *"(NP (DT a) (JJ further) (NN cut))"* should be a noun, but the word *"cut"* in the head position of the verb phrase *"(VP (VB cut) (NP (NNS costs)))"* should be a verb. This may be more frequent in Vietnamese because it is not an inflectional language i.e., the word form does not change according to tenses, word categories (e.g., nouns, verbs, and adjectives), or number (singular and plural).

The method involved three steps. First, we extracted words in the same position for each phrase category. Second, we counted the number of different POS tags of each word. Words that had more than one POS tag were determined to be multi-POS inconsistencies. For example, in the following two preposition phrases, *"(PP (E-H của) (P chúng_tôi*[1]*)) {of us}"* and *"(PP (C-H của) (P hội_nghị)) {of conference}"*, the words *"của {of}"* appear at the head positions of both phrases, but they are annotated with different POS tags, preposition (E) and conjunction (C). Therefore, they are MIs according to our method.

It should be noted that this method was applied to words that were direct children of a phrase. Embedded phrases, such as *"(PP (E của) (P chúng_tôi))"* in *"(NP (M hai) (Nc-H con) (N mèo) (PP (E của) (P chúng_tôi))) {our two cats}"*, were considered separately.

Correction method (MI_CM)

A multi-POS inconsistency detected with the MI_DM method is denoted by *"w|P1-f1|P2-f2|...|Pn-fn AC"*, where *Pi* (i = 1, 2, ..., n) is a POS tag of word *w*, *fi* is the frequency of POS tag *Pi*, and AC is applying condition of *w*. Our method of correcting the POS tag for POS inconsistency *"w|P1-f1|P2-f2|...|Pn-fn AC"* involves two steps. First, we select the POS tag with the highest frequency of all POS tags of *"w|P1-f1|P2-f2|...|Pn-fn AC"* (*Pmax*). Second, we replace POS tags *Pi* of all instances *(w|Pi)* satisfying condition *AC* with POS tag *Pmax*. For MIs, the AC of word *w* is its phrase category and position in the phrase.

For example, *"toàn bộ|L-27|P-2"* is a multi-POS inconsistency in the pre-head position of a noun phrase. The frequency of POS tag "L" is 27 and the frequency of POS tag "P" is 2. Therefore, "L" is the POS tag that was selected by the MI_CM method. We replace all POS tags *Pi* of instances *"toàn bộ|Pi"* in the pre-head positions of noun phrases with POS tag "L".

4.2 Language-specific method for classifier nouns

Detection method

As mentioned in Section 2, an Nc-noun can be

[1]We used underscore "_" to link syllables of Vietnamese compound words.

annotated with POS tag "Nc" or "N" depending on the modifier that follows that Nc-noun. Analyzing the VTB corpus revealed that Nc-nouns had two characteristics. First, an Nc-noun that is followed by the same word at each occurrence is usually annotated with the same POS tag. Second, an Nc-noun that is followed by a phrase or nothing at each occurrence is annotated with the same POS tag. Based on these two cases, we propose two methods of detecting NcIs, which we have called NcI_DM1 and NcI_DM2. They are described below.

NcI_DM1: We counted Nc-nouns in VTB that had two or more ways of POS annotation, satisfying the condition that Nc-nouns are followed by a phrase or nothing. For example, the Nc-noun *"con"* in *"(NP (M 2) (N-H con)) {2 children}"* is followed by nothing or it is followed by a prepositional phrase as in *"(NP (L các) (N-H con) (PP (E-H của) (P tôi))) {my children}"*.

NcI_DM2: We counted two-gram sequences beginning with an Nc-noun in VTB that had two or more ways of POS annotation of the Nc-noun, satisfying the conditions that two tokens were all in the same phrase and and they all had the same depth in a phrase. For example, the Nc-noun *"con"* in the two-gram *"con gái {daughter}"* was sometimes annotated "Nc", and sometimes annotated "N" in VTB; in addition, as *"con"* and *"gái"* in the structure *"(NP (Nc-H con) (N gái) (PP (E-H của) (P tôi))) {my daughter}"* were in the same phrase and have the same depth, *"con"* was an NcI.

Correction method

We denoted NcIs with *"w|P1-f1|P2-f2|...|Pn-fn AC"* similarly to MIs. We also replaced the POS tag of Nc-nouns with the highest frequency tag. The only differences were the applying conditions that varied according to the previous two cases of NcIs.

- For Nc inconsistencies detected by the NcI_DM1 method, AC is defined as follows: *w* is an Nc-noun that is followed by nothing or a phrase.

- For Nc inconsistencies detected by the NcI_DM2 method, AC is defined as follows: *w* is an Nc-noun that must be followed by a word, *m*.

5 Results and evaluation

We detected and corrected MIs and NcIs based on the two data sets, ORG and VAR_FREQ. The ORG data set was the original VTB corpus and VAR_FREQ was the original corpus with modifications to WS annotation. This setting was made similar to that used by Nguyen et al. (2012) to enable comparison.

There are a total of 128,871 phrases in the VTB corpus. The top five types of phrases are noun phrases (NPs) (representing 49.6% of the total number of phrases), verb phrases (VPs), prepositional phrases (PPs), adjectival phrases (ADJPs), and quantity phrases (QPs), representing 99.1% of the total number of phrases in the VTB corpus. We analyzed the VTB corpus based on these five types of phrases.

5.1 Results for detected POS inconsistencies

Tables 2 and 3 show the overall statistics for MIs and NcIs for each phrase category. The second and third columns in these tables indicate the numbers of inconsistencies and their instances that were detected in the ORG data set. The fourth and fifth columns indicate the numbers of inconsistencies and their instances that were detected in the VAR_FREQ data set. The rows in Table 3 indicate the number of NcIs and the number of instances detected with the NcI_DM1 and NcI_DM2 methods.

According to Table 2, most of the MIs occurred in noun phrases, representing more than 72% of the total number of MIs. All NcIs in Table 3 are also in noun phrases. There are two possible reasons for this. First, noun phrases represent the majority of phrases in VTB (represent 49.6% of the total number of phrases in the VTB corpus). Second, nouns are sub-divided into many other types (common noun (N), classifier noun (Nc), proper noun (Np), and unit noun (Nu)) (mentioned in Section 2), which may confuse annotators in annotating POS tags for nouns. In addition, the high number of NcIs in Table 3 indicate that it is difficult to distinguish between Nc and other types of nouns. Therefore, we need to have clearer annotation guidelines for this.

5.2 Evaluation of methods to detect and correct inconsistencies

We estimated the accuracy of our methods which detected and corrected inconsistencies in POS tag-

Phrase	ORG		VAR_FREQ	
	Inc	Ins	Inc	Ins
NP	792	28,423	752	27,067
VP	221	10,158	139	10,110
ADJP	64	1,302	61	1,257
QP	4	22	4	22
PP	14	5,649	13	5,628
Total	**1,095**	**45,554**	**969**	**44,084**

Table 2: Statistics for multi-POS inconsistencies for each phrase category in VTB. Number of Inconsistencies (Inc) and Number of Instances (Ins).

Detection method	ORG		VAR_FREQ	
	Inc	Ins	Inc	Ins
NcI_DM1	52	3,801	51	3,792
NcI_DM2	338	2,468	326	2,412
Total	***390***	***6,269***	***377***	***6,204***

Table 3: Statistics for Nc inconsistencies in head positions of noun phrases in VTB.

ging by manually inspecting inconsistent annotations. We manually inspected the two data sets of ORG_EVAL and ORG_POS_EVAL. To create ORG_EVAL, we randomly selected 100 sentences which contained instances of POS inconsistencies in the ORG data set. ORG_EVAL contained 459 instances of 157 POS inconsistencies. ORG_POS_EVAL was the ORG_EVAL data set with corrections made to multi-POS inconsistencies and Nc inconsistencies with our methods of correction above.

Detection: We manually checked POS inconsistencies and found that 153 cases out of 157 POS inconsistencies (97.5%) were actual inconsistencies. There were four cases that our method detected as multi-POS inconsistencies, but they were actually ambiguities in Vietnamese POS tagging. They were polysemous words whose meanings and POS tags depended on surrounding words, but did not depend on their positions in phrases. For example, the word *"sáng"* in the post-head positions of the verb phrases VP1 and VP2 below, can be a noun that means *morning* in English, or it can be an adjective that means *bright*, depending on the preceding verb.

VP1: (VP (V-H thắp) (A sáng) {lighten bright}

VP2: (VP (V-H đi) (N sáng) {go in the morning}

Correction: Table 4 shows results of comparison of the POS tags for 459 instances in ORG_EVAL and those in ORG_POS_EVAL. These results indicate that there are instances whose POS tags are incorrect in ORG_EVAL but correct in ORG_POS_EVAL (the third row in Table 4), and there are instances whose POS tags are correct in ORG_EVAL but incorrect in ORG_POS_EVAL (the fourth row in Table 4). The results in Table 4 indicate that, the number of correct POS tags in ORG_POS_EVAL (445 instances, representing 96.9% of the total number of instances) is higher than that in ORG_EVAL (415 instances, representing 90.4% of the total number of instances). This means our methods of correcting inconsistencies in POS tagging improved the quality of treebank annotations.

ORG_EVAL	ORG_POS_EVAL	No. of Instances
correct	correct	404
incorrect	correct	41
correct	incorrect	11
incorrect	incorrect	3
	Total	***459***

Table 4: Comparison of POS tags for 459 instances in ORG_EVAL with those in ORG_POS_EVAL.

PoPOS	Counts	Examples
Nc-N	385	*người {the, person}*
N-V	186	*mất mát {loss}*
N-Np	176	*Hội {association}*
N-A	144	*khó khăn {difficult}*
V-A	92	*phải {must, right}*

Table 5: Top five pairs of confusing POS tags.

5.3 Analysis of detected inconsistencies

We analyzed the detected POS inconsistencies to find the reasons for inconsistent POS annotations. We classified the detected POS inconsistencies according to pairs of their POS tags. There were a total of 85 patterns of pairs of POS tags. Table 5 lists the top five confusing patterns (PoPOS), their counts of inconsistencies (Counts), and examples. It also seemed to be extremely confusing for the annotators to distinguish types of nouns (Nc and N, and N and Np) and distinguish nouns from other types of words (such as verbs, adjectives, and pronouns).

We investigated POS inconsistencies and the annotation guidelines (Nguyen et al., 2010b; Nguyen et al., 2010a; Nguyen et al., 2010c) to find why common nouns were sometimes tagged as classifier nouns and vice versa, and verbs were sometimes tagged as common nouns and vice versa, and so on. We found that these POS inconsistencies belonged to polysemous words that were difficult to tag.

The difficulties with tagging polysemous words

were due to four main reasons: (1) The POS of a polysemous word changes according to the function of that polysemous word in each phrase category or changes according to the meaning of surrounding words. Although polysemous words are annotated with different POS tags, they do not change their word form. (2) The way polysemous words are tagged according to their context is not completely clear in the POS tagging guidelines. (3) Annotators referred to a dictionary that had been built as part of the VLSP project (Nguyen et al., 2009) (VLSP dictionary) to annotate the VTB corpus. However, this dictionary lacked various words and did not cover all contexts for the words. For example, *"hơn {more than}"* in Vietnamese is an adjective when it is the head word of an adjectival phrase, but *"hơn {over}"* is an adverb when it is the modifier of a quantifier noun (such as *"hơn 200 sinh viên {over 200 students}"*). However, the VLSP dictionary only considered *"hơn"* to be an adjective (*"tôi hơn nó hai tuổi {I am more than him two years old}"*). No cases where *"hơn"* was an adverb were mentioned in this dictionary. (4) There are several overlapping but conflicting instructions across the annotation guidelines for different layers of the treebank. For example, the combinations of affixes and words they modify to create compound words are clear in the WS guidelines, but POS tagging guidelines treat affixes as words and they are annotated as POS tags "S". For words modifying quantifier nouns, such as *"hơn and gần {over and about}"*, the POS tagging guidelines treat them as adjectives, but the bracketing guidelines treat them as adverbs. Therefore, our method detected multi-POS inconsistencies as *"hơn|A-135|R-51"*, *"gần|A-102|R-5"* at the prehead positions of noun phrases. Since the frequencies of the adjective tags were greater than those of adverb tags (fA > fR), these words were automatically assigned to adjective POS tags (A) according to our method of correction. These were POS inconsistencies that our method of correction could not be applied to, because the frequency of incorrect POS tags was higher than that of actual POS tags.

6 Evaluation of state-of-the-art parsers on VTB

We carried out experiments to evaluate two popular parsers, a syntactic parser and a dependency parser, on different versions of the VTB corpus. Some of these data sets were made the same as the data settings for WS in Nguyen et al. (2012). The other data sets contained changes in POS annotations following our methods of correcting inconsistencies presented in Section 4. We could observe how the problems with WS and POS tagging influenced the quality of Vietnamese parsing by analyzing the parsing results.

6.1 Experimental settings

Data. Nine configurations of the VTB corpus were created as follows:

- ORG: The original VTB corpus.
- BASE, STRUCT_AFFIX, STRUCT_NC, VAR_SPLIT, VAR_COMB, and VAR_FREQ correspond to different settings for WS described in Nguyen et al. (2012).
- ORG_POS: The ORG data set with corrections for multi-POS inconsistencies and Nc inconsistencies by using the methods in Section 4.1 and 4.2.
- VAR_FREQ_POS: The VAR_FREQ data set with corrections for multi-POS inconsistencies and Nc inconsistencies by using the methods in Section 4.1 and 4.2.

Each of the nine data sets was randomly split into two subsets for training and testing our parser models. The training set contained 9,443 sentences, and the testing set contained 1,000 sentences.

Tools

We used the Berkeley parser (Petrov et al., 2006) to evaluate the syntactic parser on VTB. This parser has been used in experiments in English, German, and Chinese and achieved an F1 of 90.2% on the English Penn Treebank.

We used the conversion tool built by Johansson et al. (2007) to convert VTB into dependency trees.

We used the MST parser to evaluate the dependency parsing on VTB. This parser was evaluated on the English Penn Treebank (Mcdonald et al., 2006a) and 13 other languages (Mcdonald et al., 2006b). Its accuracy achieved 90.7% on the English Penn Treebank.

We made use of the bracket scoring program EVALB, which was built by Sekine et al. (1997),

Data sets	Bracketing F-measures
ORG	72.10
BASE	72.20
STRUCT_AFFIX	72.60
STRUCT_NC	71.92
VAR_SPLIT	72.03
VAR_COMB	72.46
VAR_FREQ	72.34
ORG_POS	72.72
VAR_FREQ_POS	**73.21**

Table 6: Bracketing F-measures of Berkeley parser on nine configurations of VTB corpus.

Data set	UA	LA
ORG	50.51	46.14
BASE	53.90	50.14
STRUCT_AFFIX	54.00	50.25
STRUCT_NC	53.88	49.96
VAR_SPLIT	53.95	50.14
VAR_COMB	53.93	50.27
VAR_FREQ	54.21	50.41
ORG_POS	54.20	50.37
VAR_FREQ_POS	**57.87**	**53.19**

Table 7: Dependency accuracy of MSTParser on nine configurations of VTB corpus. Unlabeled Accuracy (UA), Labeled Accuracy (LA).

to evaluate the performance of the Berkeley parser. As an evaluation tool was included in the MST parser tool, we used it to evaluate the MST parser.

6.2 Experimental results

The bracketing F-measures of the Berkeley parser on nine configurations of the VTB corpus are listed in Table 6. The dependency accuracies of the MST parser on nine configurations of the VTB corpus are shown in Table 7. These results indicate that the quality of the treebank strongly affected the quality of the parsers.

According to Table 6, all modifications to WS inconsistencies improved the performance of the Berkeley parser except for STRUCT_NC and VAR_SPLIT. More importantly, the ORG_POS model achieved better results than the ORG model, and the VAR_FREQ_POS model achieved better results than the VAR_FREQ model, which indicates that the modifications to POS inconsistencies improved the performance of the Berkeley parser. The VAR_FREQ_POS model scored 1.11 point higher than ORG, which is a significant improvement.

Dependency accuracies of the MST parser in Table 7 indicate that all modifications to POS inconsistencies improved the performance of the MST parser. All modifications to WS inconsistencies also improved the performance of the MST parser except for STRUCT_NC. The VAR_FREQ_POS model scored 7.36 points higher than ORG, which is a significant improvement.

APSs	CCTs and Freq
A M N	NP-79|ADJP-27
A V	VP-56|ADJP-78|NP-2

Table 8: Examples of ambiguous POS sequences (APSs), their CCTs, and frequency of each CCT (Freq)

6.3 Analysis of parsing results

The results for the Berkeley parser and MST parser trained on the POS-modified versions of VTB were better than those trained on the original VTB corpus, but they were still much lower than the performance of the same parsers on the English language. We analyzed error based on the output data of the best parsing results (VAR_FREQ_POS) for the Berkeley parser, and found that the unmatched annotations between gold and test data were caused by ambiguous POS sequences in the VTB corpus.

An ambiguous POS sequence is a sequence of POS tags that has two or more constituency tags. For example, there are the verb phrase *"(VP (R đang) (A cặm_cụi) (V làm)) {* (be) painstakingly doing}"* and the adjectival phrase *"(ADJP (R rất) (A dễ) (V thực_hiện)) {very easy (to) implement}"* in the training data of VAR_FREQ_POS. As these two phrases have the same POS sequence *"R A V"*, *"R A V"* is an ambiguous POS sequence, and VP and ADJP are confusing constituency tags (CCTs). We found 42,373 occurrences of 213 ambiguous POS sequences (representing 37.02% of all phrases) in the training data of VAR_FREQ_POS. We also found 1,065 occurrences of 13 ambiguous POS sequences in the parsing results for VAR_FREQ_POS. Some examples of ambiguous POS sequences, their CCTs, and the number of occurrences of each CCT in the training data of VAR_FREQ_POS are listed in Table 8.

We classified the detected ambiguous POS sequences according to pairs of different CCTs to find the reasons for ambiguity in each pair. There were a total of 42 pairs of CCTs, whose top three pairs, along with their counts of types of ambiguous POS sequences, and examples of ambigu-

Pairs of CCTs	Counts	Examples
NP-VP	61	P V N, ...
VP-ADJP	54	R A V, A V N, ...
ADJP-NP	52	A M N, ...

Table 9: Top three pairs of confusing constituency tags

Pairs of CCTs	1	2
NP-VP	M, L ,R ,V	N, R, M, P, A
VP-ADJP	A, R	N, R
ADJP-NP	N, R	R, M, A, L

Table 10: Statistics for POS tags at pre-head position of each phrase category.

ous POS sequences are listed in Table 9. We extracted different POS tags at each position of each phrase category for each pair of CCTs, based on the ambiguous POS sequences. For example, the third row in Table 9 has "R A V" and "A V N", which are two ambiguous POS sequences that were sometimes annotated as VP and sometimes annotated as ADJP. The different POS tags that were extracted from the pre-head positions of VPs based on these two POS sequences were "R, A" and "R" was the POS tag that was extracted from the pre-head positions of ADJPs based on these two POS sequences. These POS tags are important clues to finding reasons for ambiguities in POS sequences.

Table 10 summarizes the extracted POS tags at pre-head positions for the top three pairs of CCTs. For example, the POS tags in row NP-VP and column 1 are in the pre-head positions of NP and the POS tags in row NP-VP and column 2 are in the pre-head positions of VP. By comparing these results with the structures of the pre-head positions of phrase categories in VTB bracketing guidelines (Nguyen et al., 2010c), we found many cases that were not annotated according to instructions in the VTB bracketing guidelines, such as those according to Table 10, where an adjective (A) is in the pre-head position of VP, but according to the VTB bracketing guidelines, the structure of the pre-head position of VB only includes adverb (R).

We investigated cases that had not been annotated according to the guidelines, and found two possible reasons that caused ambiguous POS sequences. First, although our methods improved the quality of the VTB corpus, some POS annotation errors remained in the VTB corpus. These POS annotation errors were cases to which our methods could not be applied (mentioned in Section 5). Second, there were ambiguities in POS sequences caused by Vietnamese characteristics, such as the adjectival phrase *"(ADJP (R đang) (N ngày_đêm) (A đau_đớn)) {* day-and-night painful}"* and the noun phrase *"(NP (R cũng) (N sinh_viên) (A giỏi)) {also good student}"* that had the same POS sequence of "R N A".

Therefore, POS annotation errors need to be eliminated from the VTB corpus to further improve its quality and that of the Vietnamese parser. We not only need to eliminate overlapping but conflicting instructions, which were mentioned in Section 5.3, from the guidelines, but we also have to complete annotation instructions for cases that have not been treated (or not been clearly treated) in the guidelines. We may also need to improve POS tag set because adverbs modifying adjectives, verbs and nouns are all presently tagged as "R", which caused ambiguous POS sequences, such as the ambiguous POS sequence "R N A" mentioned above. If we use different POS tags for the adverb *"đang"*, which modifies the adjective *"đau đớn {painful}"*, and the adverb *"cũng"*, which modifies the noun *"sinh viên {student}"*, we can eliminate ambiguous POS sequences in these cases.

7 Conclusion

We proposed several methods of improving the quality of the VTB corpus. Our manual evaluation revealed that our methods improved the quality of the VTB corpus by 6.5% with correct POS tags. Analysis of inconsistencies and the annotation guidelines suggested that: (1) better instructions should be added to the VTB guidelines to help annotators to distinguish difficult POS tags, (2) overlapping but conflicting instructions should be eliminated from the VTB guidelines, and (3) annotations that referred to dictionaries should be avoided.

To the best of our knowledge, this paper is the first report on evaluating state-of-the-art parsers used on the Vietnamese language. The results obtained from evaluating these two parsers were used as feedback to improve the quality of treebank annotations. We also thoroughly analyzed the parsing output, which revealed challenging issues in treebank annotations and in the Vietnamese parsing problem itself.

References

Anna M. D. Sciullo and Edwin Williams. 1987. *On the definition of word*. The MIT Press.

Fei Xia. 2000. *The part-of-speech tagging guidelines for the penn chinese treebank (3.0)*.

Minh Nghiem, Dien Dinh and Mai Nguyen. 2008. *Improving Vietnamese POS tagging by integrating a rich feature set and Support Vector Machines*. Proceedings of RIVF 2008, pages: 128–133.

Phe Hoang. 1998. *Vietnamese Dictionary*. Scientific & Technical Publishing.

Phuong H. Le, Azim Roussanaly, Huyen T. M. Nguyen and Mathias Rossignol. 2010. *An empirical study of maximum entropy approach for part-of-speech tagging of Vietnamese texts*. Proceedings of TALN 2010 Conference. Montreal, Canada.

Quy T. Nguyen, Ngan L.T. Nguyen and Yusuke Miyao. 2012. *Comparing Different Criteria for Vietnamese Word Segmentation*. Proceedings of 3rd Workshop on South and Southeast Asian Natural Language Processing (SANLP), pages: 53–68.

Richard Johansson and Pierre Nugues. 2007. *Extended Constituent-to-dependency Conversion for English*. Proceedings of NODALIDA, Tartu, Estonia, pages: 105–112.

Ryan Mcdonald and Fernando Pereira. 2006a. *Online Learning of Approximate Dependency Parsing Algorithms*. Proceedings of 11th Conference of the European Chapter of the Association for Computational Linguistics: EACL 2006, pages: 81–88.

Ryan Mcdonald, Kevin Lerman and Fernando Pereira. 2006b. *Multilingual Dependency Analysis with a Two-Stage Discriminative Parser*. Proceedings of Tenth Conference on Computational Natural Language Learning (CoNLL-X), Bergan, Norway, pages: 216–220.

Slav Petrov, Leon Barrett, Romain Thibaux and Dan Klein. 2006. *Learning accurate, compact, and interpretable tree annotation*. Proceedings of 21st International Conference on Computational Linguistics and the 44th annual meeting of the Association for Computational Linguistics, pages: 433–440.

Thai P. Nguyen, Luong X. Vu and Huyen T.M. Nguyen. 2010a. *VTB part-of-speech tagging guidelines*.

Thai P. Nguyen, Luong X. Vu and Huyen T.M. Nguyen. 2010b. *VTB word segmentation guidelines*.

Thai P. Nguyen, Luong X. Vu, Huyen T.M. Nguyen, Hiep V. Nguyen and Phuong H. Le. 2009. *Building a large syntactically-annotated corpus of Vietnamese*. Proceedings of Third Linguistic Annotation Workshop, pages: 182–185.

Thai P. Nguyen, Luong X. Vu, Huyen T.M. Nguyen, Thu M. Dao, Ngoc T.M. Dao and Ngan K. Le. 2010c. *VTB bracketing guidelines*.

Vietnamese grammar. 1983. Social Sciences Publishers.

Influence of preprocessing on dependency syntax annotation: speed and agreement

Arne Skjærholt
Department of Informatics, University of Oslo
arnskj@ifi.uio.no

Abstract

When creating a new resource, preprocessing the source texts before annotation is both ubiquitous and obvious. How the preprocessing affects the annotation effort for various tasks is for the most part an open question, however. In this paper, we study the effects of preprocessing on the annotation of dependency corpora and how annotation speed varies as a function of the quality of three different parsers and compare with the speed obtained when starting from a least-processed baseline.

We also present preliminary results concerning the effects on agreement based on a small subset of sentences that have been doubly-annotated.[1]

1 Introduction

It is commonly accepted wisdom in treebanking that it is preferable to preprocess data before PoS and syntax annotation, rather than having annotators work from raw text. However, the impact of preprocessing is not well studied and factors such as the lower bound on performance for preprocessing to be useful and the return on investment of increased performance are largely unknown.

Corpora and applications based on dependency syntax have become increasingly popular in recent years, and many new corpora are being created. In this work we investigate the task of syntactic annotation based on dependency grammar, and how annotation speed and inter-annotator agreement are influenced by parser performance. Our study is performed in the context of the annotation effort currently under way at the national library of Norway, tasked with creating a freely available syntactically annotated corpus of Norwegian. It is the first widely available such corpus.

[1]Code and data used to obtain these results is available at https://github.com/arnsholt/law7-annotation

1.1 Related work

The Penn Treebank project (Marcus et al., 1993) had annotators correct automatically parsed and PoS-tagged data, and they report that correcting rather than annotating from scratch is massively helpful in the PoS annotation task (from scratch took twice as long and increased error rate and disagreement by 50%), but unfortunately there is no such comparison for the syntactic bracketing task. The task of PoS annotation has been studied further by Fort and Sagot (2010), who establish the lower bound on tagger accuracy to be in the range of 60–80% for the preprocessing to be useful.

For the task of syntactic bracketing, Chiou et al. (2001) investigated some facets of the problem while developing the Penn Chinese treebank and found that when using a parser with a labelled $F_1 = 76.04$, the time spent correcting is 58% of the time spent on unassisted annotation, and a further improved parser ($F_1 = 82.14$) reduces the time to 50% of that used by unassisted annotation.

2 Experimental protocol

In this section we outline the key methodological choices made for our experiments. First we discuss what timing data we collect and the texts annotated, before describing the preprocessors used.

Environment For our experiments, four different texts were chosen for annotation: two from the *Aftenposten* (AP 06 & AP 08), and two from *Dagbladet* (DB 12 & DB 13), both daily newspapers. Key statistics for the four texts are given in Table 1. The annotation effort uses the TrEd tool[2], originally created for the Prague Dependency Treebank project. It is easily extended, and thus we used these facilities to collect the timing data. To minimise interference with the annotators, we simply recorded the time a sentence was shown on screen and accounted for outliers caused by breaks and interruptions in the analysis.

The annotation work is done by two annotators, Odin and Thor. Both are trained linguists, and

[2]http://ufal.mff.cuni.cz/tred/

Text	n	μ	s
AP 06	373	17.0	10.8
AP 08	525	16.5	9.11
DB 12	808	12.1	8.47
DB 13	648	14.6	9.15
Total	2354	34223 tokens	

Table 1: Statistics of the annotated texts. n number of sentences, μ mean length, s length standard deviation.

are full-time employees of the National Library tasked with annotating the corpus. The only additional instruction given to the annotators in conjunction with the experiment was that they try to close the TREd program when they know that they were going away for a long time, in order to minimise the number of outliers. The actual annotation proceeded as normal according to the annotation guidelines[3]. Thor annotated AP 08 and DB 13, while Odin annotated AP 06 and DB 12 as well as the first 400 sentences of DB 13 for the purposes of measuring annotator agreement.

Preprocessing In our experiments, we consider three different statistical parsers as preprocessors and compare these to a minimally preprocessed baseline. Unfortunately, it was impossible to get timing data for completely unannotated data, as TREd requires its input to be a dependency tree. For this reason our minimal preprocessing, we call it the caterpillar strategy, is attaching each word to the previous word, labelled with the most frequent dependency relation.

Of the three statistical parsers, one is trained directly on already annotated Norwegian data released by the treebank project (version 0.2) and the other two are cross-lingual parsers trained on converted Swedish and Danish data using the techniques described in Skjærholt and Øvrelid (2012). In brief, this technique involves mapping the PoS and dependency relation tagsets of the source corpora into the corresponding tagsets of the target representation, and applying structural transformations to bring the syntactic analyses into as close a correspondence as possible with the target analyses. It was also shown that for languages as closely related as Norwegian, Danish and Swedish, not delexicalising, contrary to the standard procedure in cross-lingual parsing (Søgaard, 2011; Zeman and Resnik, 2008), yields a non-negligible boost in performance.

[3]Distributed with the corpus at:
http://www.nb.no/Tilbud/Forske/Spraakbanken/Tilgjengelege-ressursar/Tekstressursar

Parser	UAS	LAS
Baseline	30.8%	3.86%
Danish	69.9%	46.7%
Swedish	77.7%	68.1%
Norwegian	86.6%	83.5%

Table 2: Parser performance. Labelled (LAS) and unlabelled (UAS) attachment scores.

All three parsers are trained using MaltParser (Nivre et al., 2007) using the liblinear learner and the nivreeager parsing algorithm with default settings. The Norwegian parser is trained on the first 90% of the version 0.2 release of the Norwegian dependency treebank with the remaining 10% held out for evaluation, while the cross-lingual parsers are trained on the training sets of Talbanken05 (Nivre et al., 2006) and the Danish Dependency Treebank (Kromann, 2003) as distributed for the CoNLL-X shared task. The parser trained on Swedish data is lexicalised, while the one trained on Danish used a delexicalised corpus.

The performance of the four different preprocessing strategies is summarised in Table 2. The numbers are mostly in line with those reported in Skjærholt and Øvrelid (2012), with a drop of a few percentage points in both LAS and UAS for all parsers, except for a gain of more than 5 points LAS for the Danish parser, due to the fixed relation labels. There are three reasons for the differences: First of all, the test corpus is different; Skjærholt and Øvrelid (2012) used the version 0.1 release of the Norwegian corpus, while we use version 0.2. Secondly, TREd requires that its input trees only have a single child of the root node, while MaltParser will attach unconnected subgraphs to the root node if the graph produced after consuming the whole input isn't connected. Finally, TREd validates dependency relation labels strictly, which revealed a few bugs in the conversion script for the Danish data. A post-processing script corrects the invalid relations and attaches multiple children of the root node to the most appropriate child of the root.

The texts given to the annotators were an amalgam of the outputs of the four parsers, such that each block of ten sentences comes from the same parser. Each chunk was randomly assigned

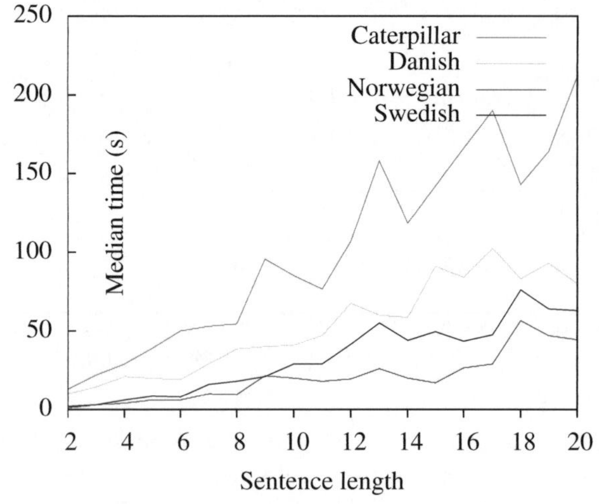

Figure 1: Median annotation time, Odin.

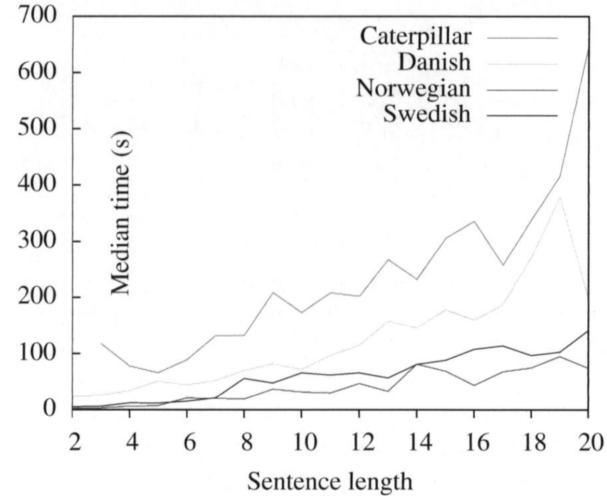

Figure 2: Median annotation time, Thor.

to a parser, in such a way that 5 chunks were parsed with the baseline strategy and the remaining chunks were evenly distributed between the remaining three parsers. This strategy ensures as even a distribution between parsers as possible, while keeping the annotators blind to parser assignments. We avoid the annotators knowing which parser was used, as this could subconciously bias their behaviour.

3 Results

Speed To compare the different parsers as preprocessors for annotation, we need to apply a summary statistic across the times for each annotator, binned by sentence length. We use the median, which is highly resistant to outliers and conceptually simpler than strategies for outlier elimination[4]. Furthermore, to ensure large enough bins, we only consider sentences of length 20 or less.

Figure 1 shows the evolution of annotation time as a function of sentence length for Odin for all four parsers, and Figure 2 the corresponding graphs for Thor. It is clear that, although Odin consistently uses less time to annotate sentences than Thor, the different parsers are ranked identically, and the relative speed-up of the higher quality parsers is similar for both annotators.

Agreement To measure agreement we study the LAS and UAS we get from comparing Odin and Thor's annotations. Artstein and Poesio (2008) argue strongly in favour of using a chance-corrected measure of agreement, but the measures they present are applicable to categorical data, not structured data such as syntactic data. Thus, simple agreement measures are the standard measures in syntax (Hajič, 2004; Miltsakaki et al., 2004; Maamouri et al., 2008). As mentioned in Section 2, only 400 sentences were doubly annotated. Ideally, we would have liked to have all the texts doubly annotated, but external constraints on the annotation effort limited us to the set at hand.

Parser	*n*	UAS	LAS
Baseline	10	99.1%	99.1%
Danish	130	96.3%	94.0%
Swedish	110	96.1%	94.4%
Norwegian	150	96.8%	95.3%

Table 3: Annotator agreement. *n* sentences, unlabelled (UAS) and labelled (LAS) attachment.

Table 3 shows the unlabelled and unlabelled accuracies on the doubly annotated dataset, along with the number of sentences in each dataset. Due to the random distribution of sentences, only a single baseline chunk was in the first 400 sentences, making it hard to draw conclusions on the quality obtained with that strategy. The imbalance is less severe for the other parsers, but the Norwegian set is still almost 50% larger than the Swedish one. The agreement on the baseline set is quite surprising, with only a single token out of 115 receiving different heads and all tokens having the same dependency relation. Unlabelled agreement is lower by about three percentage points on the three remaining datasets, with no real variation in terms

[4]Nor does it assume normality, which would be inappropriate for timing data, unlike most outlier detection methods.

of parser performance, and labelled agreement is somewhat lower again, indicating some level of disagreement over dependency relations.

4 Analysis

Our results are clearest for the question of how time used to annotate is affected by preprocessing quality. The Danish parser halves the time required to annotate sentences compared to the baseline; already an important gain. The Norwegian parser cuts the time in half again, with the Swedish parser between the two. Based on the learning curves in Skjærholt and Øvrelid (2012), a parser with performance equivalent to the Danish parser (70% UAS) can be obtained with about 50 annotated sentences, and the 80% UAS of the Swedish parser is reachable with about 200 sentences.

Given the limited amount of data available for our study of agreement, it is hard to make solid conclusions, but it does appear that head selection is virtually unchanged by parser performance, while there may be some increase in agreement on dependency relation labels, from 96.0% with the Danish parser, to 96.5% and 97.1% with the Swedish and Norwegian parsers. Agreement is extremely high for both heads and labels on the data preprocessed with the baseline parser, but based on 10 sentences, it is impossible to say whether this is a fluke or a reasonable approximation of the value we would get with a larger sample.

The unchanged agreement score suggests that the annotators are not unduly influenced by a better parser. An increase in agreement would not be an unambiguously positive result though; a positive interpretation would be that the annotators' work is closer to the Platonic ideal of a correct analysis of the corpus, but a less charitable interpretation is that the annotators are more biased by the parser. Furthermore, the very high agreement for the baseline parser is potentially worrying if the result remains unchanged by a larger sample. This would indicate that in order to get the best quality annotation, it is necessary to start from a virtually unprocessed corpus, which would require four times as much time as using a 90% UAS parser for preprocessing, based on our data.

5 Conclusions

Given the time-consuming nature of linguistic annotation, higher annotation speed is an obvious good for any annotation project as long as the annotation quality doesn't degrade unacceptably. Based on the results obtained in our study, it is clear that the speed-up to be had from a good dependency parser is important, to the extent that when annotating it is a very bad idea to not use one. Further, based on the learning curves presented in Skjærholt and Øvrelid (2012), it seems that parser adaptation with a view to preprocessing for annotation is primarily useful in the earliest stages of an annotation effort as the learning curves show that once 100 sentences are annotated, a parser trained on that data will already be competitive with a cross-lingual parser for Norwegian. Other languages may require more data, but the amount required is most likely on the same order of magnitude. If same-language data are available, a parser trained on that may last longer.

As regards annotator agreement, our results show that head selection as measured by unlabelled accuracy is unchanged by parser accuracy. Agreement as measured by labelled accuracy increases somewhat with increased parser performance, which indicates that agreement on labels increases with parser performance. The agreement results for our baseline parser are extremely high, but given that we only have ten sentences to compare, it is impossible to say if this is a real difference between the baseline and the other parsers.

5.1 Future work

There are a number of things, particularly relating to annotator agreement we would like to investigate further. Chief of these is the lack of a chance corrected agreement measure for dependency syntax. As mentioned previously, no such measure has been formulated as most agreement measures are most naturally expressed in terms of categorical assignments, which is a bad fit for syntax. However, it should be possible to create an agreement measure suitable for syntax.

We would also like to perform a deeper study of the effects of preprocessing on agreement using a proper measure of agreement. The results for our baseline strategy are based on extremely little data, and thus it is hard to draw any solid conclusions. We would also like to see if different groups of annotators are influenced differently by the parsers. Our annotators were both trained linguists, and it would be interesting to see if using lay annotators or undergraduate linguistics students changes the agreement scores.

References

Ron Artstein and Massimo Poesio. 2008. Inter-Coder Agreement for Computational Linguistics. *Computational Linguistics*, 34(4):555–596.

Fu-Dong Chiou, David Chiang, and Martha Palmer. 2001. Facilitating Treebank Annotation Using a Statistical Parser. In *Proceedings of the first international conference on Human language technology research*, pages 1–4.

Karën Fort and Benoît Sagot. 2010. Influence of Pre-annotation on POS-tagged Corpus Development. In Nianwen Xue and Massimo Poesio, editors, *Proceedings of the fourth linguistic annotation workshop*, pages 56–63, Stroudsburg. Association for Computational Linguistics.

Jan Hajič. 2004. Complex Corpus Annotation: The Prague Dependency Treebank. Jazykovedný ústav L'. Štúra, SAV.

Matthias Trautner Kromann. 2003. The Danish Dependency Treebank and the DTAG Treebank Tool. In *Proceedings of the 2nd Workshop on Treebanks and Linguistic Theories*, pages 217–220. Växjö University Press.

Mohamed Maamouri, Ann Bies, and Seth Kulick. 2008. Enhancing the Arabic Treebank : A Collaborative Effort toward New Annotation Guidelines. In *Proceedings of the 6th International Conference on Language Resources and Evaluation*, pages 3192–3196. European Language Resources Association.

Mitchell P. Marcus, Beatrice Santorini, and Mary Ann Marcinkiewicz. 1993. Building a large annotated corpus of English: The Penn Treebank. *Computational Linguistics*, 19(2):313–330.

Eleni Miltsakaki, Rashmi Prasad, Aravind Joshi, and Bonnie Webber. 2004. The Penn Discourse Treebank. In *Proceedings of the 4th International Conference on Language Resources and Evaluation*, pages 2237–2240. European Language Resources Association.

Joakim Nivre, Jens Nilsson, and Johan Hall. 2006. Talbanken05 : A Swedish Treebank with Phrase Structure and Dependency Annotation. In *Proceedings of the fifth international conference on Language Resources and Evaluation.*

Joakim Nivre, Jens Nilsson, Johan Hall, Atanas Chanev, Gülşen Eryiğit, Sandra Kübler, Svetoslav Marinov, and Erwin Marsi. 2007. MaltParser: A language-independent system for data-driven dependency parsing. *Natural Language Engineering*, 13(2):95–135.

Arne Skjærholt and Lilja Øvrelid. 2012. Impact of treebank characteristics on cross-lingual parser adaptation. In Iris Hendrickx, Sandra Kübler, and Kiril Simov, editors, *Proceedings of the 11th international workshop on treebanks and linguistic theories*, pages 187–198, Lisbon. Edições Colibri.

Anders Søgaard. 2011. Data point selection for cross-language adaptation of dependency parsers. In *Proceedings of the 49th Annual Meeting of the Association for Computational Linguistics*, pages 682–686.

Daniel Zeman and Philip Resnik. 2008. Cross-Language Parser Adaptation between Related Languages. In Anil Kumar Singh, editor, *Proceedings of the IJCNLP-08 Workshop on NLP for Less Privileged Languages*, pages 35–42, Hyderabad, India. Asian Federation of Natural Language Processing.

Continuous Measurement Scales in Human Evaluation of Machine Translation

Yvette Graham **Timothy Baldwin** **Alistair Moffat** **Justin Zobel**
Department of Computing and Information Systems, The University of Melbourne
{ygraham,tbaldwin,ammoffat,jzobel}@unimelb.edu.au

Abstract

We explore the use of continuous rating scales for human evaluation in the context of machine translation evaluation, comparing two assessor-intrinsic quality-control techniques that do not rely on agreement with expert judgments. Experiments employing Amazon's Mechanical Turk service show that quality-control techniques made possible by the use of the continuous scale show dramatic improvements to intra-annotator agreement of up to $+0.101$ in the kappa coefficient, with inter-annotator agreement increasing by up to $+0.144$ when additional standardization of scores is applied.

1 Introduction

Human annotations of language are often required in natural language processing (NLP) tasks for evaluation purposes, in order to estimate how well a given system mimics activities traditionally performed by humans. In tasks such as machine translation (MT) and natural language generation, the system output is a fully-formed string in a target language. Annotations can take the form of direct estimates of the quality of those outputs or be structured as the simpler task of ranking competing outputs from best-to-worst (Callison-Burch et al., 2012).

A direct estimation method of assessment, as opposed to ranking outputs from best-to-worst, has the advantage that it includes in annotations not only that one output is better than another, but also the degree to which that output was better than the other. In addition, direct estimation of quality within the context of machine translation extends the usefulness of the annotated data to other tasks such as quality-estimation (Callison-Burch et al., 2012).

For an evaluation to be credible, the annotations must be credible. The simplest way of establishing this is to have the same data point annotated by multiple annotators, and measure the agreement between them. There has been a worrying trend in recent MT shared tasks – whether the evaluation was structured as ranking translations from best-to-worst, or by direct estimation of fluency and adequacy – of agreement between annotators decreasing (Callison-Burch et al., 2008; Callison-Burch et al., 2009; Callison-Burch et al., 2010; Callison-Burch et al., 2011; Callison-Burch et al., 2012). Inconsistency in human evaluation of machine translation calls into question conclusions drawn from those assessments, and is the target of this paper: by revising the annotation process, can we improve annotator agreement, and hence the quality of human annotations?

Direct estimates of quality are intrinsically continuous in nature, but are often collected using an interval-level scale with a relatively low number of categories, perhaps to make the task cognitively easier for human assessors. In MT evaluation, five and seven-point interval-level scales are common (Callison-Burch et al., 2007; Denkowski and Lavie, 2010). However, the interval-level scale commonly used for direct estimation of translation quality (and other NLP annotation tasks) forces human judges to discretize their assessments into a fixed number of categories, and this process could be a cause of inconsistency in human judgments. In particular, an assessor may be repeatedly forced to choose between two categories, neither of which really fits their judgment. The continuous nature of translation quality assessment, as well as the fact that many statistical methods exist that can be applied to continuous data but not interval-level data, motivates our trial of a continuous rating scale.

We use human judgments of translation fluency as a test case and compare consistency levels when the conventional 5-point interval-level scale and a continuous visual analog scale (VAS) are used for human evaluation. We collected data via Amazon's Mechanical Turk, where the quality of annotations is known to vary considerably (Callison-Burch et al., 2010). As such, we test two quality-control techniques based on statistical significance – made possible by the use of the continuous rating scale – to intrinsically assess the quality of individual human judges. The quality-control techniques are not restricted to fluency judgments and are relevant to more general MT evaluation, as well as other NLP annotation tasks.

2 Machine Translation Fluency

Measurement of fluency as a component of MT evaluation has been carried out for a number of years (LDC, 2005), but it has proven difficult to acquire consistent judgments, even from expert assessors. Evaluation rounds such as the annual Workshop on Statistical Machine Translation (WMT) use human judgments of translation quality to produce official rankings in shared tasks, initially using an two-item assessment of fluency and adequacy as separate attributes, and more recently by asking judges to simply rank system outputs against one another according to "which translation is better". However, the latter method also reports low levels of agreement between judges. For example, the 2007 WMT reported low levels of consistency in fluency judgments in terms of both intra-annotator agreement (intra-aa), with a kappa coefficient of $\kappa = 0.54$ (moderate), and inter-annotator agreement (inter-aa), with $\kappa = 0.25$ (slight). Adequacy judgments for the same data received even lower scores: $\kappa = 0.47$ for intra-aa, and $\kappa = 0.23$ for inter-aa.

While concerns over annotator agreement have seen recent WMT evaluations move away from using fluency as an evaluation component, there can be no question that fluency is a useful means of evaluating translation output. In particular, it is not biased by reference translations. The use of automatic metrics is often criticized by the fact that a system that produces a good translation which happens not to be similar to the reference translations will be unfairly penalized. Similarly, if human annotators are provided with one or more reference sentences, they may inadvertently favor translations that are similar to those references. If fluency is judged independently of adequacy, no reference translation is needed, and the bias is removed.

In earlier work, we consider the possibility that *translation quality* is a hypothetical construct (Graham et al., 2012), and suggest applying methods of validating measurement of psychological constructs to the validation of measurements of translation quality. In psychology, a scale that employs more items as opposed to fewer is considered more valid. Under this criteria, a two-item (fluency and adequacy) scale is more valid than a single-item translation quality measure.

3 Measurement Scales

Direct estimation methods are designed to elicit from the subject a direct quantitative estimate of the magnitude of an attribute (Streiner and Norman, 1989). We compare judgments collected on a visual analog scale (VAS) to those using an interval-level scale presented to the human judge as a sequence of radio-buttons. The VAS was first used in psychology in the 1920's, and prior to the digital age, scales used a line of fixed length (usually 100mm in length), with anchor labels at both ends, and to be marked by hand with an "X" at the desired location (Streiner and Norman, 1989).

When an interval-scale is used in NLP evaluation or other annotation tasks, it is commonly presented in the form of an adjectival scale, where categories are labeled in increasing/decreasing quality. For example, an MT evaluation of fluency might specify 5 = "Flawless English", 4 = "Good English", 3 = "Non-native English", 2 = "Disfluent English", and 1 = "Incomprehensible" (Callison-Burch et al., 2007; Denkowski and Lavie, 2010).

With both a VAS and an adjectival scale, the choice of labels can be critical. In medical research, patients' ratings of their own health have been shown to be highly dependent on the exact wording of descriptors (Seymour et al., 1985). Alexandrov (2010) provides a summary of the extensive literature on the numerous issues associated with adjectival scale labels, including bias resulting from positively and negatively worded items not being true opposites of one another, and items intended to have neutral intensity in fact proving to have unique conceptual meanings.

Likert scales avoid the problems associated with adjectival labels, by structuring the question as a simple statement that the respondent registers their level of (dis)agreement with. Figure 1 shows

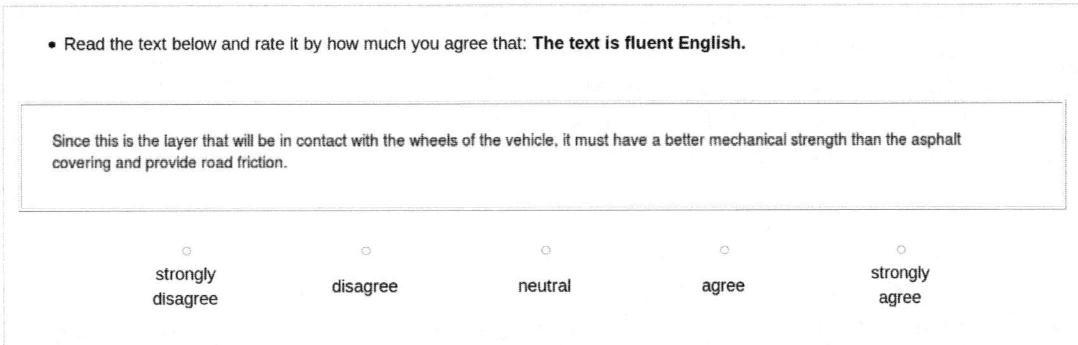

Figure 1: Amazon Mechanical Turk interface for fluency judgments with a Likert-type scale.

Figure 2: Continuous rating scale for fluency judgments with two anchors.

the Likert-type interval-level scale we use to collect fluency judgments of MT output, and Figure 2 shows an equivalent VAS using the two most extreme anchor labels, *strongly disagree* and *strongly agree*.

4 Crowd-sourcing Judgments

The volume of judgments required for evaluation of NLP tasks can be large, and employing experts to undertake those judgments may not always be feasible. Crowd-sourcing services via the Web offer an attractive alternative, and have been used in conjunction with a range of NLP evaluation and annotation tasks. Several guides exist for instructing researchers from various backgrounds on using Amazon's Mechanical Turk (AMT) (Gibson et al., 2011; Callison-Burch, 2009), and allowance for the use of AMT is increasingly being made in research grant applications, as a cost-effective way of gathering data. Issues remain in connection with low payment levels (Fort et al., 2011); nevertheless, Ethics Approval Boards are typically disinterested in projects that make use of AMT, regarding AMT as being a purchased service rather than a part of the experimentation that may affect human subjects.

The use of crowd-sourced judgments does, however, introduce the possibility of increased inconsistency, with service requesters typically having no specific or verifiable knowledge about any given worker. Hence, the possibility that a worker is acting in good faith but not performing the task well must be allowed for, as must the likelihood that some workers will quite ruthlessly seek to minimize the time spent on the task, by deliberately giving low-quality or fake answers. Some workers may even attempt to implement automated responses, so that they get paid without having to do the work they are being paid for.

For example, if the task at hand is that of assessing the fluency of text snippets, it is desirable to employ native speakers. With AMT the requester has the ability to restrict responses to only workers who have a specified skill. But that facility does not necessarily lead to confidence – there is nothing stopping a worker employing someone else to do the test for them. Devising a test that reliably evaluates whether or not someone is a native speaker is also not at all straightforward.

Amazon allow location restrictions, based on the registered residential address of the Turker, which can be used to select in favor of those likely to have at least some level of fluency (Callison-Burch et al., 2010). We initially applied this restriction to both sets of judgments in experiments, setting the task up so that only workers registered in Germany could evaluate the to-German translations, for example. However, very low response rates for languages other than to-English were problematic, and we also received a number of apparently-genuine requests from native speakers residing outside the target countries. As a result, we removed all location restrictions other than for the to-English tasks.[1]

Crowd-sourcing judgments has the obvious risk of being vulnerable to manipulation. On the other hand, crowd-sourced judgments also offer the potential of being *more* valid than those of experts, since person-in-the-street abilities might be a more useful yardstick for some tasks than informed academic judgment, and because a greater number of judges may be available.

Having the ability to somehow evaluate the quality of the work undertaken by a Turker is thus highly desirable. We would like to be able to put in place a mechanism that filters out non-native speakers; native speakers with low literacy levels; cheats; and robotic cheats. That goal is considered in the next section.

5 Judge-Intrinsic Quality Control

One common method of quality assessment for a new process is to identify a set of "gold-standard" items that have been judged by experts and whose merits are agreed, present them to the new process or assessor, and then assess the degree to which the new process and the experts "agree" on the outcomes (Snow et al., 2008; Callison-Burch et al., 2010). A possible concern is that even experts can be expected to disagree (and hence have low inter-aa levels), meaning that disagreement with the new process will also occur, even if the new process is a reliable one. In addition, the quality of the judgments collected is also assessed via agreement levels, meaning that any filtering based on a quality-control measure that uses agreement will automatically increase consistency, even to the extent of recalibrating non-expert workers' responses to more closely match expert judgments (Snow et al., 2008). Moreover, if an interval-level scale is used, standardized scores cannot be employed, so a non-expert who is more lenient than the experts, but in a reliable and systematic manner, might still have their assessments discarded.

For judgments collected on a continuous scale, statistical tests based on difference of means (over assessors) are possible. We structure our human

[1] It has also been suggested that AMT restricts Turker registration by country; official information is unclear about this.

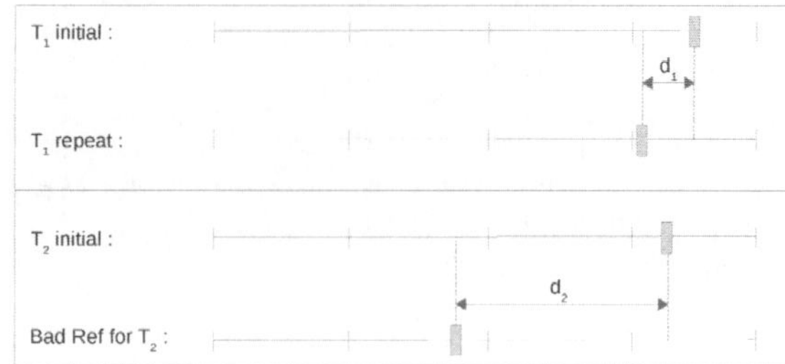

Figure 3: Intrinsic quality-control distributions for an individual judge.

intelligence tasks (HITs) on Mechanical Turk in groups of 100 in a way that allows us to control assignment of repeat item pairs to workers, so that statistical tests can later be applied to an individual worker's score distributions for repeat items. Workers were made aware of the task structure before accepting it – the task preview included a message *This HIT consists of 100 fluency assessments, you have 0 so far complete.*

We refer to the repeat items in a HIT as *ask_again* translations. In addition, we inserted a number of *bad_reference* pairs into each HIT, with a *bad_reference* pair consisting of a genuine MT system output, and a distorted sentence derived from it, expecting that its fluency was markedly worse than that of the corresponding system output. This was done by randomly selecting two words in the sentence and duplicating them in random locations not adjacent to the original word and not in the initial or sentence-final position. Any other degradation method could also be used, so long as it has a high probability of reducing the fluency of the text, and provided that it is not immediately obvious to the judges.

Insertion of *ask_again* and *bad_reference* pairs into the HITs allowed two measurements to be made for each worker: when presented with an *ask_again* pair, we expect a conscientious judge to give similar scores (but when using a continuous scale, certainly not identical), and on *bad_reference* pairings a conscientious judge should reliably give the altered sentence a lower score. The wide separation of the two appearances of an *ask_again* pair makes it unlikely that a judge would remember either the sentence or their first reaction to it, and backwards movement through the sentences comprising each HIT was not possible. In total, each HIT contained 100 sen-

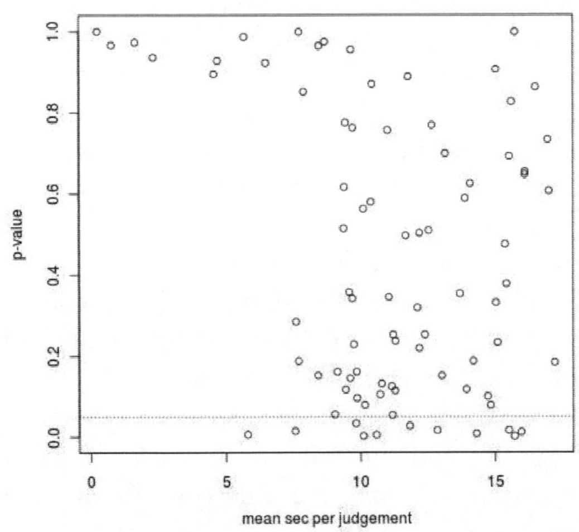

Figure 4: Welch's t-test reliability estimates plotted against mean seconds per judgment.

tences, including 10 *bad_reference* pairs, and 10 *ask_again* pairs.

Figure 3 illustrates these two types of pairs, presuming that over the course of one or more HITs each worker has assessed multiple *ask_again* pairs generating the distribution indicated by d_1, and also multiple *bad_reference* pairs, generating the distribution indicated by d_2. As an estimate of the reliability of each individual judge we apply a t-test to compare *ask_again* differences with *bad_reference* differences, with the expectation that for a conscientious worker the latter should be larger than the former. Since there is no guarantee that the two distributions of d_1 and d_2 have the same variance, we apply Welch's adaptation of the Student t-test.

The null hypothesis to be tested for each AMT worker is that the score difference for *ask_again* pairs is not less than the score difference for *bad_reference* pairs. Lower p values mean more reliable workers; in the experiments that are reported shortly, we use $p < 0.05$ as a threshold of reliability. We also applied the non-parametric Mann-Whitney test to the same data, for the purpose of comparison, since there is no guarantee that d_1 and d_2 will be normally distributed for a given assessor.

The next section provides details of the experimental structure, and then describes the outcomes in terms of their effect on overall system rankings. As a preliminary indication of Turker behavior, Figure 4 summarizes some of the data that was obtained. Each plotted point represents one AMT worker who took part in our experiments, and the horizontal axis reflects their average per-judgment time (noting that this is an imprecise measurement, since they may have taken phone calls or answered email while working through a HIT, or simply left the task idle to help obscure a lack of effort). The vertical scale is the p value obtained for that worker when the *ask_again* distribution is compared to their *bad_reference* distribution, with a line at $p = 0.05$ indicating the upper limit of the zone for which we are confident that they had a different overall response to *ask_again* pairs than they did to *bad_reference* pairs. Note the small number of very fast, very inaccurate workers at the top left; we have no hesitation in calling them unconscientious (and declining to pay them for their completed HITs). Note also the very small number of workers for which it was possible to reliably distinguish their *ask_again* behavior from their *bad_reference* behavior.

6 Experiments

HIT Structure

A sample of 560 translations was selected at random from the WMT 2012 published shared task dataset for a range of language pairs, with segments consisting of 70 translations, each assigned to a total of eight distinct HITs. The sentences were generated as image files, as recommended for judgment of translations (Callison Burch, 2009). Each HIT was presented to a worker as a set of 100 sentences including a total of 30 quality control items, with only one sentence visible on-screen at any given time. Each quality control item comprised a pair of corresponding translations, widely separated within the HIT. Three kinds of quality control pairs were used:

- *ask_again*: system output and exact repeat;
- *bad_reference*: system output and an altered version of it with noticeably lower fluency; and
- *good_reference*: system output and the corresponding human produced reference translation (as provided in the released WMT data).

Each HIT consisted of 10 groups, each containing 10 sentences: 7 "normal" translations, plus one of each type of quality control translation drawn from one of the other groups in the HIT in such a way that 40–60 judgments would be completed between the elements of any quality-control pair.

Consistency of Human Judgments

Using judgments collected on the continuous rating scale, we first examine assessor consistency based on Welch's t-test and the non-parametric Mann-Whitney U-test. In order to examine the degree to which human assessors assign consistent scores, we compute mean values of d_1 (Figure 3) when *ask_again* pairs are given to the same judge, and across pairs of judges. Three sets of results are shown: the raw unfiltered data; data filtered according to $p < 0.05$ according to the quality-control regime described in the previous section using the Welch's t-test; and data filtered using the Mann-Whitney U-test. Table 1 shows that the t-test indicates that only 13.1% of assessors meet quality control hurdle, while a higher proportion, 35.7%, of assessors are deemed acceptable.

The stricter filter, Welch's t-test, yields more consistent scores for same-judge repeat items: decreases of 4.5 (mean) and 4.2 (sd) are observed when quality control is applied. In addition, results for Welch's t-test show high levels of consistency for same-judge repeat items: an average difference of only 9.5 is observed, which is not unreasonable, given that the scale is 100 points in length and a 10-point difference corresponds to just 60 pixels on the screen.

For repeat items rated by distinct judges, both filtering methods decrease the mean difference in scores compared to the unfiltered baseline, with the two tests giving similar improvements.

When an interval-level scale is used to evaluate the data, the Kappa coefficient is commonly used to evaluate consistency levels of human judges (Callison-Burch et al., 2007), where $\Pr(a)$ is the relative observed agreement among raters, and $\Pr(e)$ is the hypothetical probability of chance agreement:

$$\kappa = \frac{\Pr(a) - \Pr(e)}{1 - \Pr(e)}$$

In order to use the Kappa coefficient to compare agreement levels for the interval-level and continuous scales, we convert continuous scale scores to a target number of interval categories. We do this primarily for a target number of five, as this best provides a comparison between scores for the 5-point interval-level scale. But we also present results for targets of four and two categories, since the continuous scale is marked at the midway and quarter points, providing implicit intervals. A two-category is also interesting if the assessment process is regarded as dichotomizing to only include for each translation whether or not the judge considered it to be "good" or "bad". Use of statistical difference of means tests on interval-level data is not recommended; but for the purpose of illustration, we also applied Welch's t-test to quality control workers that completed the interval-level HITs, with the same threshold of $p < 0.05$.

Tables 2 and 3 show intra-annotator agreement for the five-point interval scale and continuous scales, with and without quality control.[2] Results for repeat items on the interval-level scale show that quality control only alters intra-aa marginally ($\Pr(a)$ increases by 1%), and that inter-aa levels worsen ($\Pr(a)$ decreases by 6.2%). This confirms that applying statistical tests to interval-level data is not a suitable way of filtering out low quality workers.

When comparing consistency levels of assessors using the interval-level scale to those of the continuous scale, we observe marginally lower κ coefficients for both intra-aa (-0.009) and inter-aa (-0.041) for the continuous scale. However, this is likely to be in part due to the fact that the continuous scale corresponds more intuitively to 4 categories, and agreement levels for the unfiltered 4-category continuous scale are higher than those collected on the interval-level scale by $+0.023$ intra-aa and $+0.014$ inter-aa.

Applying quality-control on the continuous scale results in dramatic increases in intra-aa levels: $+0.152$ for 5-categories (5-cat), $+0.100$ for 4-categories (4-cat) and $+0.096$ for 2-categories (2-cat). When considering inter-aa levels, quality-control does not directly result in as dramatic an increase, as inter-aa levels increase by $+0.010$ for 5-cat, $+0.006$ for 4-cat and $+0.004$ for 2-cat. It is likely, however, that apparent disagreement between assessors might be due to different assessors judging fluency generally worse or better than one another. The continuous scale allows for scores to be standardized by normalizing scores with respect to the mean and standard deviation of all scores assigned by a given individual judge. We therefore transform scores of each judge into

[2] Note that the mapping from continuous scores to categories was not applied for quality control.

			same judge		distinct judges	
	workers	judgments	mean	sd	mean	sd
Unfiltered	100.0%	100.0%	14.0	18.4	28.9	23.5
Welch's t-test	13.1%	23.5%	9.5	14.2	25.2	21.0
Mann-Whitney U-test	35.7%	48.8%	13.1	17.7	25.0	22.6

Table 1: Mean and standard deviation of score differences for continuous scale with *ask_again* items within a given judge and across two distinct judges, for no quality control (unfiltered), Welch's t-test and Mann-Whitney U-test with a quality-control threshold of $p < 0.05$.

# categ-ories	5-pt. interval unfiltered		5-pt. interval filtered		continuous unfiltered		continuous filtered	
	$\Pr(a)$	κ	$\Pr(a)$	κ	$\Pr(a)$	κ	$\Pr(a)$	κ
5	60.4%	0.505	61.4%	0.517	59.7%	0.496	71.8%	0.647
4	-	-	-	-	64.6%	0.528	72.1%	0.629
2	-	-	-	-	85.2%	0.704	90.0%	0.800

Table 2: Intra-annotator (same judge) agreement levels for 5-point interval and continuous scales for unfiltered judgments and judgments of workers with $p < 0.05$ for Welch's t-test.

corresponding z-scores and use percentiles of the combined set of all scores to map z-scores to categories where a score falling in the bottom 20 th percentile corresponds to *strongly disagree*, scores between the 20 th and 40 th percentile to *disagree*, and so on. Although this method of transformation is somewhat harsh on the continuous scale, since scores no longer correspond to different locations on the original scale, it nevertheless shows an increase in consistency of $+0.05$ (5-cat), $+0.086$ (4-cat) and $+0.144$ (2-cat). However, caution must be taken when interpreting consistency for standardized scores, as can be seen from the increase in agreement observed when unfiltered scores are standardized.

Table 4 shows a breakdown by target language of the proportion of judgments collected whose scores met the significance threshold of $p < 0.05$. Results appear at first to have shockingly low levels of high quality work, especially for English and German. When running the tasks in Mechanical Turk, it is worth noting that we did not adopt statistical tests to automatically accept/reject HITs and we believe this would be rather harsh on workers. Our method of quality control is a high bar to reach and it is likely that many workers that do not meet the significance threshold would still have been working in good faith. In practice, we individually examined mean scores for reference translation, system outputs and *bad_reference* pairs, and only declined payment when there was no doubt the response was either automatic or extremely careless.

English	German	French	Spanish
10.0%	0%	57.9%	62.5%

Table 4: High quality judgments, by language.

The structure of the task and the fact that the quality-control items were somewhat hidden may have lulled workers into a false sense of complacency, and perhaps encouraged careless responses. However, even taking this into consideration, the fact that *none* of the German speaking assessors and just 10% of English speaking assessors reached our standards serves to highlight the importance of good quality-control techniques when employing services like AMT. In addition, the risk of getting low quality work for some languages might be more risky than for others. The response rate for high quality work for Spanish and French was so much higher than German and English, perhaps by chance, or perhaps the result of factors that will be revealed in future experimentation.

System Rankings

As an example of the degree to which system rankings are affected by applying quality control, for the language direction for which we achieved the highest number of high quality assessments, English-to-Spanish, we include system rankings by mean score with each measurement scale, with and without quality control and for mean z-scores

# categ-ories	5-pt. interval unfiltered		5-pt. interval qual.-controlled		continuous unfiltered		continuous qual.-controlled		cont. standrdzed. unfiltered		cont. standrdzed. qual.-controlled	
	$\Pr(a)$	κ	$\Pr(a)$	κ	$\Pr(a)$	κ	$\Pr(a)$	κ	$\Pr(a)$	κ	$\Pr(a)$	κ
5	33.0%	0.16	26.8%	0.084	29.5%	0.119	30.3%	0.128	30.2%	0.1272	33.5%	0.169
4	-	-	-	-	38.1%	0.174	38.5%	0.180	35.5%	0.1403	44.5%	0.260
2	-	-	-	-	66.5%	0.331	66.8%	0.335	75.5%	0.5097	73.8%	0.475

Table 3: Inter-annotator (distinct judge) agreement levels for 5-point interval and continuous scales for unfiltered judgments and judgments of workers with $p < 0.05$ for Welch's t-test.

5-pt. unfiltered		5-pt. qual.-controlled		continuous unfiltered		continuous qual.-controlled		z-scores continuous qual.-controlled	
Sys A	2.00	Sys A	2.00	Sys E	69.60	Sys E	74.39	Sys E	0.43
Sys B	1.98	Sys D	1.97	Sys B	61.78	Sys F	65.07	Sys B	0.16
Sys C	1.98	Sys F	1.95	Sys G	60.21	Sys G	64.51	Sys G	0.08
Sys D	1.98	Sys C	1.95	Sys F	59.38	Sys B	63.68	Sys D	0.06
Sys E	1.98	Sys E	1.95	Sys D	59.05	Sys D	63.52	Sys C	0.02
Sys F	1.97	Sys B	1.94	Sys A	57.44	Sys C	61.33	Sys F	0.01
Sys G	1.97	Sys G	1.93	Sys I	56.31	Sys A	58.43	Sys H	–0.03
Sys H	1.96	Sys H	1.90	Sys C	55.82	Sys I	57.46	Sys I	–0.07
Sys I	1.96	Sys I	1.88	Sys H	55.27	Sys H	57.04	Sys A	–0.10
Sys J	1.94	Sys J	1.81	Sys J	50.46	Sys J	50.73	Sys J	–0.23
Sys K	1.90	Sys K	1.76	Sys K	44.62	Sys K	41.25	Sys K	–0.47

Table 5: WMT system rankings based on approximately 80 randomly-selected fluency judgments per system, with and without quality control for radio button and continuous input types, based on German-English. The quality control method applied is annotators who score worsened system output and genuine system outputs with statistically significant lower scores according to paired Student's t-test.

when raw scores are normalized by individual assessor mean and standard deviation. The results are shown in Table 5. (Note that we do not claim that these rankings are indicative of actual system rankings, as only fluency of translations was assessed, using an average of just 55 translations per system.)

When comparing system rankings for unfiltered versus quality-controlled continuous scales, firstly the overall difference in ranking is not as dramatic as one might expect, as many systems retain the same rank order, with only a small number of systems changing position. This happens because random-clickers cannot systematically favor any system, and positive and negative random scores tend to cancel each other out. However, even having two systems ordered incorrectly is of concern; careful quality control, and the use of normalization of assessors' scores may lead to more consistent outcomes. We also note that incorrect system orderings may lead to flow-on effects for evaluation of automatic metrics.

The system rankings in Table 5 also show how the use of the continuous scale can be used to rank systems according to z-scores, so that individual assessor preferences over judgments can be ameliorated. Interestingly, the system that scores closest to the mean, Sys F, corresponds to the baseline system for the shared task with a z-score of 0.01.

7 Conclusion

We have compared human assessor consistency levels for judgments collected on a five-point interval-level scale to those collected on a continuous scale, using machine translation fluency as a test case. We described a method for quality-controlling crowd-sourced annotations that results in marked increases in intra-annotator consistency and does not require judges to agree with experts. In addition, the use of a continuous scale allows scores to be standardized to eliminate individual judge preferences, resulting in higher levels of inter-annotator consistency.

Acknowledgments

This work was funded by the Australian Research Council. Ondřej Bojar, Rosa Gog, Simon Gog, Florian Hanke, Maika Vincente Navarro, Pavel Pecina, and Djame Seddah provided translations of task instructions, and feedback on published HITs.

References

A. Alexandrov. 2010. Characteristics of single-item measures in Likert scale format. *The Electronic Journal of Business Research Methods*, 8:1–12.

C. Callison-Burch, C. Fordyce, P. Koehn, C. Monz, and J. Schroeder. 2007. (Meta-) evaluation of machine translation. In *Proc. 2nd Wkshp. Statistical Machine Translation*, pages 136–158, Prague, Czech Republic.

C. Callison-Burch, C. Fordyce, P. Koehn, C. Monz, and J. Schroeder. 2008. Further meta-evaluation of machine translation. In *Proc. 3rd Wkshp. Statistical Machine Translation*, pages 70–106, Columbus, Ohio.

C. Callison-Burch, P. Koehn, C. Monz, and J. Schroeder. 2009. Findings of the 2009 Workshop on Statistical Machine Translation. In *Proc. 4th Wkshp. Statistical Machine Translation*, pages 1–28, Athens, Greece.

C. Callison Burch, P. Koehn, C. Monz, K. Peterson, M. Przybocki, and O. Zaidan. 2010. Findings of the 2010 Joint Workshop on Statistical Machine Translation and Metrics for Machine Translation. In *Proc. 5th Wkshp. Statistical Machine Translation*, pages 17–53, Uppsala, Sweden.

C. Callison-Burch, P. Koehn, C. Monz, and O. Zaidan. 2011. Findings of the 2011 Workshop on Statistical Machine Translation. In *Proc. 6th Wkshp. Statistical Machine Translation*, pages 22–64, Edinburgh, Scotland.

C. Callison-Burch, P. Koehn, C. Monz, M. Post, R. Soricut, and L. Specia. 2012. Findings of the 2012 Workshop on Statistical Machine Translation. In *Proc. 7th Wkshp. Statistical Machine Translation*, pages 10–51, Montreal, Canada.

C. Callison-Burch. 2009. Fast, cheap, and creative: Evaluating translation quality using Amazon's Mechanical Turk. In *Proc. Conf. Empirical Methods in Natural Language Processing*, pages 286–295, Singapore.

M. Denkowski and A. Lavie. 2010. Choosing the right evaluation for machine translation: An examination of annotator and automatic metric performance on human judgement tasks. In *Proc. 9th Conf. Assoc. Machine Translation in the Americas (AMTA)*, Denver, Colorado.

K. Fort, G. Adda, and K. B. Cohen. 2011. Amazon Mechanical Turk: Gold mine or coal mine? *Computational Linguistics*, 37(2):413–420.

E. Gibson, S. Piantadosi, and K. Fedorenko. 2011. Using Mechanical Turk to obtain and analyze English acceptability judgments. *Language and Linguistics Compass*, 5/8:509–524.

Y. Graham, T. Baldwin, A. Harwood, A. Moffat, and J. Zobel. 2012. Measurement of progress in machine translation. In *Proc. Australasian Language Technology Wkshp.*, pages 70–78, Dunedin, New Zealand.

LDC. 2005. Linguistic data annotation specification: Assessment of fluency and adequacy in translations. Technical report, Linguistic Data Consortium. Revision 1.5.

R. A. Seymour, J. M. Simpson, J. E. Charlton, and M. E. Phillips. 1985. An evaluation of length and end-phrase of visiual analogue scales in dental pain. *Pain*, 21:177–185.

R. Snow, B. O'Connor, D. Jursfsky, and A. Y. Ng. 2008. Cheap and fast – but is it good? Evaluating non-expert annotations for natural language tasks. In *Proc. Conf. Empirical Methods in Natural Language Processing*, pages 254–263, Honolulu, Hawaii.

D. L. Streiner and G. R. Norman. 1989. *Health Measurement Scales: A Practical Guide to their Development and Use*. Oxford University Press, fourth edition.

Entailment: An Effective Metric for Comparing and Evaluating Hierarchical and Non-hierarchical Annotation Schemes

Rohan Ramanath* R. V. College of Engineering, India ronramanath@gmail.com

Monojit Choudhury **Kalika Bali** Microsoft Research Lab India {monojitc, kalikab}@microsoft.com

Abstract

Hierarchical or *nested* annotation of linguistic data often co-exists with simpler non-hierarchical or *flat* counterparts, a classic example being that of annotations used for parsing and chunking. In this work, we propose a general strategy for comparing across these two schemes of annotation using the concept of *entailment* that formalizes a correspondence between them. We use crowdsourcing to obtain query and sentence chunking and show that entailment can not only be used as an effective evaluation metric to assess the quality of annotations, but it can also be employed to filter out noisy annotations.

1 Introduction

Linguistic annotations at all levels of linguistic organization – phonological, morpho-syntactic, semantic, discourse and pragmatic, are often hierarchical or *nested* in nature. For instance, syntactic dependencies are annotated as *phrase structure* or *dependency trees* (Jurafsky and Martin, 2000). Nevertheless, the inherent cognitive load associated with nested segmentation and the sufficiency of simpler annotation schemes for building NLP applications have often lead researchers to define non-hierarchical or *flat* annotation schemes. The flat annotation, in essence, is a "flattened" version of the tree. For instance, *chunking* of Natural Language (NL) text, which is often considered an essential preprocessing step for many NLP applications (Abney, 1991; Abney, 1995), is, loosely speaking, a flattened version of the phrase structure tree. The closely related task of *Query Segmentation* is of special interest to us here, as it is the first step in further analysis and understanding of Web search queries (Hagen et al., 2011).

*The work was done during author's internship at Microsoft Research Lab India.

f	Pipe representation	*Boundary var.*
3	barbie dress up | games	0 0 1
3	barbie dress | up games	0 1 0
2	barbie | dress up | games	1 0 1
2	barbie | dress up games	1 0 0

Table 1: Example of flat segmentations from 10 Turkers. *f* is the frequency of annotations; segment boundaries are represented by |.

The task in both query and sentence chunking is to divide the string of words into contiguous substrings of words (commonly refered to as *segments* or *chunks*) such that the words from a segment are related to each other more strongly than words from different segments. It is typically assumed that the segments are syntactically and semantically coherent. Table 1 illustrates the concept of segmentation of a query. The crowdsourced annotations for this data were obtained from 10 annotators, the experimental details of which will be described in Sec. 5. We shall refer to this style of text chunking as *flat segmentation.*

Nested segmentation of a query or a sentence, on the other hand, is a recursive application of flat segmentation, whereby the longer flat segments are further divided into smaller chunks recursively. The process stops when a segment consists of less than three words or is a multiword entity that cannot be segmented further. This style of segmentation can be represented through nested parenthesization of the text, as illustrated in Table 2. These annotations were also obtained through the same crowdsourcing experiment (Sec. 5). Fig. 1 shows an alternative visualization of a nested segmentation in the form of a tree.

An important problem that arises in the context of flat segmentation is the issue of granular-

f	Bracket representation	*Boundary var.*
4	((barbie dress)(up games))	0 1 0
3	(barbie ((dress up) games))	2 0 1
2	(barbie (dress (up games)))	2 1 0
1	((barbie (dress up)) games)	1 0 2

Table 2: Example of nested segmentation from 10 Turkers. *f* is the frequency of annotations.

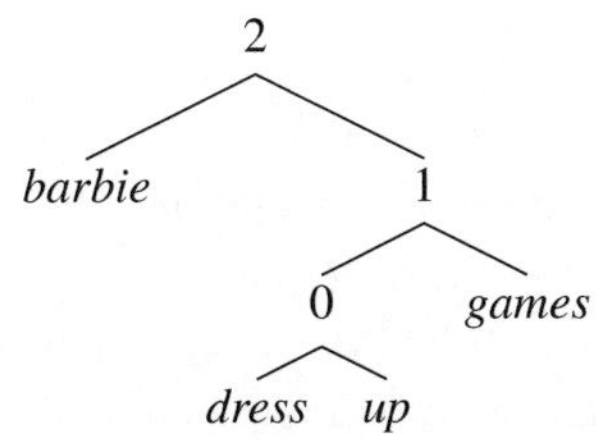

Figure 1: Tree representation of the nested segmentation: (*barbie* ((*dress up*) *games*))

ity. For instance, in the case of NL chunking, it is not clear whether the chunk boundaries should correspond to the innermost parentheses in the nested segmentation marking very short chunks, or should one annotate the larger chunks corresponding to clausal boundaries. For this reason, Inter-Annotator Agreement (IAA) for flat annotation tasks is often poor (Bali et al., 2009; Hagen et al., 2011; Saha Roy et al., 2012). However, low IAA does not necessarily imply low quality annotation, and could as well be due to the inherent ambiguity in the task definition with respect to granularity. Although we have illustrated the concept and problems of flat and nested annotations using the examples of sentence and query segmentation, these issues are generic and typical of any flat annotation scheme which tries to flatten or approximate an underlying hierarchical structure. There are three important research questions pertaining to the *linguistic annotations* of this kind:

- How to measure the true IAA and the quality of the flat annotations?
- How to compare the agreement between the flat and the nested annotations?
- How can we identify or construct the optimal or error-free flat annotations from a noisy mixture of nested and flat annotations?

In this paper, we introduce the concept of "*entailment* of a flat annotation by a nested annotation". For a given linguistic unit (a query or a sentence, for example), a nested annotation is said to *entail* a flat annotation if the structure of the latter does not contradict the more specific structure represented by the former. Based on this simple notion, which will be formalized in Sec. 3, we develop effective techniques for comparing across and evaluating the quality of flat and nested annotations, and identifying the optimal flat annotation. We validate our theoretical framework on the tasks of query and sentence segmentation. In particular, we conduct crowdsourcing based flat and nested segmentation experiments for Web search queries and sentences using Amazon Mechanical Turk (AMT)[1]. We also obtain annotations for the same datasets by trained experts which are expected to be of better quality than the AMT-based annotations. Various statistical analyses of the annotated data bring out the effectiveness of *entailment* as a metric for comparison and evaluation of flat and nested annotations.

The rest of the paper is organized as follows. Sec. 2 provides some background on the annotation tasks and related work on IAA. In Sec. 3, we introduce the notion of entailment and develop theoretical models and related strategies for assessing the quality of annotation. In Sec. 4, we introduce some strategies based on entailment for the identification of error-free annotations from a given set of noisy annotations. Sec. 5 describes the annotation experiments and results. Sec. 6 concludes the paper by summarizing the work and discussing future research directions. All the annotated datasets used in this research can be obtained freely from `http://research.microsoft.com/apps/pubs/default.aspx?id=192002` and used for non-commercial research purposes.

2 Background

Segmentation or chunking of NL text is a well-studied problem. Abney (1991; 1992; 1995) defines a chunk as a sub-tree within a syntactic phrase structure tree corresponding to Noun, Prepositional, Adjectival, Adverbial and Verb Phrases. Similarly, Bharati et al (1995) define it as Noun Group and Verb Group based only on local surface information. Chunking is an important preprocessing step towards parsing.

Like chunking, query segmentation is an important step towards query understanding and is generally believed to be useful for Web search

[1]`https://www.mturk.com/mturk/welcome`

(see Hagen et al. (2011) for a survey). Automatic query segmentation algorithms are typically evaluated against a small set of human-annotated queries (Bergsma and Wang, 2007). The reported low IAA for such datasets casts serious doubts on the reliability of annotation and the performance of the algorithms evaluated on them (Hagen et al., 2011; Saha Roy et al., 2012). To address the issue of data scarcity, Hagen et al. (2011) created a large set of manually segmented queries through crowdsourcing[2]. However, their approach has certain limitations because the crowd is already provided with a few possible segmentations of a query to choose from. Nevertheless, if large scale data has to be procured crowdsourcing seems to be the only efficient and effective model for the task, and has been proven to be so for other IR and linguistic annotations (see Lease et al. (2011) for examples). It should be noted that almost all the work on query segmentation, except (Huang et al., 2010), has considered only flat segments.

An important problem that arises in the context of *flat* annotations is the issue of granularity. In the absence of a set of guidelines that explicitly state the granularity expected, Inter-Annotator Agreement (IAA) for flat annotation tasks are often poor. Bali et al. (2009) showed that for NL chunking, annotators typically agree on major (i.e., clausal) boundaries but do not agree on minor (i.e., phrasal or intra-phrasal) boundaries. Similarly, for query segmentation, low IAA remains an issue (Hagen et al., 2011; Saha Roy et al., 2012).

The issue of granularity is effectively addressed in *nested* annotation, because the annotator is expected to mark the most atomic segments (such as named entities and multiword expressions) and then recursively combine them to obtain larger segments. Certain amount of ambiguity, that may arise because of lack of specific guidelines on the number of valid segments at the last level (i.e., topmost level of the nested segmentation tree), can also be resolved by forcing the annotator to recursively divide the sentence/query always into exactly two parts (Abney, 1992; Bali et al., 2009).

The present study is an extension of our recent work (Ramanath et al., 2013) on analysis of the effectiveness of crowdsourcing for query and sentence segmentation. We introduced a novel IAA metric based on Kripendorff's α, and showed that while the apparent agreement between the annotators in a crowdsourced experiment might be high, the chance corrected agreement is actually low for both flat and nested segmentations (as compared to gold annotations obtained from three experts). The reason for the apparently high agreement is due to an inherent bias of the crowd to divide a piece of text in roughly two equal parts. The present study extends this work by introducing a metric to compare across flat and nested segmentations that enables us to further analyze the reliability of the crowdsourced annotations. This metric is then employed to identify the optimal flat segmentation(s) from a set of noisy annotations. The study uses the same experimental setup and annotated datasets as described in (Ramanath et al., 2013). Nevertheless, for the sake of readability and self-containedness, the relevant details will be mentioned here again.

We do not know of any previous work that compares flat and nested schemes of annotation. In fact, Artstein and Poesio (2008), in a detailed survey of IAA metrics and their usage in NLP, mention that defining IAA metrics for trees (hierarchical annotations) is a difficult problem due to the existence of overlapping annotations. Vadas and Curran (2011) and Brants (2000) discuss measuring IAA of nested segmentations employing the concepts of precision, recall, and f-score. However, neither of these studies apply statistical correction for chance agreement.

3 Entailment: Definition and Modeling

In this section, we shall introduce certain notations and use them to formalize the notion of entailment, which in turn, is used for the computation of agreement between flat and nested segmentations. Although we shall develop the whole framework in the context of queries, it is applicable to sentence segmentation and, in fact, more generally to any flat and nested annotations.

3.1 Basic Definitions

Let Q be the set of all queries. A query $q \in Q$ can be represented as a sequence of $|q|$ words: $w_1 w_2 \ldots w_{|q|}$. We introduce $|q|-1$ random variables, $b_1, b_2, \ldots b_{|q|-1}$, such that b_i represents the boundary between the words w_i and w_{i+1}. A flat and nested segmentation of q, represented by F_q^j and N_q^j respectively, j varying from 1 to total number of annotations, $\mathbf{c}$, is a particular instantiation of these boundary variables as follows.

[2] http://www.webis.de/research/corpora

Definition. *Flat Segmentation*: A flat segmentation, F_q^j, can be uniquely defined by a binary assignment of the boundary variables b_i^j, where $b_i^j = 1$ iff w_i and w_{i+1} belong to two different flat segments. Otherwise, $b_i^j = 0$. Thus, q has $2^{|q|-1}$ possible flat segmentations.

Definition. *Nested Segmentation*: A nested segmentation, N_q^j, is defined as an assignment of non-negative integers to the boundary variables such that $b_i^j = 0$ iff words w_i and w_{i+1} form an atomic segment (i.e., they are grouped together), else $b_i^j = 1 + max(left_i, right_i)$, where $left_i$ and $right_i$ are the heights of the largest subtrees ending at w_i and beginning at w_{i+1} respectively.

This numbering scheme can be understood through Fig. 1. Every internal node of the binary tree corresponding to the nested segmentation is numbered according to its height. The lowest internal nodes, both of whose children are query words, are assigned a value of 0. Other internal nodes get a value of one greater than the height of its higher child. Since every internal node corresponds to a boundary, we assign the height of the node to the corresponding boundary variables. The number of unique nested segmentations of q is the corresponding *Catalan number*[3] $C_{|q|-1}$.

Note that, following Abney's (1992) suggestion for nested chunking, we define nested segmentation as a strict binary tree or binary bracketing of the query. This is not only helpful for theoretical analysis, but also necessary to ensure that there is no ambiguity related to the granularity of segments.

3.2 Entailment

Given a nested segmentation N_q^j, there are several possible ways to "flatten" it. Flat segmentations of q, where $b_i = 0$ for all i (i.e., the whole query is one segment) and $b_i = 1$ for all i (i.e., all words are in different segments) are trivially obtainable from N_q^j, and therefore, are not neither informative nor interesting. Intuitively, any flat segmentation, F_q^k, can be said to agree with N_q^j if for every flat segment in F_q^k there is a corresponding internal node in N_q^j, such that the subgraph rooted at that node *spans* (contains) all and only those words present in the flat segment (Abney, 1991).

Let us take the examples of flat and nested segmentations shown in Tables 1 and 2 to illustrate this notion. Consider two nested segmentations, $N_q^1 = ((barbie\ (dress\ up))\ games)$, $N_q^2 = (barbie\ ((dress\ up)\ games))$ and three flat segmentations, $F_q^1 = barbie \mid dress\ up \mid games$, $F_q^2 = barbie \mid dress\ up\ games$, $F_q^3 = barbie\ dress \mid up\ games$. Figure 2 diagrammatically compares the two nested segmentations (the two rows) with the three flat segmentations (columns A, B and C). There are three flat segments in F_q^1, of which the two single word segments $barbie$ and $games$ trivially coincide with the corresponding leaf nodes. The segment $dressup$ coincides exactly with the words spanned by the node marked 0 of N_q^1 (Fig. 2, top row, column A). Hence, F_q^1 can be said to be in agreement with N_q^1. On the other hand, there is no node in N_q^1, which exactly coincides with the segment $dressupgames$ of F_q^2 (Fig. 2, top row, column B). Hence, we say that N_q^1 does not agree with F_q^2.

We formalize this notion of agreement in terms of *entailment*, which is defined as follows.

Definition: *Entailment.* A nested segmentation, N_q^j is said to *entail* a flat segmentation, F_q^k, (or equivalently, F_q^k is *entailed by* N_q^j) if and only if for every multiword segment $w_{i+1}, w_{i+2}, ..., w_{i+l}$ in F_q^k, the corresponding boundary variables in N_q^j follows the constraint: $b_i > b_{i+m}$ and $b_{i+l} > b_{i+m}$ for all $1 \leq m < l$.

It can be proved that this definition of entailment is equivalent to the intuitive description provided earlier. Yet another equivalent definition of entailment is presented in the form of Algorithm 1. Due to paucity of space, the proofs of equivalence are omitted.

Definition: *Average Observed Entailment.* For the set of queries Q, and corresponding sets of $\mathbf{c}$ flat and nested segmentations, there are $|Q|\mathbf{c}^2$ pairs of flat and nested segmentations that can be compared for entailment. We define the *average observed entailment* for this annotation set as the fraction of these $|Q|\mathbf{c}^2$ annotation pairs for which the flat segmentation is entailed by the corresponding nested segmentation. We shall express this fraction as percentage.

3.3 Entailment by Random Chance

Average observed Entailment can be considered as a measure of the IAA, and hence, an indicator of the quality of the annotations. However, in order to interpret the significance of this value, we need an estimate of the average entailment that

[3] http://en.wikipedia.org/wiki/Catalan_number

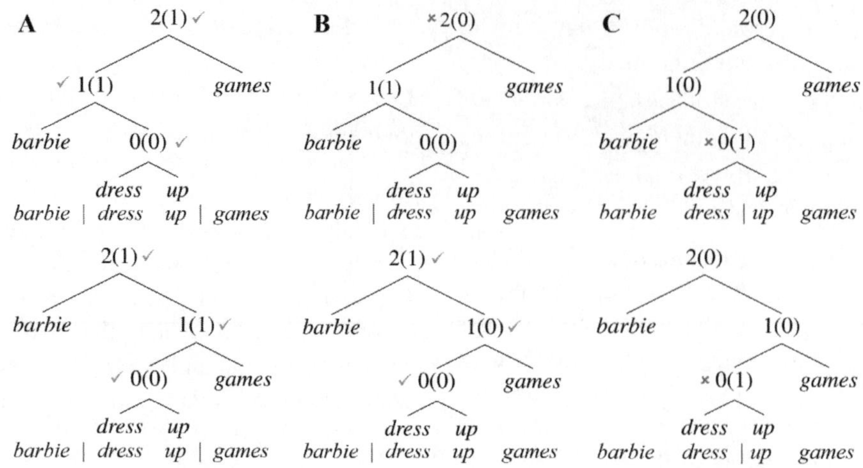

Figure 2: Every node of the tree represent boundary values, nested(flat). Column A: F_q^1 is entailed by both N_q^1 and N_q^2, Column B: F_q^2 is entailed by N_q^2 but not N_q^1, Column C: F_q^3 is entailed by neither N_q^1 nor N_q^2. The nodes (or equivalently the boundaries) violating the entailment constraint are marked a cross, and those agreeing are marked with ticks.

Algorithm 1 Algorithm: isEntail

```
procedure ISENTAIL(flat, nested)    ▷ flat, nested are lists containing boundary values
    if len(nested) ≤ 1 or len(flat) ≤ 1 then
        return True
    end if
    h ← largest element in nested
    i ← index of h
    if flat[i] = 1 then
        if ! isEntail(flat[: i], nested[: i]) or ! isEntail(flat[i+1 :], nested[i+1 :]) then
            return False
        else
            return True
        end if
    else
        while h ≠ 0 do
            nested[i] ← −nested[i]
            h ← largest element in nested
            i ← index of h
            if flat[i] = 1 then
                return False
            end if
        end while
        return True
    end if
end procedure
```

one would expect if the annotations, both flat and nested, were drawn uniformly at random from the set of all possible annotations. From our experiments we observe that trivial flat segmentations are, in fact, extremely rare, and a very large fraction of the flat annotations have two or three segments. Therefore, for computing the chance entailment, we assume that the number of segments in the flat segmentation is known and fixed, which is either 2 or 3, but all segmentations with these many segments are equally likely to be chosen. We also assume that all nested segmentations are equally likely.

When there are 2 segments: For a query q, the number of flat segmentations with two segments, i.e., one boundary, is $\binom{|q|-1}{1} = |q| - 1$. Note that for any nested segmentation N_q^j, all flat segmentations that have at least one boundary and is entailed by it must have a boundary between w_{i^*} and w_{i^*+1}, where b_{i^*} has the highest value in N_q^j. In other words, b_{i^*} is the boundary corresponding to the root of the nested tree (the proof is intuitive and is omitted). Therefore, there is *exactly one* "flat segmentation with one boundary" that is entailed by a given N_q^j. Therefore, the random chance that a nested segmentation N_q^j will entail a flat segmentation with one boundary is given by $(|q| - 1)^{-1}$ (for $|q| > 1$).

When there are 3 segments: Number of flat segmentations with two boundaries is $\binom{|q|-1}{2}$. The flat segmentation(s) entailed by N_q^j can be generated as follows. As argued above, every flat segmentation entailed by N_q^j must have a boundary at position i^*. The second boundary can be either in the left or right of i^*. But in either case, the choice of the boundary is unique which will correspond to the highest node in the left or right subtree of the root node. Thus, every nested segmentation entails at most 2 flat segmentations. However, if $i^* = 1$ or $|q| - 1$ for a N_q^j, then, respectively, the left or right subtrees do not exist. In such cases, there is only one flat segmentation entailed by N_q^j. Note that there are exactly $C_{|q|-2}$ nested segmentations for which the $i^* = 1$, and similarly another $C_{|q|-2}$ for which $i^* = |q| - 1$. Therefore, out of $C_{|q|-1} \times \binom{|q|-1}{2}$ pairs, exactly $2C_{|q|-1} - 2C_{|q|-2}$ pairs satisfy the entailment conditions. Thus, the expected probability of entailment by random chance when there are exactly two boundaries in the flat segmentation of q is:

$$\frac{2(C_{|q|-1} - C_{|q|-2})}{C_{|q|-1}\binom{|q|-1}{2}} = 2\binom{|q|-1}{2}^{-1}(1 - \frac{C_{|q|-2}}{C_{|q|-1}})$$

The values of the probability of observing a random nested segmentation entailing a flat segmentation with exactly two boundaries for $|q| = 3, 4, 5, 6, 7$ and 8 are 1, 0.4, 0.213. 0.133, 0.091 and 0.049 respectively.

3.4 Other IAA Metrics

Although entailment can be used as a measure of agreement between flat and nested segmentations, IAA within flat or within nested segmentations cannot be computed using this notion. In (Ramanath et al., 2013), we have extensively dealt with the issue of computing IAA for these cases. Krippendorff's α (Krippendorff, 2004), which is an extremely versatile agreement coefficient, has been appropriately modified to be applicable to a crowdsourced annotation scenario. $\alpha = 1$ implies perfect agreement, $\alpha = 0$ implies that the observed agreement is just as good as that by random chance, whereas $\alpha < 0$ implies that the observed agreement is less than that one would expect by random chance. Due to paucity of space we omit any further discussion on this and refer the reader to (Ramanath et al., 2013). Here, we will use the α values as an alternative indicator of IAA and therefore, the quality of annotation.

4 Optimal Segmentation

Suppose that we have a large number of flat and nested annotations coming from a noisy source such as crowdsourcing; is it possible to employ the notion of entailment to identify the annotations which are most likely to be correct? Here, we describe two such strategies to obtain the optimal (error-free) flat segmentation.

Flat Entailed by Most Nested (FEMN): The intuition behind this approach is that if a flat segmentation F_q^k is entailed by most of the nested segmentations of q, then it is very likely that F_q^k is correct. Therefore, for each flat segmentations of q, we count the number of nested segmentations of q that entail it, and the one with highest count is declared as the optimal FEMN segmentation. It is interesting to note that while computing the optimal FEMN segmentation, we never encountered a tie between two flat segmentations. The trivial flat segmentations (i.e., if the whole query is one segment or every word is in different segments) are filtered as a preprocessing step.

Iterative Voting (IV): FEMN assumes that the nested segmentations are relatively noise-free. If most of the nested segmentations are erroneous, FEMN would select an erroneous optimal flat segmentation. To circumvent this issue, we propose a more sophisticated *iterative voting* process, where we count the number of flat segmentations entailed by each nested segmentation of q, and similarly, number of nested segmentations that entail each flat segmentation. The flat and nested segmentations with the least scores are then removed from the dataset. Then we recursively apply the IV process on the reduced set of annotations until we are left with a single flat segmentation.

5 Experiments and Results

We obtained nested and flat segmentation of Web search queries through crowdsourcing as well as from trained experts. Furthermore, we also conducted similar crowdsourcing experiments for NL sentences, which helped us understand the specific challenges in annotating queries because of their apparent lack of a well-defined syntactic structure.

In this section, we first describe the experimental setup and datasets, and then present the observations and results.

5.1 Crowdsourcing Experiment

In this study we use the same set of crowdsourced annotations as described in (Ramanath et al., 2013). For the sake of completeness, we briefly describe the annotation procedure here as well. We used Amazon Mechanical Turk for the crowdsourcing experiments. Two separate Human Intelligence Tasks were designed for flat and nested segmentation. The concept of flat and nested segmentation was introduced to the Turkers with the help of two short videos[4].

When in doubt regarding the meaning of a query, the Turkers were advised to issue the query on a search engine of their choice and find out its possible interpretation(s). Only Turkers who had completed more than 100 tasks at an acceptance rate of $\geq 60\%$ were allowed to participate in the task and were paid $\$0.02$ for a flat and $\$0.06$ for a nested segmentation. Every query was annotated by 10 different annotators.

5.2 Dataset

The following sets of queries and sentences were used for annotations:

Q500, QG500: Saha Roy et al. (2012) released a dataset of 500 queries, 5 to 8 words long, for the evaluation of various segmentation algorithms. This dataset has flat segmentations from three annotators obtained under controlled experimental settings, and could be considered as *Gold* annotation. Hence, we selected this set for our experiments as well. We procured the corresponding nested segmentation for these queries from two human experts who are regular search engine users. They annotated the data under supervision and were trained and paid for the task. We shall refer to the set of flat and nested gold annotations as **QG500**, whereas **Q500** will be reserved for the dataset procured through the AMT experiments.

Q700: As 500 queries are not enough for making reliable conclusions and also, since the queries may not have been chosen specifically for the purpose of annotation experiments, we expanded the set with another 700 queries sampled from the logs of a popular commercial search engine. We picked, uniformly at random, queries that were 4 to 8 words long.

S300: We randomly selected 300 English sentences from a collection of full texts of public domain books[5] that were 5 to 15 words long, and manually checked them for well-formedness.

[4]Flat: `http://youtu.be/eMeLjJIvIh0`, Nested: `http://youtu.be/xE3rwANbFvU`

[5]`http://www.gutenberg.org`

5.3 Entailment Statistics

Table 3 reports two statistics – the values of Kripendorff's α and the average observed entailment (expressed as %) for flat and nested segmentations along with the corresponding expected values for entailment by chance. For nested segmentation, the α values were computed for two different distance metrics[6] d_1 and d_2.

As expected, the highest value of α for both flat and nested segmentation is observed for the gold annotations. An $\alpha > 0.6$ indicates a *reasonably good*[7] IAA, and thus, reliable annotations. We note that the entailment statistics follow a very similar trend as α, and for all the cases, the observed average entailment is much higher than what we would expect by random chance. These two observations clearly point to the fact that entailment is indeed a good indicator of the agreement between the nested and flat segmentations, and consequently, the reliability of the annotations. We also observe that the average entailment for **S300** is in the same ballpark as for the queries. This indicates that the apparent lack of structure in queries does not specifically influence the annotations. Along the same lines, one can also argue that the length of a text, which is higher for sentences than queries, does not affect the crowdsourced annotations. In fact, in our previous study (Ramanath et al., 2013), we show that it is the bias of the Turkers to divide a text in approximately two segments of equal size (irrespective of other factors, like syntactic structure or length), that leads to very similar IAA across different types of texts. Our current study on entailment further strengthens this fact.

Figure 3 plots the distribution of the entailment values for the three datasets. The distributions are normal-like implying that entailment is a robust metric and its average value is a usable statistic.

In order to analyze the agreement between the Turkers and the experts, we computed the average entailment between **Q500** flat annotations (from AMT) with **QG500** nested annotations, and similarly, **Q500** nested annotations with **QG500**

[6]Intuitively, for d_1 disagreements between segment boundaries are equally penalized at all the levels of nested tree, whereas for d_2 disagreements higher up the tree (i.e., close to the root) are penalized more than those at lower levels.

[7]It should be noted that there is no consensus on what is a good value of α for linguistic annotations, partly because it is dependent on the nature of the annotation task and the demand of the end applications that use the annotated data.

Dataset	Krippendorff's α			Entailment Statistics	
	Flat	*Nested*		*Observed*	*Chance*
	d_1	d_1	d_2		
Q700	0.21	0.21	0.16	49.68	12.63
Q500	0.22	0.15	0.15	56.69	19.08
QG500	0.61	0.66	0.67	87.07	11.91
S300	0.27	0.18	0.14	52.86	19.12

Table 3: α and Average Entailment Statistics

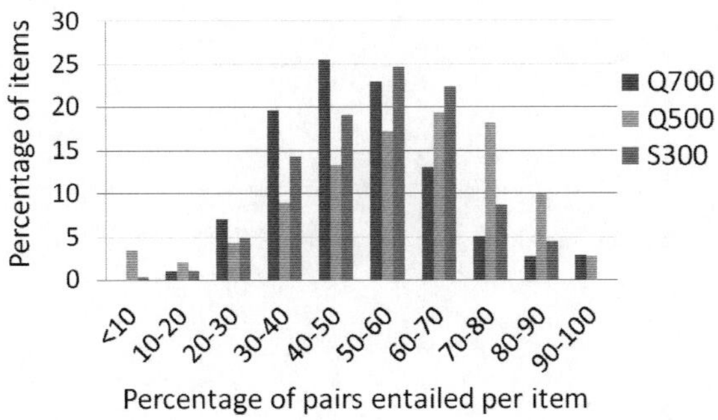

Figure 3: Distribution of the entailment values (x-axis) plotted as the % of comparable flat-nested annotation pairs.

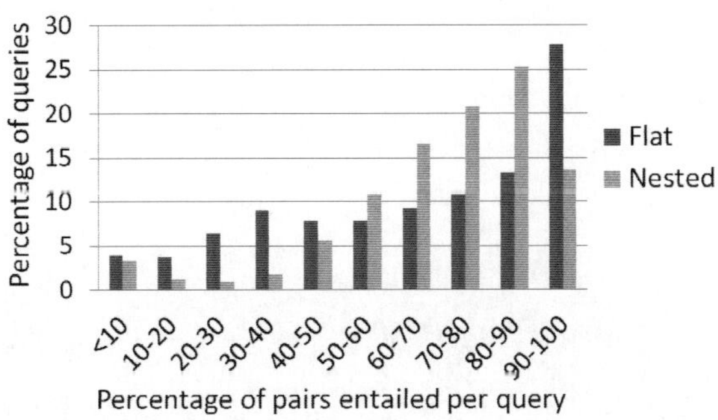

Figure 4: Distribution of percentage of entailed pairs using **QG500** as reference.

flat annotations, which turned out to be 70.42% and 63.24% respectively. The corresponding distributions are shown as *Nested* and *Flat* in Fig. 4. Thus, the flat segmentations from the Turkers seem to be more accurate than their nested segmentations, a fact also supported by the α values. This could be due to the much higher cognitive load associated with nested segmentation that demands more time and concentration that an ordinary Turker may not be willing to invest.

5.4 Optimal Segmentation Results

In order to evaluate the optimal flat segmentation selection strategies, FEMN and IV, we computed the percentage of queries in **Q500** for which the optimal flat segmentation (as obtained by applying these strategies on AMT annotations) is entailed by the corresponding nested segmentations in **QG500**. The average entailment values for FEMN and IV turns out to be 79.60% and 82.80% respectively. This shows that the strategies are indeed able to pull out the more accurate flat segmentations from the set, though, as one would expect, IV performs better than FEMN, and its chosen segmentations are almost as good as that by expert annotators.

Another experiment was conducted to precisely characterize the effectiveness of these strategies whereby we mixed the annotations from the **Q500** and **QG500**, and then applied FEMN and IV to pull out the optimal flat segmentations. We observed that for 63.71% and 91.44% of the queries, the optimal segmentation chosen by FEMN and IV respectively was indeed one of the three gold flat annotations in **QG500**. This reinforces our conclusion that IV can effectively identify the optimal flat segmentation of a query from a noisy set of flat and nested segmentations.

6 Conclusion

In this paper, we proposed entailment as a theoretical model for comparing hierarchical and non-hierarchical annotations. We present a formalization of the notion of entailment and use it for devising two strategies, FEMN and IV, for identifying the optimal flat segmentation in a noisy set of annotations. One of the main contributions of this work resides in our following experimental finding: Even though annotations obtained through crowdsourcing for a difficult task like query segmentation might be very noisy, a small fraction of the annotations are nevertheless correct; it is possible to filter out these correct annotations using the Iterative Voting strategy when both hierarchical and non-hierarchical segmentations are available from the crowd.

The proposed model is generic and we believe that the experimental findings extend beyond query and sentence segmentation to other kinds of linguistic annotations where hierarchical and non-hierarchical schemes co-exist.

Acknowledgment

Thanks to Rishiraj Saha Roy, IIT Kharagpur, for his valuable inputs during this work.

References

Steven P. Abney. 1991. *Parsing By Chunks*. Kluwer Academic Publishers.

Steven P. Abney. 1992. Prosodic Structure, Performance Structure And Phrase Structure. In *Proceedings 5th Darpa Workshop on Speech and Natural Language*, pages 425–428. Morgan Kaufmann.

Steven P. Abney. 1995. Chunks and dependencies: Bringing processing evidence to bear on syntax. *Computational Linguistics and the Foundations of Linguistic Theory*, pages 145–164.

Ron Artstein and Massimo Poesio. 2008. Inter-coder agreement for computational linguistics. *Computational Linguistics*, 34(4):555–596.

Kalika Bali, Monojit Choudhury, Diptesh Chatterjee, Sankalan Prasad, and Arpit Maheswari. 2009. Correlates between Performance, Prosodic and Phrase Structures in Bangla and Hindi: Insights from a Psycholinguistic Experiment. In *ICON '09*, pages 101 – 110.

Shane Bergsma and Qin Iris Wang. 2007. Learning Noun Phrase Query Segmentation. In *EMNLP-CoNLL '07*, pages 819–826.

Akshar Bharati, Vineet Chaitanya, and Rajeev Sangal. 1995. *Natural Language Processing: A Paninian Perspective.* Prentice.

Thorsten Brants. 2000. Inter-annotator agreement for a German newspaper corpus. In *In Proceedings of Second International Conference on Language Resources and Evaluation LREC-2000.*

Matthias Hagen, Martin Potthast, Benno Stein, and Christof Bräutigam. 2011. Query segmentation revisited. In *WWW '11*, pages 97–106.

Jian Huang, Jianfeng Gao, Jiangbo Miao, Xiaolong Li, Kuansan Wang, Fritz Behr, and C. Lee Giles. 2010. Exploring Web Scale Language Models for Search Query Processing. In *WWW '10*, pages 451–460.

Dan Jurafsky and James H Martin. 2000. *Speech & Language Processing*. Pearson Education India.

Klaus Krippendorff. 2004. *Content Analysis: An Introduction to Its Methodology.* Sage,Thousand Oaks, CA.

Matthew Lease, Vaughn Hester, Alexander Sorokin, and Emine Yilmaz, editors. 2011. *Proceedings of the ACM SIGIR 2011 Workshop on Crowdsourcing for Information Retrieval (CIR 2011).*

Rohan Ramanath, Monojit Choudhury, Kalika Bali, and Rishiraj Saha Roy. 2013. Crowd Prefers the Middle Path: A New IAA Metric for Crowdsourcing Reveals Turker Biases in Query Segmentation. In *Proceedings of ACL*. ACL.

Rishiraj Saha Roy, Niloy Ganguly, Monojit Choudhury, and Srivatsan Laxman. 2012. An IR-based Evaluation Framework for Web Search Query Segmentation. In *SIGIR '12*, pages 881–890. ACM.

David Vadas and James R. Curran. 2011. Parsing Noun Phrases in the Penn Treebank. *Comput. Linguist.*, 37(4):753–809, December.

A Framework for (Under)specifying Dependency Syntax without Overloading Annotators

Nathan Schneider[†*] **Brendan O'Connor**[†] **Naomi Saphra**[†] **David Bamman**[†]
Manaal Faruqui[†] **Noah A. Smith**[†] **Chris Dyer**[†] **Jason Baldridge**[‡]
[†]School of Computer Science, Carnegie Mellon University
[‡]Department of Linguistics, The University of Texas at Austin

Abstract

We introduce a framework for lightweight dependency syntax annotation. Our formalism builds upon the typical representation for unlabeled dependencies, permitting a simple notation and annotation workflow. Moreover, the formalism encourages annotators to underspecify parts of the syntax if doing so would streamline the annotation process. We demonstrate the efficacy of this annotation on three languages and develop algorithms to evaluate and compare underspecified annotations.

1 Introduction

Computational representations for natural language syntax are borne of competing design considerations. When designing such representations, there may be a tradeoff between parsimony and expressiveness. A range of *linguistic theories* attract support due to differing purposes and aesthetic principles (Chomsky, 1957; Tesnière, 1959; Hudson, 1984; Sgall et al., 1986; Mel'čuk, 1988, *inter alia*). Formalisms concerned with tractable computation may care chiefly about *learnability* or *parsing efficiency* (Shieber, 1992; Sleator and Temperly, 1993; Kuhlmann and Nivre, 2006). Further considerations may include *psychological* and *evolutionary plausibility* (Croft, 2001; Tomasello, 2003; Steels et al., 2011; Fossum and Levy, 2012), integration with other representations such as semantics (Steedman, 2000; Bergen and Chang, 2005), or suitability for particular applications (e.g., translation).

Here we elevate *ease of annotation* as a primary design concern for a syntactic annotation formalism. Currently, a lack of annotated data is a huge bottleneck for robust NLP, standing in the way of parsers for social media text (Foster et al., 2011) and many low-resourced languages (to name two examples). Traditional syntactic annotation projects like the Penn Treebank (Marcus et al., 1993) or Prague Dependency Treebank (Hajič, 1998) require highly trained annotators and huge amounts of effort. Lowering the cost of annotation, by making it easier and more accessible, could greatly facilitate robust NLP in new languages and genres.

To that end, we design and test new, lightweight methodologies for syntactic annotation. We propose a *formalism*, **Fragmentary Unlabeled Dependency Grammar** (FUDG) for unlabeled dependency syntax that addresses some of the most glaring deficiencies of basic unlabeled dependencies (§2), with little added burden on annotators. FUDG requires minimal theoretical commitments, and can be supplemented with a project-specific style guide (we provide a brief one for English). We contribute a simple ASCII markup language—**Graph Fragment Language** (GFL; §3)—that allows annotations to be authored using any text editor, along with tools for validating, normalizing, and visualizing GFL annotations.[1]

An important characteristic of our framework is annotator flexibility. The formalism supports this by allowing *underspecification* of structural portions that are unclear or unnecessary for the purposes of a project. Fully leveraging this power requires new algorithms for evaluation, e.g., of inter-annotator agreement, where annotations are partial; such algorithms are presented in §4.[2]

Finally, small-scale case studies (§5) apply our framework (formalism, notation, and evaluations) to syntactically annotate web text in English, news in Malagasy, and dialogues in Kinyarwanda.

2 A Dependency Grammar for Annotation

Although dependency-based approaches to syntax play a major role in computational linguistics, the nature of dependency representations is far from uniform. Exemplifying one end of the spectrum is the Prague Dependency Treebank, which articulates an elaborate dependency-based syntactic the-

*Corresponding author: nschneid@cs.cmu.edu

[1]https://github.com/brendano/gfl_syntax/

[2]Parsing algorithms are left for future work.

Found the scarriest mystery door in my school . I'M SO CURIOUS D:

```
Found** < (the scarriest mystery door*)
Found < in < (my > school)
I'M** < (SO > CURIOUS)
D:**
my = I'M
```

thers still like 1 1/2 hours till Biebs bday here :P

```
thers** < still
thers < ((1 1/2) > hours < till < (Biebs > bday))
(thers like 1 1/2 hours)
thers < here
:P**
```

Figure 1: Two tweets with example GFL annotations. (The formalism and notation are described in §3.)

ory in a rich, multi-tiered formalism (Hajič, 1998; Böhmová et al., 2003). On the opposite end of the spectrum are the structures used in dependency parsing research which organize all the tokens of a sentence into a tree, sometimes with category labels on the edges (Kübler et al., 2009). Insofar as they reflect a theory of syntax, these **vanilla dependency grammars** provide a highly reductionist view of structure—indeed, parses used to train and evaluate dependency parses are often simplifications of Prague-style parses, or else converted from constituent treebanks.

In addition to the binary dependency links of vanilla dependency representations, we offer three devices to capture certain linguistic phenomena more straightforwardly:[3]

1. We make explicit the meaningful lexical units over which syntactic structure is represented. Our approach (a) allows punctuation and other extraneous tokens to be excluded so as not to distract from the essential structure; and (b) permits tokens to be grouped into shallow multiword lexical units.[4]

2. Coordination is problematic to represent with unlabeled dependencies due to its non-binary nature. A coordinating conjunction typically joins multiple expressions (conjuncts) with equal status, and other expressions may relate to the compound structure as a unit. There are several different conventions for forcing coordinate structures into a head-modifier straightjacket (Nivre, 2005; de Marneffe and Manning, 2008; Mareček et al., 2013). Conjuncts, coordinators, and shared dependents can be distinguished with edge labels; we equivalently use a special notation, permitting the coordinate structure to be automatically transformed with any of the existing conventions.[5]

3. Following Tesnière (1959), our formalism offers a simple facility to express anaphora-antecedent relations (a subset of semantic relationships) that are salient in particular syntactic phenomena such as relative clauses, appositives, and -expressions.

Underspecification. Our desire to facilitate lightweight annotation scenarios requires us to abandon the expectation that syntactic informants provide a complete parse for every sentence. On one hand, an annotator may be *uncertain* about the appropriate parse due to lack of expertise, insufficiently mature annotation conventions, or actual ambiguity in the sentence. On the other hand, annotators may be *indifferent* to certain phenomena. This can happen for a variety of reasons:

- Some projects may only need annotations of specific constructions. For example, building a semantic resource for events may require annotation of syntactic verb-argument relations, but not internal noun phrase structure.
- As a project matures, it may be more useful to annotate only infrequent lexical items.
- Semisupervised learning from partial annotations may be sufficient to learn complete parsers (Hwa, 1999; Clark and Curran, 2006).
- Beginning annotators may wish to focus on easily understood syntactic phenomena.
- Different members of a project may wish to specialize in different syntactic phenomena, reducing training cost and cognitive load.

Rather than treating annotations as invalid unless and until they are complete trees, we formally represent and reason about partial parse structures. Annotators produce **annotations**, which encode constraints on the (inferred) **analysis**, the parse structure, of a sentence. We say that a valid annotation **supports** (is compatible with) one or more **analyses**. Both annotations and analyses are represented as graphs (the graph representation is described below in §3.2). We require that the directed edges in an *analysis* graph must form a tree over all the lexical items in the sentence.[6] Less

[3]Some of this is inspired by the conventions of Reed-Kellogg *sentence diagramming*, a graphical dependency annotation system for English pedagogy (Reed and Kellogg, 1877; Kolln and Funk, 1994; Florey, 2006).

[4]The Stanford representation supports a limited notion of multiword expressions (de Marneffe and Manning, 2008). For simplicity, our formalism treats multiwords as unanalyzed (syntactically opaque) wholes, though some multiword expressions may have syntactic descriptions (Baldwin and Kim, 2010).

[5]Tesnière (1959) and Hudson (1984) similarly use special structures for coordination (Schneider, 1998; Sangati and Mazza, 2009).

[6]While some linguistic phenomena (e.g., relative clauses, control constructions) can be represented using non-tree

stringent well-formedness constraints on the *annotation* graph leave room for underspecification.

Briefly, an annotation can be underspecified in two ways: (a) an expression may not be attached to any parent, indicating it might depend on any nondescendant in a full analysis—this is useful for annotating sentences piece by piece; and (b) multiple expressions may be grouped together in a **fudge expression** (§3.3), a constraint that the elements form a connected subgraph in the full analysis while leaving the precise nature of that subgraph indeterminate—this is useful for marking relationships between chunks (possibly constituents).

A formalism, not a theory. Our framework for dependency grammar annotation is a syntactic *formalism*, but it is not sufficiently comprehensive to constitute a *theory* of syntax. Though it standardizes the basic treatment of a few basic phenomena, simplicity of the formalism requires us to be conservative about making such extensions. Therefore, just as with simpler formalisms, language- and project-specific conventions will have to be developed for specific linguistic phenomena. By embracing underspecified annotation, however, our formalism aims to encourage efficient corpus coverage in a nascent annotation project, without forcing annotators to make premature decisions.

3 Syntactic Formalism and GFL

In our framework, a syntactic **annotation** of a sentence follows an extended dependency formalism based on the desiderata enumerated in the previous section. We call our formalism **Fragmentary Unlabeled Dependency Grammar (FUDG)**.

To make it simple to create FUDG annotations with a text editor, we provide a plain-text dependency notation called **Graph Fragment Language (GFL)**. Fragments of the FUDG graph—nodes and dependencies linking them—are encoded in this language; taken together, these fragments describe the annotation in its entirety. The ordering of GFL fragments, and of tokens within each fragment, is of no formal consequence. Since the underlying FUDG representation is transparently related to GFL constructions, GFL notation will be introduced alongside the discussion of each kind of FUDG node.[7]

structures, we find that being able to alert annotators when they inadvertently violate the tree constraint is more useful than the expressive flexibility.

[7]In principle, FUDG annotations could be created with an alternative mechanism such as a GUI, as in Hajič et al. (2001).

3.1 Tokens

We expect a tokenized string, such as a sentence or short message. The provided tokenization is respected in the annotation. For human readability, GFL fragments refer to tokens as strings (rather than offsets), so all tokens that participate in an annotation must be unambiguous in the input.[8] A token may be referenced multiple times in the annotation.

3.2 Graph Encoding

Directed arcs. As in other dependency formalisms, **dependency arcs** are directed links indicating the syntactic headedness relationship between pairs of nodes. In GFL, directed arcs are indicated with angle brackets pointing from the dependent to its head, as in `black > cat` or (equivalently) `cat < black`. Multiple arcs can be chained together: `the > cat < black < jet` describes three arcs. Parentheses help group portions of a chain: `(the > cat < black < jet) > likes < fish` (the structure `black < jet > likes`, in which `jet` appears to have two heads, is disallowed). Note that another encoding for this structure would be to place the contents of the parentheses and the chain `cat > likes < fish` on separate lines. Curly braces can be used to list multiple dependents of the same head: `{cat fish} > likes`.

Anaphoric links. These undirected links join coreferent anaphora to each other and to their antecedent(s). In English this includes personal pronouns, relative pronouns (*who*, *which*, *that*), and anaphoric *do* and *so* (*Leo loves Ulla and* ***so does*** *Max*). This introduces a bit of semantics into our annotation, though at present we do not attempt to mark non-anaphoric coreference. It also allows a more satisfying treatment of appositives and relative clauses than would be possible from just the directed tree (the third example in figures 2 and 3).

Lexical nodes. Whereas in vanilla dependency grammar syntactic links are between pairs of **token nodes**, FUDG abstracts away from the individual tokens in the input. The lowest level of a FUDG annotation consists of **lexical nodes**, i.e.,

[8]If a word is repeated within the sentence, it must be indexed in the input string in order to be referred to from a fragment. In our notation, successive instances of the same word are suffixed with `~1`, `~2`, `~3`, etc. Punctuation and other tokens omitted from an annotation do not need to be indexed.

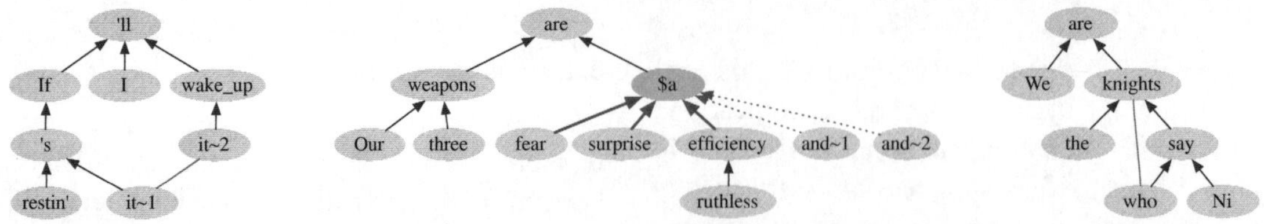

Figure 2: FUDG graphs corresponding to the examples in figure 3. The two special kinds of directed edges are for attaching conjuncts (bolded) and their coordinators (dotted) in a coordinate structure. Anaphoric links are undirected. The root node of each sentence is omitted.

```
If it~1 's restin' I 'll wake it~2 up .
  If < (it~1 > 's < restin')
  I > 'll < [wake up] < it~2
  If > 'll**
  it~1 = it~2
Our three weapons are fear and~1 surprise and~2
ruthless efficiency ...
  {Our three} > weapons > are < $a
  $a :: {fear surprise efficiency} :: {and~1 and~2}
  ruthless > efficiency
We are the knights who say ... Ni !
  We > are < knights < the
  knights < (who > say < Ni)
  who = knights
```

Figure 3: GFL for the FUDG graphs in figure 2.

lexical item occurrences. Every token node maps to 0 or 1 lexical nodes (punctuation, for instance, can be ignored).

A **multiword** is a lexical node incorporating more than one input token and is atomic (does not contain internal structure). A multiword node may group any subset of input tokens; this allows for multiword expressions which are not necessarily contiguous in the sentence (e.g., the verb-particle construction *make up* in *make the story up*). GFL notates multiwords with square brackets, e.g., `[break a leg]`.

Coordination nodes. Coordinate structures require at least two kinds of dependents: **coordinators** (i.e., lexical nodes for coordinating conjunctions—at least one per coordination node) and **conjuncts** (heads of the conjoined subgraphs—at least one per coordination node). The GFL annotation has three parts: a variable representing the node, a set of conjuncts, and a set of coordinator nodes. For instance, `$a :: {[peanut butter] honey} :: {and}` (*peanut butter and honey*) can be embedded within a phrase via the coordination node variable `$a`; *a [fresh [[peanut butter] and honey] sandwich] snack* would be formed with `{fresh $a} > sandwich > snack < a`. A graphical example of coordination can be seen in figure 2—note the bolded conjunct edges and the dotted coordinator edges. If the conjoined phrase as a whole takes modifiers, these are attached to the coordination node with regular directed arcs. For example, in *Sam really adores kittens and abhors puppies.*, the shared subject *Sam* and adverb *really* attach to the entire conjoined phrase. In GFL:

```
$a :: {adores abhors} :: {and}
Sam > $a < really
adores < kittens    abhors < puppies
```

Root node. This is a special top-level node used to indicate that a graph fragment constitutes a standalone utterance or a discourse connective. For an input with multiple utterances, the head of each should be designated with ∗∗ to indicate that it attaches to the root.

3.3 Means of Underspecification

As discussed in §2, our framework distinguishes *annotations* from full syntactic *analyses*. With respect to dependency structure (directed edges), the former may underspecify the latter, allowing the annotator to commit only to a partial analysis.

For an annotation $\mathcal{A}$, we define *support*($\mathcal{A}$) to be the set of full analyses compatible with that annotation. A full analysis is required to be a directed rooted tree over all lexical nodes in the annotation. An annotation is *valid* if its support is non-empty.

The 2 mechanisms for dependency underspecification are unattached nodes and fudge nodes.

Unattached nodes. For any node in an annotation, the annotator is free to simply leave it not attached to any head. This is interpreted as allowing its head to be any other node (including the root node), subject to the tree constraint. We call a node's possible heads its **supported parents**. Formally, for an unattached node v in annotation $\mathcal{A}$, $suppParents_{\mathcal{A}}(v) = nodes(\mathcal{A}) \setminus (\{v\} \cup descendants(v))$.

Fudge nodes. Sometimes, however, it is desirable to represent a sort of skeletal structure without filling in all the details. A **fudge expression** (FE) asserts that a group of nodes (the expression's **members**) belong together in a *connected subgraph*, while leaving the internal structure of that subgraph unspecified.[9] The notation

[9]This underspecification semantics is, to the best of our knowledge, novel, though it has been proposed that connected dependency subgraphs (known as *catenae*) are of theoretical importance in syntax (Osborne et al., 2012).

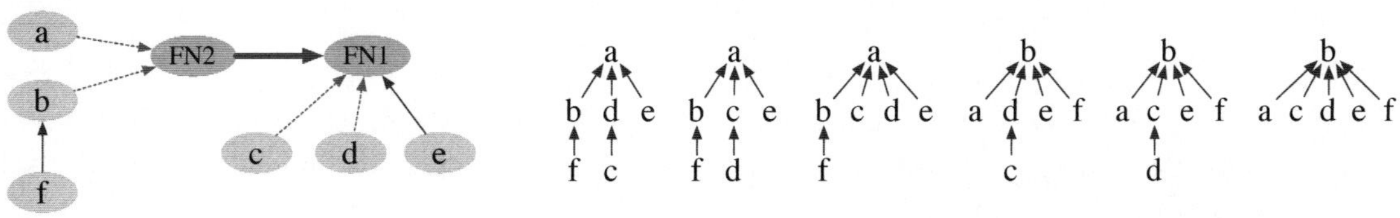

Figure 4: *Left:* An annotation graph with 2 fudge nodes and 6 lexical nodes; it can be encoded with GFL fragments `((a b)* c d) < e` and `b < f`. *Right:* All of its supported analyses: $prom(\mathcal{A}) = 6$. $com(\mathcal{A}) = 1 - \frac{\log 6}{\log 7^5} = .816$.

for this is a list of two or more nodes within parentheses: an annotation for *Few if any witches are friends with Maria.* might contain the FE `(Few if any)` so as to be compatible with the structures `Few < if < any`, `Few > if > any`, etc.—but *not*, for instance, `Few > witches < any`. In the FUDG graph, this is represented with a **fudge node** to which members are attached by special **member arcs**. Fudge nodes may be linked to other nodes: the GFL fragment `(Few if any) > witches` is compatible with `(Few < if < any) > witches`, `(Few < (if > any)) > witches`, and so forth.

Properties. Let **f** be a fudge expression. From the connected subgraph definition and the tree constraint on analyses, it follows that:

- Exactly 1 member of **f** must, in any compatible analysis, have a parent that is not a member of **f**. Call this node the **top** of the fudge expression, denoted f^*. f^* dominates all other members of **f**; it can be considered **f**'s "internal head."
- **f** does not necessarily form a full subtree. Any of its members may have dependents that are not themselves members of the fudge expression. (Such dependencies can be specified in additional GFL fragments.)

Top designation. A single member of a fudge expression may optionally be designated as its top (internal head). This is specified with an asterisk: `(Few* if any) > witches` indicates that *Few* must attach to *witches* and also dominate both *if* and *any*. In the FUDG graph, this is represented with a special **top arc** as depicted in bold in figure 4.

Nesting. One fudge expression may nest within another, e.g. `(Few (if any)) > witches`; the word analyzed as attaching to `witches` might be `Few` or whichever of `(if any)` heads the other. A nested fudge expression can be designated as top: `(Vanishingly few (if any)*)`.

Modifiers. An arc attaching a node to a fudge expression as a whole asserts that the external node should modify the *top* of the fudge expression (whether or not that top is designated in the annotation). For instance, two of the interpretations of *British left waffles on Falklands* would be preserved by specifying `British > left` and `(left waffles) < on < Falklands`. Analyses `British > left < waffles < on < Falklands` and `(British > left < on < Falklands) > waffles` would be excluded because the preposition does not attach to the head of `(left waffles)`.[10]

Multiple membership. A node may be a member of multiple fudge expressions, or a member of an FE while attached to some other node via an explicit arc. Each connected component of the FUDG graph is therefore a polytree (not necessarily a tree). The annotation graph minus all member edges of fudge nodes and all (undirected) anaphoric links must be a directed tree or forest.

Enumerating supported parents. Fudge expressions complicate the procedure for listing a node's supported parents (see above). Consider an FE **f** having some member v. v might be the top of **f** (unless some other node is so designated), in which case anything the fudge node can attach to is a potential parent of v. If some node other than v might be the top of **f**, then v's head could be any member of **f**. Below (§4.1) we develop an algorithm for enumerating supported parents for any annotation graph node.

4 Annotation Evaluation Measures

For an annotation task which allows for a great deal of latitude—as in our case, where a syntactic annotation may be full or partial—quantitative evaluation of data quality becomes a challenge. In the context of our formalism, we propose measures that address:

- **Annotation efficiency**, quantified in terms of annotator productivity (tokens per hour).
- The **amount of information** in an underspecified annotation. Intuitively, an annotation that flirts with many full analyses conveys less syntactic information than one which supports few analyses. We define an annotation's **promiscuity** to be the number of full analyses it supports, and develop an algorithm to compute it (§4.1).

[10] Not all attachment ambiguities can be precisely encoded in FUDG. For instance, there is no way to forbid an attachment to a word that lies along the path between the possible heads. The best that can be done given a sentence like *They conspired to defenestrate themselves on Tuesday.* is `They > conspired < to < defenestrate < themselves` and `(conspired* to defenestrate (on < Tuesday))`.

- **Inter-annotator agreement** between two partial annotations. Our measures for dependency structure agreement (§4.2) incorporate the notion of promiscuity.

We test these evaluations on our pilot annotation data in the case studies (§5).

4.1 Promiscuity vs. Commitment

Given a FUDG annotation of a sentence, we quantify the extent to which it underspecifies the full structure by counting the number of analyses that are compatible with the constraints in the annotation. We call this number the **promiscuity** of the annotation. Each analysis tree is rooted with the root node and must span all lexical nodes.[11]

A naïve algorithm for computing promiscuity would be to enumerate all directed spanning trees over the lexical nodes, and then check each of them for compatibility with the annotation. But this quickly becomes intractable: for n nodes, one of which is designated as the root, there are n^{n-2} spanning trees. However, we can filter out edges that are known to be incompatible with the annotation *before* searching for spanning trees. Our "upward-downward" method for constructing a graph of **supported edges** first enumerates a set of candidate top nodes for every fudge expression, then uses that information to infer a set of supported parents for every node.[12] The supported edge graph then consists of vertices $\mathit{lexnodes}(\mathcal{A}) \cup \{\quad\}$ and edges $\bigcup_{v \in \mathit{lexnodes}(\mathcal{A})} \{(v \rightarrow v') \; \forall \, v' \in \mathit{suppParents}_{\mathcal{A}}(v)\}$. From this graph we can count all directed spanning trees in cubic time using Kirchhoff's matrix tree theorem (Chaiken and Kleitman, 1978; Smith and Smith, 2007; Margoliash, 2010).[13] If some lexical node has no supported parents, this reflects conflicting constraints in the annotation, and no spanning tree will be found.

Promiscuity will tend to be higher for longer sentences. To control for this, we define a second quantity, the annotation's **commitment quotient** (commitment being the opposite of promiscuity), which normalizes for the number of possible spanning trees given the sentence length. The commitment quotient for an annotation of a sentence with $n-1$ lexical nodes and one root node is given by:

$$\mathit{com}(\mathcal{A}) = 1 - \frac{\log \mathit{prom}(\mathcal{A})}{\log n^{n-2}}$$

(the logs are to attenuate the dominance of the exponential term). This will be 1 if only a single tree is supported by the annotation, and 0 if the annotation does not constrain the structure at all. (If the constraints in the annotation are internally inconsistent, then promiscuity will be 0 and commitment undefined.) In practice, there is a tradeoff between efficiency and commitment: more detailed annotations require more time. The value of minimizing promiscuity will therefore depend on the resources and goals of the annotation project.

4.2 Inter-Annotator Agreement

FUDG can encode flat groupings and coreference at the lexical level, as well as syntactic structure over lexical items. Inter-annotator agreement can be measured separately for each of these facets. Pilot annotator feedback indicated that our initial lexical-level guidelines were inadequate, so we focus here on measuring structural agreement pending further clarification of the lexical conventions.

Attachment accuracy, a standard measure for evaluating dependency parsers, cannot be computed between two FUDG annotations if either of them underspecifies any part of the dependency structure. One solution is to consider the intersection of supported full trees, in the spirit of our promiscuity measure. For annotations $\mathcal{A}_1$ and $\mathcal{A}_2$ of sentence **s**, one annotation's supported analyses can be enumerated and then filtered subject to the constraints of the other annotation. The tradeoff between inter-annotator compatibility and commitment can be accounted for by taking their product, i.e. $\mathit{comPrec}(\mathcal{A}_1 \mid \mathcal{A}_2) = \mathit{com}(\mathcal{A}_1)\frac{|\mathit{supp}(\mathcal{A}_1) \cap \mathit{supp}(\mathcal{A}_2)|}{|\mathit{supp}(\mathcal{A}_1)|}$.

A limitation of this support-intersection approach is that if the two annotations are not compatible, the intersection will be empty. A more fine-grained approach is to decompose the comparison by lexical node: we generalize attachment accuracy with $\mathit{softComPrec}(\mathcal{A}_1 \mid \mathcal{A}_2) = \mathit{com}(\mathcal{A}_1)\frac{\sum_{\ell \in \mathbf{s}} \bigcap_{i \in \{1,2\}} \mathit{suppParents}_{\mathcal{A}_i}(\ell)}{\sum_{\ell \in \mathbf{s}} \mathit{suppParents}_{\mathcal{A}_1}(\ell)}$, computing $\mathit{com}(\cdot)$ and $\mathit{suppParents}(\cdot)$ as in the previous section. As lexical nodes may differ between the two annotations, a reconciliation step is required

[11] This measure assumes a fixed lexical analysis (set of lexical nodes) and does not consider anaphoric links. Coordinate structures are simplified into ordinary dependencies, with coordinate phrases headed by the coordinator's lexical node. If a coordination node has multiple coordinators, one is arbitrarily chosen as the head and the others as its dependents.

[12] Python code for these algorithms appears in Schneider et al. (2013) and the accompanying software release.

[13] Due to a technicality with non-member attachments to fudge nodes, for some annotations this is only an upper bound on promiscuity; see Schneider et al. (2013).

Language	Tokens	Rate (tokens/hr)
English Tweets (partial)	667	430
English Tweets (full)	388	250
Malagasy	4,184	47
Kinyarwanda	8,036	80

Table 1: Productivity estimates from pilot annotation project. All annotators were native speakers of English.

to compare the structures: multiwords proposed in only one of the two annotations are converted to fudge expressions. Tokens annotated by neither annotator are ignored. Like with the promiscuity measure, we simplify coordinate structures to ordinary dependencies (see footnote 11).

5 Case Studies

5.1 Annotation Time

To estimate annotation efficiency, we performed a pilot annotation project consisting of annotating several hundred English tweets, about 1,000 sentences in Malagasy, and a further 1,000 sentences in Kinyarwanda.[14] Table 1 summarizes the number of tokens annotated and the effort required. For the two Twitter cases, the same annotator was first permitted to do partial annotation of 100 tweets, and then spend the same amount of time doing a complete annotation of all tokens. Although this is a very small study, the results clearly suggest she was able to make much more rapid progress when partial annotation was an option.[15]

This pilot study helped us to identify linguistic phenomena warranting specific conventions: these include -expressions, comparatives, vocatives, discourse connectives, null copula constructions, and many others. We documented these cases in a 20-page style guide for English,[16] which informed the subsequent pilot studies discussed below.

5.2 Underspecification and Agreement

We annotated 2 small English data samples in order to study annotators' use of underspecification. The first is drawn from Owoputi et al.'s 2013 Twitter part-of-speech corpus; the second is from the R portion of the English Web Treebank (EWTB) (Bies et al., 2012). (Our annotators only saw the tokenized text.) Both datasets are informal and conversational in nature, and are dominated by short messages/sentences. In spite of their brevity, many of the items were deemed to contain multiple "utterances," which we define to include discourse connectives and emoticons (at best marginal parts of the syntax); utterance heads are marked with ** in figure 1.

	1Ws	MWs	Omit. Tkns	FEs	*prom* Hist. 1	>1	≥10	≥10^2	Mean *com*
T	*60 messages, 957 tokens*								
A	597	56	304	23	43	17	11	5	.96
B	644	47	266	28	37	23	12	6	.95
R	*55 sentences, 778 tokens*								
A	609	33	136	2	53	2	2	1	1.00
C ∩ D	643	19	116	114	11	44	38	21	.82
T	704	—	74	—	55	0	0	0	1

Table 2: Measures of our annotation samples. Note that annotator "D" specialized in noun phrase–internal structure, while annotator "C" specialized in verb phrase/clausal phenomena; C ∩ D denotes the combination of their annotation fragments. "T" denotes our dependency conversion of the English Web Treebank parses. (The value 1.00 was rounded up from .9994.)

Table 2 indicates the sizes of the two data samples, and gives statistics over the output of each annotator: total counts of single-word and multiword lexical nodes, tokens not represented by any lexical node, and fudge nodes; as well as a histogram of promiscuity counts and the average of commitment quotients (see §4.1). For instance, the two sets of annotations obtained for the T sample used underspecification in 17/60 and 23/60 tweets, respectively, though the promiscuity rarely exceeded 100 compatible trees per annotation. Examples can be seen in figure 1, where annotator "A" marked only the noun phrase head for *the scarriest mystery door*, opted not to choose a head within the quantity *1 1/2*, and left ambiguous the attachment of the hedge *like*. The strong but not utter commitment to the dependency structure is reflected in the mean commitment quotients for this dataset, both of which exceed 0.95.

Inter-annotator agreement (IAA) is quantified in table 3. The row marked A ~ B, for instance, considers the agreement between annotator "A" and annotator "B". Measuring IAA on the dependency structure requires a common set of lexical nodes, so a **lexical reconciliation** step ensures that (a) any token used by either annotation is present in both, and (b) no multiword node is present in only one annotation—solved by relaxing incompatible multiwords to FEs (which increases promiscuity). For T , lexical reconciliation

[14]Malagasy is a VOS Austronesian language spoken by 15 million people, mostly in Madagascar. Kinyarwanda is an SVO Bantu language spoken by 12 million people mostly in Rwanda. All annotations were done by native speakers of English. The Kinyarwanda and Malagasy annotators had basic proficiency in these languages.

[15]As a point of comparison, during the Penn Treebank project, annotators corrected the syntactic bracketings produced by a high-quality hand-written parser (Fidditch) and achieved a rate of only 375 tokens/hour using a specialized GUI interface (Marcus et al., 1993).

[16]Included with the data and software release (footnote 1).

thus reduces the commitment averages for each annotation—to a greater extent for annotator "A" (.96 in table 2 vs. .82 in table 3) because "A" marked more multiwords. An analysis fully compatible with both annotations exists for only 27/60 sentences; the finer-grained *softComPrec* measure (§4.2), however, offers insight into the balance between commitment and agreement.

Qualitatively, we observe three leading causes of incompatibilities (disagreements): obvious annotator mistakes (such as *the* marked as a head); inconsistent handling of verbal auxiliaries; and uncertainty whether to attach expressions to a verb or the root node, as with *here* in figure 1.[17] Annotators noticed occasional ambiguous cases and attempted to encode the ambiguity with fudge expressions: *again* in the tweet *maybe put it off until you feel like ~ talking again ?* is one example. More often, fudge expressions proved useful for syntactically difficult constructions, such as those shown in figure 1 as well as: *2 shy of breaking it*, *asked what tribe I was from*, *a $ 13 / day charge*, *you two*, and *the most awkward thing ever*.

5.3 Annotator Specialization

As an experiment in using underspecification for labor division, two of the annotators of R data were assigned specific linguistic phenomena to focus on. Annotator "D" was tasked with the internal structure of base noun phrases, including resolving the antecedents of personal pronouns. "C" was asked to mark the remaining phenomena—i.e., utterance/clause/verb phrase structure—but to mark base noun phrases as fudge expressions, leaving their internal structure unspecified. Both annotators provided a full lexical analysis. For comparison, a third individual, "A," annotated the same data in full. The three annotators worked completely independently.

Of the results in tables 2 and 3, the most notable difference between full and specialized annotation is that the combination of independent specialized annotations (C ∩ D) produces somewhat higher promiscuity/lower commitment. This is unsurprising because annotators sometimes overlook relationships that fall under their specialty.[18] Still, annotators reported that specialization made the task less burdensome, and the specialized annotations did prove complementary to each other.[19]

[17] Another example: Some uses of conjunctions like *and* and *so* can be interpreted as either phrasal coordinators or discourse connectives (cf. The PDTB Research Group, 2007).

[18] A more practical and less error-prone approach might be for specialists to work sequentially or collaboratively (rather than independently) on each sentence.

	com			*softComPrec*		
IAA	1	2	$N_{\lvert\cap\rvert>0}$	1|2	2|1	F_1
T (*N*=60)						
A ~ B	.82	.91	27	.57	.72	.63
R (*N*=55)						
A ~ (C ∩ D)	.95	.76	30	.64	.40	.50
A ~ T	.92	1	26	.48	.91	.63
(C ∩ D) ~ T	.73	1.00	28	.33	.93	.49

Table 3: Measures of inter-annotator agreement. Annotator labels are as in table 2. Per-annotator *com* (with lexical reconciliation) and inter-annotator *softComPrec* are aggregated over sentences by arithmetic mean.

5.4 Treebank Comparison

Though the annotators in our study were native speakers well acquainted with representations of English syntax, we sought to quantify their agreement with the expert treebankers who created the EWTB (the source of the R sentences). We converted the EWTB's constituent parses to dependencies via the PennConverter tool (Johansson and Nugues, 2007),[20] then removed punctuation.

Agreement with the converted treebank parses appears in the bottom two rows of table 3. Because the EWTB commits to a single analysis, precision scores are quite lopsided. Most of its attachments are consistent with our annotations (*softComPrec* > 0.9), but these allow many additional analyses (hence the scores below 0.5).

6 Conclusion

We have presented a framework for simple dependency annotation that overcomes some of the representational limitations of unlabeled dependency grammar and embraces the practical realities of resource-building efforts. Pilot studies (in multiple languages and domains, supported by a human-readable notation and a suite of open-source tools) showed this approach lends itself to rapid annotation with minimal training.

The next step will be to develop algorithms exploiting these representations for learning parsers. Other future extensions might include additional expressive mechanisms (e.g., multi-headedness, labels), crowdsourcing of FUDG annotations (Snow et al., 2008), or even a semantic counterpart to the syntactic representation.

[19] In fact, for only 2 sentences did "C" and "D" have incompatible annotations, and both were due to simple mistakes that were then fixed in the combination.

[20] We ran PennConverter with options chosen to emulate our annotation conventions; see Schneider et al. (2013).

Acknowledgments

We thank Lukas Biewald, Yoav Goldberg, Kyle Jerro, Vijay John, Lori Levin, André Martins, and several anonymous reviewers for their insights. This research was supported in part by the U. S. Army Research Laboratory and the U. S. Army Research Office under contract/grant number W911NF-10-1-0533 and by NSF grant IIS-1054319.

References

Timothy Baldwin and Su Nam Kim. 2010. Multiword expressions. In Nitin Indurkhya and Fred J. Damerau, editors, *Handbook of Natural Language Processing, Second Edition*. CRC Press, Taylor and Francis Group, Boca Raton, FL.

Benjamin K. Bergen and Nancy Chang. 2005. Embodied Construction Grammar in simulation-based language understanding. In Jan-Ola Östman and Mirjam Fried, editors, *Construction grammars: cognitive grounding and theoretical extensions*, pages 147–190. John Benjamins, Amsterdam.

Ann Bies, Justin Mott, Colin Warner, and Seth Kulick. 2012. English Web Treebank. Technical Report LDC2012T13, Linguistic Data Consortium, Philadelphia, PA.

Alena Böhmová, Jan Hajič, Eva Hajičová, Barbora Hladká, and Anne Abeillé. 2003. The Prague Dependency Treebank: a three-level annotation scenario. In *Treebanks: building and using parsed corpora*, pages 103–127. Springer.

Seth Chaiken and Daniel J. Kleitman. 1978. Matrix Tree Theorems. *Journal of Combinatorial Theory, Series A*, 24(3):377–381.

Noam Chomsky. 1957. *Syntactic Structures*. Mouton, La Haye.

Stephen Clark and James Curran. 2006. Partial training for a lexicalized-grammar parser. In *Proceedings of the Human Language Technology Conference of the NAACL (HLT-NAACL 2006)*, pages 144–151. Association for Computational Linguistics, New York City, USA.

William Croft. 2001. *Radical Construction Grammar: Syntactic Theory in Typological Perspective*. Oxford University Press, Oxford.

Marie-Catherine de Marneffe and Christopher D. Manning. 2008. Stanford typed dependencies manual. `http://nlp.stanford.edu/downloads/dependencies_manual.pdf`.

Kitty Burns Florey. 2006. *Sister Bernadette's Barking Dog: The quirky history and lost art of diagramming sentences*. Melville House, New York.

Victoria Fossum and Roger Levy. 2012. Sequential vs. hierarchical syntactic models of human incremental sentence processing. In *Proceedings of the 3rd Workshop on Cognitive Modeling and Computational Linguistics (CMCL 2012)*, pages 61–69. Association for Computational Linguistics, Montréal, Canada.

Jennifer Foster, Ozlem Cetinoglu, Joachim Wagner, Joseph Le Roux, Stephen Hogan, Joakim Nivre, Deirdre Hogan, and Josef van Genabith. 2011. #hardtoparse: POS Tagging and Parsing the Twitterverse. In *Proceedings of the 2011 AAAI Workshop on Analyzing Microtext*, pages 20–25. AAAI Press, San Francisco, CA.

The PDTB Research Group. 2007. The Penn Discourse Treebank 2.0 annotation manual. Technical Report IRCS-08-01, Institute for Research in Cognitive Science, University of Pennsylvania, Philadelphia, PA.

Jan Hajič. 1998. Building a syntactically annotated corpus: the Prague Dependency Treebank. In Eva Hajičová, editor, *Issues of Valency and Meaning. Studies in Honor of Jarmila Panevová*, pages 12–19. Prague Karolinum, Charles University Press, Prague.

Jan Hajič, Barbora Vidová Hladká, and Petr Pajas. 2001. The Prague Dependency Treebank: annotation structure and support. In *Proceedings of the IRCS Workshop on Linguistic Databases*, pages 105–114. University of Pennsylvania, Philadelphia, USA.

Richard A. Hudson. 1984. *Word Grammar*. Blackwell, Oxford.

Rebecca Hwa. 1999. Supervised grammar induction using training data with limited constituent information. In *Proceedings of the 37th Annual Meeting of the Association for Computational Linguistics (ACL-99)*, pages 73–79. Association for Computational Linguistics, College Park, Maryland, USA.

Richard Johansson and Pierre Nugues. 2007. Extended constituent-to-dependency conversion for English. In Joakim Nivre, Heiki-Jaan Kaalep, Kadri Muischnek, and Mare Koit, editors, *Proceedings of the 16th Nordic Conference of Computational Linguistics (NODALIDA-2007)*, pages 105–112. Tartu, Estonia.

Martha Kolln and Robert Funk. 1994. *Understanding English Grammar*. Macmillan, New York.

Sandra Kübler, Ryan McDonald, and Joakim Nivre. 2009. *Dependency Parsing*. Number 2 in Synthesis Lectures on Human Language Technologies. Morgan & Claypool, San Rafael, CA.

Marco Kuhlmann and Joakim Nivre. 2006. Mildly non-projective dependency structures. In *Proceedings of the COLING/ACL 2006 Main Conference Poster Sessions*, pages 507–514. Association for Computational Linguistics, Sydney, Australia.

Mitchell P. Marcus, Beatrice Santorini, and Mary Ann Marcinkiewicz. 1993. Building a large annotated corpus of English: the Penn Treebank. *Computational Linguistics*, 19(2):313–330.

David Mareček, Martin Popel, Loganathan Ramasamy, Jan Štěpánek, Daniel Zeman, Zdeněk Žabokrtský, and Jan Hajič. 2013. Cross-language study on influence of coordination style on dependency parsing performance. Technial Report 49, ÚFAL MFF UK.

Jonathan Margoliash. 2010. Matrix-Tree Theorem for directed graphs. `http://www.math.uchicago.edu/~may/VIGRE/VIGRE2010/REUPapers/Margoliash.pdf`.

Igor Aleksandrovič Mel'čuk. 1988. *Dependency Syntax: Theory and Practice*. SUNY Press, Albany, NY.

Joakim Nivre. 2005. Dependency grammar and dependency parsing. Technical Report MSI report 05133, Växjö University School of Mathematics and Systems Engineering, Växjö, Sweden.

Timothy Osborne, Michael Putnam, and Thomas Groß. 2012. Catenae: introducing a novel unit of syntactic analysis. *Syntax*, 15(4):354–396.

Olutobi Owoputi, Brendan O'Connor, Chris Dyer, Kevin Gimpel, Nathan Schneider, and Noah A. Smith. 2013. Improved part-of-speech tagging for online conversational text with word clusters. In *Proceedings of the 2013 Conference of the North American Chapter of the Association for Computational Linguistics: Human Language Technologies*, pages 380–390. Association for Computational Linguistics, Atlanta, Georgia, USA.

Alonzo Reed and Brainerd Kellogg. 1877. *Work on English grammar & composition*. Clark & Maynard.

Federico Sangati and Chiara Mazza. 2009. An English dependency treebank à la Tesnière. In Marco Passarotti, Adam Przepiórkowski, Savina Raynaud, and Frank Van Eynde, editors, *Proceedings of the Eigth International Workshop on Treebanks and Linguistic Theories*, pages 173–184. EDUCatt, Milan, Italy.

Gerold Schneider. 1998. *A linguistic comparison of constituency, dependency and link grammar*. Master's thesis, University of Zurich.

Nathan Schneider, Brendan O'Connor, Naomi Saphra, David Bamman, Manaal Faruqui, Noah A. Smith, Chris Dyer, and Jason Baldridge. 2013. A framework for (under)specifying dependency syntax without overloading annotators. arXiv:1306.2091 [cs.CL]. `arxiv.org/pdf/1306.2091`.

Petr Sgall, Eva Hajičová, and Jarmila Panevová. 1986. *The Meaning of the Sentence in its Semantic and Pragmatic Aspects*. Reidel, Dordrecht and Academia, Prague.

Stuart M. Shieber. 1992. *Constraint-Based Grammar Formalisms*. MIT Press, Cambridge, MA.

Daniel Sleator and Davy Temperly. 1993. Parsing English with a link grammar. In *Proceedings of the Third International Workshop on Parsing Technology (IWPT'93)*, pages 277–292. Tilburg, Netherlands.

David A. Smith and Noah A. Smith. 2007. Probabilistic models of nonprojective dependency trees. In *Proceedings of the 2007 Joint Conference on Empirical Methods in Natural Language Processing and Computational Natural Language Learning (EMNLP-CoNLL 2007)*, pages 132–140. Association for Computational Linguistics, Prague, Czech Republic.

Rion Snow, Brendan O'Connor, Daniel Jurafsky, and Andrew Ng. 2008. Cheap and fast — but is it good? Evaluating non-expert annotations for natural language tasks. In *Proceedings of the 2008 Conference on Empirical Methods in Natural Language Processing (EMNLP 2008)*, pages 254–263. Association for Computational Linguistics, Honolulu, Hawaii.

Mark Steedman. 2000. *The Syntatic Process*. MIT Press, Cambridge, MA.

Luc Steels, Jan-Ola Östman, and Kyoko Ohara, editors. 2011. *Design patterns in Fluid Construction Grammar*. Number 11 in Constructional Approaches to Language. John Benjamins, Amsterdam.

Lucien Tesnière. 1959. *Eléments de Syntaxe Structurale*. Klincksieck, Paris.

Michael Tomasello. 2003. *Constructing a Language: A Usage-Based Theory of Language Acquisition*. Harvard University Press, Cambridge, MA.

Converting Italian Treebanks: Towards an Italian Stanford Dependency Treebank

Cristina Bosco
Dipartimento di Informatica
Università di Torino
cristina.bosco@unito.it

Simonetta Montemagni
Istituto di Linguistica Computazionale "Antonio Zampolli" (ILC–CNR)
simonetta.montemagni@ilc.cnr.it

Maria Simi
Dipartimento di Informatica
Università di Pisa
simi@unipi.it

Abstract

The paper addresses the challenge of converting MIDT, an existing dependency–based Italian treebank resulting from the harmonization and merging of smaller resources, into the Stanford Dependencies annotation formalism, with the final aim of constructing a standard–compliant resource for the Italian language. Achieved results include a methodology for converting treebank annotations belonging to the same dependency–based family, the *Italian Stanford Dependency Treebank* (ISDT), and an Italian localization of the Stanford Dependency scheme.

1 Introduction

The limited availability of training resources is a widely acknowledged bottleneck for machine learning approaches for Natural Language Processing (NLP). This is also the case of dependency treebanks within statistical dependency parsing. Moreover, the availability of a treebank in a standard format strongly improves its usefulness, increasing the number of tasks for which it can be exploited and allowing the application of a larger variety of tools. It also has an impact on the reliability of achieved results, and, last but not least, it permits comparability with other resources.

This motivated a variety of initiatives devoted to the definition of standards for the linguistic annotation of corpora. Since the early 1990s, different initiatives have been devoted to the definition of standards for the linguistic annotation of corpora with a specific view to re–using and merging existing treebanks. The starting point is represented by the EAGLES (Expert Advisory Groups on Language Engineering Standards) initiative, which ended up with providing provisional standard guidelines (Leech et al., 1996), operating at the level of both content (i.e. the linguistic categories) and encoding format. More recent initiatives, e.g. LAF/GrAF (Ide and Romary, 2006; Ide and Suderman, 2007) and SynAF (Declerck, 2008) representing on–going ISO TC37/SC4 standardization activities[1], rather focused on the definition of a pivot format capable of representing diverse annotation types of varying complexity without providing specifications for the annotation of content categories (i.e., the labels describing the associated linguistic phenomena), for which standardization appeared since the beginning to be a much trickier matter. Recently, other standardization efforts such as ISOCat (Kemps-Snijders et al., 2009) tackled this latter issue by providing a set of data categories at various levels of granularity, each accompanied by a precise definition of its linguistic meaning. Unfortunately, the set of dependency categories within ISOCat is still basic and restricted. We can thus conclude that as far as content categories are concerned *de jure* standards are not suitable at the moment for being used in the harmonization and merging of real dependency treebanks.

The alternative to *de jure* standards is represented by *de facto* standards. For what concerns dependency–based annotation, which in the recent past has been increasingly exploited for a wide range of NLP–based information extraction tasks, the Stanford Dependency (SD) scheme (de Marneffe et al., 2006) is gaining popularity as a *de facto* standard. Among the contexts where SD has been applied, we can observe e.g. parsers and corpora exploited in biomedical information extraction, where it has been suggested to be a suitable unifying syntax formalism for several incompatible syntactic annotation schemes (Pyysalo et al., 2007). SD has already been applied to different languages, e.g. Finnish in the Turku treebank (Haverinen et al., 2010), Swedish in the Talbanken

[1] http://www.tc37sc4.org/

treebank[2], Chinese in the Classical Chinese Literature treebank (Seraji et al., 2012) or Persian in the Uppsala Persian Dependency Treebank (Lee and Kong, 2012).

In this paper, we describe the conversion of an existing Italian resource into the SD annotation scheme, with the final aim of developing a standard–compliant treebank, the *Italian Stanford Dependency Treebank* (ISDT). The reference resource, called *Merged Italian Dependency Treebank* (MIDT)[3] (Bosco et al., 2012), is the result of a previous effort in the direction of improving interoperability of data sets available for Italian by harmonizing and merging two existing dependency–based resources, i.e. TUT and ISST–TANL, adopting incompatible annotation schemes. The two conversion steps are visualized in Figure 1: note that in both of them the focus is on the conversion and merging of the content of linguistic annotation; for what concerns the representation format, all involved treebanks follow the CoNLL tab–separated format (Buchholz and Marsi, 2006) which nowadays represents a *de facto* standard within the international dependency parsing community. In this paper, we deal with the second step, focusing on the MIDT to ISDT conversion.

Starting from a comparative analysis of the MIDT and SD annotation schemes, we developed a methodology for converting treebank annotations belonging to the same dependency–based family based on:

- a comparative analysis of the source and target annotation schemes, carried out with respect to different dimensions of variation, ranging from head selection criteria, dependency tagset granularity to defined annotation criteria;
- the analysis of the performance of a state–of–the–art dependency parser by using as training the source and the target treebanks;
- the mapping of the MIDT annotation scheme onto the SD data categories.

[2] http://stp.lingfil.uu.se/~nivre/swedish_treebank/talbanken-stanford-1.2.tar.gz

[3] MIDT was developed within the project PARLI (http://parli.di.unito.it/project_en.html) partially funded in 2008-2012 by the Italian Ministry for University and Research, for fostering the development of new resources and tools that can operate together, and the harmonization of existing ones. MIDT is documented at http://medialab.di.unipi.it/wiki/MIDT/.

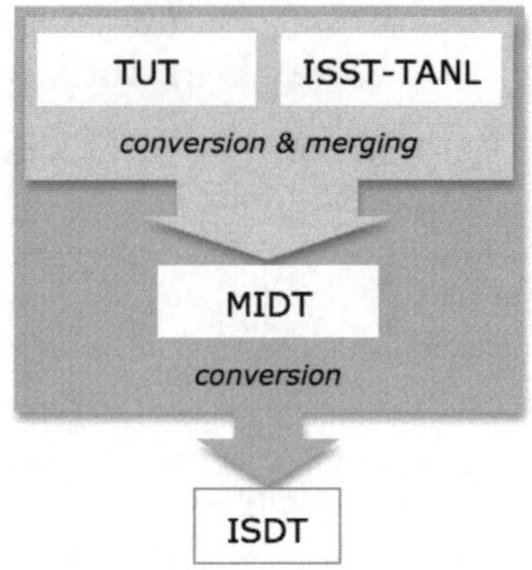

Figure 1: Merging and conversion process from TUT and ISST–TANL to MIDT and ISDT.

In this conversion process, we had to deal with the peculiarities of the Italian language: the tackled issues range from morphological richness, presence of clitic pronouns to relatively free word order and pro–drop, all properties requiring specific annotation strategies to be dealt with. Therefore, a by product of this conversion process is represented by the specialization of the SD annotation scheme with respect to Italian.

In the following sections, after briefly describing the methodology applied for the development of the MIDT resource (Section 2), we focus on a comparative analysis of the MIDT and SD annotation schemes (Section 3) followed by a description of the implemented conversion process (Section 4). Finally, we present the results obtained by training a parsing system on the newly developed resource (Section 5).

2 The starting point: MIDT

ISDT originates from the conversion towards the SD standard of the MIDT resource, whose origins and development are summarised below (for more details on this harmonization and merging step the interested reader is referred to Bosco et al. (2012)).

2.1 The ancestors: TUT and ISST–TANL

The TUT and ISST–TANL resources differ under different respects, at the level of both corpus composition and adopted annotation schemes.

For what concerns size and composition, TUT (Bosco et al., 2000)[4] currently includes 3,452 Italian sentences (i.e. 102,150 tokens in TUT native,

[4] http://www.di.unito.it/~tutreeb/

and 93,987 in CoNLL) and represents five different text genres (newspapers, Italian Civil Law Code, JRC-Acquis Corpus[5], Wikipedia and the Costituzione Italiana), while ISST–TANL includes 3,109 sentences (71,285 tokens in CoNLL format), which were extracted from the "balanced" ISST partition (Montemagni et al., 2003) exemplifying general language usage as testified in articles from newspapers and periodicals, selected to cover a high variety of topics (politics, economy, culture, science, health, sport, leisure, etc.).

As far as the annotation scheme is concerned, TUT applies the major principles of the Word Grammar theoretical framework (Hudson, 1984) using a rich set of dependency relations, but it includes *null* elements to deal with non–projective structures, long distance dependencies, equi phenomena, pro–drop and elliptical structures[6]. The ISST–TANL annotation scheme originates from FAME (Lenci et al., 2008), an annotation scheme which was developed starting from *de facto* standards and which was specifically conceived for complying with the basic requirements of parsing evaluation, and – later – for the annotation of unrestricted Italian texts.

2.2 Creating the merged MIDT resource

The challenge we tackled in the development of MIDT was to translate between different annotation schemes and merging them. We focused on the harmonization and merging of content categories. To this specific end, we defined a set of linguistic categories to be used as a "bridge" between the specific TUT and ISST–TANL schemes.

First of all, we analyzed similarities and differences of the underlying schemes, which led to identify a core of syntactic constructions for which the annotations agreed, but also to highlight variations in head selection criteria, inventory of dependency types and their linguistic interpretation, projectivity constraint and analysis of specific syntactic constructions. For instance, TUT always assigns heads on the basis of syntactic criteria, i.e. the head role is played by the function word in all constructions where one function word and one content word are involved (e.g. determiner–noun, verb–auxiliary), while in ISST–TANL head selection follows from a combination of syntactic and semantic criteria (e.g. in determiner–noun and auxiliary–verb relations the head role is played by the content word). Both schemes assume different inventories of dependency types and degrees of granularity in the representation of specific relations. Moreover, whereas ISST–TANL allows for non–projective representations, TUT assumes the projectivity constraint. Further differences are concerned with the treatment of coordination and punctuation, which are particularly problematic to deal with in the dependency framework.

As a second step, we defined a bridge annotation, i.e. the MIDT dependency tagset, following practical considerations: bridge categories should be automatically reconstructed by exploiting morpho–syntactic and dependency information contained in the original resources; for some constructions, the MIDT representation is parameterizable, i.e. the tagset provides two different options, corresponding to the TUT and ISST–TANL annotation styles (e.g. for determiner–noun or preposition–noun relations).

The final MIDT tagset contains 21 dependency tags (as opposed to the 72 tags of TUT and the 29 of ISST–TANL), including the different options provided for the same type of construction. CoNLL is used as encoding format.

3 Comparing the MIDT and SD schemes

The MIDT and SD annotation schemes are both dependency–based and therefore fall within the same broader family. This fact, however, does not guarantee *per se* an easy and linear conversion process from one to the other: as pointed out in Bosco et al. (2012), harmonizing and converting annotation schemes can be quite a challenging task, even when this process is carried out within a same paradigm and with respect to the same language. In the case at hand, this task is made easier thanks to the fact that the MIDT and SD schemes share similar design principles: for instance, in both cases preference is given a) to relations which are semantically contentful and useful to applications, or b) to relations linking content words rather than being indirectly mediated via function words (see design principles 2 and 5 respectively in de Marneffe and Manning (2008a)). Another peculiarity shared by MIDT and SD consists in the fact that they both neutralize the argument/adjunct distinction for what concerns prepositional complements, which is taken to be "largely useless

[5] `http://langtech.jrc.it/JRC-Acquis.html`

[6] The CoNLL format does not include null elements, but the projectivity constraint is maintained at the cost of a loss of information with respect to native TUT in some cases.

in practice" as de Marneffe and Manning (2008a) claim. In spite of their sharing similar design principles, there are also important differences concerning the inventory of dependency types and their linguistic interpretation, the head selection criteria as well as the treatment of specific syntactic constructions. In what follows, we summarize the main dimensions of variation between the MIDT and SD annotation schemes, with a specific view to the conversion issues they arise.

3.1 Granularity and inventory of dependency types

MIDT and SD annotation schemes assume different inventories of dependency types characterized by different degrees of granularity in the representation of specific relations: the adopted dependency tagset includes 21 dependency types in the case of MIDT and 48 in the case of SD. Interestingly however, it is not always the case that the finer grained annotation scheme – i.e. SD – is the one providing more granular distinctions: whereas this is typically the case, there are also cases in which more granular distinction are adopted in the MIDT annotation scheme.

Consider first SD relational distinctions which are neutralized at the level of the MIDT annotation. As reported in de Marneffe and Manning (2008a), so–called NP–internal relations are critical in real world applications: the SD scheme therefore includes many relations of this kind, e.g. `appos` (appositive modifier), `nn` (noun compound), `num` (numeric modifier), `number` (element of compound number) and `abbrev` (abbreviation). In MIDT all these relation types are lumped together under the general heading of `mod` (modifier). To deal with these cases, the MIDT to SD conversion has to simultaneously combine dependency and morpho–syntactic information (e.g. the morpho–syntactic category of the nodes involved in the relation), which however is not always sufficient as in the case of appositive modifiers for which further evidence is needed.

Let us consider now the reverse case, i.e. in which MIDT adopts finer–grained distinctions with respect to SD. For instance, MIDT envisages different relation types for auxiliary–verb and preposition–verb (within infinitive clauses, be they modifiers or subcategorized arguments) constructions, which are `aux` and `prep` respectively. By contrast, SD represents both cases in terms of the same relation type, i.e. `aux`. Significant differences between English and Italian justify the different strategies adopted in SD and MIDT respectively: in English, open clausal complements are always introduced by the particle 'to', whereas in Italian different prepositions can introduce them (i.e. 'a', 'di', 'da'), which are selected by the governing head. The SD representation of the element introducing infinitival complements and modifiers in terms of `aux` might not be appropriate as far as Italian is concerned and it would be preferable to have a specific relation for dealing with introducers of infinitival complements (like `complm` in the case of finite clausal complements): as reported in Section 4, we are currently evaluating different representational options with a specific view to the syntactic peculiarities of the Italian language.

Another interesting and more complex example can be found for what concerns the partitioning of the space of sentential complements. MIDT distinguishes between `mod`(ifiers) on the one hand and subcategorised `arg`(uments) on the other hand: note that whereas `arg` is restricted to clausal complements subcategorized for by the governing head, the `mod` relation covers different types of modifiers (nominal, adjectival, clausal, adverbial, etc.). By contrast, SD resorts to specific relations for dealing with sentential complements: in particular, distinct relation types are envisaged depending on e.g. whether the clause is a subcategorized complement or a modifier (see e.g. `ccomp` vs `advcl`), or whether the governor is a verb or a noun (see e.g. `xcomp` vs `infmod`), or whether the clausal complement is headed by a finite or non–finite verb (see e.g. `ccomp` vs `xcomp`). Starting from MIDT, the finer–grained distinctions adopted by SD for dealing with clausal complements can be recovered by combining dependency information with morpho-syntactic one (e.g. the mood of the verbal head of the clausal complements or the morpho–syntactic category of the governing head).

3.2 Head selection

Criteria for distinguishing the head and the dependent within relations have been widely discussed in the linguistic literature in all frameworks where the notion of syntactic head plays an important role. Unfortunately, different criteria have been proposed, some syntactic and some semantic, which do not lead to a single coherent notion of dependency (Kübler et al., 2009). Head selection thus represents an important and unavoidable dimension of variation among dependency annotation schemes, especially for what concerns constructions involving grammatical function words. MIDT and SD agree on the treatment of tricky cases such as the determiner–noun relation within nominal groups, the preposition–noun relation within prepositional phrases as well as the auxiliary–main verb relation in complex verbal groups. In both schemes, head selection follows from a combination of syntactic and semantic criteria: i.e. whereas in the determiner–noun and auxiliary–verb constructions the head role is assigned to the semantic head (noun/verb), in preposition–noun constructions the head role is played by the element which is subcategorized for by the governing head, i.e. the preposition which is the syntactic head but can also be seen as as a kind of role marker. In this area, the only but not negligible difference is concerned with subordinate clauses whose head in SD is assumed to be the verb, rather than the introducing element (whether a preposition or a subordinating conjunction) as in MIDT: in this case, the MIDT to SD conversion requires restructuring of the dependency tree.

3.3 Coordination and punctuation

In both MIDT and SD schemes, coordinate constructions are considered as asymmetric structures with a main difference: while in MIDT both the conjunction and conjuncts starting from the second one are linked to the immediately preceding conjunct, in SD the conjunction(s) and the subsequent conjunct(s) are all linked to the first one. Also the treatment of punctuation is quite problematic in the framework of a dependency annotation scheme, although this has not been specifically dealt with in the linguistic literature. Whereas MIDT has its own linguistically–motivated strategy to deal with punctuation, SD does not appear to provide explicit and detailed annotation guidelines in this respect.

3.4 MIDT- or SD–only relations

It is not always the case that a dependency type belonging to the MIDT or SD annotation scheme has a counterpart in the other. Let us start from SD relation types which are not explicitly encoded in the MIDT source annotation, due to constraints of the CoNLL representation format. This is the case of the `ref` dependency linking the relative word introducing the relative clause and its antecedent, or of the `xsubj` relation which in spite of its being part of the original TUT and ISST resources have been omitted from the most recent and CoNLL–compliant versions, which represent the starting point of in MIDT: in both cases, the "one head per dependent" constraint of the CoNLL representation format is violated. From this, it follows that ISDT won't include these dependency types. Other SD relations which were part of the MIDT's ancestors but were neutralized in MIDT are concerned with semantically–oriented distinctions which turned out to be problematic to be reliably identified in parsing in spite of their being explicitly encoded in both source annotation schemes (Bosco et al., 2012). This is the case of the indirect object relation (`iobj`) or of temporal modifiers (`tmod`).

The MIDT relation types which instead do not have a corresponding relation in SD are those that typically represent Italian–specific peculiarities. This is the case of the `clit`(ic) dependency, linking clitic pronouns to the verbal head they refer to. In MIDT, whenever appropriate clitic pronouns are assigned a label that reflects their grammatical function (e.g. "dobj" or "iobj"): this is the case of reflexive constructions (*Maria si lava* lit. 'Maria her washes' meaning that 'Maria washes herself') or of complements overtly realized as clitic pronouns (*Giovanni mi ha dato un libro* lit. 'Giovanni to–me has given a book' meaning that 'Giovanni gave me a book'). With pronominal verbs, in which the clitic can be seen as part of the verbal inflection, a specific dependency relation (`clit`) is resorted to link the clitic pronoun to the verbal head: for instance, in a sentence like *la sedia si è rotta* lit. 'the chair it is broken' meaning that 'the chair broke', the dependency linking the clitic *si* to the verbal head is `clit`.

4 The MIDT to SD conversion

The conversion process followed to generate the *Italian Stanford Dependency Treebank* (ISDT) starting from MIDT is based on the results of the comparative analysis reported in the previous section. It is organized in two different steps: the first one aimed at generating an enriched version of the MIDT resource, henceforth referred to as MIDT++, including SD–relevant distinctions neutralized in MIDT, and the second one in charge of converting the MIDT++ annotation in terms of the Stanford Dependencies as described in de Marneffe and Manning (2008b) specialized with respect to the Italian language syntactic peculiarities. Note that also the resulting ISDT resource adheres to the CoNLL tabular format.

The first step relied on previous harmonization work leading to the construction of the MIDT resource starting from the CoNLL–compliant TUT and ISST–TANL treebanks (described in Bosco et al. (2012)). During this step, we recovered from the native resources relevant distinctions that have been neutralized in MIDT, because of choices made in the design of the MIDT annotation scheme (e.g. indirect objects or temporal modifiers which are assigned an underspecified representation in MIDT, see Section 3) or simply because the harmonization of the source annotation schemes was not possible without manual revision (this is the case of appositions, explicitly annotated only in TUT).

Other issues tackled during this first pre–processing step include the treatment of coordination and multi–word expressions. Since in SD conjunctions and conjuncts, after the first one, are all linked to the first conjunct, exactly as it was in ISST–TANL, the intermediate MIDT++ is generated according to this scheme, with no conversion for ISST–TANL and by restructuring the different cascading coordination style of TUT. For what concerns multi–word expressions, we unified the multi–word repertoires of the two resources. Another area that required some pre–processing with manual revision is concerned with the annotation of the parataxis relation. The augmented resource resulting from this pre–processing step, i.e. MIDT++, is used as a "bridge" towards the SD representation format.

Starting from the results of the comparative analysis detailed in Section 3, we defined conversion patterns which can be grouped into two main classes according to whether they refer to individual dependencies (case A) or they involve dependency subtrees due to head reassignment (case B).

A) ***Structure–preserving mapping rules*** involving dependency retyping without restructuring of the tree:

A.1) ***1:1 mapping*** requiring dependency retyping only (e.g. MIDT `prep` > SD `pobj`, or MIDT `subj` > SD `nsubj`);

A.2) ***1:n mapping*** requiring finer–grained dependency retyping (e.g. MIDT `mod` > SD `abbrev` | `amod` | `appos` | `nn` | `nnp` | `npadvmod` | `num` | `number` | `partmod` | `poss` | `preconj` | `predet` | `purplcl` | `quantmod` | `tmod`);

B) ***Tree restructuring mapping rules*** involving head reassignment and dependency retyping. Focusing on dependency retyping we distinguish the following cases:

B.1) head reassignment with ***1:1 dependency mapping*** (e.g. MIDT `subj` > SD `csubj` in the case of clausal subjects);

B.2) head reassignment with ***1:n dependency mapping*** based on finer–grained distinctions (e.g. MIDT `arg` > SD `xcomp` — `ccomp`, or MIDT `mod` (with verbal head) > SD `advcl` | `infmod` | `prepc` | `purpcl`).

In what follows, we will exemplify how the abstract patterns described above have been translated into MIDT_to_SD conversion rules. The conversion of the MIDT `arg` relation, referring to clausal complements subcategorized for by the governing head, represents an interesting example of 1:n dependency mapping with tree restructuring (case B.2 above). In MIDT, clausal complements, either finite or non–finite clauses, are linked to the governing head (which can be a verb, a noun or an adjective) as `arg`(uments), with a main difference with respect to SD, i.e. that the head of the clausal complement is the word introducing it (be it a preposition or a subordinating conjunction) rather than the verb of the clausal complement. The main conversion rules to SD can be summarised as follows, where the $\Rightarrow$ separates the left from the right hand side of the rule, the notation $x \rightarrow_{dep\_label} y$ denotes that token y is governed by token x with the dependency label specifying the relation holding between the two (a MIDT tag is found on the left side of the rule, whereas an SD one occurs on the right side):

1. $\$1[S|V|A] \rightarrow_{arg} \$2[E] \rightarrow_{prep} \$3[V_{infinitive}] \Rightarrow \$1 \rightarrow_{xcomp} \$3; \$3 \rightarrow_{aux} \$2$

2. $\$1[S|V|A] \rightarrow_{arg} \$2[CS] \rightarrow_{sub} \$3[V_{finite}] \Rightarrow \$1 \rightarrow_{ccomp} \$3; \$3 \rightarrow_{complm} \$2$

In the rules, the \$ followed by a number is a variable indentifying a given dependency node. Constraints on tokens in the left–hand side of the rule

(a) MIDT representation

(b) SD representation

Figure 2: MIDT vs SD annotation of the same sentence

are reported within square brackets: they are typically concerned with the grammatical category of the token (CS stands for subordinative conjunction, E for preposition, S for noun, V for verb). Rule 1 above handles the transformation of the infinitival clause from the MIDT representation to SD. Consider as an example the MIDT dependency tree in Figure 2(a) for the sentence *Giovanni ha dichiarato ai giudici di avere pagato i terroristi*, lit. 'Giovanni told to–the judges to have paid the terrorists' 'Giovanni told the judges that he has paid the terrorists' whose SD conversion is reported in Figure 2(b). By comparing the trees, we see that head restructuring and dependency retyping have both been performed in the conversion of the infinitival clause representation: in MIDT the head of the infinitival clause is the preposition whereas in SD it is the verb; the relation linking the governing head and the head of the infinitival clause is `arg` in MIDT and `xcomp` in SD.

Currently, the conversion script implements over 100 rules which are still being tested with the final aim of finding the most appropriate representation with respect to the Italian syntactic peculiarities. The problematic area of sentential complements is still being explored to find out adequate representational solutions. Consider as an example the case of the word introducing infinitival complements: Figure 2(b) above, reporting the result of the SD conversion, shows that the same `aux` relation is used to link the preposition to the verb heading the infinitival complement as well as the auxiliary *avere* 'to have' to the main verb. This solution might not be so appropriate given the peculiarities of the Italian language, where different prepositions (lexically selected by the governing head) can introduce infinitival complements.

During the conversion step, the SD scheme has been specialized with respect to the Italian language. There are SD dependency relations which were excluded from the Italian localization of the standard scheme, either because not appropriate given the syntactic peculiarities of this language (this is the case e.g. of the `prt` relation) or because they could not be recovered from the CoNLL–compliant versions of the resources we started from (see e.g. the relations `ref` or `xsubj`). The SD tagset was also extended with new dependency types: this is the case of the `clit` relation used for dealing with clitics in pronominal verbs, or of the `nnp` relation specifically defined for compound proper nouns. Other specializations are concerned with the use of underspecified categories: rather than resorting to the most generic relation, i.e. `dep` used when it is impossible to determine a more precise dependency relation, we exploited the hierarchical organization of SD typed dependencies, i.e. we used the `comp` and `mod` relations when we could not find an appropriate relation within the set of their dependency subtypes.

5 Using ISDT as training corpus

In this section, we report the results achieved by using ISDT for training a dependency parser, namely DeSR (Dependency Shift Reduce), a transition–based statistical parser (Attardi, 2006), where it is possible to specify, through a configuration file, the set of features to use (e.g. POS tag, lemma, morphological features) and the classification algorithm (e.g. Multi-Layer Perceptron (Attardi and Dell'Orletta, 2009), Support Vector Machine, Maximum Entropy). DeSR has been trained on TUT and ISST–TANL in the framework of the evaluation campaigns Evalita, for the last time in 2011 (Bosco and Mazzei, 2012; Dell'Orletta et al., 2012). More recently DeSR has been trained and tested on MIDT: the results ob-

Table 1: Parsing results with ISDT resources

TRAINING	TEST	PARSER	LAS	LAS no punct
TUT–SDT_train	TUT–SDT_test	DeSR MLP	84.14%	85.57%
ISST–TANL–SDT_train	ISST–TANL–SDT_test	DeSR MLP	80.55%	82.11%
TUT+ISST–TANL–SDT_train	TUT+ISST–TANL–SDT_test	DeSR MLP	83.34%	84.16%
TUT+ISST–TANL–SDT_train	TUT–SDT_test	DeSR MLP	84.14%	85.79%
TUT+ISST–TANL–SDT_train	ISST–TANL–SDT_test	DeSR MLP	79.94%	81.86%

tained on both the MIDT version of the individual TUT and ISST–TANL resources and the merged resource are reported in (Bosco et al., 2012): the best scores, achieved applying a parser combination strategy and training on TUT in MIDT format, are LAS 90.11% and LAS 91.58% without punctuation.

For the experiments on the ISDT resource we used a basic and fast variant of the DeSR parser based on Multi-Layer Perceptron (MLP). In fact, the purpose of the experiment was not to optimize the parser for the new resource but to compare relative performances of the same parser on different versions of the same resources. As a result, the substantial drop in performance observed with respect to the MIDT resource is in part due to this factor, and cannot be totally attributed to the greater complexity of the SD scheme or quality of the conversion output.

Table 1 reports, in the first two rows, the values of Labeled Attachment Score (LAS, with and without punctuation) obtained against the TUT–ISDT and ISST–TANL–ISDT datasets. The different performance of the parser on the two converted datasets (TUT–ISDT and ISST–TANL–ISDT) is in line with what was observed in previous experiments with native resources and MIDT (Bosco et al., 2010; Bosco et al., 2012); therefore, the composition of the training and test corpora can still be identified as possible causes for such a difference. The results reported in rows 3–5 have been obtained by training DeSR with the larger resource including both TUT–ISDT and ISST–TANL–ISDT. As test set, we used a combination of the two test sets (row 3) and test sets from the two data sets separately (rows 4 and 5). The preliminary results achieved by using ISDT are encouraging, in line with what was obtained on the WSJ for English and reported in (Cer et al., 2010), where the best results in labeled attachment precision, achieved by a fast dependency parser (Nivre Eager feature Extract), is 81.7. For the time being, training with the larger combined resource does not seem to provide a substantial advantage, confirming results obtained with MIDT, despite the fact that in the conversion from MIDT to ISDT a substantial effort was spent to further harmonize the two resources.

6 Conclusion

In this paper, we addressed the challenge of converting MIDT, an existing dependency–based Italian treebank resulting from the harmonization and merging of smaller resources adopting incompatible annotation schemes, into the Stanford Dependencies annotation formalism, with the final aim of constructing a standard–compliant resource for the Italian language. SD, increasingly acknowledged within the international NLP community as a *de facto* standard, was selected for its being defined with a specific view to supporting information extraction tasks.

The outcome of this still ongoing effort is three–fold. Starting from a comparative analysis of the MIDT and SD annotation schemes, we developed a methodology for converting treebank annotations belonging to the same dependency–based family. Second, Italian has now a new standard–compliant treebank, i.e. the *Italian Stanford Dependency Treebank* (ISDT, 200,516 tokens)[7]: we believe that this conversion will significantly improve the usability of the resource. Third, but not least important, we specialized the Stanford Dependency annotation scheme to deal with the peculiarities of the Italian language.

7 Acknowledgements

This research was supported by a Google "gift". Giuseppe Attardi helped with the experiments with the DeSR parser, Roberta Montefusco produced the converter to the collapsed/propagated version of ISDT and in so doing helped us to reduce inconsistencies and errors in the resource.

[7]Both the MIDT and ISDT resources are released by the authors under the Creative Commons Attribution–NonCommercial-ShareAlike 3.0 Unported licence (`http://creativecommons.org/licenses/by-nc-sa/3.0/legalcode.txt`).

References

G. Attardi and F. Dell'Orletta. 2009. Reverse revision and linear tree combination for dependency parsing. In *Proceedings of of NAACL HLT (2009)*.

G. Attardi. 2006. Experiments with a multilanguage non–projective dependency parser. In *Proceedings of the CoNLL-X '06*, New York City, New York.

C. Bosco and A. Mazzei. 2012. The evalita 2011 parsing task: the dependency track. In *Working Notes of Evalita'11*, Roma, Italy.

C. Bosco, V. Lombardo, L. Lesmo, and D. Vassallo. 2000. Building a treebank for italian: a data-driven annotation schema. In *Proceedings of the LREC'00*, Athens, Greece.

C. Bosco, S. Montemagni, A. Mazzei, V. Lombardo, F. Dell'Orletta, A. Lenci, L. Lesmo, G. Attardi, M. Simi, A. Lavelli, J. Hall, J. Nilsson, and J. Nivre. 2010. Comparing the influence of different treebank annotations on dependency parsing. In *Proceedings of the LREC'10*, Valletta, Malta.

C. Bosco, M. Simi, and S. Montemagni. 2012. Harmonization and merging of two italian dependency treebanks. In *Proceedings of the LREC 2012 Workshop on Language Resource Merging*, Istanbul, Turkey.

Sabine Buchholz and Erwin Marsi. 2006. Conll-x shared task on multilingual dependency parsing. In *In Proc. of CoNLL*, pages 149–164.

D. Cer, M.C. de Marneffe, D. Jurafsky, and C.D. Manning. 2010. Parsing to stanford dependencies: Trade-offs between speed and accuracy. In *Proceedings of the LREC'10)*, Valletta, Malta.

M.C. de Marneffe and C. Manning. 2008a. The stanford typed dependencies representation. In *Coling 2008: Proceedings of the workshop on Cross-Framework and Cross-Domain Parser Evaluation*, pages 1–8, Stroudsburg, PA, USA. Association for Computational Linguistics.

M.C. de Marneffe and C.D. Manning. 2008b. Stanford typed dependencies manual. Technical report, Stanford University.

M.C. de Marneffe, B. MacCartney, and C.D. Manning. 2006. Generating typed dependency parses from phrase structure parses. In *Proceedings of 5th International Conference on Language Resources and Evaluation (LREC 2006)*.

T. Declerck. 2008. A framework for standardized syntactic annotation. In *Proceedings of the LREC'08*, Marrakech, Morocco.

F. Dell'Orletta, S. Marchi, S. Montemagni, G. Venturi, T. Agnoloni, and E. Francesconi. 2012. Domain adaptation for dependency parsing at evalita 2011. In *Working Notes of Evalita'11*, Roma, Italy.

K. Haverinen, T. Viljanen, V. Laippala, S. Kohonen, F. Ginter, and T. Salakoski. 2010. Treebanking Finnish. In *Proceedings of the 9th Workshop on Treebanks and Linguistic Theories (TLT-9)*, pages 79–90, Tartu, Estonia.

R. Hudson. 1984. *Word Grammar*. Basil Blackwell, Oxford and New York.

N. Ide and L. Romary. 2006. Representing linguistic corpora and their annotations. In *Proceedings of the LREC'06*, Genova, Italy.

N. Ide and K. Suderman. 2007. GrAF: A graph-based format for linguistic annotations. In *Proceedings of the Linguistic Annotation Workshop*, Prague, Czech Republic.

M. Kemps-Snijders, M. Windhouwer, P. Wittenburg, and S.E. Wright. 2009. Isocat: remodelling metadata for language resources. *IJMSO*, 4(4):261–276.

S. Kübler, R.T. McDonald, and J. Nivre. 2009. *Dependency Parsing*. Morgan & Claypool Publishers, Oxford and New York.

John Lee and Yin Hei Kong. 2012. A dependency treebank of classical chinese poems. In *Proceedings of the 2012 Conference of the North American Chapter of the Association for Computational Linguistics: Human Language Technologies*, pages 191–199, Montréal, Canada, June. Association for Computational Linguistics.

G. Leech, R. Barnett, and P. Kahrel. 1996. Eagles recommendations for the syntactic annotation of corpora. Technical report, EAG-TCWG-SASG1.8.

A. Lenci, S. Montemagni, V. Pirrelli, and C. Soria. 2008. A syntactic meta–scheme for corpus annotation and parsing evaluation. In *Proceedings of the LREC'00*, Athens, Greece.

S. Montemagni, F. Barsotti, M. Battista, N. Calzolari, O. Corazzari, A. Lenci, A. Zampolli, F. Fanciulli, M. Massetani, R. Raffaelli, R. Basili, M. T. Pazienza, D. Saracino, F. Zanzotto, N. Mana, F. Pianesi, and R. Delmonte. 2003. Building the Italian Syntactic-Semantic Treebank. In A. Abeillé, editor, *Building and Using syntactically annotated corpora*. Kluwer, Dordrecht.

S. Pyysalo, F. Ginter, K. Haverinen, J. Heimonen, T. Salakoski, and V. Laippala. 2007. On the unification of syntactic annotations under the Stanford dependency scheme: A case study on Bioinfer and GENIA. In *BioNLP 2007: Biological, translational, and clinical language processing*, pages 25–32, Prague.

M. Seraji, B. Megyesi, and J. Nivre. 2012. Bootstrapping a persian dependency treebank. *Special Issue of Linguistic Issues in Language Technology (LiLT) on Treebanks and Linguistic Theories*, 7.

Analyses of the Association between Discourse Relation and Sentiment Polarity with a Chinese Human-Annotated Corpus

Hen-Hsen Huang **Chi-Hsin Yu** **Tai-Wei Chang** **Cong-Kai Lin** **Hsin-Hsi Chen**
Department of Computer Science and Information Engineering
National Taiwan University, Taipei, Taiwan
{hhhuang, jsyu, twchang, cklin}@nlg.csie.ntu.edu.tw;
hhchen@ntu.edu.tw

Abstract

Discourse relation may entail sentiment information. In this work, we annotate both discourse relation and sentiment information on a moderate-sized Chinese corpus extracted from the ClueWeb09. Based on the annotation, we investigate the association between the relation type and the sentiment polarity in Chinese and interpret the data from various aspects. Finally, we highlight some language phenomena and give some remarks.

1 Introduction

A discourse relation indicates how two arguments (i.e., elementary discourse units) cohere to each other. Various discourse relations were defined according to different taxonomy (Carlson and Marcu, 2001; Carlson et al., 2002; Prasad et al., 2008). In the work of the Penn Discourse Treebank 2.0 annotation, Prasad et al. (2008) labeled four grammatical classes of connectives in English, including subordinating conjunctions, coordinating conjunctions, adverbial connectives, and implicit connectives. Besides, the sense of each connective was also tagged. They defined three levels of sense hierarchy for the connectives. The four classes on the top level are *Temporal*, *Contingency*, *Comparison*, and *Expansion*.

There are *explicit* and *implicit* uses of discourse relations. An explicit discourse relation indicates the arguments are connected with an overt discourse marker (i.e., connective). A connective joins two discourse units such as phrases, clauses, or sentences together. For example, the word *however* is a common connective that indicates a *Comparison* relation between two arguments. The sense of a discourse marker denotes how its two arguments cohere. In other words, a discourse marker presents the relation of its two arguments.

In other cases, discourse marker is absent from an implicit relation. However, readers can still infer the relation from its argument pair. To resolve implicit discourse relations, i.e., without the information from discourse markers, is more challenging (Lin et al., 2009; Zhou et al., 2010).

Hutchinson (2004) pointed out the properties of a discourse marker from three dimensions, including polarity, veridicality, and type. The polarity of a discourse marker indicates the sentiment transition of its two arguments. Veridicality, the second dimension of a discourse marker, specifies whether both the two arguments are true or not. Type, similar to the sense which is annotated in the PDTB, is the third dimension of a discourse marker.

Our previous work (Huang and Chen, 2012a; Huang and Chen, 2012b) addressed the interaction between the sentiment polarity and the discourse structure in Chinese. Consider (S1), which consists of three clauses and forms a nested discourse structure shown in Figure 1.

(S1) 管理處雖然嘗試要讓長期以來作為大台北後花園的陽明山區更回歸自然 (Although the management office tried to make the Yangmingshan area a more natural environment as the long-term garden of Taipei)，但隨著週休二日、經濟環境改善 (but due to the two-day weekend and the improved economic conditions)，遊客帶來停車、垃圾等間接影響卻更嚴重 (the issues of tourist parking, garbage, and other indirect effects become more serious)。

The second and the third clauses form a *Contingency* relation with a sentiment polarity transition from Positive to Negative. Furthermore,

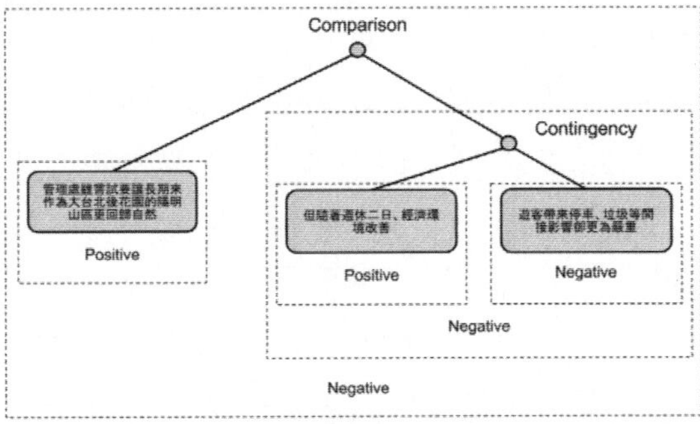

Figure 1: Discourse structure and sentiment polarities of (S1).

these two clauses also constitute one of the arguments of a *Positive-Negative Comparison* relation. As the PDTB 2.0 annotation manual suggests (Prasad, et al., 2007), a *Comparison* relation is established to emphasize the differences between two arguments. Therefore, it is expected that the two arguments of a *Comparison* relation are relatively likely to have the opposing polarity states (i.e., *Positive-Negative* or *Negative-Positive*). On the other hand, the two arguments of an *Expansion* relation are relatively likely to belong to the same polarity states (e.g., *Positive-Positive* or *Neutral-Neutral*).

Discourse relation recognition (Hernault et al., 2010; Soricut and Marcu, 2003) and sentiment analysis (Pang and Lee, 2008) have attracted much attention recently. Due to the limitation of the resources, the research on Chinese discourse relation analysis is relatively rare. In our previous work, we annotated a collection of Chinese discourse corpora, namely NTU Chinese Discourse Resources (http://nlg.csie.ntu.edu.tw/ntu-discourse/), for inter-sentential and intra-sentential discourse relation recognition (Huang and Chen, 2011; Huang and Chen, 2012a). However, no sentiment information is labeled in these corpora. In another work (Huang and Chen, 2012b), we proposed an annotation scheme to construct a Chinese discourse corpus with rich information including sentiment polarities, but the corpus is still under construction due to its complexity. Zhou and Xue (2012) did PDTB-style Chinese discourse corpus annotation, but the corpus is also not available yet.

In this paper, we annotate a moderate-sized Chinese corpus with the information of discourse relations and sentiment polarities. Total 7,638 sentences are sampled from the ClueWeb09. We review the results of annotation and analyze some language phenomena found in the corpus.

The rest of this paper is organized as follows. In Section 2, we introduce the ClueWeb corpus and a dictionary of Chinese discourse markers. In Section 3, the criteria to sample instances and the annotation scheme are shown. We analyze the language phenomena found in the annotated data and discuss the correlation between discourse relations and sentiment polarities in Section 4. Finally, we conclude the remarks in Section 5.

2 Linguistic Resources

The PDTB is a popular dataset used in the English discourse research. In contrast, no Chinese discourse corpus is publicly available at present. To construct a Chinese discourse corpus, we sample instances from a huge Chinese corpus (Yu et al., 2012). This corpus was developed based on the ClueWeb09 dataset, where Chinese material is the second largest. It contains a total of 9,598,430,559 POS-tagged sentences in 172,298,866 documents.

In this paper, only the explicit discourse relations are concerned. A dictionary of discourse markers is consulted to extract the instances of explicit discourse relations from the ClueWeb. This Chinese discourse marker dictionary is developed based on Cheng and Tian (1989), Cheng (2006) and Lu (2007). Table 1 shows an overview of the discourse marker dictionary. It contains 808 words and word pairs mapped into the PDTB four top-level classes (Cheng and Tian, 1989; Wolf and Gibson, 2005). Besides the types of discourse relations, we further classify the markers into three groups of scopes shown in the second column, including *Single word*, *Intra-sentential*, and *Inter-sentential*, according to their grammatical usages. The *Single word* group contains those individual words used as discourse markers. The *Intra-sentential* group contains pairs of words that occur inside the same sentence and denote a discourse relation. Here, a Chinese sentence is defined as a sequence of successive words that is ended by a period, a question mark, or an exclamation mark. The clauses of a sentence are delimited by commas. The *Inter-sentential* discourse markers are similar to the *Intra-sentential* ones, but the two words of a pair individually appear in different sentences. Some discourse markers can be used as both Inter-sentential and Intra-sentential. In this work, the Inter-sentential only discourse markers are excluded because we only concern the discourse relation occurring within a sentence. The third column lists the number of discourse markers for each scope under each PDTB class, and the fourth column gives some examples.

PDTB Class	Scope	# Markers	Examples
Expansion	Single word	177	另外 (besides), 抑或 (or), 不只 (not only), 例如 (such as)
	Intra-sentential	106	一方面…一方面 (on the one hand ... on the other hand), 不是…而是 (not ... but), 不只…也 (not only ... also)
	Inter-sentential	26	首先…再者 (first ... second), 或…或許 (or ... perhaps), 不只…不只 (not only ... not only)
Temporal	Single word	41	接著 (then)
	Intra-sentential	80	最初…最後 (first ... finally)
	Inter-sentential	30	最初…現在 (first ... now)
Comparison	Single word	34	即使 (even if)
	Intra-sentential	38	儘管…但 (although ... but)
	Inter-sentential	15	雖說…其實 (in spite of ... in fact)
Contingency	Single word	67	因為 (because), 如 (if), 假設 (suppose), 以免 (in order to avoid)
	Intra-sentential	180	因…而 (because ... then), 如…則 (if then), 凡…可 (any ... can)
	Inter-sentential	14	既然…於是 (since ... then), 至少…不然 (at least ... otherwise)

Table 1: Overview of a Chinese discourse marker dictionary.

3 Annotation

Based on the Chinese part of the ClueWeb09 (Yu et al., 2012), we sample a moderate-sized data with some criteria and annotate them with the information of discourse relations and sentiment polarities.

3.1 Sampling a reliable dataset

Discourse relations may be explicit or implicit, and a sentence may contain more than one discourse marker. Multiple discourse relations occurring in a sentence will make the annotation more complex. In this work, we focus on the correlation between discourse relations and sentiment polarity. To get a reliable dataset for analysis, we sample sentences based on the following three criteria.

1. A sentence should contain only two clauses.
2. A sentence should contain exact one discourse marker shown in the Chinese discourse marker dictionary. We match the discourse marker on the word level. For the *Single word* markers, the marker can appear in either of the clauses. For the pairwise markers, the first word should appear in the first clause, and the second word should appear in the second one.
3. The lengths of both clauses in a sentence are no more than 20 Chinese characters.

As shown in Figure 1, the sentiment polarity determination is more challenging when more than one discourse relation is involved in a sentence. In order to facilitate the analysis, we focus on those sentences that contain exact one discourse marker. The limitation of clause length is also applied to avoid the noise from implicit discourse relation. Based on a preliminary statistics, we find that most clauses in the Chinese part of the ClueWeb (Yu et al., 2012) are no longer than 20 Chinese characters shown in Figure 2.

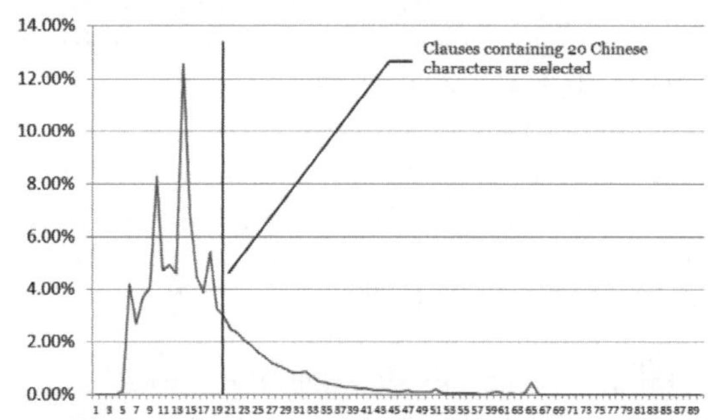

Figure 2: Length distribution in the ClueWeb.

3.2 Annotation scheme

Using the criteria described in Section 3.1, total 7,638 instances are randomly selected from the ClueWeb, and 87 native speakers annotate these instances. Each instance is shown to three annotators. The annotator labels the polarities of the first clause, the second clause, and the whole instance with *Negative*, *Neutral*, and *Positive*. In addition, the discourse relation between the two clauses is also labeled with *Temporal*, *Contingency*, *Comparison*, and *Expansion*. For each target sentence, the annotation is based on the information from the sentence only. The sentences are not given to annotators. Finally, the majority of each label is taken. For example, the polarity p_1 of the first clause in the instance (S2) is labeled as *Positive*, the polarity p_2 of the second clause is labeled as *Negative*, the resulting polarity p_w of the whole sentence is also labeled as *Negative*, and the discourse relation between the two clauses is labeled as *Comparison*.

(S2) 法國品牌的汽車在本土市場的佔有率雖然過半 (Although French brand cars share more than half of the domestic market share)，但市場份額持續萎縮 (but the market share continued to shrink)。

The inter-agreements of p_1, p_2, p_w, and discourse relation among annotators are 0.49, 0.50, 0.47, and 0.41 in Fleiss' Kappa values, respectively (all are moderate agreement). The resulting corpus is publicly available on the website of NTU Chinese Discourse Resources[1].

4 Results and Discussion

To investigate the corpus annotated with discourse relation and sentiment polarity, we firstly give an overview of results with respect to these two types of linguistic phenomena. And then, the most frequent discourse markers for each class of discourse relations are discussed. Finally, we reorganize the results to several aspects and discuss the association between discourse relations and sentiment polarities.

4.1 Overview of the annotated corpus

The distribution of the discourse relations versus the polarities of whole sentence (p_w) is shown in Table 2. Compared to the distributions of discourse relations in the Penn Discourse Treebank (Prasad et al., 2008) shown in Table 3, the explicit Chinese discourse corpus is more similar to the whole English corpus. The instances of *Expansion* form the largest set among four discourse relation classes. In Chinese, the instances of *Expansion* are even more. *Temporal* is the most infrequent relation which has close frequencies in both corpora. The different characteristic is the frequency of *Comparison* relation. In our Chinese corpus, the frequency of *Comparison* relation is about half of that in the PDTB.

In Table 2, the symbol † is used to highlight the relatively major polarity of each relation. The symbol ‡ is marked when the polarity is the majority (i.e., with a frequency greater than 50%). Near half (49.11%) of the instances belong to *Neutral*. Neutral statements are major in *Temporal* and *Expansion* classes. On the other hand, *Comparison* is the relation which is most involved in expressing sentiment, negative sentiment in particular. *Contingency* is second to *Comparison* in expressing sentiment.

[1] http://nlg.csie.ntu.edu.tw/ntu-discourse/

The distribution of the discourse relations versus (p_1, p_2), the sentiment polarity transitions between two clauses, is shown in Table 4. *Neutral-Neutral* is the most frequent polarity transition in all relations. More than half of the *Temporal* instances are *Neutral-Neutral*. The reason may be that the *Temporal* relations are usually used in the sentences that describe the objective facts of the past, present, or the future. In such sentences, the sentiments are relatively rare. On the other hand, the sentences of *Comparison* and *Contingency* occur more in the critical and analytical scenarios.

Although the most frequent transition of *Comparison* is also *Neutral-Neutral* (23.14%), the other three types of transitions, *Positive-Negative*, *Neutral-Negative*, and *Negative-Positive*, have close frequencies of 22.71%, 16.90%, and 15.72%, respectively. Moreover, *Negative* polarity is involved in all these three transitions in one of their clauses.

The relations between p_1, p_2, and p_w are also interesting. Table 5 shows the top 10 most frequent correlations of the polarities (p_1, p_2, p_w) of the first clause, the second clause, and the whole sentence. On the one hand, it is not surprising that most instances belong to (*Neutral*, *Neutral*, *Neutral*). On the other hand, it is worthy of noting that p_2 and p_w are identical in the top eight types of combinations in Table 5. In other words, the resulting sentiment polarity of a two-clause sentence is mostly consistent with the polarity of

Relation	#	%	Neu (%)	Pos (%)	Neg (%)
Temporal	849	11.12	‡60.66	22.38	16.96
Contingency	1,598	20.92	†44.74	26.97	28.29
Comparison	929	12.16	33.37	27.88	†38.75
Expansion	4,262	55.80	‡51.88	31.75	16.38
Overall	7,638	100.00	†49.11	29.24	21.65

Table 2: Distribution of discourse relations vs. polarities of whole sentences.

Relation	Only Explicit Cases		Total	
	#	%	#	%
Temporal	3,612	18.88	4,650	12.71
Contingency	3,581	18.72	8,042	21.98
Comparison	5,516	28.83	8,394	22.94
Expansion	6,424	33.58	15,506	42.38
Overall	19,133	100.00	36,592	100.00

Table 3: Distribution of discourse relations in the Penn Discourse TreeBank 2.0.

PDTB Class	#	Distribution of each type of sentiment polarity transition (p_1, p_2) (%)								
		Neu Neu	Pos Neu	Neg Neu	Neu Pos	Pos Pos	Neg Pos	Neu Neg	Pos Neg	Neg Neg
Temporal	849	‡57.01	1.53	2.12	16.37	3.53	2.36	12.72	1.06	3.30
Contingency	1,598	†35.42	3.69	5.88	13.70	10.45	2.32	11.64	1.81	15.08
Comparison	929	†23.14	2.69	2.48	8.61	3.12	15.72	16.90	22.71	4.63
Expansion	4,262	†48.33	2.86	1.92	14.24	16.19	0.59	7.86	0.63	7.37
Overall	7,638	†43.53	2.87	2.84	13.68	11.99	2.99	10.29	3.61	8.20

Table 4: Distribution of discourse relations vs. types of sentiment transitions.

p_1	p_2	p_w	Occurrences
Neutral	Neutral	Neutral	3,268
Neutral	Positive	Positive	945
Positive	Positive	Positive	908
Neutral	Negative	Negative	706
Negative	Negative	Negative	614
Positive	Negative	Negative	204
Negative	Positive	Positive	199
Negative	Neutral	Neutral	125
Positive	Neutral	Positive	121
Neutral	Positive	Neutral	99

Table 5: Most frequent (p_1, p_2, p_w) combinations.

	$p_1 = p_w$	$p_1 \neq p_w$	Total
$p_2 = p_w$	62.71%	29.79%	92.50%
$p_2 \neq p_w$	5.51%	1.99%	7.50%
Total	68.22%	31.78%	100.00%

Table 6: Correlations between (p_1,p_w) and (p_2,p_w).

the second clause. Table 6 shows the correlations of sentiment polarities between clauses and the whole sentence. Total 92.50% of instances belong to the case ($p_2 = p_w$), where the polarity of the second clause is identical to the polarity of the whole sentence. In Chinese writing, putting the important part of a sentence at the end of the sentence is very common.

4.2 Frequent discourse markers

The top discourse markers in our Chinese corpus are shown in Table 7. For each PDTB class, the five most frequent discourse markers are listed. In each row of the table, its number of occurrences and the distribution of its nine sentiment polarity transitions are given. Note that there are three polarities, i.e., *positive*, *neutral*, and *negative*. The relatively major sentiment polarity transition of each discourser maker is labeled with the symbol †. The symbol ‡ is marked when the sentiment polarity is the majority, i.e., its ratio is greater than 50%.

Some discourse markers are the top markers in more than one discourse relation such as 也 (also) and 還 (still). In the discourse marker dictionary, the word 也 (also) is defined as a discourse marker of the *Expansion* relation. However, this word is frequent in the instances of all the four relations. In different relations, the distributions of the sentiment transitions of this word differ. In other words, the word 也 (also), which is a common word in Chinese, is not only used as a discourse marker for emphasizing the *Expansion* relation, but also has various senses in other usages.

For instance, the word 也 in (S3) is a discourse marker to denote an *Expansion* relation, but it is a particle in (S4). In fact, (S4) is an instance of the implicit *Contingency* relation. We ignore all of instances of the word 也 (also) in the following analysis since it is an outlier.

(S3) 這既是對我們工作的肯定 (This is an affirmation of our work)，也是對我們的一種鼓勵和鞭策(and also our encouragement and motivation)。

(S4) 不能放開心前行 (The mind cannot be open to forward progress)，天地也變得狹小 (the world becomes narrow)。

The word 還 (still) is another ambiguous discourse marker. Besides the *Expansion* relation defined in the dictionary, it is sometimes used to denote the *Temporal* relation, especially in the negation context, e.g., 還沒 (not yet).

The two frequent discourse markers of the *Contingency* relation, 由於 (due to) and 因為 (because) share the similar sense, and their distributions of sentiment polarity transitions are more consistent than the other markers of the *Contingency* relation.

The most frequent discourse marker of the *Comparison* class is 但 (but). The other two discourse markers 卻 (but) and 但是 (but) share the similar sense, however, their polarity distributions differ significantly. Compared to the more general marker 但 (but), the second frequent marker 卻 (but) is bolder and more critical. (S5) is an example of the marker 卻 (but). As shown in our data, the marker 卻 (but) is likely to highlight the negative sentences.

PDTB Class	Discourse Markers	#	Distribution of each type of sentiment polarity transition (%)								
			Neu Neu	Pos Neu	Neg Neu	Neu Pos	Pos Pos	Neg Pos	Neu Neg	Pos Neg	Neg Neg
Temporal	之後 (and then) in Arg1	69	‡50.72	1.45	2.90	15.94	5.80	2.90	8.70	4.35	7.25
	也 (also) in Arg2	50	†44.00	2.00	2.00	18.00	6.00	0.00	20.00	0.00	8.00
	又 (again) in Arg2	49	‡71.43	0.00	0.00	12.24	2.04	0.00	10.20	4.08	0.00
	還 (still) in Arg2	46	‡58.70	0.00	0.00	10.87	8.70	0.00	17.39	0.00	4.35
	再 (again) in Arg2	38	‡78.95	2.63	0.00	10.53	0.00	0.00	2.63	0.00	5.26
Contingency	如果 (if) in Arg1	190	†42.63	4.21	11.58	14.21	3.68	3.16	10.53	1.05	8.95
	由於 (due to) in Arg1	82	†31.71	2.44	2.44	4.88	18.29	3.66	13.41	1.22	21.95
	也 (also) in Arg2	77	20.78	0.00	1.30	20.78	19.48	0.00	11.69	2.60	†23.38
	因為 (because) in Arg1	70	†28.57	4.29	7.14	7.14	10.00	2.86	18.57	4.29	17.14
	為了 (in order to) in Arg1	62	‡50.00	14.52	1.61	6.45	9.68	1.61	8.06	6.45	1.61
Comparison	但 (but) in Arg2	176	21.59	4.55	2.84	4.55	3.41	16.48	15.91	†28.98	1.70
	卻 (but) in Arg2	85	11.76	0.00	2.35	4.71	1.18	10.59	22.35	†42.35	4.71
	而 (however) in Arg2	77	†46.75	5.19	0.00	5.19	1.30	3.90	10.39	22.08	5.19
	也 (also) in Arg2	44	†31.82	0.00	2.27	6.82	15.91	13.64	18.18	2.27	9.09
	但是 (but) in Arg2	44	15.91	4.55	0.00	0.00	2.27	25.00	11.36	†40.91	0.00
Expansion	也 (also) in Arg2	603	†43.62	1.66	1.49	15.26	19.07	1.00	7.79	0.33	9.78
	還 (still) in Arg2	231	‡50.65	2.60	0.87	11.26	14.72	0.87	9.96	0.43	8.66
	說 (say) in Arg1	206	†48.54	2.43	0.49	18.45	9.22	0.00	16.50	0.49	3.88
	並 (and) in Arg2	191	‡54.45	3.14	0.52	10.47	25.65	0.00	4.19	0.00	1.57
	也 (also) in Arg1	159	†37.11	7.55	3.14	11.95	25.16	0.63	3.77	0.63	10.06

Table 7. Five most frequent discourse makers of each PDTB class in our corpus.

(S5) 這樣觸目驚心的新型犯罪 (The new type of crime is so startling)，卻在偵破前一直沒被披露(but had never been disclosed before solved)。

The other discourser marker 但是 (but) is an emphasized version of the marker 但 (but) so that it is more likely used in the stronger polarity transitions such as *Positive-Negative* and *Negative-Positive*. In addition, the sense of the marker 而 (however) is also similar to the sense of 但 (but), but it is more frequent to be used in the neutral situations. These linguistic phenomena show that the synonyms may have different sentiment usages in the real world.

4.3 Association between discourse relation and sentiment polarity

To analyze the data at a higher level, we reorganize the sentiment transitions into several transition categories from four aspects. The details are shown in Table 8. The first aspect is *Polarity Tendency*, which classifies the transitions into three categories, including *Positive-Tendency*, *Neutral*, and *Negative-Tendency*. This aspect reflects the overall polarity of both arguments. The *Negative-Positive* transition is considered as *Positive-Tendency* because the emphasis of a Chinese sentence is usually placed in the last clause. Similarly, the *Positive-Negative* transition is considered as *Negative-Tendency*. The second aspect is *Polarity Change*, which indicates if the polarities of both arguments are opposite. Only *Negative-Positive* and *Positive-Negative* are regarded as *Opposite*. All the rest transitions are treated as *NonOpposite*. The third aspect is *Direction*, which captures the movement from the first clause to the second one. *To-Positive* stands for the transitions in which the polarity of the second clause is more positive than that of the first clause. On the other hand, *To-Negative* stands for the transitions in which the polarity of the second clause is less positive than that of the first clause. *Equal* stands for the cases in which the polarities of both clauses are identical. The last aspect is *Negativity*, which regards the polarity of an argument as binary values, i.e., *Negative* and *NonNegative*. In this way, we re-classify the nine-way sentiment polarity transitions into four transitions. In other words, both the polarity states *Neutral* and *Positive* are merged into one state *NonNegative* in this aspect. Such a binary scheme is also used in some related work, in which the negative polarity is distinguished and the rest are considered Positive (Kim and Hovy, 2004; Devitt and Ahmad, 2007). For each type of each aspect, five discourse markers that occur more than 10 times in the dataset and have the highest ratio of the corresponding type are listed in the fifth column of Table 8 as significant discourse markers.

We analyze the annotations according to the four aspects, and the results are shown in Table 9. The chi-squared test is used to test the dependency between the PDTB classes of discourse markers and each aspect of sentiment transitions. The results show that no matter whether the sentiment polarity transitions are categorized into *Polarity Tendency*, *Polarity Change*, *Direction*, or *Negativity*, the classes of discourse relations are significantly dependent on the sentiment polarities of the arguments at p=0.001.

In the aspect of *Polarity Tendency*, the ratios of *Neutral* in the *Temporal* and *Expansion* relations are 57.01% and 48.33%, respectively, which are definitely higher than those of *Contingency* and *Comparison* relations. In other words, the two arguments of *Contingency* and *Comparison* relations are less likely to be neutral. The ratio of *Negative-Tendency* of the *Comparison* relation is 46.72%. It confirms the *Comparison* relation is likely to be involved in negative statements. As shown in Table 8, three of the five significant discourse markers of *Negative-Tendency* are the synonyms of 卻 (but), which are discourse markers of the *Comparison* relation. The other two markers, 否則 (otherwise) and 因 (because), are discourse markers of the *Contingency* relation. Like the word *otherwise* in English, 否則 (otherwise) is used for introducing what bad scenario will happen if something is not done. The marker 因 (because) is not only a significant discourse marker of the category *Negative-Tendency*, but also a significant marker of *Negative-Negative* from the aspect of *Negativity*. From the real data, we find this marker is often used in bad cause-and-effect statements. (S6) is an example. The usage of the other discourse marker 因為 (because), which is a synonyms of 因 (because), is more general.

(S6) 因毛巾日久不見陽光 (Because the towel is without sunlight for a long time)，容易滋生細菌和真菌 (it is easy to breed bacteria and fungi)。

The ratio of *Opposite* of *Comparison* relation from the aspect of *Polarity Change* is 38.43%. Although it is not as high as expected, it is the highest among the four PDTB classes and much higher than those of three other classes. Compared to the other classes, *Comparison* is most likely to have a pair of opposite arguments.

Four of the five significant discourse markers of Opposite in Table 8 are the synonyms of 但 (but). Expansion relation has the highest ratio of *NonOpposite*. This matches our expectation that the *Expansion* relation is used to concatenate several events which have similar properties

Aspect	Transition Category	Sentiment polarity transitions	Explanation	Significant Discourse Markers
Polarity Tendency	Positive-Tendency	Pos-Neu, Neu-Pos, Pos-Pos, Neg-Pos	The two arguments present an overall positive polarity.	不僅...也 (not only... also), 終於 (finally)，既...又 (now that...), 只要 ... 就 (as long as...), 近年 (recently)
	Neutral	Neu-Neu	Both arguments are neutral.	然後 (and then), 因此 (hence)，最後 (at the end), 故 (so)，以及 (as well as)
	Negative-Tendency	Pos-Neg, Neg-Neu, Neu-Neg, Neg-Neg	The two arguments present an overall negative polarity.	否則 (otherwise), 卻 (but), 可是 (but), 但是 (but), 因 (because)
Polarity Change	Opposite	Neg-Pos, Pos-Neg	The polarities of both arguments are opposite.	但是 (but), 雖然...但 (although...)，但 (but), 卻 (but), 不過 (but)
	NonOpposite	Neu-Neu, Pos-Neu, Neg-Neu, Neu-Pos, Pos-Pos, Neu-Neg, Neg-Neg	The polarities of both arguments are not opposite.	或 (or), 像 (as), 而且 (moreover), 如果...會 (if ... may), 表示 (say)
Direction	To-Positive	Neg-Neu, Neg-Pos, Neu-Pos	The second argument is less negative than the first one.	終於 (finally), 雖然 ... 但 (although...)，近年 (recently), 只要 ... 就 (as long as...)，看來 (seem...)
	Equal	Neg-Neg, Neu-Neu, Pos-Pos	Both arguments are the same polarity value.	不僅...更 (Not only... even), 最後 (at the end), 並且 (in addition), 故 (so), 既...也 (now that...)
	To-Negative	Pos-Neu, Pos-Neg, Neu-Neg	The second argument is less positive than the first one.	卻 (but), 但是 (but), 可是 (but), 否則 (otherwise), 即使...也 (even if...)
Negativity	NonNegative-NonNegative	Neu-Neu, Neu-Pos, Pos-Neu, Pos-Pos	Both arguments are not negative.	以及 (as well as), 未來 (in the future), 以便 (in order to), 並且 (in addition), 然後 (and then)
	NonNegative-Negative	Neu-Neg, Pos-Neg	The first argument is not negative while the second argument is negative.	卻 (but), 否則 (otherwise), 但是 (but), 即使...也 (even if...), 可是 (but)
	Negative-NonNegative	Neg-Neu, Neg-Pos	The first argument is negative while the second argument is not negative.	雖然...但 (although...), 但是 (but), 不過 (but), 終於 (finally), 但 (but)
	Negative-Negative	Neg-Neg	Both arguments are negative.	甚至 (even), 卻 (but), 因 (because), 如果...將 (if... may), 但是 (but)

Table 8: Aspects of sentiment transition.

PDTB Class	#	Polarity Tendency (%)			Polarity Change (%)		Direction(%)			Negativity (%)			
		Pos Tend	Neutral	Neg Tend	Oppo	Non Oppo	To Pos	Eq.	To Neg	NonNeg-NonNeg	NonNeg-Neg	Neg-NonNeg	Neg-Neg
Tem	849	23.79	57.01	19.20	3.42	96.58	20.85	63.84	15.31	78.45	13.78	4.48	3.30
Con	1,598	30.16	35.42	34.42	4.13	95.87	21.90	60.95	17.15	63.27	13.45	8.20	15.08
Com	929	30.14	23.14	46.72	38.43	61.57	26.80	30.89	42.30	37.57	39.61	18.19	4.63
Exp	4,262	33.88	48.33	17.79	1.22	98.78	16.75	71.89	11.36	81.63	8.49	2.51	7.37

Table 9: Statistics of sentiment transition for each PDTB class over the corpus annotated by human.

from certain perspective.

The ratio of *To-Negative* of *Comparison* relation from the aspect of *Direction* in Table 9 is 42.30%, which is significantly higher than the ratios of *To-Negative* of the other classes. This also confirms the *Comparison* relation is likely to be used to express critical opinions. Furthermore, the ratio of *Equal* of *Comparison* relations is much lower than those of other classes. This result shows the *Comparison* relation is more involved in sentiment polarity transitions.

The *Negativity* aspect in Table 9 also shows the *NonNegative-Negative* is more likely to happen than the *Negative-NonNegative* in all relations. This statistics reflects a particular phenomenon “good words ahead” in Chinese. That is, speakers tend to express a negative opinion after kind words.

The sentiment polarity flips in the instances of the two categories *Negative-NonNegative* and *NonNegative-Negative*. However, the significant discourse markers of the two categories are very different. In spite of the general marker 但是 (but), the discourse markers 卻 (but), 否則 (otherwise), 即使...也 (even if...), and 可是 (but) are often used in *NonNegative-Negative*, which usually results a negative remark. On the other hand, the discourse markers 雖然...但 (although...), 不過 (but), 終於 (finally), and 但 (but) are often used in *Negative-NonNegative*, which usually results a positive remark. For example, the discourse marker 終於 (finally), which is a discourse marker of the *Temporal* relation, is usually used when an event successfully accomplished after twists and turns such as (S7).

(S7) 歷經多次磨難的國產手機巨頭波導 (Domestic mobile phone giant Ningbo Bird after many tribulations)，終於成功轉戰汽車行業 (finally successfully fought in the automotive industry)。

5 Conclusion

To investigate the discourse relation and the sentiment polarity of Chinese discourse markers, we construct a moderate-sized corpus based on the Chinese part of ClueWeb09. In this paper, our annotation scheme and the analysis of the annotation results are shown. Total 7,638 instances are annotated by native speakers. The discourse relation distribution of the annotated data is comparable to the distribution of the well-known English discourse corpus PDTB 2.0. Through the data analysis, we validate certain human intuitions in Chinese language. Near half of instances are in neutral sentiment while the *Comparison* relation is most likely to be involved in negative sentiment. Furthermore, the high sentiment dependency between the last clause and the whole sentence is validated in the data.

The data shows the significant association between the discourse relation and the sentiment polarity. The arguments of a *Comparison* relation or a *Contingency* relation are more likely to be involved in expressing sentiment. Moreover, the *Comparison* relation often occurs in the sentences with sentiment polarity transitions, and frequently occurs in the instances with the negative sentiment. On the other hand, the arguments of the *Temporal* and the *Expansion* relations are relatively objective. The behavior of word choice between synonyms is also observed in the data. Each synonym of a sense may have its own usage in expressing sentiment.

This paper points out the ambiguities of the discourse markers in Chinese. That is, a marker may suggest more than one discourse relation. Besides, words may have both the functions of discourse connectives and non-discourse ones in their surface forms. These two issues make the interpretation of Chinese discourse markers more challenging. Determination of their correct uses and disambiguation of their discourse functions will be investigated in the future.

Acknowledgments

This research was partially supported by Excellent Research Projects of National Taiwan University under contract 102R890858 and 2012 Google Research Award.

References

Lynn Carlson and Daniel Marcu. 2001. Discourse Tagging Reference Manual. http://www.isi.edu/~marcu/discourse/tagging-ref-manual.pdf

Lynn Carlson, Daniel Marcu, and Mary Ellen Okurowski. 2002. *RST Discourse Treebank*. Linguistic Data Consortium, Philadelphia.

Shou-Yi Cheng. 2006. *Corpus-Based Coherence Relation Tagging in Chinese Discourse*. Master's Thesis, National Chiao Tung University, Hsinchu, Taiwan.

Xianghui Cheng and Xiaolin Tian. 1989. *Xian dai Han yu* (*現代漢語*), San lian shu dian (三聯書店), Hong Kong.

Ann Devitt and Khurshid Ahmad. 2007. Sentiment polarity identification in financial news: a cohesion-based approach. In *Proceedings of the 45th Annual Meeting of the Association of Computational Linguistics* (*ACL 2007*), pages 984-991, Prague, Czech Republic.

Hugo Hernault, Helmut Prendinger, David A. duVerle, and Mitsuru Ishizuka. 2010. HILDA: A Discourse Parser Using Support Vector Machine Classification. *Dialogue and Discourse*, 1(3): 1-33.

Hen-Hsen Huang and Hsin-Hsi Chen. 2011. Chinese discourse relation recognition. In *Proceedings of the 5th International Joint Conference on Natural Language Processing* (*IJCNLP 2011*). pages 1442-1446, Chiang Mai, Thailand.

Hen-Hsen Huang and Hsin-Hsi Chen. 2012a. Contingency and comparison relation labeling and structure prediction in Chinese sentences. In *Proceedings of the 13th Annual Meeting of the Special Interest Group on Discourse and Dialogue* (*SIGDIAL 2012*), pages 261-269, Seoul, South Korea.

Hen-Hsen Huang and Hsin-Hsi Chen. 2012b. An Annotation System for Development of Chinese Discourse Corpus. In *Proceedings of the 24th International Conference on Computational Linguistics* (*COLING 2012*)*: Demonstration Papers*, pages 223-230, Mumbai, India.

Ben Hutchinson. 2004. Acquiring the meaning of discourse markers. In Proceedings of the 42nd Annual Meeting of the Association for Computational Linguistics (ACL 2004), pages 684-691, Barcelona, Spain.

Soo-Min Kim and Eduard Hovy. 2004. Determining the sentiment of opinions. In *Proceedings of the 20th International Conference on Computational Linguistics* (*COLING-04*), pages 1367-1373, Geneva, Switzerland.

Ziheng Lin, Min-Yen Kan, and Hwee Tou Ng. 2009. Recognizing implicit discourse relations in the Penn Discourse Treebank. In *Proceedings of the 2009 Conference on Empirical Methods in Natural Language Processing* (*EMNLP 2009*), pages 343-351.

Shuxiang Lu. 2007. *Eight Hundred Words of The Contemporary Chinese (Xian dai Han yu Ba bai Ci)*, China Social Sciences Press.

Bo Pang and Lillian Lee. 2008. Opinion Mining and Sentiment Analysis. *Foundations and Trends in Information Retrieval*, 2(1-2): 1-135.

Rashmi Prasad, Nikhil Dinesh, Alan Lee, Eleni Miltsakaki, Livio Robaldo, Aravind Joshi, and Bonnie Webber. 2007. *The Penn Discourse Treebank 2.0 Annotation Manual*. The PDTB Research Group.

Rashmi Prasad, Nikhil Dinesh, Alan Lee, Eleni Miltsakaki, Livio Robaldo, Aravind Joshi, and Bonnie Webber. 2008. The Penn Discourse TreeBank 2.0. In *Proceedings of the 6th Language Resources and Evaluation Conference* (*LREC 2008*), pages 2961-2968, Marrakech, Morocco.

Radu Soricut and Daniel Marcu. 2003. Sentence level discourse parsing using syntactic and lexical information. In *Proceedings of Human Language Technology Conference of the North American Chapter of the Association for Computational Linguistics* (*HLT/NAACL 2003*), pages 149-156, Edmonton, Canada.

Florian Wolf and Edward Gibson. 2005. Representing Discourse Coherence: A Corpus-Based Analysis. *Computational Linguistics*, 31(2): 249-287.

Chi-Hsin Yu, Yi-jie Tang and Hsin-Hsi Chen. 2012. Development of a web-scale Chinese word N-gram corpus with parts of speech information. In *Proceedings the 8th International Conference on Language Resources and Evaluation* (*LREC 2012*), pages 320-324, Istanbul, Turkey.

Zhi-Min Zhou, Yu Xu, Zheng-Yu Niu, Man Lan, Jian Su, and Chew Lim Tan. 2010. Predicting discourse connectives for implicit discourse relation recognition. In *Proceedings of the 23rd International Conference on Computational Linguistics* (*COLING 2010*)*: Posters*, pages 1507-1514.

Yuping Zhou and Nianwen Xue. 2012. PDTB-style discourse annotation of Chinese text. In *Proceedings the 50th Annual Meeting of the Association for Computational Linguistics* (*ACL 2012*), pages 69-77, Jeju, South Korea.

Towards a Better Understanding of Discourse: Integrating Multiple Discourse Annotation Perspectives Using UIMA

Claudiu Mihăilă*, **Georgios Kontonatsios***, **Riza Theresa Batista-Navarro***,
Paul Thompson*, **Ioannis Korkontzelos and Sophia Ananiadou**
The National Centre for Text Mining,
School of Computer Science, The University of Manchester
{mihailac,kontonag,batistar,thompsop,
korkonti,ananiads}@cs.man.ac.uk

Abstract

There exist various different discourse annotation schemes that vary both in the perspectives of discourse structure considered and the granularity of textual units that are annotated. Comparison and integration of multiple schemes have the potential to provide enhanced information. However, the differing formats of corpora and tools that contain or produce such schemes can be a barrier to their integration. U-Compare is a graphical, UIMA-based workflow construction platform for combining interoperable natural language processing (NLP) resources, without the need for programming skills. In this paper, we present an extension of U-Compare that allows the easy comparison, integration and visualisation of resources that contain or output annotations based on multiple discourse annotation schemes. The extension works by allowing the construction of parallel sub-workflows for each scheme within a single U-Compare workflow. The different types of discourse annotations produced by each sub-workflow can be either merged or visualised side-by-side for comparison. We demonstrate this new functionality by using it to compare annotations belonging to two different approaches to discourse analysis, namely discourse relations and functional discourse annotations. Integrating these different annotation types within an interoperable environment allows us to study the correlations between different types of discourse and report on the new insights that this allows us to discover.

*The authors have contributed equally to the development of this work and production of the manuscript.

1 Introduction

Over the past few years, there has been an increasing sophistication in the types of available natural language processing (NLP) tools, with named entity recognisers being complemented by relation and event extraction systems. Such relations and events are not intended to be understood in isolation, but rather they are arranged to form a coherent discourse. In order to carry out complex tasks such as automatic summarisation to a high degree of accuracy, it is important for systems to be able to analyse the discourse structure of texts automatically. To facilitate the development of such systems, various textual corpora containing discourse annotations have been made available to the NLP community. However, there is a large amount of variability in the types of annotations contained within these corpora, since different perspectives on discourse have led to the development of a number of different annotation schemes.

Corpora containing discourse-level annotations usually treat the text as a sequence of coherent textual zones (e.g., clauses and sentences). One line of research has been to identify which zones are logically connected to each other, and to characterise these links through the assignment of *discourse relations*. There are variations in the complexity of the schemes used to annotate these discourse relations. For example, Rhetorical Structure Theory (RST) (Mann and Thompson, 1988) defines 23 types of discourse relations that are used to structure the text into complex discourse trees. Whilst this scheme was used to enrich the Penn TreeBank (Carlson et al., 2001), the Penn Discourse TreeBank (PDTB) (Prasad et al., 2008) used another scheme to identify discourse relations that hold between pairs of text spans. It categorises the relations into types such as "causal", "temporal" and "conditional", which can be either explicit or implicit, depending on whether or not they are represented in text using overt *discourse connectives*. In the biomedical domain, the Biomedical Discourse Relation Bank (BioDRB) (Prasad et al., 2011) annotates a similar set of relation types, whilst BioCause focusses exclusively on causality (Mihăilă et al., 2013).

A second line of research does not aim to link textual zones, but rather to classify them according to their specific function in the discourse. Examples of functional discourse annotations include whether a particular zone asserts new information into the discourse or represents a speculation or hypothesis. In scientific texts, knowing the type of information that a zone represents (e.g., background knowledge, hypothesis, experimental observation, conclusion, etc.) allows for automatic isolation of new knowledge claims (Sándor and de Waard, 2012). Several annotation schemes have been developed to classify textual zones according to their rhetorical status or general information content (Teufel et al., 1999; Mizuta et al., 2006; Wilbur et al., 2006; de Waard and Pander Maat, 2009; Liakata et al., 2012a). Related to these studies are efforts to capture information relating to discourse function at the level of events, i.e., structured representations of pieces of knowledge which, when identified, facilitate sophisticated semantic searching (Ananiadou et al., 2010). Since there can be multiple events in a sentence or clause, the identification of discourse information at the event level can allow for a more detailed analysis of discourse elements than is possible when considering larger units of text. Certain event corpora such as ACE 2005 (Walker, 2006) and GENIA-MK (Thompson et al., 2011) have been annotated with various types of functional discourse information.

It has previously been shown that considering several functional discourse annotation schemes in parallel can be beneficial (Liakata et al., 2012b), since each scheme offers a different perspective. For a common set of documents, the cited study analysed and compared functional discourse annotations at different levels of textual granularity (i.e., sentences, clauses and events), showing how the different schemes could complement each other in order to lay the foundations for a possible future harmonisation of the schemes. The results of this analysis provide evidence that it would be useful to carry out further such analyses involving other such schemes, including an investigation of how discourse relations and functional discourse annotations could complement each other, e.g., which types of functional annotations occur within the arguments of discourse relations. There are, however, certain barriers to carrying out such an analysis. For example, a comparison of annotation schemes would ideally allow the different types of annotations to be visualised simultaneously or seamlessly merged together. However, the fact that annotations in different corpora are encoded using different formats (e.g., stand-off or in-line) and different encoding schemes means that this can be problematic.

A solution to the challenges introduced above is offered by the Unstructured Information Management Architecture (UIMA) (Ferrucci and Lally, 2004), which defines a common workflow metadata format facilitating the straightforward combination of NLP resources into a workflow. Based on the interoperability of the UIMA framework, numerous researchers distribute their own tools as UIMA-compliant components (Kano et al., 2011; Baumgartner et al., 2008; Hahn et al., 2008; Savova et al., 2010; Gurevych et al., 2007; Rak et al., 2012b). However, UIMA is only intended to provide an abstract framework for the interoperability of language resources, leaving the actual implementation to third-party developers. Hence, UIMA does not explicitly address interoperability issues of tools and corpora.

U-Compare (Kano et al., 2011) is a UIMA-based workflow construction platform that provides a graphical user interface (GUI) via which users can rapidly create NLP pipelines using a drag-and-drop mechanism. Conforming to UIMA standards, U-Compare components and pipelines are compatible with any UIMA application via a common and sharable type system (i.e., a hierarchy of annotation types). In defining this type system, U-Compare promotes interoperability of tools and corpora, by exhaustively modelling a wide range of NLP data types (e.g., sentences, tokens, part-of-speech tags, named entities). This type system was recently extended to include discourse annotations to model three discourse phenomena, namely causality, coreference and meta-knowledge (Batista-Navarro et al., 2013).

In this paper, we describe our extensions to U-Compare, supporting the integration and visualisation of resources annotated according to multiple discourse annotation schemes. Our method decomposes pipelines into parallel sub-workflows, each linked to a different annotation scheme. The resulting annotations produced by each sub-workflow can be either merged within a single document or visualised in parallel views.

2 Related work

Previous studies have shown the advantages of comparing and integrating different annotation schemes on a corpus of documents (Guo et al., 2010; Liakata et al., 2010; Liakata et al., 2012b). Guo et al. (2010) compared three different discourse annotation schemes applied to a corpus of biomedical abstracts on cancer risk assessment and concluded that two of the schemes provide more fine-grained information than the other scheme. They also revealed a subsumption relation between two schemes. Such outcomes from comparing schemes are meaningful for users who wish to select the most appropriate scheme for annotating their data. Liakata et al. (2012) underline that different discourse annotation schemes capture different dimensions of discourse. Hence, there might be complementary information across different schemes. Based on this hypothesis, they provide a comparison of three annotation schemes, namely CoreSC (Liakata et al., 2012a), GENIA-MK (Thompson et al., 2011) and DiscSeg (de Waard, 2007), on a corpus of three full-text papers. Their results showed that the categories in the three schemes can complement each other. For example, the values of the *Certainty Level* dimension of the GENIA-MK scheme can be used to assign confidence values to the Conclusion, Result, Implication and Hypothesis categories of CoreSC and DiscSeg. In contrast to previous studies, our proposed approach automatically integrates multiple annotation schemes. The proposed mechanism allows users to easily compare, integrate and visualise multiple discourse annotation schemes in an interoperable NLP infrastructure, i.e., U-Compare.

There are currently a number of freely-available NLP workflow infrastructures (Ferrucci and Lally, 2004; Cunningham et al., 2002; Schäfer, 2006; Kano et al., 2011; Grishman, 1996; Baumgartner et al., 2008; Hahn et al., 2008; Savova et al., 2010; Gurevych et al., 2007; Rak et al., 2012b). Most of the available infrastructures support the development of standard NLP applications, e.g., part-of-speech tagging, deep parsing, chunking, named entity recognition and several of them allow the representation and analysis of discourse phenomena (Kano et al., 2011; Cunningham et al., 2002; Savova et al., 2010; Gurevych et al., 2007). However, none of them has demonstrated the integration of resources annotated according to multiple annotation schemes within a single NLP pipeline.

GATE (Cunningham et al., 2002) is an open source NLP infrastructure that has been used for the development of various language processing tasks. It is packaged with an exhaustive number of NLP components, including discourse analysis modules, e.g., coreference resolution. Furthermore, GATE offers a GUI environment and wrappers for UIMA-compliant components. However, GATE implements a limited workflow management mechanism that does not support the execution of parallel or nested workflows. In addition to this, GATE does not promote interoperability of language resources since it does not define any hierarchy of NLP data types and components do not formally declare their input/output capabilities.

In contrast to GATE, UIMA implements a more sophisticated workflow management mechanism that supports the construction of both parallel and nested pipelines. In this paper, we exploit this mechanism to integrate multiple annotation schemes in NLP workflows. cTAKES (Savova et al., 2010) and DKPro (Gurevych et al., 2007) are two repositories containing UIMA-compliant components that are tuned for the medical and general domain, respectively. However, both of these repositories support the representation of only one discourse phenomenon, i.e., coreference. Argo (Rak et al., 2012a; Rak et al., 2012b) is a web-based platform that allows multiple branching and merging of UIMA pipelines. It incorporates several U-Compare components and consequently, supports the U-Compare type system.

3 A UIMA architecture for processing multiple annotation schemes

In UIMA, a document, together with its associated annotations, is represented as a standardised data structure, namely the Common Analysis Structure (CAS). Each CAS can contain any number of nested sub-CASes, i.e., *Subjects of Analysis* (*Sofas*), each of which can associate a different type of annotation with the input document. In this paper, we employ this UIMA mechanism to allow the integration and comparison of multiple

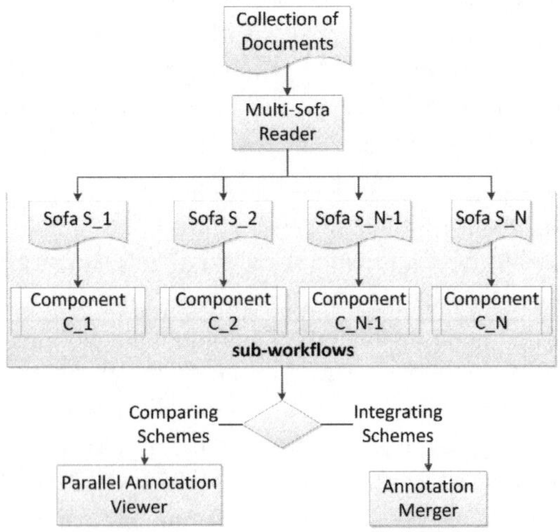

Figure 1: Integrating annotations from multiple annotation schemes in UIMA workflows

annotation schemes in a single U-Compare workflow. Assume that we have a corpus of documents which has been annotated according to n different schemes, $S_1, S_2, ..., S_{n-1}, S_n$. Also, assume that we will use a library of m text analysis components, $C_1, C_2, ..., C_{m-1}, C_m$, to enrich the corpus with further annotations.

Our implemented architecture is illustrated in Figure 1. Using multiple Sofas, we are able to split a UIMA workflow into parallel sub-workflows. Starting from a *Multi-Sofa reader*, we create n sub-workflows, i.e., Sofas, each of which is linked to a particular scheme for a different annotation type. Each sub-workflow can then apply the analysis components that are most suitable for processing the annotations from the corresponding scheme.

U-Compare offers two different modes for visualising corpora that have been annotated according to multiple schemes. In the comparison mode, the default annotation viewer is automatically split to allow annotations from different schemes to be displayed side-by-side. The second type of visualisation merges the annotations produced by the parallel sub-workflows into a single view. The most appropriate view may depend on the preferences of the user and the task at hand, e.g., identifying similarities, differences or complementary information between different schemes.

4 Application Workflows

In this section, we demonstrate two workflow applications that integrate multiple discourse annotation schemes. The first workflow exploits U-Compare's comparison mode to visualise in parallel functional discourse annotations from two schemes, namely, CoreSC (Liakata et al., 2012a) and GENIA-MK (Thompson et al., 2011). The second application integrates functional discourse annotations in the ACE 2005 corpus with discourse relations obtained by an automated tool.

4.1 Visualising functional discourse annotations from different schemes

The purpose of this workflow application is to reveal the different interpretations given by two discourse annotation schemes applied to a biomedical corpus of three full-text papers (Liakata et al., 2012b). The pipeline contains two readers that take as input the annotations (in the BioNLP Shared Task stand-off format) from the two schemes and map them to U-Compare's type system. In this way, the annotations become interoperable with existing components in U-Compare's library. U-Compare detects that the workflow contains two annotation schemes and automatically creates two parallel sub-workflows as explained earlier. Furthermore, we configure the workflow to use the comparison mode. Therefore, the annotation viewer will display the two different types of annotations based on the input schemes side-by-side. Figure 2 illustrates the parallel viewing of a document annotated according to both the CoreSC (left-hand side) and GENIA-MK (right-hand side) annotation schemes. The CoreSC scheme assigns a single category per sentence. The main clause in the highlighted sentence on the left-hand side constitutes the hypothesis that *transcription factors bind to exon-1*. Accordingly, as can be confirmed from the annotation table on the far right-hand side of the figure, the *(Hyp)othesis* category has been assigned to the sentence.

In the GENIA-MK corpus, the different pieces of information contained within the sentence have been separately annotated as structured events. One of these events corresponds to the hypothesis, but this is not the only information expressed: information about a previous experimental outcome from the authors, i.e., that exon1 is implicated in CCR3 transcription, is annotated as a sep-

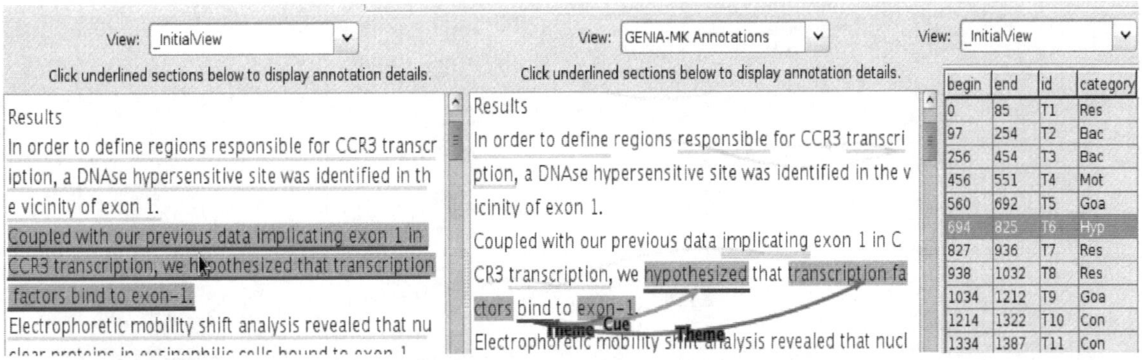

Figure 2: Comparing discourse annotations schemes in U-Compare. The pipeline uses two Sofas corresponding to the CoreSC (left panel) and GENIA-MK (right panel) schemes.

arate event. Since functional discourse information is annotated directly at the event level in the GENIA-MK corpus, the *bind* event is considered independently from the other event as representing an *Analysis*. Furthermore, the word *hypothesized* is annotated as a cue for this categorisation. There are several ways in which the annotations of the two schemes can be seen to be complementary to each other. For example, the finer-grained categorisation of analytical information in the CoreSC scheme could help to determine that the analytical *bind* event in the GENIA-MK corpus specifically represents a hypothesis, rather than, e.g., a conclusion. Conversely, the event-based annotation in the GENIA-MK corpus can help to determine exactly which part of the sentence represents the hypothesis. Furthermore, the cue phrases annotated in the GENIA-MK corpus could be used as additional features in a system trained to assign CoreSC categories. Although in this paper we illustrate only the visualisation of different types of functional discourse annotations, it is worth noting that U-Compare provides support for further processing. Firstly, unlike annotation platforms such as brat (Stenetorp et al., 2012), U-Compare allows for analysis components to be integrated into workflows in a straightforward and user-interactive manner. If, for example, it is of interest to determine the tokens (and the corresponding parts-of-speech) which frequently act as cues in *Analysis* events, syntactic analysis components (e.g., tokenisers and POS taggers) can be incorporated via a drag-and-drop mechanism. Also, U-Compare allows the annotations to be saved in a computable format using the provided Xmi Writer CAS Consumer component. This facilitates further automatic comparison of annotations.

4.2 Integrating discourse relations with functional discourse annotations

To demonstrate the integration of annotations originating from two completely different perspectives on discourse, we have created a workflow that merges traditional discourse relations with functional discourse annotations in a general domain corpus. For this application, we used the ACE 2005 corpus, which consists of 599 documents coming from broadcast conversation, broadcast news, conversational telephone speech, newswire, weblog and usenet newsgroups. This corpus contains event annotations which have been enriched by attributes such as *polarity* (positive or negative), *modality* (asserted or other), *genericity* (generic or specific) and *tense* (past, present, future or unspecified). We treat the values of these attributes as functional discourse annotations, since they provide further insight into the interpretation of the events. We created a component that reads the event annotations in the corpus and maps them to U-Compare's type system.

To obtain discourse relation annotations (which are not available in the ACE corpus) we employed an end-to-end discourse parser trained on the Penn Discourse TreeBank (Lin et al., 2012). It outputs three general types of annotations, namely, explicit relations, non-explicit relations and attribution spans. Explicit relations (i.e., those having overt discourse connectives) are further categorised into the following 16 PDTB level-2 types: Asynchronous, Synchrony, Cause, Pragmatic_cause, Contrast, Concession, Conjunction, Instantiation, Restatement, Alternative, List, Condition, Pragmatic_condition, Pragmatic_contrast, Pragmatic_concession and Excep-

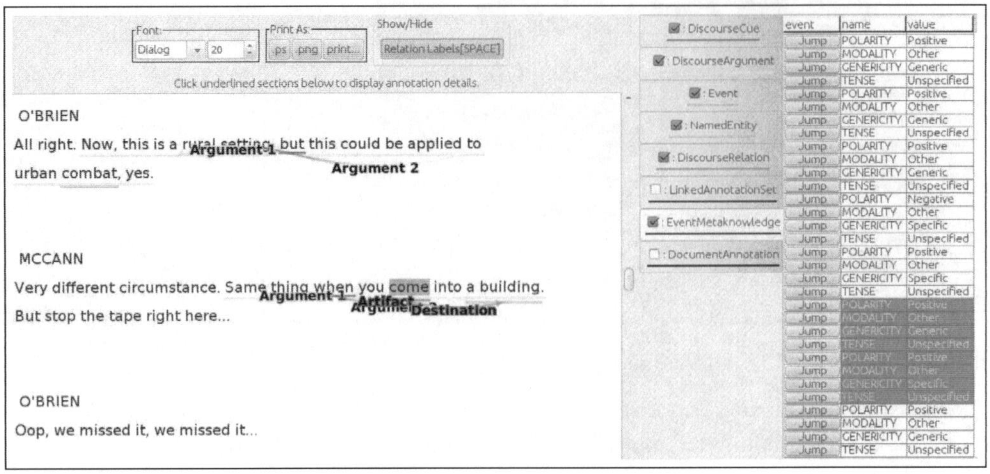

Figure 3: Integrating different discourse annotation schemes in U-Compare.

tion. Non-explicit relations, on the other hand, consist of EntRel and NoRel types, in addition to the same first 11 explicit types mentioned above.

We created a workflow consisting of the ACE corpus reader and the discourse parser (available in U-Compare as a UIMA web service). This allowed us to merge traditional discourse relations with event-based functional discourse annotations, and to visualise them in the same document (Figure 3). Furthermore, with the addition of the Xmi Writer CAS Consumer in the workflow, the merged annotations can be saved in a computable format for further processing, allowing users to perform deeper analyses on the discourse annotations. This workflow has enabled us to gain some insights into the correlations between functional discourse annotations and discourse relations.

5 Correlations between discourse relations and functional discourse annotations

Based on the merged annotation format described in the previous section, we computed cases in which at least one of the arguments of a discourse relation also contains an event. Figure 4 is a heatmap depicting the correlations between different types of discourse relations and the attribute values of ACE events that co-occur with these relations. The darker the colour, the smaller the ratio of the given discourse relation co-occurring with the specified ACE event attribute value. For instance, the *Cause* relation co-occurs mostly with *positive* events (over 95%) and the corresponding cell is a very light shade of green. These are discussed and exemplified below. In the examples, the following marking convention is used: discourse connectives are capitalised, whilst arguments are underlined. Event triggers are shown in bold, and cues relating to functional discourse categories are italicised.

For all discourse relation types, at least 50% of co-occurring events are assigned the *specific* value of the *Genericity* attribute. Specific events are those that describe a specific occurrence or situation, rather than a more *generic* situation. In general, this high proportion of *specific* events is to be expected. The types of text contained within the corpus, consisting largely of news and transcriptions of conversions, would be expected to introduce a large amount of information about specific events.

For two types of discourse relations, i.e. *Condition* and *Concession*, there are more or less equal numbers of *specific* and *generic* events. The nature of these relation types helps to explain these proportions. Conditional relations often describe how a particular, i.e., *specific*, situation will hold if some hypothetical situation is true. Since hypothetical situations do not denote specific instances, they will usually be labelled as *generic*. Concessions, meanwhile, usually describe how a specific situation holds, even though another (more generic) situation would normally hold, that would be inconsistent with this. For the *Instantiation* relation category, it may once again be expected that similar proportions of *generic* and *specific* events would co-occur within their arguments, since an instantiation describes a specific instance of a more generic situation. However, contrary to these

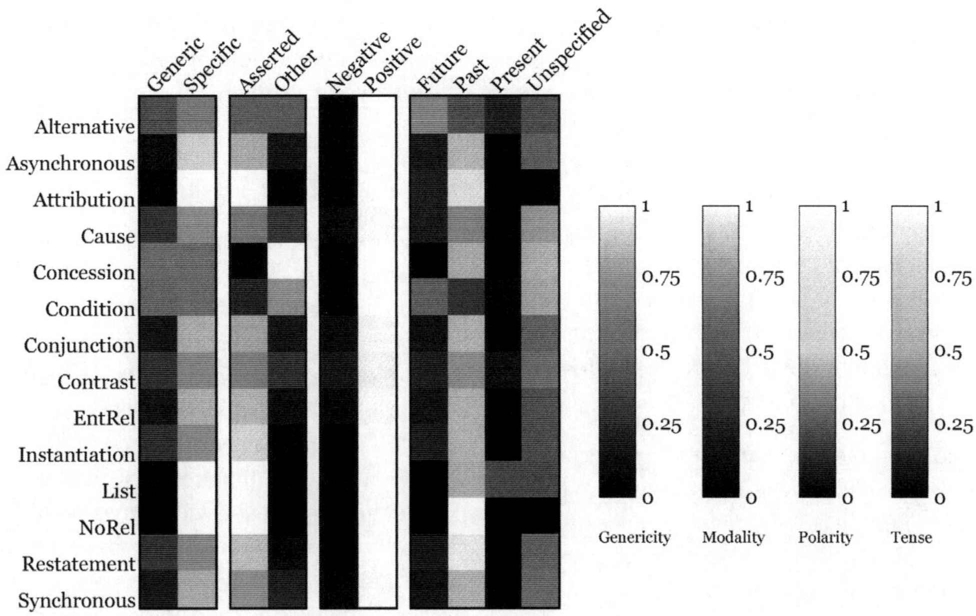

Figure 4: Heatmap showing the distribution of correlations between discourse relations and event-based functional discourse categories. A darker shade indicates a smaller percentage of instances of a discourse relation co-occurring with an event attribute.

expectations, the ratio of specific to generic events is 3:1. A reason for this is that discourse arguments corresponding to the description of a specific instance may contain several different events, as illustrated in Example (1).

(1) Toefting has been **convicted** before. In 1999 he was given a 20-day suspended **sentence** for **assaulting** a fan who berated him for playing with German club Duisburg.

In terms of the *Modality* attribute, most discourse relations correlate with definite, *asserted* events. Similarly to the *Genericity* attribute, this can be largely explained by the nature of the texts. However, there are two relation types, i.e., *Condition* and *Consession*, which have particularly high proportions of co-occurring events whose modality is *other*. Events that are assigned this attribute value correspond to those that are *not* described as though they are real occurrences. This includes, e.g., speculated or hypothetical events. The fact that *Condition* relations are usually hypothetical in nature explain why 76% of events that co-occur with such relations are assigned the *other* value for the *Modality* attribute. Example (2) illustrates a sentence containing this relation type.

(2) And I've said many times, IF we all agreed on everything, everybody *would* want to **marry** Betty and we would really be in a mess, wouldn't we, Bob.

An even higher proportion of *Concession* relations co-occurs with events whose modality is *other*. Example (3) helps to explain this. In the first clause (the generic situation), the mention of minimising civilian casualties is only described as an *effort*, rather than a definite situation. The hedging of this generic situation is necessary in order to concede that the more specific situation described in the second clause could actually be true, i.e., that a large number of civilians have already been killed. Due to the nature of news reporting, which may come from potentially unreliable sources, the *killed* event in this second clause is also hedged, through the use of the word *reportedly*.

(3) ALTHOUGH the coalition leaders have repeatedly assured that every effort would be made to minimize civilian casualties in the current Iraq war, at least 130 Iraqi civilians have been *reportedly* **killed** since the war started five days ago.

Almost 96% of events that co-occur with arguments of discourse relations have positive polarity. Indeed, for eight relation types, 100% of the corresponding events are positive. This can partly be explained by the fact that, in texts reporting news, there is an emphasis on reporting events that have happened, rather than events that did not happen. It can, however, be noted that events that co-occur with certain discourse relation types have a greater likelihood of having negative polarity. These relations include *Contrast* (9% of events having negative polarity) and Cause (5% negative events). Contrasts can include comparisons of positive and negative situations, as in Example (4), whilst for *Causes*, it can sometimes be relevant to state that a particular situation caused a specific event *not* to take place, as shown in Example (5).

(4) The message from the Israeli government is that its soldiers are *not* **targeting** journalists, BUT that journalists who travel to places where there could be live fire exchange between Israeli forces and Palestinian gunmen have a responsibility to take greater precautions.

(5) His father *didn't* want to **invade** Iraq, BECAUSE of all these problems they're having now.

For most relation types, around 60% of their co-occurring events are annotated as describing *past* tense situations. This nature of newswire and conversations mean that this is largely to be expected, since they normally report mainly on events that have already happened. The proportion of events assigned the *future* tense value is highest when they co-occur with discourse relations of type *Alternative*. In this relation type, it is often the case that one of the arguments describes a possible future alternative to a current situation, as the case in Example (6). This possible information pattern for *Alternative* relations, where one of the arguments represents a currently occurring situation, would also help to explain why, even though very few events in general are annotated as *present* tense, almost 10% of events that co-occur with *Alternative* relations describe events that are currently ongoing. As for events whose *Tense* value is *unspecified*, two of the most common discourse relation types with which they occur are *Condition* and *Concession*. As exemplified above, *Condition* relations are often hypothetical in nature, meaning that no specific tense can be assigned. The generic argument of a *Concession* relation can also remain unmarked for tense. As in Example (3), it is not clear whether the effort to minimise civilian casualties has already been initiated, or will be initiated in the future.

(6) Saddam wouldn't be destroying missiles UNLESS he thought he *was going to* be **destroyed** if he didn't.

6 Conclusions

Given the level of variability in existing discourse-annotated corpora, it is meaningful for users to identify the relative merits of different schemes. In this paper, we have presented an extension of the U-Compare infrastructure that facilitates the comparison, integration and visualisation of documents annotated according to different annotation schemes. U-Compare constructs multiple and parallel annotation sub-workflows nested within a single workflow, with each sub-workflow corresponding to a distinct scheme. We have applied the implemented method to visualise the similarities and differences of two functional discourse annotation schemes, namely CoreSC and GENIA-MK. To demonstrate the integration of multiple schemes in U-Compare, we developed a workflow that merged event annotations from the ACE 2005 corpus (which include certain types of functional discourse information) with discourse relations obtained by an end-to-end parser. Moreover, we have analysed the merged annotations obtained by this workflow and this has allowed us to identify various correlations between the two different types of discourse annotations.

Based on the intuition that there is complementary information across different types of discourse annotations, we intend to examine how the integration of multiple discourse schemes, e.g., features obtained by merging annotations, affects the performance of machine learners for discourse analysis.

7 Acknowledgements

We are grateful to Dr. Ziheng Lin (National University of Singapore) for providing us with the discourse parser used for this work. This work was partially funded by the European Community's Seventh Framework Program (FP7/2007-2013) [grant number 318736 (OSSMETER)]; Engineering and Physical Sciences Research Council [grant numbers EP/P505631/1, EP/J50032X/1]; and MRC Text Mining and Screening (MR/J005037/1).

References

Sophia Ananiadou, Sampo Pyysalo, Junichi Tsujii, and Douglas B. Kell. 2010. Event extraction for systems biology by text mining the literature. *Trends in Biotechnology*, 28(7):381 – 390.

Riza Theresa B. Batista-Navarro, Georgios Kontonatsios, Claudiu Mihăilă, Paul Thompson, Rafal Rak, Raheel Nawaz, Ioannis Korkontzelos, and Sophia Ananiadou. 2013. Facilitating the analysis of discourse phenomena in an interoperable NLP platform. In *Computational Linguistics and Intelligent Text Processing*, volume 7816 of *Lecture Notes in Computer Science*, pages 559–571. Springer Berlin Heidelberg, March.

William A. Baumgartner, Kevin Bretonnel Cohen, and Lawrence Hunter. 2008. An open-source framework for large-scale, flexible evaluation of biomedical text mining systems. *Journal of biomedical discovery and collaboration*, 3:1+, January.

Lynn Carlson, Daniel Marcu, and Mary Ellen Okurowski. 2001. Building a discourse-tagged corpus in the framework of Rhetorical Structure Theory. In *Proceedings of the Second SIGdial Workshop on Discourse and Dialogue - Volume 16*, SIGDIAL '01, pages 1–10, Stroudsburg, PA, USA. Association for Computational Linguistics.

Hamish Cunningham, Diana Maynard, Kalina Bontcheva, and Valentin Tablan. 2002. GATE: an architecture for development of robust HLT applications. In *In Recent Advanced in Language Processing*, pages 168–175.

Anita de Waard and Henk Pander Maat. 2009. Epistemic segment types in biology research articles. In *Proceedings of the Workshop on Linguistic and Psycholinguistic Approaches to Text Structuring (LPTS 2009)*.

Anita de Waard. 2007. A pragmatic structure for research articles. In *Proceedings of the 2nd international conference on Pragmatic web*, ICPW '07, pages 83–89, New York, NY, USA. ACM.

David Ferrucci and Adam Lally. 2004. Building an example application with the unstructured information management architecture. *IBM Systems Journal*, 43(3):455–475.

Ralph Grishman. 1996. TIPSTER Text Phase II architecture design version 2.1p 19 june 1996. In *Proceedings of the TIPSTER Text Program: Phase II*, pages 249–305, Vienna, Virginia, USA, May. Association for Computational Linguistics.

Yufan Guo, Anna Korhonen, Maria Liakata, Ilona Silins Karolinska, Lin Sun, and Ulla Stenius. 2010. Identifying the information structure of scientific abstracts: An investigation of three different schemes. In *Proceedings of the 2010 Workshop on Biomedical Natural Language Processing*, pages 99–107. Association for Computational Linguistics.

Iryna Gurevych, Max Mühlhäuser, Christof Müller, Jürgen Steimle, Markus Weimer, and Torsten Zesch. 2007. Darmstadt knowledge processing repository based on UIMA. In *Proceedings of the First Workshop on Unstructured Information Management Architecture at Biannual Conference of the GSCL*.

Udo Hahn, Ekaterina Buyko, Rico Landefeld, Matthias Mühlhausen, Michael Poprat, Katrin Tomanek, and Joachim Wermter. 2008. An overview of JCoRe, the JULIE lab UIMA component repository. In *LREC'08 Workshop 'Towards Enhanced Interoperability for Large HLT Systems: UIMA for NLP'*, pages 1–7, Marrakech, Morocco, May.

Yoshinobu Kano, Makoto Miwa, Kevin Cohen, Lawrence Hunter, Sophia Ananiadou, and Jun'ichi Tsujii. 2011. U-Compare: A modular NLP workflow construction and evaluation system. *IBM Journal of Research and Development*, 55(3):11.

Maria Liakata, Simone Teufel, Advaith Siddharthan, and Colin Batchelor. 2010. Corpora for the conceptualisation and zoning of scientific papers. In *Proceedings of LREC*, volume 10.

Maria Liakata, Shyamasree Saha, Simon Dobnik, Colin Batchelor, and Dietrich Rebholz-Schuhmann. 2012a. Automatic recognition of conceptualization zones in scientific articles and two life science applications. *Bioinformatics*, 28(7):991–1000.

Maria Liakata, Paul Thompson, Anita de Waard, Raheel Nawaz, Henk Pander Maat, and Sophia Ananiadou. 2012b. A three-way perspective on scientic discourse annotation for knowledge extraction. In *Proceedings of the ACL Workshop on Detecting Structure in Scholarly Discourse (DSSD)*, pages 37–46, July.

Ziheng Lin, Hwee Tou Ng, and Min-Yen Kan. 2012. A PDTB-styled end-to-end discourse parser. *Natural Language Engineering*, FirstView:1–34, 10.

William C. Mann and Sandra A. Thompson. 1988. Rhetorical Structure Theory: Toward a functional theory of text organization. *Text*, 8(3):243–281.

Claudiu Mihăilă, Tomoko Ohta, Sampo Pyysalo, and Sophia Ananiadou. 2013. BioCause: Annotating and analysing causality in the biomedical domain. *BMC Bioinformatics*, 14(1):2, January.

Yoko Mizuta, Anna Korhonen, Tony Mullen, and Nigel Collier. 2006. Zone analysis in biology articles as a basis for information extraction. *International Journal of Medical Informatics*, 75(6):468 – 487. Recent Advances in Natural Language Processing for Biomedical Applications Special Issue.

Rashmi Prasad, Nikhil Dinesh, Alan Lee, Eleni Miltsakaki, Livio Robaldo, Aravind Joshi, and Bonnie Webber. 2008. The Penn Discourse TreeBank 2.0. In Nicoletta Calzolari, Khalid Choukri, Bente Maegaard, Joseph Mariani, Jan Odjik, Stelios

Piperidis, and Daniel Tapias, editors, *In Proceedings of the 6th International Conference on language Resources and Evaluation (LREC)*, pages 2961–2968.

Rashmi Prasad, Susan McRoy, Nadya Frid, Aravind Joshi, and Hong Yu. 2011. The biomedical discourse relation bank. *BMC Bioinformatics*, 12(1):188.

Rafal Rak, Andrew Rowley, and Sophia Ananiadou. 2012a. Collaborative development and evaluation of text-processing workflows in a UIMA-supported web-based workbench.

Rafal Rak, Andrew Rowley, William Black, and Sophia Ananiadou. 2012b. Argo: an integrative, interactive, text mining-based workbench supporting curation. *Database: The Journal of Biological Databases and Curation*, 2012.

Ágnes Sándor and Anita de Waard. 2012. Identifying claimed knowledge updates in biomedical research articles. In *Proceedings of the Workshop on Detecting Structure in Scholarly Discourse*, ACL '12, pages 10–17, Stroudsburg, PA, USA. Association for Computational Linguistics.

Guergana Savova, James Masanz, Philip Ogren, Jiaping Zheng, Sunghwan Sohn, Karin Kipper-Schuler, and Christopher Chute. 2010. Mayo clinical text analysis and knowledge extraction system (cTAKES): architecture, component evaluation and applications. *Journal of the American Medical Informatics Association*, 17(5):507–513.

Ulrich Schäfer. 2006. Middleware for creating and combining multi-dimensional nlp markup. In *Proceedings of the 5th Workshop on NLP and XML: Multi-Dimensional Markup in Natural Language Processing*, pages 81–84. ACL.

Pontus Stenetorp, Sampo Pyysalo, Goran Topić, Tomoko Ohta, Sophia Ananiadou, and Jun'ichi Tsujii. 2012. brat: a web-based tool for NLP-assisted text annotation. In *Proceedings of the Demonstrations Session at EACL 2012*, Avignon, France, April. Association for Computational Linguistics.

Simone Teufel, Jean Carletta, and Marc Moens. 1999. An annotation scheme for discourse-level argumentation in research articles. In *Proceedings of the ninth conference on European chapter of the Association for Computational Linguistics*, EACL '99, pages 110–117, Stroudsburg, PA, USA. Association for Computational Linguistics.

Paul Thompson, Raheel Nawaz, John McNaught, and Sophia Ananiadou. 2011. Enriching a biomedical event corpus with meta-knowledge annotation. *BMC Bioinformatics*, 12(1):393.

Christopher Walker. 2006. ACE 2005 Multilingual Training Corpus.

W John Wilbur, Andrey Rzhetsky, and Hagit Shatkay. 2006. New directions in biomedical text annotation: definitions, guidelines and corpus construction. *BMC Bioinformatics*, 7(1):356.

Making UIMA Truly Interoperable with SPARQL

Rafal Rak and Sophia Ananiadou
National Centre for Text Mining
School of Computer Science, University of Manchester
{rafal.rak,sophia.ananiadou}@manchester.ac.uk

Abstract

Unstructured Information Management Architecture (UIMA) has been gaining popularity in annotating text corpora. The architecture defines common data structures and interfaces to support interoperability of individual processing components working together in a UIMA application. The components exchange data by sharing common type systems—schemata of data type structures—which extend a generic, top-level type system built into UIMA. This flexibility in extending type systems has resulted in the development of repositories of components that share one or several type systems; however, components coming from different repositories, and thus not sharing type systems, remain incompatible. Commonly, this problem has been solved programmatically by implementing UIMA components that perform the alignment of two type systems, an arduous task that is impractical with a growing number of type systems. We alleviate this problem by introducing a conversion mechanism based on SPARQL, a query language for the data retrieval and manipulation of RDF graphs. We provide a UIMA component that serialises data coming from a source component into RDF, executes a user-defined, type-conversion query, and deserialises the updated graph into a target component. The proposed solution encourages ad hoc conversions, enables the usage of heterogeneous components, and facilitates highly customised UIMA applications.

1 Introduction

Unstructured Information Management Architecture (UIMA) (Ferrucci and Lally, 2004) is a framework that supports the interoperability of media-processing software components by defining common data structures and interfaces the components exchange and implement. The architecture has been gaining interest from academia and industry alike for the past decade, which resulted in a multitude of UIMA-supporting repositories of analytics. Notable examples include METANET4U components (Thompson et al., 2011) featured in U-Compare[1], DKPro (Gurevych et al., 2007), cTAKES (Savova et al., 2010), BioNLP-UIMA Component Repository (Baumgartner et al., 2008), and JULIE Lab's UIMA Component Repository (JCoRe) (Hahn et al., 2008).

However, despite conforming to the UIMA standard, each repository of analytics usually comes with its own set of *type systems*, i.e., representations of data models that are meant to be shared between analytics and thus ensuring their interoperability. At present, UIMA does not facilitate the alignment of (all or selected) types between type systems, which makes it impossible to combine analytics coming from different repositories without an additional programming effort. For instance, NLP developers may want to use a sentence detector from one repository and a tokeniser from another repository only to learn that the required input `Sentence` type for the tokeniser is defined in a different type system and namespace than the output `Sentence` type of the sentence detector. Although both `Sentence` types represent the same concept and may even have the same set of features (attributes), they are viewed as two distinct types by UIMA.

Less trivial incompatibility arises from the same concept being encoded as structurally different types in different type systems. Figures 1 and 2 show fragments of some of existing type systems;

[1] http://nactem.ac.uk/ucompare/

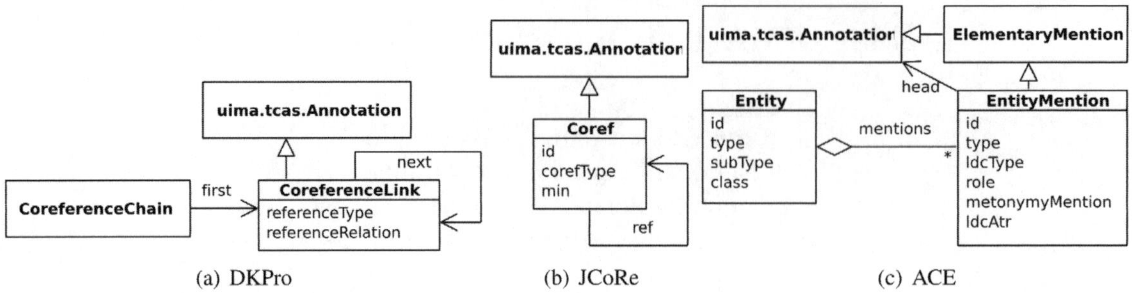

Figure 1: UML diagrams representing fragments of type systems that show differences in encoding coreferences.

specifically, they show the differences in encoding *coreferences* and *events*, respectively. For instance, in comparison to the JCoRe type system in Figure 1(b), the DKPro type system in Figure 1(a) has an additional type that points to the beginning of the linked list of coreferences.

Conceptually similar types in two different type systems may also be incompatible in terms of the amount of information they convey. Compare, for instance, type systems in Figure 2 that encode a similar concept, event. Not only are they structurally different, but the cTAKES type system in Figure 2(a) also involves a larger number of features than the other two type systems. Although, in this case, the alignment of any two structures cannot be carried out without a loss or deficiency of information, it may still be beneficial to do so for applications that consist of components that either fulfill partially complete information or do not require it altogether.

The available type systems vary greatly in size, their modularity, and intended applicability. The DKPro UIMA software collection, for instance, includes multiple, small-size type systems organised around specific syntactic and semantic concepts, such as part of speech, chunks, and named entities. In contrast, the U-Compare project as well as cTAKES are oriented towards having a single type system. Respectively, the type systems define nearly 300 and 100 syntactic and semantic types, with U-Compare's semantic types biased towards biology and chemistry and cTAKES's covering clinical domain. Most of the U-Compare types extend a fairly expressive higher-level type, which makes them universally applicable, but at the same time, breaks their semantic cohesion. The lack of modularity and the all-embroiling types suggest that the U-Compare type system is developed primarily to work with the U-Compare application.

The Center for Computational Pharmacology (CCP) type system (Verspoor et al., 2009) is a radically different approach to the previous systems. It defines a closed set of top-level types that facilitate the use of external resources, such as databases and ontologies. This gives the advantage of having a nonvolatile type system, indifferent to changes in the external resources, as well as greater flexibility in handling some semantic models that would otherwise be impossible to encode in a UIMA type system. On the other hand, such an approach shifts the handling of interoperability from UIMA to applications that must resolve compatibility issues at runtime, which also results in the weakly typed programming of analytics. Additionally, the UIMA's native indexing of annotation types will no longer work with such a type system, which prompts an additional programming effort from developers.

The aforementioned examples suggest that establishing a single type system that could be shared among all providers is unlikely to ever take place due to the variability in requirements and applicability. Instead, we adopt an idea of using a *conversion* mechanism that enables aligning types across type systems. The conversion has commonly been solved programmatically by creating UIMA analytics that map all or (more likely) selected types between two type systems. For instance, U-Compare features a component that translates some of the CPP types into the U-Compare types. The major drawback of such a solution is the necessity of having to implement an analytic which requires programming skills and becomes an arduous task with an increasing number of type systems. In contrast, we propose a conversion based *entirely* on developers' writing a query in the well established SPARQL language,

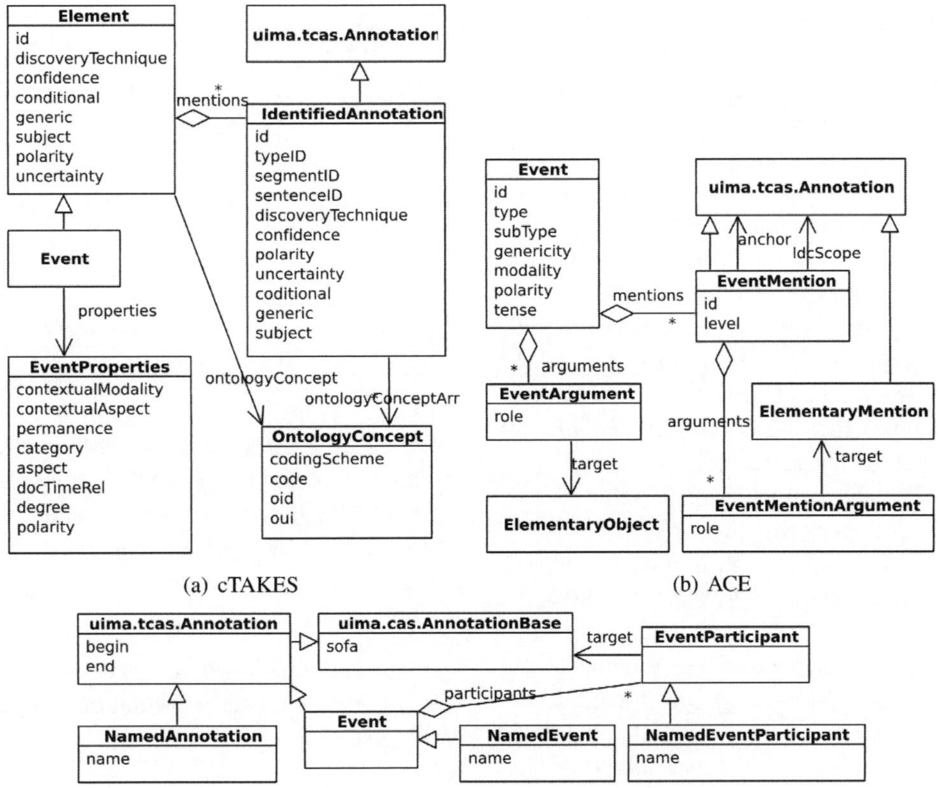

(a) cTAKES

(b) ACE

(c) Events Type System

Figure 2: UML diagrams representing fragments of type systems that show differences in encoding event structures.

an official W3C Recommendation[2]. Our approach involves 1) the serialisation of UIMA's internal data structures to RDF[3], 2) the execution of a user-defined, type-conversion SPARQL query, and 3) the deserialisation of the results back to the UIMA structure.

The remainder of this paper is organised as follows. The next section presents related work. Section 3 provides background information on UIMA, RDF and SPARQL. Section 4 discusses the proposed representation of UIMA structures in RDF, whereas Section 5 examines the utility of our method. Section 6 details the available implementation, and Section 7 concludes the paper.

2 Related Work

In practice, type alignment or conversion is the creation of new UIMA feature structures based on the existing ones. Current efforts in this area mostly involve solutions that are essentially (cascaded) finite state transducers, i.e., an input stream of existing feature structures is being matched against developers' defined patterns, and if a match is found, a series of actions follows and results in one or more output structures.

TextMarker (Kluegl et al., 2009) is currently one of the most comprehensive tools that defines its own rule-based language. The language capabilities include the definition of new types, annotation-based regular expression matching and a rich set of condition functions and actions. Combined with a built-in lexer that produces basic token annotations, TextMarker is essentially a self-contained, UIMA-based annotation tool.

Hernandez (2012) proposed and developed a suite of tools for tackling the interoperability of components in UIMA. The suite includes uima-mapper, a conversion tool designed to work with a rule-based language for mapping UIMA annotations. The rules are encoded in XML, and–contrary to the previous language that relies solely on its own syntax—include XPath expressions for patterns, constraints, and assigning values to new

[2]http://www.w3.org/TR/2013/REC-sparql11-overview-20130321

[3]http://www.w3.org/RDF/

feature structures. This implies that the input of the conversion process must be encoded in XML.

PEARL (Pazienza et al., 2012) is a language for projecting UIMA annotations onto RDF repositories. Similarly to the previous approaches, the language defines a set of rules triggered upon encountering UIMA annotations. The language is designed primarily to work in CODA, a platform that facilitates population of ontologies with the output of NLP analytics. Although it does not directly facilitate the production or conversion of UIMA types, the PEARL language shares similarities to our approach in that it incorporates certain RDF Turtle, SPARQL-like semantics.

Contrary to the aforementioned solutions, we do not define any new language or syntax. Instead, we rely completely on an existing data query and manipulation language, SPARQL. By doing so, we shift the problem of conversion from the definition of a new language to representing UIMA structures in an existing language, such that they can be conveniently manipulated in that language.

A separate line of research pertains to the formalisation of textual annotations with knowledge representations such as RDF and OWL[4]. Buyko *et al.* (2008) link UIMA annotations to the reference ontology OLiA (Chiarcos, 2012) that contains a broad vocabulary of linguistic terminology. The authors claim that two conceptually similar type systems can be aligned with the reference ontology. The linking involves the use of OLiA's associated annotation and linking ontology model pairs that have been created for a number of annotation schemata. Furthermore, a UIMA type system has to define additional features for each linked type that tie a given type to an annotation model. In effect, in order to convert a type from an arbitrary type system to another similar type system, both systems must be modified and an annotation and linking models must be created. Such an approach generalises poorly and is unsuitable for impromptu type system conversions.

3 Background

3.1 UIMA Overview

UIMA defines both structures and interfaces to facilitate interoperability of individual processing components that share type systems. Type systems may be defined in or imported by a processing component that produces or modifies annotations in a *common annotation structure* (CAS), i.e., a CAS is the container of actual data bound by the type system.

[4]http://www.w3.org/TR/owl2-overview/

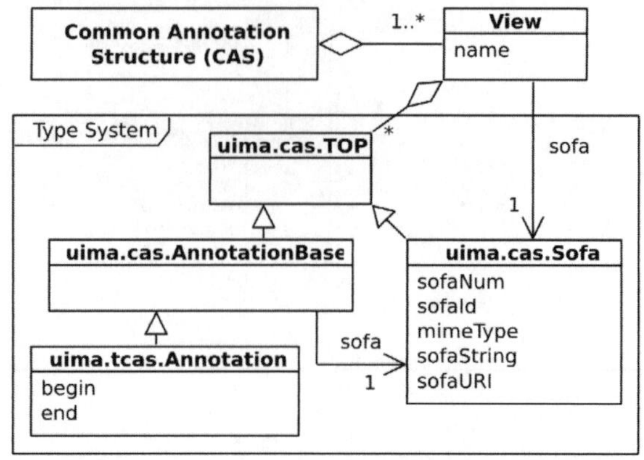

Figure 3: UML diagram representing relationships between CASes, views, and feature structures in UIMA. The shown type system is a fragment of the built-in UIMA type system.

Types may define multiple primitive *features* as well as references to *feature structures* (data instances) of other types. The single-parent inheritance of types is also possible. The resulting structures resemble those present in modern object-oriented programming languages.

Feature structures stored in a CAS may be grouped into several *views*, each of which having its own *subject of analysis* (Sofa). For instance, one view may store annotations about a Sofa that stores an English text, whereas another view may store annotations about a different Sofa that stores a French version of the same text. UIMA defines built-in types including primitive types (boolean, integer, string, etc.), arrays, lists, as well as several complex types, e.g., `uima.tcas.Annotation` that holds a reference to a Sofa the annotation is asserted about, and two features, begin and end, for marking boundaries of a span of text. The relationships between CASes, views, and several prominent built-in types are shown in Figure 3.

The built-in complex types may further be extended by developers. Custom types that mark a fragment of text usually extend `uima.tcas.Annotation`, and thus inherit the reference to the subject of analysis, and the begin and end features.

UIMA element/representation	RDF resource
CAS	<uima:aux:CAS>
Access to CAS's views	rdfs:member or rdf:_1, rdf:_2, ...
View	<uima:aux:View>
View's name	<uima:aux:View:name>
View's Sofa	<uima:aux:View:sofa>
Access to view's feature structures	rdfs:member or rdf:_1, rdf:_2, ...
Access to feature structure's sequential number	<uima:aux:seq>
Type uima.tcas.Annotation	<uima:ts:uima.tcas.Annotation>
Feature uima.tcas.Annotation:begin	<uima:ts:uima.cas.Annotation:begin>
Access to uima.cas.ArrayBase elements	rdfs:member or rdf:_1, rdf:_2, ...

Table 1: UIMA elements and their corresponding RDF resource representations

3.2 RDF and SPARQL

Resource Description Framework (RDF) is a method for modeling concepts in form of making statements about resources using triple subject-predicate-object expressions. The triples are composed of *resources* and/or *literals* with the latter available only as objects. Resources are represented with valid URIs, whereas literals are values optionally followed by a datatype. Multiple interlinked subject and objects ultimately constitute *RDF graphs*.

SPARQL is a query language for fetching data from RDF graphs. Search patterns are created using RDF triples that are written in RDF Turtle format, a human-readable and easy to manipulate syntax. A SPARQL triple may contain *variables* on any of the three positions, which may (and usually does) result in returning multiple triples from a graph for the same pattern. If the same variable is used more than once in patterns, its values are bound, which is one of the mechanisms of constraining results.

Triple-like patterns with variables are simple, yet expressive ways of retrieving data from an RDF graph and constitute the most prominent feature of SPARQL. In this work, we additionally utilise features of SPARQL 1.1 Update sublanguage that facilitates graph *manipulation*.

4 Representing UIMA in RDF

We use RDF Schema[5] as the primary RDF vocabulary to encode type systems and feature structures in CASes. The schema defines resources such as rdfs:Class, rdf:type (to denote a membership of an instance to a particular class) and rdfs:subClassOf (as a class inheritance property)[6]. It is a popular description language for expressing a hierarchy of concepts, their instances and relationships, and forms a base for such semantic languages as OWL.

The UIMA type system structure falls naturally into this schema. Each type is expressed as rdfs:Class and each feature as rdfs:Property accompanied by appropriate rdfs:domain and rdfs:range statements. Feature structures (instances) are then assigned memberships of their respective types (classes) through rdf:type properties.

A special consideration is given to the type ArrayBase (and its extensions). Since the order of elements in an array may be of importance, feature structures of the type ArrayBase are also instances of the class rdf:Seq, a sequence container, and the elements of an array are accessed through the properties rdf:_1, rdf:_2, etc., which, in turn, are the subproperties of rdfs:member. This enables querying array structures with preserving the order of its members. Similar, enumeration-property approach is used for views that are members of CASes and feature structures that are members of views. The order for the latter two is defined in the internal indices of a CAS and follows the order in which the views and feature structures were added to those indices.

We also define several auxiliary RDF resources to represent relationships between CASes, views and feature structures (cf. Figure 3). We introduced the scheme name "uima" for the URIs of

5 http://www.w3.org/TR/rdf-schema/

6 Following RDF Turtle notation we denote prefixed forms of RDF resources as prefix:suffix and their full forms as <fullform>

```
PREFIX rdfs: <http://www.w3.org/2000/01/rdf-schema#>
INSERT {
  _:newSentence a <uima:ts:our.Sentence> ;
    <uima:ts:uima.tcas.Annotation:begin> ?begin ;
    <uima:ts:uima.tcas.Annotation:end> ?end .
  ?view rdfs:member _:newSentence .
}
WHERE {
  ?view a <uima:aux:View> ;
    rdfs:member ?sentence .
  ?sentence a <uima:ts:their.Sentence> ;
    <uima:ts:uima.tcas.Annotation:begin> ?begin ;
    <uima:ts:uima.tcas.Annotation:end> ?end .
}
```

Figure 4: Complete SPARQL query that converts the sentence type in one type system to a structurally identical type in another type system.

the UIMA-related resources. The fully qualified names of UIMA types and their features are part of the URI paths. The paths are additionally prefixed by "`ts:`" to avoid a name clash against the aforementioned auxiliary CAS and view URIs that, in turn, are prefixed with "`aux:`". Table 1 summarises most of the UIMA elements and their corresponding representations in RDF.

5 Conversion Capabilities

In this section we examine the utility of the proposed approach and the expressiveness of SPARQL by demonstrating several conversion examples. We focus on technical aspects of conversions and neglect issues related to a loss or deficiency of information that is a result of differences in type system conceptualisation (as discussed in Introduction).

5.1 One-to-one Conversion

We begin with a trivial case where two types from two different type systems have exactly the same names and features; the only difference lies in the namespace of the two types. Figure 4 shows a complete SPARQL query that converts (copies) `their.Sentence` feature structures to `our.Sentence` structures. Both types extend the `uima.tcas.Annotation` type and inherit its begin and end features. The WHERE clause of the query consists of patterns that match CASes' views and their feature structures of the type `their.Sentence` together with the type's begin and end features.

For each solution of the WHERE clause (each retrieved tuple), the INSERT clause then creates a new sentence of the target type `our.Sentence` (the `a` property is the shortcut of `rdf:type`)

```
INSERT {
?eventUri a gen:NamedEvent ;
  gen:NamedEvent:name ?type ;
  tcas:Annotation:begin ?anchorBegin ;
  tcas:Annotation:end ?anchorEnd ;
  gen:Event:participants ?arrayUri .
?arrayUri a cas:FSArray, rdf:Seq ;
  ?argumentIdxUri _:participant .
_:participant a gen:NamedEventParticipant ;
  gen:NamedEventParticipant:name ?role ;
  gen:EventParticipant:target ?target .
?view rdfs:member ?eventUri .
}
WHERE {
?view a aux:View ;
  rdfs:member ?event .
?event a ace:Event ;
  ace:Event:type ?type ;
  ace:Event:mentions ?mentions .
?mentions rdfs:member ?mention .
?mention a ace:EventMention ;
  ace:EventMention:arguments ?arguments ;
  ace:EventMention:anchor ?anchor ;
  aux:seq ?mentionSeq .
?anchor tcas:Annotation:begin ?anchorBegin ;
  tcas:Annotation:end ?anchorEnd .
?arguments rdfs:member ?argument ;
  ?argumentIdxUri ?argument .
?argument ace:EventMentionArgument:role ?role ;
  ace:EventMentionArgument:target ?target ;
  aux:seq ?argumentSeq .

BIND(URI(CONCAT("tmp:", STR(?mentionSeq)))
    AS ?eventUri)
BIND(URI(CONCAT("tmp:", STR(?mentionSeq), "#array"))
    AS ?arrayUri)
}
```

Figure 5: SPARQL query that aligns different conceptualisations of event structures between two type systems. Prefix definitions are not shown.

and rewrites the begin and end values to its features. The *blank node* `_:sentence` is going to be automatically re-instantiated with a unique resource for each matching tuple making each sentence node distinct. The last line of the INSERT clause ties the newly created sentence to the view, which is UIMA's equivalent of indexing a feature structure in a CAS.

5.2 One-to-many Conversion

In this use case we examine the conversion of a container of multiple elements to a set of disconnected elements. Let us consider event types from the ACE and Events type systems as shown in Figures 2(b) and 2(c), respectively. A single `Event` structure in the ACE type system aggregates multiple `EventMention` structures in an effort to combine multiple text evidence supporting the same event. The `NamedEvent` type in the Events type system, on the other hand, makes no such provision and is agnostic to the fact that multiple mentions may refer to the same event.

To avoid confusion, we will refer to the types using their RDF prefixed notations, "`ace:`" and "`gen:`", to denote the ACE and "generic" Events type systems, respectively.

The task is to convert all `ace:Events` and their `ace:EventMentions` into `gen:NamedEvents`. There is a couple of nuances that need to be taken into consideration. Firstly, although both `ace:EventMention` and `gen:NamedEvent` extend `uima.tcas.Annotation`, the begin and end features have different meanings for the two event representations. The `gen:NamedEvent`'s begin and end features represent an anchor/trigger, a word in the text that initiates the event. The same type of information is accessible from `ace:EventMention` via its `anchor` feature instead. Secondly, although it may be tempting to disregard the `ace:Event` structures altogether, they contain the `type` feature whose value will be copied to `gen:NamedEvent`'s `name` feature.

The SPARQL query that performs that conversion is shown in Figure 5. In the WHERE clause, for each `ace:Event`, patterns select `ace:EventMentions` and for each `ace:EventMention`, `ace:EventMentionArguments` are also selected. This behaviour resembles triply nested *for* loop in programming languages. Additionally, `ace:Event`'s type, `ace:EventMention`'s anchor begin and end values, and `ace:EventMentionArgument`'s role and target are selected. In contrast to the previous example, we cannot use blank nodes for creating event resources in the INSERT clause, since the retrieved tuples share event URIs for each `ace:EventMentionArgument`. Hence the last two `BIND` functions create URIs for each `ace:EventMention` and its array of arguments, both of which are used in the INSERT clause.

Note that in the INSERT clause, if several `gen:NamedEventParticipants` share the same `gen:NamedEvent`, the definition of the latter will be repeated for each such participant. We take advantage of the fact that adding a triple to an RDF graph that already exists in the graph has no effect, i.e., an insertion is simply ignored and no error is raised. Alternatively, the query could be rewritten as two queries, one that creates `gen:NamedEvent` definitions and another that creates `gen:NamedEventParticipant` definitions.

```
INSERT {
?mentionUri a ace:EntityMention ;
  tcas:Annotation:begin ?begin ;
  tcas:Annotation:end ?end ;
  ace:EntityMention:type ?type ;
  ace:EntityMention:role ?relation .
?mentions a cas:FSArray, rdf:Seq ;
  ?mentionMemberUri ?mentionUri .
?entityUri a ace:Entity ;
  ace:Entity:mentions ?mentions .
?view rdfs:member ?entityUri .
}
WHERE {
?view a <uima:View> ;
  rdfs:member ?chain .
?chain a dkpro:CoreferenceChain ;
  dkpro:CoreferenceChain:first/
     dkpro:CoreferenceLink:next* ?link ;
  <uima:aux:seq> ?chainSeq .
?link <uima:aux:seq> ?linkSeq ;
  dkpro:CoreferenceLink:referenceType ?type ;
  dkpro:CoreferenceLink:referenceRelation ?relation ;
  tcas:Annotation:begin ?begin ;
  tcas:Annotation:end ?end .

BIND(URI(CONCAT("entity:", STR(?chainSeq)))
     AS ?entityUri)
BIND(URI(CONCAT("mention:", STR(?linkSeq)))
     AS ?mentionUri)
BIND(URI(CONCAT(STR(?entityUri), "#mentions"))
     AS ?mentions)
BIND(URI(CONCAT(str(rdf:), "_", str(?linkSeq)))
     AS ?mentionMemberUri) .
}
```

Figure 6: SPARQL query that converts coreferences expressed as linked lists to an array representation. Prefix definitions are not shown.

To recapitulate, RDF and SPARQL support one-to-many (and many-to-one) conversions by storing only unique triple statements and by providing functions that enable creating arbitrary resource identifiers (URIs) that can be shared between retrieved tuples.

5.3 Linked-list-to-Array Conversion

For this example, let us consider two types of structures for storing coreferences from the DKPro and ACE type systems, as depicted in Figures 1(a) and 1(c), respectively.

The idea is to convert DKPro's chains of links into ACE's entities that aggregate entity mentions, or—using software developers' vocabulary—to convert a linked list into an array. The SPARQL query for this conversion is shown in Figure 6.

The WHERE clause first selects all `dkpro:CoreferenceChain` instances from views. Access to `dkpro:CoreferenceLink` instances for each chain is provided by a *property path*. Property paths are convenient shortcuts for navigating through nodes of an RDF graph. In this case, the property path expands to the chain's `first` feature/property followed by any number (signified by the asterisk) of links' `next` feature/property. The pattern with this path will result in returning all links that are accessible from the originating chain; however, according to the SPARQL specification, the order of links is not guaranteed to be preserved, which in coreference-supporting applications is usually of interest. A solution is to make use of the property `<uima:aux:seq>` that points to the sequential number of a feature structure and is unique in the scope of a single CAS. Since feature structures are serialised into RDF using deep-first traversal, the consecutive link structures for each chain will have their sequence numbers monotonically increasing. These sequence numbers are translated to form `rdf:_nn` properties (*nn* standing for the number), which facilitates the order of elements in the `ace:Entity` array of mentions[7]. It should be noted, however, that using the sequence number property will work only if the links of a chain are not referred to from another structure. There is another, robust solution (not shown due to space limitation and complexity) that involves multiple INSERT queries and temporary, supporting RDF nodes. RDF nodes that are not directly relevant to a CAS and its feature structures are ignored during the deserialisation process, and thus it is safe to create any number of such nodes.

6 Tool Support

We have developed a UIMA analysis engine, SPARQL Annotation Editor, that incorporates the serialisation of a CAS into RDF (following the protocol presented in Section 4), the execution of a user-defined SPARQL query, and the deserialisation of the updated RDF graph back to the CAS. The RDF graph (de)serialisation and SPARQL query execution is implemented using Apache Jena[8], an open-source framework for building Semantic Web applications.

To further assist in the development of type-conversion SPARQL queries, we have provided two additional UIMA components, RDF Writer and RDF Reader. RDF Writer serialises CASes to files that can then be used with SPARQL query engines, such as Jena Fuseki (part of the Apache Jena project), to develop and test conversion queries. The modified RDF graphs can be imported back to a UIMA application using RDF Reader, an RDF deserialisation component.

The three components are featured in Argo (Rak et al., 2012), a web-based workbench for building and executing UIMA workflows.

7 Conclusions

The alignment of types between different type systems using SPARQL is an attractive alternative to existing solutions. Compared to other solutions, our approach does not introduce a new language or syntax; to the contrary, it relies entirely on a well-defined, standardised language, a characteristic that immediately broadens the target audience. Likewise, developers who are unfamiliar with SPARQL should be more likely to learn this well-maintained and widely used language than any other specialised and not standardised syntax.

The expressiveness of SPARQL makes the method superior to the rule-based techniques, mainly due to SPARQL's inherent capability of random data access and simple, triple-based querying. At the same time, the semantic cohesion of data is maintained by a graph representation.

The proposed solution facilitates the rapid alignment of type systems and increases the flexibility in which developers choose processing components to build their UIMA applications. As well as benefiting the design of applications, the conversion mechanism may also prove helpful in the development of components themselves. To ensure interoperability, developers usually adopt an existing type system for a new component. This essential UIMA-development practice undeniably increases the applicability of such a component; however, at times it may also result in having the ill-defined representation of the data produced by the component. The availability of an easy-to-apply conversion tool promotes constructing fine-tuned type systems that best represent such data.

Acknowledgments

This work was partially funded by the MRC Text Mining and Screening grant (MR/J005037/1).

[7] The `rdf:_nn` properties are not required to be consecutive in an RDF container

[8] http://jena.apache.org/

References

W A Baumgartner, K B Cohen, and L Hunter. 2008. An open-source framework for large-scale, flexible evaluation of biomedical text mining systems. *Journal of biomedical discovery and collaboration*, 3:1+.

E Buyko, C Chiarcos, and A Pareja-Lora. 2008. Ontology-based interface specifications for a nlp pipeline architecture. In *Proceedings of the Sixth International Conference on Language Resources and Evaluation (LREC'08)*, Marrakech, Morocco.

C Chiarcos. 2012. Ontologies of linguistic annotation: Survey and perspectives. In *Proceedings of the Eighth International Conference on Language Resources and Evaluation (LREC'12)*, pages 303–310.

D Ferrucci and A Lally. 2004. UIMA: An Architectural Approach to Unstructured Information Processing in the Corporate Research Environment. *Natural Language Engineering*, 10(3-4):327–348.

Iryna Gurevych, Max Mühlhäuser, Christof Müller, Jürgen Steimle, Markus Weimer, and Torsten Zesch. 2007. Darmstadt Knowledge Processing Repository Based on UIMA. In *Proceedings of the First Workshop on Unstructured Information Management Architecture at Biannual Conference of the Society for Computational Linguistics and Language Technology*, Tübingen, Germany.

U Hahn, E Buyko, R Landefeld, M Mühlhausen, M Poprat, K Tomanek, and J Wermter. 2008. An Overview of JCORE, the JULIE Lab UIMA Component Repository. In *Proceedings of the Language Resources and Evaluation Workshop, Towards Enhanc. Interoperability Large HLT Syst.: UIMA NLP*, pages 1–8.

N Hernandez. 2012. Tackling interoperability issues within UIMA workflows. In *Proceedings of the Eight International Conference on Language Resources and Evaluation (LREC'12)*, Istanbul, Turkey. European Language Resources Association (ELRA).

P Kluegl, M Atzmueller, and F Puppe. 2009. TextMarker: A Tool for Rule-Based Information Extraction. In *Proceedings of the Biennial GSCL Conference 2009, 2nd UIMA@GSCL Workshop*, pages 233–240. Gunter Narr Verlag.

M T Pazienza, A Stellato, and A Turbati. 2012. PEARL: ProjEction of Annotations Rule Language, a Language for Projecting (UIMA) Annotations over RDF Knowledge Bases. In *Proceedings of the Eight International Conference on Language Resources and Evaluation (LREC'12)*, Istanbul, Turkey. European Language Resources Association (ELRA).

R Rak, A Rowley, W Black, and S Ananiadou. 2012. Argo: an integrative, interactive, text mining-based workbench supporting curation. *Database : The Journal of Biological Databases and Curation*, page bas010.

G K Savova, J J Masanz, P V Ogren, J Zheng, S Sohn, K C Kipper-Schuler, and C G Chute. 2010. Mayo clinical Text Analysis and Knowledge Extraction System (cTAKES): architecture, component evaluation and applications. *Journal of the American Medical Informatics Association : JAMIA*, 17(5):507–513.

P Thompson, Y Kano, J McNaught, S Pettifer, T K Attwood, J Keane, and S Ananiadou. 2011. Promoting Interoperability of Resources in META-SHARE. In *Proceedings of the IJCNLP Workshop on Language Resources, Technology and Services in the Sharing Paradigm (LRTS)*, pages 50–58.

K Verspoor, W Baumgartner Jr, C Roeder, and L Hunter. 2009. Abstracting the Types away from a UIMA Type System. *From Form to Meaning: Processing Texts Automatically.*, pages 249–256.

Importing MASC into the ANNIS linguistic database: A case study of mapping GrAF

Arne Neumann
EB Cognitive Science and SFB 632
University of Potsdam
neumana@uni-potsdam.de

Nancy Ide
Department of Computer Science
Vassar College
ide@cs.vassar.edu

Manfred Stede
EB Cognitive Science and SFB 632
University of Potsdam
stede@uni-potsdam.de

Abstract

This paper describes the importation of Manually Annotated Sub-Corpus (MASC) data and annotations into the linguistic database ANNIS, which allows users to visualize and query linguistically-annotated corpora. We outline the process of mapping MASC's GrAF representation to ANNIS's internal format relANNIS and demonstrate how the system provides access to multiple annotation layers in the corpus. This access provides information about inter-layer relations and dependencies that have been previously difficult to explore, and which are highly valuable for continued development of language processing applications.

1 Introduction

Over the past decade, corpora with multiple layers of linguistic annotation have been developed in order to extend the range of empirically-based linguistic research and enable study of inter-layer interactions. Recently created corpora include OntoNotes (Pradhan et al., 2007), the Groningen Meaning Bank (Basile et al., 2012), and the Manually Annotated Sub-Corpus (MASC)[1] (Ide et al., 2010). Typically, such corpora are represented in idiosyncratic in-house formats, and developers provide special software to access and query the annotations (for example, the OntoNotes "db tool" and Groningen's GMB Explorer). Access without the use of developer-supplied software often requires significant programming expertise, and as a result, it is not easy–or even possible–for others to add to or modify data and annotations in the resource.

This paper describes the importation of MASC data and annotations into the linguistic database ANNIS[2] (Chiarcos et al., 2008; Zeldes et al., 2009), which was designed to visualize and query linguistically-annotated corpora. Unlike most other corpora with multi-layer annotations, no special software has been developed for access to MASC. Instead, all MASC data and annotations are represented in GrAF (Ide and Suderman, 2007), the XML serialization of the abstract model for annotations defined by ISO TC37 SC4's Linguistic Annotation Framework (ISO/LAF) (Ide and Suderman, In press). GrAF is intended to serve as a generic "pivot" format that is isomorphic to annotation schemes conforming to the abstract model and therefore readily mappable to schemes used in available systems. We outline the process of mapping GrAF to ANNIS's internal format relANNIS and demonstrate how the system provides access to multiple annotation layers in MASC.

2 The ANNIS Infrastructure

The ANNIS system is a linguistic database geared toward the requirements of querying multi-layer annotated corpora, and providing various visualization means for layers with different structural properties. In particular, the annotation types supported are spans, DAGs with labelled edges, and pointing relations between terminals or non-terminals. For illustration, Figure 1 shows a screenshot where various parallel annotations of the same data are provided: dependency trees, constituent trees (here with "secondary edges" in dotted lines), and a grid view for annotations that assign labels to token spans. In addition, ANNIS offers a "discourse view" giving the complete text with coreference relations indicated by color and underlining. In the top of the screenshot, it can be noted that the system also stored video (and au-

[1] www.anc.org/MASC

[2] http://www.sfb632.uni-potsdam.de/annis/

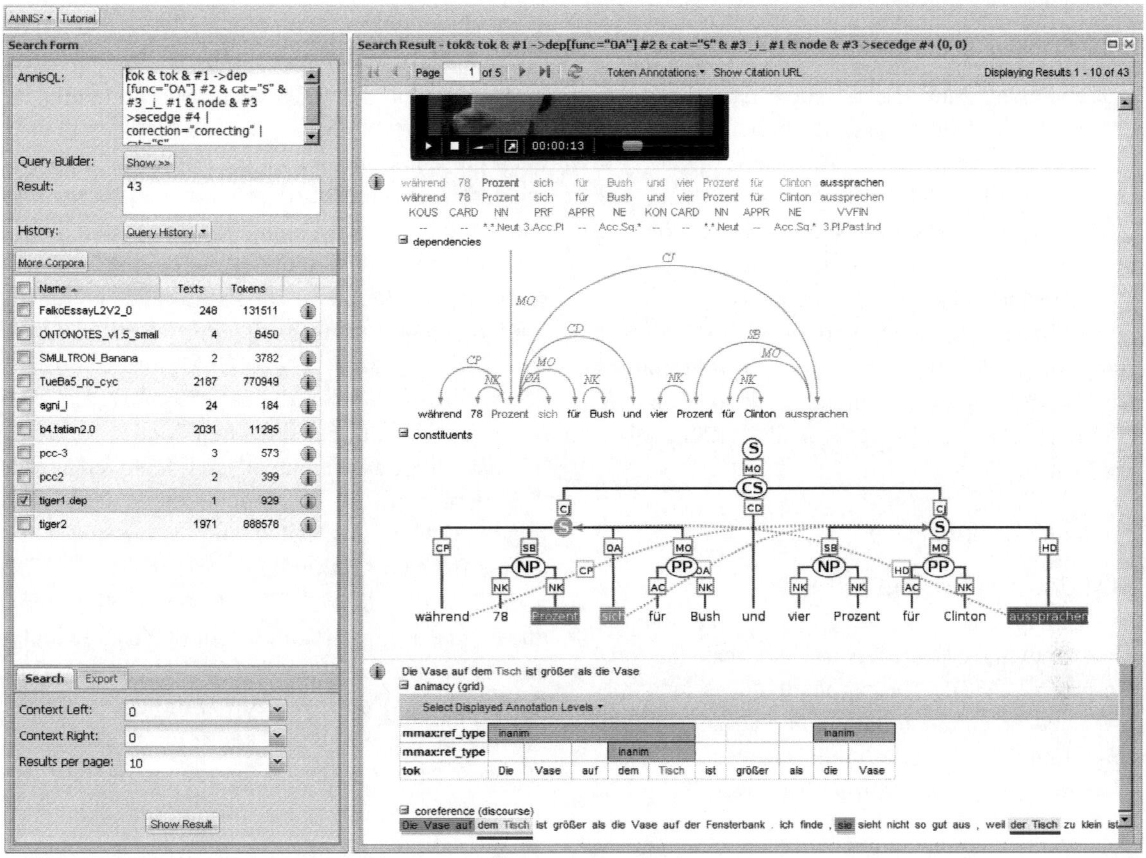

Figure 1: Screenshot of ANNIS2

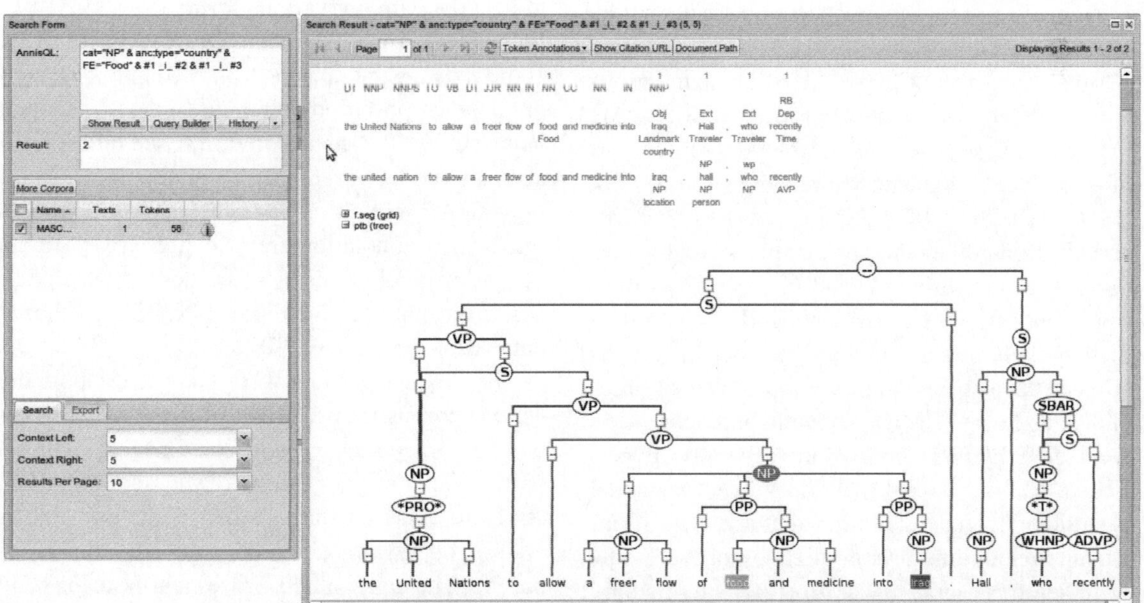

Figure 2: Querying MASC in ANNIS2 for an NP that includes both a *food* frame element and a *location* named entity

dio) data, but that aspect shall not concern us in this paper.

The system is web-based; the user interface is written in Java and ExtJS. The backend is PostgreSQL[3]. In general, all components are open source under the Apache License 2.0, and you can download ANNIS from the above-mentioned URL. We offer two versions: A server version, and the more lightweight "ANNIS kickstarter", which can be installed locally, e.g., on laptops.

ANNIS is complemented by SaltNPepper, a framework for converting annotations stemming from various popular annotation tools (MMAX, EXMARaLDA, annotate/Synpathy, RSTTool) – see Section 4.

3 MASC and GrAF

MASC is a fully open, half-million word corpus covering nineteen diverse genres of American English drawn from the Open American National Corpus (OANC)[4]. The corpus includes manually produced or hand-validated annotations for multiple linguistic layers, including morphosyntax (two different annotations), shallow parse (noun and verb chunks), Penn Treebank syntax, and named entities. Portions of the corpus are also annotated for FrameNet frames, opinion, PropBank predicate-arguments, and WordNet 3.1 word senses. Discourse-level annotation, including coreference, clauses, and discourse markers, will be available in fall, 2013.

Like the OANC, all MASC annotations are rendered in standoff form using GrAF, the graph-based format developed as a part of the ISO Linguistic Annotation Framework (ISO/LAF)(ISO 24612, 2012). GrAF is an XML serialization of the LAF abstract model for annotations, a formalization of models used across multiple applications for associating (linking) information, including not only directed-acyclic graphs (DAGs) but also ER diagrams, the Universal Modeling Language (UML), semantic and neural networks, RDF/OWL, and, more generally, hyperlinked data on the World Wide Web. The model is sufficiently general to represent any type of linguistic annotation; any serialization of the model can therefore serve as a *pivot* or intermediary among diverse annotation formats that conform to the abstract model. Thus, any sufficiently well-formed annotation scheme should be isomorphic to a GrAF representation of the same information. Problems arise only when a scheme does not specify information explicitly but rather embeds the interpretation in processing software rather than in the representation itself; for transduction to GrAF, this information must be made explicit in the representation.

Funding for MASC did not allow for extensive software development; the expectation is that by rendering the corpus in the ISO standard GrAF format, access could rely on GrAF-aware software developed by others, or transduction from GrAF to appropriate alternative formats would be trivial. We have already developed and deployed means to import linguistic data represented in GrAF into UIMA, GATE, and NLTK, and we provide transducers from GrAF to inline XML and the CoNLL IOB format.[5] Additionally, a GrAF-to-RDF transducer is near completion, which will enable inclusion of MASC in the Linguistic Linked Open Data (LLOD) cloud[6]. The incorporation of a GRAF transducer for ANNIS provides another example of the flexibility afforded via the GrAF representation.

4 Mapping GrAF to ANNIS via SaltNPepper

Pepper is a software framework that converts linguistic data among various formats, e.g. CoNLL, EXMARaLDA, PAULA, TigerXML, RSTTool and TreeTagger (Zipser et al., 2011). It is built upon the graph-based Salt meta model (Zipser and Romary, 2010), which is in turn based on the LAF abstract model for linguistic annotation. Mapping GrAF to Salt extends the range of formats into which annotations represented in GrAF can be automatically transduced to those to which Salt has been mapped, including ANNIS's relational database format relANNIS.

The following steps were taken to import the MASC corpus into ANNIS: first, the MASC corpus data was extracted with the GrAF API[7]. Second, a mapping between GrAF and Salt data structures was created. Most of the conversion is straightforward, since both models are graph-based. The only added processing is to provide

[3] `http://www.postgresql.org/`
[4] `www.anc.org/OANC`

[5] Available from `http://www.anc.org/MASC`.
[6] `http://linguistics.okfn.org/resources/llod/`
[7] `http://sourceforge.net/projects/iso-graf/`

explicit edge labels in the Salt representation for ordered constiuents: in GrAF, directed edges from one to several other nodes by default represent sets of ordered constituents and need not be explicitly labeled as such, whereas in Salt, the role of all edges must be specified explicitly. Explicit labels in ANNIS are required in order to generate the appropriate visualizations automatically (e.g. trees for syntactic hierarchies and arc diagrams for syntactic dependencies).

Finally, the code was structured as a plug-in for Pepper and parameterized to make it usable for GrAF-formatted corpora other than MASC. It will be included in the next SaltNPepper release. The code is currently available from our software repository[8].

5 MASC in ANNIS: Examples

The ANNIS Query Language (AQL) allows users to search for specific token values and annotations as well as relationships between them, even across annotation level boundaries.[9] Token values are represented as text between quotes (e.g. `"men"`), while annotations are specified as attribute-value pairs (e.g. `pos="NN"`, a part-of-speech attribute with the value NN). A query for an annotation will return all elements with that annotation. Where necessary, namespaces[10] can be added to any element to disambiguate, e.g., `ptb:cat="NP"` signifies all annotation attribute-value pairs (attribute: `cat`, value: NP) that are in the `ptb` (Penn Treebank) namespace.

Relations among elements are specified by back-referencing incremental variable numbers, e.g. #1, #2 etc. Linguistically motivated operators bind the elements together; e.g. `#1 > #2` means that the first element dominates the second in a tree. Operators can express overlap and adjacency between annotation spans, as well as recursive hierarchical relations that hold between nodes (such as elements in a syntactic tree).

The following examples show AQL queries that combine annotations from different layers:

1. A VP that dominates a PP which contains a named person at its right border:

```
cat="VP" & cat="PP" & NER="person" &
#1>#2 & #2_r_#3
```

2. a VP of passive form in past tense that includes a mention of a FrameNet frame element:

```
cat="VP" & voice="passive" &
tense="SimPas" & FE="Event" & #1_i_#2
& #1_i_#3 & #1_i_#4
```

Figure 2 shows the results of a search for an NP that includes both a named entity of the type *country* and a FrameNet frame element of the type *Food*:

```
cat="NP" & anc:type="country" &
FE="Food" & #1 _i_ #2 & #1 _i_ #3
```

6 Summary and Outlook

We explained the mapping of the MASC multilayer corpus to the ANNIS database by interpreting the GrAF format via the Pepper framework. Both MASC and ANNIS are freely available; a portion of MASC will also be added to the online demo version of ANNIS. We are also making the Pepper converter module for GrAF available.

Version 3 of ANNIS is currently under development[11]. Besides a new front-end and a REST-based API, it offers improved tokenization support (annotation on the level of subtokens; conflicting tokenizations) and handles dialogue corpora with simultaneous speakers as well as time-aligned audio/video data.

The ability to query across multiple annotation levels opens up significant new possibilities for exploring linguistically annotated data. Most commonly, language models are developed using information from at most one or two linguistic layers; ANNIS enables user to explore interdependencies that have been previously difficult to detect. By providing tools and data that are entirely free for use by the community, the ANNIS and MASC efforts contribute to the growing trend toward transparent sharing and openness of linguistic data and tools.

[8] https://korpling.german.hu-berlin.de/svn/saltnpepper/PepperModules/GrAFModules/

[9] Note that ANNIS does not allow searching for arbitrary strings from the primary data, but only for pre-identified segments such as tokens, named entities, etc.

[10] A namespace groups one or more types of annotation into a logical unit, e.g all annotations produced by a specific tool or project.

[11] Early development releases can be found at http://www.sfb632.uni-potsdam.de/annis/annis3.html

Acknowledgments

MASC and GrAF development was supported by US NSF award CRI-0708952. The work of A.N. and M.S. was supported by Deutsche Forschungsgemeinschaft as part of the Collaborative Research Center "Information Structure" (SFB 632) at Univ. Potsdam and HU Berlin.

References

Valerio Basile, Johan Bos, Kilian Evang, and Noortje Venhuizen. 2012. Developing a large semantically annotated corpus. In *Proceedings of the Eight International Conference on Language Resources and Evaluation (LREC 2012)*, pages 3196–3200, Istanbul, Turkey.

Christian Chiarcos, Stefanie Dipper, Michael Götze, Ulf Leser, Anke Lüdeling, Julia Ritz, and Manfred Stede. 2008. A flexible framework for integrating annotations from different tools and tag sets. *Traitement Automatique des Langues (TAL)*, 49(2).

Nancy Ide and Keith Suderman. 2007. GrAF: A graph-based format for linguistic annotations. In *Proceedings of the First Linguistic Annotation Workshop*, pages 1–8, Prague.

Nancy Ide and Keith Suderman. In press. The Linguistic Annotation Framework: A Standard for Annotation Interchange and Merging. *Language Resources and Evaluation*.

Nancy Ide, Collin Baker, Christiane Fellbaum, and Rebecca Passonneau. 2010. The Manually Annotated Sub-Corpus : A community resource for and by the people. In *Proceedings of the The 48th Annual Meeting of the Association for Computational Linguistics*, Uppsala, Sweden.

ISO 24612. 2012. *Language Resource Management – Linguistic Annotation Framework*. International Standards Organization, Geneva, Switzerland.

Sameer S. Pradhan, Eduard Hovy, Mitch Marcus, Martha Palmer, Lance Ramshaw, and Ralph Weischedel. 2007. OntoNotes: A unified relational semantic representation. In *ICSC '07: Proceedings of the International Conference on Semantic Computing*, pages 517–526, Washington, DC, USA. IEEE Computer Society.

Amir Zeldes, Julia Ritz, Anke Lüdeling, and Christian Chiarcos. 2009. ANNIS: A search tool for multi-layer annotated corpora. In *Proceedings of Corpus Linguistics 2009*.

Florian Zipser and Laurent Romary. 2010. A model oriented approach to the mapping of annotation formats using standards. In *Proceedings of the Workshop on Language Resource and Language Technology Standards, LREC 2010*, pages 7–18, Malta.

Florian Zipser, Amir Zeldes, Julia Ritz, Laurent Romary, and Ulf Leser. 2011. Pepper: Handling a multiverse of formats. In *33. Jahrestagung der Deutschen Gesellschaft für Sprachwissenschaft*, Göttingen.

Generic noun phrases and annotation of coreference and bridging relations in the Prague Dependency Treebank

Anna Nedoluzhko
Faculty of Mathematics and Physics, Charles University in Prague
nedoluzko@ufal.mff.cuni.cz

Abstract

This paper discusses the problem of annotating coreference relations with generic expressions in a large scale corpus. We present and analyze some existing theories of genericity, compare them to the approaches to generics that are used in the state-of-the-art coreference annotation guidelines and discuss how coreference of generic expressions is processed in the manual annotation of the Prague Dependency Treebank. After analyzing some typical problematic issues we propose some partial solutions that can be used to enhance the quality and consistency of the annotation.

1 Introduction

One of the most problematic issues of annotating coreference in large scale corpora is processing coreference of generic expressions. The decision to annotate generic noun phrases produces a significant decrease of inter-annotator agreement. On the other hand, neglecting coreference relations between generic expressions causes a significant loss of information on the text coherence that is primordially the reason for annotating coreference relations at all. It also causes the inconsistency of annotation guidelines: due to relatively vague definition of genericity, it is almost impossible to exclude *all* coreference relations between generics from the annotation.

In the Prague Dependency Treebank (henceforth PDT), we tried to distinguish coreference relations between nominal expressions with specific and generic reading. Comparing the inter-annotator agreement for these groups shows that the agreement for noun coreference with specific reading is significantly higher than the agreement for the coreference of generic NPs (F1-measure 0.705 for specific NPs and 0.492 for generics[1]). Moreover, the manual analysis of the cases of disagreement of specific NPs coreference demonstrates that most cases of disagreement are those where NPs in question may be interpreted generically.

Having formulated a set of criteria which help identifying generic expressions, there still remains a wide range of typical examples which can have generic interpretation, though not necessarily. In this paper, we try to delimit the set of generic NPs presenting the overview of some existing theories of genericity (Sections 2 and 3.1) and compare them to the stand-of-the-art coreference annotation guidelines (Section 3.2). Then we present our approach to annotating coreference with generic noun phrases in PDT where we apply the presented theories to coreference and bridging relations annotation (Section 4). We analyze typical problematic issues (Section 5) and discuss some possible solutions (Section 6).

2 What are generics and can they corefer?

Generic reference is a term commonly used in linguistic semantics to describe noun-phrase reference to kinds of things (Carlson 2005). In different languages, generic reference may be expressed by noun phrases with definite and indefinite articles and with determinerless expressions quite generally. In languages without articles, the determinerless form is typically used (Carlson 2005, Hlavsa 1975; Padučeva 1985, etc.).

[1] F1-measure for generics is closer to inter-annotator agreement for bridging relations (0.460 for all annotated data).

Compare some typical examples for generic noun reference (different uses of *a/the dog(s)*) in English, German and Czech:

English: *Dogs bark – The dog has evolved from the Jackal – A dog knows when it is time for his walk*[2].

German: *Hunde beißen. Der Hund stammt vom Schakal ab. Ein Hund weiß// Hunde wissen, wenn es Zeit für seinen Spaziergang ist.*

Czech (non-article language): *Psi štěkají. – Pes je šelma.*

The examples above demonstrate that generic noun phrases cannot be recognized by their forms (this fact was pointed out in Lyons 1999, Carlson 2005, etc.). While in English the plural form of the definite can only marginally have generic reference, in German, which is closely related to English, the plural definite may imply generic reference quite easily. In Romance languages, the form of bare plural with generics is prohibited (Delfitto 2006) and even in languages without articles, generics with determiners are not so rare (see e.g. common examples with Czech in Nedoluzhko 2003)[3]. This leads to a suggestion that genericity is not a primitive category of semantic or syntactic description.

Theoretical studies like Carlson (1980) appeal to typical examples with noun phrases referring to specific objects. A discussion on his approach (Paducheva 1985, Delfitto 2006, Lyons 1999) concerns theoretical issues that are analyzed in similar typical cases.

When analyzing real corpus examples we encounter a lot of cases indicating that not all generic expressions are generic in the same way. Problems with processing generic expressions arise also from the lack of a universally accepted theory of genericity which would be applicable to the real texts analysis.

Generic reading is possible not only with referring nouns, but also with mass nouns, group nouns, abstract nouns, quantifiers and deverbatives. Look at the example (1). Everyone should probably agree that *the homeless* is a generic expression, but is the same true about *the homeless population*?

(1) *Your comments implied we had discovered that the principal cause of homelessness is to be found in the large numbers of mentally ill and substance-abusing people in the homeless population. [...] The study shows that nearly 40% of the homeless population is made up of women and children and that only 25% of the homeless exhibits some combination of drug, alcohol and mental problems*[4].

Another relevant question is if generic expressions referring to the same kind can be considered coreferent in the same sense as noun phrases with a specific reading. According to Carlson's (1980) and Lyons' (1999) claim, generics refer to classes in the similar way as proper names refer to unique entities. In this sense, coreference of generic expressions appears to be obvious. On the other hand, Carlson's observations seem to be quite language-specific. Arguing against a quantificational analysis of bare plurals with generic meaning, he claims that the sentence *Miles wants to meet policemen* cannot be assigned a reading according to which "there are certain policemen that Miles wants to meet," whereas this interpretation is naturally available in the case of *Miles wants to meet some policemen*. This is not the case of languages without articles where plural forms can be assigned any reading regardless of the use of the quantifier[5]. Generally, we suppose that quantificational (or predicative) interpretation of generic expressions in different languages is not impossible (see for example almost obligatory predicative reading of *Czech exporters in* (7)). However, this fact does not necessarily exclude the coreference relation between them. Eventually, the discourse deixis as reference to events is also often considered and annotated as coreference.

3 Recent research on generics

We believe that it would not be a strong exaggeration to claim that theoretical and computational linguistics have different goals as concerns their approach to genericity. The challenge of linguistic research is to find out more about the essence of genericity. The aim of annotating is to

[2] However, Carlson – Pelletier (1995) do not consider *a dog* in the last sentence to be generic, because it cannot be combined with kind-level predicates.

[3] It may be possible to determine generics in sentences with so-called "kind-level predicates" (Carlson 2005), they interact with aspectual distinctions in verbs (Lyons 1999) etc, but these approaches are not applicable to real-text data.

[4] The example comes from the Prague English Dependency Treebank (PEDT, Hajič et al. 2009)

[5] Actually, even in English not all bare plurals should necessarily refer to kinds. In modern journalistic texts, the tendency to omit articles appears to be quite strong.

make the group of generics as clear as possible, in order to reach higher agreement and better results of automatic processing.

It is also generally known that the features of an annotation must be adapted to the task it is designed for. However, the existing large-scale annotated corpora (especially those prepared on university basis) are often meant to be multipurpose. They serve both as train data for (different!) automatic tasks and as a rich manually annotated material for linguistic research.

In what follows, we complete the theoretical overview (started in section 2), present the annotation approach and look for the common points.

3.1 Linguistic research

There is a rich variety of linguistic approaches to genericity. Even as concerns the terminology with generics, it is quite inconsistent and cannot be relied on with much certainty. According to different researchers, generic NPs are considered to be either referring to classes (Carlson – Pelletier 1995, Mendoza 2004) or non-referring (rather predicating) classifications over kinds (Paducheva 1985), beeing able to have specific and non-specific interpretation (Mendoza 2004, Smelev 1996) and divided from non-specific NPs as a separate group (Carlson – Pelletier 2005, Paducheva 1985).

Carlson (1980) represents the most influential approach to genericity that has been elaborated in the framework of formal semantics and generative grammar. Calson's hypothesis is that generics are kind-referring expressions, roughly names for kinds, as opposed to individual-referring expressions that refer to individuals or groups of individuals. In his approach, there is a difference between generic reference and individual non-specific reference, i.e. reference to an open set of individual objects. For example, NP *lions that have toothaches* is not generic, its reference is individual (i.e. non-generic) and non-specific, which can be demonstrated by the fact that it cannot be substituted by the definite NP *the lion that has toothache* (such NP can have only individual reading). However, the problem with this criterion is that it is clearly language-specific (it cannot be applied at all to Czech, for instance).

3.2 Annotation coreference with generic expression

Let's now have a look on how generic NPs are processed in annotation projects with anaphoric and coreference annotation.

In some projects, e.g. ARRAU and other corpora based on the MATE coreference annotation scheme (Poesio 2004), genericity is marked as a part of lexico-semantical information of the noun (an attribute `generic-yes/no/undersp` is applied to each noun). This information is contemplated in the annotation of identical coreference. Identical coreference for generics is also annotated in AnCora (Recasens 2010) and PDT (Nedoluzhko 2011).

In other projects, annotation of coreference with generic NPs may be excluded from annotation schemes that are geared towards a reliable annotation of large text quantities. For example, generics are not annotated for coreference in Ontonotes (Pradhan et al. 2007), TüBA-DZ (Hinrichs et al. 2004) and PoCoS (Krasavina-Chiarchos 2007).

However, even if an annotation scheme explicitly says that coreference of generic NPs is not annotated, there are some borderline cases where coreference can still be annotated quite systematically. So, TüBA annotates coreference with the nominal expression if it appears repeatedly in the text with the same interpretation. In Ontonotes, the explicit anaphora with *it* in the anaphoric position is commonly annotated for coreference:

> (2) *Still, <u>any change in East Germany</u> has enormous implications, for both East and West. <u>It</u> raises the long-cherished hopes of many Germans for reunification*[6].

Furthermore, systematic exclusion of generic expressions from the annotation will force the coders not to mark the cases like (3) and (4)[7]. From the point of view of applied tasks and automatic coreference resolvers it will lead to the loss of relevant information and to an essential complification of automatic tools.

> (3) *The sterilizing gene is expressed just before the pollen is about to develop and it deactivates the anthers of every flower in <u>the plant</u>. Mr. Leemans said this genetic manipulation doesn't hurt the growth <u>of that plant</u>.*

> (4) *A workshop needs to be planned carefully. Otherwise <u>it</u> may turn in a disaster.*

As far as we know, there are no significant projects for annotating coreference separately for

[6] This example is taken from PEDT, to which the Ontonotes coreference was applied.

[7] Examples come from PEDT.

generic, unspecific non-generic and specific expressions.

4 Coreference annotation in Prague Dependency Treebank

In this section we describe how generic expressions (or more precisely, what we decided to consider generic expressions) are annotated in the Prague Dependency Treebank.

Annotation of coreference and discourse relations is a project related to the Prague Dependency Treebank 2.5 (PDT; Bejček et al. 2011). It represents a new manually annotated layer of language description, above the existing layers of the PDT (morphology, analytic syntax and tectogrammatics) and it captures linguistic phenomena from the perspective of discourse structure and coherence. This special layer of the treebank consists of annotation of nominal coreference and bridging relations (Nedoluzhko et al. 2009), discourse connectives, discourse units linked by them and semantic relations between these units (Mladová 2011).

Considering the fact that Czech has no definite article (hence no formal possibility to exclude non-anaphoric coreference), our annotation is aimed at coreference relations regardless to their anaphoricity.

Coreference relations are marked for noun phrases with specific and generic reference separately – coreference of specific noun phrases – type SPEC, coreference of generic noun phrases – type GEN[8]. Bridging relations, which mark some semantic relations between non-coreferential entities, are also annotated in PDT. The following types of bridging relations are distinguished: PART-OF (e.g. *room - ceiling*), SUBSET (*students - some students*) and FUNCT (*state - president*) traditional relations, CONTRAST for coherence relevant discourse opposites (*this year - last year*), ANAF for explicitly anaphoric relations without coreference or one of the semantic relations mentioned above (*rainbow - that word*) and the further underspecified group REST[9].

As seen from the point of view of the annotated groups, generic NPs are explicitly marked only with the second element of the coreference relation. However, this distinction remains unregistered by bridging relations. Moreover, it appears to be possible (and even not so uncommon) that a coreference relation was annotated between a generic and a non-generic noun phrase. These cases are interpreted as either (linguistically) ambiguous or insufficiently classified by the guidelines. For example, in (5), the specific noun phrase *tento národ* (*=this nation*) is coreferent with generic plural *Romy* (*=the Gipsies*):

> (5) *Nic z toho se však nevyrovná míře neštěstí, které Romy postihlo v letech druhé světové války. Spolu se Židy byli označeni za méněcennou rasu a stali se objektem patologických fašistických opatření, jejichž cílem byla úplná genocida tohoto národa.* (= *Nothing of this, however, compares to the misfortune that befell the Gipsies during the Second World War. Together with the Jews, they were called an inferior race and became the object of pathological fascist measures, their purpose being the complete genocide of the nation.*)

Annotation rules for generics in PDT are described in detail in sections 4.1-4.3.

4.1 Type coreference of generic NPs

Coreference relations between the same types are annotated as coreference of generic NPs (attribute `coref_text, type GEN`). Cf. (6) where antecedent generic *drug* is pronominalized in the anaphoric position:

> (6) *<u>Droga</u> je tedy tak účinná, že ten, kdo <u>ji</u> užívá, se snadno dostane do „pohody" kouřením nebo šňupáním.* (= *<u>The drug</u> is so effective that the person who takes <u>it</u> can easily achieve the state of "coolness" by smoking or snorting.*)

The "generic coreference" is more frequent for plural forms (7):

> (7) *Nová striktní omezení vlády SR proti <u>českým exportérům</u>. Již několik dnů je všeobecně známo, že ochranářská opatření slovenské vlády proti <u>českým exportérům</u> se dotýkají zejména oblasti obchodu s potravinami a zemědělskými produkty.* (= *The new Slovak government's strict restrictions on <u>Czech exporters</u>. It's commonly known for several days that protective measures of Slovakia's government against <u>Czech exporters</u> apply mostly to the trade of food and agricultural products.*)

[8] The reason for this decision is the lack of semantic information assigned to nouns themselves, as it is done e.g. for Gnome in MATE sceme (Poesio 2004).

[9] For detailed classification of identity coreference and bridging relations used in PDT, see e.g. Nedoluzhko et al. 2011.

Textual coreference of type GEN is also annotated for the majority of abstract nouns (see more detail in Section 5.5), cf. (8):

(8) *Tímto faktorem je podnikatel-inovátor, který se snaží o zisk, a proto logicky nemůže existovat ve stavu statiky, která nezná ani zisk, ani ztrátu.* (= *This factor is the enterpreneur-innovator, who is trying to gain profit, and hence, logically, cannot exist in a static state, where there is no profit or loss.*)

4.2. Classes and subclasses

The relation "category – sub-category" is marked as a bridging relation of the SUBSET type. Cf. (9).

(9) *I když konzervativní Anglie jeho čin odsoudila, ... Británie se pro žvýkačku stala bránou do Evropy. Ještě jeden milník si zaslouží zmínku – zrod bublinové žvýkačky* (= *Although conservative England did not accept it, ... for the gum, Britain has become the gateway to Europe. Another milestone is worth mentioning, that is the birth of a bubble gum.*)

Annotating the SUBSET relation with generic expressions appears to be quite a serious problem. This relation has a different meaning compared to the SUBSET relation of noun phrases with specific reading. However, such relations may be quite relevant for cohesion.

4.3 The relation "type – entity"

If a specific mention is used in the text after a generic mention (or the contrary), the relation between them is annotated as a bridging relation of the SUBSET type. Cf. (10):

(10) *Nový VW Golf je vybaven motorem o síle... Dostali jsme možnost se novým golfem projet.* (= *The new VW Golf is equipped with an engine power ... We had an opportunity to ride a new golf.*)

Similar, but not the same is the relation between a set of specific objects and a non-specific element in (11):

(11) *[volontéři] Absolvovali školení v první pomoci pro člověka v nouzi . [...]Když dítě zavolá, dostane buď radu hned, nebo si s ním volontér domluví další hovor.* (=*The volunteers have been trained in first aid for people in need. [...] When a child calls, it will get get an advice immediately, or a volunteer will arrange a meeting with him.*)

5 Problem cases with generics in PDT

Although the cases presented in sections 4.1-4.3 do not look very reliable, they are still considered to be relatively clear as compared to what follows in 5.1 -5.6. The decisions made in annotation guidelines for these cases are often case-sensitive, might be in some cases contra-intuitive, and they result in high inter-annotator disagreement.

5.1 Non-generic non-specific NPs

In case of non-generic non-specific noun phrases, when antecedent and anaphoric noun phrases have the same t-lemmas and the same scope, but anaphoric NP does not have a determiner, coreference of type GEN is annotated. Although this kind of relation does not contribute much to text coherence, we still tend to mark this relation, also for the reason that the border between what should be annotated and what should not is not always easy to determine.

(12) *Když si dítě bude přát, aby se o jeho problému nikdo z rodiny nebo školy nedozvěděl, musíme to respektovat, vysvětluje Jana Drtilová . [...] Většinou se stává, že dítě ani nechce, aby se rodina dozvěděla, že se nám ozval. Linka by neměla rodinu nahrazovat, ale doplňovat.* (= *If a child desires that no one from the family or school would find out about his problems, we have to respect that, says Jana Drtilova. [...] It is usually the case that the child does not even want for the family to know that he contacted us. The hotline should not replace the family, but to supplement it.*)

There are also cases of non-specific non-generic NPs the referential value of which is provided by syntactic factors. These are so-called contexts with removed assertiveness, e.g. sentences with modal verbs (*can, want, need*), imperative sentences, future tense, questions, negations, disjunctions, irreality, uncertainty and so on. Non-specific NPs are often used with performative verbs, propositional attitudes (*want, think, consider*) and some constructions as e.g. in English *such as*, in Czech *jde o* (=lit. *It is about*), *takový X* (=*such* X), etc. These contexts can give a non-specific reading to an expression, even if it actually has a specific meaning. Cf (13), where

(13) *Ale jedna věc je jistá - palác bude stavebně předáván letos na podzim. [...] Provoz tak obrovské budovy přijde ročně na desítky milionů korun.* (=lit. *But one thing is certain – the reconstruction of the palace will be finished this fall.* [...] *It will cost tens of millions crowns, to run such a huge building.*)

5.2 Borderline cases between coreference of specific and generic NPs

In some cases, it is hard to decide if a noun phrase has a specific or a generic reading. Mostly, both interpretations are possible. There are no firm rules for an unambiguous assignment of the types in those cases; the type is chosen on the basis of the available context and the annotator's consideration. Uncertainty of the choice between generic and specific reference is common with some typical groups of noun phrases, first of all with those that have or may have modifications. Cf. *pořad* (=*TV show*) in (14) that may have a temporal modification. The obligatoriness of this modification influences the annotator's decision if (s)he should read it as a generic or a specific NP. For this case, the specific reading was chosen.

(14) *K tématu pořadu TV NOVA TABU "Zrak za bílou hůl" byl přizván ke konzultaci Oldřich Čálek. Kateřina Hamrová, dramaturgyně pořadu, TV NOVA.* (= *To consult the topic of the TV NOVA show TABU "Vision for a white cane", Ulrich Čálek was invited. Catherine Hamrová, the dramatist of the show, TV NOVA*)

Also, for example for (15), *the detergent Toto* can be understood as a specific (a name for a detergent brand) or generic (the type of the detergent of such brand). Also in this case, the specific reference is preferred in PDT:

(15) *U detergentu Toto jsme například řešili problém s udržením stálé kvality, protože jednotlivé partie byly nevyvážené. Investovali jsme dva miliony korun do nákupu pásových vah, zpřesnili dávkování a jakost pracího prášku stabilizovali.* (=*For example, with the Toto detergent we face problems with maintaining consistent quality... We invested two million crowns... and stabilized the quality of the detergent.*)

5.3 Borderline cases between coreference of generic NPs and zero relation

There is also a borderline between the cases of coreference of the generic NPs and the cases where it makes no sense to mark a coreferential relation. We do not annotate "generic coreference" if noun phrases have different scope (i.e. they refer to different sets of objects), e.g. *ženy* (= *women*) – *ženy v 19. století* (= *women in 19th century*). In this case, the bridging relation of the type SUBSET is annotated instead. In other problematic cases, annotators usually apply to their intuition and the text coherence. If both say no, no coreference is annotated.

5.4 Coreference with measure NPs and other NPs with a 'container' meaning

In PDT, a special group of numerals and nouns with a 'container' meaning is singled out. They have the modification in their valency frames denoting the content (people, things, substance etc.) of a container expressed by the governing noun. These 'container' expressions are e.g. nouns and numerals denoting groups, number or amount, sets, collections, portions, etc. (*skupina lidí* (=*group of people*), *počet akcií* (=*number of stocks*), *stádo krav* (=*herd of cows*), *dostatek financí* (=*abundance of finance*), *milióny židů* (=*millions of Jews*), *sklenice piva* (=*glass of beer*), *deset procent obyvatel* (=*ten percent of population*)).

The PDT convention on annotating coreference by NPs with a 'container' meaning follows the maximum-scope rule, i.e., if possible, the governing ('container') node is linked by a coreference link (16). The modifications of containers may be coreferential themselves independently of the 'containers' (17)

(16) *Absolutní většina lidí závislých na heroinu je příliš mladá na to, aby si #PersPron pamatovala rozklad a zesláblost generace sedmdesátých let, takže odvrácenou stránku „fantastického" života si #PersPron mnohdy vůbec neuvědomí.* (=*Absolute majority of people addicted to heroin is too young to remember the decomposition and enfeeblement of the generation of seventies, so they* (lit. '*she*' referring to '*majority*') *do not realize the downside of the "fantastic" life.*)

(17) *V běžném vzorku sedmdesátých let byla pouze 3–4 procenta čisté suroviny. b. Nyní jsou k dostání balíčky obsahující až 80 procent čistého heroinu.* (=*In an average sam-*

ple from the seventies, there were only 3-4 percent of pure raw material. Currently, one can get packages containing up to 80 percent of pure heroin.)

Coreference of 'containers' can be problematic from the point of view of their generic or specific interpretation. Nouns referring to groups may refer generically to the elements belonging to that group or specifically to the group itself. In the following example, there has been a disagreement between annotators concerning the generic/specific reading of the NP *skupina* (=*group*). We believe that this kind of disagreement could be solved by separating the group of non-specific non-generic references.

(18) *Podle výzkumů ve vyspělých zemích se ukazuje, že lidí, kteří potřebují speciální služby, je daleko víc. U nás by tuto skupinu tvořilo asi tak 70000 osob. Jsou to hlavně starší lidé se zbytky zraku a slabozrací. Tato skupina stojí úplně mimo a má tak život ještě více ztížený, protože mnozí o těchto službách ani nevědí.* (=*According to the research in the developed countries, there are many more people who need special services. In our country, the group of such people would count about 70,000 individuals. They are mainly older people sighted and visually impaired. This group is completely off, their life being even more difficult, because they don't even know about many of these services.*)

More complicated are the cases where coreference chains for 'containers' and their modifications intersect. In (19), a coreference link for *the strikers* in b. should lead to *three and a half thousand workers* but in c., the number of strikers changes, so the container modification *workers* should be marked as coreferent with *the strikers* in b. For such cases, coreference of type GEN is used in PDT.

(19) a. *Tři a půl tisíce dělníků vyhlásili stávku.* b. *Stávkující žádají zvýšení platů o šest procent.* c. *Do 8. března se počet stávkujících může zdvojnásobit.* (a. *Three and a half thousand workers went on strike.* b. *The strikers demand six percent of salary increase.* c. *By 8 March, the number of strikers may double.*)

However, in this case, the problem is rather specific. Here, *počet stávkujících* (=*the number of strikers*) does not actually refer to the strikers (as it would e.g. in *tisíc stávkujících* (=*thousand strikers*) but to the number itself and that is the reason for coreference annotation to *strikers*. In such cases, *the number* does not serve as a 'container' in proper sense.

5.5 Coreference with abstract nouns

Processing coreference of abstract nouns seems to be in some respects close to that of generics. Abstract nouns do not refer to a type, but to a notion. However, this notion is unique in the same way as type is unique to the generic expression which refers to it. Moreover, abstract nouns are close to predicative and quantificational interpretation and there are no formal rules distinguishing them from concrete NPs and deverbatives. They also result in high ambiguity when annotated for coreference.

There have been several changes in the guidelines for the annotation of coreference and bridging relations with abstract nouns. Finally, we decided to distinguish between "specific" and "generic" abstracts. If subjects to annotation have complements with specific reference, or they have unambiguously specific reference themselves, coreference between them is annotated as textual coreference, type SPEC (20). In case of even a little doubt, we annotate textual coreference, type GEN (8).

(20) *Ve specifických podmínkách české ekonomiky růst nezaměstnanosti v letech 1991–1993 značně zaostal za poklesem HDP. [...] Nejméně dvouprocentní růst české ekonomiky již letos.* (=*In the specific conditions of the Czech economy the growth of unemployment... This year at least a two percent growth of the Czech economy.*)

5.6 Coreference with verbal nouns

With verbal nouns, both specifying and generic reference are possible as well. Textual coreference with verbal nouns is annotated according to the following strategy:

- If both verbal nouns are specific, they refer to a specific situation and their possible arguments are coreferential, the relation between them is annotated as textual coreference, type SPEC, cf. (21);
- If both verbal nouns are generic, or rather if their arguments are generic, the relation between them is annotated as textual coreference, type GEN. Cf. (22);
- If both verbal nouns are specific, but their arguments are not coreferential, coreferen-

tial relation between them is not annotated.;

- If one verbal noun is specific and the other is generic, coreferential relation between them is not annotated.

(21) *Vedení Pojišťovny Investiční a Poštovní banky nás upozornilo, že jejich pojišťovna nebyla zařazena mezi ty, které umožňují úrazové připojištění, ač tuto službu poskytují. Omlouváme se za toto nedopatření, dotyčná redaktorka byla pokutována.* (=*The Insurance Investment and the Post Bank management has notified us that their insurance company was not included among those that allow casualty insurance, although it provides this service. We apologize for this oversight, the editor who made the mistake was fined.*)

(22) *Rychlé, avšak i bezpečné vypořádání. Rychlost vypořádání burzovních obchodů v čase odpovídá podle Jiřího Béra potřebám.* (= *Fast, yet safe transaction. According to Jiřího Bér's opinion, the speed of transaction corresponds to the needs.*)

However, such instructions are quite ambiguous themselves, because, firstly, it is not always clear, what a specific verbal noun means and, secondly and most importantly, verbal nouns may have more than one argument, one of them being generic and other – specific (Pergler 2010). Moreover, deverbatives themselves may refer to specific events that has already happened (thus tending to type SPEC if coreferent) or to hypothetic or typical ones (then, in case of coreference, marked as GEN).

6 Discussion

Processing coreference of generic expressions, even in manual annotation, raises a number of problems, both theoretical and the applied, like complification of coreference resolving. As we have seen, the problem of generics is very language-specific. Each resolving system trying to process coreference for generics will have to be oriented towards the specific linguistic description of the language in question. But even so, there are many possibilities of expressing generic expressions in every language, thus making the formal problem of extracting generics even in one separate language extremely difficult.

Generic expressions are analyzed relatively in more detail for English (Carlson 1980, Carlson - Pelletier 1995). However, this research relies heavily on language forms, it is not based on a large-scale corpus and it seems to be too theoretical to be easily adapted to a large corpus (manual or automatic) processing. On the other hand, Carlson's classification of the reference reading of nouns could be used in practice for the distinction between generic and non-specific non-generic NPs. Using our experience, we believe that it would make the annotation more consistent: there would be less ambiguity between specific and generic readings. However, being helpful in resolving the cases from section 5.1, this decision would not resolve the majority of the remaining problematic cases. There still remain borderline cases with specific noun expressions with possible valency frames (see 5.2), coreference with abstract and verbal nouns and so on. Separating the group of NPs with non-specific reading, the coders should concentrate on quite specific semantic issues when annotating. Moreover, annotating more groups of nouns is always a costly and time-consuming task.

From the theoretical point of view, one could imagine a scale: from noun expressions with concrete meaning and specific reading (say named entities) up to abstract nouns and deverbatives with generic reading. However, such an approach will not help to process generic NPs in large-scale corpora.

7 Conclusion

In this paper, we discussed the problem of annotating coreference with generic expressions. Considering theoretical approaches has revealed that they tend to be very language specific. State-of-the-art in annotating coreference relations for generic NPs needs unification but this is complicated, as the formal representation of genericity differs dramatically from language to language and can be hardly unified. We have presented an approach to annotation of generic expressions in PDT and analyzed some typical problematic examples. We consider this issue to be far from being solved. Both, theoretical research and large data approaches should be further investigated.

Acknowledgments

We gratefully acknowledge support from the Grant Agency of the Czech Republic (grants P406/12/0658 and P406/2010/0875).

References

Eduard Bejček, Jan Hajič, Jarmila Panevová, Jan Popelka, Lenka Smejkalová, Pavel Straňák, Magda Ševčíková, Jan Štěpánek, Josef Toman and Zdeněk Žabokrtský. 2011. *Prague Dependency Treebank 2.5.* Data/software, Charles University in Prague, MFF, ÚFAL, Praha, Czech Republic (http://ufal.mff.cuni.cz/pdt2.5/).

Greg Carlson. 1980. *Reference to kinds in English.* New York: Garland.

Greg Carlson. 2005. Generic Reference. In *The Encyclopedia of Language and Linguistics, 2nd Ed. Elsevier.*

Greg Carlson and F.J. Pelletier (eds.). 1995. *The Generic Book.* Chicago: University of Chicago Press.

Denis Delfitto. 2006. Bare plurals. In Martin Everaert and Henk van Riemsdijk (eds.) *The Blackwell Companion to Syntax.* Blackwell Publishing, pp. 214-259.

Erhard Hinrichs, Sandra Kübler, Karin Naumann, Heike Telljohann, Julia Trushkina und Heike Zinsmeister. 2004. Recent Developments in Linguistic Annotations of the TüBa–D/Z Treebank. In *Proceedings of the third workshop on treebanks and linguistic theories (TLT 2004).* Tübingen.

Jan Hajič, Silvie Cinková, Kristýna Čermáková, Lucie Mladová, Anja Nedolužko, Petr Pajas, Jiří Semecký, Jana Šindlerová, Josef Toman, Kristýna Tomšů, Matěj Korvas, Magdaléna Rysová, Kateřina Veselovská, Zdeněk Žabokrtský. 2009. *Prague English Dependency Treebank 1.0.* Institute of Formal and Applied Linguistics. Charles University in Prague.

Zdeněk Hlavsa. 1975. *Denotace objektu a její prostředky v současné češtině.* (*Object denotation and its means in current Czech*). Prague, Czech Republic.

Olga Krasavina and Christian Chiarcos. 2007. PoCoS – Potsdam Coreference Scheme. In *Proceedings of ACL 2007*, Prague, Czech Republic.

Christopher Lyons. 1999. *Definiteness.* Cambridge: Cambridge University Press.

Lucie Mladová. 2011. Annotating Discourse in Prague Dependency Treebank. In *Workshop of Annotation of Discourse Relations in Large Corpora at the conference Corpus Linguistics 2011 (CL 2011).* Birmingham, Great Britain, July 2011.

Anna Nedoluzhko, Jiří Mírovský, Radek Ocelák, Jiří Pergler. 2009. Extended Coreferential Relations and Bridging Anaphora in the Prague Dependency Treebank. In *Proceedings of the 7th Discourse Anaphora and Anaphor Resolution Colloquium (DAARC 2009).* Goa, India, 2009, pp. 1–16.

Anna Nedoluzhko. 2003. Ukazovací zájmeno "ten" a generické jmenné fráze v češtině. In *IV. mezinárodní setkání mladých lingvistů Olomouc 2003: Jazyky v kontaktu, jazyky v konfliktu.* Olomouc: Univerzita Palackého v Olomouci, pp. 85 – 96.

Anna Nedoluzhko. 2011. *Rozšířená textová koreference a asociační anafora. Koncepce anotace českých dat v Pražském závislostním korpusu.* Prague, ÚFAL.

Elena V. Paducheva. 1985. *Vyskazyvanie i ego sootnesennost s dejstviteľnosťju.* Moskva.

Jiří Pergler. 2010. *Koreferenční řetězce s nespecifickou a generickou referencí v češtině (Coreferential chains with non-specific and generic reference in Czech).* Unpublished bachelor thesis. Prague.

Massimo Poesio. 2004. The MATE/GNOME Proposals for Anaphoric Annotation, Revisited. In *Proceedings of SIGDIAL.*

Sameer S. Pradhan, Eduard Hovy, Mitch Marcus, Martha Palmer, Lance Ramshaw, and Ralph Weischedel. 2007. Ontonotes: A unified relational semantic representation. In *Proceedings of the International Conference on Se-mantic Computing (ICSC-07).* Washington, DC, pp. 517–526.

Marta Recasens and Antònia Martí. 2010. AnCora-CO: Coreferentially annotated corpora for Spanish and Catalan. In *Language Resources and Evaluation.*

Uriel Weinreich. 1966. On the Semantic Structure of Language. In *Universals of Language*, 2nd ed. Cambridge, Mass.

Annotating Anaphoric Shell Nouns with their Antecedents

Varada Kolhatkar
Department of Computer Science
University of Toronto
varada@cs.toronto.edu

Heike Zinsmeister
Institut für Maschinelle Sprachverarbeitung
Universität Stuttgart
zinsmeis@ims.stuttgart-uni.de

Graeme Hirst
Department of Computer Science
University of Toronto
gh@cs.toronto.edu

Abstract

Anaphoric shell nouns such as *this issue* and *this fact* conceptually encapsulate complex pieces of information (Schmid, 2000). We examine the feasibility of annotating such anaphoric nouns using crowdsourcing. In particular, we present our methodology for reliably annotating antecedents of such anaphoric nouns and the challenges we faced in doing so. We also evaluated the quality of crowd annotation using experts. The results suggest that most of the crowd annotations were good enough to use as training data for resolving such anaphoric nouns.

1 Introduction

Anaphoric shell nouns (ASNs) such as *this fact*, *this possibility*, and *this issue* are common in all kinds of text. They are called *shell nouns* because they provide nominal conceptual shells for complex chunks of information representing abstract concepts such as *fact*, *proposition*, and *event* (Schmid, 2000). An example is shown in (1).

(1) Despite decades of education and widespread course offerings, **the survival rate for out-of-hospital cardiac arrest remains a dismal 6 percent or less worldwide**.

This fact prompted the American Heart Association last November to simplify the steps of CPR to make it easier for lay people to remember and to encourage even those who have not been formally trained to try it when needed.

Here, the ASN *this fact* encapsulates the clause marked in bold from the preceding paragraph.

ASNs play an important role in organizing a discourse. First, they are used metadiscursively to talk about the current discourse. In (1), the author *characterizes* the information presented in the context by referring to it as a *fact* — a thing that is indisputably the case. Second, they are used as cohesive devices in a discourse. In (1), for example, *this fact* on the one hand refers to the proposition marked in bold, and on the other, faces forward and serves as the starting point of the following paragraph. Finally, as Schmid (2000) points out, like conjunctions *so* and *however*, ASNs may function as topic boundary markers and topic change markers.

Despite their importance, ASNs have not received much attention in Computational Linguistics. Although there has been some effort to annotate certain anaphors with similar properties, i.e., demonstratives and the pronoun *it* (Byron, 2003; Artstein and Poesio, 2006), in contrast to ordinary nominal anaphora, there are not many annotated corpora available that could be used to study ASNs. Indeed, many questions of annotation of ASNs must still be answered. For example, the extent to which native speakers themselves agree on the resolution of such anaphors, i.e., on the precise antecedents, remains unclear.

An essential first step in this field of research is therefore to clearly establish the extent of inter-annotator agreement on antecedents of ASNs as a measure of feasibility of the task. In this paper, we describe our methodology for annotating ASNs using crowdsourcing, a cheap and fast way of obtaining annotation. We also describe how we evaluated the feasibility of the task and the quality of the annotation, and the challenges we faced in doing so, both with regard to the task itself and the crowdsourcing platform we use. The results suggest that most of the crowd-annotations were good enough to use as training data for ASN resolution.

2 Related work

There exist only few annotated corpora of anaphora with non-nominal antecedents (Dipper and Zinsmeister, 2011). The largest one of these, the ARRAU corpus (Poesio and Artstein, 2008), contains 455 anaphors pointing to non-nominal antecedents, but only a few instances are ASNs. Kolhatkar and Hirst (2012) annotated antecedents of the same type as we do, but restricted their efforts to the ASN *this issue*.[1] In addition, there are corpora annotated with event anaphora in which verbal instances are identified as proxies for non-nominal antecedents (Pradhan et al., 2007; Chen et al., 2011; Lee et al., 2012).

For the task of identifying non-nominal antecedents as free spans of text, there is no standard way of reporting inter-annotator agreement. Some studies report only observed percentage agreement with results in the range of about 0.40–0.55 (Vieira et al., 2002; Dipper and Zinsmeister, 2011). The studies differed with respect to number of annotators, types of anaphors, and language of the corpora. Artstein and Poesio (2006) discuss Krippendorff's alpha for chance-corrected agreement. They considered antecedent strings as bags of words and computed the degree of difference between them by different distance measures (e.g. Jaccard, Dice). The bag-of-words approach is rather optimistic in the sense that even two non-overlapping strings are very likely to share at least a few words. Kolhatkar and Hirst (2012) followed a different approach by using Krippendorff's unitizing alpha ($_u\alpha$) which considers the longest common subsequence of different antecedent options (Krippendorff, 2013). They reported high chance-corrected $_u\alpha$ of 0.86 for two annotators but in a very restricted domain.

There has been some prior effort to annotate anaphora and coreference using *Games with a Purpose* as a method of crowdsourcing (Chamberlain et al., 2009; Hladká et al., 2009). Another, less time-consuming approach of crowdsourcing is using platforms such as Amazon Mechanical Turk[2]. It has been shown that crowdsourced data can successfully be used as training data for NLP tasks (Hsueh et al., 2009).

[1]Another data set reported in the literature could have been relevant for us: Botley's (2006) corpus contained about 462 ASN instances signaled by shell nouns; but this data is no longer available (S. Botley, p.c.).

[2]`https://mturk.com/mturk/`

Class	Description	Examples
factual	states of affairs	***fact***, ***reason***
linguistic	linguistic acts	***question***, *report*
mental	thoughts and ideas	***issue***, ***decision***
modal	subjective judgements	***possibility***, *truth*
eventive	events	*act*, *reaction*
circumstantial	situations	*situation*, *way*

Table 1: Schmids categorization of shell nouns. The nouns in boldface are used in this research.

3 The Anaphoric Shell Noun Corpus

Our goal is to obtain annotated data for ASN antecedents that could be used to train a supervised machine learning system to resolve ASNs. For that, we created the **A**naphoric **S**hell **N**oun (ASN) corpus.

Schmid (2000) provides a list of 670 English nouns which are frequently used as shell nouns. He divides them into six broad semantic classes: *factual*, *mental*, *linguistic*, *modal*, *circumstantial*, and *eventive*. Table 1 shows this classification, along with example shell nouns for each category.

To begin with, we considered articles containing occurrences of these 670 shell nouns from the New York Times (NYT) corpus (about 711,046 occurrences).[3] To create a corpus of a manageable size for annotation, we considered first 10 highly frequent shell nouns distributed across each of Schmid's shell noun categories from Table 1 and extracted ASN instances by searching for the pattern {*this* shell_noun} in these articles.[4]

To examine the feasibility of the annotation, we systematically annotated sample data ourselves, which contained about 15 examples of each of these 10 highly frequent shell nouns. The annotation process revealed that not all ASN instances are easy to resolve. The instances with shell nouns from the circumstantial and eventive categories, in particular, had very long and unclear antecedents. So we excluded these categories in this research and work with six shell nouns from the other four categories: *fact*, *reason*, *issue*, *decision*, *question*, and *possibility*. To create the ASN corpus, we extracted about 500 instances for each of these six shell nouns. After removing duplicates and instances with a non-abstract sense (e.g., *this is-*

[3]`http://www.ldc.upenn.edu/Catalog/catalogEntry.jsp?catalogId=LDC2008T19`

[4]Schmid (2000) provides patterns for anaphoric shell nouns, and *this*-NP is the most prominent pattern among them.

sue with a publication-related sense), we were left with 2,822 ASN instances.

4 ASN Annotation Challenges

ASN antecedent annotation is a complex task, as it involves deeply understanding the discourse and interpreting it. Here we point out two main challenges associated with the task.

What to annotate? The question of 'what to annotate' as mentioned by Fort et al. (2012) is not straightforward for ASN antecedents, as the notion of *markables* is complex compared to ordinary nominal anaphora: the units on which the annotation work should focus are heterogeneous.[5] Moreover, due to this heterogeneous nature of annotation units, there is a huge number of markables (e.g., all syntactic constituents given by a syntactic parse tree). So there are many options to choose from, while only a few units are actually to be annotated. Moreover, there is no one-to-one correspondence between the syntactic type of an antecedent and the semantic type of its referent (Webber, 1991). For instance, a semantic type such as *fact* can be expressed with different syntactic shapes such as a clause, a verb phrase, or a complex sentence. Conversely, a syntactic shape, such as a clause, can function as several semantic types, including *fact*, *proposition*, and *event*.

Lack of the notion of the *right* answer It is not obvious how to define clear and detailed annotation guidelines to create a gold-standard corpus for ASN antecedent annotation due to our limited understanding of the nature and interpretation of such antecedents. The notion of the *right* answer is not well-defined for ASN antecedents. Indeed most people will be hard-pressed to say whether or not to include the clause *Despite decades of education and widespread course offerings* in the antecedent of *this fact* in example (1). The main challenge is to identify the conditions when two different candidates for annotation should be considered as representing essentially the same concept, which raises deep philosophical issues that we do not propose to solve in this paper. For our purposes, we believe, this challenge could only be possibly tackled by the requirements of downstream applications of ASN resolution.

[5]Occasionally, ASN antecedents are non-contiguous spans of text, but in this work, we ignore them for simplicity.

5 Annotation Methodology

Considering the difficulties of ASN annotation discussed above, there were two main challenges involved in the annotation process: first, to find annotators who can annotate data reliably with minimal guidelines, and second, to design simple annotation tasks that will elicit data useful for our purposes. Now we discuss how we dealt with these challenges.

Crowdsourcing We wanted to examine to what extent non-expert native speakers of English with minimal annotation guidelines would agree on ASN antecedents. We explored the possibility of using *crowdsourcing*, which is an effective way to obtain annotations for natural language research (Snow et al., 2008). In particular, we explored the use of CrowdFlower[6], a crowdsourcing platform that in turn uses various worker channels such as Amazon Mechanical Turk. CrowdFlower offers a number of features.

First, it offers a number of integrated *quality-control* mechanisms. For instance, it throws gold questions randomly at the annotators, and annotators who do not answer them correctly are not allowed to continue. To further minimize spammers, it also offers a training phase before the actual annotation. In this phase, every annotator is presented with a few gold questions. Only those annotators who get the gold questions right get admittance to do the actual annotation.

Second, CrowdFlower chooses a unique answer for each annotation unit based on the majority vote of the trusted annotators. For each annotator, it assigns a trust level based on how she performs on the gold examples. The unique answer is computed by adding together the trust scores of annotators, and then picking the answer with the highest sum of trusts (CrowdFlower team, p.c.). It also assigns a *confidence* score (denoted as c henceforth) for each answer, which is a normalized score of the summation of the trusts. For example, suppose annotators A, B, and C with trust levels 0.75, 0.75, and 1.0 give answers *no*, *yes*, *yes* respectively for a particular instance. Then the answer *yes* will score 1.75 and answer *no* will score 0.75 and *yes* will be chosen as the crowd's answer with $c = 0.7$ (i.e., $1.75/(1.75 + 0.75)$). We use these confidence scores in our analysis of inter-annotator agreement below.

[6]`http://crowdflower.com/`

Finally, CrowdFlower also provides detailed annotation results including demographic information and trustworthiness of each annotator.

Design of the annotation tasks With the help of well-designed gold examples, CrowdFlower can get rid of spammers and ensures that only reliable annotators perform the annotation task. But the annotation task must be well-designed in the first place to get a good quality annotation. Following the claim in the literature that with crowdsourcing platforms simple tasks do best (Madnani et al., 2010; Wang et al., 2012), we split our annotation task into two relatively simple sequential annotation tasks. First, identifying the broad region of the antecedent, i.e., not the precise antecedent but the region where the antecedent lies, and second, identifying the precise antecedent, given the broad region of the antecedent. Now we will discuss each of our annotation tasks in detail.

5.1 CrowdFlower experiment 1

The first annotation task was about identifying the broad region of ASN antecedents without actually pinpointing the precise antecedents. We defined the broad region as the sentence containing the ASN antecedent, as the shell nouns we have chosen tend to have antecedents that lie within a single sentence. We designed a CrowdFlower experiment where we presented to the annotators ASNs from the ASN corpus with three preceding paragraphs as context. Sentences in the vicinity of ASNs were each labelled: four sentences preceding the anaphor, the sentence containing the anaphor, and two sentences following the anaphor. This choice was based on our pilot annotation: the antecedents very rarely occur more than four sentences away from the anaphor. The annotation task was to pinpoint the sentence in the presented text that contained the antecedent for the ASN and selecting the appropriate sentence label as the correct answer. If no labelled sentence in the presented text contained the antecedent, we suggested to the annotators to select *None*. If the antecedent spanned more than one sentence, then we suggested to them to select *Combination*. We also provided a link to the complete article from which the text was drawn in case the annotators wanted to have a look at it.

Settings We asked for 8 judgements per instance and paid 8 cents per annotation unit. Our job contained in total 2,822 annotation units with 168 gold units. As we were interested in the verdict of native speakers of English, we limited the allowed demographic region to English-speaking countries.

5.2 CrowdFlower experiment 2

This annotation task was about pinpointing the exact antecedent text of the ASN instances. We designed a CrowdFlower experiment, where we presented to the annotators ASN instances from the ASN corpus with highlighted ASNs and the sentences containing the antecedents, the output of experiment 1. One way to pinpoint the exact antecedent string is to ask the annotators to mark free spans of text within the antecedent sentence, similar to Byron (2003) and Artstein and Poesio (2006). However, CrowdFlower quality-control mechanisms require multiple-choice annotation labels. So we decided to display a set of labelled candidates to the annotators and ask them to choose the answer that best represents the ASN antecedent. A practical requirement of this approach is that the number of options to be displayed be only a handful in order to make it a feasible task for online annotation. But as we noted in Section 4, the number of markables for ASN antecedents is large. If, for example, we define markables as all syntactic constituents given by the Stanford parser[7], there are on average 49.5 such candidates per sentence in the ASN corpus. It is not practical to display all these candidates and to ask CrowdFlower annotators to choose one answer from this many options. Also, some potential candidates are clearly not appropriate candidates for a particular shell noun. For instance, the NP constituent *the survival rate* in example (1) is not an appropriate candidate for the shell noun *fact* as generally facts are propositions. So the question is whether it is possible to restrict this set of candidates by discarding unlikely ones.

To deal with this question, we used supervised machine learning methods trained on easy, non-anaphoric unlabelled examples of shell nouns (e.g., *the fact that X*). In this paper, we will focus on the annotation and will treat these methods as a black box. In brief, the methods reduce the large search space of ASN antecedent candidates to a size that is manageable for crowdsourcing annotation, without eliminating the most likely candi-

[7] `http://nlp.stanford.edu/software/lex-parser.shtml`

dates. We displayed the 10 most-likely candidates given by these methods. In addition, we made sure not to display two candidates with only a negligible difference. For example, given two candidates, *X* and *that X*, which differ only with respect to the introductory *that*, we chose to display only the longer candidate *that X*.

In a controlled annotation, with detailed guidelines, such difficulties of selecting between minor variations could be avoided. However, such detailed annotation guidelines still have to be developed.

Settings As in experiment 1, we asked for 8 judgements per instance and paid 6 cents per annotation unit. But for this experiment we considered only 2,323 annotation units with 151 gold units, only high-confidence units ($c \geq 0.5$) from experiment 1. This task turned out to be a suitable task for crowdsourcing as it offered a limited number of options to choose from, instead of asking the annotators to mark arbitrary spans of text.

6 Agreement

Our annotation tasks pose difficulties in measuring inter-annotator agreement both in terms of the task itself and the platform used for annotation. In this section, we describe our attempt to compute agreement for each of our annotation tasks and the challenges we faced in doing so.

6.1 CrowdFlower experiment 1

Recall that in this experiment, annotators identify the sentence containing the antecedent and select the appropriate sentence label as their answer. We know from our pilot annotation that the distribution of such labels is skewed: most of the ASN antecedents lie in the sentence preceding the anaphor sentence. We observed the same trend in the results of this experiment. In the ASN corpus, the crowd chose the preceding sentence 64% of the time, the same sentence 13% of the time, and long-distance sentences 23% of the time.[8] Considering the skewed distribution of labels, if we use traditional agreement coefficients, such as Cohen's κ (1960) or Krippendorff's α (2013), expected agreement is very high, which in turn results in a low reliability coefficient (in our case $\alpha = 0.61$) that does not necessarily reflect the true reliability of the annotation (Artstein and Poesio, 2008).

	F	*R*	*I*	*D*	*Q*	*P*	*all*
$c < .5$	8	8	36	21	13	7	16
$.5 \leq c < .6$	6	6	13	8	7	5	8
$.6 \leq c < .8$	24	25	31	31	22	27	27
$.8 \leq c < 1.$	22	23	11	14	19	25	18
$c = 1.$	40	38	9	26	39	36	31
Average *c*	.83	.82	.61	.72	.80	.83	.76

Table 2: CrowdFlower confidence distribution for CrowdFlower experiment 1. Each column shows the distribution in percentages for confidence of annotating antecedents of that shell noun. The final row shows the average confidence of the distribution. Number of ASN instances = 2,822. *F = fact*, *R = reason*, *I = issue*, *D = decision*, *Q = question*, *P = possibility*.

One way to measure the reliability of the data, without taking chance correction into account, is to consider the distribution of the ASN instances with different levels of CrowdFlower confidence. Table 2 shows the percentages of instances in different confidence level bands for each shell noun as well as for all instances. For example, for the shell noun *fact*, 8% of the total number of *this fact* instances were annotated with $c < 0.5$. As we can see, most of the instances of the shell nouns *fact*, *reason*, *question*, and *possibility* were annotated with high confidence. In addition, most of them occurred in the band $0.8 \leq c \leq 1$. There are relatively few instances with low confidence for these nouns, suggesting the feasibility of reliable antecedent annotation for these nouns. By contrast, the mental nouns *issue* and *decision* had a large number of low-confidence ($c < 0.5$) instances, bringing in the question of reliability of antecedent annotation of these nouns.

Given these results with different confidence levels, the primary question is what confidence level should be considered acceptable? For our task, we required that at least four trusted annotators out of eight annotators should agree on an answer for it to be acceptable.[9] We will talk about acceptability later in Section 7.

6.2 CrowdFlower experiment 2

Recall that this experiment was about identifying the precise antecedent text segment given the sentence containing the antecedent. It is not clear what the best way to measure the amount of such

[8]This confirms Passonneau's (1989) observation that non-nominal antecedents tend to be close to the anaphors.

[9]We chose this threshold after systematically examining instances with different confidence levels.

	Jaccard			Dice		
	D_o	D_e	α	D_o	D_e	α
A&P	.53	.95	.45	.43	.94	.55
Our results	.47	.96	.51	.36	.92	.61

Table 3: Agreement using Krippendorff's α for CrowdFlower experiment 2. A&P = Artstein and Poesio (2006).

agreement is. Agreement coefficients such as Cohen's κ underestimate the degree of agreement for such annotation, suggesting disagreement even between two very similar annotated units (e.g., two text segments that differ in just a word or two). We present the agreement results in three different ways: Krippendorff's α with distance metrics Jaccard and Dice (Artstein and Poesio, 2006), Krippendorff's unitizing alpha (Krippendorff, 2013), and CrowdFlower confidence values.

Krippendorff's α using Jaccard and Dice To compare our agreement results with previous efforts to annotate such antecedents, following Artstein and Poesio (2006), we computed Krippendorff's α using distance metrics Jaccard and Dice. The general form of coefficient α is:

$$\alpha = 1 - \frac{D_o}{D_e} \tag{1}$$

where D_o and D_e are observed and expected disagreements respectively. $\alpha = 1$ indicates perfect reliability and ${}_u\alpha = 0$ indicates the absence of reliability. When ${}_u\alpha < 0$, either the sample size is very small or the disagreement is systematic. Table 3 shows the agreement results. Our agreement results are comparable to Artstein and Poesio's agreement results. They had 20 annotators annotating 16 anaphor instances with segment antecedents, whereas we had 8 annotators annotating 2,323 ASN instances. As Artstein and Poesio point out, expected disagreement in case of such antecedent annotation is close to maximal, as there is little overlap between segment antecedents of different anaphors and therefore α pretty much reflects the observed agreement.

Krippendorff's *unitizing* α (${}_u\alpha$) Following Kolhatkar and Hirst (2012), we use ${}_u\alpha$ for measuring reliability of the ASN antecedent annotation task. This coefficient is appropriate when the annotators work on the same text, identify the units in the text that are relevant to the given research

	F	*R*	*I*	*D*	*Q*	*P*	*all*
$c < .5$	11	17	32	31	14	28	21
$.5 \le c < .6$	12	12	19	23	9	19	15
$.6 \le c < .8$	36	33	34	32	30	36	33
$.8 \le c < 1.$	24	22	10	10	21	13	18
$c = 1.$	17	16	5	3	26	4	13
Average c	.74	.71	.60	.59	.77	.62	.68

Table 4: CrowdFlower confidence distribution for CrowdFlower experiment 2. Each column shows the distribution in percentages for confidence of annotating antecedents of that shell noun. The final row shows the average confidence of the distribution. Number of ASN instances = 2,323. *F* = *fact*, *R* = *reason*, *I* = *issue*, *D* = *decision*, *Q* = *question*, *P* = *possibility*.

question, and then label the identified units (Krippendorff, p.c.). The general form of coefficient ${}_u\alpha$ is the same as in equation 1. In our context, the annotators work on the same text, the ASN instances. We define an *elementary annotation unit* (the smallest separately judged unit) to be a word token. The annotators identify and locate ASN antecedents for the given anaphor in terms of sequences of elementary annotation units.

${}_u\alpha$ incorporates the notion of distance between strings by using a distance function which is defined as the square of the distance between the non-overlapping tokens in our case. The distance is 0 when the annotated units are exactly the same, and is the summation of the squares of the unmatched parts if they are different. We compute observed and expected disagreement as explained by Krippendorff (2013, Section 12.4). For our data, ${}_u\alpha$ was 0.54.[10] ${}_u\alpha$ was lower for the mental nouns *issue* and *decision* and the modal noun *possibility* compared to other shell nouns.

CrowdFlower confidence results We also examined different confidence levels for ASN antecedent annotation. Table 4 gives confidence results for all instances and for each noun. In contrast with Table 2, the instances are more evenly distributed here. As in experiment 1, the mental nouns *issue* and *decision* had many low confidence instances. For the modal noun *possibility*, it was easy to identify the sentence containing the antecedent, but pinpointing the precise antecedent

[10]Note that ${}_u\alpha$ reported here is just an approximation of the actual agreement as in our case the annotators chose an option from a set of predefined options instead of marking free spans of text.

turned out to be difficult.

Now we discuss the nature of disagreement in ASN annotation.

Disagreement in experiment 1 There were two primary sources of disagreement in experiment 1. First, the annotators had problems agreeing on the answer *None*. We instructed them to choose *None* when the sentence containing the antecedent was not labelled. Nonetheless, some annotators chose sentences that did not precisely contain the actual antecedent but just hinted at it. Second, sometimes it was hard to identify the precise antecedent sentence as the antecedent was either present in the blend of all labelled sentences or there were multiple possible answers, as shown in example (2).

(2) Any biography of Thomas More has to answer one fundamental question. Why? Why, out of all the many ambitious politicians of early Tudor England, did only one refuse to acquiesce to a simple piece of religious and political opportunism? What was it about More that set him apart and doomed him to a spectacularly avoidable execution?

The innovation of Peter Ackroyd's new biography of More is that he places the answer to **this question** outside of More himself.

Here, the author formulates the question in a number of ways and any question mentioned in the preceding text can serve as the antecedent of the anaphor *this question*.

Hard instances Low agreement can indicate different problems: unclear guidelines, poor-quality annotators, or difficult instances (e.g., not well understood linguistic phenomena) (Artstein and Poesio, 2006). We can rule out the possibility of poor-quality annotators for two reasons. First, we consider 8 diverse annotators who work independently. Second, we use CrowdFlower's quality-control mechanisms and hence allow only trustworthy annotators to annotate our texts. Regarding instructions, we take inter-annotator agreement as a measure for feasibility of the task, and hence we keep the annotation instruction as simple as possible. This could be a source of low agreement. The third possibility is hard instances. Our results show that the mental nouns *issue* and *decision* had many low-confidence instances, suggesting the difficulty associated with the interpretation of these nouns (e.g., the very idea of what counts as an issue is fuzzy). The shell noun *decision* was harder because most of its instances were court-decision related articles, which were in general hard to understand.

Different strings representing similar concepts As noted in Section 4, the main challenge with the ASN annotation task is that different antecedent candidates might represent the same concept and it is not trivial to incorporate this idea in the annotation process. When five trusted annotators identify the antecedent as *but X* and three trusted annotators identify it as merely *X*, since CrowdFlower will consider these two answers to be two completely different answers, it will give the answer *but X* a confidence of only about 0.6. $_u\alpha$ or α with Jaccard and Dice will not consider this as a complete disagreement; however, the coefficients will register it as a difference. In other words, the difference functions used with these coefficients do not respond to semantics, paraphrases, and other similarities that humans might judge as inconsequential. One way to deal with this problem would be clustering the options that reflect essentially the same concepts before measuring the agreement. Some of these problems could also be avoided by formulating instructions for marking antecedents so that these differences do not occur in the identified antecedents. However, crowdsourcing platforms require annotation guidelines to be clear and minimal, which makes it difficult to control the annotation variations.

7 Evaluation of Crowd Annotation

CrowdFlower experiment 2 resulted in 1,810 ASN instances with $c > 0.5$. The question is how good are these annotations from experts' point of view.

To examine the quality of the crowd annotation we asked two judges A and B to evaluate the *acceptability* of the crowd's answers. The judges were highly-qualified academic editors: A, a researcher in Linguistics and B, a translator with a Ph.D. in History and Philosophy of Science. From the crowd-annotated ASN antecedent data, we randomly selected 300 instances, 50 instances per shell noun. We made sure to choose instances with borderline confidence ($0.5 \leq c < 0.6$), medium confidence ($0.6 \leq c < 0.8$), and high confidence ($0.8 \leq c \leq 1.0$). We asked the judges to rate the acceptability of the crowd-answers based on the extent to which they provided interpretation of the corresponding anaphor. We gave them four options: *perfectly* (the crowd's answer is perfect and the judge would have chosen the same antecedent), *reasonably* (the crowd's answer is acceptable and is close to their answer),

		Judge B				
		P	*R*	*I*	*N*	Total
Judge A	*P*	**171**	44	11	7	233
	R	12	**27**	7	4	50
	I	2	4	**6**	1	13
	N	1	2	0	**1**	4
	Total	186	77	24	13	300

Table 5: Evaluation of ASN antecedent annotation. *P = perfectly*, *R = reasonably*, *I = implicitly*, *N = not at all*

implicitly (the crowd's answer only implicitly contains the actual antecedent), and *not at all* (the crowd's answer is not in any way related to the actual antecedent).[11] Moreover, if they did not mark *perfectly*, we asked them to provide their antecedent string. The two judges worked on the task independently and they were completely unaware of how the annotation data was collected.

Table 5 shows the confusion matrix of the ratings of the two judges. Judge B was stricter than Judge A. Given the nature of the task, it was encouraging that most of the crowd-antecedents were rated as *perfectly* by both judges (72% by A and 62% by B). Note that *perfectly* is rather a strong evaluation for ASN antecedent annotation, considering the nature of ASN antecedents themselves. If we weaken the acceptability criteria and consider the antecedents rated as *reasonably* to be also acceptable antecedents, 84.6% of the total instances were acceptable according to both judges.

Regarding the instances marked *implicitly*, most of the times the crowd's answer was the closest textual string of the judges' answer. So we again might consider instances marked *implicitly* as acceptable answers.

For a very few instances (only about 5%) either of the judges marked *not at all*. This was a positive result and suggests success of different steps of our annotation procedure: identifying broad region, identifying the set of most likely candidates, and identifying precise antecedent. As we can see in Table 5, there were 7 instances where the judge A rated *perfectly* while the judge B rated *not at all*, i.e., completely contradictory judgements. When we looked at these examples, they were rather hard and ambiguous cases. An example is shown in (3). The *whether* clause marked in the preceding sentence is the crowd's answer. One of our judges rated this answer as *perfectly*, while the other rated it as *not at all*. According to her the correct antecedent is *whether Catholics who vote for Mr. Kerry would have to go to confession.*

(3) Several Vatican officials said, however, that any such talk has little meaning because the church does not take sides in elections. But the statements by several American bishops that Catholics who vote for Mr. Kerry would have to go to confession have raised the question in many corners about **whether this is an official church position**.

The church has not addressed **this question** publicly and, in fact, seems reluctant to be dragged into the fight..."

There was no notable relation between the annotator's rating and the confidence level: many instances with borderline confidence were marked *perfectly* or *reasonably*, suggesting that instances with $c \geq 0.5$ were reasonably annotated instances, to be used as training data for ASN resolution.

8 Conclusion

In this paper, we addressed the fundamental question about feasibility of ASN antecedent annotation, which is a necessary step before developing computational approaches to resolve ASNs. We carried out crowdsourcing experiments to get native speaker judgements on ASN antecedents. Our results show that among 8 diverse annotators who worked independently with a minimal set of annotation instructions, usually at least 4 annotators converged on a single ASN antecedent. The result is quite encouraging considering the nature of such antecedents.

We asked two highly-qualified judges to independently examine the quality of a sample of crowd-annotated ASN antecedents. According to both judges, about 95% of the crowd-annotations were acceptable. We plan to use this crowd-annotated data (1,810 instances) as training data for an ASN resolver. We also plan to distribute the annotations at a later date.

Acknowledgements

We thank the CrowdFlower team for their responsiveness and Hans-Jörg Schmid for helpful discussions. This material is based upon work supported by the United States Air Force and the Defense Advanced Research Projects Agency under Contract No. FA8650-09-C-0179, Ontario/Baden-Württemberg Faculty Research Exchange, and the University of Toronto.

[11] Before starting the actual annotation, we carried out a training phase with 30 instances, which gave an opportunity to the judges to ask questions about the task.

References

Ron Artstein and Massimo Poesio. 2006. Identifying reference to abstract objects in dialogue. In *Proceedings of the 10th Workshop on the Semantics and Pragmatics of Dialogue*, pages 56–63, Potsdam, Germany.

Ron Artstein and Massimo Poesio. 2008. Inter-coder agreement for computational linguistics. *Computational Linguistics*, 34(4):555–596, December.

Simon Philip Botley. 2006. Indirect anaphora: Testing the limits of corpus-based linguistics. *International Journal of Corpus Linguistics*, 11(1):73–112.

Donna K. Byron. 2003. Annotation of pronouns and their antecedents: A comparison of two domains. Technical report, University of Rochester. Computer Science Department.

Jon Chamberlain, Udo Kruschwitz, and Massimo Poesio. 2009. Constructing an anaphorically annotated corpus with non-experts: Assessing the quality of collaborative annotations. In *Proceedings of the 2009 Workshop on The People's Web Meets NLP: Collaboratively Constructed Semantic Resources*, pages 57–62, Suntec, Singapore, August. Association for Computational Linguistics.

Bin Chen, Jian Su, Sinno Jialin Pan, and Chew Lim Tan. 2011. A unified event coreference resolution by integrating multiple resolvers. In *Proceedings of 5th International Joint Conference on Natural Language Processing*, pages 102–110, Chiang Mai, Thailand, November.

Jacob Cohen. 1960. A coefficient of agreement for nominal scales. *Educational and Psychological Measurement*, 20(1):37.

Stefanie Dipper and Heike Zinsmeister. 2011. Annotating abstract anaphora. *Language Resources and Evaluation*, 69:1–16.

Karën Fort, Adeline Nazarenko, and Sophie Rosset. 2012. Modeling the complexity of manual annotation tasks: a grid of analysis. In *24th International Conference on Computational Linguistics*, pages 895–910.

Barbora Hladká, Jiří Mírovský, and Pavel Schlesinger. 2009. Play the language: Play coreference. In *Proceedings of the Association of Computational Linguistics and International Joint Conference on Natural Language Processing 2009 Conference Short Papers*, pages 209–212, Suntec, Singapore, August. Association for Computational Linguistics.

Pei-Yun Hsueh, Prem Melville, and Vikas Sindhwani. 2009. Data quality from crowdsourcing: A study of annotation selection criteria. In *Proceedings of the NAACL HLT 2009 Workshop on Active Learning for Natural Language Processing*, pages 27–35, Boulder, Colorado, June. Association for Computational Linguistics.

Varada Kolhatkar and Graeme Hirst. 2012. Resolving "this-issue" anaphora. In *Proceedings of the 2012 Joint Conference on Empirical Methods in Natural Language Processing and Computational Natural Language Learning*, pages 1255–1265, Jeju Island, Korea, July. Association for Computational Linguistics.

Klaus Krippendorff. 2013. *Content Analysis: An Introduction to Its Methodology*. Sage, Thousand Oaks, CA, third edition.

Heeyoung Lee, Marta Recasens, Angel Chang, Mihai Surdeanu, and Dan Jurafsky. 2012. Joint entity and event coreference resolution across documents. In *Proceedings of the 2012 Joint Conference on Empirical Methods in Natural Language Processing and Computational Natural Language Learning*, pages 489–500, Jeju Island, Korea, July. Association for Computational Linguistics.

Nitin Madnani, Jordan Boyd-Graber, and Philip Resnik. 2010. Measuring transitivity using untrained annotators. In *Proceedings of the NAACL HLT 2010 Workshop on Creating Speech and Language Data with Amazon's Mechanical Turk*, pages 188–194, Los Angeles, June. Association for Computational Linguistics.

Rebecca J. Passonneau. 1989. Getting at discourse referents. In *Proceedings of the 27th Annual Meeting of the Association for Computational Linguistics*, pages 51–59, Vancouver, British Columbia, Canada, June. Association for Computational Linguistics.

Massimo Poesio and Ron Artstein. 2008. Anaphoric annotation in the ARRAU corpus. In *Proeedings of the Sixth International Conference on Language Resources and Evaluation (LREC'08)*, Marrakech, Morocco, May. European Language Resources Association (ELRA).

Sameer S. Pradhan, Lance A. Ramshaw, Ralph M. Weischedel, Jessica MacBride, and Linnea Micciulla. 2007. Unrestricted coreference: Identifying entities and events in OntoNotes. In *Proceedings of the International Conference on Semantic Computing*, pages 446–453, September.

Hans-Jörg Schmid. 2000. *English Abstract Nouns As Conceptual Shells: From Corpus to Cognition*. Topics in English Linguistics 34. De Gruyter Mouton, Berlin.

Rion Snow, Brendan O'Connor, Daniel Jurafsky, and Andrew Ng. 2008. Cheap and fast – but is it good? evaluating non-expert annotations for natural language tasks. In *Proceedings of the 2008 Conference on Empirical Methods in Natural Language Processing*, pages 254–263, Honolulu, Hawaii, October. Association for Computational Linguistics.

Renata Vieira, Susanne Salmon-Alt, Caroline Gasperin, Emmanuel Schang, and Gabriel Othero. 2002. Coreference and anaphoric relations of demonstrative noun phrases in multilingual corpus. In *Proceedings of the 4th Discourse Anaphora and Anaphor Resolution Conference (DAARC 2002)*, pages 385–427, Lisbon, Portugal, September.

Aobo Wang, Cong Duy Vu Hoang, and Min-Yen Kan. 2012. Perspectives on crowdsourcing annotations for natural language processing. In *Language Resources and Evaluation*, volume in press, pages 1–23. Springer.

Bonnie Lynn Webber. 1991. Structure and ostension in the interpretation of discourse deixis. In *Language and Cognitive Processes*, pages 107–135.

Applicative Structures and Immediate Discourse in the Turkish Discourse Bank

Işın Demirşahin, Adnan Öztürel, Cem Bozşahin, and Deniz Zeyrek
Department of Cognitive Science, Informatics Institute
Middle East Technical University
{disin,ozturel,bozsahin,zeyrek}@metu.edu.tr

Abstract

Various discourse theories have argued for data structures ranging from the simplest trees to the most complex chain graphs. This paper investigates the structure represented by the explicit connectives annotated in the multiple-genre Turkish Discourse Bank (TDB). The dependencies that violate tree-constraints are analyzed. The effects of information structure in the surface form, which result in seemingly complex configurations with underlying simple dependencies, are introduced; and the structural implications are discussed. The results indicate that our current approach to local discourse structure needs to accommodate properly contained arguments and relations, and partially overlapping as well as shared arguments; deviating further from simple trees, but not as drastically as a chain graph structure would imply, since no genuine cases of structural crossing dependencies are attested in TDB.

1 Introduction

A variety of structures for discourse representation has been proposed, including successive trees of varying sizes connected and occasionally intertwined at the peripheries (Hobbs, 1985), a single tree structure (Rhetorical Structure Theory, RST, Mann & Thompson, 1988), entity chains (Knott *et al.* 2001), tree-adjoining grammars (Discourse-Lexicalized Tree Adjoining Grammar, D-LTAG, Webber, 2004), directed acyclic graphs (Lee *et al.*, 2006, 2008) and chain graphs (Wolf & Gibson, 2005).

The simplest of these structures is a tree, which treats discourse structure simpler than sentence-level syntax. The most complex representation, chain graphs that allow for crossing dependencies and other tree-violations, treats discourse as more complex than sentence level. We know since the work of Shieber (1985) and Joshi (1985) that sentence-level structures require more than context-free power, but not to the extent of dealing with general graphs, or with strings that grow out of constant control. It is of general interest to discover whether such complexity occurs in natural discourses, because we would like to know how far discourse structures deviate from applicative semantics. (Applicative structures are binary operations on data; for example a connective's meaning depending only on two arguments. A system is applicative if it only makes use of function application, but not e.g. graph reduction or general function composition. The concepts are distinct but related: function application can be linked to applicative structures by currying.) If more complex structures are found, we must go above applicative semantics, and we must worry about function compositions and graph reductions, which are known to require more computational power.

2 Turkish Discourse Bank

Turkish Discourse Bank (TDB) is the first large-scale publicly available language resource with discourse level annotations for Turkish built on a ~ 400,000-word sub-corpus of METU Turkish Corpus (MTC) (Say *et al.*, 2002), annotated in the style of Penn Discourse Tree Bank (PDTB) (Prasad *et al.*, 2008). The TDB Relations are annotated for explicit discourse connectives, which link two spans of text that can be interpreted as Abstract Objects (Asher, 1993). Connectives are annotated together with their modifiers and arguments,and with supplementary materials for the arguments (Zeyrek & Webber, 2008; Zeyrek et al., 2010). The first release of TDB is available at http://medid.ii.metu.edu.tr/.

As in PDTB, the connectives in TDB come from a variety of syntactic classes (Zeyrek & Webber, *ibid*). The coordinating and subordinating conjunctions such as *ve* 'and' and *için* 'for' and 'in order to', respectively, are considered structural connectives, meaning that they take both arguments structurally. Discourse adverbials and phrasal expressions that are built by combining a discourse-anaphoric element with a subordinating conjunction are considered to be anaphoric connectives, meaning that they only take the argument that is syntactically related, and the other argument is interpreted anaphorically. In PDTB and TDB style, the syntactically related argument is called the second argument (Arg2), and the other argument is called the first argument (Arg1), for both structural and anaphoric connectives. The syntactic class of the discourse connective will be included in the further releases of TDB along with the sense of the discourse relations, and some morphological features for the arguments of subordinating conjunctions (Demirşahin *et al.*, 2012).

3 Discourse Relation Configurations in Turkish

Lee *et al.* (2006) identified *independent relations* and *fully embedded relations* as conforming to the tree structure, and *shared arguments*, *properly contained arguments*, *pure crossing*, and *partially overlapping arguments* as departures from the tree structure in PDTB. Although most departures from the tree structure can be accounted for by non-structural explanations, such as anaphora and attribution, Lee *et al.* (2006, 2008) state that shared arguments may have to be accepted in discourse structure.

Aktaş *et al.* (2010) identified similar structures in TDB, adding *nested relations* that do not violate tree structure constraints, as well as *properly contained relations* that introduce further deviations from trees. Following their terminology, we will reserve the word *relation* to discourse relations (or coherence relations), and use the term *configuration* to refer to relations between discourse relations.

1.1 Independent, Fully Embedded and Nested Relations

The first release of TDB consists of 8,484 explicit relations. The argument spans of some discourse connectives do not overlap with those of any other connectives in the corpus. We call them *independent relations*. All others are called *non-independent relations*. We have identified 2,548 non-independent configurations consisting of 3,474 unique relations, meaning that 5,010 relations (59.05%) are independent. Table 1 shows the distribution of 2,548 non-independent configurations.

Configuration	#	%
Full Embedding	695	27.28
Nested Relations	138	5.42
Total Non-violating Configurations	**833**	**32.69**
Shared Argument	489	19.19
Prop. Cont. Argument	194	7.61
Prop. Cont. Relation	1018	39.95
Pure Crossing	2	0.08
Partial Overlap	12	0.47
Total Violating Configurations	**1715**	**67.31**
Total	**2548**	**100.00**

Table 1: Distribution of non-independent configurations

Since full embedding and nested relations conform to tree structure, these configurations will not be discussed further. The following subsections discuss the suitability of explanations involving anaphora and attribution to tree-violating configurations. Those that cannot be completely explained away must be accommodated by the discourse structure.

1.2 Shared Arguments

Lee *et al.* (2006, 2008) state that *shared argument* is one of the configurations that cannot be explained away, and should be accommodated by discourse structure. Similarly, Egg & Redeker (2008) admit that even in a corpus annotated within RST Framework, which enforces tree structure by annotation guidelines, there is a genre-specific structure that is similar to the shared arguments in Lee *et al.* (2006).

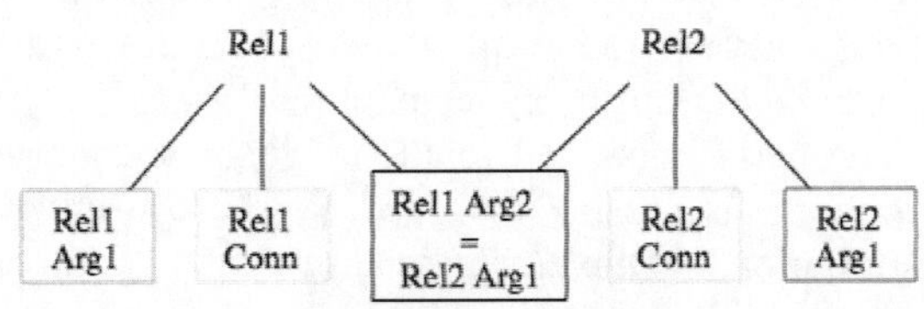

Figure 1 - Shared Argument

Of the 489 shared arguments in TDB, 331 belong to anaphoric discourse relations (i.e. relations in which at least one of the connectives involved is either a discourse adverbial or a phrasal expression) (67.69%). In the remaining 158 relations (32.31%), arguments are shared by structural connectives. (1) is an example of a shared argument.

(1) 00001131-2&3

(a) *Vazgeçmek kolaydı, ertelemek de.* Ama **tırmanmaya başlandı mı bitirilmeli!** Çünkü her seferinde acımasız bir geriye dönüş vardı.

"*It was easy to give up, so was to postpone.* But **once you start climbing you have to go all the way!** Because there was a cruel comeback everytime."

(b) Vazgeçmek kolaydı, ertelemek de. Ama *tırmanmaya başlandı mı bitirilmeli!* Çünkü **her seferinde acımasız bir geriye dönüş vardı.**

"It was easy to give up, so was to postpone. But *once you start climbing you have to go all the way!* Because **there was a cruel comeback everytime.**"

All examples are from TDB; the first line indicates the file name (00077211 in (1)), and the browser index of the connectives involved in the configuration (2 & 3 in (1)). The first arguments (Arg1) of the connectives are in *italic,* the second arguments (Arg2) are in **bold.** The connectives themselves are underlined. For the sake of simplicity, the modifiers of the connectives are displayed as part of the connective, and the shared tags are omitted when they are immaterial to the configuration being discussed.

In (1), the first argument of *but* (relation 2) annotated in (a) completely overlaps with the first argument of *because* (relation 3), annotated in (b) on the same text for comparison. The result is a shared argument configuration.

1.3 Properly Contained Relations and Arguments

In TDB there are 1,018 properly contained relations, almost half of which (471 relations; 46.27%) are caused by anaphoric relations.

Properly contained relations where anaphoric connectives are not involved can be caused by attribution, complement clauses, and relative clauses. (2) is a relation within a relative clause (a), which is part of another relation in the matrix clause (b). The result is a properly contained relation.

(2) 00001131-27&28

(a) Sabah çok erken saatte **bir önceki akşam gün batmadan** hemen önce *astığı* çamaşırları toplamaya çıkıyordu ve doğal olarak da gün batmadan o günkü çamaşırları asmak için geliyordu.

"She used to go out to gather the clean laundry *she had hung to dry* right before **the sun went down the previous evening**, and naturally she came before sunset to hang the laundry of the day."

(b) *Sabah çok erken saatte bir önceki akşam gün batmadan hemen önce astığı çamaşırları toplamaya çıkıyordu* ve **doğal olarak da gün batmadan o günkü çamaşırları asmak için geliyordu.**

"*She used to go out to gather the clean laundry she had hung to dry the previous evening right before the sun went down,* and **naturally she came before sunset to hang the laundry of the day.**"

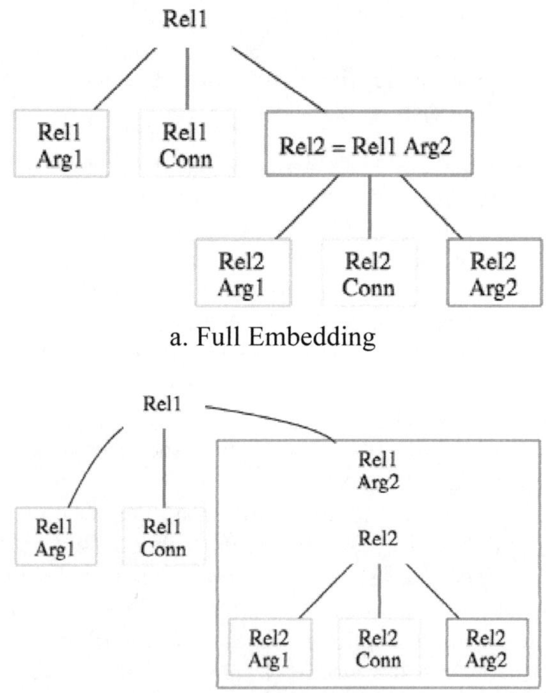

a. Full Embedding

b. Properly Contained Relation

Figure 2 - Properly Contained Relation vs. Full Embedding

Sometimes a verb of attribution is the only element that causes proper containment. Lee *et al.* (2006) argue that since the relation between the verb of attribution and the owner of the attribution is between an abstract object and an entity, and not between two abstract objects, it is not a relation on the discourse level. Therefore, those stranded verbs of attribution should not be regarded as tree-structure violations. In (3) the properly contained relations occur in a quote, but the intervening materials are more than just verbs of attribution. Because the intervening materials in (3) are whole sentences that participate in complex discourse structures, we believe that (3) is different than the case proposed by Lee *et al.* (2006) and should be considered a genuine case of properly contained relation.

(3) 00003121-10, 11&13

(a) "Evet, küçük amcamdı o, nur içinde yatsın, yetmişlik bir rakıyı devirip ipi sek sek geçmeye kalkmış; kaptan olan amcam ise kocaman bir gemiyi sulara gömdü. Aylardan kasımdı, ben çocuktum, çok iyi anımsıyorum, fırtınalı bir gecede, Karadeniz'in batısında batmışlardı. *Kaptandı*, ama **yüzme bilmezdi amcam**. Bir namaz tahtasına sarılmış olarak kıyıya vurduğunda kollarını zor açmışlar, yarı yarıya donmuş. *Belki de o anda Tanrı'ya yakarıp yardım istiyordu*, çünkü **çok dindar bir adamdı**. Ama artık değil; küp gibi içip meyhanelerde keman çalıyor." Sonra da Nesli'nin ilgiyle çatılmış alnına bakıp gülüyor: "Çok istavritsin!"

"Yes, he was my younger uncle, may he rest in peace, he tried to hop on the tightrope after quaffing down a bottle of raki; my other uncle who was a captain, on the other hand, sank a whole ship. It was October, I was a child, I remember it vividly, in a stormy night, they sank by the west of the Black Sea. *He was a captain*, but **he couldn't swim**, my uncle. When he washed ashore holding onto a piece of driftwood, they pried open his arms with great difficulty, he was half frozen. *Maybe at that moment he was begging God for help*, because **he was a very religious man**. But not anymore, now he hits the bottle and plays the violin in taverns." Then he sees Nesli's interested frown and laughs: "You're so gullible!"

(b) *"Evet, [...] Ama artık değil; küp gibi içip meyhanelerde keman çalıyor."* Sonra da **Nesli'nin ilgiyle çatılmış alnına bakıp gülüyor: "Çok istavritsin!"**

"Yes, [...]But not anymore, now he hits the bottle and plays the violin in taverns." Then **he sees Nesli's interested frown and laughs: "You're so gullible!"**

Whereas attribution can be discarded as a non-discourse relation, a discourse model based on discourse connectives should be able to accommodate partially contained relations resulting from relations within complements of verbs and relative clauses.

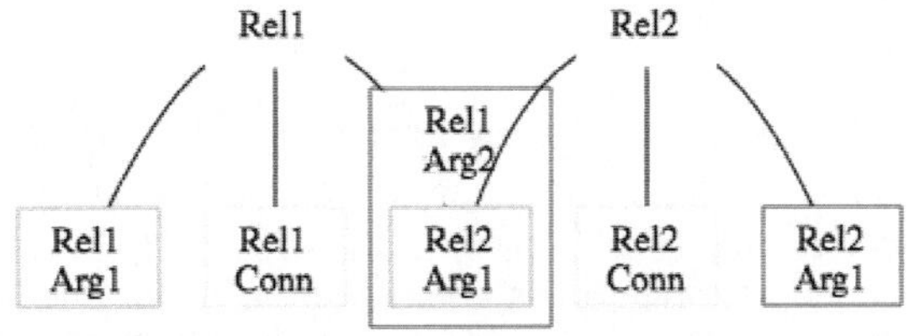

Figure 3 - Properly Contained Argument

As in properly contained relations, properly contained arguments may arise when an abstract object that is external to a quote is in a relation with an abstract object in a quote. Likewise, a discourse relation within the complement of a verb or a relative clause can cause properly contained arguments. Anaphoric connectives account for the 129 (66.49%) of the 194 properly contained arguments in TDB.

1.4 Partial Overlap

There are only 12 partial overlaps in TDB, and 3 of them involve anaphoric relations.

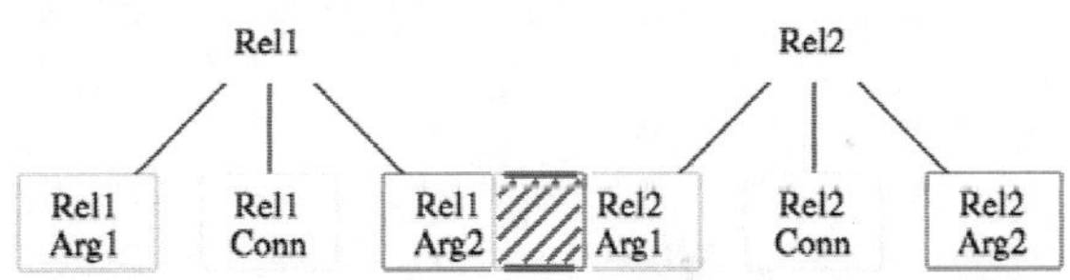

Figure 4 - Partial Overlap

In (4), the argument span of *in order to* partially overlaps with the argument span of *to.* This is a partial overlap of the arguments of two structural connectives.

(4) 20630000-44&45

(a) *Hükümetin, 1998'de kapatılan kumarhaneleri,* **kaynak sorununa çözüm bulmak** amacıyla *yeniden açmak için harekete geçmesi,* tartışma yarattı.

"The fact that *the governtment took action in order to reopen the casinos that were closed down in 1998* in order to **come up with a solution to the resource problem** caused arguments."

(b) *Hükümetin,* **1998'de kapatılan kumarhaneleri, kaynak sorununa çözüm bulmak amacıyla yeniden açmak** için *harekete geçmesi,* tartışma yarattı.

"The fact that *the governtment took action* in order to **reopen the casinos that were closed down in 1998 in order to come up with a solution to the resource problem** caused arguments."

The first argument of relation 44 (a) properly contains the first argument of 45 (b), whereas the second argument of (b) properly contains the second argument of (a). This double containment results in a complicated structure that will be analyzed in detail in §3.5.

In (5) the second argument of *but* (relation 42 (a)) contains only one of the two conjoined clauses, whereas the first argument of *after* (relation 43 (b)) contains both of them. The most probable cause for this difference in annotations is the combination of "blind annotation" with the "minimality principle." This principle guides the participants to annotate the minimum text span required to interpret the relation. Since the annotators cannot see previous annotations, they have to assess the minimum span of an argument again when they annotate the second relation. Sometimes the minimal span for one relation is annotated differently than the minimal span required for the other, resulting in partial overlaps.

(5) 00001131-42&43

(a) *Yine istediği kişiyi bir türlü görememişti*, ama **aylarca sabrettikten sonra gözetlediği bir kadın soluğunu daralttı**, tüyleri diken diken oldu.

"Once again he couldn't see the person he wanted to see, but **after waiting patiently for months, a woman he peeped at took his breath away,** gave him goose bumps".

(b) Yine istediği kişiyi bir türlü görememişti, ama **aylarca sabrettikten** sonra *gözetlediği bir kadın soluğunu daralttı, tüyleri diken diken oldu.*

"Once again he couldn't see the person he wanted to see, but after **waiting patiently for months**, *a woman he peeped at took his breath away, gave him goose bumps."*

1.5 Pure Crossing

There are only 2 pure crossing examples in the current release of TDB, a number so small that it is tempting to treat them as negligible. However, the inclusion of pure crossing would result in the most dramatic change in discourse structure, raising the complexity level to chain graph and making discourse structure markedly more complex than sentence level grammar. Therefore, we would like to discuss both examples in detail.

(6) 00010111-54&55

(a) Sonra *ansızın sesler gelir*. Ayak sesleri. Birilerinin ya işi vardır, aceleyle yürürler, ya koşarlar. O zaman **kız katılaşır ansızın**. Oğlan da katılaşır ve her koşunun gizli bir isteği var.

"And then *suddenly there is a sound.* Footsteps. Someone has an errand to run, they walk hurriedly or run. Then **the girl stiffens suddenly.** The boy stiffens, too; and every run has a hidden wish."

(b) Sonra ansızın sesler gelir. Ayak sesleri. *Birilerinin ya işi vardır, aceleyle yürürler, ya koşarlar.* O zaman kız katılaşır ansızın. Oğlan da katılaşır ve **her koşunun gizli bir isteği var.**

"And then suddenly there is a sound. Footsteps. *Someone has an errand to run, they walk hurriedly or run.* Then the girl stiffens suddenly. The boy stiffens, too; and **every run has a hidden wish."**

In (6), the discourse relation encoded by *then* is not only anaphoric -and therefore not determinant in terms of discourse structure- but also the crossing annotation does not necessarily arise from the coherence relation of the connective's arguments. It is more likely imposed by lexical cohesive elements (Halliday & Hasan, 1976), as the annotators apparently made use of the repetitions of *ansızın* 'suddenly' and *koş* 'run' in the text when they could not interpret the intended meaning.

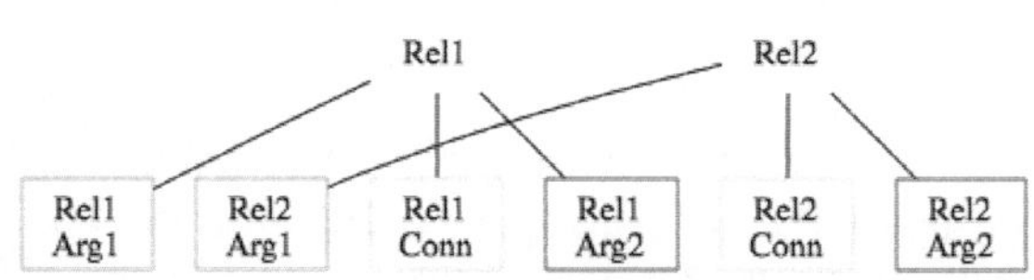

Figure 5 - Pure Crossing

The other example, given in (7), is not anaphoric. It is more interesting as it points to a peculiar structure similar to (4) in §3.4, a surface crossing which is frequent in the subordinating conjunctions of Turkish.

(7) 20510000-31,32&34

(a) *Ceza*, **Telekom'un iki farklı internet alt yapısı pazarında tekel konumunu kötüye kullandığı** için ve uydu istasyonu işletmeciliği pazarında artık tekel hakkı kalmadığı halde rakiplerinin faaliyetlerini zorlaştırdığı için *verildi*.

"The penalty was given because **Telekom abused its monopoly status in the two different internet infrastructure markets** and because it caused difficulties with its rivals' activities although it did not have a monopoly status in the satellite management market anymore."

(b) Ceza, Telekom'un *iki farklı internet alt yapısı pazarında tekel konumunu kötüye kullandığı* için ve **uydu istasyonu işletmeciliği pazarında artık tekel hakkı kalmadığı halde rakiplerinin faaliyetlerini zorlaştırdığı** için verildi.

"The penalty was given because *Telekom abused its monopoly status in the two different internet infrastructure markets* and because **it caused difficulties with its rivals' activities although it did not have a monopoly status in the satellite management market anymore.**"

(c) *Ceza,* Telekom'un iki farklı internet alt yapısı pazarında tekel konumunu kötüye kullandığı için ve **uydu istasyonu işletmeciliği pazarında artık tekel hakkı kalmadığı halde rakiplerinin faaliyetlerini zorlaştırdığı** için *verildi.*

"The penalty was given because Telekom abused its monopoly status in the two different internet infrastructure markets and because **it caused difficulties with its rivals' activities although it did not have a monopoly status in the satellite management market anymore."**

A closer inspection reveals that the pure crossings in (7) are caused by two distinct reasons.

The first reason is the repetition of the subordinator *için* 'because'. Had there been only the rightmost subordinator, the relation would be a simple case of Full Embedding, where *ve* 'and' in (b) connects the two reasons for the penalty, while the rightmost subordinator connects the combined reasons to the matrix clause (see Figure 6). However, since both subordinators were present, they were annotated separately. They share their first arguments, and take different spans as their second arguments, which are also connected by *ve* 'and', resulting in an apparent pure crossing.

Our alternative analysis is that *ve* 'and' actually takes the subordinators *için* 'because' in its scope, and it should be analyzed similar to an assumed single-subordinator case. This kind of annotation was not available in TDB because the annotation guidelines state that the discourse connectives at the peripheries of the arguments should be left out. Machine Learning can help us spot these instances.

The second reason for crossing is the *wrapping* of the first arguments of (a) and (c) around the subordinate clause. This crossing is in fact not a configuration-level dependency, but a relation-level surface phenomenon confined within the relation anchored by *için* 'because', without underlying complex discourse semantics. Example (8) is a simpler case where the surface crossing within the relation can be observed.

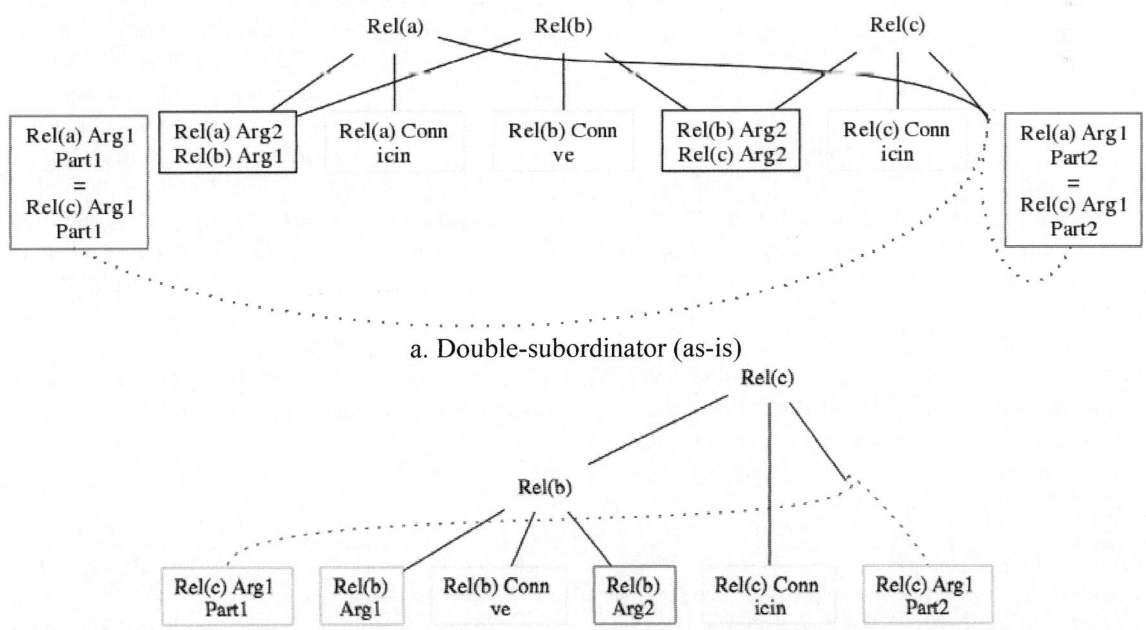

b. Single-subordinator (hypothetical)

Figure 6 - Configuration for (7) as is, and the hypothetical single-subordinator version

(8) 10380000-3

1882'de İstanbul Ticaret Odası, **bir zahire ve ticaret borsası kurulması** <u>için</u> *girişimde bulunuyor* ama sonuç alamıyor.

"In 1882, İstanbul Chamber of Commerce makes an attempt <u>for</u> **founding a Provisions and Commodity Exchange Market** but cannot obtain a result."

Subordinators in Turkish form adverbial clauses (Kornfilt, 1997), so they can occupy any position that is legitimate for a sentential adverb.

Wrapping in discourse seems to be motivated information-structurally. In the unmarked position, the subordinate clause comes before the matrix clause and introduces a theme. However, the discourse constituents can occupy different positions or carry non-neutral prosodic features to express different information structures (Demirşahin, 2008). In (7), wrapping takes *ceza* 'penalty' away from the rheme and makes it part of the theme, at the same time bringing the causal discourse relation into the rheme.

As is clear from the gloss in (7) and its stringset, this is function application, where *ceza verildi* 'penalty was given' wraps in the first argument as a whole. Double occurrence of the "connective" within the wrapped-in argument is causing the apparent crossing, but there is in fact one discourse relation.

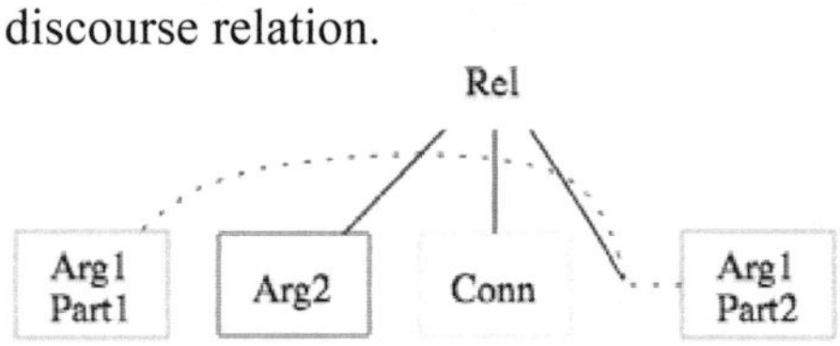

Figure 7 - Wrapping

Wrapping in discourse is almost exclusive to subordinating conjunctions, possibly due to their adverbial freedom in sentence-level syntax. The subordinators make up 468 of the total of 479 wrapping cases identified in TDB. However, there are also four cases of coordinating conjunctions with wrapping. Two of them result in surface crossing as in (9), and the other two build a nested-like structure, as in (10) and (11). The latter two are both parentheticals.

(9) 10690000-32

Bezirci'nin *sonradan elimize geçen* <u>ve</u> **1985'lerde yaptığı** antoloji hazırlığında, [...]

"In the preparation for an anthology **which Bezirci made during 1985's** <u>and</u> *which came into our possession later*[...]"

In (9) *ve* 'and' links two relative clauses, one of which seems to be embedded in the other. It should be noted that the first part of Arg1 (*Bezirci-nin*) has an ambiguous suffix. The suffix could be the agreement marker of the relative clause, as reflected in the annotation, or it could be the genitive marked complement of the genitive-possessive construction *Bezirci'nin antoloji hazırlığı* 'Bezirci's anthology preparation'. The latter analysis does not cause wrapping.

(10) 00003121-26

Biz yasalar karşısında evli sayılacak, ama *gerçekte evli iki insan gibi değil de* (**evlilikler sıradanlaşıyordu** <u>çünkü</u>**, tekdüze ve sıkıcıydı**; biz farklı olacaktık), *aynı evi paylaşan iki öğrenci gibi yaşayacaktık.*

"We would be married under the law, but *in reality we would live like two students sharing the same house rather than two married people* (<u>because</u> **marriages were getting ordinary, (they were) monotonous and boring**; we would be different)."

(11) 00008113-10

Masa ya da duvar saatleri bulunmayan, ezan seslerini her zaman duyamayıp zamanı öğrenmek için *erkeklerin (***evde oldukları** <u>zaman</u>**, tabii***) cep saatiyle doğanın ışık saatine ve kendi içgüdüleriyle tahminlerine bel bağlayan* birçok aile, yaşamlarını bu top sesine göre ayarlarlardı.

"Lots of families who didn't have a table clock or a wall clock and couldn't always hear the prayer calls, who *relied upon the men's pocket watch (*<u>when</u> **they were home, of course***) and their instincts and guesses* to learn the time adjusted their lives according to this cannon shot."

Both (10) and (11) are parentheticals, resulting in a double-wrapping-like construction (Figure 8). However, parentheticals move freely in the clause and occupy various positions, so we believe that this construction should be taken as a peculiarity of the parenthetical, rather than the structural connectives involved in the relation.

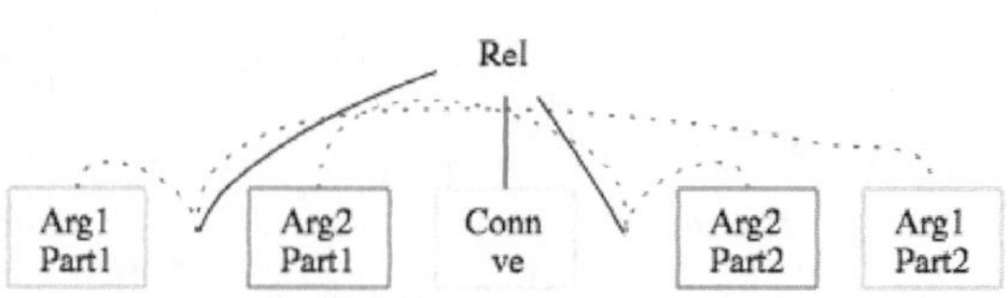

Figure 8 - Double-wrap-like Parenthetical Construction for (10)

4 Conclusion

In this paper we presented possible deviations from the tree structure in the first release of TDB. Following Lee *et al.* (2006, 2008) and Aktaş *et al.* (2010). We have scanned the corpus for shared arguments, properly contained relations and arguments, partial overlaps, and pure crossings. Overall, about half of these configurations can be accounted for by anaphoric relations, i.e. they are not applicative structures (see Table 2). Note that if one of the relations in a configuration is anaphoric, we treat the configuration as anaphoric.

Configuration	Structural	Anaphoric	Total
Shared Argument	158	331	489
	32.31%	67.69%	100.00%
Prop. Cont. Arg.	65	129	194
	33.51%	66.49%	100.00%
Prop. Cont. Rel.	547	471	1018
	53.73%	46.27%	100.00%
Pure Crossing	1	1	2
	50.00%	50.00%	100.00%
Partial Overlap	9	3	12
	75.00%	25.00%	100.00%
Total	780	935	1715
	45.48%	54.52%	100.00%

Table 2: Distribution of anaphoric relations among tree-violating configurations

In addition to the shared arguments that were accepted in discourse structure by Lee *et al.*, we have also come up with partially contained relations arising from verbal complements and relative clauses. These structures can be treated differently in other frameworks; for instance in RST, they are treated as discourse constituents taking part in coherence relations. However, for the connective-based approach adopted in this study, they need to be accommodated as deviations from tree structure.

The few partial overlaps we have encountered could mostly be explained away by wrapping and by different interpretations of annotation guidelines by the annotators, especially the minimality principle. Recall that wrap has applicative semantics. Of the two pure crossing examples we have found, one was also anaphoric, whereas the other could be explained in terms of information-structurally motivated relation-level surface crossing, rather than configuration-level crossing dependency. In other words, if we leave the processing of information structure to other processes, the need for more elaborate annotation disappears. In Joshi's (2011) terminology, immediate discourse in the TDB appears to be an applicative structure, which, unlike syntax, seems to be in no need of currying.

As a result, we can state that pure crossing (i.e. crossing of the arguments of structural connectives) is not genuinely attested in the current release of TDB. The annotation scheme need not be enriched to allow more complex algorithms to deal with unlimited use of crossing. There seems to be a reason in every contested case to go back to the annotation, and revise it in ways to keep the applicative semantics, without losing much of the connective's meaning.

In summary, our preliminary analysis shows that discourse structure may have to accommodate partial containment and wrap in addition to shared arguments. TDB has an applicative structure.

Taking into account that *independent relations*, *fully embedded relations* and *nested relations* are frequent in discourse structure, and that the discourse structure should accommodate shared arguments and partial containments; we are currently inclined to think of discourse structure as Hobbs (1985) does: local trees of various sizes connected and occasionally intertwined at the edges. Further complications within trees are an open field for further studies.

References

Berfin Aktaş, Cem Bozşahin, Deniz Zeyrek. 2010. Discourse Relation Configurations in Turkish and an Annotation Environment. *Proc. LAW IV - The Fourth Linguistic Annotation Workshop.*

Nicholas Asher. 1993. *Reference to Abstract Objects in Discourse.* Kluwer Academic Publishers.

Işın Demirşahin. 2008. Connective Position, Argument Order and Information Structure of Discourse Connectives in Written Turkish Texts. Unpublished MS Thesis, Cognitive Science Program, Middle East Technical University.

Işın Demirşahin, Ayışığı Sevdik-Çallı, Hale Ögel Balaban, Ruket Çakıcı and Deniz Zeyrek. 2012. Turkish Discourse Bank: Ongoing Developments. *Proc. LREC 2012. The First Turkic Languages Workshop.*

Markus Egg, Gisela Redeker. 2010. How Complex is Discourse Structure? *Proc. 7th International Conference on Language Resources and Evaluation (LREC 2010)* pp. 1619–23.

Michael A. K. Halliday, Ruqaiya Hasan. 1976. *Cohesion in English.* London: Longman

Jerry R. Hobbs. 1985. On the Coherence and Structure of Discourse. *Report CSLI-85-37, Center for Study of Language and Information.*

Aravind K. Joshi. 1985. How Much Context-sensitivity is Necessary for Characterizing Structural Descriptions: Tree Adjoining Grammars. In David Dowty, Lauri Karttunen and Arnold Zwicky (eds.) *Natural Language Parsing*. Cambridge University Press.

Aravind K. Joshi. 2011. Some Aspects of Transition from Sentence to Discourse. Keynote address, Informatics Science Festival, Middle East Technical University, Ankara, June 9.

Alistair Knott, Jon Oberlander, Michael O'Donnel, Chris Mellish. 2001. Beyond elaboration: The interaction of relations and focus in coherent text. In Ted Sanders, Joost Schilperoord and Wilbert Spooren (Eds.), *Text Representation: Linguistic and psycholinguistic aspects* (181-196): John Benjamins Publishing.

Jacqueline Kornfilt. 1997. *Turkish.* New York: Routledge.

Alan Lee, Rashmi Prasad, Aravind K. Joshi, Nikhil Dinesh, Bonnie Webber. 2006. Complexity of dependencies in discourse: are dependencies in discourse more complex than in syntax? *Proc. 5th Workshop on Treebanks and Linguistic Theory (TLT'06).*

Alan Lee, Rashmi Prasad, Aravind K. Joshi, Bonnie Webber. 2008. Departures from tree structures in discourse. *Proc. Workshop on Constraints in Discourse III.*

William C. Mann, Sandra A. Thompson. 1988. Rhetorical structure theory: Toward a functional theory of text organization. *Text, 8(3),* 243-281.

Rashmi Prasad, Nikhil Dinesh, Alan Lee, Eleni Miltsakaki, Livio Robaldo, Aravind K. Joshi, Bonnie Webber. 2008. The Penn Discourse Treebank 2.0. *Proc. LREC'08 - The sixth international conference on Language Resources and Evaluation.*

Bilge Say, Deniz Zeyrek, Kemal Oflazer, and Umut Özge. 2002. Development of a Corpus and a Treebank for Present-day Written Turkish. *Proc. Eleventh International Conference on Turkish Linguistics (ICTL 2002).*

Stuart Shieber. 1985. Evidence against the Context-Freeness of Natural Language. *Linguistics and Philosophy*: 8:333-343.

Bonnie Webber. 2004. D-LTAG: Extending Lexicalized TAG to Discourse. *Cognitive Science,* 28(5), 751-779.

Florian Wolf, Edward Gibson. 2005. Representing discourse coherence: a corpus-based study. *Computational Linguistics* 31: 249–87.

Deniz Zeyrek, Bonnie Webber. 2008. A Discourse Resource for Turkish: Annotating Discourse Connectives in the METU Turkish Corpus. *Proc. 6 th Workshop on Asian Language Resources, The Third International Joint Conference on Natural Language Processing (IJNLP).*

Deniz Zeyrek, Işın Demirşahin, Ayışığı Sevdik-Çallı, Hale Ögel Balaban, İhsan Yalçınkaya, Ümit Deniz Turan. 2010. The annotation scheme of Turkish discourse bank and an evaluation of inconsistent annotations. *Proc. 4th Linguistic Annotation Workshop (LAW IV).*

TURKSENT: A Sentiment Annotation Tool for Social Media

Gülşen Eryiğit
Dep. of Computer Eng.
Istanbul Technical University
gulsen.cebiroglu@itu.edu.tr

Fatih Samet Çetin and **Meltem Yanık**
Dep. of Information Technology
Turkcell Global Bilgi
fatih.cetin@global-bilgi.com.tr
meltem.yanik@global-bilgi.com.tr

Tanel Temel
Dep. of Information Technology
Turkcell Global Bilgi
tanel.temel@global-bilgi.com.tr

İlyas Çiçekli
Dep. of Computer Eng.
Hacettepe University
ilyas@cs.hacettepe.edu.tr

Abstract

In this paper, we present an annotation tool developed specifically for manual sentiment analysis of social media posts. The tool provides facilities for general and target based opinion marking on different type of posts (i.e. comparative, ironic, conditional) with a web based UI which supports synchronous annotation. It is also designed as a SaaS (Software as a Service). The tool's outstanding features are easy and fast annotation interface, detailed sentiment levels, multi-client support, easy to manage administrative modules and linguistic annotation capabilities.

1 Introduction

Today, monitoring social media is a vital need for companies and it has a high commercial value. So almost all companies have social media accounts and departments for following the social media about their business sectors. In recent decade, the studies on sentiment analysis has gained high popularity and several academic (Pang and Lee, 2007; Liu, 2012) and commercial (Radian6, 2013; Lithium, 2013) projects emerged in this field. Although there are many works (Bosco et al., 2013; Wiebe et al., 2005) on creating sentiment corpora, up to our knowledge there are no publicly available and professional sentiment annotation tools.

A huge contact center communicates with the customers for different trade marks on behalf of them and provides detailed CRM[1], impact and competitor analysis reports. With this purpose, they employ thousands of customer representatives among which an increasing percentage should deal with social media monitoring, the new channel of communication. In such an environment, the monitoring should be done via professional and synchronous UIs (user interfaces) where the performance of each human agent has high importance. Most of the current commercial monitoring tools leaks the following features:

- a detailed sentiment analysis interface for feature based and comparative opinion declarations,
- an effective and synchronous annotation interface,
- on-demand data loading,
- linguistic annotation modules,
- detailed data analyses for corpus creation (to be used in supervised machine learning).

The aim of our work is to fulfill all of the above listed requirements and provide a platform for effective annotation of social media data. The tool has the following sentiment and linguistic annotation layers:

- general and target based sentiment
- text normalization
- named entity
- morphology
- syntax

The sentiment annotation module of TURKSENT may operate multilingually whereas the linguistic annotation module is initially configured

[1] CRM: Customer Relationship Management

specific to Turkish following the work in ITU Treebank Annotation Tool (Eryiğit, 2007). It is also possible to adapt this part to other languages by plugging relevant linguistic adapters (for semi-automatic annotation).

TURKSENT will be freely available for academic projects as a SaaS.

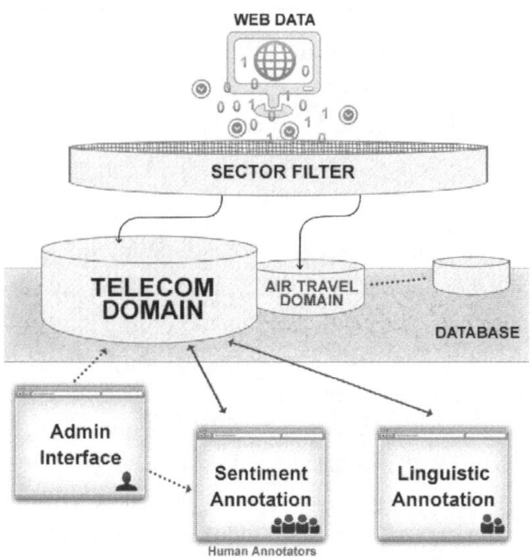

Figure 1: Application Flow

2 Architecture

Figure 1 gives an idea about the flow of our application. In our system, the web data is monitored continuously. It is first of all filtered according to the target sector by the "sector filter" and it is then stored in the relevant database domains. In our system, each domain represents a workspace which consists of the related sector data (collected via web or uploaded manually to the system), an administrator and a bunch of human annotators.

2.1 Sentiment Annotation

Our choice of SaaS design has the following goals:

- Platform independence (No special machine or no special operating system)
- Accessibility (Accessible from anywhere anytime by multiple users)
- No installation effort (Browser based application)
- No need to deploy updates to clients

Figure 2 gives a sample sentiment annotation screen-shot on an example Tweet ("Samsung Galaxy S4's hardware features are amazing but software is not stable as Iphone"). The upper half of the screen (up to the table) show the general sentiment part which is tagged as ***both***[2] (the ambivalent smiley). General sentiment tagging means identifying the sentimental class regardless of a target. In other words, extracting dominant sentimental class of an instance. In this stage the annotator is also expected to select an appropriate comment category and sentence type.

The lower half is for target based sentiment annotation. These deep sentiments are represented as tuples consisting of the brand, product/service, feature and sentiment tags. For example, the first tuple in the sample Tweet will be composed as the following: <Samsung, Galaxy S4, hardware, positive> which means the hardware feature of the Samsung Brand's product Galaxy S4 had a positive impact on the Tweet's author.

2.2 Linguistic Annotation

Recent researches on sentiment analysis show that it is not possible to really understand the sentiment of a sentence without any natural language processing (NLP). And the addition of NLP features to these systems increases the success ratios of the automatic analyzers dramatically. In order to be able to prepare a sentiment corpus, being able to annotate the focus data within the same platform is an important issue. Furthermore, the web data has severe differences when compared to formal natural language text and it needs additional preprocessing before linguistic phases. With this need, we added a linguistic annotation interface to our application which is basically a reimplementation and adaptation of a previous academic study (Eryiğit, 2007) according to our needs.

In this layer, the linguistic expert annotator is asked to first normalize the instances (i.e. misspellings, exaggerations, web jargon), and then determine the entities (ex: "Galaxy S4"), select the appropriate postag categories for words and annotate the syntactic parts of a post. It is also possible to operate this layer semi-automatically by using the pretrained linguistic tools and outputting their

[2]Other options are: positive, negative and neutral(no sentimental expression at all).

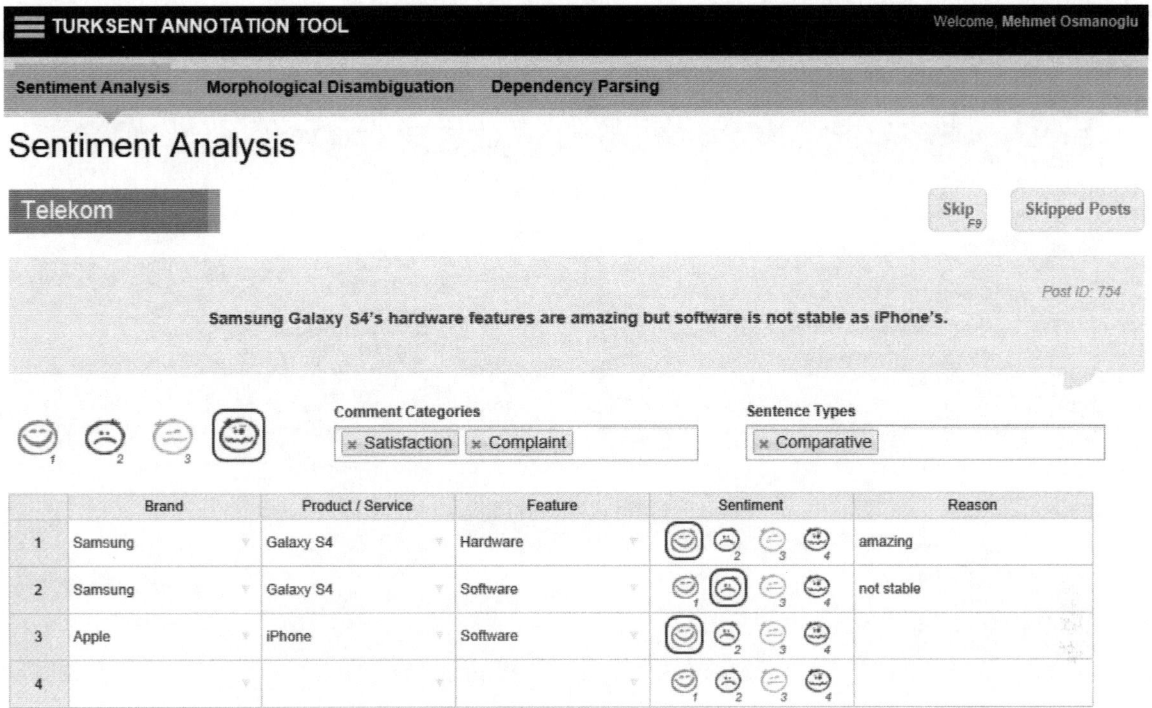

Figure 2: Sentiment annotation

results to the human experts and taking their corrections. This speed-up procedure is only available for Turkish now, but the tool is developed as a pluggable architecture to support further studies on other languages. Figure 3 shows some sample screenshots for the linguistic layer.

2.3 Administrative Operations

TURKSENT has a simple and easy-to-use admin interface. A user who has administration rights has the ability to perform the actions listed below:

- Creating a workspace (with a focus data and annotator group)
- Determining the data subsets for linguistic annotation
- Controlling/Changing the ongoing annotations
- Defining configurable items (sentence types, comment categories, product/service list, feature list, brand list)
- Defining linguistic tags (pos tags, named entity types, dependency types)

3 Usability

The usability is seriously taken into account during the design and development of our application. The spent time per post is a high concern within big operations. End-user software tests are accomplished and observed for each step. On the final UI design, every action can be done via keyboard without the need of mouse usage. Almost every text areas has strong auto-completion feature in itself. While an annotator is working on an issue, it is possible to deliver any idea-suggestion to the administrator within seconds. And if an annotator need to browse his/her previous annotations, can easily search and find within them.

4 Conclusion

In this work, we presented a professional sentiment annotation tool TURKSENT which supports synchronous annotations on a web-based platform. The study is a part of an automatic sentiment analysis research project. That is why, it both aims to manually annotate the sentiments of web posts and to create a sentiment corpus also annotated linguistically (to be used in automatic

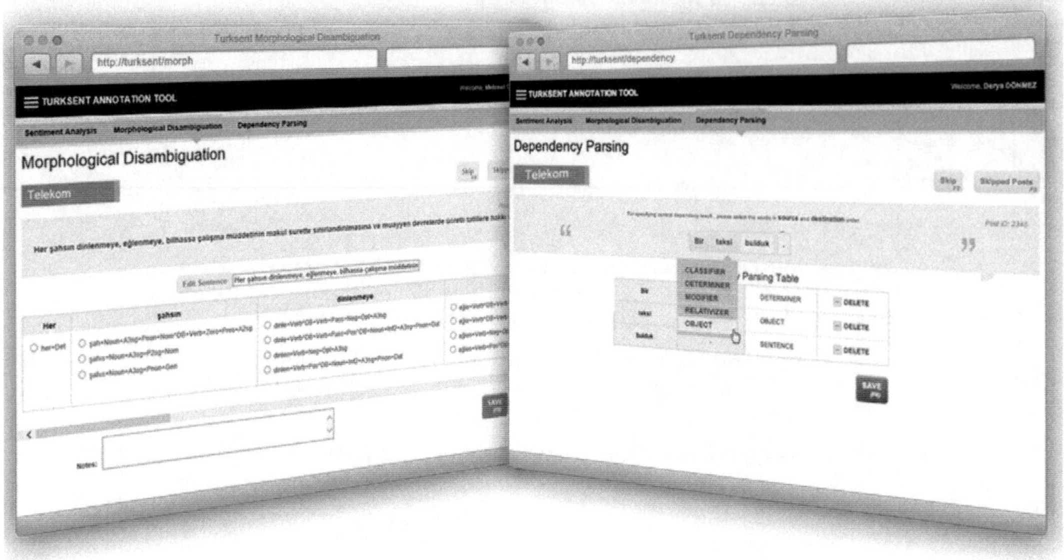

Figure 3: Linguistic Annotations

sentiment analysis). With this purpose it consists different layers of annotation specific to web data. It serves as a SaaS and designed as dynamic as possible for future use on different sectors and languages.

Acknowledgment

This work is accomplished as a part of a TUBITAK-TEYDEB (The Scientific and Technological Research Council of Turkey - Technology and Innovation Funding Programs Directorate) project (grant number: 3120605) in "Turkcell Global Bilgi" Information Technology Department. The authors want to thank Derya Dönmez and Mehmet Osmanoğlu for design and implementation.

References

Cristina Bosco, Viviana Patti, and Andrea Bolioli. 2013. Developing corpora for sentiment analysis and opinion mining: the case of irony and senti-tut. *Intelligent Systems*.

Gülşen Eryiğit. 2007. ITU Treebank Annotation Tool. In *Proceedings of the ACL workshop on Linguistic Annotation (LAW 2007)*, Prague, 24-30 June.

Lithium. 2013. Lithium. `http://www.lithium.com/`.

Bing Liu. 2012. *Sentiment Analysis and Opinion Mining*. Synthesis Lectures on Human Language Technologies. Morgan and Claypool Publishers.

Bo Pang and Lillian Lee. 2007. Opinion mining and sentiment analysis. *Foundations and Trends in Information Retrieval*, 2(1-2):1–135.

Radian6. 2013. Radian 6. `http://www.salesforcemarketingcloud.com/products/social-media-listening/`.

Janyce Wiebe, Theresa Wilson, and Claire Cardie. 2005. Annotating expressions of opinions and emotions in language. *Language Resources and Evaluation*, 39(2-3):165–210.

Tweet Conversation Annotation Tool
with a Focus on an Arabic Dialect, Moroccan Darija

Stephen Tratz[†], **Douglas Briesch**[†], **Jamal Laoudi**[‡], and **Clare Voss**[†]
†Army Research Laboratory, Adelphi, MD 20783
‡ArtisTech, Inc., Fairfax, VA 22030
{stephen.c.tratz.civ,douglas.m.briesch.civ,jamal.laoudi.ctr,clare.r.voss.civ}@mail.mil

Abstract

This paper presents the DATOOL, a graphical tool for annotating conversations consisting of short messages (i.e., tweets), and the results we obtain in using it to annotate tweets for Darija, an historically unwritten Arabic dialect spoken by millions but not taught in schools and lacking standardization and linguistic resources.

With the DATOOL, a native-Darija speaker annotated hundreds of mixed-language and mixed-script conversations at approximately 250 tweets per hour. The resulting corpus was used in developing and evaluating Arabic dialect classifiers described briefly herein.

The DATOOL supports downstream discourse analysis of tweeted "conversations" by mapping extracted relations such as, *who tweets to whom in which language,* into graph markup formats for analysis in network visualization tools.

1 Overview

For historically unwritten languages, few textual resources exist for developing NLP applications such as machine translation engines. Even when audio resources are available, difficulties arise when converting sound to text (Robinson and Gadelii, 2003). Increasingly, however, with the widespread use of mobile phones, these languages are being written in social media such as Twitter. Not only can these languages be written in multiple scripts, but conversations, and even individual messages, often involve multiple languages. To build useful textual resources for documenting and translating these languages (e.g., bilingual dictionaries), tools are needed to assist in language annotation for this noisy, multiscript, multilingual form of communication.

This paper presents the Dialect Annotation Tool (DATOOL), a graphical tool for annotating conversations consisting of short messages (i.e., tweets), and the results we obtain in using it to annotate tweets for Darija, an historically unwritten North African Arabic dialect spoken by millions but not taught in schools and lacking in standardardization and linguistic resources. The DATOOL can retrieve the conversation for each tweet on a user's timeline or via Apollo (Le et al., 2011) and display the discourse, enabling annotators to make more informed decisions. It has integrated classifiers for automatically annotating data so a user can either verify or alter the automatically-generated annotations rather than start from scratch. The tool can also export annotated data to GEPHI (Bastian et al., 2009), an open source network visualization tool with many layout algorithms, which will facilitate future "code-switching" research.

2 Tool Description

2.1 Version 1.0

The first version of the tool is depicted in Figure 1. It is capable of loading a collection of tweets and extracting the full conversations they belong to. Each conversation is displayed within its own block in the conversation display table. An annotator can mark multiple tweets as Darija (or other language) by selecting multiple checkboxes in the lefthand side of the table. Also, if a tweet is written in multiple languages, the annotator can annotate the different sections using the *Message* text box below the conversation display table.

The tool also calculates user and collection level summary statistics, which it displays below the main annotation section.

We worked with a Darija-speaking annotator during the tool's development, who provided valuable feedback, helping to shape the overall design of the tool and improve its functionality.

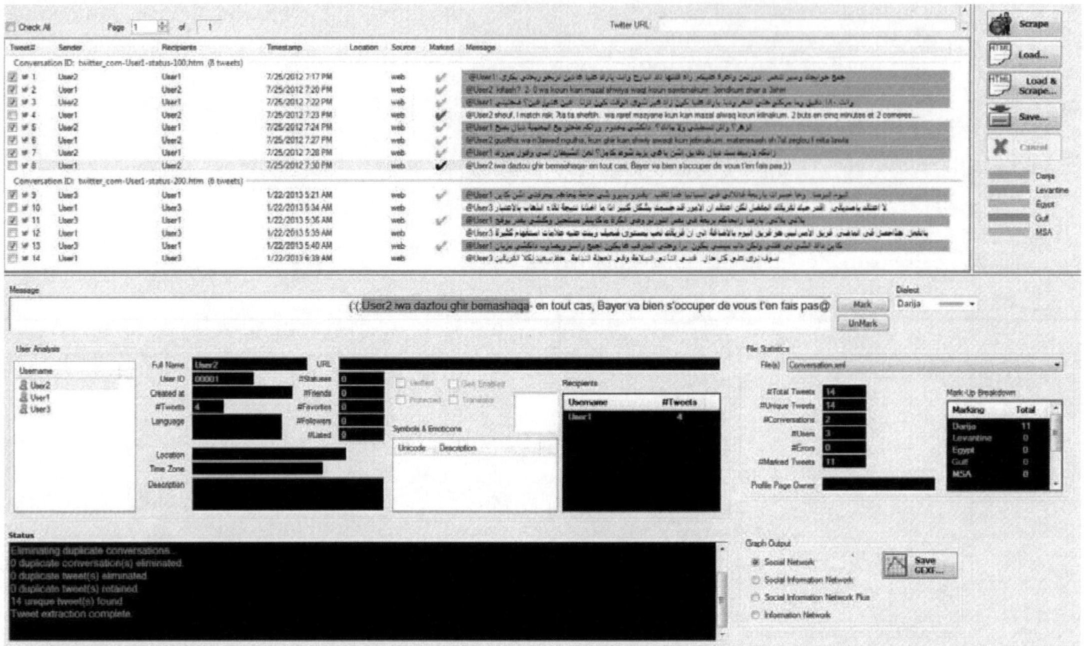

Figure 1: The Dialect Annotation Tool (DATOOL) displaying a possible Twitter conversation.

Data Annotation Using version 1.0, the annotator marked up 3013 tweets from 3 users for the presence of the Darija (approximately 1,000 per user), averaging about 250 tweets per hour. Of the 1,400 tweets with Arabic script, 1,013 contained Darija. This annotated data is used to evaluate the Arabic dialect classifier discussed in Section 3.

2.2 Version 2.0

The second version of the tool contains the additional ability to invoke pre-trained classification models to automatically annotate tweets. The tool displays the classifier's judgment confidence next to each tweet, and the user can set a minimal confidence threshold, below which automatic annotations are hidden. Figure 2 illustrates the new classification functionality.

2.3 XML Output

The DATOOL stores data in an XML-based format that can be reloaded for continuing or revising annotation. It can also export four different views of the data in Graph Exchange XML Format (GEXF), a format that can be read by GEPHI. In the *social network* view, users are represented by nodes, and tweets are represented as directed edges between the nodes. The *information network* view displays tweets as nodes with directed edges between time-ordered tweets within a conversation. In the *social-information network* view, both users and tweets are represented by nodes, and there are directed edges both from tweet senders to their tweets and from tweets to recipients. The *social-information network plus* view provides all the information of both the social network and the information network.

3 Classifier

For the second version of the DATOOL, we integrated an Arabic dialect classifier capable of distinguishing among Darija, Egyptian, Gulf, Levantine and MSA with the goal of improving the speed and consistency of the annotation process.

Though language classification is sometimes viewed as a solved problem (McNamee, 2005), with some experiments achieving over 99% accuracy (Cavnar and Trenkle, 1994), it is significantly more difficult when distinguishing closely-related languages or short texts (Vatanen et al., 2010; da Silva and Lopes, 2006). The only language classification work for distinguishing between these closely-related Arabic dialects that we are aware of was performed by Zaidan and Callison-Burch (2013). They collected web commentary data written in MSA, Egyptian, Levantine, and Gulf and performed dialect identification experiments, their strongest classifier achiev-

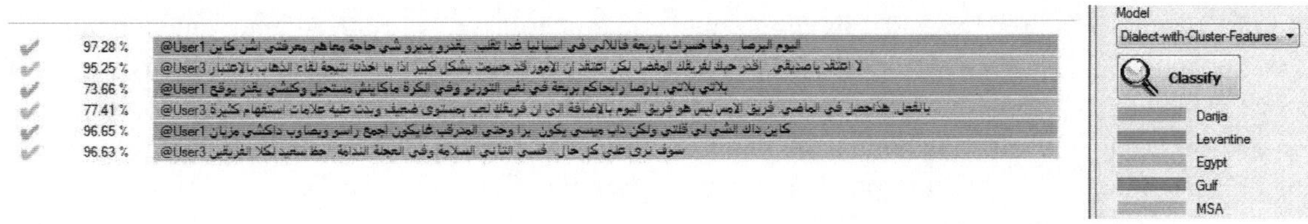

Figure 2: Screenshot showcasing the automatic classification output, including confidence values.

ing 81.0% accuracy.

3.1 Training Data

Since Zaidan and Callison-Burch's dataset includes no Darija, we collected Darija examples from the following sources to augment their dataset: Moroccan jokes from `noktazwina.com`, web pages collected using Darija-specific query terms with a popular search engine, and 37,538 Arabic script commentary entries from `hespress.com` (a Moroccan news website).

Nearly all the joke (N=399) and query term (N=874) data contained Darija. By contrast, the commentary data was mostly MSA. To extract a subset of the commentary entries most likely to contain Darija, we applied an iterative, semi-supervised approach similar to that described by Tratz and Sanfilippo (2007), in which the joke and query term data were treated as initial seeds and, in each iteration, a small portion of commentary data with the highest Darija scores were added to the training set. After having run this process to its completion, we examined 131 examples at intervals of 45 from the resulting ranked list of commentary. The 62nd example was the first of these to have been incorrectly classified as containing Darija. We thus elected to assume all examples up to the 61st of the 131 contain Darija, for a total of 2,745 examples (61*45=2,745). As an additional check, we examined two more commentary entries from each of the 61 blocks, finding that 118 of 122 contain Darija.

3.2 Initial Classifier

The integrated dialect classifier is a Maximum Entropy model (Berger et al., 1996) that we train using the LIBLINEAR (Fan et al., 2008) toolkit. In preprocessing, Arabic diacritics are removed, all non-alphabetic and non-Arabic script characters are converted to whitespace, and sequences of any repeating character are collapsed to a single character. The following set of feature templates are applied to each of the resulting whitespace-separated tokens:

- The full token
- 'Shape' of the token—all consonants are replaced by the letter *C*, alefs by *A*, and *waws* and *yehs* by *W*
- First character plus the last character (if length ≥ 2)
- Character unigrams, bigrams, and trigrams
- The last character of the token plus the first character of the next token
- Prefixes of length 1, 2, and 3
- Indicators that token starts with *mA* and
  - ends with *$*
  - the next token ends with *$*
  - is length 5 or greater

3.3 LDA Model

As an exploratory effort, we investigated using Latent Direchlet Allocation (LDA) (Blei et al., 2003) as a method of language identification. Unfortunately, using the aforementioned feature templates, LDA produced topics that corresponded poorly with the training data labels. But, after several iterations of feature engineering, the topics began to reflect the dialect distinctions. Our final LDA model feature templates are listed below.

- The full token
- Indicators that the token contains
  - *theh*; *thal*; *zah*; *theh*, *thal*, **or** *zah*
- Indicators the token is of length 5+ and starts with
  - *hah* plus *yeh*, *teh*, *noon*, or *alef*
  - *seen* plus *yeh*, *teh*, *noon*, or *alef*
  - *beh* plus *yeh*, *teh*, *noon*, or *alef*
  - *ghain* plus *yeh*, *teh*, or *noon*
  - or *kaf* plus *yeh*, *teh*, or *noon*
- Indicators that token starts with *mA* and
  - ends with *$*
  - the next token ends with *$*
  - is length 5 or greater

The following features produced using the LDA model for each document are given to the Maximum Entropy classifier: 1) indicator of the most-likely cluster, 2) product of scores for each pair of clusters.

3.4 Classifier Evaluation

We evaluated the versions of the classifier by applying them to the annotated data discussed in

Section 2.1. The initial classifier without the LDA-derived features achieved 96.9% precision and 24.1% recall. The version with LDA-derived features achieved 97.2% precision and 44.1% recall, a substantial improvement. Upon review, we concluded that most cases where the classifier "incorrectly" selected the Darija label were due to errors in the gold standard.

4 Analysis of Annotated Conversations

Visualization of Darija in Conversations

The DATOOL may recover the conversation in which a tweet occurs, providing the annotator with the tweet's full, potentially-multilingual context. To visualize the distribution of Darija[1] by script in ≈1K tweets from each user's conversations, the DATOOL transforms and exports annotated data into a GEXF information network (cf. Figure 3), which can be displayed in GEPHI.[2] Currently, GEPHI displays at most one edge between any two nodes—GEPHI automatically augments the edge's weight for each additional copy of the edge.

The Darija in this user's conversations, unlike our two other users, is predominantly Romanized. With more data, we plan to assess the impact of one user's script and language choice on others.

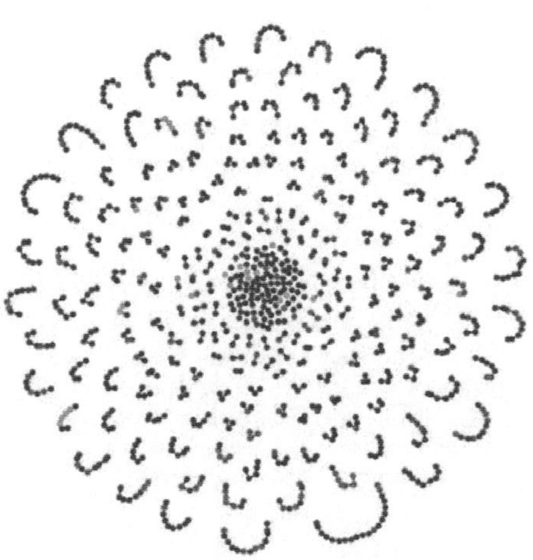

Figure 3: Information network visualization. *Red*—contains Romanized Darija; *green*—contains Arabic-script Darija; *blue*—no Darija.

Code-Switching

The alternation of Darija with non-Darija in the information network (red and green nodes vs. blue nodes) within conversations is consistent with well-known code-switching among Arabic speakers, extending spoken discourse into informal writing (Bentahila and Davies, 1983; Redouane, 2005). Code-switching also appears within our tweet corpus where Romanized Darija frequently alternates with French. Given the prevalence of code-switching within tweets, future work will entail training a Roman-script classifier at the token level.[3] Since our DATOOL already supports token-level as well as multi-token, tweet-internal annotation in the mid-screen *Message* box, our current corpus provides a seed set for this effort.

5 Conclusion and Future Work

The DATOOL now supports semi-automated annotation of tweet conversations for Darija. As we scale the process of building low-resource language corpora, we will document its impact on annotation time when few native speakers are available, a condition also relevant and critical to preserving endangered languages. We have begun extending the classifier to support additional Arabic script languages (e.g., Farsi, Urdu), leveraging resources from others (Bergsma et al., 2012).

Many other open questions remain regarding the annotation process, the visualizations, and the human expert. Which classified examples should the language expert review? When should an annotator adjust the confidence threshold in the DATOOL? For deeper linguistic analysis and code-switching prediction, would seeing participants and tweets, turn by turn, in network diagrams such as Figure 4 help experts understand new patterns emerging in tweet conversations?

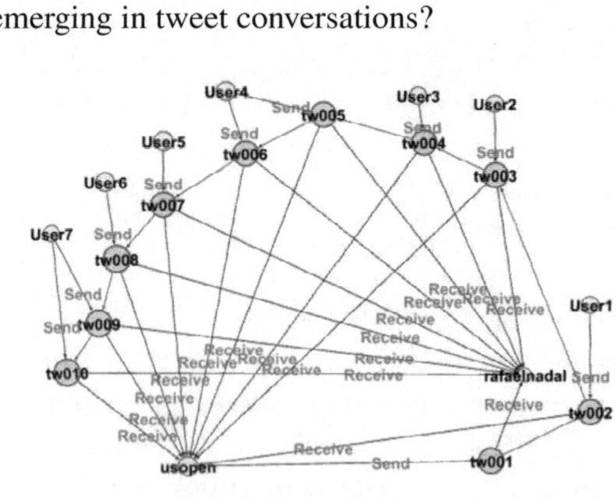

Figure 4: Social-Information Network Plus.

[1] In our initial annotation work, words and tweets in languages other than Darija received no markup.

[2] GEPHI's Force Atlas layout automatically positions subgraphs by size, with larger ones further away from the center.

[3] As described in Section 3, our current classifier works at the tweet level and only on Arabic-script tweets.

Acknowledgments

We would like to thank Tarek Abdelzaher for all his feedback regarding our work and guidance in using Apollo. We would also like to thank our reviewers for their valuable comments and suggestions.

References

Mathieu Bastian, Sebastien Heymann, and Mathieu Jacomy. 2009. Gephi: An Open Source Software for Exploring and Manipulating Networks. In *International AAAI Conference on Weblogs and Social Media*.

Abdelali Bentahila and Eirlys E Davies. 1983. The Syntax of Arabic-French Code-Switching. *Lingua*, 59(4):301–330.

Adam L. Berger, Vincent J. Della Pietra, and Stephen A. Della Pietra. 1996. A Maximum Entropy Approach to Natural Language Processing. *Computational Linguistics*, 22(1):39–71.

Shane Bergsma, Paul McNamee, Mossaab Bagdouri, Clayton Fink, and Theresa Wilson. 2012. Language Identification for Creating Language-Specific Twitter Collections. In *Proceedings of the 2012 Workshop on Language in Social Media (LSM 2012)*, pages 65–74.

David Blei, Andrew Ng, and Michael Jordan. 2003. Latent dirichlet allocation. *The Journal of Machine Learning Research*, 3:993–1022.

William B Cavnar and John M Trenkle. 1994. N-gram-based text categorization. *Ann Arbor MI*, 48113(2):161–175.

Joaquim Ferreira da Silva and Gabriel Pereira Lopes. 2006. Identification of document language is not yet a completely solved problem. In *Computational Intelligence for Modelling, Control and Automation, 2006 and International Conference on Intelligent Agents, Web Technologies and Internet Commerce, International Conference on*, pages 212–212. IEEE.

Rong-En Fan, Kai-Wei Chang, Cho-Jui Hsieh, Xiang-Rui Wang, and Chih-Jen Lin. 2008. LIBLINEAR: A Library for Large Linear Classification. *Journal of Machine Learning Research*, 9:1871–1874.

Hieu Khac Le, Jeff Pasternack, Hossein Ahmadi, M. Gupta, Y. Sun, Tarek F. Abdelzaher, Jiawei Han, Dan Roth, Boleslaw K. Szymanski, and Sibel Adali. 2011. Apollo: Towards factfinding in participatory sensing. In *IPSN*, pages 129–130.

Paul McNamee. 2005. Language identification: A solved problem suitable for undergraduate instruction. *Journal of Computing Sciences in Colleges*, 20(3):94–101.

Rabia Redouane. 2005. Linguistic constraints on codeswitching and codemixing of bilingual Moroccan Arabic-French speakers in Canada. In *ISB4: Proceedings of the 4th International Symposium on Bilingualism*, pages 1921–1933.

Clinton Robinson and Karl Gadelii. 2003. Writing Unwritten Languages, A Guide to the Process. *http://portal.unesco.org/education/en/ev.php-URL_ID=28300&URL_DO=DO_TOPIC&URL_SECTION=201.html*, UNESCO, Paris, France. December.

Stephen Tratz and Antonio Sanfilippo. 2007. A High Accuracy Method for Semi-supervised Information Extraction. In *Human Language Technologies 2007: The Conference of the North American Chapter of the Association for Computational Linguistics; Companion Volume, Short Papers*, pages 169–172.

Tommi Vatanen, Jaakko J Väyrynen, and Sami Virpioja. 2010. Language identification of short text segments with n-gram models. In *Proceedings of the Seventh International Conference on Language Resources and Evaluation LREC'10*.

Omar Zaidan and Chris Callison-Burch. 2013. Arabic dialect identification. *Computational Linguistics (To Appear)*.

Relation Annotation for Understanding Research Papers

Yuka Tateisi† Yo Shidahara‡ Yusuke Miyao† Akiko Aizawa†
†National Institute of Informatics, Tokyo, Japan
{yucca,yusuke,aizawa}@nii.ac.jp
‡Freelance Annotator
yo.shidahara@gmail.com

Abstract

We describe a new annotation scheme for formalizing relation structures in research papers. The scheme has been developed through the investigation of computer science papers. Using the scheme, we are building a Japanese corpus to help develop information extraction systems for digital libraries. We report on the outline of the annotation scheme and on annotation experiments conducted on research abstracts from the IPSJ Journal.

1 Introduction

Present day researchers need services for searching research papers. Search engines and publishing companies provide specialized search services, such as Google Scholar, Microsoft Academic Search, and Science Direct. Academic societies provide archives of journal articles and/or conference proceedings such as the ACL Anthology. These services focus on simple keyword-based searches as well as extralinguistic relations among research papers, authors, and research topics. However, because contemporary research is becoming increasingly complicated and interrelated, intelligent content-based search systems are desired (Banchs, 2012). A typical query in computational linguistics could be *what tasks have CRFs been used for?*, which includes the elements of a typical schema for searching research papers; researchers want to find relationships between a technique and its applications (Gupta and Manning, 2011). Answers to this query can be found in various forms in published papers, for example,
(1) CRF-based POS tagging has achieved state-of-the-art accuracy.
(2) CRFs have been successfully applied to sequence labeling problems including POS tagging and named entity recognition.
(3) We apply feature reduction to CRFs and show its effectiveness in POS tagging.
(4) This study proposes a new method for the efficient training of CRFs. The proposed method is evaluated for POS tagging tasks.

Note that the same semantic relation, i.e., the use of CRFs for POS tagging, is expressed by various syntactic constructs: internal structures of the phrase in (1), clause-level structures in (2), inter-clause structures in (3), and discourse-level structures in (4). This implies that an integrated framework is required to represent semantic relations for phrase-level, clause-level, inter-clause level, and discourse-level structures. Another interesting fact is that we can recognize various fragments of information from single texts. For example, from sentence (1), we can identify *CRF is applied to POS tagging*, *state-of-the-art accuracy is achieved for POS tagging*, and *CRFs achieve high POS tagging accuracy*, all of which is valuable content for different search requests. This indicates that we need a framework that can cover (almost) all content in a text.

In this paper we describe a new annotation scheme for formalizing typical schemas for representing relations among concepts in research papers, such as techniques, resources, and effects. Our study aims to establish a framework for representing the semantics of research papers to help construct intelligent search systems. In particular, we focus on the formalization of typical schemas that we believe exemplify common query characteristics.

From the above observations, we have developed the following criteria for our proposed framework: use the same scheme for annotating contents in all levels of linguistic structures, annotate (almost) all contents presented in texts, and capture relations necessary for surveying research papers. We investigated 71 computer science abstracts (498 sentences) and defined an annotation scheme comprising 16 types of semantic relations.

Computer science is particularly suitable for our purpose because it is primarily concerned with abstract concepts rather than concrete entities, which are typically the primary focus of empirical sciences such as physics and biology. In addition, computer and computational methods can be applied to an extraordinarily wide range of topics; computer science papers might discuss a bus timetable (for automatic optimization), a person's palm (as a device for projecting images), or looking over another person s shoulder (to obtain passwords). Therefore, to annotate all computer science papers, we cannot develop predefined entity ontologies, which is the typical approach taken in biomedical text mining (Kim et al., 2011).

However, most computer science papers have characteristic schemata: the papers describe a problem, postulate a method, apply the method to the problem using particular data or devices, and perform experiments to evaluate the method. The typical schemata clearly represent the structure of interests in this research field. Therefore, we can focus on typical schemata, such as *application of a method to a problem* and *evaluation of a method for a task*. As we will demonstrate in this paper, the proposed annotation scheme can cover almost all content, from phrase levels to discourse levels, in computer science papers.

Note that this does not necessarily mean that our framework can only be applied to computer science literature. The characteristics of the schemata described above are universal in contemporary science and engineering, and many other activities in human society. Thus, the framework presented in this study can be viewed as a starting point for research focusing on representative schemata of human activities.

2 Related Work

Traditionally, research on searching research papers has focused more on the social aspects of papers and their authors, such as citation links and co-authorship analysis implemented in the aforementioned services. Recently, research on content-based analysis of research papers has been emerging.

For example, methods of document zoning have been proposed for research papers in biomedicine (Mizuta et al., 2006; Agarwal and Yu, 2009; Liakata et al., 2010; Guo et al., 2011; Varga et al., 2012), and chemistry and computational linguistics (Teufel et al., 2009). Zoning provides a sentence-based information structure of papers to help identify the components such as the proposed method and the results obtained in the study. As such, zoning can narrow down the sections of a paper in which the answer to a query can be found. However, zoning alone cannot always capture the relation between the concepts described in the sections as it focuses on relation at a sentence level. For example, the examples (1), (2), (3) in the previous section require intra-sentence analysis to capture the relation between *CRF* and *POS tagging*. Our annotation scheme, which can be seen as conplementary to zoning, attempts to provide a structure for capturing the relationship between concepts at a finer-grained level than a sentence.

Establishing semantic relations among scientific papers has also been studied. For example, the ACL Anthology Searchbench (Schäfer et al., 2011) provides querying by predicate-argument relations. The system accepts specifications of subject, predicate, and object, and searches for texts that semantically match the query using the results from an HPSG parser. It can also search by topics automatically extracted from the papers. Gupta and Manning (2011) proposed a method for extracting *Focus*, *Domain*, and *Technique* from papers in the ACL anthology: *Focus* is a research article's main contribution, *Domain* is an application domain, and *Technique* is a method or a tool used to achieve the *Focus*. The change in these aspects over time is traced to measure the influence of research communities on each other. Fukuda et al. (2012) developed a method of technical trend analysis that can be applied to both patent applications and academic papers, using the distribution of named entities. However, as processes and functions are key concepts in computer science, elements are often described in a unit with its own internal structures which include data, systems, and other entities as substructures. Thus, technical concepts such as technique cannot be captured fully by extracting named entities. Gupta and Manning (2011) analyzed the internal structures of concepts syntactically using a dependency parser, but did not further investigate the structure semantically.

In addition to the methodological aspects of research, i.e., what techniques are applied to what domain, a research paper can include other information that we also want to capture, such as how the author evaluates current systems and methods or the previous efforts of others. An attempt to identify the evaluation and other *meta*-aspects of scientific papers was made by Thompson et al. (2011), which, on top of the biomedical events annotated in the GENIA event corpus (Kim et al., 2008), annotated meta-knowledge such as the certainty level of the author, polarity (positive–negative), and manner (strong–weak) of events, as well as source (whether the event is attributed to the current study or previous studies), along with the clue mentioned in the text. For in-domain relations within and between the events, they relied on the underlying GENIA annotation, which maps events and their participants to a subset of Gene Ontology (The Gene Ontology Consortium, 2000), a standard ontology in genome science.

We cannot assume the existence of standard domain ontology in the variety of domains to which computer systems are applied, as was mentioned in Section 1. On the other hand, using domain-general linguistic frameworks, such as FrameNet (Ruppenhofer et al., 2006) or the Lexical Conceptual Structure (Jackendoff, 1990) is also not satisfactory for our purpose. These frameworks attempt to identify the relations lexicalized by verbs and their case arguments; however, they do not consider discourse or other levels of linguistic representation. In addition, relying on a linguistic theory requires that annotators understand linguistics. Most computer scientists, the best candidates for performing the annotation task, would not have the necessary knowledge of linguistics and would require training, which would increase costs for corpus annotation.

3 Annotation Scheme

The principle is to employ a uniform structure to represent semantic relations in scientific papers in phrase-level, clause-level, inter-clause level, and discourse-level structures. For this purpose, a bottom-up strategy that identifies relations between the entities mentioned is used. This strategy is similar to dependency parsing/annotation, which identifies the relations between constituents to find the overall structure of sentences.

We did not want the relations to be unconditionally concrete and domain-specific, because, as mentioned in the previous section, new concepts and relations that may not be expressed by pre-defined (concrete, domain-specific) concepts and relations may be created. For the same reason, we did not set specific entity types on the basis of domain ontology. We simply classified entities as "general object," "specific object," and "measurement."

In this paper, we propose a novel strategy for parallel preconditioning of large scale linear systems by means of a two-level approximate inverse technique with AISM method. According to the numerical results on an origin 2400 by using MPI, the proposed parallel technique of computing the approximate inverse makes the speedup of about 136.72 times with 16 processors.

Figure 1: Sample Abstract

To illustrate our scheme, consider the two-sentence abstract[1] shown in Figure 1[2].

In the first sentence, we can read that a method called *two-level approximate inverse* is used for parallel preconditioning (1), the preconditioning is applied to large-scale linear systems, the AISM method is a subcomponent or a substage of the two-level technique, and the author claims that the use of two-level approximate inverse is a novel strategy.

In the second sentence, we can read that the author has conducted a numerical experiment, the experiment was conducted on an origin 2400 (a computer system), message Passing Interface (MPI, a standardized method for message passing) was used in the experiment, the proposed parallel technique was 136.72 times quicker than existing methods, and the speedup was achieved using 16 processors.

In addition, by comparing the two sentences, we can determine that *the proposed parallel technique* in the second sentence refers to the parallel preconditioning using two-level approximate inverse mentioned in the first sentence. Consequently, we can infer the author's claim that the parallel preconditioning using two-level approximate inverse achieved 136.72 times speedup.

We define binary relations including `APPLY_TO`(*A*, *B*) (A method *A* is applied to achieve the purpose *B* or used for doing *B*), `EVALUATE`(*A*, *B*) (*A* is evaluated as

[1]Linjie Zhang, Kentaro Moriya and Takashi Nodera. 2008. Two-level Parallel Computation for Approximate Inverse with AISM Method. IPSJ Journal, 48 (6): 2164-2168.

[2]Although the annotation was done for abstracts in Japanese, we present examples in English except where we discuss issues that we believe are specific to Japanese.

APPLY_TO(*two-level approximate inverse, parallel preconditioning*)
APPLY_TO(*parallel preconditioning, large scale linear systems*)
SUBCONCEPT(*AISM method, two-level approximate inverse*)
EVALUATE(*two-level approximate inverse, novel*)
RESULT(*numerical results, 136.72 times speedup*)
CONDITION(*origin 2400, 136.72 times speedup*)
APPLY_TO(*MPI, numerical results*)
EVALUATE(*the proposed parallel technique, 136.72 times speedup*)
CONDITION(*16 processors, 136.72 times speedup*)
EQUIVALENCE(*the proposed parallel technique, two-level approximate inverse*)

Figure 2: Relations Found in the Sentences in Figure 1

B), SUBCONCEPT(*A*, *B*) (*A* is a part of *B*), RESULT(*A*, *B*) (The result of experiment *A* is *B*), CONDITION(*A*, *B*) (The condition *A* holds in situation *B*), and EQUIVALENCE(*A*, *B*) (*A* and *B* refer to the same entity), with which we can express the relations mentioned in the example, as shown in Figure 2.

Note that it is *the use of two-level approximate inverse for parallel preconditioning*(*A*) that the author claims to be novel. However, the relation in *A* is already represented by the first APPLY_TO relation. Consequently, it is sufficient to annotate the EVALUATE relation between *two-level approximate inverse* and *novel*. This is approximately equivalent to paraphrasing *the use of two-level approximate inverse for parallel preconditioning is novel* as *two-level approximate inverse used for parallel preconditioning is novel*. The same holds for the equivalence relation involving *the proposed method*.

Expressing the content as the set of relations facilitates discovery of a concept that plays a particular role in the work. For example, if a reader wants to know the method for achieving parallel preconditioning, X, which satisfies the relation APPLY_TO(*X, parallel preconditioning*) must be searched for. By using the APPLY_TO relations mentioned in Figure 2 and inference on an *is-a* relation expressed by the SUBCONCEPT, we can obtain the result that *AISM method* is used for *parallel preconditioning*.

After a series of trial annotations on 71 abstracts from the IPSJ Journal (a monthly peer-reviewed journal published by the Information Processing Society of Japan), the following tag set was fixed. The annotation was conducted by the two of the authors of this paper.

3.1 Entity and Relation Types

The current tag set has 16 relation types and three entity types. An entity is whatever can be an argument or a participant in a relation. Entity types are OBJECT, MEASURE, or TERM, as shown in Table 1. Note that, unlike most schemes where the term *entity* refers to a nominal (named entity), in our scheme, almost all syntactic types of content words can be an entity, including numbers, verbs, adjectives, adverbs, and even some auxiliaries. The 16 types of relations are shown in Table 2. They are binary relations are directed from *A* to *B*.

Type	Definition	Example
OBJECT	the name of concrete entities such as a system, a person, and a company	Origin 2400, SGI
MEASURE	value, measurement, necessity, obligation, expectation, and possibility	novel, 136.72
TERM	any other	

Table 1: Entity Tags

All relations except EVALUATE COMPARE, and ATTRIBUTE can hold between any types of entity. EVALUATE and COMPARE relations hold between an entity (of any type) and an entity of the MEASURE type. The entities involved in an ATTRIBUTE relation must not be of the MEASURE type.

The INPUT and OUTPUT relations were introduced to deal with the distinction between the data and method used in computer systems. We extend the use of the scheme to annotate the inner structure of sentences and predicates, by establishing the relations between verbs and their case elements. For example, in *automatically generated test data*, obviously *test data* is an output of the action of *generate*, and *automatically* is the manner of generation. We annotate the *test data* as an OUTPUT and *automatically* as an ATTRIBUTE of *generate*. In another example, *a protocol that combines biometrics and zero-knowledge proof*, the protocol is the product of an action of combining biometrics and zero-

Type	Definition	Example
APPLY_TO(*A*, *B*)	A method *A* is applied to achieve the purpose *B* or used for conducting *B*	CRF_A-based $tagger_B$
RESULT(*A*, *B*)	*A* results in *B* in the sense that *B* is either an experimental result, a logical conclusion, or a side effect of *A*	$experiment_A$ shows the $increase_B$ in F-score compared to the baseline
PERFORM(*A*, *B*)	*A* is the agent of an intentional action *B*	a frustrated $player_A$ of a $game_B$
INPUT(*A*, *B*)	*A* is the input of a system or a process *B*, *A* is something obtained for *B*	$corpus_A$ for $training_B$
OUTPUT(*A*, *B*)	*A* is the output of a system or a process*B*, *A* is something generated from *B*	an $image_a$ $displayed_B$ on a palm
TARGET(*A*, *B*)	*A*is the target of an action *B*, which does not suffer alteration	to $drive_B$ a bus_A
ORIGIN(*A*, *B*)	*A* is the starting point of action *B*	to $drive_B$ from $Shinjuku_A$
DESTINATION(*A*, *B*)	*A* is the ending point of action *B*	an image $displayed_B$ on a $palm_A$
CONDITION(*A*, *B*)	The condition *A* holds in situation *B*, e.g, time, location, experimental condition	a $survey_B$ conducted in $India_a$
ATTRIBUTE(*A*, *B*)	*A* is an attribute or a characteristic of *B*	$accuracy_A$ of the $tagger_B$
STATE(*A*, *B*)	*A* is the sentiment of a person *B* other than the author, e.g. a user of a computer system or a player of a game	a $frustrated_A$ $player_B$ of a game
EVALUATE(*A*, *B*) COMPARE(*C*, *B*)	*A* is evaluated as *B* in comparison to *C*	experiment shows an $increase_B$ in $F-score_A$ compared to the $baseline_C$
SUBCONCEPT(*A*, *B*)	*A* *is-a*, or is a *part-of* *B*	a $corpus_A$ such as PTB_a
EQUIVALENCE(*A*, *B*)	terms *A* and *B* refer to the same entity: definition, abbreviation, or coreference	DoS_B $(denial-of-service_A)$ attack
SPLIT(*A*, *B*)	a term is split by parenthetical expressions into *A* and *B*	DoS_B (denial-of-service) $attack_A$

Table 2: Relation Tags

knowledge proof. Therefore, both *biometrics* and *zero-knowledge proof* are annotated as INPUTs of *combines*, and *protocol* is annotated as OUTPUT of *combines*. This scheme is not only used for computer-related verbs, but is further extended to any verb phrases or phrases with nominalized verbs. In *change in a situation*, *situation* is annotated as both INPUT and OUTPUT of *change*. It is as if we regard *change* as a machine that changes something, and when we input a situation, the *change-machine* processes it and output a different situation. Similarly, in *evolution of mobile phones*, *mobile phones* is annotated as both INPUT and OUTPUT of *evolution*. Here we regard *evolution* as a machine, and when we input (old-style) mobile phones, the *evolution-machine* processes them and outputs (new-style) mobile phones. We have found that a wide variety of predicates can be interpreted using these relations.

3.2 Other Features

Although we aim to annotate all possible relations mentioned, some conventions are introduced to reduce the workload.

First, we do not annotate the structure within entities. No nested entities are allowed, and compound words are treated as a single word. In addition, polarity (negation) is not expressed as a relation but as a part of an entity. We assume that the internal structure of entities can be analyzed by mechanisms such as technical term recognition. On the other hand, nested and crossed relations are allowed.

Second,, we do not annotate words that indicate the existence of relations. This is because the relations are usually indicated by case markers and punctuation [3] and marking them up was found to be a considerable mental workload. In addition, words and phrases that directly represent the relations themselves are not annotated as entities. For example, in *CG iteration was applied to the problem*, we directly *CG relation* and *the problem* directly with APPLY_TO and skip the phrase *was applied to*.

Third, relations other than EQUIVALENCE and SUBCONCEPT are annotated within a sentence. We assume that the discourse-level relation can be inferred by the composition of relations.

In addition, the annotation of frequent verbs and their case elements was examined in the trial process. Verbs were classified, according to the pattern of the annotated relation with the case elements. For example, verbs semantically similar to *assemble* and *compile* form a class. The semantic role of the direct object of these verbs varies by context. For example, the materials in phrases like *compile source codes* or the product in phrases like

[3]This is in the case with Japanese. In languages such as English, there may be no trigger words, as the semantic relations are often expressed by the structure of sentences.

compile the driver from the source codes. In our scheme, the former is the `INPUT` of the verb, and the latter is the `OUTPUT` of the verb. Another example is the class of verbs that includes *learn* and *obtain*. The direct object (what is learned) is the `INPUT` to the system but is also the result or an output of the learning process. In such cases, we decided that both `INPUT` and `OUTPUT` should be annotated between the verb and its object.

Other details of annotation fixed in the process of trial annotation include:
1) The span of entities, which is determined to be the longest possible sequences delimited by case suffix (*-ga*,*-wo*, etc.) in the case of nominals and to separate the *-suru* suffix of verbs and the *-da* suffix of adjectives but retain other conjugation suffixes;
2) How to annotate evaluation sentences involving nouns derived from adjectives that imply evaluation and measurement, such as *necessity*, *difficulty*, and *length*. The initial agreement was that we would consider that they lose `MEASURE`-ness when nominalized; however, with the similarity of Japanese expressions *hitsuyou/mondai de aru* (is necessary/problematic) and *hitsuyou/mondai ga aru*(there is a necessity/problem), there was confusion about which word should be the `MEASURE` argument necessary for the `EVALUATE` relation. It was determined that, for example, in *hitsuyou/mondai de aru*, *de aru*, a copula, is ignored and *hitsuyou/mondai* is the `MEASURE`. In *hitsuyou/mondai ga aru*, *aru* is the `MEASURE`;
3) How to annotate phrases like *the tagger was better in precision*, where it can be understood that *the system* is evaluated as being *better in precision*. While what is actually measured in the evaluation process described in the paper is the precision (an attribute) of the tagger and the sentence has almost the same meaning as *the tagger's precision was better*, the surface (syntactic) subject of *is better* is *the tagger*. This can lead to two possibilities for the target of the `EVALUATE` relation. We decided that the `EVALUATE` relation holds between *precision* and *better*, and the `ATTRIBUTE` relation holds between *precision* and *tagger*, as illustrated in Figure 3.

A set of annotation guidelines was compiled as the result of the trial annotation, including the classifications and the pattern of annotation on frequent verbs and their arguments.

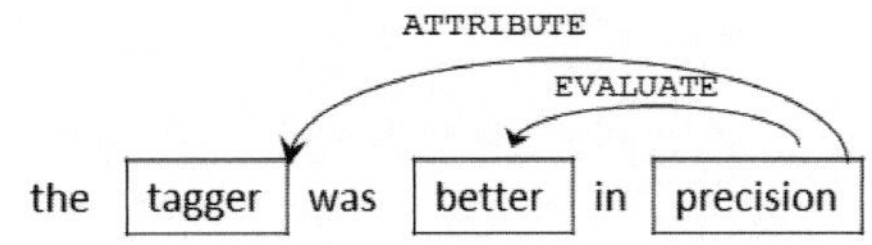

Figure 3: Annotation of *the tagger was better in precision*

Entity			Relation		
	Conunt	%		Conunt	%
Total	1895	100.0	Total	2269	100.0
OK	1658	87.5	OK	1110	48.9
Type	56	3.0	Type	250	11.0
Span	67	3.5	Direction	6	0.3
			Direction+Type	106	4.7
None	114	6.0	None	797	35.1

Table 3: Tag Counts

4 Annotation Experiment

We conducted an experiment on another 30 abstracts (197 sentences) from the IPSJ Journal. The two annotators who participated in the development of the guidelines annotated the abstracts independently, and inter-annotator discrepancy was checked. The annotation was performed manually using the brat annotation tool(Stenetorp et al., 2012). No automatic preprocessing was performed. Figure 4 shows the annotation results for the abstract shown in Figure 1. The 30 pairs of annotation results were aligned automatically; The results are shown in Tables 3, 4, and 5.

Table 3 shows the matches between the two annotators. "Total" denotes the count of entities/relations that at least one annotator found, "OK" denotes complete matches, "Type" denotes cases where two annotations on the same span have different entity/relation types, "Span" denotes entities where two annotations partially overlap, "Direction" denotes the count of relations where (only) the direction is different, and "Direction+Type"denotes relations where the same pair of entities were in different types of relation and in opposite directions, and "None" denotes cases where no counterpart was found in the other result.

Tables 4 and 5 are the confusion matrices for entity type and relation type, respectively. The differences in the span and direction are ignored. Agreement in F-score calculated in the same manner as in Brants (2000) for each relation is shown in column F, with the overall (micro-average) F-score shown in the bottom row of column F.

If we assume the number of cases that none of

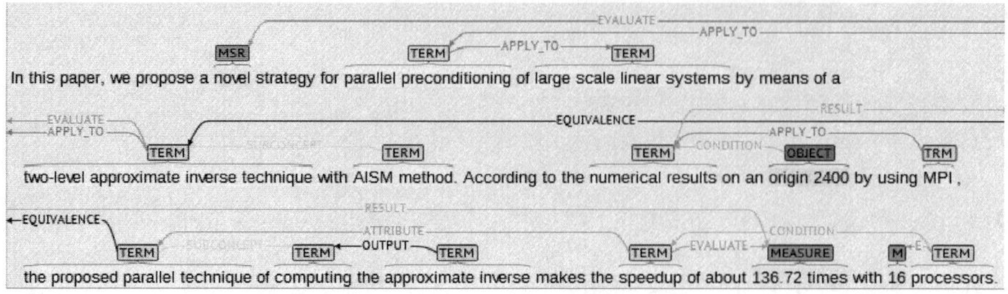

Figure 4: Annotation Results with brat

	TERM	OBJECT	MEASURE	NONE	Total	F(%)
TERM	1458	2	38	14	1512	94.9
OBJECT	0	17	0	0	17	94.4
MEASURE	28	0	238	18	284	83.8
None	74	0	8	X	82	
Total	1560	19	284	32		93.0

Table 4: Confusion Matrix for Entity

the annotators recognized (the value of the cell X in the tables) to be zero, the observed agreement and Cohen's κ coefficient are 90.3% and 70.0% for entities, and 49.3% and 43.5% for relations, respectively. If we ignore the count for the cases where one annotator did not recognize the entity/relation ("None" rows and columns in the tables), the observed agreement and κ are 96.1% and 89.3% for entities, and 76.1% and 74.3% for relations, respectively. The latter statistics indicate the agreement on types for entities/relations that both annotators recognized.

These results show that entity annotation was consistent between the annotators but the agreement for relation annotation varied, depending on the relation type. Table 5 shows that agreement for `DESTINATION`, `ORIGIN`, `EVALUATE`, and `SPLIT` was reasonably high, but was low for `CONDITION` and `TARGET`. The rise in agreement (simple and κ) by excluding cases where only one annotator recognized the relation indicate that the problem is recognition, rather than classification, of relations[4].

From the investigation of the annotated text, the following was found:

(1) `ATTRIBUTE/CONDITION` decision was inconsistent in phrases involving `EVALUATE` relation, such as *the disk space is smaller for the image* (Figure 5). The `EVALUATE` relation between *the disk space* and *smaller* was agreed; however, the two annotators recognized different relations between *the image* and other words. One annotator recognized the `ATTRIBUTE` relation between *the disk space* and *the image* ("the disk space *as a feature of* the image is smaller"). The other recognized the `CONDITION` relation between *the image* and *smaller* ("the disk space is smaller *in the case of* the image").

(2) We were not in complete agreement about skipping phrases that directly represent a relation. The expressions to be skipped in the 71 trial abstracts were listed in the guidelines; however, it is difficult to exhaust all such expressions.

(3) In the case of some verbs, an argument can be `INPUT` and `OUTPUT` simultaneously (Section 3.1). We agreed that an object that undergoes alteration in a process should be tagged as both `INPUT` and `OUTPUT` but one that does not undergo alteration or which is just moved is the `TARGET`. Conflicts occurred for verbs that denote prevention of some situations such as *prevent*, *avoid*, and *suppress*, as illustrated in Figure 6. One annotator claimed that the possibility of DoS attacks is reduced to zero; hence the argument of the verb should be annotated with `INPUT` and `OUTPUT`. The other claims that since the DoS attack itself does not change, it is a `TARGET`.

(4) In a coordination expression, logical inference may be implicitly stated. For example, in *it requires the linguistic knowledge and is costly*, the reason for *costly* is likely to be the need for linguistic knowledge, i.e., employment of an expert linguist. However, the relation is not readily apparent. We wanted to capture the relation in such cases, but the disagreement shows that it is difficult to judge such a relation consistently.

(5) The decision on whether to split expressions like *XX dekiru* and *XX kanou* (can/able to *XX*) was also problematic. The guideline was to split them. This contradicts the decision for the compound words in general that we do not split them; however, we determined that *dekiru/kanou* cases had

[4] The same observation was true for entities

	APP	ATT	COMP	COND	DEST	EQU	EVAL	IN	ORIG	OUT	PER	RES	SPL	STA	SUB	TAR	None	Total	F(%)
APPLY_TO	136	9	0	2	1	1	2	10	1	0	0	3	0	0	1	0	65	231	53.0
ATTRIBUTE	14	154	0	19	6	0	9	5	1	0	7	1	0	0	3	0	28	247	59.7
COMPARE	0	0	6	1	0	0	0	0	0	0	0	0	0	0	0	0	4	11	54.5
CONDITION	4	11	1	77	0	0	1	4	0	0	0	5	0	0	0	0	49	152	48.7
DESTINATION	6	0	0	0	39	0	0	0	0	1	0	0	0	0	0	0	4	50	77.2
EQUIVALENCE	4	1	0	1	0	54	0	0	0	0	0	0	0	0	4	0	23	87	60.0
EVALUATE	0	11	0	0	0	0	215	3	0	9	0	0	0	0	0	1	41	280	76.1
INPUT	12	2	0	0	0	1	4	96	0	11	0	0	0	0	0	9	15	150	58.7
ORIGIN	0	0	0	0	0	0	0	0	16	0	0	0	0	0	0	0	2	18	78.0
OUTPUT	2	1	0	3	0	0	4	23	0	141	0	0	0	0	0	18	37	229	56.5
PERFORM	1	0	0	0	0	0	0	0	0	0	19	0	0	0	0	0	2	22	74.5
RESULT	8	1	0	0	0	0	1	1	0	0	0	38	0	0	0	0	22	71	54.3
SPLIT	0	0	0	0	0	0	0	0	0	0	0	0	2	0	0	0	0	2	80.0
STATE	0	0	0	0	0	0	0	0	0	0	0	0	0	0	0	0	0	0	0
SUBCONCEPT	14	10	0	3	0	4	5	0	0	2	0	0	0	0	81	0	34	153	58.1
TARGET	6	2	1	3	2	0	7	12	0	14	1	0	0	0	0	42	6	96	47.7
None	75	67	3	55	3	33	37	23	5	92	2	22	1	0	37	10	X	465	
Total	282	269	11	164	51	93	285	177	23	270	29	69	3	0	126	80	332		59.8

Table 5: Confusion Matrix for Relation

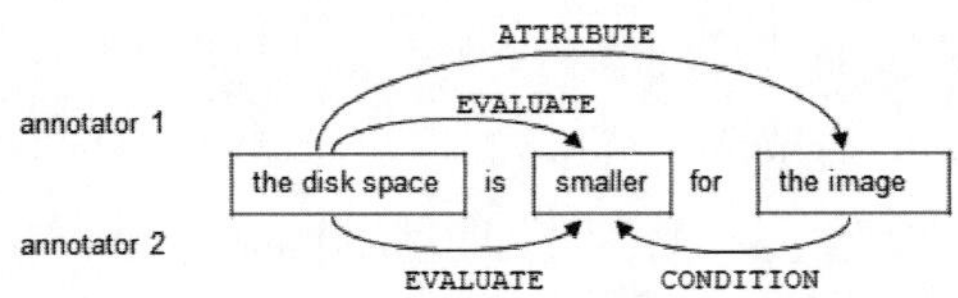

Figure 5: `ATTRIBUTE/CONDITION` Disagreement

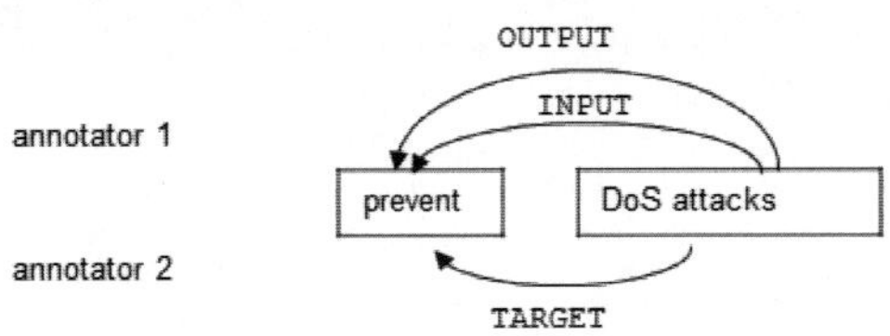

Figure 6: `INPUT/OUTPUT/TARGET` Disagreement

to be exceptions because the possibility of *XX* is expressed by *dekiru/kanou* and it seemed natural to relate *XX* and *dekiru/kanou* with `EVALUATE`. Unfortunately, confusion about splitting them remains.

5 Conclusions

We set up a scheme to annotate the content of research papers comprehensively. Sixteen semantic relations were defined, and guidelines for annotating semantic relations between concepts using the relations were established. The experimental results on 30 abstracts show that fairly good agreement was achieved, and that while entity- and relation-type determination can be performed consistently, determining whether a relation exists between particular pairs of entities remains problematic. We also found several discrepancy patterns that should be resolved and included in a future revision of the guidelines.

Traditionally, in semantic annotation of texts in the science/engineering domains, corpus creators focus on specific types of entities or events in which they are interested. On the other hand, we did not assume such specific types of entities or events, and we attempted to design a scheme that annotates more general relations in computer science/engineering domain.

Although the annotation is conducted for computer science abstracts in Japanese, we believe the scheme can be used for other languages, or for the broader science/engineering domains. The annotated corpus can provide data for constructing comprehensive semantic relation extraction systems. This would be challenging but worthwhile since such systems are in great demand. Such relation extraction systems will be the basis for content-based retrieval and other applications, including paraphrasing and translation.

The abstracts annotated in the course of the experiment have been cleaned up and are available on request. We are planning to increase the volume and make the corpus widely available.

In the future, we will assess machine-learning performance and incorporate the relation extraction mechanisms into search systems. Comparison of the annotated structure and the structures that can be given by existing semantic theories could be an interesting theoretical subject for future research.

Acknowledgments

This study was partially supported by the Japan Ministry of Education, Culture, Sports, Science and Technology Grant-in-Aid for Scientific Research (B) No. 22300031.

References

Shashank Agarwal and Hong Yu. 2009. Automatically classifying sentences in full-text biomedical articles into introduction, methods, results and discussion. *Bioinformatics*, 25(23):3174–3180.

Rafael E. Banchs, editor. 2012. *Proceedings of the ACL-2012 Special Workshop on Rediscovering 50 Years of Discoveries*. Association for Computational Linguistics.

Thorsten Brants. 2000. Inter-annotator agreement for a German newspaper corpus. In *Proceedings of the Second International Conference on Language Resources and Evaluation*.

Satoshi Fukuda, Hidetsugu Nanba, and Toshiyuki Takezawa. 2012. Extraction and visualization of technical trend information from research papers and patents. In *Proceedings of the 1st International Workshop on Mining Scientific Publications*.

Yufan Guo, Anna Korhonen, and Thierry Poibeau. 2011. A weakly-supervised approach to argumentative zoning of scientific documents. In *Proceedings of the 2011 Conference on Empirical Methods in Natural Language Processing*, pages 273–283.

Sonal Gupta and Christopher D Manning. 2011. Analyzing the dynamics of research by extracting key aspects of scientific papers. In *Proceedings of 5th IJCNLP*.

Ray Jackendoff. 1990. *Semantic Structures*. The MIT Press.

Jin-Dong Kim, Tomoko Ohta, and Jun ichi Tsujii. 2008. Corpus annotation for mining biomedical events from literature. *BMC Bioinformatics*, 9.

Jin-Dong Kim, Sampo Pyysalo, Tomoko Ohta, Robert Bossy, Ngan Nguyen, and Jun'ichi Tsujii. 2011. Overview of bionlp shared task 2011. In *Proceedings of BioNLP Shared Task 2011 Workshop*, pages 1–6.

Maria Liakata, Simone Teufel, Advaith Siddharthan, and Colin Batchelor. 2010. Corpora for conceptualisation and zoning of scientific papers. In *Proceedings of LREC 2010*.

Yoko Mizuta, Anna Korhonen, Tony Mullen, and Nigel Collier. 2006. Zone analysis in biology articles as a basis for information extraction. *International Journal of Medical Informatics*, 75(6):468–487.

Josef Ruppenhofer, Michael Ellsworth, Miriam R.L. Petruck, Christopher R. Johnson, and Jan Scheffczyk. 2006. *FrameNet II: Extended Theory and Practice*. International Computer Science Institute.

Ulrich Schäfer, Bernd Kiefer, Christian Spurk, Jörg Steffen, and Rui Wang. 2011. The ACL anthology searchbench. In *Proceedings of the ACL-HLT 2011 System Demonstrations*, pages 7–13.

Pontus Stenetorp, Sampo Pyysalo, Goran Topić, Tomoko Ohta, Sophia Ananiadou, and Jun'ichi Tsujii. 2012. brat: a web-based tool for NLP-assisted text annotation. In *Proceedings of the Demonstrations Session at EACL*.

Simone Teufel, Advaith Siddharthan, and Colin Batchelor. 2009. Towards discipline-independent argumentative zoning: evidence from chemistry and computational linguistics. In *Proceedings of the 2009 Conference on Empirical Methods in Natural Language Processing*, pages 1493–1502.

The Gene Ontology Consortium. 2000. Gene ontology: tool for the unification of biology. *Nature Genetics*, 25(1):25–29.

Paul Thompson, Raheel Nawaz, John McNaught, and Sophia Ananiadou. 2011. Enriching a biomedical event corpus with meta-knowledge annotation. *BMC Bioinformatics*, 12.

Andrea Varga, Daniel Preotiuc-Pietro, and Fabio Ciravegna. 2012. Unsupervised document zone identification using probabilistic graphical models. In *Proceedings of LREC 2012*, pages 1610–1617.

Developing Parallel Sense-tagged Corpora with Wordnets

Francis Bond, Shan Wang,
Eshley Huini Gao, Hazel Shuwen Mok, Jeanette Yiwen Tan
Linguistics and Multilingual Studies, Nanyang Technological University
bond@ieee.org

Abstract

Semantically annotated corpora play an important role in natural language processing. This paper presents the results of a pilot study on building a sense-tagged parallel corpus, part of ongoing construction of aligned corpora for four languages (English, Chinese, Japanese, and Indonesian) in four domains (story, essay, news, and tourism) from the NTU-Multilingual Corpus. Each subcorpus is first sense-tagged using a wordnet and then these synsets are linked. Upon the completion of this project, all annotated corpora will be made freely available. The multilingual corpora are designed to not only provide data for NLP tasks like machine translation, but also to contribute to the study of translation shift and bilingual lexicography as well as the improvement of monolingual wordnets.

1 Introduction

Large scale annotated corpora play an essential role in natural language processing (NLP). Over the years with the efforts of the community part-of-speech tagged corpora have achieved high quality and are widely available. In comparison, due to the complexity of semantic annotation, sense tagged parallel corpora develop slowly. However, the growing demands in more complicated NLP applications such as information retrieval, machine translation, and text summarization suggest that such corpora are in great need. This trend is reflected in the construction of two types of corpora: (i) parallel corpora: FuSe (Cyrus, 2006), SMULTRON (Volk et al., 2010), CroCo (Čulo et al., 2008), German-English parallel corpus (Padó and Erk, 2010), Europarl corpus (Koehn, 2005), and OPUS (Nygaard and Tiedemann, 2003; Tiedemann and Nygaard, 2004; Tiedemann, 2009, 2012) and (ii) sense-tagged monolingual corpora: English corpora such as Semcor (Landes et al., 1998); Chinese corpora, such as the crime domain of Sinica Corpus 3.0 (Wee and Mun, 1999), 1 million word corpus of People's Daily (Li et al., 2003), three months' China Daily (Wu et al., 2006); Japanese corpora, such as Hinoki Corpus (Bond et al., 2008) and Japanese SemCor (Bond et al., 2012) and Dutch Corpora such as the Groningen Meaning Bank (Basile et al., 2012). Nevertheless, almost no parallel corpora are sense-tagged. With the exception of corpora based on translations of SemCor (Bentivogli et al., 2004; Bond et al., 2012) sense-tagged corpora are almost always monolingual.

This paper describes ongoing work on the construction of a sense-tagged parallel corpus. It comprises four languages (English, Chinese, Japanese, and Indonesian) in four domains (story, essay, news, and tourism), taking texts from the NTU-Multilingual Corpus (Tan and Bond, 2012). For these subcorpora we first sense tag each text monolingually and then link the concepts across the languages. The links themselves are typed and tell us something of the nature of the translation. The annotators are primarily multilingual students from the division of linguistics and multilingual studies (NTU) with extensive training. In this paper we introduce the planned corpus annotation and report on the results of a completed pilot: annotation and linking of one short story: *The Adventure of the Dancing Men* in Chinese, English and Japanese. All concepts that could be were aligned and their alignments annotated.

The paper is structured as follows. Section 2 reviews existing parallel corpora and sense tagged corpora that have been built. Section 3 introduces the resources that we use in our annotation project. The annotation scheme for the multilingual corpora is laid out in Section 4. In Section 5 we report in detail the results of our pilot study. Section 6 presents our discussion and future work.

2 Related Work

In recent years, with the maturity of part-of-speech (POS) tagging, more attention has been paid to the practice of getting parallel corpora and sense-tagged corpora to promote NLP.

2.1 Parallel Corpora

Several research projects have reported annotated parallel corpora. Among the first major efforts in this direction is FuSe (Cyrus, 2006), an English-German parallel corpus extracted from the EUROPARL corpus (Koehn, 2005). Parallel sentences were first annotated mono-lingually with POS tags and lemmas; related predicates (e.g. a verb and its nominalization are then linked). SMULTRON (Volk et al., 2010) is a parallel treebank of 2,500 sentences from different genres: a novel, economy texts from several sources, a user manual and mountaineering reports. Most of the corpus is German-English-Swedish parallel text, with additional texts in French and Spanish. CroCo (Čulo et al., 2008) is a German-English parallel and comparable corpus of a dozen texts from eight genres, totaling approximately 1,000,000 words. Each sentence is annotated with phrase structures and grammatical functions, and words, chunks and phrases are aligned across parallel sentences. This resource is limited to two languages, English and German, and is not systematically linked to any semantic resource. Padó and Erk (2010) have conducted a study of translation shifts on a German-English parallel corpus of 1,000 sentences from EUROPARL annotated with semantic frames from FrameNet and word alignments. Their aim was to measure the feasibility of frame annotation projection across languages.

The above corpora have been used for studying translation shift. Plain text parallel corpora are also widely used in NLP. The Europarl corpus collected the parallel text in 11 official languages of the European Union (i.e. Danish, German, Greek, English, Spanish, Finnish, French, Italian, Dutch, Portuguese, and Swedish) from proceedings of the European Parliament. Each language is composed of about 30 million words (Koehn, 2005). Newer versions have even more languages. OPUS v0.1 contains the documentation of the office package OpenOffice with a collection of 2,014 files in English and five translated texts, namely, French, Spanish, Swedish, German and Japanese. This corpus consists of 2.6 million words (Nygaard and Tiedemann, 2003; Tiedemann and Nygaard, 2004; Tiedemann, 2012). However, when we examined the Japanese text, we found the translations are often from different versions of the software and not synchronized very well.

2.2 Sense Tagged Corpora

Surprisingly few languages have sense tagged corpora. In English, Semcor was built by annotating texts from the Brown Corpus using the sense inventory of WordNet 1.6 (Fellbaum, 1998) and has been mapped to subsequent WordNet versions (Landes et al., 1998). The Defense Science Organization (DSO) corpus annotated the 191 most frequent and ambiguous nouns and verbs from the combined Brown Corpus and Wall Street Journal Corpus using WordNet 1.5. The 191 words comprise of 70 verbs with an average sense number of 12 and 121 nouns with an average sense number of 7.8. The verbs and nouns respectively account for approximately 20% of all verbs and nouns in any unrestricted English text (Ng and Lee, 1996). The WordNet Gloss Disambiguation Project uses Princeton WordNet 3.0 (PWN) to disambiguate its own definitions and examples.[1]

In Chinese, Wee and Mun (1999) reported the annotation of a subset of Sinica Corpus 3.0 using HowNet. The texts are news covering the crime domain with 30,000 words. Li et al. (2003) annotated the semantic knowledge of a 1 million word corpus from *People's Daily* with dependency grammar. The corpus include domains such as politics, economy, science, and sports. (Wu et al., 2006) described the sense tagged corpus of Peking University. They annotated three months of the People's Daily using the Semantic Knowledge-base of Contemporary Chinese (SKCC)[2]. SKCC describes the features of a word through attribute-value pairs, which incorporates distributional information.

In Japanese, the Hinoki Corpus annotated 9,835 headwords with multiple senses in Lexeed: a Japanese semantic lexicon (Kasahara et al., 2004) To measure the conincidence of tags and difficulty degree in identifying senses, each word was annotated by 5 annotators (Bond et al., 2006).

[1] `http://wordnet.princeton.edu/glosstag.shtml`

[2] `http://ccl.pku.edu.cn/ccl_sem_dict/`

We only know of two multi-lingual sense-tagged corpora. One is MultiSemCor, which is an English/Italian parallel corpus created based on SemCor (Landes et al., 1998). MultiSemCor is made of 116 English texts taken from SemCor with their corresponding 116 Italian translations. There are 258,499 English tokens and 267,607 Italian tokens. The texts are all aligned at the word level and content words are annotated with POS, lemma, and word senses. It has 119,802 English words semantically annotated from SemCor and 92,820 Italian words are annotated with senses automatically transferred from English (Bentivogli et al., 2004). Japanese SemCor is another translation of the English SemCor, whose senses are projected across from English. It takes the same texts in MultiSemCor and translates them into Japanese. Of the 150,555 content words, 58,265 are sense tagged either as monosemous words or by projecting from the English annotation (Bond et al., 2012). The low annotation rate compared to MultiSemCor reflects both a lack of coverage in the Japanese wordnet and the greater typological difference.

Though many efforts have been devoted to the construction of sense tagged corpora, the majority of the existing corpora are monolingual, relatively small in scale and not all freely available. To the best of our knowledge, no large scale sense-tagged parallel corpus for Asian languages exists. Our project will fill this gap.

3 Resources

This section introduces the wordnets and corpora we are using for the annotation task.

3.1 Wordnets

Princeton WordNet (PWN) is an English lexical database created at the Cognitive Science Laboratory of Princeton University. It was developed from 1985 under the direction of George A. Miller. It groups nouns, verbs, adjective and adverbs into synonyms (synsets), most of which are linked to other synsets through a number of semantic relations. (Miller, 1998; Fellbaum, 1998). The version we use in this study is 3.0.

A number of wordnets in various languages have been built based on and linked to PWN. The Open Multilingual Wordnet (OMW) project[3] currently provides 22 wordnets (Bond and Paik, 2012; Bond and Foster, 2013). The Japanese and Indonesian wordnets in our project are from OMW provided by the creators (Isahara et al., 2008, Nurril Hirfana et al., 2011).

The Chinese wordnet we use is a heavily revised version of the one developed by Southeast University (Xu et al., 2008). This was automatically constructed from bilingual resources with minimal hand-checking. It has limited coverage and is somewhat noisy, we have been revising it and use this revised version for our annotation.

3.2 Multilingual Corpus

The NTU-multilingual corpus (NTU-MC) is compiled at Nanyang Technological University. It contains eight languages: English (eng), Mandarin Chinese (cmn), Japanese (jpn), Indonesian (ind), Korean, Arabic, Vietnamese and Thai (Tan and Bond, 2012). We selected parallel data for English, Chinese, Japanese, and Indonesian from NTU-MC to annotate. The data are from four genres, namely, short story (two Sherlock Holmes' Adventures), essay (Raymond, 1999), news (Kurohashi and Nagao, 2003) and tourism (Singapore Tourist Board, 2012). The corpus sizes are shown in Table 1. We show the number of words and concepts (open class words tagged with synsets) only for English, the other languages are comparable in size.

4 Annotation Scheme for Multilingual Corpora

The annotation task is divided into two phases: monolingual sense annotation and multilingual concept alignment.

4.1 Monolingual Sense Annotation

First, the Chinese, Japanese and Indonesian corpora were automatically tokenized and tagged with parts-of-speech. Secondly, concepts were tagged with candidate synsets, with multiword expressions allowing a skip of up to 3 words. Any match with a wordnet entry was considered a potential concept.

These were then shown to annotators to either select the appropriate synset, or point out a problem. The interface for doing sense annotation is shown in Figure 1.

In Figure 1, the concepts to be annotated are shown as red and underlined. When clicking on

[3] `http://www.casta-net.jp/~kuribayashi/multi/`

Genre	Text	Sentences				Words	Concepts
		Eng	Cmn	Jpn	Ind	Eng	Eng
Story	The Adventure of the Dancing Men	599	606	698	–	11,200	5,300
	The Adventure of the Speckled Band	599	612	702	–	10,600	4,700
Essay	The Cathedral and the Bazaar	769	750	773	–	18,700	8,800
News	Mainichi News	2,138	2,138	2,138	–	55,000	23,200
Tourism	Your Singapore (web site)	2,988	2,332	2,723	2,197	74,300	32,600

Table 1: Multilingual corpus size

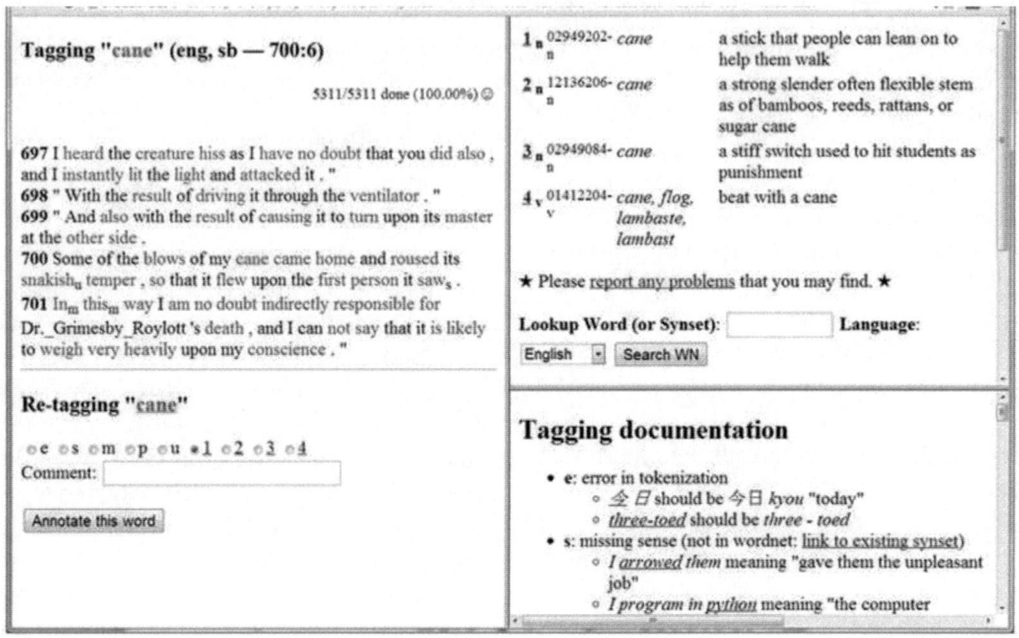

Figure 1: Tagging the sense of *cane*.

a concept, its WordNet senses appear to the right of a screen. The annotator chooses between these senses or a number of meta-tags: **e, s, m, p, u.** Their meaning is explained below.

e error in tokenization
今 日 should be 今日
<u>three-toed</u> should be *three - toed*

s missing sense (not in wordnet)
I program in <u>python</u> "the computer language"
COMMENT: add link to existing synset
<`06898352-n` "programming language"

m bad multiword
(i) if the lemma is a multiword, this tag means it is not appropriate
(ii) if the lemma is single-word, this tag means it should be part of a multiword

p POS that should not be tagged (article, modal, preposition, . . .)

u lemma not in wordnet but POS open class (tagged automatically)
COMMENT: add or link to existing synset

Missing senses in the wordnets were a major issue when tagging, especially for Chinese and Japanese. We allowed the annotators to add candidate new senses in the comments; but these were not made immediately available in the tagging interface. As almost a third of the senses were missing in Chinese and Japanese, this slowed the annotators down considerably.

Our guidelines for adding new concepts or linking words to existing cover four cases:

= When a word is a synonym of an existing word, add =synset to the comment: e.g. for laidback, it is a synonym of `02408011-a` "laid-back, mellow", so we add =`02408011-a` to the comment for laidback.

< When a word is a hyponym/instance of

an existing word, mark it with <synset: For example, *python* is a hyponym of `06898352-n` ***programming language***, so we add `<06898352-n` to *python*

! Mark antonyms with !synset.

~ If you cannot come up with a more specific relationship, just say the word is related in some way to an existing synset with ~synset; and add more detail in the comment.

Finally, we have added more options for the annotators: **prn** (pronouns) and seven kinds of named entities: **org** (organization); **loc** (location); **per** (person); **dat** (date/time); **num** (number); **oth** (other) and the super type **nam** (name). These basically follow Landes et al. (1998, p207), with the addition of number, date/time and name. Name is used when automatically tagging, it should be specialized later, but is useful to have when aligning. Pronouns include both personal and indefinite-pronouns. Pronouns are not linked to their monolingual antecedents, just made available for cross-lingual linking.

4.2 Multilingual Concept Alignment

We looked at bitexts: the translated text and its source (in this case English). Sentences were already aligned as part of the NTU-Multilingual Corpus. The initial alignment was done automatically: concepts that are tagged with the same synset or related synsets (one level of hyponymy) are directly linked. Then the sentence pairs are presented to the annotator, using the interface shown in Figure 2.

In the alignment interface, when you hover over a concept, its definition from PWN is shown in a pop-up window at the top. Clicking concepts in one language and then the other produces a candidate alignment: the annotator then choses the kind of alignment. After concepts are aligned they are shown in the same color. Both *bell* and 门铃 *ménlíng* "door bell" have the same synset, so they are linked with =. Similarly, *Watson* and 华生 *Huáshēng* "Watson" refer to the same person, so they are also connected with =. However, *ring* in the English sentence is a noun while the corresponding Chinese word 响 *xiǎng* "ring" is a verb; so they are linked with the weaker type ~.

We found three issues came up a lot during the annotation: (i) Monolingual tag errors; (ii) multiword expression not tagged; (iii) Pronouns not tagged.

(i) In some cases, the monolingual tag was not the best choice. Looking at the tagging in both languages often made it easier to choose between similar monolingual tags, and the annotators found themselves wanting to retag a number of entries.

(ii) It was especially common for it to become clear that things should have been tagged as multiword expressions. Consider *kuchi-wo hiraku* "speak" in (1).

(1) Said he suddenly

a.

ホームズが		突然	口	を	開く
ho-muzu	ga	totsuzen	kuchi	wo	hiraku
Holmes	NOM	suddenly	mouth	ACC	open

"Holmes opens his mouth suddenly"

This was originally tagged as "open mouth" but in fact it is a multiword expression with the meaning "say", and is parallel in meaning to the original English text. As this concept is lexicalized, the annotator grouped the words together and tagged the new concept to the synset `00941990-v` "express in speech". The concepts were then linked together with ˜. It is hard for the monolingual annotator to consistently notice such multiword expressions: however, the translation makes them more salient.

(iii) It was often the case that an open class word in one language would link to a closed class word in the other, especially to a pronoun. We see this in (1) where *he* in English links to *ho-muzu* "Holmes" in Japanese. In order to capture these correspondences, we allowed the annotator to also tag named entities, pronouns and interrogatives. From now on we will tag these as part of the initial monolingual alignment.

We tagged the links between concepts with the types shown in Table 2.

5 Pilot Study Results

A pilot study was conducted using the first story text: *The Adventure of the Dancing Men*, a Sherlock Holmes short story (Conan Doyle, 1905). The Japanese version was translated by Otokichi Mikami and Yu Okubu;[4] we got the translated version of Chinese from a website which later disappeared. Using English text as the source language, the Japanese and Chinese texts were aligned and

[4]`http://www.aozora.gr.jp/cards/000009/card50713.html`

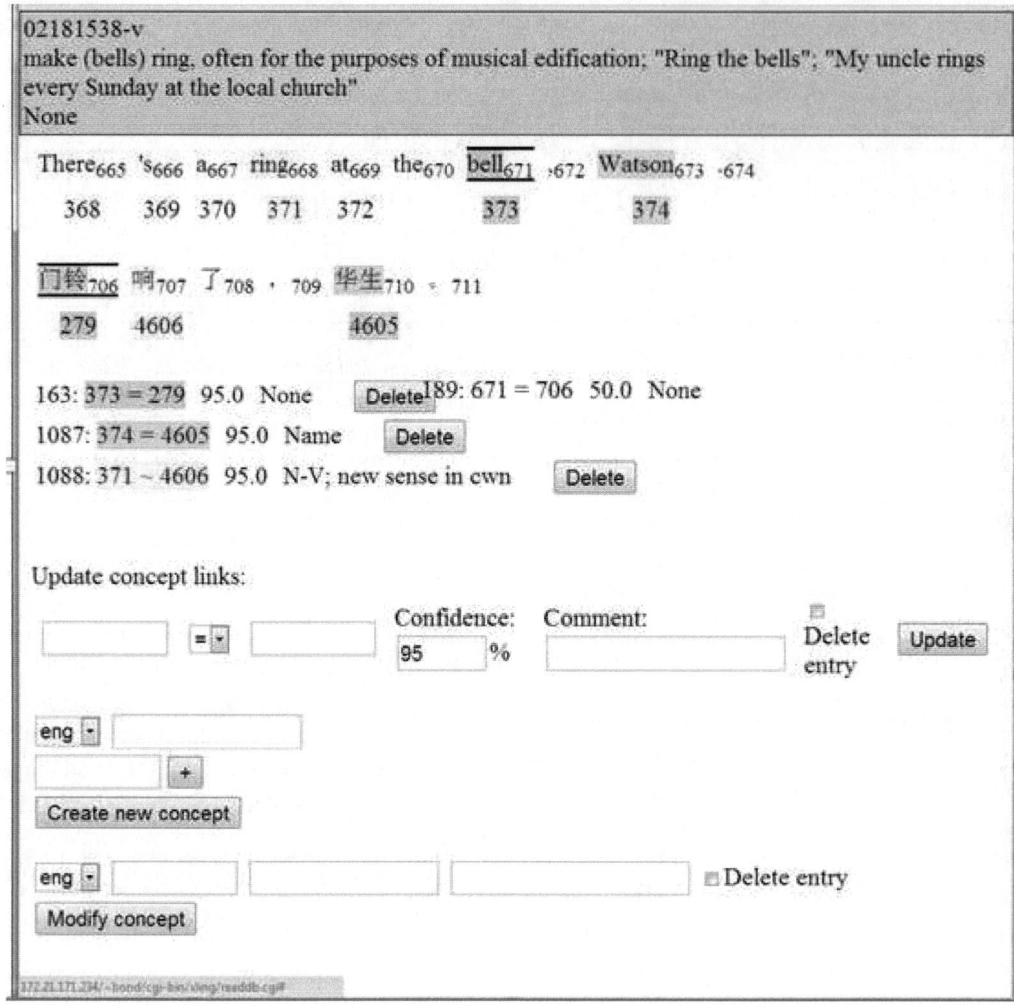

Figure 2: Interface for aligning concepts.

manually sense-tagged with reference to their respective wordnets. The number of words and concepts for each language is shown in Table 3.

	English	Chinese	Japanese
Sentences	599	680	698
Words	11,198	11,325	13,483
Concepts	5,267	4,558	4,561

Excluding candidate concepts rejected by the annotators.

Table 3: Concepts in Dancing Men

The relationships between words were tagged using the symbols in in Table 2. The difficult cases are similar relation and translation equivalent relation. Due to translation styles and language divergence, some concepts with related meaning cannot be directly linked. We give examples in (2) through (4).

(2) "How on earth do you know that?" I asked.

a. 「いったい 、 どうして その こと=を
「 ittai 、 doushite sono koto=wo
" on+earth , why that thing=ACC
？ 」 と 私=は 聞き=返す
？ 」 to watashi=wa kiki=kaesu
? " QUOT me=TOP ask=return

"Why on earth do you know that thing?" I ask in return.

In (2), compared to *ask* in English, the Japanese *kikikaesu* has the additional meaning of "in return": it is a hyponym. We marked their relation as $\sim$ (similar in meaning).

We introduced a new class $\approx$ to indicate combinations of words or phrases that are translation equivalents of the original source but are not lexicalized enough to be linked in the wordnet. One example is shown in (3).

(3) be content with my word

	Type	Example
=	same concept	*say* ↔言う *iu* "say"
⊃	hypernym	*wash* ↔洗い落とす *araiotosu* "wash out"
$\supset^2$	2nd level	*dog* ↔ 動物 *doubutsu* "animal"
⊂	hyponym	*sunlight* ↔光 *hikari* "light"
$\subset^n$	nth level	
∼	similar	*notebook* ↔ メモ帳 *memochou* "notepad" *dull$_a$* ↔ くすむ *kusumu* "darken"
≈	equivalent	*be content with my word* ↔ わたくし の 言葉 を 信じ-て "believe in my words"
!	antonym	*hot* ↔寒く=ない *samu=ku nai* "not cold"
#	weak ant.	*not propose to invest* ↔ 思いとどまる *omoi=todomaru* "hold back"

Table 2: Translation Equivalence Types

a. わたくし=の 言葉=を 信じ=て
watakushi=no kotoba=wo shinji=te
me=of word=ACC believe=ing
"believe in my words"

In this case *shinjite* "believe" is being used to convey the same pragmatic meaning as *content with* but they are not close enough in meaning that we want to link them in the lexicon.

(4) shows some further issues in non-direct translation.

(4) I am sure that I shall say$_h$ no$_i$thing$_j$ of the kind$_k$.

a. いやいや 、 そんな こと は
iyaiya , sonna$_k$ koto$_j$ wa
by+no+means , that+kind$_k$+of thing$_j$ TOP
言わ-ん よ
iwa$_h$-n$_i$ yo
say$_h$-NEG$_i$ yo
"no no, I will not say that kind of thing"

Say$_h$ no$_i$thing$_j$ of the kind$_k$ becomes roughly "not$_i$ say$_h$ that kind$_k$ of thing$_j$". All the elements are there, but they are combined in quite a different structure and some semantic decomposition would be needed to link them. Chinese and Japanese do not use negation inside the NP, so this kind of difference is common. Tagging was made more complicated by the fact that determiners are not part of wordnet, so it is not clear which parts of the expression should be tagged.

Though there are many difficult cases, the most common case was for two concepts to share the same synset and be directly connected. For example, *notebook* is tagged with the synset `06415419-n`, defined as "a book with blank pages for recording notes or memoranda". In the Japanese version, this concept is translated into 備忘録 *bibouroku* "notebook", with exactly the same synset (`06415419-n`). Hence, we linked the words with the = symbol.

The number of link types after the first round of cross-lingual annotation (eng-jpn, eng-cmn) is summarized in Table 4. In the English-Japanese and English-Chinese corpora, 51.38% and 60.07% of the concepts have the same synsets: that is, slightly over half of the concepts can be directly translated. Around 5% of the concepts in the two corpora are linked to words close in the hierarchy (hyponym/hypernym). There were very few antonyms (0.5%). Similar relations plus translation equivalents account for 42.85% and 34.74% in the two corpora respectively. These parts are the most challenging for machine translation.

In this first round, when the annotator attempted to link concepts, it was sometimes the case that the translation equivalent was a word not excluded from wordnet by design. Especially common was cases of common nouns in Japanese and Chinese being linked to pronouns in English. In studying how concepts differ across languages, we consider these of interest. We therefore expanded our tagging effort to include pronouns.

6 Discussion and Future Work

The pilot study showed clearly that cross-lingual annotation was beneficial not just in finding interesting correspondences across languages but also in improving the monolingual annotation. In particular, we found many instances of multiword expressions that had been missed in the monolingual annotation. Using a wordnet to sense tag a corpus is extremely effective in improving the quality of the wordnet, and tagging and linking parallel text

Type	Eng-Jpn		Eng-Cmn	
linked	2,542		2,535	
=	1,416	51.58	1,712	60.07
$\sim$	990	36.07	862	30.25
$\approx$	186	6.78	128	4.49
$\supset$	75	2.73	94	3.30
$\supset^2$	8	0.81	13	1.51
$\subset$	63	2.30	39	1.37
$\subset^2$	10	1.01	18	2.09
!	1	0.04	2	0.07
#	14	0.51	13	0.46
unlinked	2,583		1,898	

Table 4: Analysis of links

is an excellent way to improve the quality of the monolingual annotation. Given how many problems we found in both wordnet and corpus when we went over the bilingual annotation, we hypothesize that perhaps one of the reasons WSD is currently so difficult is that the gold standards are not yet fully mature. They have definitely not yet gone through the series of revisions that many syntactic corpora have, even though the tagging scheme is far harder.

For this project, we improved our annotation process in two major ways:

(i) We expanded the scope of the annotation to include pronouns and named entities interrogatives. These will now be tagged from the monolingual annotation stage.

(ii) We improved the tool to make it possible to add new entries directly to the wordnets, so that they are available for tagging the remaining text. Using the comments to add new sense was a bad idea: synset-ids were cut and pasted, often with a character missing, and annotators often mistyped the link type. In addition, for words that appeared many times, it was tedious to redo it for each word. We are now testing an improved interface where annotators add new words to the wordnet directly, and these then become available for tagging. As a quality check, the new entries are reviewed by an expert at the end of each day, who has the option of amending the entry (and possibly re-tagging).

We are currently tagging the remaining texts shown in Table 1, with a preliminary release scheduled for September 2013. For this we are also investigating ways of improving the automatic cross-lingual annotation: using word level alignments; using global translation models and by relaxing the mapping criteria (in particular allowing linking across parts of speech through derivational links). When we have finished, we will also link the Japanese to the Chinese, using English as a pivot. Finally, we will go through the non-aligned concepts, and analyze why they cannot be aligned.

In future work we intend to also add structural semantic annotation to cover issues such as quantification. Currently we are experimenting with Dependency Minimal Recursion Semantics (DMRS: Copestake et al., 2005; Copestake, 2009) and looking at ways to also constrain these cross-linguistically (Frermann and Bond, 2012).

An interesting further extension would be to look at a level of discourse marking. This would be motivated by those translations which cannot be linked at a lower level. In this way we would become closer to the Groningen Meaning Bank, which annotates POS, senses, NE, thematic roles, syntax, semantics and discourse (Basile et al., 2012).

7 Conclusions

This paper presents preliminary results from an ongoing project to construct large-scale sense-tagged parallel corpora. Four languages are chosen for the corpora: English, Chinese, Japanese, and Indonesia. The annotation scheme is divided into two phrases: monolingual sense annotation and multilingual concept alignment. A pilot study was carried out in Chinese, English and Japanese for the short story *The Adventure of the Dancing Men*. The results show that in the English-Japanese and English-Chinese corpora, over half of the concepts have the same synsets and thus can be easily translated. However, 42.85% and 34.74% of the concepts in the two corpora cannot be directly linked, which suggests it is hard for machine translation. All annotated corpora will be made freely available through the NTU-MC, in addition, the changes made to the wordnets will be released through the individual wordnet projects.

Acknowledgments

This research was supported in part by the MOE Tier 1 grant *Shifted in Translation — An Empirical Study of Meaning Change across Languages*.

References

Valerio Basile, Johan Bos, Kilian Evang, and Noortje Venhuizen. 2012. Developing a large semantically annotated corpus. In *Proceedings of the Eighth International Conference on Language Resources and Evaluation (LREC 2012)*, pages 3196–3200. Istanbul, Turkey.

Luisa Bentivogli, Pamela Forner, and Emanuele Pianta. 2004. Evaluating cross-language annotation transfer in the MultiSemCor corpus. In *20th International Conference on Computational Linguistics: COLING-2004*, pages 364–370. Geneva.

Francis Bond, Timothy Baldwin, Richard Fothergill, and Kiyotaka Uchimoto. 2012. Japanese SemCor: A sense-tagged corpus of Japanese. In *Proceedings of the 6th Global WordNet Conference (GWC 2012)*, pages 56–63. Matsue.

Francis Bond and Ryan Foster. 2013. Linking and extending an open multilingual wordnet. In *51st Annual Meeting of the Association for Computational Linguistics: ACL-2013*. Sofia.

Francis Bond, Sanae Fujita, and Takaaki Tanaka. 2006. The Hinoki syntactic and semantic treebank of Japanese. *Language Resources and Evaluation*, 40(3–4):253–261. URL `http://dx.doi.org/10.1007/s10579-007-9036-6`, (Special issue on Asian language technology; re-issued as DOI s10579-008-9062-z due to Springer losing the Japanese text).

Francis Bond, Sanae Fujita, and Takaaki Tanaka. 2008. The Hinoki syntactic and semantic treebank of Japanese. *Language Resources and Evaluation*, 42(2):243–251. URL `http://dx.doi.org/10.1007/s10579-008-9062-z`, (Re-issue of DOI 10.1007/s10579-007-9036-6 as Springer lost the Japanese text).

Francis Bond and Kyonghee Paik. 2012. A survey of wordnets and their licenses. In *Proceedings of the 6th Global WordNet Conference (GWC 2012)*. Matsue. 64–71.

Arthur Conan Doyle. 1905. *The Return of Sherlock Homes*. George Newnes, London. Project Gutenberg `www.gutenberg.org/files/108/108-h/108-h.htm`.

Ann Copestake. 2009. Slacker semantics: Why superficiality, dependency and avoidance of commitment can be the right way to go. In *Proceedings of the 12th Conference of the European Chapter of the ACL (EACL 2009)*, pages 1–9. Athens.

Ann Copestake, Dan Flickinger, Carl Pollard, and Ivan A. Sag. 2005. Minimal Recursion Semantics. An introduction. *Research on Language and Computation*, 3(4):281–332.

Oliver Čulo, Silvia Hansen-Schirra, Stella Neumann, and Mihaela Vela. 2008. Empirical studies on language contrast using the English-German comparable and parallel CroCo corpus. In *Proceedings of Building and Using Comparable Corpora, LREC 2008 Workshop, Marrakesh, Morocco*, volume 31, pages 47–51.

Lea Cyrus. 2006. Building a resource for studying translation shifts. In *Proceedings of The Second International Conference on Language Resources and Evaluation (LREC-2006)*.

Christine Fellbaum, editor. 1998. *WordNet: An Electronic Lexical Database*. MIT Press.

Lea Frermann and Francis Bond. 2012. Cross-lingual parse disambiguation based on semantic correspondence. In *50th Annual Meeting of the Association for Computational Linguistics: ACL-2012*, pages 125–129. Jeju, Korea.

Hitoshi Isahara, Francis Bond, Kiyotaka Uchimoto, Masao Utiyama, and Kyoko Kanzaki. 2008. Development of the Japanese WordNet. In *Sixth International conference on Language Resources and Evaluation (LREC 2008)*. Marrakech.

Kaname Kasahara, Hiroshi Sato, Francis Bond, Takaaki Tanaka, Sanae Fujita, Tomoko Kanasugi, and Shigeaki Amano. 2004. Construction of a Japanese semantic lexicon: Lexeed. In *IPSG SIG: 2004-NLC-159*, pages 75–82. Tokyo. (in Japanese).

Philipp Koehn. 2005. Europarl: A parallel corpus for statistical machine translation. In *MT Summit X*.

Sadao Kurohashi and Makoto Nagao. 2003. Building a Japanese parsed corpus — while improving the parsing system. In Anne Abeillé, editor, *Treebanks: Building and Using Parsed Corpora*, chapter 14, pages 249–260. Kluwer Academic Publishers.

Shari Landes, Claudia Leacock, and Christiane Fellbaum. 1998. Building semantic concordances. In Fellbaum (1998), chapter 8, pages 199–216.

Mingqin Li, Juanzi Li, Zhendong Dong, Zuoying Wang, and Dajin Lu. 2003. Building a large Chinese corpus annotated with semantic dependency. In *Proceedings of the second SIGHAN workshop on Chinese language processing-Volume 17*, pages 84–91. Association for Computational Linguistics.

George Miller. 1998. Foreword. In Fellbaum (1998), pages xv–xxii.

Nurril Hirfana Mohamed Noor, Suerya Sapuan, and Francis Bond. 2011. Creating the open Wordnet Bahasa. In *Proceedings of the 25th Pacific Asia Conference on Language, Information and Computation (PACLIC 25)*, pages 258–267. Singapore.

Hwee Tou Ng and Hian Beng Lee. 1996. Integrating multiple knowledge sources to disambiguate word sense: An exemplar-based approach. In *Proceedings of the 34th annual meeting on Association for Computational Linguistics*, pages 40–47.

Lars Nygaard and Jörg Tiedemann. 2003. OPUS — an open source parallel corpus. In *Proceedings of the 13th Nordic Conference on Computational Linguistics*.

Sebastian Padó and Katrin Erk. 2010. Translation shifts and frame-semantic mismatches: A corpus analysis. Ms: `http://www.nlpado.de/~sebastian/pub/papers/ijcl10_pado_preprint.pdf`.

Eric S. Raymond. 1999. *The Cathedral & the Bazaar*. O'Reilly.

Singapore Tourist Board. 2012. Your Singapore. Online: `www.yoursingapore.com`. [Accessed 2012].

Liling Tan and Francis Bond. 2012. Building and annotating the linguistically diverse NTU-MC (NTU-multilingual corpus). *International Journal of Asian Language Processing*, 22(4):161–174.

Jörg Tiedemann. 2009. News from OPUS — a collection of multilingual parallel corpora with tools and interfaces. In N. Nicolov, K. Bontcheva, G. Angelova, and R. Mitkov, editors, *Recent Advances in Natural Language Processing*, volume 5, pages 237–248. John Benjamins, Amsterdam/Philadelphia.

Jörg Tiedemann. 2012. Parallel data, tools and interfaces in OPUS. In *Proceedings of the Eight International Conference on Language Resources and Evaluation (LREC'12)*, pages 2214–2218.

Jörg Tiedemann and Lars Nygaard. 2004. The OPUS corpus — parallel and free. In *In Proceeding of the 4th International Conference on Language Resources and Evaluation (LREC-4)*.

Martin Volk, Anne Göhring, Torsten Marek, and Yvonne Samuelsson. 2010. SMULTRON (version 3.0) — The Stockholm MULtilingual parallel TReebank. `http://www.cl.uzh.ch/research/paralleltreebanks_en.html`.

Gan Kok Wee and Tham Wai Mun. 1999. General knowledge annotation based on how-net. *Computational Linguistics and Chinese Language Processing*, 4(2):39–86.

Yunfang Wu, Peng Jin, Yangsen Zhang, and Shiwen Yu. 2006. A chinese corpus with word sense annotation. In *Computer Processing of Oriental Languages. Beyond the Orient: The Research Challenges Ahead*, pages 414–421. Springer.

Renjie Xu, Zhiqiang Gao, Yuzhong Qu, and Zhisheng Huang. 2008. An integrated approach for automatic construction of bilingual Chinese-English WordNet. In *3rd Asian Semantic Web Conference (ASWC 2008)*, pages 302–341.

Animacy Annotation in the Hindi Treebank

Itisree Jena, Riyaz Ahmad Bhat, Sambhav Jain and Dipti Misra Sharma
Language Technologies Research Centre, IIIT-Hyderabad, India
{itisree|riyaz.bhat|sambhav.jain}@research.iiit.ac.in, dipti@iiit.ac.in

Abstract

In this paper, we discuss our efforts to annotate nominals in the Hindi Treebank with the semantic property of animacy. Although the treebank already encodes lexical information at a number of levels such as morph and part of speech, the addition of animacy information seems promising given its relevance to varied linguistic phenomena. The suggestion is based on the theoretical and computational analysis of the property of animacy in the context of anaphora resolution, syntactic parsing, verb classification and argument differentiation.

1 Introduction

Animacy can either be viewed as a biological property or a grammatical category of nouns. In a strictly biological sense, all living entities are animate, while all other entities are seen as inanimate. However, in its linguistic sense, the term is synonymous with a referent's ability to act or instigate events volitionally (Kittilä et al., 2011). Although seemingly different, linguistic animacy can be implied from biological animacy. In linguistics, the manifestation of animacy and its relevance to linguistic phenomena have been studied quite extensively. Animacy has been shown, cross linguistically, to control a number of linguistic phenomena. Case marking, argument realization, topicality or discourse salience are some phenomena, highly correlated with the property of animacy (Aissen, 2003). In linguistic theory, however, animacy is not seen as a dichotomous variable, rather a range capturing finer distinctions of linguistic relevance. Animacy hierarchy proposed in Silverstein's influential article on "animacy hierarchy" (Silverstein, 1986) ranks nominals on a scale of the following gradience: *1st pers > 2nd pers > 3rd anim > 3rd inanim*. Several such hierarchies of animacy have been proposed following (Silverstein, 1986), one basic scale taken from (Aissen, 2003) makes a three-way distinction as *humans > animates > inanimates*. These hierarchies can be said to be based on the likelihood of a referent of a nominal to act as an agent in an event (Kittilä et al., 2011). Thus higher a nominal on these hierarchies higher the degree of agency/control it has over an action. In morphologically rich languages, the degree of control/agency is expressed by case marking. Case markers capture the degree of control a nominal has in a given context (Hopper and Thompson, 1980; Butt, 2006). They rank nominals on the continuum of control as shown in (1)[1]. Nominals marked with Ergative case have highest control and the ones marked with Locative have lowest.

$$Erg > Gen > Inst > Dat > Acc > Loc \quad (1)$$

Of late the systematic correspondences between animacy and linguistic phenomena have been explored for various NLP applications. It has been noted that animacy provides important information, to mention a few, for anaphora resolution (Evans and Orasan, 2000), argument disambiguation (Dell'Orletta et al., 2005), syntactic parsing (Øvrelid and Nivre, 2007; Bharati et al., 2008; Ambati et al., 2009) and verb classification (Merlo and Steven-

[1]Ergative, Genitive, Instrumental, Dative, Accusative and Locative in the given order.

son, 2001). Despite the fact that animacy could play an important role in NLP applications, its annotation, however, is not usually featured in a treebank or any other annotated corpora used for developing these applications. There are a very few annotation projects that have included animacy in their annotation manual, following its strong theoretical and computational implications. One such work, motivated by the theoretical significance of the property of animacy, is (Zaenen et al., 2004). They make use of a coding scheme drafted for a paraphrase project (Bresnan et al., 2002) and present an explicit annotation scheme for animacy in English. The annotation scheme assumes a three-way distinction, distinguishing Human, Other animates and Inanimates. Among the latter two categories '*Other animates*' is further sub-categorized into Organizations and Animals, while the category of '*Inanimates*' further distinguishes between concrete and non-concrete, and time and place nominals. As per the annotation scheme, nominals are annotated according to the animacy of their referents in a given context. Another annotation work that includes animacy for nominals is (Teleman, 1974), however, the distinction made is binary between human and non-human referents of a nominal in a given context. In a recent work on animacy annotation, Thuilier et al. (2012) have annotated a multi-source French corpora with animacy and verb semantics, on the lines of (Zaenen et al., 2004). Apart from the manual annotation for animacy, lexical resources like wordnets are an important source of this information, if available. These resources usually cover animacy, though indirectly (Fellbaum, 2010; Narayan et al., 2002). Although a wordnet is an easily accessible resource for animacy information, there are some limitations on its use, as discussed below:

1. *Coverage*: Hindi wordnet only treats common nouns while proper nouns are excluded (except famous names) see Table 1. The problem is severe where the domain of text includes more proper than common nouns, which is the case with the Hindi Treebank as it is annotated on newspaper articles.

2. *Ambiguity*: Since words can be ambiguous, the animacy listed in wordnet can only be used in presence of a high performance word sense disambiguation system. As shown in Table 2, only 38.02% of nouns have a single sense as listed in Hindi Wordnet.

3. *Metonymy or Complex Types*: Domains like newspaper articles are filled with metonymic expressions like courts, institute names, country names etc, that can refer to a building, a geographical place or a group of people depending on the context of use. These words are not ambiguous per se but show different aspects of their semantics in different contexts (logically polysemous). Hindi wordnet treats these types of nouns as inanimate.

Nominals in HTB	*Hindi WordNet*	*Coverage*
78,136	65,064	83.27%

Table 1: Coverage of Hindi WordNet on HTB Nominals.

HTB Nominals with WN Semantics	*Single Unique Sense in Hindi WordNet*
65,064	24,741 (38.02%)

Table 2: Nominals in HTB with multiple senses

Given these drawbacks, we have included animacy information manually in the annotation of the Hindi Treebank, as discussed in this work. In the rest, we will discuss the annotation of nominal expressions with animacy and the motivation for the same, the discussion will follow as: Section 2 gives a brief overview of the Hindi Treebank with all its layers. Section 3 motivates the annotation of nominals with animacy, followed by the annotation efforts and issues encountered in Section 4. Section 5 concludes the paper with a discussion on possible future directions.

2 Description of the Hindi Treebank

In the following, we give an overview of the Hindi Treebank (HTB), focusing mainly on its dependency layer. The Hindi-Urdu Treebank (Palmer et al., 2009; Bhatt et al., 2009) is a multi-layered and multi-representational treebank. It includes three levels of annotation, namely two syntactic levels and one lexical-semantic level. One syntactic level is a dependency layer which follows the CPG (Begum et al., 2008), inspired by the Pāṇinian grammatical theory of Sanskrit. The other level is annotated with phrase structure inspired by the Chomskyan approach to syntax (Chomsky, 1981) and follows a binary branching representation. The third layer of annotation, a purely lexical semantic one, encodes the semantic relations following the English PropBank (Palmer et al., 2005).

In the dependency annotation, relations are mainly verb-centric. The relation that holds between a verb and its arguments is called a *kaṛaka* relation. Besides *kaṛaka* relations, dependency relations also exist between nouns (genitives), between nouns and their modifiers (adjectival modification, relativization), between verbs and their modifiers (adverbial modification including subordination). CPG provides an essentially syntactico-semantic dependency annotation, incorporating *kaṛaka* (e.g., agent, theme, etc.), *non-kaṛaka* (e.g. possession, purpose) and other (part of) relations. A complete tag set of dependency relations based on CPG can be found in (Bharati et al., 2009), the ones starting with 'k' are largely Pāṇinian *kaṛaka* relations, and are assigned to the arguments of a verb. Figure 1 encodes the dependency structure of (5), the preterminal node is a part of speech of a lexical item (e.g. NN,VM, PSP). The lexical items with their part of speech tags are further grouped into constituents called chunks (e.g. NP, VGF) as part of the sentence analysis. The dependencies are attached at the chunk level, marked with '*drel*' in the SSF format. k1 is the agent of an action (खाया 'eat'), whereas k2 is the object or patient.

(5) *संध्या ने सेब खाया ।*
Sandhya-*Erg* apple-*Nom* eat-*Perf*
'Sandhya ate an apple.'

```
<Sentence  id = "1">
Offset  Token   Tag  Feature structure
  1     ((      NP   <fs name='NP' drel='k1:VGF'>
  1.1   संध्या    NNP  <fs af='संध्या,n,f,sg,3,o,0,0'>
  1.2   ने       PSP  <fs af='ने,psp,,,,,'>
        ))
  2     ((      NP   <fs name='NP2' drel='k2:VGF'>
  2.1   सेब      NN   <fs af='सेब,n,m,sg,3,d,0,0'>
        ))
  3     ((      VGF  <fs name='VGF'>
  3.1   खाया     VM   <fs af='खा,v,m,sg,any,,yA,yA'>
        ))
</Sentence>
```

Figure 1: Annotation of an Example Sentence in SSF.

Despite the fact that the Hindi Treebank already features a number of layers as discussed above, there have been different proposals to enrich it further. Hautli et al. (2012) proposed an additional layer to the treebank, for the deep analysis of the language, by incorporating the *functional structure* (or f-structure) of Lexical Functional Grammar which encodes traditional syntactic notions such as subject, object, complement and adjunct. Dakwale et al. (2012) have also extended the treebank with anaphoric relations, with a motive to develop a data driven anaphora resolution system for Hindi. Given this scenario, our effort is to enrich the treebank with the animacy annotation. In the following sections, we will discuss in detail, the annotation of the animacy property of nominals in the treebank and the motive for the same.

3 Motivation: In the Context of Dependency Parsing

Hindi is a morphologically rich language, grammatical relations are depicted by its morphology via case clitics. Hindi has a morphologically split-ergative case marking system (Mahajan, 1990; Dixon, 1994). Case marking is dependent on the aspect of a verb (progressive/perfective), transitivity (transitive/intransitive) and the type of a nominal (definite/indefinite, animate/inanimate). Given this peculiar behavior of case marking in Hindi, arguments of a verb (e.g. transitive) have a number of possible configurations with respect to the case marking as shown in the statistics drawn from the Hindi Treebank released for MTPIL Hindi Dependency parsing shared task (Sharma et al., 2012) in Table 3. Almost in 15% of the transitive clauses, there is no morphological case marker on any of the arguments of a verb which, in the context of data driven parsing, means lack of an explicit cue for machine learning. Although, in other cases there is a case marker, at least on one argument of a verb, the ambiguity in case markers (one-to-many mapping between case markers and grammatical functions as presented in Table 4) further worsens the situation (however, see Ambati et al. (2010) and Bhat et al. (2012) for the impact of case markers on parsing Hindi/Urdu). Consider the examples from

(6a-e), the instrumental *se* is extremely ambiguous. It can mark the instrumental adjuncts as in (6a), source expressions as in (6b), material as in (6c), comitatives as in (6d), and causes as in (6e).

	K2-Unmarked	*K2-Marked*
K1-Unmarked	1276	741
K1-Marked	5373	966

Table 3: Co-occurrence of Marked and Unmarked verb arguments (core) in HTB.

	ने/ne (Ergative)	को/ko (Dative)	से/se (Instrumental)	में/meN (Locative)	पर/par (Locative)	का/kaa (Genitive)
k1(agent)	7222	575	21	11	3	612
k2(patient)	0	3448	451	8	24	39
k3(instrument)	0	0	347	0	0	1
k4(recipient)	0	1851	351	0	1	4
k4a(experiencer)	0	420	8	0	0	2
k5(source)	0	2	1176	12	1	0
k7(location)	0	1140	308	8707	3116	19
r6(possession)	0	3	1	0	0	2251

Table 4 : Distribution of case markers across case function.

(6a) मोहन ने चाबी से ताला खोला ।
Mohan-*Erg* key-*Inst* lock-*Nom* open
'Mohan opened the lock with a key.'

(6b) गीता ने दिल्ली से सामान
Geeta-*Erg* Delhi-*Inst* luggage-*Nom*
मंगवाया ।
procure
'Geeta procured the luggage from Delhi.'

(6c) मूर्तिकार ने पत्थर से मूर्ति बनायी ।
sculptor-*Erg* stone-*Inst* idol-*Nom* make
'The sculptor made an idol out of stone.'

(6d) राम की श्याम से बात हुई ।
Ram-*Gen* Shyaam-*Inst* talk-*Nom* happen
'Ram spoke to Shyaam.'

(6e) बारिश से कई फसलें तबाह
rain-*Inst* many crops-*Nom* destroy
हो गयीं ।
happen-*Perf*
'Many crops were destroyed due to the rain.'

(7) चिड़िया दाना चुग रही है ।
bird-*Nom* grain-*Nom* devour-*Prog*
'A bird is devouring grain.'

A conventional parser has no cue for the disambiguation of instrumental case marker *se* in examples (6a-e) and similarly, in example (7), it's hard for the parser to know whether 'bird' or 'grain' is the agent of the action 'devour'. Traditionally, syntactic parsing has largely been limited to the use of only a few lexical features. Features like POS-tags are way too coarser to provide deep information valuable for syntactic parsing while on the other hand lexical items often suffer from lexical ambiguity or out of vocabulary problem. So in oder to assist the parser for better judgments, we need to complement the morphology somehow. A careful observation easily states that a simple world knowledge about the nature (e.g. living-nonliving, artifact, place) of the participants is enough to disambiguate. For Swedish, Øvrelid and Nivre (2007) and Øvrelid (2009) have shown improvement, with animacy information, in differentiation of core arguments of a verb in dependency parsing. Similarly for Hindi, Bharati et al. (2008) and Ambati et al. (2009) have shown that even when the training data is small simple animacy information can boost dependency parsing accuracies, particularly handling the differentiation of core arguments. In Table 5, we show the distribution of animacy with respect to case markers and dependency relations in the annotated portion of the Hindi Treebank. The high rate of co-occurrence between animacy and dependency relations makes a clear statement about the role animacy can play in parsing. Nominals marked with dependency relations as k1 '*agent*', k4 '*recipient*', k4a '*experiencer*' are largely annotated as *human* while k3 '*instrument*' is marked as *inanimate*, which confirms our conjecture that with animacy information a parser can reliably predict linguistic patterns. Apart from parsing, animacy has been reported to be beneficial for a number of natural language applications (Evans and Orasan, 2000; Merlo and Stevenson, 2001). Following these computational implications of animacy, we started encoded this property of nominals explicitly in our treebank. In the next section, we will present these efforts followed by the inter-annotator agreement studies.

		Human	Other-Animates	Inanimate
k1	ने/ne (Erg)	2321	630	108
	को/ko (Dat/Acc)	172	8	135
	से/se (Inst)	6	0	14
	में/me (Loc)	0	0	7
	पर/par (Loc)	0	0	1
	का/kaa (Gen)	135	2	99
	ϕ (Nom)	1052	5	3072
k2	ने/ne (Erg)	0	0	0
	को/ko (Dat/Acc)	625	200	226
	से/se (Inst)	67	0	88
	में/me (Loc)	2	0	6
	पर/par (Loc)	5	0	37
	का/kaa (Gen)	15	0	14
	ϕ (Nom)	107	61	2998
k3	ने/ne (Erg)	0	0	0
	को/ko (Dat/Acc)	0	0	0
	से/se (Inst)	2	0	199
	में/me (Loc)	0	0	0
	पर/par (Loc)	0	0	0
	का/kaa (Gen)	0	0	0
	ϕ (Nom)	0	0	20
k4	ने/ne (Erg)	0	0	0
	को/ko (Dat/Acc)	597	0	13
	से/se (Inst)	53	0	56
	में/me (Loc)	0	0	0
	पर/par (Loc)	0	0	0
	का/kaa (Gen)	0	0	0
	ϕ (Nom)	7	0	8
k4a	ने/ne (Erg)	0	0	0
	को/ko (Dat/Acc)	132	0	8
	से/se (Inst)	4	0	2
	में/me (Loc)	0	0	0
	पर/par (Loc)	0	0	0
	का/kaa (Gen)	1	0	0
	ϕ (Nom)	56	0	1
k5	ने/ne (Erg)	0	0	0
	को/ko (Dat/Acc)	0	0	0
	से/se (Inst)	7	0	460
	में/me (Loc)	0	0	1
	पर/par (Loc)	0	0	0
	का/kaa (Gen)	0	0	0
	ϕ (Nom)	0	0	2
k7	ने/ne (Erg)	0	0	0
	को/ko (Dat/Acc)	4	0	0
	से/se (Inst)	3	0	129
	में/me (Loc)	0	1977	1563
	पर/par (Loc)	66	0	1083
	का/kaa (Gen)	0	0	8
	ϕ (Nom)	5	0	1775
r6	ने/ne (Erg)	0	0	0
	को/ko (Dat/Acc)	0	0	0
	से/se (Inst)	1	0	0
	में/me (Loc)	0	0	0
	पर/par (Loc)	0	0	0
	का/kaa (Gen)	156	80	605
	ϕ (Nom)	13	3	25

Table 5: Distribution of semantic features with respect to case markers and dependency relations [a].

[a] k1 'agent', k2 'patient', k3 'instrument', k4 'recipient', k4a 'experiencer', k5 'source', k7 'location', r6 'possession'

4 Animacy Annotation

Following Zaenen et al. (2004), we make a three-way distinction, distinguishing between *Human*, *Other Animate* and *In-animate* referents of a nominal in a given context. The animacy of a referent is decided based on its sentience and/or control/volitionality in a particular context. Since, prototypically, agents tend to be animate and patients tend to be inanimate (Comrie, 1989), higher animates such as humans, dogs etc. are annotated as such in all contexts since they frequently tend to be seen in contexts of high control. However, lower animates such as insects, plants etc. are annotated as '*In-animate*' because they are ascribed less or no control in human languages like inanimates (Kittilä et al., 2011). Non-sentient referents, except intelligent machines and vehicles, are annotated as '*In-animate*' in all contexts. Intelligent machines like robots and vehicles, although, lack any sentience, they possess an animal like behavior which separates them from inanimate nouns with no animal resemblance, reflected in human language as control/volitionality. These nouns unlike humans and other higher animates are annotated as per the context they are used in. They are annotated as '*Other animate*' only in their agentive roles. Nominals that vary in sentience in varying contexts are annotated based on their reference in a given context as discussed in Subsection 4.2. These nominals include country names referring to geographical places, teams playing for the country, governments or their inhabitants; and organizations including courts, colleges, schools, banks etc. Unlike Zaenen et al. (2004) we don't further categorize '*Other Animate*' and '*In-animate*' classes. We don't distinguish between *Organizations* and *Animals* in '*Other Animate*' and *Time* and *Place* in '*In-animates*'.

The process of animacy annotation in the Hindi Treebank is straight forward. For every chunk in a sentence, the animacy of its head word is captured in an '*attribute-value*' pair in SSF format, as shown in Figure 3. Hitherto, around 6485 sentence, of the Hindi Treebank, have been annotated with the animacy information.

<Sentence id = "1">

Offset	Token	Tag	Feature structure
1	((	NP	<fs name='NP' drel='k1:VGF'
			semprop='human'>
1.1	मोहन	NNP	<fs af='मोहन,n,m,sg,3,d,0,0'>
1.2	ने	PSP	<fs af='ने,psp,,,,,' name='ने'>
	))		
2	((	NP	<fs name='NP2' drel='k4:VGF'
			semprop='other-animate'>
2.1	बिल्ली	NN	<fs af='बिल्ली,n,f,sg,3,d,0,0'>
2.2	को	PSP	<fs af='को,psp,,,,,' name='को'>
	))		
3	((	NP	<fs name='NP3' drel='k3:VGF'
			semprop='inanimate'>
3.1	बोतल	NN	<fs af='बोतल ,n,f,sg,3,d,0,0'>
3.2	से	PSP	<fs af='से,psp,,,,,'>
	))		
4	((	NP	<fs name='NP4' drel='k2:VGF'
			semprop='inanimate'>
4.1	दूध	NN	<fs af='दूध,n,m,sg,3,d,0,0'>
	))		
5	((	VGF	<fs name='VGF'>
5.1	पिलाया	VM	<fs af='पिला,v,m,sg,any,,yA,yA'>
	))		

</Sentence>

Figure 3: Semantic Annotation in SSF.

(8) *मोहन ने बिल्ली को बोतल से दूध*
Mohan-*Erg* cat-*Dat* bottle-*Inst* milk-*Nom*
पिलाया ।
drink-*Perf*
'Mohan fed milk to the cat with a bottle.'

In the following, we discuss some of the interesting cross linguistic phenomena which added some challenge to the annotation.

4.1 Personification

Personification is a type of meaning extension whereby an entity (usually non-human) is given human qualities. Personified expressions are annotated, in our annotation procedure, as *Human*, since it is the sense they carry in such contexts. However, to retain their literal sense, two attributes are added. One for their context bound sense (metaphorical) and the other for context free sense (literal). In example (9), *waves* is annotated with literal animacy as *In-animante* and metaphoric animacy as *Human*, as shown in Figure 4 (offset 2).

<Sentence id = "1">

Offset	Token	Tag	Feature structure
1	((	NP	<fs name='NP' drel='k7p:VGF' >
1.1	सागर	NNC	<fs af='सागर,n,m,sg,3,d,0,0'>
1.2	तट	NN	<fs af='तट,n,m,sg,3,d,0,0'>
1.3	पर	PSP	<fs af='पर,psp,,,,,'>
	))		
2	((	NP	<fs name='NP2' drel='k1:VGF'
			semprop='inanimate'
			metaphoric='human'>
2.1	लहरें	NN	<fs af='लहरें,n,f,pl,3,d,0,0'>
	))		
3	((	VGF	<fs name='VGF'>
3.1	नाच	VM	<fs af='नाच,v,any,any,any,,0,0'>
3.2	रही	VAUX	<fs af='रही,v,f,sg,any,,ya,ya'>
3.3	हैं	AUX	<sf AF='हैं,v,any,pl,1,,he,he'>
	))		

</Sentence>

Figure 4: Semantic Annotation in SSF.

(9) *सागर तट पर लहरें नाच रही हैं* ।
sea coast-*Loc* waves-*Nom* dance-*Prog*
'Waves are dancing on the sea shore.'

4.2 Complex Types

The Hindi Treebank in largely built on newspaper corpus. Logically polysemous expressions (metonymies) such as *government*, *court*, *newspaper* etc. are very frequent in news reporting. These polysemous nominals can exhibit contradictory semantics in different contexts. In example (10a), *court* refers to a *person* (judge) or a *group of persons* (jury) while in (10b) it is a *building* (see Pustejovsky (1996) for the semantics of complex types). In our annotation procedure, such expressions are annotated as per the sense or reference they carry in a given context. So, in case of (10a) *court* will be annotated as *Human* while in (10b) it will be annotated as *In-animante*.

(10a) *अदालत ने मुकदमे का फैसला*
court-*Erg* case-*Gen* decision-*Nom*
सुनाया ।
declare-*Perf*
'The court declared its decision on the case.'

(10b) मैं अदालत में हूँ ।
I-*Nom* court-*Loc* be-*Prs*
'I am in the court.'

4.3 Inter-Annotator Agreement

We measured the inter-annotator agreement on a set of 358 nominals ($\sim$50 sentences) using Cohen's kappa. We had three annotators annotating the same data set separately. The nominals were annotated in context i.e., the annotation was carried considering the role and reference of a nominal in a particular sentence. The kappa statistics, as presented in Table 6, show a significant understanding of annotators of the property of animacy. In Table 7, we report the confusion between the annotators on the three animacy categories. The confusion is high for '$Inanimate$' class. Annotators don't agree on this category because of its fuzziness. As discussed earlier, although '$Inanimate$' class enlists biologically inanimate entities, some entities may behave like animates in some contexts. They may be sentient and have high linguistic control in some contexts. The difficulty in deciphering the exact nature of the reference of these nominals, as observed, is the reason behind the confusion. The confusion is observed for nouns like organization names, lower animates and vehicles. Apart from the linguistically and contextually defined animacy, there was no confusion, as expected, in the understanding of biological animacy.

$Annotators$	κ
ann1-ann2	0.78
ann1-ann3	0.82
ann2-ann3	0.83
Average κ	0.811

Table 6: Kappa Statistics

	Human	*Other-animate*	*Inanimate*
Human	71	0	14
Other-animate	0	9	5
Inanimate	8	10	241

Table 7: Confusion Matrix

5 Conclusion and Future Work

In this work, we have presented our efforts to enrich the nominals in the Hindi Treebank with animacy information. The annotation was followed by the inter-annotator agreement study for evaluating the confusion over the categories chosen for annotation. The annotators have a significant understanding of the property of animacy as shown by the higher values of Kappa (κ). In future, we plan to continue the animacy annotation for the whole Hindi Treebank. We also plan to utilize the annotated data to build a data driven automatic animacy classifier (Øvrelid, 2006). From a linguistic perspective, an annotation of the type, as discussed in this paper, will also be of great interest for studying information dynamics and see how semantics interacts with syntax in Hindi.

6 Acknowledgments

The work reported in this paper is supported by the NSF grant (Award Number: CNS 0751202; CFDA Number: 47.070). [2]

References

Judith Aissen. 2003. Differential object marking: Iconicity vs. economy. *Natural Language & Linguistic Theory*, 21(3):435–483.

B.R. Ambati, P. Gade, S. Husain, and GSK Chaitanya. 2009. Effect of minimal semantics on dependency parsing. In *Proceedings of the Student Research Workshop*.

B.R. Ambati, S. Husain, J. Nivre, and R. Sangal. 2010. On the role of morphosyntactic features in Hindi dependency parsing. In *Proceedings of the NAACL HLT 2010 First Workshop on Statistical Parsing of Morphologically-Rich Languages*, pages 94–102. Association for Computational Linguistics.

R. Begum, S. Husain, A. Dhwaj, D.M. Sharma, L. Bai, and R. Sangal. 2008. Dependency annotation scheme for Indian languages. In *Proceedings of IJCNLP*. Citeseer.

Akshar Bharati, Samar Husain, Bharat Ambati, Sambhav Jain, Dipti Sharma, and Rajeev Sangal. 2008. Two semantic features make all the difference in parsing accuracy. *Proceedings of ICON*, 8.

[2]Any opinions, findings, and conclusions or recommendations expressed in this material are those of the author(s) and do not necessarily reflect the views of the National Science Foundation.

A. Bharati, D.M. Sharma, S. Husain, L. Bai, R. Begum, and R. Sangal. 2009. AnnCorra: TreeBanks for Indian Languages Guidelines for Annotating Hindi TreeBank (version–2.0).

R.A. Bhat, S. Jain, and D.M. Sharma. 2012. Experiments on Dependency Parsing of Urdu. In *Proceedings of TLT11 2012 Lisbon Portugal*, pages 31–36. Ediçes Colibri.

R. Bhatt, B. Narasimhan, M. Palmer, O. Rambow, D.M. Sharma, and F. Xia. 2009. A multi-representational and multi-layered treebank for hindi/urdu. In *Proceedings of the Third Linguistic Annotation Workshop*, pages 186–189. Association for Computational Linguistics.

Joan Bresnan, Jean Carletta, Richard Crouch, Malvina Nissim, Mark Steedman, Tom Wasow, and Annie Zaenen. 2002. Paraphrase analysis for improved generation, link project.

Miriam Butt. 2006. The dative-ergative connection. *Empirical issues in syntax and semantics*, 6:69–92.

N. Chomsky. 1981. Lectures on Government and Binding. *Dordrecht: Foris.*

Bernard Comrie. 1989. *Language universals and linguistic typology: Syntax and morphology*. University of Chicago press.

Praveen Dakwale, Himanshu Sharma, and Dipti M Sharma. 2012. Anaphora Annotation in Hindi Dependency TreeBank. In *Proceedings of the 26th Pacific Asia Conference on Language, Information, and Computation*, pages 391–400, Bali,Indonesia, November. Faculty of Computer Science, Universitas Indonesia.

Felice Dell'Orletta, Alessandro Lenci, Simonetta Montemagni, and Vito Pirrelli. 2005. Climbing the path to grammar: A maximum entropy model of subject/object learning. In *Proceedings of the Workshop on Psychocomputational Models of Human Language Acquisition*, pages 72–81. Association for Computational Linguistics.

R.M.W. Dixon. 1994. *Ergativity*. Number 69. Cambridge University Press.

Richard Evans and Constantin Orasan. 2000. Improving anaphora resolution by identifying animate entities in texts. In *Proceedings of the Discourse Anaphora and Reference Resolution Conference (DAARC2000)*, pages 154–162.

Christiane Fellbaum. 2010. *WordNet*. Springer.

A. Hautli, S. Sulger, and M. Butt. 2012. Adding an annotation layer to the Hindi/Urdu treebank. *Linguistic Issues in Language Technology*, 7(1).

Paul J Hopper and Sandra A Thompson. 1980. Transitivity in grammar and discourse. *Language*, pages 251–299.

Seppo Kittilä, Katja Västi, and Jussi Ylikoski. 2011. *Case, Animacy and Semantic Roles*, volume 99. John Benjamins Publishing.

A.K. Mahajan. 1990. *The A/A-bar distinction and movement theory*. Ph.D. thesis, Massachusetts Institute of Technology.

Paola Merlo and Suzanne Stevenson. 2001. Automatic verb classification based on statistical distributions of argument structure. *Computational Linguistics*, 27(3):373–408.

Dipak Narayan, Debasri Chakrabarty, Prabhakar Pande, and Pushpak Bhattacharyya. 2002. An experience in building the indo wordnet-a wordnet for hindi. In *First International Conference on Global WordNet, Mysore, India*.

Lilja Øvrelid and Joakim Nivre. 2007. When word order and part-of-speech tags are not enough – Swedish dependency parsing with rich linguistic features. In *Proceedings of the International Conference on Recent Advances in Natural Language Processing (RANLP)*, pages 447–451.

Lilja Øvrelid. 2006. Towards robust animacy classification using morphosyntactic distributional features. In *Proceedings of the Eleventh Conference of the European Chapter of the Association for Computational Linguistics: Student Research Workshop*, pages 47–54. Association for Computational Linguistics.

Lilja Øvrelid. 2009. Empirical evaluations of animacy annotation. In *Proceedings of the 12th Conference of the European Chapter of the Association for Computational Linguistics (EACL)*.

M. Palmer, D. Gildea, and P. Kingsbury. 2005. The proposition bank: An annotated corpus of semantic roles. volume 31, pages 71–106. MIT Press.

M. Palmer, R. Bhatt, B. Narasimhan, O. Rambow, D.M. Sharma, and F. Xia. 2009. Hindi Syntax: Annotating Dependency, Lexical Predicate-Argument Structure, and Phrase Structure. In *The 7th International Conference on Natural Language Processing*, pages 14–17.

J. Pustejovsky. 1996. The Semantics of Complex Types. *Lingua*.

Dipti Misra Sharma, Prashanth Mannem, Joseph van-Genabith, Sobha Lalitha Devi, Radhika Mamidi, and Ranjani Parthasarathi, editors. 2012. *Proceedings of the Workshop on Machine Translation and Parsing in Indian Languages*. The COLING 2012 Organizing Committee, Mumbai, India, December.

Michael Silverstein. 1986. Hierarchy of features and ergativity. *Features and projections*, pages 163–232.

Ulf Teleman. 1974. *Manual för grammatisk beskrivning av talad och skriven svenska*. Studentlitteratur.

Juliette Thuilier, Laurence Danlos, et al. 2012. Semantic annotation of French corpora: animacy and verb semantic classes. In *LREC 2012-The eighth international conference on Language Resources and Evaluation*.

Annie Zaenen, Jean Carletta, Gregory Garretson, Joan Bresnan, Andrew Koontz-Garboden, Tatiana Nikitina, M Catherine O'Connor, and Tom Wasow. 2004. Animacy Encoding in English: why and how. In *Proceedings of the 2004 ACL Workshop on Discourse Annotation*, pages 118–125. Association for Computational Linguistics.

Automatic Named Entity Pre-Annotation for Out-of-Domain Human Annotation

Sophie Rosset[α], **Cyril Grouin**[α], **Thomas Lavergne**[α,β], **Mohamed Ben Jannet**[α,β,γ,δ]
Jérémy Leixa[ε], **Olivier Galibert**[γ], **Pierre Zweigenbaum**[α].
[α]LIMSI–CNRS [β]Université Paris-Sud [γ]LNE
[δ]LPP, Université Sorbonne Nouvelle [ε]ELDA
{rosset,grouin,lavergne,ben-jannet,pz}@limsi.fr
leixa@elda.org, olivier.galibert@lne.fr

Abstract

Automatic pre-annotation is often used to improve human annotation speed and accuracy. We address here out-of-domain named entity annotation, and examine whether automatic pre-annotation is still beneficial in this setting. Our study design includes two different corpora, three pre-annotation schemes linked to two annotation levels, both expert and novice annotators, a questionnaire-based subjective assessment and a corpus-based quantitative assessment. We observe that pre-annotation helps in all cases, both for speed and for accuracy, and that the subjective assessment of the annotators does not always match the actual benefits measured in the annotation outcome.

1 Introduction

Human corpus annotation is a difficult, time-consuming, and hence costly process. This motivates research into methods which reduce this cost (Leech, 1997). One such method consists of automatically pre-annotating the corpus (Marcus et al., 1993; Dandapat et al., 2009) using an existing system, e.g., a POS tagger, syntactic parser, named entity recognizer, according to the task for which the annotations aim to provide a gold standard. The pre-annotations are then corrected by the human annotators. The underlying hypothesis is that this should reduce annotation time while possibly at the same time increasing annotation completeness and consistency.

We study here corpus pre-annotation in a specific setting, *out-of-domain named entity annotation*, in which we examine specific questions that we present below. We produced corpora and annotation guidelines for named entities which are both hierarchical and compositional (Grouin et al., 2011),[1] and which we used in contrastive studies of news texts in French (Rosset et al., 2012). We want to rely on the same named entity definitions for studies on two types of data we did not cover: parliament debates (*Europarl* corpus) and regional, contemporary written news (*L'Est Républicain*), both in French. To help the annotation process we could reuse our system (Dinarelli and Rosset, 2011), but needed first to examine whether a system trained on one type of text (our first Broadcast News data) could be used to produce a useful pre-annotation for different types of text (our two corpora).

We therefore set up the present study in which we aim to answer the following questions linked to this point and to related annotation issues:

- can a system trained on data from one specific domain be useful on data from another domain in a pre-annotation task?
- does this pre-annotation help human annotators or bias them?
- what importance can we give to the annotators' subjective assessment of the usefulness of the pre-annotation?
- can we observe differences in the use of pre-annotation depending on the level of expertise of human annotators?

Moreover, as the aforementioned annotation scheme is based on two annotation levels (*entities* and *components*), we want to answer these questions taking into account these two levels.

We first examine related work on pre-annotation (Section 2), then present our corpora and annotation task (Section 3). We describe and discuss experiments in Section 4, and make subjective and

[1] Corpora, guidelines and tools are available through ELRA under references ELRA-S0349 and ELRA-W0073.

quantitative observations in Sections 5 and 6. Finally, we conclude and present some perspectives in Section 7.

2 Related Work

Facilitating human annotations has been the topic of a large amount of research. Two different approaches can be distinguished: active learning (Ringger et al., 2007; Settles et al., 2008) and pre-annotation (Marcus et al., 1993; Dandapat et al., 2009). Our work falls into the latter type.

Pre-annotation can be used in several ways. The first is to provide annotations to be corrected by human annotators (Fort and Sagot, 2010). A variant consists of merging multiple automatic annotations before having them corrected by human curators to produce a gold-standard (Rebholz-Schuhmann et al., 2011). The second type consists of providing clues to help human annotators perform the annotation task (Mihaila et al., 2013).

This work addresses the first type, a single-system pre-annotation with human correction. An objective is to examine whether a system trained on one type of text can be useful to pre-annotate texts of a different type. Most previous studies have been performed on well-behaved tasks such as part-of-speech tagging on in-domain data, i.e., the model used for pre-annotating the target data had been trained on similar data. For instance, Fort and Sagot (2010) provide a precise evaluation of the usefulness of pre-annotation and compare the impact of different quality levels in POS taggers on the Penn TreeBank corpus. They first trained different models on the training part of the corpus and applied them to the test corpus. The pre-annotated test corpus was then corrected by humans. They reported gains in accuracy and inter-annotator agreement. The study focused on the minimal quality (accuracy threshold) of automatic annotation that would prove useful for human annotation. They reported a gain for human annotation when accuracy ranged from 66.5% to 81.6%. On the contrary, for a semantic-frame annotation task, Rehbein et al. (2009) observed no significant gain in quality and speed of annotation even when using a state-of-the-art system.

Generally speaking, annotators find the pre-annotation stage useful (Rehbein et al., 2009; South et al., 2011; Huang et al., 2011). Annotation managers consider that a bias may occur depending on how much human annotators trust the pre-annotation (Rehbein et al., 2009; Fort and Sagot, 2010; South et al., 2011). In their frame-semantic argument structure annotation, Rehbein et al. (2009) addressed a specific question considering a two-level annotation scheme: is the pre-annotation of frame assignment (low-level annotation) useful for annotating semantic roles (high-level annotation)? Although for the low-level annotation task they observed a significant difference in quality of final annotation, for the high-level task they found no difference.

Most of these studies used a pre-annotation system trained on the same kind of data as those which were to be annotated manually. Nevertheless some system-oriented studies have focused on the results obtained by systems trained on one type of corpus and applied to another type of corpus, e.g., for a Latin POS tagger (Poudat and Longrée, 2009; Skjærholt, 2011) or for a CoNLL named entity tagger for German (Faruqui and Padó, 2010) for which the authors noticed noticed a reduction of the F-measure when going from in-domain (newswire data, F=0.782 for their best system) to out-of-domain (Europarl data, F=0.656).

One of our objectives is then to examine whether a system trained on one type of text can be useful to pre-annotate texts of a different type. We set up experiments to study precisely the possible induced bias and whether the level of experience of the annotators would make a difference in such a context. In this study, we used two different kinds of corpora, which were both different from the corpus used to train the pre-annotation system.

3 Task and corpus description

3.1 Task

In this work, we used the structured named entity definition we proposed in a previous study (Grouin et al., 2011): entities are both hierarchical (types have subtypes) and compositional (types and components are included in entities) as in Figure 1.

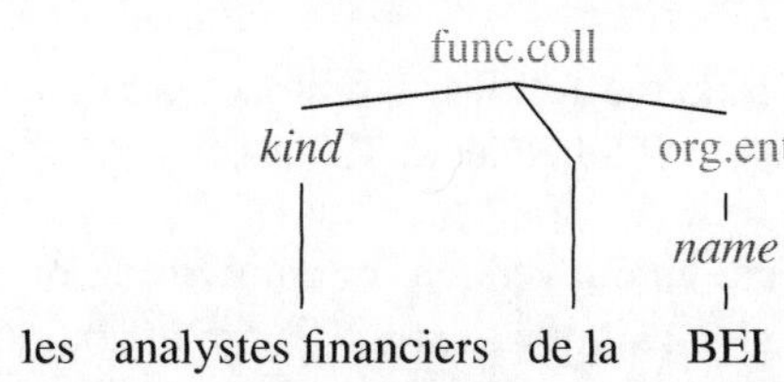

Figure 1: Multi-level annotation of entity subtypes (red tags) and components (*blue* tags): *the financial analysts of the EBI*

This taxonomy of entity types is composed of 7 types (*person, location, organization, amount, time, production* and *function*) and 32 sub-types (individual person *pers.ind* vs. group of persons *pers.coll*; administrative organization *org.adm* vs. services *org.ent*; etc.). Types and subtypes constitute the first level of annotation.

Within these categories, components are second-level elements (*kind, name, first.name*, etc.), and can never be used outside the scope of a type or subtype element.

3.2 Corpora

Two French corpora were sampled from larger ones:

Europarl: Prepared speech (*Parliament Debates—Europarl*): 15,306 word extract;

Press: Local, contemporary written news (*L'Est Républicain*): 11,146 word extract.

These corpora were automatically annotated using the system described in (Dinarelli and Rosset, 2011). This system relies on a Conditional Random Field (CRF) model for the detection of components and on a probabilistic context-free grammar (PCFG) model for types and sub-types. These models have been trained on Broadcast News data. This system achieved a Slot Error Rate (Makhoul et al., 1999) of 37.0% on Broadcast conversation and 29.7% on Broadcast news, and ranked first in the Quaero evaluation campaign (Galibert et al., 2011).

4 Experiments

In this section we present the protocol we designed to study the usefulness of pre-annotation under different conditions, and its overall results.

4.1 Protocol

We defined the following protocol, similar to the one used in Rehbein et al. (2009).

Corpora. Four versions of our two corpora were prepared: (i) raw text, (ii) pre-annotation of types, (iii) pre-annotation of components, and (iv) full pre-annotation of both types and components. Each of these four versions was split into four quarters.

Annotators. Eight human annotators were involved in this task. Among them, four are considered as expert annotators (they annotated corpora in the previous years) while the four remaining ones are novice annotators (this was the first time they annotated such corpora; they were given training sessions before starting actual annotation). We defined four pairs of annotators, where each pair was composed of an expert and a novice annotator.

Quarter allocation. We allocated each corpus quarter in such a way that each pair of annotators processed, in each corpus, material from each one of the four pre-annotated versions (see Table 3). The same allocation was made in both corpora.

4.2 Results

For each corpus part, a reference was built based on a majority vote by confronting all annotations. The resulting reference corpus is presented in Table 1.

Corpus		# comp.	# types	# entities	# words
Press	Q1	481	310	791	3047
	Q2	367	246	673	2628
	Q3	495	327	822	2971
	Q4	413	282	695	2600
Europarl	Q1	362	259	621	3926
	Q2	309	221	530	3809
	Q3	378	247	625	3604
	Q4	413	299	712	3967

Table 1: General description of the reference annotations: number of components, types, entities (the sum of components and types), and words

Table 2 presents the performance of the automatic pre-annotation system against the reference corpus. We used the well known F-measure and in addition the Slot Error Rate as it allows to weight different error classes (deletions, insertions, type or frontier errors). Fort and Sagot (2010) reported a gain in human annotation when pre-annotation accuracy ranged from 66.5% to 81.6%. Given their results we can hope for a gain in both accuracy and annotation time when using pre-annotation.

Table 3 presents all results obtained by each annotators given each pre-annotation condition (raw, components, types and full) in terms of precision, recall and F-measure.

Corpus	#	Raw text R	Raw text P	Raw text F	Components R	Components P	Components F	Types R	Types P	Types F	Full R	Full P	Full F
Press	Q1	0.874	0.777	0.823	0.876	0.741	0.803	0.824	0.870	**0.846**	0.852	0.800	0.825
		0.810	0.766	0.788	0.815	0.777	0.796	0.645	0.724	0.683	0.844	0.785	**0.813**
	Q2	0.765	0.796	0.780	0.870	0.773	0.819	0.822	0.801	0.812	0.917	0.773	**0.839**
		0.558	0.654	0.602	0.826	0.775	**0.800**	0.815	0.777	0.795	0.816	0.752	0.783
	Q3	0.835	0.715	0.771	0.888	0.809	0.847	0.884	0.796	0.837	0.887	0.859	**0.873**
		0.792	0.689	0.736	0.904	0.780	**0.837**	0.876	0.771	0.820	0.780	0.827	0.803
	Q4	0.802	0.757	0.779	0.845	0.876	0.860	0.900	0.702	0.789	0.914	0.840	**0.876**
		0.794	0.727	0.759	0.696	0.715	0.705	0.812	0.701	0.752	0.802	0.757	**0.779**
Europarl	Q1	0.809	0.728	0.766	0.800	0.568	0.665	0.776	0.862	**0.817**	0.754	0.720	0.736
		0.754	0.720	**0.736**	0.720	0.609	0.660	0.687	0.607	0.644	0.736	0.638	0.683
	Q2	0.776	0.792	**0.784**	0.782	0.617	0.690	0.797	0.645	0.713	0.821	0.526	0.641
		0.563	0.498	0.529	0.802	0.619	**0.699**	0.698	0.553	0.617	0.769	0.566	0.652
	Q3	0.747	0.459	0.569	0.749	0.624	0.681	0.805	0.800	**0.803**	0.735	0.744	0.739
		0.732	0.598	0.658	0.736	0.717	0.726	0.822	0.738	**0.777**	0.808	0.734	0.769
	Q4	0.742	0.624	0.678	0.874	0.760	**0.813**	0.732	0.480	0.580	0.743	0.608	0.669
		0.721	0.566	0.634	0.695	0.652	**0.672**	0.707	0.600	0.649	0.738	0.603	0.664

Table 3: Overall recall, precision and F-measure for each pair of annotators *(blue: pair #1, ocre: pair #2, green: pair #3, white: pair #4)* on each corpus quarter *(Q1, Q2, Q3, Q4)*, depending on the kind of pre-annotation *(raw text, only components, only types, full pre-annotation)*. Expert annotator is on the upper line of each quarter, novice annotator is on the lower line. Boldface indicates the best F-measure for each novice and expert annotator among all pre-annotation tasks in a given corpus quarter

Corpus		Components F	Components SER	Types F	Types SER	Full F	Full SER
Press	Q1	72.4	37.9	63.5	46.3	68.9	41.0
	Q2	77.2	32.2	66.8	43.5	73.1	36.6
	Q3	76.1	34.1	68.3	41.7	73.1	36.9
	Q4	76.1	33.3	63.3	45.7	71.0	38.2
Europarl	Q1	61.9	49.9	57.5	55.4	60.1	52.2
	Q2	61.2	51.3	54.6	54.3	58.5	52.5
	Q3	61.6	50.1	53.3	55.7	58.2	52.2
	Q4	57.1	57.0	48.1	59.7	53.3	58.1
Broad.		88.3	29.1	73.1	39.1	73.2	33.1

Table 2: F-measure and Slot Error Rate achieved by the automatic system on each kind of annotation and on in-domain broadcast data

We also computed inter-annotator agreement (IAA) for each corpus considering two groups of annotators, *experts* and *novices*. We consider that the inter-annotator agreement is somewhere between the F-measure and the standard IAA considering as *markables* all the units annotated by at least one of the annotators (Grouin et al., 2011). We computed Scott's Pi (Scott, 1955), and Cohen's Kappa (Cohen, 1960). The former considers one model for all annotators while the latter considers one model per annotator. In our case, these two values are almost the same, which means that the proportions and kinds of annotations are very similar across experts and novices. Figure 2 shows the IAA (Cohen's Kappa and F-measure) obtained on the two corpora given the four pre-annotation conditions (no pre-annotation, components, types, and full pre-annotation). As we can see, IAA is systematically higher for the *Press* corpus than for the *Europarl* corpus, which can be linked to the higher performance of the automatic pre-annotation system on this corpus. We also can see that pre-annotation always improves agreement and that full pre-annotation yields the best result. We observe that, as expected, pre-annotation leads human annotators to obtain higher consistency.

5 Subjective assessment

An important piece of information in any annotation campaign is the feelings of the annotators about the task. This can give interesting clues about the expected quality of their work and on the usefulness of the pre-annotation step. We asked the annotators a few questions concerning several features of this project, such as the annotation

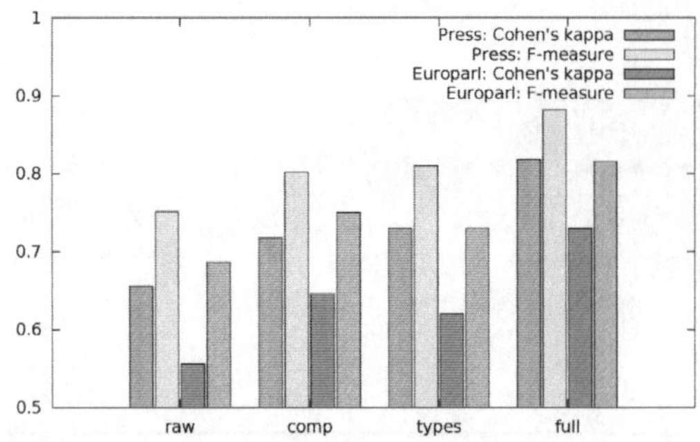

Figure 2: Cohen's Kappa (red and blue) and F-measure (green and pink) measuring agreement of experts and novices on Press and Europarl corpora in four pre-annotation conditions. Each measure compares the concatenated annotations of the four experts with the four novices.

manual, or how they assessed the benefits of pre-annotation in the different corpora (Section 5.1). Another important point is the experience of the annotators, which we also examine in the light of theirs answers to the questionnaire (Section 5.2).

5.1 Questionnaire

The questionnaire submitted to the annotators contained 4 questions, dealing with their feedback on the annotation process:

1. According to you, which level of pre-annotation has been the most helpful during the annotation process? Types, components, or both?

2. To what extent would you say that pre-annotation helped you in terms of precision and speed? Did it produce many errors you had to correct?

3. If you had to choose between the Europarl corpus and the Press corpus, could you say that one has been easier to annotate than the other?

4. Concerning the annotation manual, are there topics that you would like to change, or correct? In the same way, which named entities caused you the most difficulties to deal with?

All 8 annotators answered these questions. We summarize below what we found in their answers.

5.1.1 Level of pre-annotation

Most of the annotators preferred the corpora that were pre-annotated with types only. The reason, for the most part, is that a pre-annotation of types allows the annotator to work faster on their files, because guessing the components from the types is easier than guessing types from components.[2] Indeed, the different types of entities defined in the manual always imply the same components, be they specific (to one entity type) or transverse (common to several entity types). On the contrary, a transverse component, such as <kind>, can be part of any type of named entity. The other reason for this choice of pre-annotation concerns the readability brought to the corpora. An annotation with types only is easier to read than an annotation with components, and less exhausting after many hours of work on the texts.

5.1.2 Gain in precision and speed

What motivated the answers to the second question mainly concerns the accuracy of the different pre-annotation methods. While all of them presented errors that needed to be corrected, the pre-annotation of types was the one that they felt presented the smaller number of errors. Thus, annotators spent less time reviewing the corpora in search of errors, compared to the other pre-annotated corpora (with components, and with both types and components), where more errors had to be spotted and corrected. This search for incorrect pre-annotations impacted the time spent on each corpus. Indeed, most annotators declared that pre-annotation with types was quicker to deal with than other pre-annotation schemes.

5.1.3 Corpus differences

About one half of the annotators agreed that the Europarl corpus had been more difficult to annotate. Despite obvious differences in register, sentence structure and vocabulary between the two corpora, Europarl seemed more redundant and complex than the other corpus. For instance, one of the annotators declared:

> *The Europarl corpus is more difficult to annotate in the sense that the existing types and components do not always match the realities found in the corpus, either because their definitions*

[2]This feeling is supported by results about ambiguity presented in Fort et al. (2012).

cannot apply exactly, or because the required types and components are missing (mainly for frequencies: "five times per year").

The other half of the annotators did not feel any specific difficulties in annotating one corpus or the other. According to them, both corpora are the same in terms of register and sentence structure.

5.1.4 Improvements in guidelines

All of the annotators were unanimous in thinking that two points need to be modified in the manual. First of all, the distinction between the <org.adm> and <org.ent> subtypes is too difficult to apprehend, above all in the Europarl corpus where these entities are too ambiguous to be annotated correctly. Secondly, the distinction between the <pers> and <func> types has also been difficult to deal with. The other remarks about potential changes mainly concerned the introduction of explicit rules for frequencies, which are recurrent in the Europarl corpus.

5.2 Experience

As mentioned earlier in Section 4.1, we will now see if the differences in experience between annotators impacted their difficulty in annotating the corpora. First of all, when we look at the answers given to question 3, we notice that both novice and expert annotators consider the Europarl corpus the most difficult to annotate. Most of their answers deal with the redundancy and the formal register of the data. Moreover, as everyone answered in question 4, both <func> and <org> entities have to be modified to be easier to understand and to use. This unanimous opinion about what needs to be reviewed in the manual allows us to think that the annotators' level of experience has a low impact on their apprehension of the corpora, both *Europarl* and *Press*. To confirm this, we can look at the answers given to questions 1 and 2, as indicated in the previous paragraph. As has been explained, every annotator correctly pointed at the many errors found in pre-annotation, regardless of their experience. Besides, the assessment of the benefits of pre-annotation is the same for almost everyone, regardless of their experience too: both novice and expert annotators agree that pre-annotation with type adds efficiency and speed to annotation.

To conclude, according to our observations based on the questionnaire, we cannot assert that there has been a difference between novice and expert annotators. Both groups agreed on the same difficulties, pointed at the same errors, and criticized the same entities, saying that their definitions needed to be clarified.

6 Quantitative observations

In this section we provide results of quantitative observations in order to support, or not, the annotators' subjective assessment.

6.1 Corpus statistics

The annotators reported different feelings depending on the corpora. Some of them reported that the Europarl corpus was more difficult to annotate, with more complex sentence structures, or usage of fewer proper nouns.

To explore these differences, we computed some statistics over the two original, un-annotated corpora (which are much larger than the samples annotated in this experiment) as well as over the original broadcast news corpus used to train the pre-annotation system. Each of these corpora contains several million words.

Table 4 reports simple statistics about sentences in the three corpora. Based on these statistics, while the *Europarl* (Euro) corpus is very similar to the original *Broadcast News* (BN), the *Press* corpus shows differences: sentences are 20% shorter, with fewer but larger chunks, confirming the impression of simpler, less convoluted sentences.

	BN	Press	Euro
Mean sentence length	30.2	23.9	29.7
Mean chunk count	10.9	6.7	10.4
Mean chunk length	2.7	3.6	2.8

Table 4: Sentence summary of the three corpora

Looking more closely at the contents of these sentences, Figure 3 summarizes the proportions of grammatical word classes. The sentiment of extensive naming of entities in the *Press* corpus is confirmed by the four times higher rate of proper nouns. On the other hand, entities are more often referred to using nouns with an optional adjective in the *Europarl* corpus, leading to a more frequent usage of the latter.

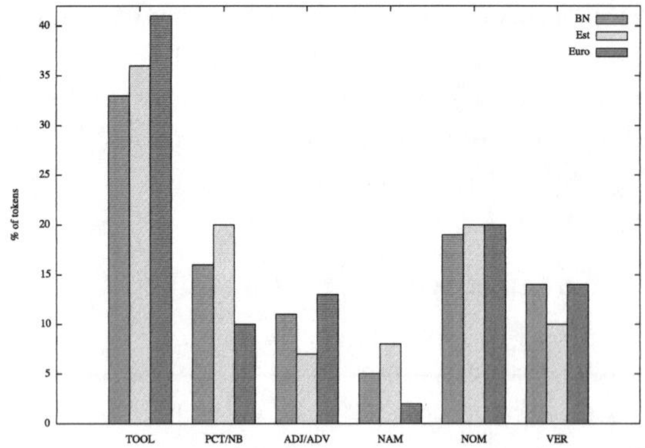

Figure 3: Frequency of word classes in the three corpora (BN = Broadcast News, Est = Press, Euro = Europarl). TOOL = grammatical words, PCT/NB = punctuation and numbers, ADJ/ADV = adjectives and adverbs, NAM = proper name, NOM = noun, VER = verb.

6.2 Influence of pre-annotation on the behaviour of annotators

As already mentioned, it is often reported that a bias may occur depending on human confidence in the pre-annotation (Fort and Sagot, 2010; Rehbein et al., 2009; South et al., 2011). An important unknown is always the influence of pre-annotation on the behaviour of annotators, and at which point pre-annotation induces more errors than it helps. This may obviously depend on pre-annotation quality. Table 5 summarizes the error rates of the automatic annotator in the studied data (*Press* + *Europarl*) and in comparison to in-domain data. *Insertions* (Ins) are extra annotations, *deletions* (Del) missing annotations, and *substitutions* (Subs) are annotations that are incorrect in type, boundaries, or both. We can see that

Domain	Pre-annotation	Ins	Del	Subs
Out	Components	4.4%	33.6%	7.8%
	Types	7.0%	36.2%	12.7%
	Full	5.5%	34.6%	9.7%
In	Full	3.7%	23.4%	10.6%

Table 5: Pre-annotation errors and comparison with in-domain (Broadcast News) data

going out-of-domain increased deletions, probably through a lack of knowledge of domain vocabulary. But it did not influence the other error rates significantly. It is also noticeable that deletion is the type of error most produced by the system, with every third entity missed. Automatic, full pre-annotation of *Press* + *Europarl* obtains a precision of 0.79 and a recall of 0.56.

Human annotator performance can then be measured over the same three error types (Table 6). We

Pre-annotation	Ins	Del	Subs
Raw	8.9%	18.9%	12.8%
Components	5.9%	16.7%	11.3%
Types	7.1%	16.5%	12.0%
Full	7.1%	16.5%	10.1%

Table 6: Mean human annotation error levels for each pre-annotation scheme

can see that annotation quality was systematically improved by pre-annotation, with the best global result obtained by full pre-annotation. In addition there was no increase in deletions (had the human stopped looking at the unannotated text) or insertions (had the human always trusted the system) as might have been feared. This may be a side effect of the high deletion rate, making it obvious to the human that the system was missing things. In any case, the annotation was clearly beneficial in our experiment with no ill effects seen in error rates compared to the gold standard.

6.3 Is pre-annotation useful and to whom?

All annotators asserted that pre-annotation is useful, specifically with types. In this section, we provide observations concerning variations in annotation both in terms of accuracy (F-measure is used) and duration.

	Raw	Comp.	Types	Full
Experts	0.748	0.786	0.778	0.791
Novices	0.682	0.737	0.721	0.742

Table 7: Mean F-measure of experts and novices, for each pre-annotation scheme

	Raw	Comp.	Types	Full
Experts	109.0	52.5	64.0	39.13
Novices	151.7	135.5	117.9	103.88

Table 8: Mean duration (in minutes) of annotation for experts and novices, for each pre-annotation scheme (two corpus quarters)

Tables 7 and 8 confirm the hypothesis that automatic pre-annotation helps annotators to annotate faster and to be more efficient. All pre-annotation levels (components, types and both) seem to be helpful for both experts and novices. Experts reached a higher accuracy (F=0.791) and they were more than twice faster with components or full pre-annotation. Similarly, novices performed better when working on a full pre-annotation (F=0.742) and reached a faster working time (48mn less than with no pre-annotation). This last observation contradicts the annotators' reported experience: the annotators felt more comfortable and faster with a types-only pre-annotation than with full pre-annotation (see Section 5.1.2). The results show that full pre-annotation was the best choice for both quality and speed.

These results confirm that pre-annotation is useful, even with a moderate level of performance of the system. Does it help to annotate components and types equally? To answer this question, we computed the F-measure of novices and experts for both components and types separately (see Figure 4).

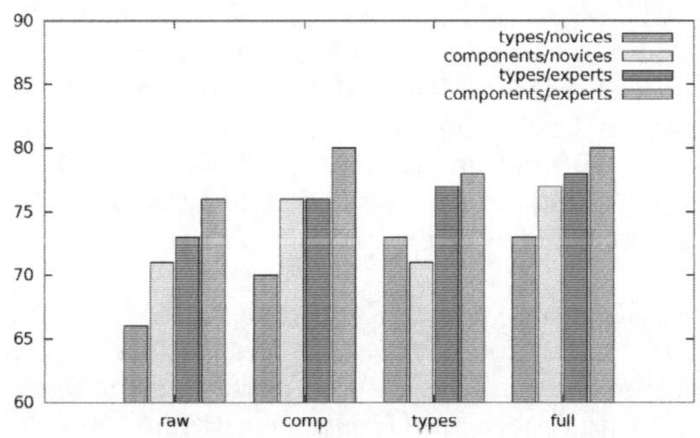

Figure 4: Mean F-measure on each pre-annotation level for expert and novice annotators

For experts we can see that all pre-annotation levels allow them to improve their performance on both types and components. However for novices, pre-annotation with types does not improve their performance in labeling components. We also notice that pre-annotation in both types and components allows experts and novices to reach their best performance for both types and components.

7 Conclusion and Perspectives

Conclusion. In this paper, we studied the interest of a pre-annotation process for a complex annotation task with only an out-of-domain annotation system available. We also designed our experiments to check whether the level of experience of the annotators made a difference in such a context. The experiment produced in the end a high-quality gold standard (8-way merge including 2 versions without pre-annotation) which enabled us to measure quantitatively the performance of every pre-annotation scheme.

We noticed that the pre-annotation system proved relatively precise for such a complex task, with 79% correct pre-annotations, but with a poor recall at 56%. This may be a good operating point for a pre-annotation system to reduce bias though.

In our quantitative experiments we found that the fullest pre-annotation helped most, both in terms of quality and annotation speed, even though the quality of the pre-annotation system varied depending on the annotation layer. This contradicted the feelings of the annotators who thought that a type-only pre-annotation was the most efficient. This shows that in such a setting self-evaluation cannot be trusted. On the other hand their remarks about the problems in the annotation guide itself seemed rather pertinent.

When it comes to experts vs. novices, we noted that their behaviour and remarks were essentially identical. Experts were both better and faster at annotating, but had similar reactions to pre-annotation and essentially the same feelings.

In conclusion, even with an out-of-domain system, a pre-annotation step proves extremely useful in both annotation speed and annotation quality, and at least in our setting, with a reasonably precise system (at the expense of recall) no bias was detectable. In addition, no matter what the annotators feel, as long as precision is good enough, the more pre-annotations the better. Pre-filtering either of our two levels did not help.

Perspectives. Based upon this conclusion, we plan to use automatic pre-annotation in further annotation work, beginning with the present corpora. As a first use, we plan to propose a few changes to the annotation principles in the guidelines we used. To annotate existing corpora with these changes, automatic pre-annotation will be useful.

As a second piece of future work, we plan to annotate new corpora with the existing annotation framework. We also plan to add new types of named entities (e.g., events) to extend the annotation of existing annotated corpora, using the pre-annotation process to reduce the overall workload.

Acknowledgments

This work has been partially funded by OSEO under the Quaero program and by the French ANR VERA project.

References

Jacob Cohen. 1960. A coefficient of agreement for nominal scales. *Educational and Psychological Measurement*, 20(1):37–46.

Sandipan Dandapat, Priyanka Biswas, Monojit Choudhury, and Kalika Bali. 2009. Complex linguistic annotation – no easy way out! A case from Bangla and Hindi POS labeling tasks. In *Proc of 3rd Linguistic Annotation Workshop (LAW-III)*, pages 10–18, Suntec, Singapore, August. ACL.

Marco Dinarelli and Sophie Rosset. 2011. Models cascade for tree-structured named entity detection. In *Proc of IJCNLP*, pages 1269–1278, Chiang Mai, Thailand.

Manaal Faruqui and Sebastian Padó. 2010. Training and evaluating a German named entity recognizer with semantic generalization. In *Proc of Konvens*, Saarbrücken, Germany.

Karën Fort and Benoît Sagot. 2010. Influence of pre-annotation on POS-tagged corpus development. In *Proc of 4th Linguistic Annotation Workshop (LAW-IV)*, pages 56–63, Uppsala, Sweden. ACL.

Karën Fort, Adeline Nazarenko, and Sophie Rosset. 2012. Modeling the complexity of manual annotation tasks: a grid of analysis. In *Proceedings of COLING 2012*, pages 895–910, Mumbai, India, December. The COLING 2012 Organizing Committee.

Olivier Galibert, Sophie Rosset, Cyril Grouin, Pierre Zweigenbaum, and Ludovic Quintard. 2011. Structured and extended named entity evaluation in automatic speech transcriptions. In *Proc of IJCNLP*, Chiang Mai, Thailand.

Cyril Grouin, Sophie Rosset, Pierre Zweigenbaum, Karën Fort, Olivier Galibert, and Ludovic Quintard. 2011. Proposal for an extension of traditional named entities: From guidelines to evaluation, an overview. In *Proc of 5th Linguistic Annotation Workshop (LAW-V)*, pages 92–100, Portland, OR. ACL.

Minlie Huang, Aurélie Névéol, and Zhiyong Lu. 2011. Recommending MeSH terms for annotating biomedical articles. *Journal of the American Medical Informatics Association*, 18(5):660–7.

Geoffrey Leech. 1997. Introducing corpus annotation. In Roger Garside, Geoffrey Leech, and Tony McEnery, editors, *Corpus annotation: Linguistic information from computer text corpora*, pages 1–18. Longman, London.

John Makhoul, Francis Kubala, Richard Schwartz, and Ralph Weischedel. 1999. Performance measures for information extraction. In *Proc. of DARPA Broadcast News Workshop*, pages 249–252.

Mitchell P Marcus, Mary Ann Marcinkiewicz, and Beatrice Santorini. 1993. Building a large annotated corpus of English: the Penn TreeBank. *Computational Linguistics*, 19(2):313–330.

Claudiu Mihaila, Tomoko Ohta, Sampo Pyysalo, and Sophia Ananiadou. 2013. Biocause: Annotating and analysing causality in the biomedical domain. *BMC Bioinformatics*, 14:2.

Céline Poudat and Doninique Longrée. 2009. Variations langagières et annotation morphosyntaxique du latin classique. *Traitement Automatique des Langues*, 50(2):129–148.

Dietrich Rebholz-Schuhmann, Antonio Jimeno, Chen Li, Senay Kafkas, Ian Lewin, Ning Kang, Peter Corbett, David Milward, Ekaterina Buyko, Elena Beisswanger, Kerstin Hornbostel, Alexandre Kouznetsov, René Witte, Jonas B Laurila, Christopher JO Baker, Cheng-Ju Kuo, Simone Clematide, Fabio Rinaldi, Richárd Farkas, György Móra, Kazuo Hara, Laura I Furlong, Michael Rautschka, Mariana Lara Neves, Alberto Pascual-Montano, Qi Wei, Nigel Collier, Md Faisal Mahbub Chowdhury, Alberto Lavelli, Rafael Berlanga, Roser Morante, Vincent Van Asch, Walter Daelemans, José L Marina, Erik van Mulligen, Jan Kors, and Udo Hahn. 2011. Assessment of NER solutions against the first and second CALBC silver standard corpus. *J Biomed Semantics*, 2.

Ines Rehbein, Josef Ruppenhofer, and Caroline Sporleder. 2009. Assessing the benefits of partial automatic pre-labeling for frame-semantic annotation. In *Proc of 3rd Linguistic Annotation Workshop (LAW-III)*, pages 19–26, Suntec, Singapore. ACL.

Eric Ringger, Peter McClanahan, Robbie Haertel, George Busby, Marc Carmen, James Carroll, Kevin Seppi, and Deryle Lonsdale. 2007. Active learning for part-of-speech tagging: Accelerating corpus annotation. In *Proc of Linguistic Annotation Workshop (LAW)*, pages 101–108. ACL.

Sophie Rosset, Cyril Grouin, Karën Fort, Olivier Galibert, Juliette Kahn, and Pierre Zweigenbaum. 2012. Structured named entities in two distinct press corpora: Contemporary broadcast news and old newspapers. In *Proc of 6th Linguistic Annotation Workshop (LAW-VI)*, pages 40–48, Jeju, South Korea. ACL.

William A Scott. 1955. Reliability of content analysis: The case of nominal scale coding. *Public Opinion Quaterly*, 19(3):321–325.

Burr Settles, Mark Craven, and Lewis Friedland. 2008. Active learning with real annotation costs. In *Proc of the NIPS Workshop on Cost-Sensitive Learning*.

Arne Skjærholt. 2011. More, faster: Accelerated corpus annotation with statistical taggers. *Journal for Language Technology and Computational Linguistics*, 26(2):151–163.

Brett R South, Shuying Shen, Robyn Barrus, Scott L DuVall, Özlem Uzuner, and Charlene Weir. 2011. Qualitative analysis of workflow modifications used to generate the reference standard for the 2010 i2b2/VA challenge. In *Proc of AMIA*.

Abstract Meaning Representation for Sembanking

Laura Banarescu SDL lbanarescu@sdl.com

Claire Bonial Linguistics Dept. Univ. Colorado claire.bonial@colorado.edu

Shu Cai ISI USC shucai@isi.edu

Madalina Georgescu SDL mgeorgescu@sdl.com

Kira Griffitt LDC kiragrif@ldc.upenn.edu

Ulf Hermjakob ISI USC ulf@isi.edu

Kevin Knight ISI USC knight@isi.edu

Philipp Koehn School of Informatics Univ. Edinburgh pkoehn@inf.ed.ac.uk

Martha Palmer Linguistics Dept. Univ. Colorado martha.palmer@colorado.edu

Nathan Schneider LTI CMU nschneid@cs.cmu.edu

Abstract

We describe Abstract Meaning Representation (AMR), a semantic representation language in which we are writing down the meanings of thousands of English sentences. We hope that a sembank of simple, whole-sentence semantic structures will spur new work in statistical natural language understanding and generation, like the Penn Treebank encouraged work on statistical parsing. This paper gives an overview of AMR and tools associated with it.

1 Introduction

Syntactic treebanks have had tremendous impact on natural language processing. The Penn Treebank is a classic example—a simple, readable file of natural-language sentences paired with rooted, labeled syntactic trees. Researchers have exploited manually-built treebanks to build statistical parsers that improve in accuracy every year. This success is due in part to the fact that we have a single, whole-sentence parsing task, rather than separate tasks and evaluations for base noun identification, prepositional phrase attachment, trace recovery, verb-argument dependencies, etc. Those smaller tasks are naturally solved as a by-product of whole-sentence parsing, and in fact, solved better than when approached in isolation.

By contrast, semantic annotation today is balkanized. We have separate annotations for named entities, co-reference, semantic relations, discourse connectives, temporal entities, etc. Each annotation has its own associated evaluation, and training data is split across many resources. We lack a simple readable sembank of English sentences paired with their whole-sentence, logical meanings. We believe a sizable sembank will lead to new work in statistical natural language understanding (NLU), resulting in semantic parsers that are as ubiquitous as syntactic ones, and support natural language generation (NLG) by providing a logical semantic input.

Of course, when it comes to whole-sentence semantic representations, linguistic and philosophical work is extensive. We draw on this work to design an Abstract Meaning Representation (AMR) appropriate for sembanking. Our basic principles are:

- AMRs are rooted, labeled graphs that are easy for people to read, and easy for programs to traverse.
- AMR aims to abstract away from syntactic idiosyncrasies. We attempt to assign the same AMR to sentences that have the same basic meaning. For example, the sentences "he described her as a genius", "his description of her: genius", and "she was a genius, according to his description" are all assigned the same AMR.
- AMR makes extensive use of PropBank framesets (Kingsbury and Palmer, 2002; Palmer et al., 2005). For example, we represent a phrase like "bond investor" using the frame "invest-01", even though no verbs appear in the phrase.
- AMR is agnostic about how we might want to derive meanings from strings, or vice-versa. In translating sentences to AMR, we do not dictate a particular sequence of rule applications or provide alignments that reflect such rule sequences. This makes sembanking very fast, and it allows researchers to explore their own ideas about how strings

are related to meanings.

- AMR is heavily biased towards English. It is not an Interlingua.

AMR is described in a 50-page annotation guideline.[1] In this paper, we give a high-level description of AMR, with examples, and we also provide pointers to software tools for evaluation and sembanking.

2 AMR Format

We write down AMRs as rooted, directed, edge-labeled, leaf-labeled graphs. This is a completely traditional format, equivalent to the simplest forms of feature structures (Shieber et al., 1986), conjunctions of logical triples, directed graphs, and PENMAN inputs (Matthiessen and Bateman, 1991). Figure 1 shows some of these views for the sentence "The boy wants to go". We use the graph notation for computer processing, and we adapt the PENMAN notation for human reading and writing.

LOGIC format:

$\exists$ w, b, g:
instance(w, want-01) $\wedge$ instance(g, go-01) $\wedge$
instance(b, boy) $\wedge$ arg0(w, b) $\wedge$
arg1(w, g) $\wedge$ arg0(g, b)

AMR format (based on PENMAN):

```
(w / want-01
  :arg0 (b / boy)
  :arg1 (g / go-01
          :arg0 b))
```

GRAPH format:

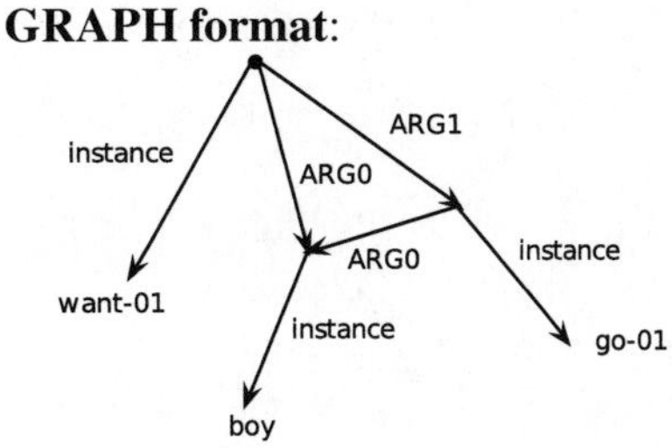

Figure 1: Equivalent formats for representating the meaning of "The boy wants to go".

3 AMR Content

In neo-Davidsonian fashion (Davidson, 1969), we introduce variables (or graph nodes) for entities, events, properties, and states. Leaves are labeled with concepts, so that "(b / boy)" refers to an instance (called b) of the concept boy. Relations link entities, so that "(d / die-01 :location (p / park))" means there was a death (d) in the park (p). When an entity plays multiple roles in a sentence, we employ re-entrancy in graph notation (nodes with multiple parents) or variable re-use in PENMAN notation.

AMR concepts are either English words ("boy"), PropBank framesets ("want-01"), or special keywords. Keywords include special entity types ("date-entity", "world-region", etc.), quantities ("monetary-quantity", "distance-quantity", etc.), and logical conjunctions ("and", etc).

AMR uses approximately 100 relations:

- **Frame arguments, following PropBank conventions.** :arg0, :arg1, :arg2, :arg3, :arg4, :arg5.

- **General semantic relations.** :accompanier, :age, :beneficiary, :cause, :compared-to, :concession, :condition, :consist-of, :degree, :destination, :direction, :domain, :duration, :employed-by, :example, :extent, :frequency, :instrument, :li, :location, :manner, :medium, :mod, :mode, :name, :part, :path, :polarity, :poss, :purpose, :source, :subevent, :subset, :time, :topic, :value.

- **Relations for quantities.** :quant, :unit, :scale.

- **Relations for date-entities.** :day, :month, :year, :weekday, :time, :timezone, :quarter, :dayperiod, :season, :year2, :decade, :century, :calendar, :era.

- **Relations for lists.** :op1, :op2, :op3, :op4, :op5, :op6, :op7, :op8, :op9, :op10.

AMR also includes the inverses of all these relations, e.g., :arg0-of, :location-of, and :quant-of. In addition, every relation has an associated reification, which is what we use when we want to modify the relation itself. For example, the reification of :location is the concept "be-located-at-91".

Our set of concepts and relations is designed to allow us represent all sentences, taking all words into account, in a reasonably consistent manner. In the rest of this section, we give examples of how AMR represents various kinds of words, phrases, and sentences. For full documentation, the reader is referred to the AMR guidelines.

[1]AMR guideline: amr.isi.edu/language.html

Frame arguments. We make heavy use of PropBank framesets to abstract away from English syntax. For example, the frameset "describe-01" has three pre-defined slots (:arg0 is the describer, :arg1 is the thing described, and :arg2 is what it is being described as).

```
(d / describe-01
  :arg0 (m / man)
  :arg1 (m2 / mission)
  :arg2 (d / disaster))

The man described the mission as a disaster.
The man's description of the mission:
  disaster.
As the man described it, the mission was a
  disaster.
```

Here, we do not annotate words like "as" or "it", considering them to be syntactic sugar.

General semantic relations. AMR also includes many non-core relations, such as :beneficiary, :time, and :destination.

```
(s / hum-02
  :arg0 (s2 / soldier)
  :beneficiary (g / girl)
  :time (w / walk-01
          :arg0 g
          :destination (t / town)))

The soldier hummed to the girl as she
  walked to town.
```

Co-reference. AMR abstracts away from co-reference gadgets like pronouns, zero-pronouns, reflexives, control structures, etc. Instead we re-use AMR variables, as with "g" above. AMR annotates sentences independent of context, so if a pronoun has no antecedent in the sentence, its nominative form is used, e.g., "(h / he)".

Inverse relations. We obtain rooted structures by using inverse relations like :arg0-of and :quant-of.

```
(s / sing-01
  :arg0 (b / boy
          :source (c / college)))

The boy from the college sang.

(b / boy
  :arg0-of (s / sing-01)
  :source (c / college))

the college boy who sang ...

(i / increase-01
  :arg1 (n / number
          :quant-of (p / panda)))

The number of pandas increased.
```

The top-level root of an AMR represents the focus of the sentence or phrase. Once we have selected the root concept for an entire AMR, there are no more focus considerations—everything else is driven strictly by semantic relations.

Modals and negation. AMR represents negation logically with :polarity, and it expresses modals with concepts.

```
(g / go-01
  :arg0 (b / boy)
  :polarity -)

The boy did not go.

(p / possible
  :domain (g / go-01
            :arg0 (b / boy))
  :polarity -))

The boy cannot go.
It's not possible for the boy to go.

(p / possible
  :domain (g / go-01
            :arg0 (b / boy)
            :polarity -))

It's possible for the boy not to go.

(p / obligate-01
  :arg2 (g / go-01
          :arg0 (b / boy))
  :polarity -)

The boy doesn't have to go.
The boy isn't obligated to go.
The boy need not go.

(p / obligate-01
  :arg2 (g / go-01
          :arg0 (b / boy)
          :polarity -))

The boy must not go.
It's obligatory that the boy not go.

(t / think-01
  :arg0 (b / boy)
  :arg1 (w / win-01
          :arg0 (t / team)
          :polarity -))

The boy doesn't think the team will win.
The boy thinks the team won't win.
```

Questions. AMR uses the concept "amr-unknown", in place, to indicate wh-questions.

```
(f / find-01
  :arg0 (g / girl)
  :arg1 (a / amr-unknown))

What did the girl find?

(f / find-01
  :arg0 (g / girl)
  :arg1 (b / boy)
  :location (a / amr-unknown))

Where did the girl find the boy?
```

```
(f / find-01
  :arg0 (g / girl)
  :arg1 (t / toy
          :poss (a / amr-unknown)))

Whose toy did the girl find?
```

Yes-no questions, imperatives, and embedded wh-clauses are treated separately with the AMR relation :mode.

Verbs. Nearly every English verb and verb-particle construction we have encountered has a corresponding PropBank frameset.

```
(l / look-05
  :arg0 (b / boy)
  :arg1 (a / answer))

The boy looked up the answer.
The boy looked the answer up.
```

AMR abstracts away from light-verb constructions.

```
(a / adjust-01
  :arg0 (g / girl)
  :arg1 (m / machine))

The girl adjusted the machine.
The girl made adjustments to the machine.
```

Nouns. We use PropBank verb framesets to represent many nouns as well.

```
(d / destroy-01
  :arg0 (b / boy)
  :arg1 (r / room))

the destruction of the room by the boy ...
the boy's destruction of the room ...
The boy destroyed the room.
```

We never say "destruction-01" in AMR. Some nominalizations refer to a whole event, while others refer to a role player in an event.

```
(s / see-01
  :arg0 (j / judge)
  :arg1 (e / explode-01))

The judge saw the explosion.

(r / read-01
  :arg0 (j / judge)
  :arg1 (t / thing
          :arg1-of (p / propose-01))

The judge read the proposal.

(t / thing
  :arg1-of (o / opine-01
             :arg0 (g / girl)))

the girl's opinion
the opinion of the girl
what the girl opined
```

Many "-er" nouns invoke PropBank framesets. This enables us to make use of slots defined for those framesets.

```
(p / person
  :arg0-of (i / invest-01))

investor

(p / person
  :arg0-of (i / invest-01
             :arg1 (b / bond)))

bond investor

(p / person
  :arg0-of (i / invest-01
             :manner (s / small)))

small investor

(w / work-01
  :arg0 (b / boy)
  :manner (h / hard))

the boy is a hard worker
the boy works hard
```

However, a treasurer is not someone who treasures, and a president is not (just) someone who presides.

Adjectives. Various adjectives invoke PropBank framesets.

```
(s / spy
  :arg0-of (a / attract-01))

the attractive spy

(s / spy
  :arg0-of (a / attract-01
             :arg1 (w / woman)))

the spy who is attractive to women
```

"-ed" adjectives frequently invoke verb framesets. For example, "acquainted with magic" maps to "acquaint-01". However, we are not restricted to framesets that can be reached through morphological simplification.

```
(f / fear-01
  :arg0 (s / soldier)
  :arg1 (b / battle-01))

The soldier was afraid of battle.
The soldier feared battle.
The soldier had a fear of battle.
```

For other adjectives, we have defined new framesets.

```
(r / responsible-41
  :arg1 (b / boy)
  :arg2 (w / work))

The boy is responsible for the work.
The boy has responsibility for the work.
```

While "the boy responsibles the work" is not good English, it is perfectly good Chinese. Similarly, we handle *tough*-constructions logically.

```
(t / tough
  :domain (p / please-01
            :arg1 (g / girl)))
```

```
Girls are tough to please.
It is tough to please girls.
Pleasing girls is tough.
```

"please-01" and "girl" are adjacent in the AMR, even if they are not adjacent in English. "-able" adjectives often invoke the AMR concept "possible", but not always (e.g., a "taxable fund" is actually a "taxed fund").

```
(s / sandwich
  :arg1-of (e / eat-01
             :domain-of (p / possible)))
```

```
an edible sandwich
```

```
(f / fund
  :arg1-of (t / tax-01))
```

```
a taxable fund
```

Pertainym adjectives are normalized to root form.

```
(b / bomb
  :mod (a / atom))
```

```
atom bomb
atomic bomb
```

Prepositions. Most prepositions simply signal semantic frame elements, and are themselves dropped from AMR.

```
(d / default-01
  :arg1 (n / nation)
  :time (d2 / date-entity
          :month 6))
```

```
The nation defaulted in June.
```

Time and location prepositions are kept if they carry additional information.

```
(d / default-01
  :arg1 (n / nation)
  :time (a / after
          :op1 (w / war-01)))
```

```
The nation defaulted after the war.
```

Occasionally, neither PropBank nor AMR has an appropriate relation, in which case we hold our nose and use a :prep-X relation.

```
(s / sue-01
  :arg1 (m / man)
  :prep-in (c / case))
```

```
The man was sued in the case.
```

Named entities. Any concept in AMR can be modified with a :name relation. However, AMR includes standardized forms for approximately 80 named-entity types, including person, country, sports-facility, etc.

```
(p / person
  :name (n / name
          :op1 "Mollie"
          :op2 "Brown"))
```

```
Mollie Brown
```

```
(p / person
  :name (n / name
          :op1 "Mollie"
          :op2 "Brown")
  :arg0-of (s / slay-01
             :arg1 (o / orc)))
```

```
the orc-slaying Mollie Brown
Mollie Brown, who slew orcs
```

AMR does not normalize multiple ways of referring to the same concept (e.g., "US" versus "United States"). It also avoids analyzing semantic relations inside a named entity—e.g., an organization named "Stop Malaria Now" does not invoke the "stop-01" frameset. AMR gives a clean, uniform treatment to titles, appositives, and other constructions.

```
(c / city
  :name (n / name
          :op1 "Zintan"))
```

```
Zintan
the city of Zintan
```

```
(p / president
  :name (n / name
          :op1 "Obama"))
```

```
President Obama
Obama, the president ...
```

```
(g / group
  :name (n / name
          :op1 "Elsevier"
          :op2 "N.V.")
  :mod (c / country
         :name (n2 / name
                 :op1 "Netherlands"))
  :arg0-of (p / publish-01))
```

```
Elsevier N.V., the Dutch publishing group...
Dutch publishing group Elsevier N.V. ...
```

Copula. Copulas use the :domain relation.

```
(w / white
  :domain (m / marble))
```

```
The marble is white.
```

```
(l / lawyer
  :domain (w / woman))
```

```
The woman is a lawyer.
```

```
(a / appropriate
  :domain (c / comment)
  :polarity -))
```

```
The comment is not appropriate.
```

```
The comment is inappropriate.
```

Reification. Sometimes we want to use an AMR relation as a first-class concept—to be able to modify it, for example. Every AMR relation has a corresponding reification for this purpose.

```
(m / marble
  :location (j / jar))

the marble in the jar ...

(b / be-located-at-91
  :arg1 (m / marble)
  :arg2 (j / jar)
  :polarity -)
  :time (y / yesterday))

The marble was not in the jar yesterday.
```

If we do not use the reification, we run into trouble.

```
(m / marble
  :location (j / jar
              :polarity -)
  :time (y / yesterday))

yesterday's marble in the non-jar ...
```

Some reifications are standard PropBank framesets (e.g., "cause-01" for :cause, or "age-01" for :age).

This ends the summary of AMR content. For lack of space, we omit descriptions of comparatives, superlatives, conjunction, possession, determiners, date entities, numbers, approximate numbers, discourse connectives, and other phenomena covered in the full AMR guidelines.

4 Limitations of AMR

AMR does not represent inflectional morphology for tense and number, and it omits articles. This speeds up the annotation process, and we do not have a nice semantic target representation for these phenomena. A lightweight syntactic-style representation could be layered in, via an automatic post-process.

AMR has no universal quantifier. Words like "all" modify their head concepts. AMR does not distinguish between real events and hypothetical, future, or imagined ones. For example, in "the boy wants to go", the instances of "want-01" and "go-01" have the same status, even though the "go-01" may or may not happen.

We represent "history teacher" nicely as "(p / person :arg0-of (t / teach-01 :arg1 (h / history)))". However, "history professor" becomes "(p / professor :mod (h / history))", because "profess-01" is not an appropriate frame. It would be reasonable in such cases to use a NomBank (Meyers et al., 2004) noun frame with appropriate slots.

5 Creating AMRs

We have developed a power editor for AMR, accessible by web interface.[2] The AMR Editor allows rapid, incremental AMR construction via text commands and graphical buttons. It includes online documentation of relations, quantities, reifications, etc., with full examples. Users log in, and the editor records AMR activity. The editor also provides significant guidance aimed at increasing annotator consistency. For example, users are warned about incorrect relations, disconnected AMRs, words that have PropBank frames, etc. Users can also search existing sembanks for phrases to see how they were handled in the past. The editor also allows side-by-side comparison of AMRs from different users, for training purposes.

In order to assess inter-annotator agreement (IAA), as well as automatic AMR parsing accuracy, we developed the *smatch* metric (Cai and Knight, 2013) and associated script.[3] Smatch reports the semantic overlap between two AMRs by viewing each AMR as a conjunction of logical triples (see Figure 1). Smatch computes precision, recall, and F-score of one AMR's triples against the other's. To match up variables from two input AMRs, smatch needs to execute a brief search, looking for the variable mapping that yields the highest F-score.

Smatch makes no reference to English strings or word indices, as we do not enforce any particular string-to-meaning derivation. Instead, we compare semantic representations directly, in the same way that the MT metric Bleu (Papineni et al., 2002) compares target strings without making reference to the source.

For an initial IAA study, and prior to adjusting the AMR Editor to encourage consistency, 4 expert AMR annotators annotated 100 newswire sentences and 80 web text sentences. They then created consensus AMRs through discussion. The average annotator vs. consensus IAA (smatch) was 0.83 for newswire and 0.79 for web text. When newly trained annotators doubly annotated 382 web text sentences, their annotator vs. annotator IAA was 0.71.

[2] AMR Editor: amr.isi.edu/editor.html
[3] Smatch: amr.isi.edu/evaluation.html

6 Current AMR Bank

We currently have a manually-constructed AMR bank of several thousand sentences, a subset of which can be freely downloaded,[4] the rest being distributed via the LDC catalog.

In initially developing AMR, the authors built consensus AMRs for:

- 225 short sentences for tutorial purposes
- 142 sentences of newswire (*)
- 100 sentences of web data (*)

Trained annotators at LDC then produced AMRs for:

- 1546 sentences from the novel "The Little Prince"
- 1328 sentences of web data
- 1110 sentences of web data (*)
- 926 sentences from Xinhua news (*)
- 214 sentences from CCTV broadcast conversation (*)

Collections marked with a star (*) are also in the OntoNotes corpus (Pradhan et al., 2007; Weischedel et al., 2011).

Using the AMR Editor, annotators are able to translate a full sentence into AMR in 7-10 minutes and postedit an AMR in 1-3 minutes.

7 Related Work

Researchers working on whole-sentence semantic parsing today typically use small, domain-specific sembanks like GeoQuery (Wong and Mooney, 2006). The need for larger, broad-coverage sembanks has sparked several projects, including the Groningen Meaning Bank (GMB) (Basile et al., 2012a), UCCA (Abend and Rappoport, 2013), the Semantic Treebank (ST) (Butler and Yoshimoto, 2012), the Prague Dependency Treebank (Böhmová et al., 2003), and UNL (Uchida et al., 1999; Uchida et al., 1996; Martins, 2012).

Concepts. Most systems use English words as concepts. AMR uses PropBank frames (e.g., "describe-01"), and UNL uses English WordNet synsets (e.g., "200752493").

Relations. GMB uses VerbNet roles (Schuler, 2005), and AMR uses frame-specific PropBank relations. UNL has a dedicated set of over 30 frequently used relations.

Formalism. GMB meanings are written in DRT (Kamp et al., 2011), exploiting full first-order logic. GMB and ST both include universal quantification.

Granularity. GMB and UCCA annotate short texts, so that the same entity can participate in events described in different sentences; other systems annotate individual sentences.

Entities. AMR uses 80 entity types, while GMB uses 7.

Manual versus automatic. AMR, UNL, and UCCA annotation is fully manual. GMB and ST produce meaning representations automatically, and these can be corrected by experts or crowds (Venhuizen et al., 2013).

Derivations. AMR and UNL remain agnostic about the relation between strings and their meanings, considering this a topic of open research. ST and GMB annotate words and phrases directly, recording derivations as (for example) Montague-style compositional semantic rules operating on CCG parses.

Top-down verus bottom-up. AMR annotators find it fast to construct meanings from the top down, starting with the main idea of the sentence (though the AMR Editor allows bottom-up construction). GMB and UCCA annotators work bottom-up.

Editors, guidelines, genres. These projects have graphical sembanking tools (e.g., Basile et al. (2012b)), annotation guidelines,[5] and sembanks that cover a wide range of genres, from news to fiction. UNL and AMR have both annotated many of the same sentences, providing the potential for direct comparison.

8 Future Work

Sembanking. Our main goal is to continue sembanking. We would like to employ a large sembank to create shared tasks for natural language understanding and generation. These tasks may additionally drive interest in theoretical frameworks for probabilistically mapping between graphs and strings (Quernheim and Knight, 2012b; Quernheim and Knight, 2012a; Chiang et al., 2013).

Applications. Just as syntactic parsing has found many unanticipated applications, we expect sembanks and statistical semantic processors to be used for many purposes. To get started, we are exploring the use of statistical NLU and NLG in

[4] amr.isi.edu/download.html

[5] UNL guidelines: www.undl.org/unlsys/unl/unl2005

a semantics-based machine translation (MT) system. In this system, we annotate bilingual Chinese/English data with AMR, then train components to map Chinese to AMR, and AMR to English. A prototype is described by Jones et al. (2012).

Disjunctive AMR. AMR aims to canonicalize multiple ways of saying the same thing. We plan to test how well we are doing by building AMRs on top of large, manually-constructed paraphrase networks from the HyTER project (Dreyer and Marcu, 2012). Rather than build individual AMRs for different paths through a network, we will construct highly-packed disjunctive AMRs. With this application in mind, we have developed a guideline[6] for disjunctive AMR. Here is an example:

```
(o / *OR*
  :op1 (t / talk-01)
  :op2 (m / meet-03)
  :OR (o2 / *OR*
        :mod (o3 / official)
        :arg1-of (s / sanction-01
                   :arg0 (s2 / state))))

official talks
state-sanctioned talks
meetings sanctioned by the state
```

AMR extensions. Finally, we would like to deepen the AMR language to include more relations (to replace :mod and :prep-X, for example), entity normalization (perhaps wikification), quantification, and temporal relations. Ultimately, we would like to also include a comprehensive set of more abstract frames like "Earthquake-01" (:magnitude, :epicenter, :casualties), "CriminalLawsuit-01" (:defendant, :crime, :jurisdiction), and "Pregnancy-01" (:father, :mother, :due-date). Projects like FrameNet (Baker et al., 1998) and CYC (Lenat, 1995) have long pursued such a set.

References

O. Abend and A. Rappoport. 2013. UCCA: A semantics-based grammatical annotation scheme. In *Proc. IWCS*.

C. Baker, C. Fillmore, and J. Lowe. 1998. The Berkeley FrameNet project. In *Proc. COLING*.

V. Basile, J. Bos, K. Evang, and N. Venhuizen. 2012a. Developing a large semantically annotated corpus. In *Proc. LREC*.

[6] Disjunctive AMR guideline: amr.isi.edu/damr.1.0.pdf

V. Basile, J. Bos, K. Evang, and N. Venhuizen. 2012b. A platform for collaborative semantic annotation. In *Proc. EACL demonstrations*.

A. Böhmová, J. Hajič, E. Hajičová, and B. Hladká. 2003. The Prague dependency treebank. In *Treebanks*. Springer.

A. Butler and K. Yoshimoto. 2012. Banking meaning representations from treebanks. *Linguistic Issues in Language Technology*, 7.

S. Cai and K. Knight. 2013. Smatch: An accuracy metric for abstract meaning representations. In *Proc. ACL*.

D. Chiang, J. Andreas, D. Bauer, K. M. Hermann, B. Jones, and K. Knight. 2013. Parsing graphs with hyperedge replacement grammars. In *Proc. ACL*.

D. Davidson. 1969. The individuation of events. In N. Rescher, editor, *Essays in Honor of Carl G. Hempel*. D. Reidel, Dordrecht.

M. Dreyer and D. Marcu. 2012. Hyter: Meaning-equivalent semantics for translation evaluation. In *Proc. NAACL*.

B. Jones, J. Andreas, D. Bauer, K. M. Hermann, and K. Knight. 2012. Semantics-based machine translation with hyperedge replacement grammars. In *Proc. COLING*.

H. Kamp, J. Van Genabith, and U. Reyle. 2011. Discourse representation theory. In *Handbook of philosophical logic*, pages 125–394. Springer.

P. Kingsbury and M. Palmer. 2002. From TreeBank to PropBank. In *Proc. LREC*.

D. B. Lenat. 1995. Cyc: A large-scale investment in knowledge infrastructure. *Communications of the ACM*, 38(11).

R. Martins. 2012. Le Petit Prince in UNL. In *Proc. LREC*.

C. M. I. M. Matthiessen and J. A. Bateman. 1991. *Text Generation and Systemic-Functional Linguistics*. Pinter, London.

A. Meyers, R. Reeves, C. Macleod, R. Szekely, V. Zielinska, B. Young, and R. Grishman. 2004. The NomBank project: An interim report. In *HLT-NAACL 2004 workshop: Frontiers in corpus annotation*.

M. Palmer, D. Gildea, and P. Kingsbury. 2005. The Proposition Bank: An annotated corpus of semantic roles. *Computational Linguistics*, 31(1).

K. Papineni, S. Roukos, T. Ward, and W.-J. Zhu. 2002. Bleu: a method for automatic evaluation of machine translation. In *ACL*, Philadelphia, PA.

S. Pradhan, E. Hovy, M. Marcus, M. Palmer, L. Ramshaw, and R. Weischedel. 2007. Ontonotes: A unified relational semantic representation. *International Journal of Semantic Computing (IJSC)*, 1(4).

D. Quernheim and K. Knight. 2012a. DAGGER: A toolkit for automata on directed acyclic graphs. In *Proc. FSMNLP*.

D. Quernheim and K. Knight. 2012b. Towards probabilistic acceptors and transducers for feature structures. In *Proc. SSST Workshop*.

K. Schuler. 2005. *VerbNet: A broad-coverage, comprehensive verb lexicon*. Ph.D. thesis, University of Pennsylvania.

S. Shieber, F. C. N. Pereira, L. Karttunen, and M. Kay. 1986. Compilation of papers on unification-based grammar formalisms. Technical Report CSLI-86-48, Center for the Study of Language and Information, Stanford, California.

H. Uchida, M. Zhu, and T. Della Senta. 1996. UNL: Universal Networking Language—an electronic language for communication, understanding and collaboration. Technical report, IAS/UNU Tokyo.

H. Uchida, M. Zhu, and T. Della Senta. 1999. A gift for a millennium. Technical report, IAS/UNU Tokyo.

N. Venhuizen, V. Basile, K. Evang, and J. Bos. 2013. Gamification for word sense labeling. In *Proc. IWCS*.

R. Weischedel, E. Hovy, M. Marcus, M. Palmer, R. Belvin, S. Pradhan, L. Ramshaw, and N. Xue. 2011. OntoNotes: A large training corpus for enhanced processing. In J. Olive, C. Christianson, and J. McCary, editors, *Handbook of Natural Language Processing and Machine Translation*. Springer.

Y. W. Wong and R. J. Mooney. 2006. Learning for semantic parsing with statistical machine translation. In *Proc. HLT-NAACL*.

The Benefits of a Model of Annotation

Rebecca J. Passonneau
Center for Computational Learning Systems
Columbia University
becky@ccls.columbia.edu

Bob Carpenter
Department of Statistics
Columbia University
carp@alias-i.com

Abstract

This paper presents a case study of a difficult and important categorical annotation task (word sense) to demonstrate a probabilistic annotation model applied to crowdsourced data. It is argued that standard (chance-adjusted) agreement levels are neither necessary nor sufficient to ensure high quality gold standard labels. Compared to conventional agreement measures, application of an annotation model to instances with crowdsourced labels yields higher quality labels at lower cost.

1 Introduction

The quality of annotated data for computational linguistics is generally assumed to be good enough if a few annotators can be shown to be consistent with one another. Metrics such as pairwise agreement and agreement coefficients measure consistency among annotators. These descriptive statistics do not support inferences about corpus quality or annotator accuracy, and the absolute values one should aim for are debatable, as in the review by Artstein and Poesio (2008). We argue that high chance-adjusted inter-annotator agreement is neither necessary nor sufficient to ensure high quality gold-standard labels. Agreement measures reveal little about differences among annotators, and nothing about the certainty of the *true* label, given the observed labels from annotators. In contrast, a probabilistic model of annotation supports statistical inferences about the quality of the observed and inferred labels.

This paper presents a case study of a particularly thorny annotation task that is of widespread interest, namely word-sense annotation. The items that were annotated are occurrences of selected words in their sentence contexts, and the annotation labels are WordNet senses (Fellbaum, 1998). The annotations, collected through crowdsourcing, consist of one WordNet sense for each item from up to twenty-five different annotators, giving each word instance a large set of labels. Note that application of an annotation model does not require this many labels for each item, and crowdsourced annotation data does not require a probabilistic model. This case study, however, does demonstrate a mutual benefit.

A highly certain ground truth label for each annotated instance is the ultimate goal of data annotation. Many issues, however, make this complicated for word sense annotation. The number of different senses defined for a word varies across lexical resources, and pairs of senses within a single sense inventory are not equally distinct (Ide and Wilks, 2006; Erk and McCarthy, 2009). A previous annotation effort using WordNet sense labels demonstrates a great deal of variation across words (Passonneau et al., 2012b). On over 116 words, chance-adjusted agreement ranged from very high to chance levels. As a result, the ground truth labels for many words are questionable. On a random subset of 45 of the same words, the crowdsourced data presented here (available as noted below) yields a certainty measure for each ground truth label indicating high certainty for most instances.

2 Chance-Adjusted Agreement

Current best practice for collecting and curating annotated data involves iteration over four steps, or variations of them: 1) design or redesign the annotation task, 2) write or revise guidelines instructing annotators how to carry out the task, possibly with some training, 3) have two or more annotators work independently to annotate a sample of data, and 4) measure the interannotator agreement on the data sample. Once the desired agreement has been obtained, a gold standard dataset is created where each item is annotated by one annotator. As noted in the introduction, how much agreement is sufficient has been much discussed (Artstein and Poesio, 2008; di Eugenio and Glass, 2004; di Eugenio, 2000; Bruce and Wiebe, 1998). The quality of the gold standard is not explicitly measured. Nor is the accuracy of the annotators. Since there are many ways to be inaccurate, and only one way to be accurate, it is assumed that if annotators agree, then the annotation must be accurate. This is often but not always correct. If two annotators do not agree well, this method does not identify whether one annotator is more accurate than the other. For the individual items they disagree on, no information is gained about the true label.

To get a high level sense of the limitations of agreement metrics, we briefly discuss how they are computed and what they tell us. For a common notation, let $i \in 1{:}I$ represent the set of all items, $j \in 1{:}J$ all the annotators, $k \in 1{:}K$ all the label classes in a categorical labeling scheme (e.g., word senses), and $y_{i,j} \in 1{:}K$ the observed labels from annotator j for item i (assuming every annotator labels every item exactly once; we relax this restriction later).

Agreement: Pairwise agreement $A_{m,n}$ between two annotators $m, n \in 1{:}J$ is defined as the proportion of items $1{:}I$ for which the annotators supplied the same label,

$$A_{m,n} = \tfrac{1}{I} \textstyle\sum_{i=1}^{I} \mathbb{I}(y_{i,m} = y_{i,n}),$$

where the indicator function $\mathbb{I}(s) = 1$ if s is true and 0 otherwise. $A_{m,n}$ is thus the maximum likelihood estimate that annotator m and n will agree.

Pairwise agreement can be extended to the entire pool of annotators by averaging over all $\binom{J}{2}$ pairs,

$$A = \tfrac{1}{\binom{J}{2}} \textstyle\sum_{m=1}^{J} \sum_{n=m+1}^{J} A_{m,n}.$$

By construction, $A_{m,n} \in [0, 1]$ and $A \in [0, 1]$. Pairwise agreement does not take into account the proportion of observed annotation values from 1:K. As a simple expected chance of agreement, it provides little information about the resulting data quality.

Chance-Adjusted Agreement: An agreement coefficient, such as Cohen's κ (Cohen, 1960) or Krippendorff's α (Krippendorff, 1980), measures the proportion of observed agreements that are above the proportion expected by chance. Given an estimate $A_{m,n}$ of the probability that two annotators $m, n \in 1{:}J$ will agree on a label and an estimate of the probability $C_{m,n}$ that they will agree by chance, the chance-adjusted interannotator agreement coefficient $\mathcal{IA}_{m,n} \in [-1, 1]$ is defined by

$$\mathcal{IA}_{m,n} = \tfrac{A_{m,n} - C_{m,n}}{1 - C_{m,n}}.$$

For Cohen's κ statistic, chance agreement is defined to take into account the prevalence of the individual labels in $1{:}K$. Specifically, it is defined to be the probability that a pair of labels drawn at random for two annotators agrees. There are two common ways to define this draw. The first assumes each annotator draws uniformly at random from her set of labels. Letting $\psi_{j,k} = \frac{1}{I} \sum_{i=1}^{I} \mathbb{I}(y_{i,j} = k)$ be the proportion of the label k in annotator j's labels, this notion of chance agreement for a pair of annotators m, n is estimated as the sum over $1{:}K$ of the products of their proportions ψ:

$$C_{m,n} = \textstyle\sum_{k=1}^{K} \psi_{m,k} \times \psi_{n,k}.$$

Another computation of chance agreement in wide use assumes each annotator draws uniformly at random from the pooled set of labels from all annotators (Krippendorff, 1980). Letting ϕ_k be the proportion of label k in the entire set of labels, this alternative estimate, $C'_{m,n} = \sum_{k=1}^{K} \phi_k^2$, does not depend on the identity of the annotators m and n.

An inter-annotator agreement statistic like κ suffers from multiple shortcomings. (1) Agreement statistics are intrinsically pairwise, although one can compare to a voted consensus or average over multiple pairwise agreements. (2) In agreement-based analyses, two wrongs make a right; if two annotators both make the same mistake, they agree. If annotators are 80% accurate on a binary task, chance agreement on the wrong category occurs at a 4% rate. (3) Chance-adjusted agreement reduces to simple agreement as chance agreement approaches zero. When chance agreement is high, even high-accuracy annotators can have low chance-adjusted agreement. For example, in a binary task with 95% prevalence of one category, two 90% accurate annotators have a chance-adjusted agreement of $\frac{0.9-(.95^2+.05^2)}{1-(.95^2+.05^2)} = -.053$. Thus high chance-adjusted inter-annotator agreement is not a necessary condition for a high-quality corpus. (4) Inter-annotator agreement statistics implicitly assume annotators are unbiased; if they are biased in the same direction, as we show they are for the sense data considered here, then agreement is an overestimate of their accuracy. In the extreme case, in a binary labeling task, two adversarial annotators who always provide the wrong answer have a chance-adjusted agreement of 100%. (5) Item-level effects such as difficulty can inflate levels of agreement-in-error. For example, hard-to-identify names in a named-entity corpus have correlated false negatives among annotators, leading to higher agreement-in-error than would otherwise be expected. (6) Inter-annotator agreement statistics are rarely computed with confidence intervals, which can be quite wide even under optimistic assumptions of no annotator bias or item-level effects. In a sample of MASC word sense data, 100 annotations by 80% accurate annotators produce a 95% interval for accuracy of +/- 6%. Agreement statistics have even wider error bounds. This introduces enough uncertainty to span the rather arbitrary decision boundaries for acceptable agreement.

Model-Based Inference: In contrast to agreement metrics, application of a model of annotation can provide information about the certainty of parameter estimates. The model of annotation presented in the next section includes as parameters the true categories of items in the corpus, and also the prevalence of each label in the corpus and each annotator's accuracies and biases by category.

3 A Probabilistic Annotation Model

A probabilistic model provides a recipe to randomly "generate" a dataset from a set of model parameters and constants.[1] The utility of a mathematical model lies in its ability to support meaningful inferences from data, such as the true prevalence of a category. Here we apply the probabilistic model of annotation introduced in (Dawid and Skene, 1979); space does not permit detailed discussion here of the inference process (this will be provided in a separate paper that is currently in preparation). Dawid and Skene used their model to determine a consensus among patient histories taken by multiple doctors. We use it to estimate the consensus judgement of category labels based on word sense annotations provided by multiple Mechanical Turkers. Inference is driven by accuracies and biases estimated for each annotator on a per-category basis.

n	ii_n	jj_n	y_n
1	1	1	4
2	1	3	1
3	192	17	5
⋮	⋮	⋮	⋮

Table 1: *Table of annotations y indexed by word instance ii and annotator jj.*

Let K be the number of possible labels or categories for an item, I the number of items to annotate, J the number of annotators, and N the total number of labels provided by annotators, where each annotator may label each instance zero or more times. Each annotation is a tuple consisting of an item $ii \in 1{:}I$, an annotator $jj \in 1{:}J$, and a label $y \in 1{:}K$. As illustrated in Table 1, we assemble the annotations in a database-like table where each row is an annotation, and the values in each column are indices over the item, annotator, and label. For example, the first two rows show that on item 1, annotators 1 and 3 assigned labels 4 and 1, respectively. The third row says that for item 192 annotator 17 provided label 5.

Dawid and Skene's model includes parameters

- $z_i \in 1{:}K$ for the true category of item i,
- $\pi_k \in [0, 1]$ for the probability that an item is of category k, subject to $\sum_{k=1}^{K} \pi_k = 1$, and
- $\theta_{j,k,k'} \in [0, 1]$ for the probabilty that annotator j will assign the label k' to an item whose true category is k, subject to $\sum_{k'=1}^{K} \theta_{j,k,k'} = 1$.

The generative model first selects the true category for item i according to the prevalence of categories, which is given by a Categorical distribution,[2]

$$z_i \sim \mathsf{Categorical}(\pi).$$

[1] In a Bayesian setting, the model parameters are themselves modeled as randomly generated from a prior distribution.

[2] The probability of n successes in m trials has a binomial distribution, with each trial (m=1) having a Bernoulli distribution. Data with more than two values has a multinomial

Word	*Pos*	*Senses*	α	*Agreement*
curious	adj	3	0.94	0.97
late	adj	7	0.84	0.89
high	adj	7	0.77	0.91
different	adj	4	0.13	0.60
severe	adj	6	0.05	0.32
normal	adj	4	0.02	0.38
strike	noun	7	0.89	0.93
officer	noun	4	0.85	0.91
player	noun	5	0.83	0.93
date	**noun**	**8**	**0.48**	**0.58**
island	noun	2	0.10	0.78
success	noun	4	0.09	0.39
combination	noun	7	0.04	0.73
entitle	verb	3	0.99	0.99
mature	verb	6	0.86	0.96
rule	verb	7	0.85	0.90
add	**verb**	**6**	**0.55**	**0.72**
help	**verb**	**8**	**0.26**	**0.58**
transfer	verb	9	0.22	0.42
ask	**verb**	**7**	**0.10**	**0.37**
justify	verb	5	0.04	0.82

Table 2: *Agreement results for MASC words with the three highest and lowest α scores, by part of speech, along with additional words discussed in the text (boldface).*

The observed labels y_n are generated based on annotator $jj[n]$'s responses $\theta_{jj[n],\, z[ii[n]]}$ to items $ii[n]$ whose true category is $zz[ii[n]]$,

$$y_n \sim \mathsf{Categorical}(\theta_{jj[n],\, z[ii[n]]}).$$

We use additively smoothed maximum likelihood estimation (MLE) to stabilize inference. This is equivalent to maximum a posteriori (MAP) estimation in a Bayesian model with Dirichlet priors,

$$\theta_{j,k} \sim \mathsf{Dirichlet}(\alpha_k) \qquad \pi \sim \mathsf{Dirichlet}(\beta).$$

The unsmoothed MLE is equivalent to the MAP estimate when α_k and β are unit vectors. For our experiments, we added a tiny fractional count to unit vectors, corresponding to a very small degree of additive smoothing applied to the MLE.

4 MASC Word Sense Sentence Corpus

MASC (Manually Annotated SubCorpus) is a very heterogeneous 500,000 word subset of the Open American National Corpus (OANC) with 16 types of annotation.[3] MASC contains a separate word sense sentence corpus for 116 words nearly evenly balanced among nouns, adjectives and verbs (Passonneau et al., 2012a). Each sentence is drawn from the MASC corpus, and exemplifies a particular word form annotated for a WordNet sense. To motivate our aim, which is to compare MASC word sense annotations with the annotations we collected through crowdsourcing, we review the MASC word sense corpus and some of its limitations.

College students from Vassar, Barnard, and Columbia were trained to carry out the MASC word sense annotation (Passonneau et al., 2012a). Most annotators stayed with the project for two to three years. Along with general training in the annotation process, annotators trained for each word on a sample of fifty sentences to become familiar with the sense inventory through discussion with Christiane Fellbaum, one of the designers of WordNet, and if needed, to revise the sense inventory for inclusion in subsequent releases of WordNet. After the pre-annotation sample, annotators worked independently to label 1,000 sentences for each word using an annotation tool that presented the WordNet senses and example usages, plus four variants of *none of the above*. Passonneau et al. describe the training and annotation tools in (2012b; 2012a). For each word, 100 of the total sentences were annotated by three or four annotators for assessment of inter-annotator reliability using pairwise agreement and Krippendorff's α.

The MASC agreement measures varied widely across words. Table 2 shows for each part of speech the words with the three highest and three lowest α scores, along with additional words exemplified below (boldface).[4] The α values in column 2 range from a high of 0.99 (for *entitle*, verb, 3 senses) to a low of 0.02 (*normal*, adjective, 3 senses). Pairwise agreement (column 3) has similarly wide variation. Passonneau et al. (2012b) argue that the differences were due in part to the different words: each word is a new annotation task.

The MASC project deviated from the best practices described in section 2 in that there was no iteration to achieve some threshold of agreement. All annotators, however, had at least two phases of training. Table 2 illustrates that annotators can agree on words with many senses, but at the same time, there are many words with low agreement.

distribution (a generalization of the binomial). Each trial then results in one of k outcomes with a categorical distribution.

[3]Both corpora are available from http://www.anc.org. The crowdsourced MASC words and labels will also be available for download.

[4]This table differs from a similar one Passonneau et al. give in (2012b) due to completion of more words and other updates.

Even with high agreement, the measures reported in Table 2 provide no information about word instance quality.

5 Crowdsourced Word Sense Annotation

Amazon Mechanical Turk is a venue for crowdsourcing tasks that is used extensively in the NLP community (Callison-Burch and Dredze, 2010). Human Intelligence Tasks (HITs) are presented to turkers by requesters. For our task, we used 45 randomly selected MASC words, with the same sentences and WordNet senses the trained MASC annotators used. Given our 1,000 instances per word, for a category whose prevalence is as low as 0.10 (100 examples expected), the 95% interval for observed examples, assuming examples are independent, will be 0.10 ± 0.06. One of our future goals for this data is to build item difficulty into the annotation model, so we collected 20 to 25 labels per item to get reasonable confidence intervals for the true label. This will also sharpen our estimates of the true category significantly, as estimated error goes down as $1/\sqrt{n}$ with n independent annotations; confidence intervals must be expanded as correlation among annotator responses increases due to annotator bias or item-level effects such as difficulty or subject matter.

In each HIT, turkers were presented with ten sentences for each word, with the word's senses listed below each sentence. Each HIT had a short paragraph of instructions indicating that turkers could expect their time per HIT to decrease as their familiarity with a word's senses increased (we wanted multiple annotations per turker per word for tighter estimates of annotator accuracies and biases).

To insure a high proportion of instances with high quality inferred labels, we piloted the HIT design and payment regimen with two trials of two and three words each, and discussed both with turkers on the Turker Nation message board. The final procedure and payment were as follows. To avoid spam workers, we required turkers to have a 98% lifetime approval rating and to have successfully completed 20,000 HITs. Our HITs were automatically approved after fifteen minutes. We considered manual approval and programming a more sophisticated approval procedure, but both were deemed too onerous given the scope of our task. Instead, we monitored performance of turkers across HITs by comparing each individual turker's labels to the current majority labels. Turkers with very poor performance were warned to take more care, or be blocked from doing further HITs. Of 228 turkers, five were blocked, with one subsequently unblocked. The blocked turker data is included in our analyses and in the full dataset, which will be released in the near future; the model-based approach to annotation is effective at adjusting for inaccurate annotators.

6 Annotator Accuracy and Bias

Through maximum likelihood estimation of the parameters of the Dawid and Skene model, annotators' accuracies and error biases can be estimated. Figure 1a) shows confusion matrices in the form of heatmaps that plot annotator responses by the estimated true labels for four of the 57 annotators who contributed labels for *add-v* (the affixes -v and -n represent part of speech). This word had a reliability of α=0.56 for four trained MASC annotators on 100 sentences and pairwise agreement=0.73. Figure 1b) shows heatmaps for four of the 49 annotators on *help-v*, which had a reliability of α=0.26 for the MASC annotators, with pairwise agreement=0.58. As indicated in the figure keys, darker cells have higher probabilities. Perfect accuracy of annotator responses (agreement with the inferred reference label) would yield black squares on the diagonal, with all the off-diagonal squares in white.

The two figures show that the turkers were generally more accurate on *add-v* than on *help-v*, which is consistent with the differences in the MASC agreement on these two words. In contrast to the knowledge gained from agreement metrics, inference based on the annotation model provides estimates of bias towards specific category values. Figure 1a shows the bias of these annotators to overuse WordNet sense 1 for *help-v*; bias appears in the plots as an uneven distribution of grey boxes off the main diagonal. Further, there were no assignments of senses 6 or 8 for this word. The figures provide a succinct visual summary that there were more differences across the four annotators for *help-v* than for *add-v*, with more bias towards overuse of not only sense 1, but also senses 2 (annotators 8 and 41) and 3 (annotator 9). When annotator 8 uses sense 1, the true label is often sense 6, thus illustrating how annotators provide information about the true label even from inaccurate responses.

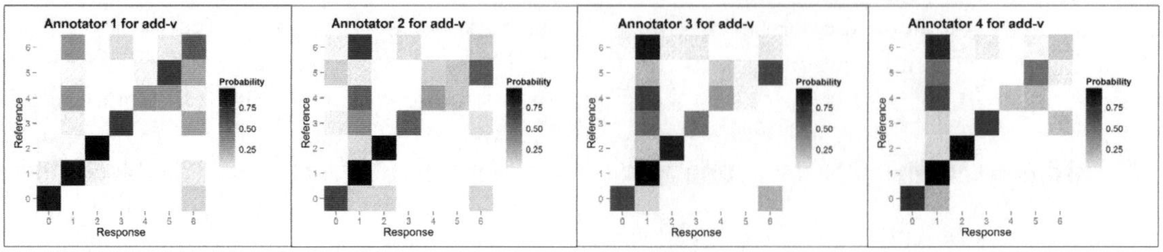

(a) *Four of 57 annotators for add-v*

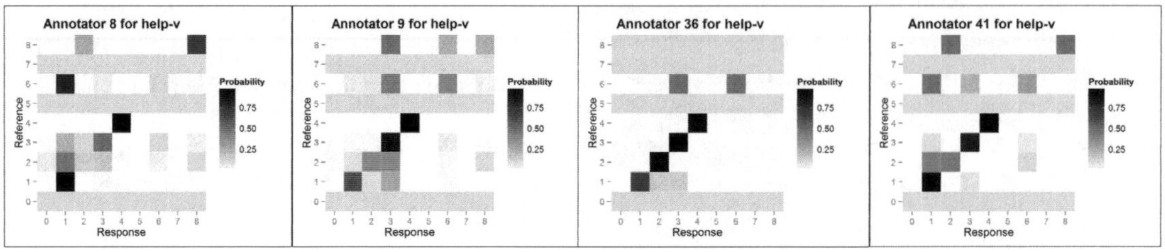

(b) *Four of 49 annotators for help-v*

Figure 1: *Heatmaps of annotators' accuracies and biases*

For the 45 words, average accuracies per word ranged from 0.05 to 0.86, with most words showing a large spread. Examination of accuracies by sense shows that accuracy was often highest for the more frequent senses. Accuracy for *add-v* ranged from 0.25 to 0.73, but was 0.90 for sense 1, 0.79 for sense 2, and much lower for senses 6 (0.29) and 7 (0.19). For *help-v*, accuracy was best on sense 1 (0.73), which was also the most frequent, but it was also quite good on sense 4 (0.64), which was much less frequent. Accuracies on senses of *help-v* ranged from 0.11 (senses 5, 7, and other) to 0.73 (sense 1).

7 Estimates for Prevalence and Labels

That the Dawid and Skene model allows annotators to have distinct biases and accuracies should match the intuitions of anyone who has performed annotation or collected annotated data. The power of their parameterization, however, shows up in the estimates their model yields for category prevalence (rate of each category) and for the true labels on each instance. Figure 2 contrasts five ways to estimate the sense prevalence of MASC words, two of which are based on models estimated via MLE. The MLE estimates each have an associated probability, thus a degree of certainty, with more certain estimates derived from the larger sets of crowdsourced labels (AMT MLE). MASC Freq is a simple ratio. Majority voted labels tend to be superior to single labels, but do not take annotators' biases into account.

The plots for the four words in Figure 2 are ordered by their α scores from four trained MASC annotators (see Table 2). There is a slight trend for the various estimates to diverge less on words where agreement is higher. The notable result, however, is that for each word, the plot demonstrates one or more senses where the AMT MLE estimate differs markedly from all other estimates. For *add-v*, the AMT MLE estimate for sense 1 is much lower (0.51) than any of the other measures (0.61-0.64). For *date-n*, the AMT MLE estimate for sense 4 is much closer to the other estimates than AMT Maj, which sugggests that some AMT annotators are baised against sense 4. The AMT MLE estimates for senses 6 and 7 are quite distinct. For *help-v*, the AMT MLE estimates for senses 1 and 6 are also very distinct. For *ask-v*, there are more differences across all estimates for senses 2 and 4, with the AMT MLE estimate neither the highest nor the lowest.

The estimates of label quality on each item are perhaps the strongest reason for turning to model-based approaches to assess annotated data. For the same four words discussed above, Table 3 shows the proportion of all instances that had an estimated true label where the label probability was greater than or equal to 0.99. For these words with α scores ranging from 0.10 (*ask-v*) to 0.55 (*add-v*), the proportion of very high quality inferred true labels ranges from 81% to 94%. Even for *help-v*, of the remaining 19% of instances, 13% have probabilities greater than 0.75. Table 3 also shows

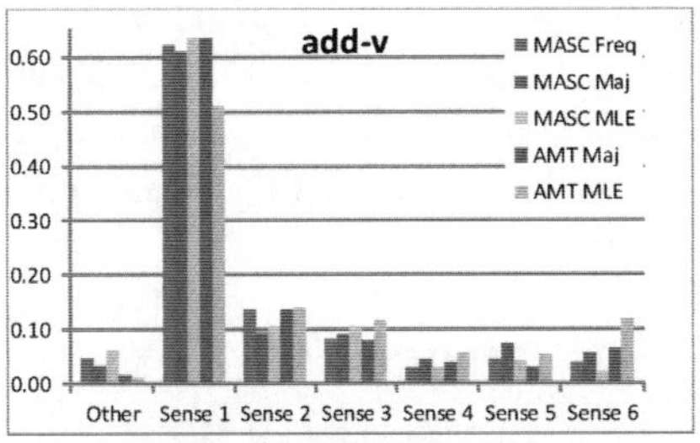

(a) *add-v* ($\alpha = 0.55$, agreement=0.72)

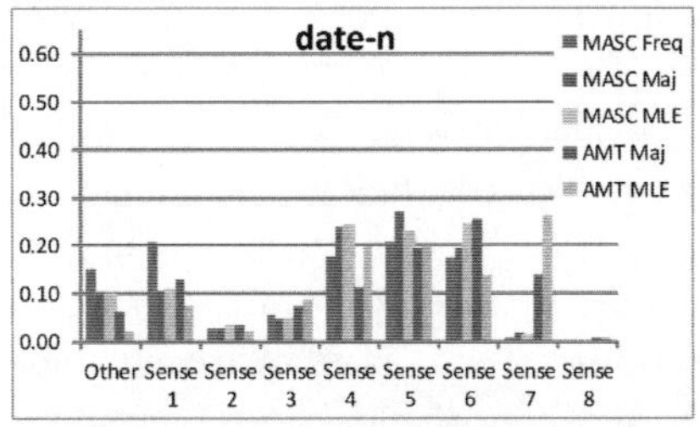

(b) *date-n* ($\alpha = 0.48$, agreement=0.58)

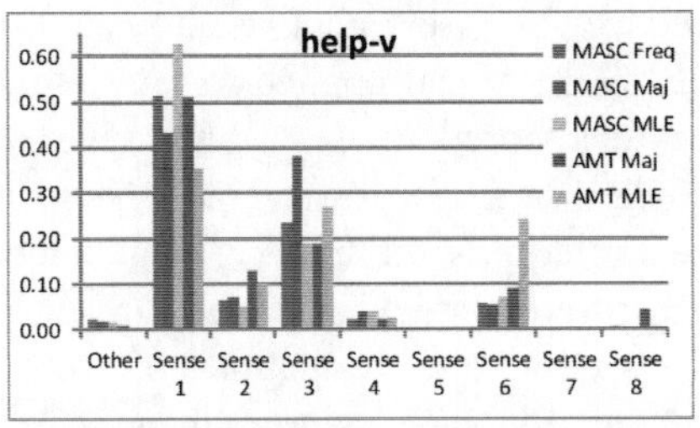

(c) *help-v* ($\alpha = 0.26$, agreement=0.58)

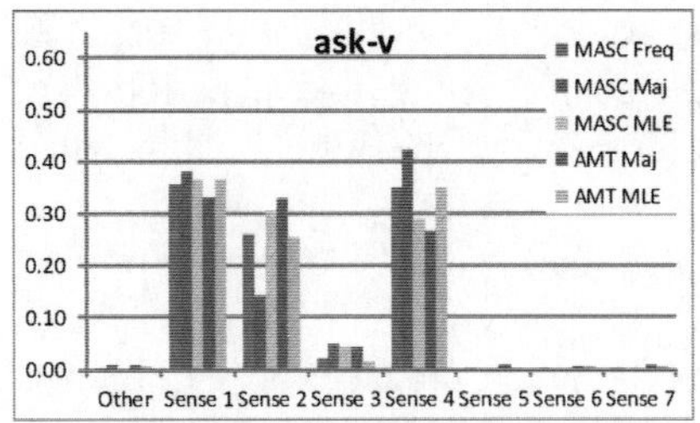

(d) *ask-v* ($\alpha = 0.10$, agreement=0.37)

Figure 2: *Prevalence estimates for 4 MASC words;* (MASC Freq) *frequency of each sense in* $\approx 1,000$ *singly-annotated instances from the trained MASC annotators;* (MASC Maj) *frequency of majority vote sense in* $\approx$100 *instances annotated by four trained MASC annotators;* (MASC MLE) *estimated probability of each sense in the same 100 instances annotated by four MASC annotators, using MLE;* (AMT Maj) *frequency of each majority vote sense for* $\approx$ 1000 *instances annotated by* $\approx$ 25 *turkers;* (AMT MLE) *estimated probability of each sense in the same* $\approx$1000 *instances annotated by* $\approx$25 *turkers, using MLE*

Sense k	≥ 0.99	Prop.
0	9	0.01
1	461	0.48
2	135	0.14
3	107	0.11
4	50	0.05
5	50	0.05
6	93	0.10
SubTot	905	0.94
Rest	62	0.06

(a) *add-v*: **94%**

Sense k	≥ 0.99	Prop.
0	19	0.02
1	68	0.07
2	19	0.02
3	83	0.09
4	173	0.18
5	190	0.20
6	133	0.14
7	236	0.25
8	5	0.01
SubTot	926	0.97
Rest	33	0.03

(b) *date-n*: **97%**

Sense k	≥ 0.99	Prop.
0	0	0.00
1	279	0.30
2	82	0.09
3	201	0.21
4	24	0.03
5	0	0.00
6	169	0.18
7	0	0.00
8	5	0.01
SubTot	760	0.81
Rest	180	0.19

(c) *help-v*: **81%**

Sense k	≥ 0.99	Prop.
0	6	0.01
1	348	0.36
2	177	0.18
3	9	0.01
4	251	0.26
5	0	0
6	0	0
7	6	0.01
8	6	0.01
SubTot	803	0.83
Rest	163	0.17

(d) *ask-v*: **83%**

Table 3: *Proportion of high quality labels per word*

that the high quality labels for each word are distributed across many of the senses. Of the 45 words studied here, 22 had α scores less than 0.50 from the trained annotators. For 42 of the same 45 words, 80% of the inferred true labels have a probability higher than 0.99.

In contrast to current best practices, an annotation model yields far more information about the most essential aspect of annotation efforts, namely how much uncertainty is associated with each gold standard label, and how the uncertainty is distributed across other possible label categories for each instance. An equally important benefit comes from a comparison of the cost per gold standard label. Over the course of a five-year period that included development of the infrastructure, the undergraduates who annotated MASC words were paid an estimated total of $80,000 for 116 words $\times$ 1000 sentences per word, which comes to a unit cost of $0.70 per ground truth label. In a 12 month period with 6 months devoted to infrastructure and trial runs, we paid 224 turkers a total of $15,000 for 45 words $\times$ 1000 sentences per word, for a unit cost of $0.33 per ground truth label. In short, the AMT data cost less than half the trained annotator data.

8 Related Work

The model proposed by Dawid and Skene (1979) comes out of a long practice in epidemiology to develop gold-standard estimation. Albert and Dodd (2008) give a relevant discussion of disease prevalence estimation adjusted for accuracy and bias of diagnostic tests. Like Dawid and Skene (1979), Smyth (1995) used unsupervised methods to model human annotation of craters on images of Venus. In the NLP literature, Bruce and Wiebe (1999) and Snow et al. (2008) use gold-standard data to estimate Dawid and Skene's model via maximum likelihood; Snow et al. show that combining noisy crowdsourced annotations produced data of equal quality to five distinct published gold standards. Rzhetsky et al. (2009) and Whitehill et al. (2009) estimate annotation models without gold-standard supervision, but neither models annotator biases, which are critical for estimating true labels. Klebanov and Beigman (2009) discuss censoring uncertain items from gold-standard corpora. Sheng et al. (2008) apply similar models to actively select the next label to elicit from annotators. Smyth et al. (1995), Rogers et al. (2010), and Raykar et al. (2010) all discuss the advantages of learning and evaluation with probabilistically annotated corpora. By now crowdsourcing is so widespread that NAACL 2010 sponsored a workshop on "Creating Speech and Language Data With Amazons Mechanical Turk" and in 2011, TREC added a crowdsourcing track.

9 Conclusion

The case study of word sense annotation presented here demonstrates that in comparison to current practice for assessment of annotated corpora, an annotation model applied to crowdsourced labels provides more knowledge and higher quality gold standard labels at lower cost. Those who would use the corpus for training benefit because they can differentiate high from low confidence labels. Cross-site evaluations of word sense disambiguation systems could benefit because there are more evaluation options. Where the most probable label is relatively uncertain, systems can be penalized less for an incorrect but close response (e.g., log loss). Systems that produce sense rankings for each instance could be scored using metrics that compare probability distributions, such as Kullbach-Leibler divergence (Resnik and Yarowsky, 2000). Wider use of annotation models should lead to more confidence from users in corpora for training or evaluation.

Acknowledgments

The first author was partially supported by from NSF CRI 0708952 and CRI 1059312, and the second by NSF CNS-1205516 and DoE DE-SC0002099. We thank Shreya Prasad for data collection, Mitzi Morris for feedback on the paper, Marilyn Walker for advice on Mechanical Turk, and Nancy Ide, Keith Suderman, Tim Brown and Mitzi Morris for help with the sentence data.

References

Paul S. Albert and Lori E. Dodd. 2008. On estimating diagnostic accuracy from studies with multiple raters and partial gold standard evaluation. *Journal of the American Statistical Association*, 103(481):61–73.

Ron Artstein and Massimo Poesio. 2008. Inter-coder agreement for computational linguistics. *Computational Linguistics*, 34(4):555–596.

Rebecca F. Bruce and Janyce M. Wiebe. 1998. Word-sense distinguishability and inter-coder agreement. In *Proceedings of Empirical Methods in Natural Language Processing*.

Rebecca F. Bruce and Janyce M. Wiebe. 1999. Recognizing subjectivity: a case study of manual tagging. *Natural Language Engineering*, 1(1):1–16.

Chris Callison-Burch and Mark Dredze. 2010. Creating speech and language data with Amazon's Mechanical Turk. In *Proceedings of the NAACL HLT 2010 Workshop on Creating Speech and Language Data with Amazon's Mechanical Turk*, pages 1–12.

Jacob Cohen. 1960. A coefficient of agreement for nominal scales. *Educational and Psychological Measurement*, 20:37–46.

A. P. Dawid and A. M. Skene. 1979. Maximum likelihood estimation of observer error-rates using the EM algorithm. *Journal of the Royal Statistical Society. Series C (Applied Statistics)*, 28(1):20–28.

Barbara di Eugenio and Michael Glass. 2004. The kappa statistic: A second look. *Computational Linguistics*, 30(1):95–101.

Barbara di Eugenio. 2000. On the usage of kappa to evaluate agreement on coding tasks. In *Proceedings of the Second International Conference on Language Resources and Evaluation (LREC)*.

Katrin Erk and Diana McCarthy. 2009. Graded word sense assignment. In *Proceedings of the Conference on Empirical Methods in Natural Language Processing*.

Christiane Fellbaum. 1998. *WordNet: An Electronic Lexical Database*. MIT Press, Cambridge, MA.

Nancy Ide and Yorick Wilks. 2006. Making sense about sense. In *Word Sense Disambiguation: Algorithms and Applications*, pages 47–74. Springer Verlag.

Beata Beigman Klebanov and Eyal Beigman. 2009. From annotator agreement to noise models. *Computational Linguistics*, 35(4):495–503.

Klaus Krippendorff. 1980. *Content analysis: An introduction to its methodology*. Sage Publications, Beverly Hills, CA.

Rebecca J. Passonneau, Collin F. Baker, Christiane Fellbaum, and Nancy Ide. 2012a. The MASC word sense corpus. In Nicoletta Calzolari (Conference Chair), Khalid Choukri, Thierry Declerck, Mehmet Uur Doan, Bente Maegaard, Joseph Mariani, Jan Odijk, and Stelios Piperidis, editors, *Proceedings of the Eight International Conference on Language Resources and Evaluation (LREC'12)*, Istanbul, Turkey. European Language Resources Association (ELRA).

Rebecca J. Passonneau, Vikas Bhardwaj, Ansaf Salleb-Aouissi, and Nancy Ide. 2012b. Multiplicity and word sense: evaluating and learning from multiply labeled word sense annotations. *Language Resources and Evaluation*, 46(2):219–252.

Vikas C. Raykar, Shipeng Yu, Linda H. Zhao, Gerardo Hermosillo Valadez, Charles Florin, Luca Bogoni, and Linda Moy. 2010. Learning from crowds. *Journal of Machine Learning Research*, 11:1297–1322.

Philip Resnik and David Yarowsky. 2000. Distinguishing systems and distinguishing senses: New evaluation methods for word sense disambiguation. *Natural Language Engineering*, 5(3):113–133.

Simon Rogers, Mark Girolami, and Tamara Polajnar. 2010. Semi-parametric analysis of multi-rater data. *Statistical Computing*, 20:317–334.

Andrey Rzhetsky, Hagit Shatkay, and W. John Wilbur. 2009. How to get the most out of your curation effort. *PLoS Computational Biology*, 5(5):1–13.

Victor S. Sheng, Foster Provost, and Panagiotis G. Ipeirotis. 2008. Get another label? improving data quality and data mining using multiple, noisy labelers. In *Proceedings of the Fourteenth ACM International Conference on Knowledge Discovery and Data Mining (KDD)*.

Padhraic Smyth, Usama Fayyad, Michael Burl, Pietro Perona, and Pierre Baldi. 1995. Inferring ground truth from subjectively-labeled images of Venus. In *Advances in Neural Information Processing Systems 7*, pages 1085–1092. MIT Press.

Rion Snow, Brendan O'Connor, Daniel Jurafsky, and Andrew Y. Ng. 2008. Cheap and fast - but is it good? evaluating non-expert annotations for natural language tasks. In *Proceedings of Empirical Methods in Natural Language Processing (EMNLP)*, pages 254–263, Honolulu.

Jacob Whitehill, Paul Ruvolo, Tingfan Wu, Jacob Bergsma, and Javier Movellan. 2009. Whose vote should count more: Optimal integration of labels from labelers of unknown expertise. In *Proceedings of the 24th Annual Conference on Advances in Neural Information Processing Systems*.

Ranking the annotators: An agreement study on argumentation structure

Andreas Peldszus
Applied Computational Linguistics
University of Potsdam
peldszus@uni-potsdam.de

Manfred Stede
Applied Computational Linguistics
University of Potsdam
stede@uni-potsdam.de

Abstract

We investigate methods for evaluating agreement among a relatively large group of annotators who have not received extensive training and differ in terms of ability and motivation. We show that it is possible to isolate a reliable subgroup of annotators, so that aspects of the difficulty of the underlying task can be studied. Our task is to annotate the argumentative structure of short texts.

1 Introduction

Scenarios for evaluating annotation experiments differ in terms of the difficulty of the task, the number of annotators, and the amount of training that annotators receive. For simple tasks, crowdsourcing involving very many annotators has recently attracted attention.[1] For more difficult tasks, the standard setting still is to work with two or a few more annotators, train them well, and compute agreement, usually in terms of the kappa measure. In this paper, we study a different scenario, which may be called 'classroom annotation': The group of annotators is bigger (in our example, 26), and there are no extensive training sessions: Students receive detailed written guidelines, there is a brief QA period, and annotation starts. In such a setting, one has to expect some agreement problems that are due to different abilities and different motivation of the students. Our goal is to develop methods for systematically studying the annotation results in such groups, to identify more or less competent subgroups, yet at the same time also learn about the difficulty of various aspects of the underlying annotation task. To this end, we investigate ways of ranking and clustering annotators.

Our task is the annotation of argumentation in short texts, which is somewhat similar to marking the rhetorical structure, e.g. in terms of RST (Mann and Thompson, 1988; Carlson et al., 2003). Thus we are dealing with a relatively difficult task involving text interpretation. We devised an annotation scheme (which is more fully described elsewhere), and in order to study the feasibility, first ran experiments with short hand-crafted texts that collectively cover all the relevant phenomena. This is the setting we report in this paper. A separate step for future work is guideline revision on the basis of the results, and then applying the scheme to authentic argumentative text (e.g., user generated content on various websites).

2 A theory of argumentation structure

Following up on Toulmin's (1958) influential analysis of argument, Freeman (1991; 2011) worked on integrating those ideas into the argument diagraming techniques of the informal logic tradition. Freeman's central idea is to model argumentation as a hypothetical dialectical exchange between a proponent, who presents and defends claims, and a challenger (the 'opponent'), who critically questions them in a regimented fashion. Every move in such a *basic dialectical situation* corresponds to a structural element in the argument diagram. The analysis of an argumentative text is thus conceived as finding the corresponding critical question of the challenger that is answered by a particular segment of the text.

Since the focus of this paper is on the evaluation methodology, we provide here only a brief sketch of the scheme; for a detailed description with many examples, see Peldszus and Stede (to appear). Premises and conclusions are propositions expressed in the text segments. We can graphically present an argument as an argument diagram, with propositions as nodes and the various relations as arrows linking either two nodes or

[1] See, for instance, Snow et al. (2008) or Bhardwaj et al. (2010) for strategies to analyse and cope with diverging performance of annotators in that scenario.

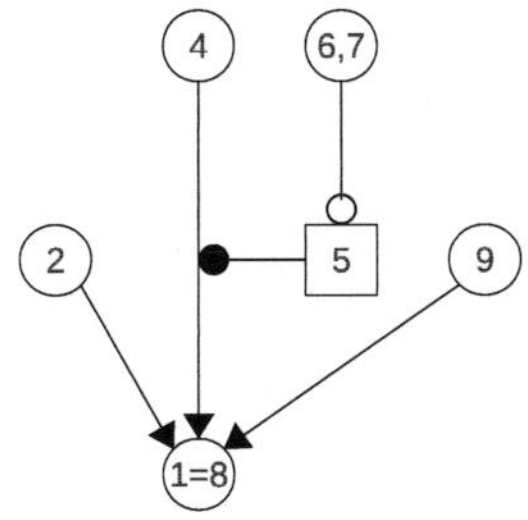

Figure 1: Example of an argumentation structure annotation for a short text

a node and a link[2]. See figure 1 for an example. Notice that segments in favor of the proponent's position are drawn in circles, whereas the challenger's perspective is given in boxes. The root of an argument tree is the central statement made in the text. In the example, it is expressed both in segment 1 and in segment 8; the = indicates that the annotator judges the contributions of the two segments as equivalent, which can happen for any node in the tree. Segments 2, 4, and 9 provide *support* to the central statement, which is the most simple configuration.

(1) [*We should tear the building down.*]$_1$ [*It is full of asbestos.*]$_2$

Support can be serial (transitive), when a supporting statement in turn receives support from another one. E.g., example (1) could be continued with ... [*The report of the commission made that very clear.*]$_3$.

If an argument involves multiple premises that support the conclusion only if they are taken together, we have a *linked* structure in Freeman's terminology. On its own none of the linked premises would be able to support the conclusion. In the basic dialectical situation, a linked structure is induced by the challenger's question as to why a premise is relevant to the claim. The proponent then answers by presenting another premise explicating the connection. Building linked structure is thus to be conceived as completing an argument. As an example, consider the following continuation of example (1) ... [*All buildings with hazardous materials should be demolished.*]$_3$. Linked support is shown in the diagram by connecting the premises before they link to the conclusion.

Two more configurations, which turn up in Figure 1, are the attacking relations (all with a circled arrowhead): *undercut* and *rebuttal*. The former (segment 5) denies the relevance of a stated relation, here: the support that 4 lends to 1=8. The opponent does not dispute the truth of 4 itself but challenges the idea that it can in fact lend support to 1=8. We draw it as an attack arrow pointing at the relation in question. In contrast, a rebuttal directly challenges the truth of a statement. In the example, the annotator first decided that segments 6 and 7 play a joint role for the argumentation (this is the step of *merging* two segments) and then marked them as the proponent's rebuttal of the challenger's statement 5.

3 Annotation Experiment

3.1 Guidelines

We developed annotation guidelines based on the theory presented in Section 2. The guidelines (6 pages) contain text examples and the corresponding graphs for all basic structures, and they present different combinations of attack and counter-attack. The annotation process is divided into three steps: First, one segment is identified as the central claim of the text. The annotator then chooses the dialectical role (proponent or opponent) for all remaining segments. Finally, the argumentative function of each segment (is it supporting or attacking) and the corresponding subtypes have to be determined, as well as the targeted segment.

3.2 Data

Applying the scheme demands a detailed, deep understanding of the text, which is why we choose to first evaluate this task on short and controlled instances of argumentation. For this purpose we built a set of 23 constructed German texts, where each text consists of only five discourse segments. While argumentative moves in authentic texts are often surrounded by material that is not directly relevant to the argumentation, such as factual background information, elaborations or rhetorical decoration, in the constructed texts all segments are clearly argumentative, i.e. they either presents the central claim, a reason, an objection or a counter-attack. Merging segments and identifying restatements is thus not necessary. The texts cover several combinations of the basic constructs in different linearisations, typically one central claim, two (simple, combined or exemplifying) premises, one objection (rebutting a premise, rebutting the conclusion or undercutting the link be-

[2]When an artificial node is introduced in such places, a standard tree representation results.

tween them) and a possible reaction (rebutting or undercutting counter-attacks, or a new reason that renders the objection uncountered). A (translated) example of a micro text is given in (2). In the questionaire the order of the texts has been randomized.

(2) [*Energy-saving light bulbs contain a considerable amount of toxic substances.*]$_1$ [*A customary lamp can for instance contain up to five milligrams of quicksilver.*]$_2$ [*For this reason, they should be taken off the market,*]$_3$ [*unless they are virtually unbreakable.*]$_4$ [*This, however, is simply not case.*]$_5$

3.3 Procedure

The annotation experiment was carried out in the context of an undergraduate university course with 26 students, participation was obligatory. The annotators only received minimal training: A short introduction (5 min.) was given to set the topic. After studying the guidelines (~30 min.) and a very brief question-answering, the subjects annotated the 23 texts (~45 min.), writing their analysis as an argumentative graph in designated areas of the questionaire.

4 Evaluation

4.1 Preparations

Since the annotators were asked to assign one and only one function to each segment, every node in the argumentative graph has exactly one out-going arc. The graph can thus be reinterpreted as a list of segment labels.

Every segment is labeled on different levels: The 'role'-level specifies the dialectical role (proponent or opponent). The 'typegen'-level specifies the general type, i.e. whether the segment presents the central claim (thesis) of the text, supports or attacks another segment. The 'type'-level additionally specifies the kind of support (normal or example) and the kind of attack (rebutter or undercutter). Whether a segment's function holds only in combination with that of another segment (combined) or not (simple) is represented on the 'combined'-level.[3] The target is finally specified by the segment identifier (1 . . . 5) or relation identifier ($a \dots d$) on the 'target'-level.

The labels of each separate level can be merged to form a complex tagset. We interpret the result as a hierarchical tagset as it is presented in Figure 2.[4] The label 'PSNC(3)' for example stands for a proponent's segment, giving normal support to segment 3 in combination with another segment, while 'OAUS(b)' represents an opponent's segment, undercutting a relation b, not combined.

Due to space and readability constraints, we focus the detailed discussion of the experiment's result on the 'role+type'-level. Still, general results will be reported for all levels.

Another question that arises before evaluation, especially in our setting, is how to deal with missing annotations, since measuring inter-annotator agreement with a κ-like coefficient requires a decision of every annotator (or at least the same number of annotators) on each item. One way to cope with this is to exclude annotators with missing annotations, another to exclude items that have not been annotated by every subject. In our experiment only 11 of the 26 subjects annotated every segment. Another 10 annotated at least 90% of the segments, five annotated less. Excluding some annotators would be possible in our setting, but keeping only 11 of 26 is unacceptable. Excluding items is also inconvenient given the small dataset. We thus chose to mark segments with missing annotations as such in the data, augmenting the tagset with the label '?' for missing annotations. We are aware of the undesired possibility that two annotators 'agree' on not assigning a category to a segment. Still, we can decide to only exclude those annotators who omitted many decisions, and to measure agreement for the remaining ones, thereby reducing the risk of false agreement.

4.2 IAA over all annotators

The agreement in terms of Fleiss's κ (Fleiss, 1971)[5] of all annotators on the different levels is shown in Table 1. For the complex levels we additionally report Krippendorff's α (Krippendorff, 1980) as a weighted measure of agreement. We use the distance between two tags in the tag hierarchy to weigh the confusion (similar to Geertzen and Bunt (2006)), in order to capture the intuition that confusing, e.g., PSNC with PSNS is less severe than confusing it with OAUS.

According to the scale of Krippendorff (1980),

[3] This is roughly equivalent to Freeman's 'linked premises'.

[4] Notice that this hierarchy is implicit in the annotation process, yet the annotators were neither confronted with a decision-tree version nor the labels of this tag hierarchy.

[5] A generalisation of Scott's π (Scott, 1955) for more than two annotators, as Artstein and Poesio (2008) pointed out.

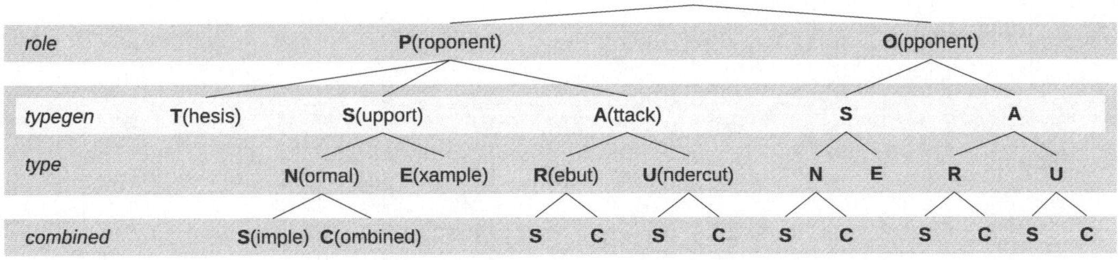

Figure 2: The hierarchy of segment labels.

level	#cats	κ	A_O	A_E	α	D_O	D_E
role	2	0.521	0.78	0.55			
typegen	3	0.579	0.72	0.33			
type	5	0.469	0.61	0.26			
comb	2	0.458	0.73	0.50			
target	(9)	0.490	0.58	0.17			
role+typegen	5	0.541	0.66	0.25	0.534	0.28	0.60
role+type	9	0.450	0.56	0.20	0.500	0.33	0.67
role+type+comb	15	0.392	0.49	0.16	0.469	0.38	0.71
role+type+comb+target	(71)	0.384	0.44	0.08	0.425	0.45	0.79

Table 1: Agreement for all 26 annotators on 115 items for the different levels. The number of categories on each level (without '?') is shown in the second column (possible target categories depend on text length). We report Fleiss's κ with the associated observed (A_O) and expected agreement (A_E). Weighted scores were calculated using Krippendorff's α, with observed (D_O) and expected disagreement (D_E).

the annotators in our experiment did neither achieve reliable ($\kappa \geq 0.8$) nor marginally reliable ($0.67 \leq \kappa < 0.8$) agreement. On the scale of Landis and Koch (1977), most results can be interpreted to show moderate correlation ($0.4 < \kappa \leq 0.6$), only the two most complex levels fall out. Considering weighted scores for those complex levels, all fall into the window of moderate correlation.

While typical results in discourse structure tagging usually reach or exceed the 0.7 threshold[6], we expected lower results for three reasons: first the minimal training of the naive annotators only based on the guidelines, second the varying commitment to the task of the annotators in the constrained setting and finally the nature of the task, which requires a precise specification of the annotators interpretation of the texts.

When it comes to investigation of the reasons of disagreement, the informativeness of a single inter-annotator agreement value is limited. We want to identify sources of disagreement in both the set of annotators as well as the categories. To

cat.	$\Delta\kappa$	n	A_O	A_E
PT	+0.265	572	0.91	0.69
PSE	+0.128	112	0.97	0.93
PSN	+0.082	1075	0.79	0.54
OAR	−0.027	430	0.86	0.75
PAR	−0.148	173	0.92	0.89
OSN	−0.198	153	0.93	0.90
OAU	0.229	172	0.92	0.89
PAU	−0.240	138	0.93	0.91
OSE	−0.451	2	0.99	0.99

Table 3: Krippendorff's category definition diagnostic for the level 'role+type', base κ=0.45.

this end, contingency tables (confusion matrices) are studied, which show the number of category agreements and confusions for a pair of annotators. However, the high number of annotators in our study makes this strategy infeasible, as there are 325 different pairs of annotators. One solution to still get an overview of typical category confusions, is to build an aggregated confusion matrix, which sums up the values of category pairs across all 325 normal confusion matrices. As proposed in Cinková et al. (2012), we derive a confusion probability matrix from this aggregated matrix, which is shown in Table 2. It specifies the conditional probability that one annotator will annotate an item with $\text{category}_{\text{column}}$, given that another has chosen $\text{category}_{\text{row}}$, so the rows sum up to 1. The diagonal cells display the probability of agreement for each category.

[6]Agreement of professional annotators on 16 rhetorical relations was κ=0.64 in the beginning and 0.82 after extensive training (Carlson et al., 2003). Agreement on 'argumentative zones' is reported κ=0.71 for trained annotators with detailed guidelines, another study for untrained annotators with only minimalistic guidelines reported values varying between 0.35 and 0.72 (depending on the text), see Teufel (2010).

	PT	PSN	PSE	PAR	PAU	OSN	OSE	OAR	OAU	?
PT	0.625	0.243	0.005	0.003	0.002	0.006	0.000	0.030	0.007	0.078
PSN	0.123	0.539	0.052	0.034	0.046	0.055	0.001	0.052	0.021	0.078
PSE	0.024	0.462	0.422	0.007	0.008	0.000	0.000	0.015	0.001	0.061
PAR	0.007	0.164	0.004	0.207	0.245	0.074	0.000	0.156	0.072	0.071
PAU	0.007	0.264	0.005	0.290	0.141	0.049	0.000	0.117	0.075	0.052
OSN	0.016	0.292	0.000	0.081	0.046	0.170	0.004	0.251	0.075	0.065
OSE	0.000	0.260	0.000	0.000	0.000	0.260	0.000	0.240	0.140	0.100
OAR	0.033	0.114	0.004	0.070	0.044	0.102	0.001	0.339	0.218	0.076
OAU	0.017	0.101	0.000	0.069	0.061	0.066	0.002	0.469	0.153	0.063
?	0.179	0.351	0.031	0.066	0.041	0.055	0.001	0.157	0.061	0.057

Table 2: Confusion probability matrix over all 26 annotators for the level 'role+type'.

category pair	$\Delta\kappa$	A_O	A_E
OAR+OAU	+0.048	0.61	0.22
PAR+PAU	+0.026	0.59	0.21
OAR+OSN	+0.018	0.58	0.22
PSN+PSE	+0.012	0.59	0.23
OAR+PAR	+0.007	0.58	0.22
PSN+OSN	+0.007	0.59	0.24
PAR+OSN	+0.005	0.57	0.21

Table 4: Krippendorff's category distinction diagnostic for the level 'role+type', base κ=0.45.

Krippendorff (1980) proposed another way to investigate category confusions by systematically comparing the agreement on the original category set with the agreement on a reduced category set. There are two different methods to collapse categories: The first is the *category definition test*, where all but the one category of interest are collapsed together, yielding a binary category distinction. When measuring the agreement with this binary distinction only confusions between the category of interest and the rest count, but no confusions between the collapsed categories. If agreement increases for the reduced set compared to the original set, that category of interest is better distinguished than the rest of the categories. As Table 3 shows, the highest distinguishability is found for PT, PSN and PSE. Rebutters are better distinguished for the opponent role than for the proponent role. Undercutters seem equally problematic for both roles. The extreme value for OSE is not surprising, given that this category was not supposed to be found in the dataset and was only used twice. It shows, though, that the results of this test have to be interpreted with caution for rare categories, since in these cases the collapsed rest always leads to a very high chance agreement.

The other of Krippendorff's diagnostics is the *category distinction test*, where two categories are collapsed in order to measure the impact of confusions between them on the overall agreement value. The higher the difference, the greater the confusion between the two collapsed categories. Table 4 shows the result for some category pairs. The highest gain is found between rebutting and undercutting attacks on the opponents side: Given the base κ=0.45, the +0.048 increase means a potential improvement of 10% if these confusions could be reduced. However, distingishing rebutters and undercutters often depends on interpretation and we consider it unlikely to reach perfect agreement on that decision.

4.3 Comparison with gold data

We now compare the result of the annotation experiment with the gold annotation. For each annotator and for each level of annotation, we calculated the F1 score, macro-averaged over the categories of that level. Figure 3 shows the distribution of those values as boxplots. We observe varying degrees of difficulty on the basic levels: While the scores on the 'role' and 'typegen' are relatively dense between 0.8 and 0.9, the distribution is much wider and also generally lower for 'type', 'comb' and 'target'. Especially remarkable is the drop of the median when comparing 'typegen' with 'type': For the simpler level, all values of the better half of annotators lie above 0.85, but for the more complex level, which also requires the distinction between rebutters and undercutters, the median drops to 0.67. The figure also shows the pure F1 score for identifying the central claim (PT). While the larger part of the annotators performs well in this task, there are still some below 0.7. This is remarkable, since identifying one segment as the central claim of a five-segment text does not appear to be a challenging task.

4.4 Ranking and clustering the annotators

Until now we have mainly investigated the tagset as a factor in measuring agreement. The widespread distribution of annotator scores in the comparison with gold data however showed that

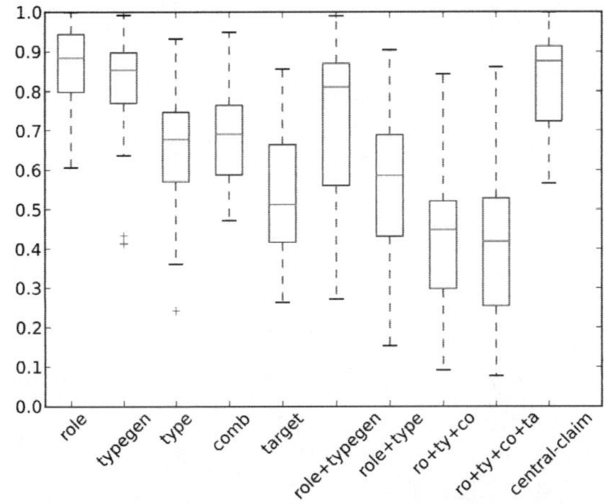

Figure 3: Comparison with gold annotation: For each level we show a boxplot of the F1 scores of all annotators (each score macro-averaged over categories of that level). Also, we present the F1 score for the recognition of the central claim.

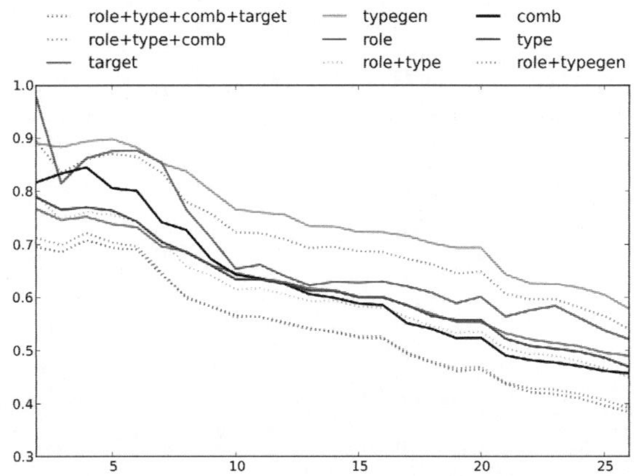

Figure 4: Agreement in κ on the different levels for the n-best annotators ordered by their F1 score in identifying the central claim.

their performance differs greatly. As described in Section 3.3, participation in the study was obligatory for our subjects (students in class). We thus want to make sure that the differences in performance are a result of the annotator's varying commitment to the task, rather than a result of possible ambiguities or flaws of the guidelines. The inter-annotator agreement values presented in Table 1 are not so helpful for answering this question, as they only provide us with an average measure, but not with an upper and lower bound of what is achievable with our annotators. Consequently, the goal of this section is to give structure to the set of annotators, to impose a (partial) order on it or even divide it into different groups and investigate their characteristic confusions.

Central claim: During the conversion of the written graphs into segment label squences, it became obvious that certain annotators nearly always chose the first segment of the text as the central claim, even in cases where it was followed by a consecutive clause with a discourse marker. Therefore, our first heuristic was to impose an order on the set of annotators according to their F1 score in identifying the central claim. This not only identifies those outliers but can additionally serve as a rough indicator of text understanding. Although this ordering requires gold data, producing gold data for the central claim of a text is relatively simple and using them only gives minimal bias in the evaluation (in contrast to e.g. 'role+type' F1 score as a sorting criterion). With this ordering we can then calculate agreement on different subsets of the annotators, e.g. only for the two best annotators, for the ten best or for all. Figure 4 shows κ on the different levels for all n-best groups of annotators: From the two best to the six best annotators the results are quite stable. The six best annotators achieve an encouraging κ=0.74 on the 'role+type' level and likewise satisfactory κ=0.69 for the full task, i.e. on the maximally complex 'role+type+comb+target' level. For increasingly larger n-best groups, the agreement decreases steadily with only minor fluctuations. Although the central claim F1 score proves to be a useful sorting criterion here, it might not work as well for authentic texts, due to the possibility of restated, or even implicit central claims.

Category distributions: Investigating the annotator bias is also a promising way to impose structure onto the group of annotators. A look on the individual distribution of categories per annotator quickly reveals that there are some deviations. Table 5 shows the individual distributions for the 'role+type'-level, as well as the average annotator distribution and that found in the gold data. We focus on three peculiarities here. First, both annotators A18 and A21 refrain from classifying segments as attacking. Although they make the distinction between the roles, they give only supporting segments. Checking the annotations shows that they must have mixed the concepts of dialectical role and argumentative function. Another example is the group of A04, A20 and A23, who refrain from using proponent attacks. Al-

anno	PT	PSN	PSE	PAR	PAU	OSN	OSE	OAR	OAU	?	Δ^{gold}	$\Delta^{\varnothing}$
A01	23	40	5	13	0	6	0	24	0	4	17	15.6
A02	22	33	7	8	11	3	0	23	1	7	17	16.9
A03	23	40	6	4	12	5	0	16	9	0	7	11.8
A04	21	52	6	1	0	0	0	14	11	10	25	20.5
A05	23	42	5	15	2	5	0	20	3	0	10	14.2
A06	24	39	6	6	9	7	0	15	9	0	7	10.9
A07	22	41	1	12	8	5	0	13	8	5	13	9.4
A08	23	35	6	6	14	6	1	17	7	0	9	13.3
A09	23	43	2	6	7	7	0	15	12	0	9	10.8
A10	23	51	3	3	4	8	0	8	15	0	21	21.2
A11	21	41	3	2	1	1	0	22	9	15	21	16.6
A12	23	42	6	15	5	3	0	13	4	4	13	11.7
A13	23	40	4	16	0	7	0	17	8	0	14	13.3
A14	19	33	6	10	4	4	0	11	8	20	26	20.2
A15	19	37	2	6	7	3	0	18	3	20	20	16.9
A16	20	31	4	7	10	7	0	14	5	17	22	16.9
A17	22	53	2	4	3	0	0	20	6	5	17	15.1
A18	23	51	5	0	0	34	1	0	1	0	39	40.4
A19	24	41	7	13	2	5	0	20	3	0	10	14.5
A20	21	41	4	0	1	2	0	31	5	10	22	18.2
A21	16	40	0	1	0	20	0	0	1	37	52	44.8
A22	22	34	7	5	10	6	0	17	9	5	12	10.3
A23	23	52	0	1	0	0	0	32	6	1	24	27.1
A24	23	41	6	6	9	5	0	22	3	0	4	11.8
A25	23	38	4	5	15	0	0	7	23	0	24	27.1
A26	23	44	5	8	4	4	0	21	3	3	9	10.2
∅	22.0	41.3	4.3	6.7	5.3	5.9	0.1	16.5	6.6	6.3		
gold	23	42	6	6	8	5	0	19	6	0		

Table 5: Distribution of categories for each annotator in absolute numbers for the 'role+type' level. The last two rows display gold and average annotator distribution for comparison. The two rightmost columns specify for each annotator the total difference to gold or average distribution $\Delta^{gold/\varnothing} = \frac{1}{2}\sum_{c}\Delta_c^{gold/\varnothing}$.

though they make the distinction between the argumentative functions of supporting and attacking, they do not systematically attribute counterattacks to the proponent. Finally, as pointed out before, there are several annotators with a different amount of missing annotations. Note, that missing annotations must not necessarily signal an unmotivated annotator (who skips an item if deciding on it is too tedious). It could very well also be a diligent but slow annotator. Still, missing annotations lead to lower agreement in most cases, so filtering out the severe cases might be a good idea. Most of the annotators showing deviations in category distribution could be identified, if annotators are sorted by deviation from average distribution $\Delta^{\varnothing}$, which is shown in the last column of Table 5. Filtering out the 7 worst annotators in terms of $\Delta^{\varnothing}$, the resulting κ increases from 0.45 to 0.54 on the 'role+type'-level, which is nearly equal to the 0.53 achieved when using the same size of annotator set in the central claim ordering. Although this ordering suffices to detect outliers in the set of annotators without relying on gold data, it still has two drawbacks: It only maximizes to the average and will thus not garantuee best agreement scores for the smaller n-best sets. Furthermore a more general critique on total orders of annotators: There are various ways in which a group agrees or disagrees simultaneously that might not be linearized this way. Luckily, a better solution is at hand.

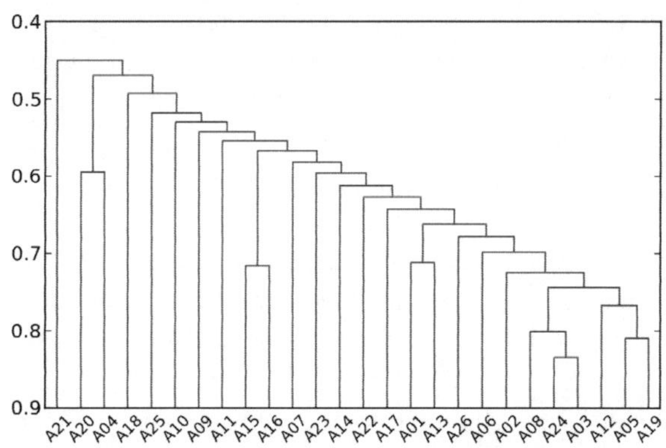

Figure 5: Clustering of the annotators (on the x-axis) for the 'role+type' level. The y-axis specifies the distance between the clusters, i.e. the κ reached by the annotators of both clusters.

Agglomerative hierarchical clustering: We apply hierarchical clustering in order to investigate the structure of agreement in the set of annotators. The clusters are initialized as singletons for each annotator. Then agreement is calculated for all possible pairs of those clusters. The pair of clusters with highest agreement is merged. This procedure is iterated until there is only one cluster left. In contrast to normal clustering, the linkage criterion does not determine the distance between complex clusters indirectly as function of the distance between singleton clusters, but directly measures agreement for the unified set of annotators of both clusters. Figure 5 shows the clustering on the 'role+type'-level. It not only gives an impression of the possible range of agreement, but also allows us to check for ambiguities in the guidelines: If there were stable alternative readings in the guidelines, we would expect multiple larger clusters that can only be merged at a lower level of κ. As the Figure shows, the clustering grows steadily, maximally incorporating clusters of two annotators, so we do not see the threat of ambiguity in the guidelines. Furthermore, the clustering conforms with central claim ordering in picking out the same set of six reliable and good annotators (with an average F1 of 0.76 for 'role+type' and of 0.67 for the full task compared to gold) and it conforms with both orderings in picking out similar sets of worst annotators.

With this clustering we now have the possibility to investigate the agreement for subgroups of annotators. Since the growth of the clusters is rather linear, we choose to track the confusion over the best path of growing clusters, i.e. starting from the best scoring {A24,A03} cluster to the maximal cluster. It would be interesting to see the change in Krippendorff's category distinction diagnostic for selected confusion pairs. However, this value not only depends on the amount of confusion but also on the frequency of that categories[7], which cannot be assume to be identical for different sets of annotators. We thus investigate the confusion rate conf_{c_1,c_2}, i.e. the ratio of confusing assigments pairs $|c_1 \circ c_2|$ in the total set of agreeing and confusing assignments pairs for these two categories:

$$\text{conf}_{c_1,c_2} = \frac{|c_1 \circ c_2|}{|c_1 \circ c_1| + |c_1 \circ c_2| + |c_2 \circ c_2|}$$

Figure 6 shows the confusion rate for selected category pairs over the path from the best scoring to the maximal cluster. The confusion between rebutters and undercutters is already at a high level for the best six best annotators, but increases when worse annotators enter the cluster. A constant and relatively low confusion rate has PSN+PAU, which means that distinguishing counter-attacks from new premises is equally 'hard' for all annotators. Distinguishing normal and example support,

[7]20% confusion of frequent categories have a larger impact on agreement than that of less frequent categories.

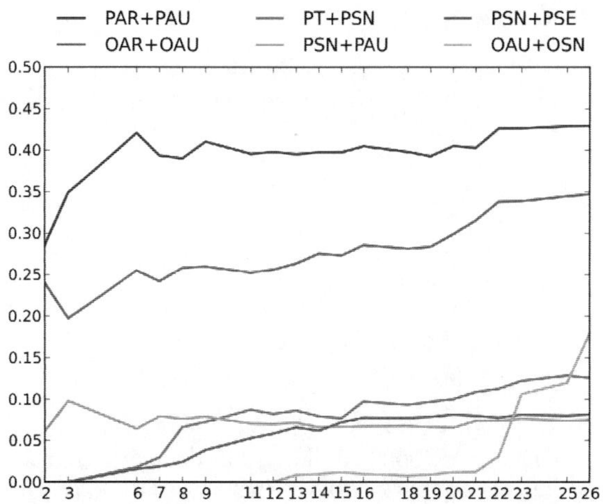

Figure 6: Confusion rate for selected category pairs in the growing clusters, with the numbers of annotators in the cluster on the x axis.

as well as central claims and supporting segments is not a problem for the six best annotators. It becomes slightly more confusing for more annotators, yet ends at a relatively low level around 0.08 and 0.13 respectively. Confusing undercutters and support on the opponents side is only a problem of the low-agreeing annotators, the confusion rate is nearly 0 for the first 21 annotators on the cluster path. Finally note, that there is no confusion typical for the high-agreeing annotators only.

5 Conclusions

We presented methods to systematically study the agreement in a larger group of annotators. To this end, we evaluated an annotation study, where 26 untrained annotators marked the argumentation structure of small texts. While the overall agreement showed only moderate correlation (as one could expect from naive annotators in a text interpretation task) we could identify a subgroup of annotators reaching a reliable level of agreement and good F1 scores in comparison with gold data by different ranking and clustering approaches and investigated which category confusions were characteristic for the different subgroups.

Acknowledgments

We thank the anonymous reviewers for their helpful comments. The first author was supported by a grant from Cusanuswerk and the second author by Deutsche Forschungsgemeinschaft (SFB 632).

References

Ron Artstein and Massimo Poesio. 2008. Inter-coder agreement for computational linguistics. *Computational Linguistics*, 34(4):555–596, December.

Vikas Bhardwaj, Rebecca J. Passonneau, Ansaf Salleb-Aouissi, and Nancy Ide. 2010. Anveshan: a framework for analysis of multiple annotators' labeling behavior. In *Proceedings of the Fourth Linguistic Annotation Workshop*, LAW IV '10, pages 47–55, Stroudsburg, PA, USA. Association for Computational Linguistics.

Lynn Carlson, Daniel Marcu, and Mary Ellen Okurowski. 2003. Building a discourse-tagged corpus in the framework of Rhetorical Structure Theory. In Jan van Kuppevelt and Ronnie Smith, editors, *Current Directions in Discourse and Dialogue*. Kluwer, Dordrecht.

Silvie Cinková, Martin Holub, and Vincent Kríž. 2012. Managing uncertainty in semantic tagging. In *Proceedings of the 13th Conference of the European Chapter of the Association for Computational Linguistics*, EACL '12, pages 840–850, Stroudsburg, PA, USA. Association for Computational Linguistics.

Joseph L. Fleiss. 1971. Measuring nominal scale agreement among many raters. *Psychological Bulletin*, 76(5):378–382.

James B. Freeman. 1991. *Dialectics and the Macrostructure of Argument*. Foris, Berlin.

James B. Freeman. 2011. *Argument Structure: Representation and Theory*. Argumentation Library (18). Springer.

Jeroen Geertzen and Harry Bunt. 2006. Measuring annotator agreement in a complex hierarchical dialogue act annotation scheme. In *Proceedings of the 7th SIGdial Workshop on Discourse and Dialogue*, SigDIAL '06, pages 126–133, Stroudsburg, PA, USA. Association for Computational Linguistics.

Klaus Krippendorff. 1980. *Content Analysis: An Introduction to its Methodology*. Sage Publications, Beverly Hills, CA.

J Richard Landis and Gary G. Koch. 1977. The measurement of observer agreement for categorial data. *Biometrics*, 33(1):159–174, March.

William Mann and Sandra Thompson. 1988. Rhetorical structure theory: Towards a functional theory of text organization. *TEXT*, 8:243–281.

Andreas Peldszus and Manfred Stede. to appear. From argument diagrams to automatic argument mining: A survey. *International Journal of Cognitive Informatics and Natural Intelligence*, 7(1).

William A. Scott. 1955. Reliability of content analysis: The case of nominal scale coding. *Public Opinion Quarterly*, 19(3):321–325.

Rion Snow, Brendan O'Connor, Daniel Jurafsky, and Andrew Y. Ng. 2008. Cheap and fast—but is it good? Evaluating non-expert annotations for natural language tasks. In *Proceedings of the Conference on Empirical Methods in Natural Language Processing*, EMNLP '08, pages 254–263, Stroudsburg, PA, USA. Association for Computational Linguistics.

Simone Teufel. 2010. *The Structure of Scientific Articles: Applications to Citation Indexing and Summarization*. CSLI Studies in Computational Linguistics. CSLI Publications.

Stephen Toulmin. 1958. *The Uses of Argument*. Cambridge University Press, Cambridge.

Leveraging Crowdsourcing for Paraphrase Recognition

Martin Tschirsich
Department of Computer Science,
TU Darmstadt
m.tschirsich@gmx.de

Gerold Hintz
Department of Computer Science,
TU Darmstadt
gerold.hintz@googlemail.com

Abstract

Crowdsourcing, while ideally reducing both costs and the need for domain experts, is no all-purpose tool. We review how paraphrase recognition has benefited from crowdsourcing in the past and identify two problems in paraphrase acquisition and semantic similarity evaluation that can be solved by employing a smart crowdsourcing strategy. First, we employ the CrowdFlower platform to conduct an experiment on sub-sentential paraphrase acquisition with early exclusion of low-accuracy crowdworkers. Second, we compare two human intelligence task designs for evaluating phrase pairs on a semantic similarity scale. While the first experiment confirms our strategy successful at tackling the problem of missing gold in paraphrase generation, the results of the second experiment suggest that, for both semantic similarity evaluation on a continuous and a binary scale, querying crowdworkers for a semantic similarity value on a multi-grade scale yields better results than directly asking for a binary classification.

1 Introduction

Paraphrase recognition[1] means to analyse whether two texts are paraphrastic, i.e. “a pair of units of text deemed to be interchangeable” (Dras, 1999). It has numerous applications in information retrieval, information extraction, machine translation and plagiarism detection. For instance, an internet search provider could recognize *"murder of the 35th U.S. president"* and *"assassination of John F. Kennedy"* to be paraphrases of each other and thus yield the same result. Paraphrase recognition is an open research problem and, even though having progressed immensely in recent years (Socher et al., 2011), state of the art performance is still below the human reference.

In this research, we analyse how *crowdsourcing* can contribute to paraphrase recognition. Crowdsourcing is the process of outsourcing a vast number of small, simple tasks, so called *HITs*[2], to a distributed group of unskilled workers, so called *crowdworkers*[3]. Reviewing current literature on the topic, we identify two problems in paraphrase acquisition and semantic similarity evaluation that can be solved by employing a smart crowdsourcing strategy. First, we propose how to reduce paraphrase generation costs by early exclusion of low-accuracy crowdworkers. Second, we compare two HIT designs for evaluating phrase pairs on a continuous semantic similarity scale. In order to evaluate our crowdsourcing strategies, we conduct our own experiments via the CrowdFlower[4] platform.

The rest of the paper is structured as follows. Section 2 first gives an overview of related work and lines out current approaches. We then proceed to our own experiments on crowdsourcing paraphrase acquisition (3.3) and semantic similarity evaluation (3.4). Section 4 and 5 conclude the study and propose future work in the area of paraphrase recognition and crowdsourcing.

2 Literature Review

Many research fields rely on paraphrase recognition and contribute to it, as there are many related concepts. These include inference rule discovery for question-answering and information retrieval (Lin and Pantel, 2001), idiom or multiword ex-

[1] the terms *paraphrase detection* and *paraphrase identification* might be used instead

[2] *Human Intelligence Tasks*

[3] often referred to as *turkers*

[4] http://crowdflower.com

pression acquisition (Fellbaum et al., 2006) and identification (Boukobza and Rappoport, 2009), machine translation evaluation (Snover et al., 2009), textual entailment recognition, and many more.

2.1 Paraphrase Definition

The notion of a paraphrase is closely related to the concepts of *semantic similarity* and *word ontology* and an exact definition is not trivial. Often, complex annotation guidelines and aggregated expert agreements decide whether phrases are to be considered paraphrastic or not (Dolan and Brockett, 2005). Formal definitions based e.g. on a domain theory and derivable facts (Burrows et al., 2013) have little practical relevance in paraphrase recognition. In terms of the semantic similarity relations *'equals'*, *'restates'*, *'generalizes'*, *'specifies'* and *'intersects'* (Marsi and Krahmer, 2010), *'paraphrase'* is equated with *'restates'*.

It is important to note that in the context of crowdsourcing, we, as well as most authors, rely on the crowdworker's intuition of what a paraphrase is. Usually, only a limited list of examples of desired valid paraphrases is given to the crowdworker as a reference.

2.2 Paraphrase Recognition

According to Socher et al. (2011), paraphrase recognition "determines whether two phrases of arbitrary length and form capture the same meaning". Paraphrase recognition is mostly understood as a binary classification process, although recently, some authors proposed a continuous semantic similarity measure (Madnani et al., 2012).

Competing paraphrase recognition approaches are often compared by their performance on the Microsoft Research Paraphrase Corpus (MSRPC). Until 2011, simple features such as n-gram overlap, dependency tree overlap as well as dependency tree edit distance produced the best results in terms of accuracy and F-measure values. However, algorithms based solely on such features can not identify semantic equivalence of synonymous words or phrases. Therefore, some authors subsequently integrated Wordnet synonyms as well as other corpus-based semantic similarity measures. The work of Madnani et al. (2012) based on the TERP machine translation evaluation metric (Snover et al., 2009) using synonyms and subsentential paraphrases presents the current state of the art for paraphrase detection on the MSRPC

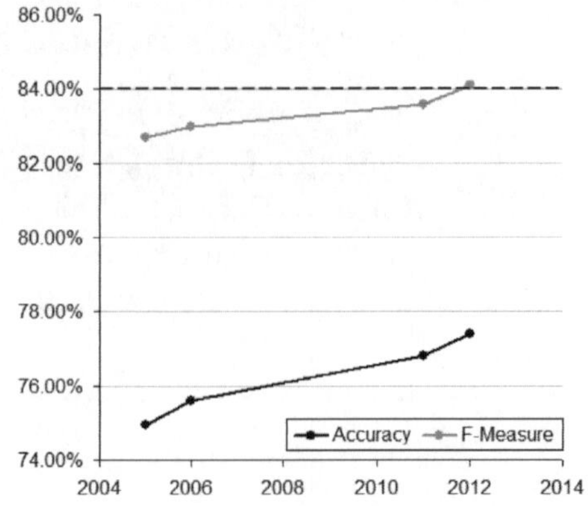

Figure 1: Highest ranking accuracy and F-measure over time for paraphrase recognition on the MSRPC with an inter-rater agreement amongst human annotators of 84%

with an accuracy of 77.4% and F-measure of 84.1%. The inter-rater agreement amongst human annotators of 84% on the MSRPC can be considered as an upper bound for the accuracy that could be obtained using automatic methods (Fernando and Stevenson, 2008).

As has become apparent, modern paraphrase recognition algorithms are evaulated on and incorporate semantic similarity measures trained on acquired paraphrases. Therefore, we subsequently give an overview over established paraphrase acquisition approaches.

2.3 Paraphrase Acquisition

Paraphrase acquisition[5] is the process of collecting or generating phrase-paraphrase pairs, often for a given set of phrases. All strategies require a subsequent verification of the acquired paraphrases, either done by experts or trusted crowdworkers.

2.3.1 Sentential Paraphrases

Most literature on paraphrase acquisition deals with sentential or sentence-level paraphrases. Bouamor et al. (2012) identify five strategies such as the translation based methods (Zhou et al., 2006) using parallel corpora or alignment of topic-clustered news articles (Dolan and Brockett, 2005).

Via Crowdsourcing In an outstanding approach, Chen and Dolan (2011) collected paraphrases by asking crowdworkers to describe short

[5] also referred to as *paraphrase generation*

videos. A more cost-effective multi-stage crowdsourcing framework was presented by Negri et al. (2012) with the goal to increase lexical divergence of the collected paraphrases.

2.3.2 Sub-Sentential Paraphrases

Incorporating sub-sentential paraphrases in machine translation metrics also used for paraphrase detection has proven effective (Madnani et al., 2012). A large corpus consisting of more than 15 million sub-sentential paraphrases was assembled by Bannard and Callison-Burch (2005) using a pivot-based paraphrase acquisition method.

Via Crowdsourcing Buzek et al. (2010) acquired paraphrases of sentence parts problematic for translation systems using AMAZON MECHANICAL TURK. Bouamor et al. (2012) collected sub-sentential paraphrases in the context of a web-based game.

2.3.3 Passage-level paraphrases

Passage-level paraphrase acquisition has been treated within the context of the evaluation lab on uncovering plagiarism, authorship, and social software misuse (PAN) (Potthast et al., 2010): Burrows et al. (2013) acquired passage-level paraphrases for the WEBIS-CPC-11 corpus via crowdsourcing.

2.4 Semantic Similarity Evaluation

Paraphrase verification can be said to be a manual semantic similarity evaluation done by experts or trusted crowdworkers, most often on a binary scale. However, Madnani et al. (2012) believe that "binary indicators of semantic equivalence are not ideal and a continuous value [...] indicating the degree to which two pairs are paraphrastic is more suitable for most approaches". They propose averaging a large number of binary crowdworker judgements or, alternatively, a smaller number of judgements on an ordinal scale as in the SEMEVAL-2012 Semantic Textual Similarity (STS) task (Agirre et al., 2012). A continuous semantic similarity score is also used to weigh the influence of sub-sentential paraphrases used by the TERP metric.

3 Our Experiments

3.1 The CrowdFlower Platform

CROWDFLOWER is a web service for HIT providers, abstracting from the actual platform on which these tasks are run. A web interface, incorporating a graphical editor as well as the CROWDFLOWER MARKUP LANGUAGE[6] (CML), can be used to model these tasks. CROWDFLOWER provides fine-grained controls over how these tasks are executed, for instance, by restricting crowdworkers to live in specific countries or by limiting the number of HITs a single worker is allowed to complete.

Furthermore, CROWDFLOWER provides a sophisticated system to verify the correctness of the collected data, aiming at early detection and exclusion of spammers and low-accuracy workers from the job: *gold items*. Gold items consist of a HIT, e.g. a pair of paraphrases *together with* one or more possible valid answers. Once gold items are present in the dataset, workers are prompted to answer these correctly before being eligible to work on the actual data. Additionally, during the run of a job, CROWDFLOWER uses hidden gold items to revise the trustworthiness of a human worker.

3.2 Human Intelligence Task Design

Apart from gold items, the actual HIT design has the biggest impact on the quality of the collected data. Correct instructions as well as good examples have a great influence on data quality. By using CML validation features, bad user input can be prevented from being collected in the first place. Care must also be taken not to introduce an artificial bias by offering answer choices of different (time-)complexity. Within our experiments, we followed common human interface design principles such as colour coding answer options.

3.3 Crowdsourcing Sub-Sentential Paraphrase Acquisition

The biggest challenge in paraphrase acquisition via crowdsourcing is the low and varying accuracy of the crowdworkers: "The challenge [...] is automatic quality assurance; without such means the crowdsourcing paradigm is not effective, and without crowdsourcing the creation of test corpora is unacceptably expensive for realistic order of magnitudes" (Burrows et al., 2013).

We propose a new crowdsourcing strategy that allows for early detection of low-accuracy workers during the generation stage. This prevents these unwanted crowdworkers from completing

[6]CML documentation: `http://crowdflower.com/docs/cml`

HITs that would almost certainly not be validated later on. We focus on the acquisition of sub-sentential paraphrases for a given set of phrases, where pivot-based paraphrase acquisition methods might not be applicable. Transferring our observations to other types of paraphrases should be unproblematic.

3.3.1 Phrase-Paraphrase Generation

For this simple baseline strategy, we asked the crowdworker to generate a short phrase along with its paraphrase (p_1, p_2) while providing a small set of examples.

3.3.2 Two-Staged Paraphrase Generation

This is the traditional crowdsourcing strategy. In a first *generation* stage, we presented the crowdworker with a phrase p_1 and asked for its paraphrase p_2. In a second *validation* stage, two or three workers were asked to verify each generated phrase-paraphrase pair until an unambiguous agreement was reached. As the answers in the validation stage are binary, gold-items were added to improve the accuracy of the collected validation judgements. Negri et al. (2012) showed that after such a validation stage, expert raters agreed in 92% of the cases with the aggregated crowdworker judgements. However, the generation stage is without gold and we cannot exclude low accuracy workers early enough not to cost money. We used the regular expression verifier provided by CROWDFLOWER to ensure that the generated paraphrases contain at least one word and are not equal to the given phrases. Other than this however, the worker could enter any text.

Input Phrases As input data, we required meaningful chunks. For this, any *constituent* of a sentence can be used. A small number of examples suggested that verb phrases have a high potential of yielding interesting paraphrases, as they often have to be replaced as an isolated unit *("get a flu" → "catch a cold")*. Therefore, we extracted verb phrases of two to five words from a source corpus. For this, we used the POS tagger of NLTK[7] (A Maxent Treebank POS tagger trained on Penn Treebank) and a simple chunking grammar parser.

Offering a Choice of Input Phrase A crowdworker might not always be able to come up with a paraphrase for a given phrase. If a worker receives one chunk at a time, he has to deal with it no matter how unfeasible it is for paraphrasing. One solution to this problem would be to offer a back-out option, in which a worker could declare a unit as *unsolvable* and possibly explain why. This however could easily be exploited by human workers, resulting in many unsolved items. An alternative solution is to offer workers a choice of the input phrase they want to paraphrase. We designed a HIT with a set of three different input phrases of which they have to pick one to paraphrase. If one of these options is repeatedly declined by multiple workers, we can declare it as *bad*, without having a worker pass on a unit. However, it turned out that less than 1% proved *unsolvable* and we therefore deemed such measures unnecessary.

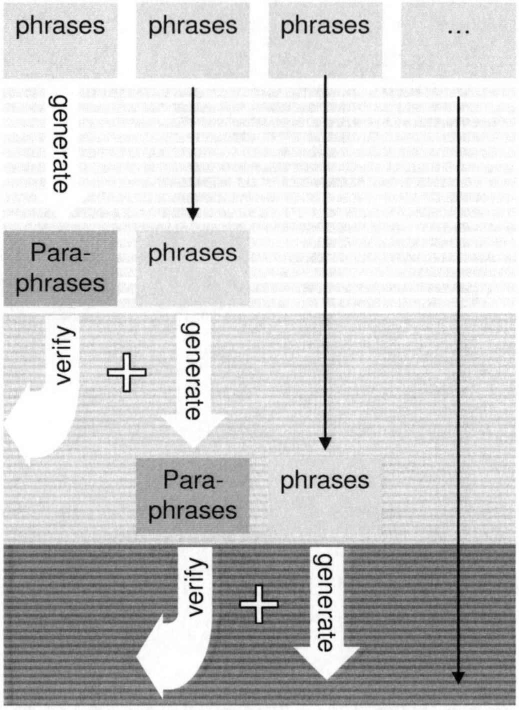

Figure 2: Illustration of the multi-stage paraphrase generation process

3.3.3 Multi-Staged Paraphrase Generation

We improved the traditional two-stage approach by combining the generation and verification steps. The task to decide whether a given pair is a paraphrase is combined with the task of paraphrasing a chunk. The matching of verification and generation items is arbitrary. Figure 2 illustrates this approach. After an initial *generate* stage, subsequent stages are combined *verify/generate* jobs. The benefit of this approach is that verification of

[7]NATURAL LANGUAGE TOOLKIT (NLTK): http://nltk.org/

phrase pairs allows the usage of gold-items. We can now assess the trustworthiness of a crowdworker through gold, and we indirectly *infer* their ability to *paraphrase* from their ability to decide if two items are paraphrases. The aim of this process is to reduce the number of incorrect paraphrases being generated in the first place, and thus improve the efficiency of the CROWDFLOWER task.

In contrast to Negri et al. (2012), we did not restrict access to the later stages of this job to high-accuracy workers of previous stages since our intermingled gold-items are expected to filter out low-accuracy workers in each succeeding stage. Therefore, we expect to attract contributors from a bigger pool of possibly cheaper workers.

3.3.4 Evaluation

While only 28% of the collected pairs were validated after the traditional two-staged paraphrase generation, this percentage increased to 80% in the second validation stage belonging to the multi-stage approach. Although the experiment was conducted on a small number of phrases, this result is a good indicator that our hypothesis is correct and that a combined generation and verification stage with gold items can reduce costs by early exclusion of low-accuracy workers.

Lexical divergence measures (TERP) decline, but this is expected after filtering out possibly highly divergent non-paraphrastic pairs. While our generation costs per non-validated sub-sentential paraphrase were around the same as those reported by Buzek et al. (2010) (0.024$), the costs for validated sub-sentential paraphrases were not much higher (0.06$). Negri et al. (2012) report costs of 0.27$ per sentential paraphrase, however these costs are difficult to compare, also because we did not optimize for lexical divergence.

3.4 Crowdsourcing Semantic Similarity Evaluation

We conducted an experiment in order to determine how to optimally query continuous semantic similarity scores from crowdworkers. The two different examined methods originally proposed by Madnani et al. (2012) are binary and senary[8] semantic similarity evaluation. Paraphrases were taken from the MSRPC. Optimality was defined by two different criteria: First, we analysed how well the (binary) paraphrase classification by domain experts on the MSRPC can be reproduced from our collected judgements. Second, we analysed how consistent our collected judgements are. Since we could not find any reference corpus for semantic similarity evaluation apart from the SEMEVAL-2012 STS gold that was also acquired via crowdsourcing, we resorted to training a machine learning classifier and comparing relative performance on the collected training data.

3.4.1 Binary Semantic Similarity

Crowdworkers were asked to give a binary classification of two phrases as either paraphrastic or non-paraphrastic. Binary decisions were enforced since no third option was given. Three examples of valid paraphrases were given.

A minimum of 20 judgements each for 207 phrase pairs were collected for 0.01$ per judgement. In order to deter spammers and the most inaccurate workers, we converted 14% of the phrase pairs - those with high expected inter-rater agreement - to gold items. Low inter-rater agreement on a phrase pair hinted at medium, high inter-rater agreement hinted at low or high semantic similarity. Trusted crowdworkers had an average gold accuracy of 93% on these gold items.

3.4.2 Senary Semantic Similarity

Crowdworkers were asked to give a senary classification of two phrases. The six classes were equivalent to those defined by the SemEval STS task. A short annotation guide consisting of one example per category was provided.

A minimum of 8 judgements each for 667 phrase pairs were collected for 0.02$ per judgement. In order to deter spammers and the most inaccurate workers, we converted 13% of the phrase pairs to gold items. Gold items were accepted as long as the judgement lay within an acceptable range of an expected similarity value.

3.4.3 Input Aggregation and Normalization

The following two phrase pairs demonstrate the relationship between binary inter-rater agreement and aggregated senary semantic similarity:

1. „It appears that many employers accused of workplace discrimination will be considered guilty until they can prove themselves innocent," he said.

   Employers accused of workplace discrimination now are considered guilty until they can prove themselves innocent.

[8] senary: $\{0, 1, 2, 3, 4, 5\}$ as opposed to binary $\{0, 1\}$.

Name	Stage	# Phrase Pairs	TERP
Phrase-Paraphrase Generation	Generation	100	0.89
Two-Staged Generation	1. Generation	378	0.85
	2. Validation	109 (28%)	0.68
Multi-Staged Generation	3. Generation + Gold	165	0.72
	4. Validation	134 (**80%**)	0.64

Table 1: Two-staged (1. - 2.) and multi-staged (1. - 4.) paraphrase generation results. Percentage values denote the amount of validated pairs relative to the preceding generation stage.

2. Sixteen days later, as superheated air from the shuttle's reentry rushed into the damaged wing, "there was no possibility for crew survival," the board said.

   Sixteen days later, as superheated air from the shuttle's re-entry rushed into the damaged wing, there was no possibility for crew survival, the board said.'

The binary inter-rater agreement for the first phrase pair is low (10%), so crowdworkers seemingly could not decide between paraphrastic and non-paraphrastic. Accordingly, the averaged senary semantic similarity takes an intermediate value (3.4).

The binary inter-rater agreement for the second phrase pair however is very high (100%), so we expect the sentences to be either clearly non-paraphrastic or clearly paraphrastic. A maximal averaged senary semantic similarity value of 5.0 confirms this intuition.

In order to make aggregated binary and senary input comparable, we scaled the binary judgements so that the sampled average and variance matched that of the senary judgements. These semantic similarities are strongly correlated (3a) with Pearson coefficient of 0.81 and seem to respect the MSRPC expert annotator rating with positive correlation between aggregated semantic similarity and binary MSRPC classification.

With reference to Denkowski and Lavie (2010), we used the following aggregation and normalization techniques:

Straight Average The aggregated semantic similarity is the average of all collected judgements. This is our baseline approach.

Judge Normalization To compensate for different evaluation standards, each judge's judgements are scaled so that its sample average and variance matches that of the average (3b).

Judge Outlier Removal Removing judges whose inter-rater agreement with the average is less than 0.5; motivated by Agirre et al. (2012): "Given the high quality of the annotations among the turkers, we could alternatively use the correlation between the turkers itself to detect poor quality annotators".

Weighted Voting Each judge's judgements are weighted by its inter-rater agreement with the average.

We also wanted to know whether limiting the amount of possible HITs or judgements per crowdworker could increase the quality of the collected judgements. However, while high-throughput crowdworkers showed lower variance in their agreement compared to crowdworkers with a small number of completed HITs, correlation between the number of completed HITs and agreement was very weak (3c) with Pearson coefficient of 0.01.

3.4.4 Machine Learning Evaluation

We trained the UKP machine learning classifier originally developed for the Semantic Textual Similarity (STS) task at SemEval-2012 (Bär et al., 2012) on the averaged binary and senary judgements for 207 identical phrase pairs. Since we were not interested in the performance of the machine learning classifier but in the quality of the collected data, we measured the relative performance of the learned model on the training data. The number of training examples remained constant. This was repeated multiple times while varying the number of judgements used in the aggregation of the semantic similarity values. We observed that with increasing number of judgements, the correlation coefficient converges seemingly against an upper bound (binary: 0.68 for 20 judgements, senary: 0.741 for 8 judgements). The

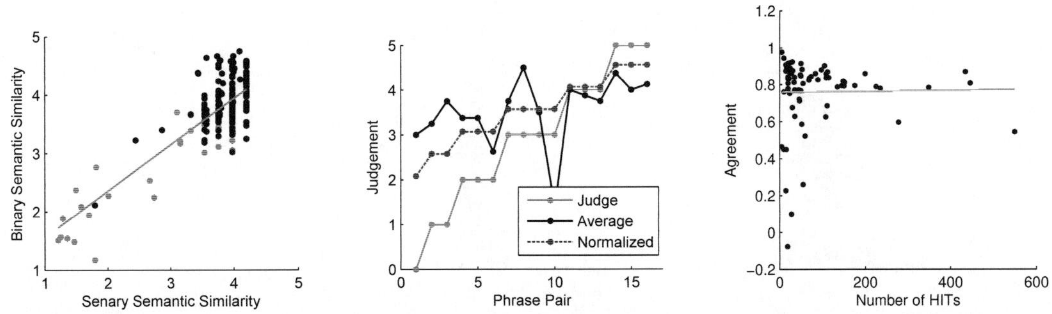

(a) Correlation between aggregated senary and binary semantic similarity (black = paraphrases according to MSRPC)

(b) Judge normalization

(c) The activity of a crowdworker does not correlate with agreement to the average

Figure 3: Input aggregation and normalization

machine learning classifier performs best when trained on semantic similarity data collected on a senary scale (4). Even if we only take the first three senary judgements per phrase pair into account, it is still superior to 20 binary judgements although the total amount of information queried from the crowdworkers is much smaller.

In a second step, we compared the performance while employing different input normalization techniques on the whole set of 667 phrase pairs with senary judgements. While all techniques increased the trained classifier's performance, weighted voting performed best (2).

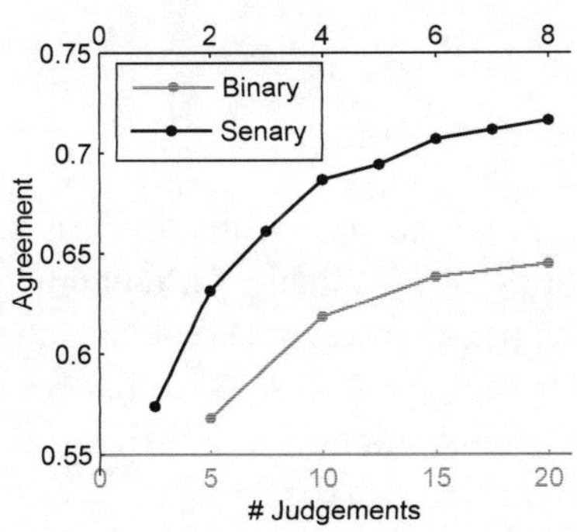

Figure 4: Machine learning results (agreement = correlation with training data)

3.4.5 MSRPC Evaluation

In addition to the machine learning evaluation, we compared our results to the binary semantic similarity classification given by the MSRPC expert annotators. In order to do so, we had to find an optimal threshold in $[0, 5]$ splitting our semantic similarity range in two, dividing paraphrastic from non-paraphrastic phrase pairs. Again, this was repeated multiple times while varying the number of judgements used in the aggregation of the semantic similarity values. However, this time we did not simply take the first n judgements each, but averaged over different possible sampling combinations. We measured percentage agreement with MSRPC and the optimal threshold for non-weighted and weighted judgements, since weighted voting performed best in the machine learning evaluation (5c).

Technique	Correlation
Straight Average	0.716
Judge Outlier Removal	0.719
Judge Normalization	0.721
Weighted Voting	**0.722**

Table 2: Input normalization results

Surprisingly, even for binary paraphrastic-non-paraphrastic classification, querying a senary semantic similarity value from crowdworkers yields better results than directly asking for a binary classification. However, the results also indicate that in both cases, input normalization plays an important role and agreement could be improved by more sophisticated or combined input normalization techniques as well as by collecting additional judgements.

A semantic similarity of 3.1 (senary) (5a) respectively 3.5 (binary) (5b) corresponds optimally to the paraphrastic-non-paraphrastic threshold chosen by the MSRPC expert annotators. Costs per evaluated phrase pair were at 0.16$

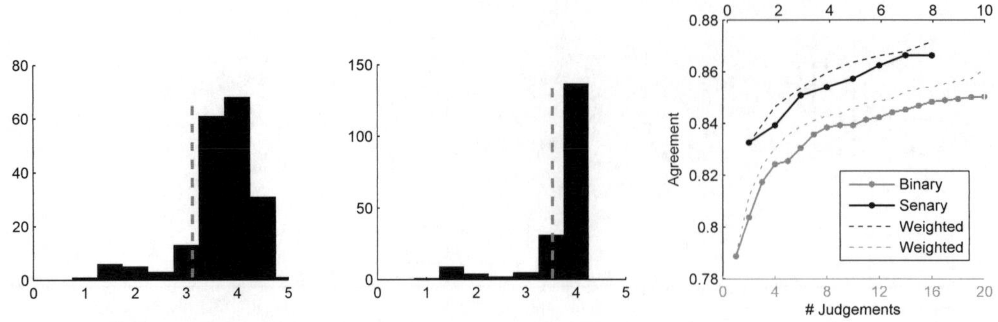

(a) Optimal threshold for senary semantic similarity is 3.1

(b) Optimal threshold for binary semantic similarity is 3.5

(c) Average agreement with MSRPC with optimal threshold per number of judgements

Figure 5: MSRPC evaluation (agreement = percentual agreement with aggregated judgements)

(senary, 8 judgements) compared to 0.20$ for the SEMEVAL-2012 STS task (senary, 5 judgements). However, we did not examine how this and possible further cost reduction impacts agreement with MSRPC.

4 Conclusion

We presented a multi-stage crowdsourcing approach tackling the problem of missing gold in paraphrase generation. This approach has shown to work very well for sub-sentential paraphrase generation and we strongly believe that it will work equally well for sentential paraphrase generation, resulting in significantly reduced costs of paraphrase corpus creation.

We also compared different crowdsourcing approaches towards semantic similarity evaluation, showing that for both semantic similarity evaluation on a continuous and a binary scale, querying an ordinal senary semantic similarity value from crowdworkers yields better results than directly asking for a binary classification.

5 Future Work

Our goal to sub-sentential paraphrase generation was cost minimization by early removal of low-accuracy workers. Apart from being grammatical and paraphrastic, we did not enforce other quality constraints on the collected data. A combination of our multi-stage approach with that of Negri et al. (2012) could prove successful if both cost and quality, i.e. lexical divergence between phrase-paraphrase pairs, are to be optimized.

There is also room for reducing the cost of the verification stage e.g. by automatically filtering out paraphrases before presenting them to a crowdworker using e.g. lexical divergence, length of the sentence or other measures as it was done by Burrows et al. (2013).

Another interesting question we could not answer due to budget constraints is: Can the crowd replace the expert and if yes, how many crowdworkers are needed to do so reliably? One possible way to answer this question for paraphrase evaluation would be to collect semantic similarity judgements for the whole MSRPC and to see how many judgements per phrase are needed to reliably reproduce the MSRPC classification results with an inter-rater agreement of 84% for the whole corpus.

Acknowledgements

The authors would like to thank Chris Biemann of TU Darmstadt, Germany, for pointing us to the problem of paraphrase evaluation via crowdsourcing leading to this research as well as his supervision and helpful suggestions. We also thank our reviewers for their feedback.

References

Eneko Agirre, Daniel Cer, Mona Diab, and Aitor Gonzalez-Agirre. 2012. Semeval-2012 task 6: A pilot on semantic textual similarity. In **SEM 2012: The First Joint Conference on Lexical and Computational Semantics – Volume 1: Proceedings of the main conference and the shared task, and Volume 2: Proceedings of the Sixth International Workshop on Semantic Evaluation (SemEval 2012)*, pages 385–393, Montréal, Canada, 7-8 June. Association for Computational Linguistics.

Colin Bannard and Chris Callison-Burch. 2005. Paraphrasing with bilingual parallel corpora. In *Proceedings of the 43rd Annual Meeting on Association for Computational Linguistics*, ACL '05, pages 597–604, Stroudsburg, PA, USA. Association for Computational Linguistics.

Daniel Bär, Chris Biemann, Iryna Gurevych, and Torsten Zesch. 2012. Ukp: Computing semantic textual similarity by combining multiple content similarity measures. In *Proceedings of the 6th International Workshop on Semantic Evaluation, held in conjunction with the 1st Joint Conference on Lexical and Computational Semantics*, pages 435–440, Montreal, Canada, Jun.

Houda Bouamor, Aurélien Max, Gabriel Illouz, and Anne Vilnat. 2012. A contrastive review of paraphrase acquisition techniques. In *Proceedings of the Eight International Conference on Language Resources and Evaluation (LREC'12)*, Istanbul, Turkey, may.

Ram Boukobza and Ari Rappoport. 2009. Multi-word expression identification using sentence surface features. In *Proceedings of the 2009 Conference on Empirical Methods in Natural Language Processing*, pages 468–477, Singapore, August. Association for Computational Linguistics.

Steven Burrows, Martin Potthast, and Benno Stein. 2013. Paraphrase Acquisition via Crowdsourcing and Machine Learning. *Transactions on Intelligent Systems and Technology (ACM TIST) (to appear)*.

Olivia Buzek, Philip Resnik, and Benjamin B. Bederson. 2010. Error driven paraphrase annotation using mechanical turk. In *Proceedings of the NAACL HLT 2010 Workshop on Creating Speech and Language Data with Amazon's Mechanical Turk*, CSLDAMT '10, pages 217–221, Stroudsburg, PA, USA. Association for Computational Linguistics.

David L. Chen and William B. Dolan. 2011. Collecting highly parallel data for paraphrase evaluation. In *Proceedings of the 49th Annual Meeting of the Association for Computational Linguistics*, pages 190–200, Portland, Oregon, USA, June.

Michael Denkowski and Alon Lavie. 2010. Exploring normalization techniques for human judgments of machine translation adequacy collected using amazon mechanical turk. In *Proceedings of the NAACL HLT 2010 Workshop on Creating Speech and Language Data with Amazon's Mechanical Turk*, CSLDAMT '10, pages 57–61, Stroudsburg, PA, USA. Association for Computational Linguistics.

William B. Dolan and Chris Brockett. 2005. Automatically constructing a corpus of sentential paraphrases. In *Third International Workshop on Paraphrasing (IWP2005)*. Asia Federation of Natural Language Processing.

Mark Dras. 1999. *Tree Adjoining Grammar and the Reluctant Paraphrasing of Text.* Ph.D. thesis, Macquarie University.

Christiane Fellbaum, Alexander Geyken, Axel Herold, Fabian Koerner, and Gerald Neumann. 2006. Corpus-based Studies of German Idioms and Light Verbs. *International Journal of Lexicography*, 19(4):349–360, December.

Samuel Fernando and Mark Stevenson. 2008. A semantic similarity approach to paraphrase detection. In *Proceedings of the 11th Annual Research Colloquium of the UK Special Interest Group for Computational Linguistics*.

Dekang Lin and Patrick Pantel. 2001. Discovery of inference rules for question-answering. *Nat. Lang. Eng.*, 7(4):343–360, December.

Nitin Madnani, Joel Tetreault, and Martin Chodorow. 2012. Re-examining machine translation metrics for paraphrase identification. In *Proceedings of the 2012 Conference of the North American Chapter of the Association for Computational Linguistics: Human Language Technologies*, NAACL HLT '12, pages 182–190, Stroudsburg, PA, USA. Association for Computational Linguistics.

Erwin Marsi and Emiel Krahmer. 2010. Automatic analysis of semantic similarity in comparable text through syntactic tree matching. In *Proceedings of the 23rd International Conference on Computational Linguistics (Coling 2010)*, pages 752–760, Beijing, China, August. Coling 2010 Organizing Committee.

Matteo Negri, Yashar Mehdad, Alessandro Marchetti, Danilo Giampiccolo, and Luisa Bentivogli. 2012. Chinese whispers: Cooperative paraphrase acquisition. In *Proceedings of the Eight International Conference on Language Resources and Evaluation (LREC'12)*, Istanbul, Turkey, may.

Martin Potthast, Alberto Barrón-Cedeño, Andreas Eiselt, Benno Stein, and Paolo Rosso. 2010. Overview of the 2nd international competition on plagiarism detection. *Notebook Papers of CLEF*, 10.

Matthew G Snover, Nitin Madnani, Bonnie Dorr, and Richard Schwartz. 2009. Ter-plus: Paraphrase, semantic, and alignment enhancements to translation edit rate. *Machine Translation*, 23(2):117–127.

Richard Socher, Eric H. Huang, Jeffrey Pennington, Andrew Y. Ng, and Christopher D. Manning. 2011. Dynamic Pooling and Unfolding Recursive Autoencoders for Paraphrase Detection. In *Advances in Neural Information Processing Systems 24*.

Liang Zhou, Chin-Yew Lin, and Eduard Hovy. 2006. Re-evaluating machine translation results with paraphrase support. In *Proceedings of the 2006 Conference on Empirical Methods in Natural Language Processing*, EMNLP '06, pages 77–84, Stroudsburg, PA, USA. Association for Computational Linguistics.

Investigation of annotator's behaviour using eye-tracking data

Ryu Iida **Koh Mitsuda** **Takenobu Tokunaga**
Department of Computer Science, Tokyo Institute of Technology
{ryu-i,mitsudak,take}@cl.cs.titech.ac.jp

Abstract

This paper presents an analysis of an annotator's behaviour during her/his annotation process for eliciting useful information for natural language processing (NLP) tasks. Text annotation is essential for machine learning-based NLP where annotated texts are used for both training and evaluating supervised systems. Since an annotator's behaviour during annotation can be seen as reflecting her/his cognitive process during her/his attempt to understand the text for annotation, analysing the process of text annotation has potential to reveal useful information for NLP tasks, in particular semantic and discourse processing that require deeper language understanding. We conducted an experiment for collecting annotator actions and eye gaze during the annotation of predicate-argument relations in Japanese texts. Our analysis of the collected data suggests that obtained insight into human annotation behaviour is useful for exploring effective linguistic features in machine learning-based approaches.

1 Introduction

Text annotation is essential for machine learning (ML)-based natural language processing (NLP) where annotated texts are used for both training and evaluating supervised systems. This annotation-then-learning approach has been broadly applied to various NLP tasks, ranging from shallow processing tasks, such as POS tagging and NP chunking, to tasks requiring deeper linguistic information, such as coreference resolution and discourse relation classification, and has been largely successful for shallow NLP tasks in particular. The key to this success is how useful information can be effectively introduced into ML algorithms as features. With shallow NLP tasks, surface information like words and their POS within a window of a certain size can be easily employed as useful features. In contrast, in semantic and discourse processing, such as coreference resolution and discourse structure analysis, it is not trivial to employ as features deeper linguistic knowledge and human linguistic intuition that are indispensable for these tasks. In order to improve system performance, past attempts have integrated deeper linguistic knowledge through manually constructed linguistic resources such as WordNet (Miller, 1995) and linguistic theories such as Centering Theory (Grosz et al., 1995). They partially succeed in improving performance, but there is still room for further improvement (duVerle and Prendinger, 2009; Ng, 2010; Lin et al., 2010; Pradhan et al., 2012).

Unlike past attempts relying on heuristic feature engineering, we take a cognitive science approach to improving system performance. In stead of employing existing resources and theories, we look into human behaviour during annotation and elicit useful information for NLP tasks requiring deeper linguistic knowledge. Particularly we focus on annotator eye gaze during annotation. Because of recent developments in eye-tracking technology, eye gaze data has been widely used in various research fields, including psycholinguistics and problem solving (Duchowski, 2002). There have been a number of studies on the relations between eye gaze and language comprehension/production (Griffin and Bock, 2000; Richardson et al., 2007). Compared to the studies on language and eye gaze, the role of gaze in general problem solving settings has been less studied (Bednarik and Tukiainen, 2008; Rosengrant, 2010; Tomanek et al., 2010). Since our current interest, text annotation, can be considered a problem solving as well as language comprehension task, we refer to them when defining our problem setting. Through analysis of annotators' eye-tracking data, we aim at finding useful information which can be employed as features in ML algorithms.

This paper is organised as follows. Section 2 presents the details of the experiment for collecting annotator behavioural data during annotation as well as details on the collected data. Section 3 explains the structure of the annotation process for a single annotation instance. Section 4 provides a detailed analysis of human annotation processes, suggesting usages of those results in NLP. Section 5 reviews the related work and Section 6 concludes and discusses future research directions.

2 Data collection

2.1 Materials and procedure

We conducted an experiment for collecting annotator actions and eye gaze during the annotation of predicate-argument relations in Japanese texts. Given a text in which candidates of predicates and arguments were marked as *segments* (i.e. text spans) in an annotation tool, the annotators were instructed to add links between correct predicate-argument pairs by using the keyboard and mouse. We distinguished three types of links based on the case marker of arguments, i.e. *ga* (nominative), *o* (accusative) and *ni* (dative). For elliptical arguments of a predicate, which are quite common in Japanese texts, their antecedents were linked to the predicate. Since the candidate predicates and arguments were marked based on the automatic output of a parser, some candidates might not have their counterparts.

We employed a multi-purpose annotation tool *Slate* (Kaplan et al., 2012), which enables annotators to establish a link between a predicate segment and its argument segment with simple mouse and keyboard operations. Figure 1 shows a screenshot of the interface provided by *Slate*. Segments for candidate predicates are denoted by light blue rectangles, and segments for candidate arguments are enclosed with red lines. The colour of links corresponds to the type of relations; red, blue and green denote nominative, accusative and dative respectively.

In order to collect every annotator operation, we modified *Slate* so that it could record several important annotation events with their time stamp. The recorded events are summarised in Table 1.

Event label	Description
create_link_start	creating a link starts
create_link_end	creating a link ends
select_link	a link is selected
delete_link	a link is deleted
select_segment	a segment is selected
select_tag	a relation type is selected
annotation_start	annotating a text starts
annotation_end	annotating a text ends

Table 1: Recorded annotation events

Figure 2: Snapshot of annotation using Tobii T60

Annotator gaze was captured by the Tobii T60 eye tracker at intervals of 1/60 second. The Tobii's display size was $1,280 \times 1,024$ pixels and the distance between the display and the annotator's eye was maintained at about 50 cm. The five-point calibration was run before starting annotation. In order to minimise the head movement, we used a chin rest as shown in Figure 2.

We recruited three annotators who had experiences in annotating predicate-argument relations. Each annotator was assigned 43 texts for annotation, which were the same across all annotators. These 43 texts were selected from a Japanese balanced corpus, BCCWJ (Maekawa et al., 2010). To eliminate unneeded complexities for capturing eye gaze, texts were truncated to about 1,000 characters so that they fit into the text area of the annotation tool and did not require any scrolling. It took about 20–30 minutes for annotating each text. The annotators were allowed to take a break whenever she/he finished annotating a text. Before restarting annotation, the five-point calibration was run every time. The annotators accomplished all assigned texts after several sessions for three or more days in total.

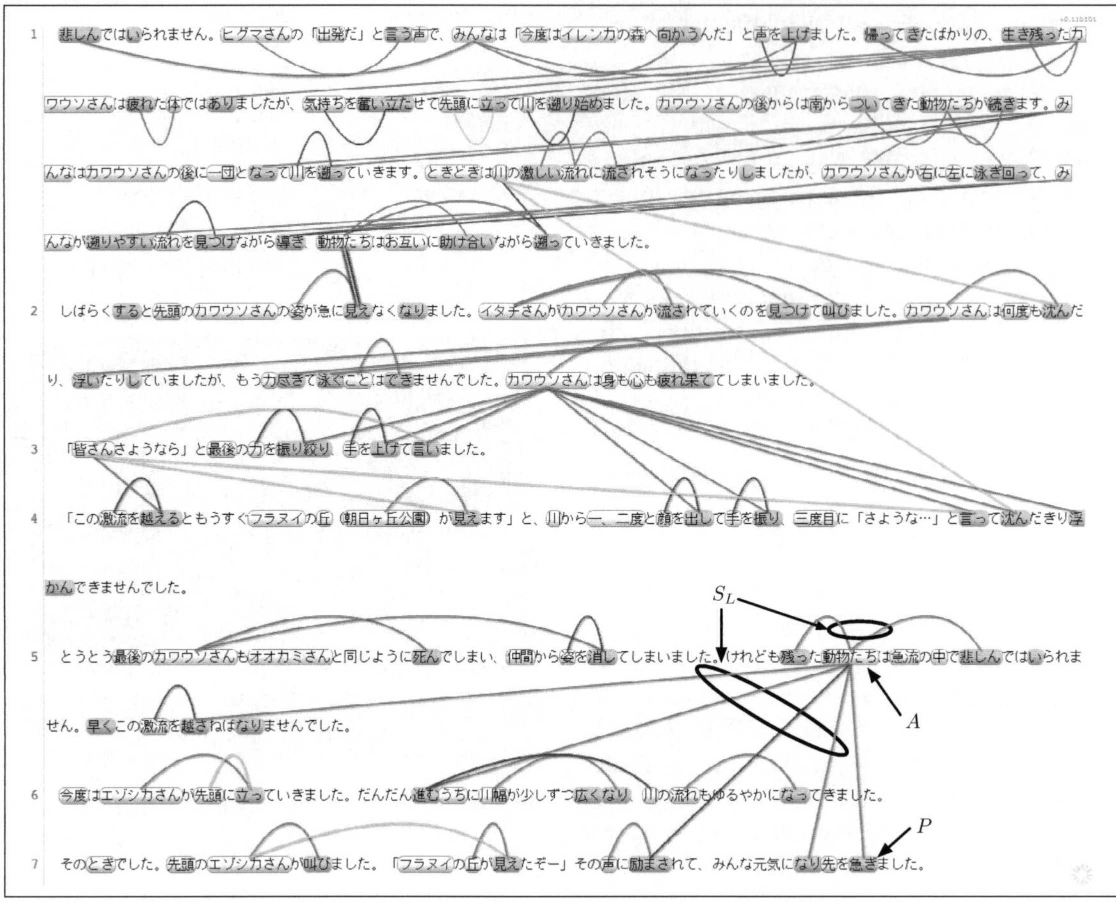

Figure 1: Screenshot of the annotation tool *Slate*

2.2 Results

The number of annotated links between predicates and arguments by three annotators A_0, A_1 and A_2 were 3,353 (A_0), 3,764 (A_1) and 3,462 (A_2) respectively. There were several cases where the annotator added multiple links with the same link type to a predicate, e.g. in case of conjunctive arguments; we exclude these instances for simplicity in the analysis below. The number of the remaining links were 3,054 (A_0), 3,251 (A_1) and 2,996 (A_2) respectively. In addition, because our analyses explained in Section 4 require an annotator's fixation on both a predicate and its argument, the number of these instances were reduced to 1,776 (A_0), 1,430 (A_1) and 1,795 (A_2) respectively. The details of the instances for our analysis are summarised in Table 2. These annotation instances were used for the analysis in the rest of this paper.

case	A_0	A_1	A_2	total
ga (nominative)	1,170	904	1,105	3,179
o (accusative)	383	298	421	1,102
ni (dative)	223	228	269	720
total	1,776	1,430	1,795	5,001

Table 2: Results of annotation by each annotator

3 Anatomy of human annotation

From a qualitative analysis of the annotator's behaviour in the collected data, we found the annotation process for predicate-argument relations could be decomposed into the following three stages.

1. An annotator reads a given text and understands its contents.

2. Having fixed a target predicate, she/he searches for its argument in the set of preceding candidate arguments considering a type of relations with the predicate.

3. Once she/he finds a probable argument in a text, she/he looks around its context in order to confirm the relation. The confirmation is finalised by creating a link between the predicate and its argument.

The strategy of searching for arguments after fixing a predicate would reflect the linguistic knowledge that a predicate subcategorises its arguments. In addition, since Japanese is a head-final language, a predicate basically follows its arguments. Therefore searching for each argument within a sentence can begin at the same position, i.e. the predicate, toward the beginning of the sentence, when the predicate-first search strategy is adopted.

The idea of dividing a cognitive process into different functional stages is common in cognitive science. For instance, Just and Carpenter (1985) divided a problem solving process into three stages: *searching*, *comparison* and *confirmation*. In their task, given a picture of two cubes with a letter on each surface, a participant is instructed to judge whether they can be the same or not. Since one of the cubes is relatively rotated in a certain direction and amount, the participant needs to mentally rotate the cubes for matching. Russo and Leclerc (1994) divided a visual decision making process into three stages: *orientation*, *evaluation* and *verification*. In their experiment, participants were asked to choose one of several daily food products that were visually presented. The boundaries of the above three stages were identified based on the participants' eye gaze and their verbal protocols. Malcolm and Henderson (2009) applied the idea to a visual search process, dividing it into *initiation*, *scanning* and *verification*. Gidlöf et al. (2013) discussed the difference between a decision making process and a visual search process in terms of the process division. Although the above studies deal with the different cognitive processes, it is common that the first stage is for capturing an overview of a problem, the second is for searching for a tentative solution, and the third is for verifying their solution.

Our division of the annotation process conforms with this idea. Particularly, our task is similar to the decision making process as defined by Russo and Leclerc (1994). Unlike these past studies, however, the beginning of an orientation stage[1] is not clear in our case, since we collected the data in a natural annotation setting, i.e. a single annotation session for a text includes creation of multiple links. In other words, the first stage might correspond to multiple second and third stages. In addition, in past research on decision making, a single object is chosen, but our annotation task involves two objects to consider, i.e. a predicate and an argument.

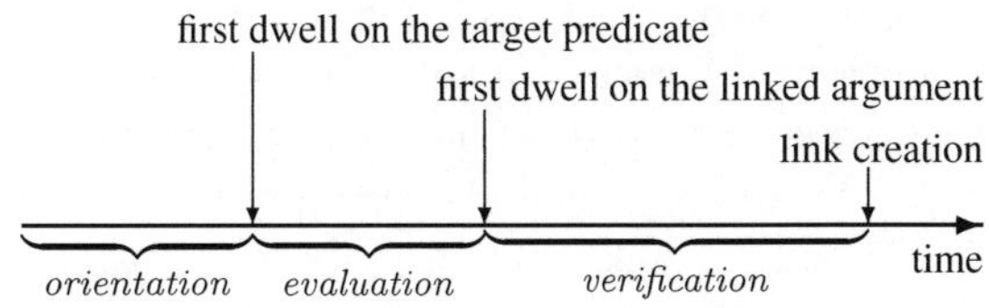

Figure 3: Division of an annotation process

Considering these differences and the proposals of previous studies (Russo and Leclerc, 1994; Gidlöf et al., 2013), we define the three stages as follows. As explained above, we can not identify the beginning of an orientation stage based on any decisive clue. We define the end of an orientation stage as the onset of the first dwell[2] on a predicate being considered. The succeeding evaluation stage starts at the onset of the first dwell on the predicate and ends at the onset of the first dwell on the argument that is eventually linked to the predicate. The third stage, a verification stage, starts at the onset of the first dwell on the linked argument and ends at the creation of the link between the predicate and argument. These definitions and the relations between the stages are illustrated in Figure 3.

The time points indicating the stage boundaries can be identified from the recorded eye gaze and tool operation data. First, gaze fixations were extracted by using the Dispersion-Threshold Identification (I-DT) algorithm (Salvucci and Goldberg, 2000). Based on a rationale that the eye movement velocity slows near fixations, the I-DT algorithm identifies fixations as clusters of consecutive gaze points within a particular dispersion. It has two parameters, the dispersion threshold that defines the maximum distance between gaze points belonging to the same cluster, and the duration threshold that constrains the minimum fixation duration. Considering the experimental configurations, i.e. (i) the display size and its resolution, (ii) the distance between the display and the annotator's eyes, and (iii) the eye-tracker resolution, we set the dispersion threshold to 16 pixels. Following Richardson et al. (2007), we set the duration threshold to 100 msec. Based on fixations, a dwell on a segment was defined as a series of fixations that consecutively stayed on the same segment where

[1] We follow the wording by Russo and Leclerc (1994).

[2] A dwell is a collection of one or several fixations within a certain area of interest, a segment in our case.

two consecutive fixations were not separated by more than 100 msec. We allowed a horizontal error margin of 16 pixels (one-character width) for both sides of a segment when identifying a dwell. Time points of link creation were determined by the "create_link_start" event in Table 1.

Among these three stages, the evaluation stage would be most informative for extracting useful features for ML algorithms, because an annotator identifies a probable argument for a predicate under consideration during this stage. Analysing annotator eye gaze during this stage could reveal useful information for predicate-argument analysis. It is, however, insufficient to regard only fixated arguments as being under the annotator's consideration during the evaluation stage. The annotator captures an overview of the current problem during the previous orientation stage, in which she/he could remember several candidate arguments in her/his short-term memory, then moves on to the evaluation stage. Therefore, all attended arguments are not necessarily observed through gaze dwells. As we explained earlier, we have no means to identify a rigid duration of an orientation stage, thus it is difficult to identify a precise set of candidate arguments under the annotator's consideration in the evaluation stage. For this purpose, we need a different experimental design so that every predicate-argument relation is annotated at a time in the same manner as the above decision making studies conducted. Another possibility is using an annotator's verbal protocols together with her/his eye gaze as done in Russo and Leclerc (1994).

On the other hand, in the verification stage a probable argument has been already determined and its validity confirmed by investigating its competitors. We would expect considered competitors are explicitly fixated during this stage. Since we have a rigid definition of the verification stage duration, it is possible to analyse the annotator's behaviour during this stage based on her/his eye gaze. For this reason, we concentrate on the analysis of the verification stage of annotation henceforth.

4 Analysis of the verification stage

Given the set of annotation instances, i.e. predicate, argument and case triplets, we categorise these instances based on the annotator's behaviour during the verification stage. We focus on two factors for categorising annotation instances: (i) the distance of a predicate and if its argument is either near or far, and (ii) whether annotator gaze dwelled on other arguments than the eventually linked argument before creating the link. We call the former factor *Near/Far* distinction, and the latter *Concentrated/Distracted* distinction.

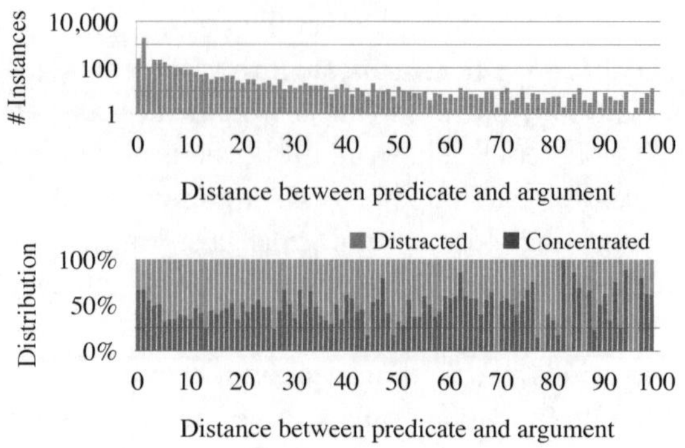

Figure 4: Distance of predicate and argument

To decide the *Near/Far* distinction, we investigated the distribution of distances of predicates and their argument. The result is shown in the upper graph of Figure 4, where the x-axis is the character-based distance and the y-axis shows the number of instances in each distance bin. Figure 4 demonstrates that the instances concentrate at the bin of distance 1. This reflects the frequently occurring instances where a one-character case maker follows an argument, and immediately precedes its predicate. The lower graph in Figure 4 shows the ratio of *Distracted* instances to *Concentrated* at each bin. The distribution indicates that there is no remarkable relation between the distance and *Concentrated/Distracted* distinction. The correlation coefficient between the distance and the number of *Concentrated* instances is -0.26. We can conclude that the distance of a predicate and its argument does not impact the *Concentrated/Distracted* distinction. Considering the above tendency, we set the distance threshold to 22, the average distance of all annotation instances; instances with a distance of less than 22 are considered *Near*.

These two factors make four combinations in total, i.e. *Near-Concentrated* (NC), *Near-Distracted* (ND), *Far-Concentrated* (FC) and *Far-Distracted* (FD). We analysed 5,001 instances shown in Table 2 to find three kinds of tendencies, which are described in the following sections.

case	*Near*	*Far*	total
ga (nominative)	2,201 (0.44)	978 (0.90)	3,179 (0.64)
o (accusative)	1,042 (0.34)	60 (0.05)	1,102 (0.22)
ni (dative)	662 (0.22)	58 (0.05)	720 (0.14)

Table 3: Distribution of cases over *Near/Far*

	NC	ND	FC	FD
ga	0.40	0.47	0.92	0.90
o, ni	0.60	0.53	0.08	0.10

Table 4: Distribution of arguments across four categories

4.1 Predicate-argument distance and argument case

We hypothesise that an annotator changes her/his behaviour with regard to the case of the argument. The argument case in Japanese is marked by a case marker which roughly corresponds to the argument's semantic role, such as Agent and Theme. We therefore analysed the relationship between the *Near/Far* distinction and argument case. The results are shown in Table 3. The table shows the distribution of argument cases, illustrating that *Near* instances are dispersed over three cases, while *Far* instances are concentrated in the *ga* (nominative) case. In other words, *ga*-arguments tend to appear far from their predicate. This tendency reflects the characteristic of Japanese where a nominative argument tends to be placed in the beginning of a sentence; furthermore, *ga*-arguments are often omitted to make ellipses. In our annotation guideline, a predicate with an elliptical argument should be linked to the referent of the ellipsis, which would be realised at a further distant position in the preceding context. In contrast, *o* (accusative) and *ni* (dative) arguments less frequently appeared as *Far* instances because they are rarely omitted due to their tighter relation with arguments. This observation suggests that each case requires an individual specific treatment in the model of predicate argument analysis; the model searches for *o* and *ni* arguments close to its predicate, while it considers all preceding candidates for a *ga* argument.

Table 4 shows the break down of the *Near/Far* columns with regards to the *Concentrated/Distracted* distinction, demonstrating that the *Concentrated/Distracted* distinction does not impact the distribution of the argument types.

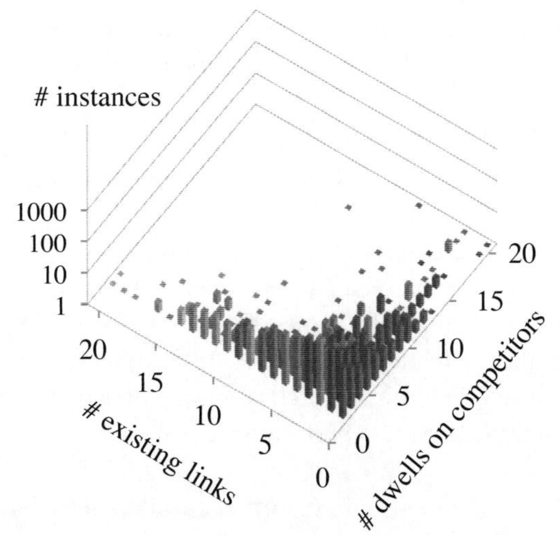

Figure 5: Relationship between the number of dwells on competitors and already-existing links

4.2 Effect of already-existing links

In the *Concentrated* instances, an annotator can verify if an argument is correct without inspecting its competitors. As illustrated in Figure 1, already annotated arguments are marked by explicit links to their predicate. These links make the arguments visually as well as cognitively salient in an annotator's short-term memory because they have been frequently annotated in the preceding annotation process. Thus, we expected that both types of saliency help to confirm the predicate-argument relation under consideration. For instance, when searching for an argument of predicate P in Figure 1, argument A that already has six links (S_L) is more salient than other competitors.

To verify this hypothesis, we examined the relation of the number of already-existing links and the number of dwells on competitors, which is shown in Figure 5. In this analysis, we used only *Far* instances because the *Near* arguments tended to have less already-existing links as they were under current interest. Figure 5 shows a three-dimensional declining slope that peaks around the intersection for instances with the fewest number of links and dwells on competitors. It reveals a mostly symmetrical relation between existing links and dwells on competitors for instances with a lower number of existing links, but that this symmetry brakes for instances with a higher number of existing links, visible by the conspicuous hole toward the left of the figure. This suggests that visual and cognitive saliency reduces annotators' cognitive load, and thus contributes to efficiently confirming the correct argument.

This result implies that the number of already-existing links of a candidate argument would reflect its saliency, thus more linked candidates should be preferred in the analysis of predicate-argument relations. Although we analysed the verification stage, the same effect could be expected in the evaluation stage as well. Introducing such information into ML algorithms may contribute to improving system performance.

4.3 Specificity of arguments and dispersal of eye gaze

Existing Japanese corpora annotated with predicate-argument relations (Iida et al., 2007; Kawahara et al., 2002) have had syntactic heads (nouns) of their projected NPs related their predicates. Since Japanese is a head-final language, a head noun is always placed in the last position of an NP. This scheme has the advantage that predicate-argument relations can be annotated without identifying the starting boundary of the argument NP under consideration. The scheme is also reflected in the structure of automatically constructed Japanese case frames, e.g. Sasano et al. (2009), which consist of triplets in the form of ⟨*Noun, Case, Verb*⟩. *Noun* is a head noun extracted from its projected NP in the original text. We followed this scheme in our annotation experiments.

However, a head noun of an argument does not always have enough information. A nominaliser which often appears in the head position in an NP does not have any semantic meaning by itself. For instance, in the NP "*benkyô suru koto* (to study/studying)", the head noun "*koto*" has no specific semantic meaning, corresponding to an English morpheme "to" or "-ing". In such cases, inspecting a whole NP including its modifiers is necessary to verify the validity of the NP for an argument in question. We looked at our data to see if annotators actually behaved like this.

For analysis, the annotation instances were distinguished if an argument had any modifier or not (column "w/o mod" and "w/ mod" in Table 5). The "w/ mod" instances are further divided into two classes: "within NP" and "out of NP", the former if all dwells remain "within" the region of the argument NP or the later if they go "out of" the region. Note that our annotation scheme creates a link between a predicate and the head of its argument as described earlier. Thus, a *Distracted* instance does not always mean an "out of NP" instance, since a distracted dwell might still remains on a segment within the NP region despite not being its head. Table 5 shows the distribution of the instances over this categorisation.

	w/o mod	w/ mod		total
		within NP	out of NP	
Concentrated	1,562	1190	–	2,752
Distracted	1,168	242	839	2,249

Table 5: Relation of argument modifiers and gaze dispersal

We found that the number of instances is almost the same between *Concentrated* and *Distracted*, i.e. (2752 : 2249 = 0.55 : 0.45). In this respect, both *Concentrated* and *Distracted* instances can be treated in the same way in the analysis of predicate-argument relations. A closer look at the break down of the "w/ mod" category, however, reveals that almost 22% of the *Distracted* arguments with any modifier attracted gaze dwells within the NP region. This fact suggests that we need to treat candidate arguments differently depending on if they have modifiers or not. In addition to argument head information, we could introduce information of modifiers into ML algorithms as features that characterise a candidate argument more precisely.

5 Related work

Recent developments in the eye-tracking technology enables various research fields to employ eye-gaze data (Duchowski, 2002).

Bednarik and Tukiainen (2008) analysed eye-tracking data collected while programmers debug a program. They defined areas of interest (AOI) based on the sections of the integrated development environment (IDE): the source code area, the visualised class relation area and the program output area. They compared the gaze transitions among these AOIs between expert and novice programmers to find different transition patterns between them. Since the granularity of their AOIs is coarse, it could be used for evaluating a programmer's expertise, but hardly explains why the expert transition pattern realises a good programming skill. In order to find useful information for language processing, we employed smaller AOIs at the character level.

Rosengrant (2010) proposed an analysis method named *gaze scribing* where eye-tracking data is combined with a subject's thought process derived by the think-aloud protocol (TAP) (Ericsson and Simon, 1984). As a case study, he analysed a process of solving electrical circuit problems on the computer display to find differences of problem solving strategy between novice and expert subjects. The AOIs are defined both at a macro level, i.e. the circuit, the work space for calculation, and a micro level, i.e. electrical components of the circuit. Rosengrant underlined the importance of applying gaze scribing to the solving process of other problems. Although information obtained from TAP is useful, it increases her/his cognitive load, and thus might interfere with her/his achieving the original goal.

Tomanek et al. (2010) utilised eye-tracking data to evaluate the degree of difficulty in annotating named entities. They are motivated by selecting appropriate training instances for active learning techniques. They conducted experiments in various settings by controlling characteristics of target named entities. Compared to their named entity annotation task, our annotation task, annotating predicate-argument relations, is more complex. In addition, our experimental setting is more natural, meaning that all possible relations in a text were annotated in a single session, while each session targeted a single named entity (NE) in a limited context in the setting of Tomanek et al. (2010). Finally, our fixation target is more precise, i.e. words, rather than a coarse area around the target NE.

We have also discussed evaluating annotation difficulty for predicate-argument relations by using the same data introduced in this paper (Tokunaga et al., 2013). Through manual analysis of the collected data, we suggested that an annotation time necessary for annotating a single predicate-argument relation was correlated with the agreement ratio among multiple human annotators.

6 Conclusion

This paper presented an analysis of an annotator's behaviour during her/his annotation process for eliciting useful information for NLP tasks. We first conducted an experiment for collecting three annotators' actions and eye gaze during their annotation of predicate-argument relations in Japanese texts. The collected data were analysed from three aspects: (i) the relationship of predicate-argument distances and argument's cases, (ii) the effect of already-existing links and (iii) specificity of arguments and dispersal of eye gaze. The analysis on these aspects suggested that obtained insight into human annotation behaviour could be useful for exploring effective linguistic features in ML-based approaches.

As future work, we need to further investigate the data from other aspects. There are advantages to manual analysis, such as done in this paper. Mining techniques for finding unknown but useful information may also be advantageous. Therefore, we are planning to employ mining techniques for finding useful gaze patterns for various NLP tasks.

In this paper, we suggested useful information that could be incorporated into ML algorithms as features. It is necessary to implement these features in a specific ML algorithm and evaluate their effectiveness empirically.

Our analysis was limited to the verification stage of annotation, in which a probable argument of a predicate was confirmed by comparing it with other competitors. The preceding evaluation stage should be also analysed, since it is the stage where annotators search for a correct argument of a predicate in question, thus probably includes useful information for computational models in identifying predicate-argument relations. For the analysis of the evaluation stage, a different design of experiments would be necessary, as already mentioned, employing single annotation at a time scheme as Tomanek et al. (2010) did, or using an annotator's verbal protocol together as Russo and Leclerc (1994), and Rosengrant (2010) did.

Last but not least, data collection and analysis in different annotation tasks are indispensable. It is our ultimate goal to establish a methodology for collecting an analysing annotators' behavioural data during annotation in order to elicit effective features for ML-based NLP.

References

Roman Bednarik and Markku Tukiainen. 2008. Temporal eye-tracking data: Evolution of debugging strategies with multiple representations. In *Proceedings of the 2008 symposium on Eye tracking research & applications (ETRA '08)*, pages 99–102.

Andrew T. Duchowski. 2002. A breadth-first survey of eye-tracking applications. *Behavior Research Meth-*

ods, Instruments, and Computers, 34(4):455–470.

David duVerle and Helmut Prendinger. 2009. A novel discourse parser based on support vector machine classification. In *Proceedings of the Joint Conference of the 47th Annual Meeting of the ACL and the 4th International Joint Conference on Natural Language Processing of the AFNLP*, pages 665–673.

K. Anders Ericsson and Herbert A. Simon. 1984. *Protocol Analysis – Verbal Reports as Data –*. The MIT Press.

Kerstin Gidlöf, Annika Wallin, Richard Dewhurst, and Kenneth Holmqvist. 2013. Using eye tracking to trace a cognitive process: Gaze behaviour during decision making in a natural environment. *Journal of Eye Movement Research*, 6(1):1–14.

Zenzi M. Griffin and Kathryn Bock. 2000. What the eyes say about speaking. *Psychological Science*, 11(4):274–279.

Barbara J. Grosz, Aravind K. Joshi, and Scott Weinstein. 1995. Centering: A framework for modeling the local coherence of discourse. *Computational Linguistics*, 21(2):203–225.

Ryu Iida, Mamoru Komachi, Kentaro Inui, and Yuji Matsumoto. 2007. Annotating a Japanese text corpus with predicate-argument and coreference relations. In *Proceeding of the ACL Workshop 'Linguistic Annotation Workshop'*, pages 132–139.

Marcel Adam Just and Patricia A. Carpenter. 1985. Cognitive coordinate systems: Accounts of mental rotation and individual differences in spatial ability. *Psychological Review*, 92(2):137–172.

Dain Kaplan, Ryu Iida, Kikuko Nishina, and Takenobu Tokunaga. 2012. Slate – a tool for creating and maintaining annotated corpora. *Journal for Language Technology and Computational Linguistics*, 26(2):89–101.

Daisuke Kawahara, Sadao Kurohashi, and Kôiti Hasida. 2002. Construction of a Japanese relevance-tagged corpus (in Japanese). In *Proceedings of the 8th Annual Meeting of the Association for Natural Language Processing*, pages 495–498.

Ziheng Lin, Hwee Tou Ng, and Min-Yen Kan. 2010. A PDTB-styled end-to-end discourse parser. Technical Report TRB8/10, School of Computing, National University of Singapore.

Kikuo Maekawa, Makoto Yamazaki, Takehiko Maruyama, Masaya Yamaguchi, Hideki Ogura, Wakako Kashino, Toshinobu Ogiso, Hanae Koiso, and Yasuharu Den. 2010. Design, compilation, and preliminary analyses of balanced corpus of contemporary written Japanese. In *Proceedings of the Eigth International Conference on Language Resources and Evaluation (LREC 2010)*, pages 1483–1486.

George L. Malcolm and John M. Henderson. 2009. The effects of target template specificity on visual search in real-world scenes: Evidence from eye movements. *Journal of Vision*, 9(11):8:1–13.

George A. Miller. 1995. WordNet: A lexical database for English. *Communications of the ACM*, 38:39–41.

Vincent Ng. 2010. Supervised noun phrase coreference research: The first fifteen years. In *Proceedings of the 48th Annual Meeting of the Association for Computational Linguistics (ACL 2010)*, pages 1396–1411.

Sameer Pradhan, Alessandro Moschitti, Nianwen Xue, Olga Uryupina, and Yuchen Zhang. 2012. CoNLL-2012 shared task: Modeling multilingual unrestricted coreference in OntoNotes. In *Joint Conference on EMNLP and CoNLL – Shared Task*, pages 1–40.

Daniel C. Richardson, Rick Dale, and Michael J. Spivey. 2007. Eye movements in language and cognition: A brief introduction. In Monica Gonzalez-Marquez, Irene Mittelberg, Seana Coulson, and Michael J. Spivey, editors, *Methods in Cognitive Linguistics*, pages 323–344. John Benjamins.

David Rosengrant. 2010. Gaze scribing in physics problem solving. In *Proceedings of the 2010 symposium on Eye tracking research & applications (ETRA '10)*, pages 45–48.

J. Edward Russo and France Leclerc. 1994. An eye-fixation analysis of choice processes for consumer nondurables. *Journal of Consumer Research*, 21(2):274–290.

Dario D. Salvucci and Joseph H. Goldberg. 2000. Identifying fixations and saccades in eye-tracking protocols. In *Proceedings of the 2000 symposium on Eye tracking research & applications (ETRA '00)*, pages 71–78.

Ryohei Sasano, Daisuke Kawahara, and Sadao Kurohashi. 2009. The effect of corpus size on case frame acquisition for discourse analysis. In *Proceedings of Human Language Technologies: The 2009 Annual Conference of the North American Chapter of the Association for Computational Linguistics (NAACL-HLT 2009)*, pages 521–529.

Takenobu Tokunaga, Ryu Iida, and Koh Mitsuda. 2013. Annotation for annotation - toward eliciting implicit linguistic knowledge through annotation -. In *Proceedings of the 9th Joint ISO - ACL SIGSEM Workshop on Interoperable Semantic Annotation (ISA-9)*, pages 79–83.

Katrin Tomanek, Udo Hahn, Steffen Lohmann, and Jürgen Ziegler. 2010. A cognitive cost model of annotations based on eye-tracking data. In *Proceedings of the 48th Annual Meeting of the Association for Computational Linguistics (ACL 2010)*, pages 1158–1167.

Enunciative and modal variations in newswire texts in French: From guideline to automatic annotation

Marine Damiani
MoDyCo, UMR 7114, Université Paris Ouest
marinedamiani@gmail.com

Delphine Battistelli
STIH, EA 4509, Université Paris Sorbonne
delphine.battistelli@paris-sorbonne.fr

Abstract

In this paper we present the development of a corpus of French newswire texts annotated with enunciative and modal commitment information. The annotation scheme we propose is based on the detection of predicative cues - referring to an enunciative and/or modal variation - and their scope at a sentence level. We describe how we have improved our annotation guideline by using the evaluation (in terms of precision, recall and F-Measure) of a first round of annotation produced by two expert annotators and by our automatic annotation system.

1 Introduction

This paper concerns the design of a reference corpus that can be used to evaluate an automatic annotation system of enunciative and modal commitment in newswire texts in French. This complex linguistic phenomenon refers to the fact that a situation can be presented as certain, or only possible/probable, by an enunciator who can be the author of the text but who can also be another enunciator (explicitly named or not) from whom the author reports some content that he has heard, read, imagined, etc. Different kinds of linguistic cues are involved. In addition to the need to identify and semantically classify these cues, one has to deal with the question of their scope. This question is even more complex as many cues can be present together in a sentence, thus complexifying the interpretation of the interaction of different scopes (see Example 1.).

1. M. Arabi **a exprimé**^{cue1} [**le souhait**^{cue2} [d'aider la Syrie à surmonter cette phase]$_{scope2}$]$_{scope1}$] // [Mr. Arabi **expressed**^{cue1} [**a desire**^{cue2} [to help Syria overcome this phase.]$_{scope2}$]$_{scope1}$

Another major difficulty concerns the fact that evidential and modal characteristics are very similar (see for example a noun like *desire*). Our work addresses the question of annotating these cues and their semantic scope. Unlike most other approaches, we have chosen not to treat these two kinds of characteristics separately, since both are implicated in what is called enunciative commitment. We will focus here on our practice for the development of a reference corpus.

After a brief presentation of the theoretical background (section 2), we describe which kinds of linguistic cues are considered and what kind of semantic scopes are then encountered (section 3). Our annotation procedure aims to delimit textual segments that are semantically impacted by the presence of enunciative and modal cues. In this light, we will focus only on what we will describe below as *predicative cues*. Then we will explain how we have improved our annotation guideline by using the evaluation of a first round of annotation produced for the same task by two expert annotators and by our automatic annotation system (section 4).

2 The phenomenon of enunciative and modal commitment

In the field of linguistics, the notion of modality can be considered from an enunciative perspective (see Bally, 1932 Benveniste, 1966; Culioli, 1973). From this perspective, which is the one we adopt here, the construction of an utterance (or a text) has to take into account certain language operations such as predication or operations of commitment, the expression of which leaves a certain number of surface linguistic traces (or cues). The enunciator's degree of commitment to a predicative content is marked in the utterance by different kinds of linguistic traces. In other words, it can be said that in discourse the enunciator expresses different degrees of commitment to the truth of the propositional content.

Very close to this issue is thus the long tradition of tracking veridicality in discourse. Whether – in the most recent work - under the term of "factuality degrees of events" (Sauri and Pustejovsky, 2012), "event veridicality" (De Marneffe et al., 2012), "detection of uncertainty" (CoNLL-2010 Shared Task) or "attributions" and "private states" (Wilson and Wiebe, 2005), this notion refers to the relationship between language and reader commitment. In our approach, we do not attempt to access the notion of veridicality directly but rather via the organization of the text into different textual segments that have different enunciative and modal validation contexts. However, the cues we have to take into account to achieve this goal are mostly the same as in veridicality studies (modal verbs, reported speech verbs, verb of propositional attitude, hedging adverbs, and so on). Moreover, beyond traditional lexical cues, we also include in our work other cues such as morphological inflection (e.g. inflection of the French conditional tense), syntactic constructions such as subordinate clauses of condition or prepositional constructions (e.g. *according to X, at first sight…*). Furthermore, we have to take into account the fact that a lot of cues are embedded (as seen in Example 1 with *express* and a *desire*). If we want to interpret the enunciative and modal context of the textual segment *to help Syria overcome this phase*, we have to consider the fact that it is embedded in the segment *a desire to help Syria overcome this phase*. From this point of view our work is related to Kilicoglu (2012) who studied "embedding predications". Thus, we do not only consider the type of cues we find in text but also the way they interact. This methodology also enables us to consider cues that play a role at a discursive level. This question of discursive markers is discussed in (Charolles et al., 2005).

Although modality markers in French - in their close relationship with the markers of evidentiality - have been systematically described (see for example Gosselin, 2010; Le Querler, 2004) there is still no reference corpus proposing the annotation of enunciative and modal characteristics as a discursive delimitation task and this is the goal we seek to achieve. This problem of identifying modal cues related to a scope was initially researched in biomedical texts (Vincze et al., 2008). This applicative task made it possible to renew the linguistic approach to modality by adopting a more concrete approach, focusing first on the variety of cues that can be identified in a text. This perspective also enables the issue of the influence of textual genre on modality markers to be addressed.

In the next section, we present the way we propose to annotate this enunciative and modal commitment variation in text in terms of cues and scopes.

3 Annotating enunciative and modal commitment in term of cues and scope

Our annotation goal is to define in which enunciative and modal context a propositional content occurs. Observation of the cues in our corpus showed that there are two kinds of cues: predicative cues that lead to the opening of a new textual segment (this kind of cue has the syntactic property of governing another textual segment, e.g. cue1 in Example 2.) and what we called modifier cues (mainly adverbs and some adjectives, e.g. cue2 in Example 2.). The identification of predicative cues (and their scope) leads to split the text into different textual segments and then the identification of modifier cues influence the validation context of the textual segment previously identified.

2. Paul **veut**^{cue1} *sûrement*^{cue2} que [Mary vienne.]$_{scope}$ // Paul *certainly*^{cue1} **wants**^{cue2} [Mary to come]$_{scope}$.

The annotation task we present here consists in annotating these *predicative cues* (that lead to modify the level of enunciative and/or modal commitment of a textual segment) and their *scope*. The scope of a predicative cue corresponds to the textual segment impacted by the variation in the level of enunciative and/or modal commitment. Table 1 presents the four classes of predicative cues that we consider and for each of them gives some examples of the syntactic components that can be under the scope of the cue.

Cues	Scope
Verbs	**Direct and/or indirect object**
Reporting verb, modal verbs	*Paul* ***promet***^{cue} *qu'[il viendra]*$_{scope}$/ *Paul* ***promises***^{cue} *that [he will come]*$_{scope}$ *Paul* ***veut***^{cue}*[venir]*$_{scope}$/ *Paul* ***wants***^{cue} *[to come]*$_{scope}$
Nouns	**Noun complements, relative clause**
Predicative nouns	*C'est* ***son souhait***^{cue} *[d'être impliqué]*$_{scope}$ */ It is* ***his wish***^{cue} *[to be involved]* $_{scope}$
Morphological	**All the verb complements**
Future, conditional	*John* ***viendra***^{cue} *[plus tard]* $_{scope}$ / *John* ***will***^{cue} *[come later]* $_{scope}$
Syntactic	**Main clause**
Subordinate clauses of condition	*[Mary refuse de donner son approbation]* $_{scope}$ ***à moins que Paul accepte***^{cue} / *[Mary refuses to give her approval]* $_{scope}$ ***unless Paul accepts***^{cue}
Prepositional construction	***D'apres Paul***^{cue}, *[Mary va venir]* $_{scope}$ /***According to Paul***^{cue}, *[Mary is coming]* $_{scope}$

Table 1: Cues and associated scopes

As can be seen, depending on the type of predicative cue, the syntactic dependents we consider in the scope vary. This description of what we consider as a predicative cue and how to delimit the corresponding scope is reported in the first version of an annotation guideline. In order to refine our descriptions and measure their relevance on the corpus, the following section presents the inter-annotator agreement between two expert annotators and the first results of the automatic system for the same annotation task. This evaluation process should lead to the production of a more precise guideline that can reveal fine discursive shades and also stimulate reflection on how best to deal with syntactic and semantic information in the automatic annotation system.

4 Annotation and evaluation process

Our final goal is to develop an automatic annotation system that produces the annotation of enunciative and modal cues and their scope in newswire texts. In this light, we have to build a guideline of our annotation aim and a reference corpus that can be used to evaluate the system.

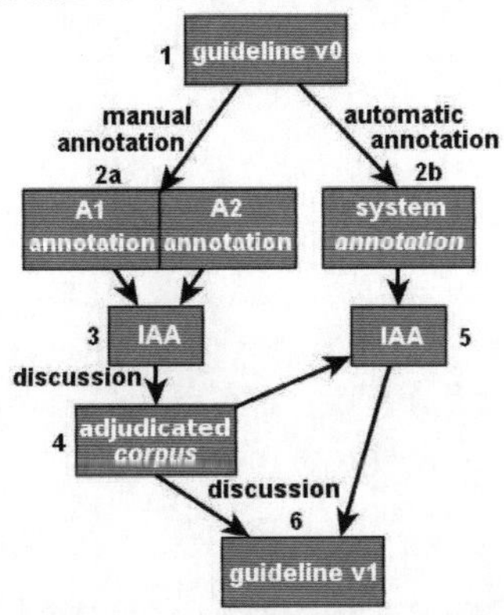

Figure 1.Workflow of guideline improvement

Figure 1 illustrates the steps in the workflow applied to improve our annotation guideline. For this purpose, two annotators (henceforth A1 and A2), both of them experts in linguistics, worked together to build a guideline and then the reference corpus[1]. First of all, the two annotators defined the annotation goals together (see step 1 in Figure 1). Then they annotated separately a corpus of 20 newswire texts (see step 2a in Figure 3). This corpus contains 256 predicative cues and their associated scopes (see Table 2).

# Sent	Total	Verbs	Nouns	Morpho	Syntactic
199	256	210	4	11	31

Table 2: Corpus statistics

[1] Our annotation process is based on Morante and Daelemans (2012).

This manual annotation task was carried out using the Glozz Annotation Tool (Widlöcher and Mathet, 2012) that relies on the URS (Unit-Relation-Schema) meta model and produces an xml output. The model permits to annotate textual units that can be embedded or not (in our case the predicative cues and their scope) and relations (for us, the opening relation links the predicative cue to its scope).

After this first annotation round, inter-annotator agreement was calculated (see table 3). The results show that the agreement between the two annotators is high for the cues but not very good for the scopes. By comparing the two sets of annotations in detail, we observed in our corpus that some textual segments can be either included or excluded from the scope depending on the annotator's interpretation. Example (3) shows the scope annotation proposed by annotator A1. As we can see, the textual segment *qui a débuté lundi* is included in the scope by this annotator but it is excluded in the annotation proposed by A2. In this particular case, we consider that both interpretations are acceptable since we cannot say for sure if this segment is presented from the viewpoint of the journalist or from the viewpoint of the source *un de ses avocats*. The same phenomenon is often observed with temporal adverbials that cannot be interpreted unambiguously as being a part of the scope or not. In these two kinds of cases the annotator needs to use the context and his linguistic background to decide. This raises the issue - already mentioned in Farkas et al. (2010) as to whether it is advisable to set a strict boundary for the scope.

We propose to address this issue by evaluating the scope annotation both strictly and more flexibly. In the flexible interpretation we distinguish the segments that are detected with an exact match boundary from those that are detected with different boundaries but that are still correct in the interpretation (as in example 3).

3. [Le procès devant un tribunal militaire d'un blogueur égyptien arrêté pour avoir critiqué l'armée, **qui a débuté lundi**, a été ajourné à dimanche]$_{scope}$, **a indiqué**^{cue} mardi un de ses avocats. // [The trial before a military court of an Egyptian blogger arrested for criticizing the army, **which began on Monday**, has been postponed to Sunday]$_{scope}$, **said**^{cue} one of his lawyers on Tuesday.

To measure the distinction of using strict or flexible boundaries for scope, we propose to distinguish the scope evaluation (for strict scope boundaries) from the weighted scope evaluation (for flexible boundaries).

Flexible boundaries are calculated with a 0.5 factor as follows:

$$Weighted\ Precision = \frac{SB + 0.5\ \times FB}{Ref}$$

$$Weighted\ Recall = \frac{SB + 0.5\ \times FB}{Rel}$$

- *SB (strict boundaries)*: the number of entities with a strict scope boundary
- *FB (flexible boundaries)*: the number of entities with a flexible scope boundary
- *Ref*: the number of reference entities (*i.e.* ideally identified)
- *Rel*: the number of relevant entities (*i.e.* correctly identified)

The distinction between the evaluation of scope and weighted scope revealed that in a significant number of cases (in this experimentation about 10 %) the two annotators disagreed in their annotation but that both interpretations were correct. This observation helped us to rethink our annotation goals and based on the result of inter-annotator agreement, the two annotators produced a common adjudicated version of their annotation[2] (step 4 in Figure 1). This new annotated version is the result of a reflection on the two annotators' disagreements and considers the context to delimit scope boundaries.

Adjudicated /System		**precision**	**recall**	**F1**
Cues		0.85	0.86	0.86
Scopes		0.79	0.72	0.76
Weighted Scopes		0.84	0.77	0.80
SB	**FB**	**Rel**	**Ref**	
185	22	256	234	

Table 3: IAA: the annotations of annotator A1 are evaluated against the annotations of annotator A2

Adjudicated /System		**precision**	**recall**	**F1**
Cues		0.83	0.85	0.84
Scopes		0.52	0.59	0.55
Weighted Scopes		0.67	0.76	0.71
SB	**FB**	**Rel**	**Ref**	
59	33	100	113	

Table 4: System evaluation: annotations from the system are evaluated against the adjudicated version

In a second step, we evaluated the first annotation version of our automatic system (step 2b in Figure 1) on a subset of the corpus against the annotation of the adjudicated version (see table 4). The subset corpus contains 100 cues and their associated scopes. Our automatic annotation system is based on the analysis dependency syntactic parser combined with scope detection rules (see Battistelli and Damiani, 2013). The results of this evaluation show that the detection of cues is good, as with the manual annotation, while the scope detection is not as good. This can be explained partly by the fact that the syntactic parser analysis produces some analysis errors (tagging or parsing errors, wrong syntactic attachment especially with coordinating conjunctions). Moreover, this evaluation shows that with an automatic system, distinguishing strict and flexible boundaries can highlight the results in another way. Indeed, if we look at the scope evaluation, the F-measure is not really satisfactory. If we take into account only this measure, it could be concluded that our system is not efficient. However, with the measure of weighted scope we see that while in many cases the scope did not match exactly with the reference corpus, it was not wrong either. This phenomenon of scope boundaries that are not easily decidable represents 10% of disagreement in the IAA (ie 22 cases) and 30% in the system evaluation (ie 33 cases), and has to be taken into account to improve the guideline and the annotation system. This first annotation experiment on a small corpus helped us to define new annotation goals that must be integrated both in the new version of the guideline (step 6 in Figure 1) and in the automatic annotation system.

5 Conclusion

In this paper, we have focused on a methodology to produce a reference corpus proposing the annotation of enunciative and modal commitment information as a discursive delimitation task. The annotation scheme we propose is based on the detection of predicative cues and their scopes. The results of the evaluation presented here show that the most challenging task is not to find the predicative cues but to delimit their scopes and beyond this delimitation question to define how to assess whether a scope is correct or not. Next step of our work is to launch a larger annotation campaign involving more human annotators and a bigger corpus. In this second step, our model will integrate modifier cues such as hedging adverbs that modify the semantic value of the textual segments that have been first delimited and introduce discursive cues that can impact more than a single sentence At last, in order to make our work available for the community our guideline and reference corpus will soon be available on *Chronolines* project website[3].

[2] This adjudicated version is available for consultation: http://vmoaxc.1fichier.com/predicative_cue_scope.zip

[3] http://www.chronolines.fr/

References

Bally, C. 1932. *Linguistique générale et Linguistique française*. Paris : Leroux, 2éd. (1944), Berne.

Battistelli, D. and Damiani, M. 2013. *Analyzing modal and enunciative discursive heterogeneity: how to combine semantic resources and a syntactic parser analysis*. In IWCS 2013 Workshop: WAMM, Potsdam.

Benveniste, E. 1966. *Problèmes de linguistique générale, 1*, Paris : Gallimard.

Charolles, M., Le Draoulec, A., Péry-Woodley, M. P. and Sarda, L. 2005. *Temporal and spatial dimensions of discourse organisation*. Journal of French Language Studies, 15(2), 115.

Culioli, A. 1973. *Sur quelques contradictions en linguistique. Communications*, 20(1), 83-91.

De Marneffe, M. C., Manning, C. D. and Potts, C. 2012. *Did it happen? The pragmatic complexity of veridicality assessment*. Computational Linguistics 38(2):301-333.

Farkas R., Vincze V., Móra G, Csirik J. and Szarvas G. 2010. *The CoNLL 2010 Shared Task: Learning to Detect Hedges and their Scope in Natural Language Text*. In Proceedings of the 2010 Conference on Computational Natural Language Learning.

Kilocoglu, H.H. 2012. *Embedding predications*. PhD Dissertation, Concordia University, Montreal.

Morante, R. and Daelemans, W. 2012. *ConanDoyle-neg: Annotation of negation in Conan Doyle stories*. In Proceedings of the Eighth International Conference on Language Resources and Evaluation (LREC).

Sauri, R. and Pustejovsky, J. 2012. *Are You Sure That This Happened? Assessing the Factuality Degree of Events in Text*. Computational Linguistics, 38(2):261-299.

Widlöcher A. and Mathet Y. 2012. *The Glozz Platform: A Corpus Annotation and Mining Tool*. In Proceedings of the 2012 ACM symposium on Document engineering, 171-180.

Wilson, T. and Wiebe, J. 2005. *Annotating Attributions and Private States*. In ACL 2005 Workshop: Frontiers in Corpus Annotation II: Pie in the Sky, 53-60.

Annotating the Interaction between Focus and Modality: the case of exclusive particles

Amália Mendes[*], Iris Hendrickx[*†], Agostinho Salgueiro[*], Luciana Ávila[*‡]

* Centro de Linguística da Universidade de Lisboa

† Center for Language Studies, Radboud University Nijmegen

‡ PosLin-Universidade Federal de Minas Gerais / Capes

{amalia.mendes,iris}@clul.ul.pt, agostinhomms@gmail.com, lucianabeatrizavila@gmail.com

Abstract

We discuss in this paper a proposal to integrate the annotation of contexts with focus-sensitive expressions (namely the Portuguese exclusive adverb *só* 'only') in a modality scheme. We describe some properties of contexts involving both exclusive particles and modal triggers and discuss how to integrate this with an existing annotation scheme implemented for European Portuguese. We present the results of the application of this annotation scheme to a sample of 100 sentences.

1 Introduction

Modality in language has been studied extensively (see Portner (2009) for an overview). In recent years, the study of modality has been associated with a trend in Information Extraction applications that aim to identify personal opinions in sentiment analysis and opinion mining (Wiebe et al., 2005), to identify events which are factual, probable or uncertain, as well as speculation and negation. This trend has lead to the development of several practical annotation schemes for modality (Sauri et al., 2006; Szarvas et al., 2008; Baker et al., 2010, Matsuyoshi et al., 2010).

Most of these annotation schemes focus on the annotation of modal elements like modal verbs or adverbs, but in the present study we go one step deeper and discuss the complex interaction between modality and focus in Portuguese. Our notion of modality focuses on the expression of the opinion and attitude of the speaker or the agent towards the proposition (Palmer, 1986). This attitude or opinion towards a state or event can assume diverse values. For example, the speaker (or subject) may consider something to be possible, probable or certain (epistemic modality), he might be obliged or allowed to do it (deontic modality), or he wants or fears it (volitive modality). Frequently, several modal expressions interact to compose the overall modal meaning of the sentence. Non modal elements can also directly influence the modality type and alter the meaning of the sentence. One such element, rather well studied, is the negation marker (Morante, 2010; Morante and Sporleder, 2012). In this paper however we discuss the element *focus*, taken as a means to "give prominence to meaning-bearing elements in an expression." (Krifka, 1995:240). The prominent constituent is called the *focus*, while the complement notion is called the *background*. We are especially concerned with the interaction between modality and a subtype of focus-sensitive expressions named exclusive particles (Beaver and Clark, 2008), and, for the purposes of this paper, we will center our discussion on the adverb *só* 'only'.

Our goal is to study closely how exclusive particles affect and alter the modal meaning of the sentence. By performing a systematic annotation of these interactions in examples drawn from a large corpus we better comprehend the role that these particles play and the different type of effects that exclusive particles can have.

Most annotation schemes for modality focus on English but resources are now being developed for other languages including Portuguese. Hendrickx et al. (2012b) have previously developed an annotation scheme for European Portuguese and applied it to a corpus of 2000 sentences. Ávila & Mello (2013) presented an annotation scheme for Brazilian Portuguese speech data, applied to information units. Here we look at the interaction between focus-sensitive adverbs and modality and discuss how to integrate these findings in the annotation scheme of Hendrickx et al. (2012a).

The structure of the paper is as follows. In section 2, we review related work in the field of modality, its annotation in texts, focus-sensitive expressions and the semantics of the exclusives. The discussion of the specific contexts with adverb *só* and a modality trigger is presented in section 3. We analyze the interaction between triggers and this specific adverb, focusing on the scope of the adverb and its influence over the modal value of the sentence. In section 4.1, we briefly summarize the annotation scheme for modality in Portuguese developed by Hendrickx et al. (2012a). We then demonstrate the implementation of our findings about adverb *só* in this annotation scheme in section 4.2. We discuss the results of the annotation of a sample of 100 sentences in 4.3 and conclude in section 5.

2 Related work

The literature on modality proposes different typologies. In linguistics, most modal systems are based on the contrast between epistemic and deontic modality. While the epistemic value is stable across typologies, the other values that are contrasted with it vary considerably. Some proposals distinguish between epistemic, participant-internal and participant-external modality (Van der Auwera and Plungian, 1998), or between epistemic, speaker-oriented modality and agent-oriented modality (Bybee et al., 1994). Other values generally considered are, for example, volition, related to the notions of will, hope and wish; evaluation, concerning the speaker's evaluation of facts and situations; and commissives, used by the speaker to express his commitment to make something happen (Palmer, 1986). Although most of the literature is centered on verbal expressions of modality (mostly semi-auxiliary verbs like *may*, *should*, *can*), studies on adverbs and modality have also been carried out for English (cf. Hoye, 1997).

In the literature on practical corpus annotation of modality, the attention focuses on the distinction between factual and non-factual information, as many NLP applications need to know what is presented as factual and certain and what is presented as non-factual or probable. Opposed to the theoretical typologies of modality, these schemes describe in detail which elements in the text are actually involved in the expression of modality and their roles. These are the subject of the modality (source) and the elements in its scope (target/scope/focus). Other schemes (Baker et al., 2010; Matsuyoshi et al., 2010; Sauri et al., 2006) also determine the relation between sentences in text, identifying temporal and conditional relations between events or the evaluation of the degree of relevance of some information within a text, rather than classifying modal values.

Rooth (1992) claims that the effects of focus on semantics can be said to be the introduction of a set of alternatives that contrasts with the ordinary semantic meaning of a sentence and that there are lexical items and construction specific-rules that refer directly to the notion of focus. The phenomenon of focalization is taken to be a grammatical feature that semantically conveys (i) newness/information update; (ii) answering the 'current question'; (iii) contrast; (iv) invocation of alternatives. In terms of semantic annotation, Matsuyoshi et al. (2010) propose an annotation scheme for representing extended modality of event mentions in Japanese. This scheme includes seven components among them the Focus, which represents the focus of negation, inference or interrogative.

There are no works on the annotation of focus and its relation with modality in Portuguese, in any of its variants. This is an attempt to put the two notions together and propose a scheme that describes the scope of exclusive particles and its impact on the meaning of the expressed modality.

3 Interaction between adverbs and modal value

In this section, we discuss in detail the possible interactions between the adverb *só* and modal expressions in the text. We extracted our examples from the online search platform of the Corpus de Referência do Português Contemporâneo (CRPC)[1], a highly diverse corpus of 312 million words covering a large variety of textual genres and Portuguese varieties (Généreux et al., 2012).

The adverb *só* is considered a focus-sensitive particle (Beaver & Clark, 2008; Aloni et al., 1999), defined as a word which semantics "involves essential reference to the information structure of the sentence containing it" (Aloni et al., 1999:1).

The meaning of *only* consists of asserting that no proposition from the set of relevant contrasts other than the one expressed is true (von Fintel, 1994). The standard views on exclusive particles consider that "the position of focal accent identi-

[1]http://alfclul.clul.ul.pt/CQPweb/crpcweb23/index.php

fies the constituent associated with *only*" (Dryer, 1994:2). Dryer (1994) and Schwarzschild (1997), on the other hand, assume that general principles of discourse could explain focus-sensitivity.

Exclusives can also downtone, by underlining the fact that this proposition "is not the strongest that in principle might have been the case", a function called Mirative (Beaver & Clark 2008: 250).

Constructions with exclusives involve a positive and a negative component: the positive is called the *prejacent* and, in sentence (1a), it is equivalent to 'he wants to go home'; the negative is called the *universal* and corresponds in (1a) to 'he does not want to do anything else'.

(1) a. Ele *só quer* ir para casa.
'He only wants to go home.'

b. As actividades de campanha eleitoral *só podem* ser financiadas por subvenção estatal.
'The activities of the election campaign can only be financed by public funding.'

We will discuss in the following subsections some properties of constructions with exclusives and modal triggers.

3.1 Scope of the exclusive particle

Exclusives give prominence to a constituent in the sentence, called the focus. In sentence (1a), *só* has scope over the modal trigger (*quer* 'wants') and its target (*ir para casa* 'to go home'). The scope of *só* can also be a smaller constituent inside the target. In (1b), *só* has scope over the by-phrase (*por subvenção estatal* 'by public funding'), and in (2), over a temporal adjunct. The adverb *só* could also occur immediately before the temporal adjunct keeping the same focus reading as in (2) (*só depois de construído o novo palácio da justiça*).

(2) O presidente respondeu que tal só deverá acontecer *depois de construído o novo palácio da justiça.*
'The president answered that it should/can only happen after the new courthouse is built.'

Two other possibilities are illustrated in (3) and (4): in (3), the focus is the subject *tu* 'you' and in (4) is the quantifier *7* 'seven':

(3) Só *tu* eras capaz de fazer juntar tanta gente.
'Only you could bring together so many people.'

(4) Claro que só podem estar *7* jogadores em campo. 'Obviously there can only be 7 players in the field.'

As these examples show, the exclusive particle is not necessarily contiguous to its focus. The analysis of a sample of the occurrences of the exclusive *só* with a modal trigger in the CRPC corpus shows that in most cases *só* has scope over a specific constituent, rather than over the full target of the modal trigger.

There can be ambiguity in the scope of the exclusive particle *só* in certain contexts. This is the case when the focus can be interpreted as the full target of the modal trigger or as a specific constituent inside the target. We illustrate such cases in sentence (5): this sentence can be interpreted as 'the only thing I'm capable of doing is to ask a metaphysical question' or 'the only question I'm capable of asking is a metaphysical one'.

(5) Só sou capaz de colocar ao Sr. Ministro uma questão metafísica.
'I'm only capable of asking a metaphysical question to Mr. Minister.'

However, in most contexts, there seems to be one preferential interpretation, in spite of the underlying ambiguity.

3.2 From possibility to necessity

In contexts where the verb *poder* has an epistemic reading, the exclusive can restrict the set of possibilities to the one presented in the sentence (x and only x), as illustrated in (6).

(6) Isto só pode ter sido um acidente.
'This can only have been an accident'

By restricting the set of possible situations to one, the adverb leads to an overall reading of the sentence as expressing epistemic necessity. Sentence (6) has indeed an equivalent modal meaning to (7) and to a double negative polarity (over the modal verb and over its target), as in (8).

(7) Isto tem de ter sido um acidente.
'It had to be an accident'

(8) Isto não pode não ter sido um acidente.
'It could not not have been an accident'

The scope of the focus-sensitive particle plays an important role on whether an epistemic trigger may be interpreted as having a necessity reading or not (cf. 3.2). Contrary to (6), the interpretation of (9) is one of epistemic possibility, although the particle *só* is present. In this case, the particle has scope over a specific constituent, the temporal adjunct, which establishes a condition over the modal trigger. But in (9b), without the temporal adjunct, the scope of *só* is coincident with the target of the modal trigger and the interpretation is one of necessity, as paraphrased by 'the member of parliament MFL has to be right'.

(9) a. Ora, a Sr.ª Deputada MFL *só pode* ter razão *quando acertar nalguma previsão*.
'Well, the member of parliament MFL may only be right when at least one of her forecasts turn out correct.'

b. Ora, a Sr.ª Deputada MFL *só pode* ter razão.
'Well, the member of parliament MFL can only be right.'

This restriction holds for stative targets, as in (9a), and also for eventive targets, although in this case the possibility or necessity reading is also determined by the tense of the verbal predicate. The necessity reading is only associated to eventive targets temporally located in the past, and is not available, for example, in the sentence *ele só pode ir ao cinema* 'he may only go to the cinema', where the target is temporally located in the future.

It seems that when the target of the modal trigger is a state or a past event, the exclusive particle leads to a necessity reading instead of a possibility reading, as long as the scope of *só* is the full target of the modal trigger and not a different constituent. However, we need to assess these factors against more corpus data.

If we compare (6) with a related declarative sentence (cf. *isto foi um acidente* 'it was an accident'), we see that the declarative has an assertive value over the situation it denotes, while (6) establishes a set of possibilities and strongly asserts a single one, in what is considered by Moreira (2005) as a case of overmodalization.

The verb *dever* 'have to' can occur in contexts similar to (6), as exemplified in (10). However, the sentence with *dever* expresses the most probable event and does not entail an epistemic necessity reading, contrary to (6) with verb *poder*.

(10) Isso só deve ter sido um acidente.
'This was probably only an accident'

In (10), the sentence merely states that this is probably what happened. The fact that the necessity reading does not arise from (10), contrary to (6), follows from the differences that exist between the possibility and the probability reading. The possibility reading in (6) denotes one particular event out of a set of possible ones and (6) singles out one possibility as the only valid one, affecting the truth-value of the set of alternatives considered. Sentence (10) denotes that this particular event is more probable to be true than other alternatives. So, in this sentence the exclusive strengthens the value of this probability but does not establish it as a single one. It is consequently a scalar use of the exclusive, in the sense that there is an ordering of propositions from weaker to stronger.

3.3 Contexts where *só* is required

Contrary to sentences (6), where the adverb *só* can be present or not (with effects on the interpretation), in sentences like (11), with the same modal verb, the adverb is required.

(11) Sr. Deputado, só pode estar a brincar!
'Congressman, you must be kidding!'

These are discursive contexts with a distinctive prosody consisting of a rising tone, marked in writing by the punctuation. The modal interpretation of (11) is one of epistemic necessity, as in (6). However, the equivalent sentence without *só* is not acceptable (**Sr. Deputado, pode estar a brincar*! 'Congressman, you can be kidding'). Contrary to (6), the speaker does not consider that a set of possibilities exist, from which one is singled out, but rather takes only into consideration the situation that the sentence denotes (to be kidding) and emphasizes it.

3.4 *Só* in ambiguous modal contexts

The presence of *só* can resolve ambiguity at the modal value level. For example, sentence (11a) might be interpreted as expressing a possibility or an internal capacity of the law itself. However, in sentence (12b), the presence of the adverb *só* blocks the participant internal reading. Sentence (12b) does not mean that this is the only property of the law but rather that it is inevitable that it reduces injustice. It has the same necessity value as (6).

(12) a. A nova lei pode reduzir a injustiça.
'The new legislation can reduce injustice'

b. A nova lei só pode reduzir a injustiça.
'The new legislation can only reduce injustice'

3.5 Weak alternative

Besides highlighting one alternative, the exclusive particle can also mark this alternative as weaker than expected. This is frequently the case with deontic modality, as illustrated in (13): the process to participate is presented as surprisingly easy.

(13) Para participar só tem de contactar a organização através dos telefones 96... ou 91...
'To participate, you only have to contact the organization through the phone numbers…'

3.6 Contrastive value

The epistemic subvalues belief and knowledge are expressed by main verbs like *achar* 'to believe' and *saber* 'to know'. When the adverb *só* occurs in these contexts, it has mainly a discursive function: it establishes a contrast with something that was previously said in the conversation. We exemplify such conversational contexts in (14):

(14) A: Eu não acho que ele seja corrupto.
'I don't think he is corrupted'

B: Eu *só sei* que ele fez grandes depósitos em offshores.
'I only know that he made big deposits in offshores'

The different contexts discussed in this section show that the interpretation of *só* with modal trigger is complex and varies according to the lexical trigger and its value, but also to the linguistic context and to pragmatic factors.

4 Corpus Annotation

In this section, we first report on the annotation scheme previously implemented for Portuguese, in 4.1. We then discuss how to integrate our findings regarding the adverb *só* 'only', in 4.2, and report on the results of the annotation of a sample corpus in 4.3.

4.1 Annotation scheme for Portuguese

The annotation scheme for Portuguese presented in Hendrickx et al. (2012a) follow a theoretically-oriented perspective, but also addresses certain modal values that are important for practical applications in Information Extraction. The annotation is not restricted to modal verbs and instead covers several parts of speech with modal value: nouns, adjectives and adverbs. Tense, however, is not included, although it has an important part in the modal interpretation of sentences. Also, only modal events are annotated, not entities. The approach is very similar to the approach taken in the OntoSem (Mcshane et al., 2005) annotation scheme for modality (Nirenburg and McShane, 2008).

Seven main modal values are considered (epistemic, deontic, participant-internal, volition, evaluation, effort and success), and several subvalues, based on the modality litterature, but also on studies focused on corpus annotation and information extraction (e.g. (Palmer, 1986; van der Auwera and Plungian, 1998; Baker et al., 2010)). There are five sub-values for epistemic modality: knowledge, belief, doubt, possibility and interrogative. Contexts traditionally considered of the modal type "evidentials" (i.e, supported by evidence) are annotated as epistemic belief. Two subvalues are identified for deontic modality: deontic obligation and deontic permission (this includes what is sometimes considered participant-external modality, as in van der Auwera and Plungian (1998)). Participant-internal modality is subdivided into necessity and capacity. Four other values are included: evaluation, volition and, following Baker et al. (2010), effort and success.

The annotation scheme comprises several components to be tagged: (a) the trigger, i.e, the lexical element conveying the modal value – we choose to tag the smallest possible unit (noun, verb, etc.); (b) the target, expressed typically by a clause and tagged maximally to include all relevant parts; (c) the source of the event mention (speaker or writer) and (d) the source of the modality (agent or experiencer), to distinguish between the person who is producing the sentence with modal value and the person who is 'undergoing' the modality. The trigger receives two attributes: Modal value (selection out of 13 possible values); and Polarity (positive or negative). The polarity attribute regards the value of the trigger and not of the full sentence.

This scheme has been applied to the manual annotation of a corpus sample of approximately 2000 sentences using the MMAX2 annotation software tool[2] (Müller and Strube, 2006). Sentences were extracted from the online search platform of written corpus CRPC.

4.2 Annotation of contexts with the adverb *só*

We will discuss in this subsection how to integrate our findings regarding the exclusive adverb *só* in modal contexts into an annotation scheme. For this purpose, we revised the modality scheme of Hendrickx et al. (2012b) to address the annotation of focus-sensitive particles in

[2] http://mmax2.sourceforge.net/

modal contexts. Instead of considering focus as an independent scheme, we treat it inside modality, inspired by the approach taken regarding polarity. The existence of a focus-sensitive particle is marked with an attribute of the trigger called "focus". This attribute has, for now, three possible values: none, exclusive, additive (for particles like *também* 'also'). The list can be enlarged in the future to address other categories of focus-sensitive particles. The focus particle does not typically have scope over the modal trigger, but rather over other components of the modal scheme (like the target or the source of modality). However, we decided to mark focus information in the trigger component, inspired by the approach of Miwa et al. (2012), since we are considering it as the main element that subsumes the total information regarding the modal event.

The component "focus cue" was added to the modal scheme to identify the focus-sensitive particle in the text. The scope of the focus-sensitive particle is an important aspect to consider in the annotation (cf. 3.1) and we decided to mark the scope of the particle with an extra component named "focus scope". The "focus cue" and the "focus scope" markables are linked to the trigger and, consequently, to the modal event. We illustrate in (15) the focus scope component of the annotation, as well as the features in the trigger component that are associated to the focus-sensitive particle.

(15) Há quem defenda que os medicamentos *só devem* ser usados *numa primeira fase do tratamento*.
'Some people argue that medical drugs should only be used in the first stage of the treatment.'

Trigger: devem
  Modal value: deontic_obligation
  Focus: exclusive
Focus cue: só
Focus scope: numa primeira fase do tratamento

There may be ambiguity regarding the scope of the focus particle (cf. 3.4) and a feature "ambiguity" is attributed to the focus scope component to deal with such cases. We mark the scope constituent according to the most natural interpretation and fill in the ambiguity feature if more than one interpretation is possible, as illustrated in (16).

(16) Portanto, *só temos de* votar a proposta 525-C, do PSD.
'So, we only have to vote proposal 525-C, of PSD.'

Trigger: temos de
  Modal value: deontic_obligation
  Focus: exclusive
Focus cue: só
Focus scope: a proposta 525-C, do PSD
  Ambiguity: votar a proposta 525-C, do PSD

When there are two consecutive modal triggers, we only give information on the focus-sensitive particle in the annotation of the first trigger. For example, in (17), the first trigger (*deverá*) is annotated with features "focus" and "focus cue", and the modal set includes the "focus scope" component. The second modal trigger (*poder*) is part of the target component of the first trigger and is consequently under the scope of its focus related features.

(17) O plantel do Estrela da Amadora *só deverá poder* voltar a contar com o guardião Tiago durante a próxima semana.
'The team of Estrela da Amadora shall only be able to count again on the goalkeeper Tiago during next week.'

In what concerns the necessity reading with *poder*, we believe that the regularities that we discussed in 3.2 allow us to recover the adequate modal value without the need of any special feature but the annotation discussed in the next section will prove if this is indeed the case or if a special feature has to be devised to handle these cases.

The non-optional nature of *só* in contexts as the one illustrated in (10) can be dealt with by selecting both *só* and the modal verb as a composite trigger. This solution would handle the fact that *só* is required in these contexts and would help identifying constructions which have a specific prosodic pattern. The modal value epistemic_necessity would be, in this case, attributed to both elements. We do not propose this solution, however, for cases like (6) and (18b) because *só* is optional in those contexts and the necessity reading follows from the compositional nature of the exclusive, the modal trigger and the target.

In contexts like (13), the exclusive singles out one alternative and also comments on the fact that it is weaker than expected (for example, easier in (13)). However, there is no change in the modal value and the annotation scheme can be applied. To cope with these cases, we added the attribute "focus value" in the trigger component, and consider for now 3 possible values: none, mirative (Beaver and Clark, 2008) and contrastive (as in sentence (14)).

4.3 Results of the annotation

This scheme has been applied, using MMAX2 software, to the manual annotation of a corpus sample of 100 sentences extracted from the online search platform of written corpus CRPC. The 100 sentences all contain the focus particle *só* in the context of a verbal modal trigger, and are not syntactically annotated. We considered, for this purpose, 5 modal verbs: *poder* 'can/may', *dever* 'must', *ter de* 'have to', *ser capaz de* 'be able to', *querer* 'want', most of them covering more than one modal value. We selected a higher number of sentences with *poder*, *dever* and *ter de* because these modal verbs have proved to be more complex and would therefore provide a good test for our annotation scheme. The sentences were selected from a randomly ordered list, and cover different text types. Table 1 presents the distribution of modal values in our sample, taking into consideration only modal events that include the focus-sensitive particle *só*: we observed that deontic obligation and epistemic possibility are the most frequent values.

Modal value	Freq.
Deontic obligation	37
Epistemic possibility	30
Participant-internal capacity	15
Volition	13
Deontic permission	5
Total	100

Table 1: Frequency information about the modal values encountered in the corpus sample.

All ambiguous cases regarding modal value involve the verb *poder* 'can/may', which can denote readings of deontic permission, epistemic possibility and participant-internal capacity. The other four modal verbs are never marked as having more than one modal reading in the context. The most frequent ambiguity in this sample involves the two modal values: epistemic possibility and deontic permission. In three cases, the annotator marked the trigger as having a deontic permission reading, and considered it ambiguous (ambiguity feature of the trigger) with an epistemic possibility value. In two other contexts, the opposite choice was made: epistemic possibility was the marked value and deontic permission was annotated as a possible alternative value. The other four cases of modal ambiguity involve epistemic possibility and participant-internal capacity: in two cases, the former was selected as the most salient value, while the opposite choice was made in the other two cases.

The most frequent constituents in the scope of the exclusive in our annotation are temporal adjuncts, with a total of 27 cases. The verb *dever* stands out, with 14 occurrences, out of the total of 27. The second most frequent type of focus (freq. 23) corresponds to cases where the exclusive has scope over the whole target of the modal trigger. The two most frequent verbs with this type of focus are *querer* and *ter de* (in fact, all but two occurrences of *querer* are of this kind). The two most paradigmatic modal verbs, *poder* and *dever*, never occur with the whole target as focus, but rather favour cases where *só* has scope over different constituents of the sentence. There is a large set of possible constituents which receive the focus of the exclusives: subjects (7), objects (9), quantifiers (5), predicative adjectives (1), by-phrases in passive constructions (3), temporal adjuncts (27), locative adjuncts (1), conditional clauses (5), prepositional phrases (7), and adverbial phrases (3). While *dever* shows a preference for the construction with a temporal adjunct, the verb *poder* presents low frequencies of a large set of these possibilities.

There are 5 cases of ambiguity in the scope of the focus particle, 2 with *ter de* 'have to', 2 with *ser capaz de* 'to be able to' and one with *poder* 'can'. This is perhaps a surprisingly low number compared to our comments in subsection 3.1. Although focus scope is potentially extremely ambiguous, it turns out that the linguistic context seems to lead to one specific interpretation regarding the constituent under focus. In the 5 ambiguous cases, the scope of the focus particle can be understood as a specific constituent included in the target of the modal trigger, or it can be the whole event denoted by the target.

The interpretation of the exclusive and the verb *poder* as a case of epistemic necessity occurs a single time in our annotation, with a stative target in the future tense. No case of contrastive value (cf. (14)) was encountered, but this is certainly due to the fact that we annotated single sentences out of context, and also to the fact that we didn't select knowledge verbs, which typically allow this value. Also, no case of non-optional exclusive particle was found in our set of sentences. We did, however, identify 7 contexts with *ter de* and 3 contexts with *querer,* which denote a weaker alternative than expected and were marked with the value "mirative".

Overall, the proposed solution for handling the complex annotation of the interaction between exclusive particles and modality captured all cases we encountered in our small sample of 100 sentences. However, the annotation of more data is required to evaluate if our modal scheme can deal with the discursive values assumed by the exclusive in certain contexts.

Two different human annotators performed the annotation of a subset of 50 sentences with *só* independently. We conducted a small study to measure the inter-annotator agreement (IAA) for this annotation task. Such a study gives us information about the feasibility of the annotation scheme and about the level of detail of our guidelines. We computed IAA using the kappa-statistic (Cohen, 1960) for each field in the annotation[3]. The trigger achieved a kappa value of 0.85, while the modal value attained a value of 0.83. Although the task involved a higher level of complexity due to the annotation of both modal and focus information, the results are in line with the ones reported in Hendrickx et al. (2012b) and, for English, in Matsuyoshi et al. (2010). We also measured the kappa value for the target component, which attained 0.64. For the focus scope an inter-annotator agreement of 0.63 is achieved. These are lower scores than the ones achieved for trigger and modal value, which is due to small differences in the delimitation of the constituents between the two annotators (for example, the inclusion or not of an adjunct).

5 Conclusion

In this paper, we have presented a detailed analysis of the interaction between the exclusive *só* and modal expressions occurring in texts.

As Portner puts it "It seems that modality is not something that one simply observes, but rather something that one discovers, perhaps only after careful work." (Portner, 2009:1) and this is what we have attempted in this study.

We presented the extension of a modality scheme developed for Portuguese to account for focus-sensitive particles in modal contexts and our experience in annotating a sample of 100 sentences with this extended scheme. Data show that this is a complex issue that needs to consider the modal value, the linguistic context and each modal trigger. The annotation confirms the dual nature of exclusives, due to the fact that in certain contexts they both signal one of the possible alternatives and describe it as weaker that would be expected by the participants. The scope of the focus particle plays an important role in the meaning of the sentence since it adds a condition to the modal value and can affect the global meaning of the sentence. Discursive aspects have also to be taken into consideration and evaluated against our annotation scheme.

As a next step we aim to study a context larger than the sentence for the annotation of the interaction between modals and exclusives. We plan to proceed with the analysis of the interaction of *só* in a larger number of modal contexts and also to enlarge the analysis to other adverbs of the same type, like *apenas* and *unicamente*. Another objective is to explore the combined effects of polarity, modality and this type of adverbs, and to later contrast the results with other Romance languages, as well as English.

Acknowledgments

This work was in part supported by FCT (PEst-OE-LIN-UI0214-2013). Luciana Ávila was supported by grant CAPES (BEX-Proc. nº 9537-12-0). The authors would like to thank the anonymous reviewers for their helpful comments.

References

Maria Aloni, David Beaver, and Brady Clark. 1999. Focus and Topic Sensitive Operators. In Paul Dekker (ed.), *Proceedings of the Twelfth Amsterdam Colloquium*, ILLC, University of Amsterdam, Amsterdam, The Netherlands.

Luciana Beatriz Ávila, and Heliana Mello. 2013. Challenges in modality annotation in a Brazilian Portuguese spontaneous speech corpus. In *Proceedings of WAMM-IWCS2013*, Potsdam, Germany.

Kathrin Baker, Michael Bloodgood, Bonnie Dorr, Nathaniel W. Filardo, Lori Levin, and Christine Piatko. 2010. A modality lexicon and its use in automatic tagging. In *Proceedings of LREC'10*, Valletta, Malta. ELRA, 1402-1407.

Kathryn Baker, Bonnie Dorr, Michael Bloodgood, Chris Callison-Burch, Nathaniel Filardo, Christine Piatko, Lori Levin, and Scott Miller. 2012. Use of Modality and Negation in Semantically-Informed

[3] Note that we are very strict in the computation, only full string matches are counted as agreement.

Syntactic MT. *Computational Linguistics*. 38(2): 411-438

David Beaver and Brady Z. Clark. 2008. *Sense and Sensitivity. How Focus Determines Meaning*. Wyley-Blackwell, Oxford, UK.

Joan L. Bybee, Revere Perkins, and William Pagliuca. 1994. *The evolution of grammar: Tense, aspect and modality in the languages of the world*. University of Chicago Press, Chicago, USA.

Jacob Cohen. 1960. A coefficient of agreement for nominal scales. *Education and Psychological Measurement*, 20:37-46.

Philip W. Davis. 2009. The constitution of focus. Available at: http://www.philipwdavis.com/sands03.pdf. Accessed: March 28, 2013.

Matthew S. Dryer. 1994. The pragmatics of association with only. Paper presented at the 1994 Winter Meeting of the L.S.A. Boston, Massachussets, USA.

Richárd Farkas, Veronika Vincze, György Móra, János Csirik, and György Szarvas. 2010. The conll-2010 shared task: Learning to detect hedges and their scope in natural language text. In *Proceedings of the Fourteenth Conference on Computational Natural Language Learning*, ACL, 1-12.

Michel Généreux, Iris Hendrickx, and Amália Mendes. 2012. Introducing the Reference Corpus of Contemporary Portuguese On-Line". In *Proceedings of the Eighth International Conference on Language Resources and Evaluation* - LREC 2012, Istanbul, May 21-27, 2012, pp. 2237-2244.

Iris Hendrickx, Amália Mendes, Silvia Mencarelli, and Agostinho Salgueiro. 2012a. *Modality Annotation Manual*, version 1.0. Centro de Linguística da Universidade de Lisboa, Lisboa, Portugal.

Iris Hendrickx, Amália Mendes, and Silvia Mencarelli. 2012b. Modality in Text: a Proposal for Corpus Annotation. In *Proceedings of the Eighth International Conference on Language Resources and Evaluation* - LREC 2012, Istanbul, May 21-27, 2012, pp. 1805-1812.

Leo Hoye. 1997. *Adverbs and Modality in English*. Longman, London, UK.

Manfred Krifka. 1995. Focus and the Interpretation of Generic Sentences. In Gregory N. Carlson and Francis Jeffry Pelletier (eds). *The Generic Book*. The University of Chicago Press, Chicago, USA, 238-264.

Suguru Matsuyoshi, Megumi Eguchi, Chitose Sao, Koji Murakami, Kentaro Inui, and Yuji Matsumoto. 2010. Annotating event mentions in text with modality, focus, and source information. In *Proceedings of LREC'10*, Valletta, Malta. ELRA.

Marjorie McShane, Sergei Nirenburg, Stephen Beale, and Thomas O'Hara. 2005. Semantically rich human-aided machine annotation. In *Proceedings of the Workshop on Frontiers in Corpus Annotations II*: Pie in the Sky, 68-75. ACL.

Makoto Miwa, Paul Thompson, John McNaught, Douglas B Kell and Sophia Ananiadou. 2012. Extracting semantically enriched events from biomedical literature. *BMC Bioinformatics* 13:108.

Roser Morante. 2010. Descriptive analysis of negation cues in biomedical texts. In *Proceedings of LREC'10*, Valletta, Malta. ELRA, 1429-1436.

Roser Morante and Caroline Sporleder. 2012. Modality and Negation: An Introduction to the Special Issue. *Computational Linguistics*, 38(2):223-260.

Benjamim Moreira. 2005. *Estudo de alguns marcadores enunciativos do português*. PhD Dissertation. Universidade de Santiago de Compostela, Faculdade de Filologia, Santiago de Compostela, Spain.

Christoph Müller and Michael Strube. 2006. Multilevel annotation of linguistic data with MMAX2. In *Corpus Technology and Language Pedagogy*: New Resources, New Tools, New Methods, 197-214. Peter Lang.

Sergei Nirenburg and Marjorie McShane. 2008. Annotating modality. Technical report, University of Maryland, Baltimore County, March 19, 2008.

Fátima Oliveira. 1988. *Para uma semántica e pragmática de DEVER e PODER*. Ph.D. thesis, Universidade do Porto, Porto, Portugal.

Frank R. Palmer. 1986. *Mood and Modality*. Cambridge textbooks in linguistics. Cambridge University Press.

Paul Portner. 2009. *Modality*. Oxford University Press, Oxford, UK.

Mats Rooth. 1992. A theory of focus interpretation. *Natural Language Semantics* 1: 75-116.

Roser Saurí, Marc Verhagen, and James Pustejovsky. 2006. Annotating and recognizing event modality in text. In *Proceedings of the 19th International FLAIRS Conference*.

Roger Schwarzschild. 1997. Why some foci must associate. Unpublished ms. Rutgers University.

György Szarvas, Veronika Vincze, Ricárd Farkas, and János Csirik. 2008. The BioScope corpus: annotation for negation, uncertainty and their scope in biomedical texts. *BioNLP 2008: Current Trends in Biomedical Natural Language Processing*, Columbus, Ohio, USA, 38-45.

Paul Thompson, Giulia Venturi, John Mcnaught, Simonetta Montemagni, and Sophia Ananiadou. 2008. Categorising modality in biomedical texts. In *Proceedings of the LREC 2008 Workshop on*

Building and Evaluating Resources for Biomedical Text Mining, Marrakech, Morocco, 27-34.

Johan Van der Auwera and Vladimir A. Plungian. 1998. Modality's semantic map. *Linguistic Typology*, 2(1): 79-124.

Veronika Vincze, György Szarvas, Móra György, Tomoko Ohta, and Richárd Farkas. 2011. Linguistic scope-based and biological event-based speculation and negation annotations in the bioscope and genia event corpora. *Journal of Biomedical Semantics*, 2(5).

Kai-Uwe Von Fintel, 1994. *Restriction on Quantifier Domains*. UMass Amherst dissertation, Amherst, Massachussets, USA.

Janyce Wiebe, Theresa Wilson, and Claire Cardie. 2005. Annotating expressions of opinions and emotions in language. *Language Resources and Evaluation*, 39:165-210.

Author Index

Association for Computational Linguistics
209 N. Eighth Street
Stroudsburg, Pennsylvania 18360